Flex 4 Cookbook

Flex 4 Cookbook

Joshua Noble, Todd Anderson, Garth Braithwaite,
Marco Casario, and Rich Tretola

O'REILLY®

Beijing · Cambridge · Farnham · Köln · Sebastopol · Taipei · Tokyo

Flex 4 Cookbook

by Joshua Noble, Todd Anderson, Garth Braithwaite, Marco Casario, and Rich Tretola

Published by O'Reilly Media, Inc., 1005 Gravenstein Highway North, Sebastopol, CA 95472.

O'Reilly books may be purchased for educational, business, or sales promotional use. Online editions are also available for most titles (*http://my.safaribooksonline.com*). For more information, contact our corporate/institutional sales department: 800-998-9938 or *corporate@oreilly.com*.

Editor: Mary E. Treseler

Development Editor: Linda LaFlamme

Production Editor: Kristen Borg

Copyeditor: Rachel Head

Proofreader: Kiel Van Horn

Indexer: Ellen Troutman Zaig

Cover Designer: Karen Montgomery

Interior Designer: David Futato

Illustrator: Robert Romano

Printing History:

May 2010:   First Edition.

RepKover.

This book uses RepKover™, a durable and flexible lay-flat binding.

ISBN: 978-0-596-80561-6

[M]

1273588214

Table of Contents

Preface xv

1. **Flex and ActionScript Basics** 1
    1.1 Create a Flex Project in Flash Builder   2
    1.2 Create a Flex Library Project in Flash Builder   7
    1.3 Set Compiler Options in Flash Builder   8
    1.4 Compile a Flex Project Without Flash Builder   11
    1.5 Add an Event Listener in MXML   13
    1.6 Create Typed Vectors   15
    1.7 Use Event Bubbling   16
    1.8 Use Custom Events and Dispatch Data with Events   18
    1.9 Listen for a Keyboard Event   19
    1.10 Define Optional Parameters for Methods   20
    1.11 Define and Implement an Interface   21
    1.12 Access the Parent of a Flex Component   23

2. **Containers** 25
    2.1 Position Children Within a Container   26
    2.2 Dynamically Add and Remove Children   28
    2.3 Reorder Child Elements of a Container   31
    2.4 Display Children Using Data Items   33
    2.5 Use a Custom Item Renderer in a DataGroup   36
    2.6 Use Multiple Item Renderers in a DataGroup   39
    2.7 Enable Scrolling in a Container   41
    2.8 Scale Children of a Container   46
    2.9 Apply Skins to a Container   48
    2.10 Set the Background Image of a BorderContainer   53
    2.11 Use a Control Bar   55
    2.12 Modify Layout of Content Elements in a Panel   57
    2.13 Track Mouse Position Within a Container   60
    2.14 Drag and Drop Between Visual Containers   62

2.15 Drag and Drop Between Data Containers   66
2.16 Add a Spark Layout Container to a MX Navigation Container   70
2.17 Create a Spark-Based ViewStack   72

3. Layout **79**
3.1 Position Children Linearly   80
3.2 Switch Layout Management at Runtime   81
3.3 Align and Size Children Within a Layout   83
3.4 Lay Out Children Using Rows and Columns   86
3.5 Size Children Uniformly   89
3.6 Lazily Create and Recycle Children   90
3.7 Create a Custom Layout   93
3.8 Measure and Alter the Container Size   95
3.9 Dynamically Change the Child Depth in the Layout   98
3.10 Use Matrix3D to Apply Transformations Within a Layout   100
3.11 Use TransformOffsets to Apply Transformations Within a Layout   102
3.12 Create a Custom 3D Layout   105
3.13 Programmatically Scroll Within a Layout   108
3.14 Determine the Visibility of Elements in a Sequence-Based Layout   112

4. Graphics **115**
4.1 Size and Position a Graphic Element   117
4.2 Use Path to Draw a Shape with Stroke and Fill   118
4.3 Display Text in a Graphic Element   122
4.4 Display Bitmap Data in a Graphic Element   124
4.5 Display Gradient Text   127
4.6 Apply Bitmap Data to a Graphic Element as a Mask   128
4.7 Create a Custom Shape Element   130
4.8 Create a Custom Standalone Graphic Component   134
4.9 Define and Reuse Graphic Symbols   136

5. Components **139**
5.1 Handle a Button's Click Event   139
5.2 Create a Button Bar   142
5.3 Load a External SWF   144
5.4 Use a Calendar Date Input   145
5.5 Create Event Handlers for Menu-Based Controls   148
5.6 Display an Alert in an Application   149
5.7 Display a Custom Pop Up in a Custom Component   151
5.8 Detect a Mouse Click Outside a Pop Up to Close It   153
5.9 Using s:Scroller to Create a Scrollable Container   154
5.10 Handle focusIn and focusOut Events   155
5.11 Open a DropDownList with a Keyboard Shortcut   156

5.12 Grouping Radio Buttons   158
5.13 Submit a Flex Form to a Server-Side Script   160

6. Skinning and Styles **163**
6.1   Create a Skin for s:Button   163
6.2   Apply a Repeating Background Image to an Application   166
6.3   Create a Skin for s:ButtonBar and s:ButtonBarButton   167
6.4   Skin an s:DropDownList   169
6.5   Skin a Spark Container   172
6.6   Change the Appearance of Components Using Styles   174
6.7   Apply Skins and Properties to Spark and MX Components with CSS   175
6.8   Create a Button Component with an Icon   177
6.9   Add Custom Style Properties   179
6.10 Partially Embed Fonts with CSS   181

7. Text and TextFlows **183**
7.1   Create a TextFlow Object   184
7.2   Generate a TextFlow Object from Another Source   185
7.3   Create Links in a TextFlow   187
7.4   Add Graphic Elements to a TextFlow   188
7.5   Bind a Value to a s:TextInput Control   190
7.6   Create a Custom Selection Style   191
7.7   Style Links Within a TextFlow   193
7.8   Locate Elements Within a TextFlow   194
7.9   Determine All Fonts Installed on a User's Computer   196
7.10 Display Vertical Text in a TextArea   197
7.11 Set the Selection in a TextArea   199
7.12 Control the Appearance of the Selected Text   201
7.13 Copy a Character as a Bitmap   202
7.14 Create Linked Containers in a TextFlow   205
7.15 Use a Custom Format Resolver   206
7.16 Skin the TextArea Control   210
7.17 Create Multiple Text Columns   211
7.18 Highlight the Last Character in a TextFlow   212

8. Lists and ItemRenderers **215**
8.1   Create an Item Renderer for a Spark List   216
8.2   Create an Editable List   217
8.3   Scroll to an Item in a Spark List   219
8.4   Change the Layout of a Spark List   219
8.5   Create a Nested List   220
8.6   Set XML Data for a Spark List   223
8.7   Allow Only Certain Items in a Spark List to Be Selectable   226

8.8 Format and Validate Data Added in a Spark List Item Editor   228
8.9 Create a Right-Click Menu for a Spark List   233
8.10 Enable Dragging in a Spark List   235
8.11 Customize the Drop Indicator of a Spark List   238
8.12 Display Asynchronously Loaded Data in a Spark List   242

9. DataGrid **247**
9.1 Create Custom Columns for a DataGrid   247
9.2 Specify Sort Functions for DataGrid Columns   251
9.3 Filter Items in a DataGrid   252
9.4 Create Custom Headers for a DataGrid   255
9.5 Handle Events from a DataGrid   258
9.6 Enable Drag and Drop in a DataGrid   262
9.7 Edit Items in a DataGrid   264
9.8 Search Within a DataGrid and Autoscroll to the Match   265
9.9 Generate a Summary for Flat Data by Using a Grouping Collection 268
9.10 Create an Async Refresh for a Grouping Collection   271

10. Video **275**
10.1 Create a Basic Video Player   275
10.2 Display Video Playback Progress   276
10.3 Create a Skinned Video Player   278
10.4 Display Streaming Video   281
10.5 Display the Bytes Loaded of a Video   282
10.6 Create a Basic Video Player Using the Open Source Media
      Framework   283
10.7 Access and Display Cue Points Embedded in a Video File   284
10.8 Create a Wrapper for the Open Source Media Framework   287
10.9 Display Captions with the Open Source Media Framework   288

11. Animations and Effects **293**
11.1 Dynamically Set a Filter for a Component   294
11.2 Call an Animation in MXML and in ActionScript   295
11.3 Create Show and Hide Effects for a Component   297
11.4 Define Keyframes for an Animation   299
11.5 Create Parallel Series or Sequences of Effects   300
11.6 Pause, Reverse, and Restart an Effect   302
11.7 Set Effects for Adding a Component to or Removing One from a
      Parent Component   303
11.8 Create Custom Animation Effects   306
11.9 Use the DisplacementMapFilter Filter in a Flex Effect   308
11.10 Use the Convolution Filter to Create an Animation   312
11.11 Use Pixel Bender to Create a Transition   317

12. Collections **321**

  12.1 Add, Remove, or Retrieve Data from an ArrayList   321

  12.2 Retrieve and Sort Data from an ArrayCollection   323

  12.3 Filter an ArrayCollection   325

  12.4 Determine When an Item Within an ArrayCollection Is Modified   326

  12.5 Create a GroupingCollection   327

  12.6 Create a Hierarchical Data Provider for a Control   330

  12.7 Navigate a Collection Object and Save Your Position   334

  12.8 Create a HierarchicalViewCollection Object   337

  12.9 Filter and Sort an XMLListCollection   340

  12.10 Sort on Multiple Fields in a Collection   342

  12.11 Sort on Dates in a Collection   343

  12.12 Create a Deep Copy of an ArrayCollection   345

  12.13 Use Data Objects with Unique IDs   347

13. Data Binding **349**

  13.1 Bind to a Property   351

  13.2 Bind to a Function   352

  13.3 Create a Bidirectional Binding   355

  13.4 Bind to Properties by Using ActionScript   356

  13.5 Use Bindable Property Chains   360

  13.6 Bind to Properties on a XML Source by Using E4X   362

  13.7 Create Customized Bindable Properties   364

  13.8 Bind to a Generic Object   368

  13.9 Bind to Properties on a Dynamic Class   370

14. Validation, Formatting, and Regular Expressions **377**

  14.1 Use Validators and Formatters with TextInput Controls   378

  14.2 Create a Custom Formatter   381

  14.3 Use Regular Expressions to Create an International Zip Code Validator   382

  14.4 Validate Combo Boxes and Groups of Radio Buttons   385

  14.5 Show Validation Errors by Using ToolTips in a Form   387

  14.6 Use Regular Expressions for Locating Email Addresses   390

  14.7 Use Regular Expressions for Matching Credit Card Numbers   391

  14.8 Use Regular Expressions for Validating ISBNs   391

  14.9 Create Regular Expressions by Using Explicit Character Classes   392

  14.10 Use Character Types in Regular Expressions   393

  14.11 Match Valid IP Addresses by Using Subexpressions   395

  14.12 Use Regular Expressions for Different Types of Matches   396

  14.13 Match Ends or Beginnings of Lines with Regular Expressions   398

  14.14 Use Back-References   398

  14.15 Use a Look-Ahead or Look-Behind   400

15. Working with Services and Server-Side Communication **403**

15.1 Configure a HTTPService 404

15.2 Use RESTful Communication Between Flex Applications 406

15.3 Communicate with a Service That Returns JSON-Formatted Data 408

15.4 Configure Services for an Application Using BlazeDS 411

15.5 Configure and Connect to a RemoteObject 415

15.6 Use Publish/Subscribe Messaging for Chat Applications 418

15.7 Use the IExternalizable Interface for Custom Serialization 424

15.8 Track Results from Multiple Simultaneous Service Calls 425

15.9 Register a Server-Side Data Type Within a Flex Application 427

15.10 Communicate with a WebService 429

15.11 Add a SOAP Header to a Request to a WebService 431

15.12 Parse a SOAP Response from a WebService 432

15.13 Communicate Securely with AMF by Using SecureAMFChannel 433

15.14 Send and Receive Binary Data via a Binary Socket 435

15.15 Communicate Using a XMLSocket 436

15.16 Navigate a XML Document in E4X 437

15.17 Use Regular Expressions in E4X Queries 439

15.18 Add a XMLList to a XML Object 440

15.19 Handle Namespaces in XML Returned by a Service 441

15.20 Encode an ActionScript Data Object as XML 442

15.21 Decode XML from a Web Service into Strongly Typed Objects 444

16. Browser Communication **447**

16.1 Link to an External URL 447

16.2 Work with FlashVars 448

16.3 Invoke JavaScript Functions from Flex 450

16.4 Invoke ActionScript Functions from JavaScript 451

16.5 Change the HTML Page Title via BrowserManager 453

16.6 Parse the URL via BrowserManager 454

16.7 Deep-Link to Data via BrowserManager 456

16.8 Deep-Link Containers via BrowserManager 458

17. Modules and Runtime Shared Libraries **461**

17.1 Create a Runtime Shared Library 462

17.2 Use Cross-Domain Runtime Shared Libraries 465

17.3 Optimize a Runtime Shared Library 467

17.4 Create a MXML-Based Module 468

17.5 Create an ActionScript-Based Module 470

17.6 Use ModuleLoader to Load Modules 472

17.7 Use ModuleManager to Load Modules 474

17.8 Load Modules from Different Servers 477

17.9 Communicate with a Module 479

    17.10 Use Query Strings to Pass Data to Modules   484
    17.11 Use Linker Reports to Optimize Modules   486

18. AIR Basics **489**
    18.1 Create and Run an AIR Application with Flash Builder 4   489
    18.2 Sign and Export an AIR Application   492
    18.3 Sign an AIR File with a Trusted Certificate   495
    18.4 Targeting a Specific Version of AIR   497
    18.5 Set the Application ID   497
    18.6 Set the Application Name and Filename   498
    18.7 Set the Application Version   500
    18.8 Edit the Application Description and Copyright Information   501
    18.9 Edit the Initial Window Settings   503
    18.10 Set the Installation Folder for an Application   505
    18.11 Set the Default Programs Menu Folder   506
    18.12 Set a Custom Application Icon   507
    18.13 Allow an AIR Application to Interact with the Browser   509
    18.14 Set the Application to Handle All Updates   510
    18.15 Determine the Application Version at Runtime   512
    18.16 Create Multilingual AIR Installations   512
    18.17 Create Applications with Update Capabilities   514
    18.18 Create Applications with Update Capabilities with a Custom
        Interface   520
    18.19 Package an Application in a Native Installer (.exe, .dmg, .rpm)   528
    18.20 Include Native Code Within Your AIR Application   529

19. Working with Data in AIR **535**
    19.1 Safeguard Files with the Encrypted Local Store   535
    19.2 Migrate Serialization Changes   538
    19.3 Create an In-Memory Database   540
    19.4 Encrypt a Database with a Password   541
    19.5 Use Parameters in Queries   544
    19.6 Include a Database in an Application   550
    19.7 Store Simple Relationships with an Object Relational Mapping   551

20. Operating System Integration with AIR **559**
    20.1 Close All Open Windows at Once   560
    20.2 Add a Drop Shadow for a Custom Chrome Window   561
    20.3 Use Deferred Rendering with Clipboard Data   567
    20.4 Create Custom Clipboard Data Formats   568
    20.5 Assign Keyboard Shortcuts to Menu Items   572
    20.6 Notify the User Through the Dock (Mac) and the Taskbar
        (Windows)   573

20.7   Register Custom File Types   576
20.8   Open a File with Its Default Application   579
20.9   Check for Mounted and Unmounted Drives   583
20.10   Obtain a List of Available External Drives   584
20.11   Tell the Operating System That a File Has Been Downloaded from the Web   591
20.12   Deploy an AIR Application as a Native Installer   592
20.13   Create a HTTP Proxy Using the ServerSocket Class   599

21. Charting **607**
21.1   Create a Chart   607
21.2   Add Effects to Charts   610
21.3   Select Regions of a Chart   613
21.4   Format Tick Marks for a Chart   615
21.5   Create a Custom Label for a Chart   617
21.6   Create a Drill-Down Effect for a Column Chart   619
21.7   Skin Chart Items   622
21.8   Use ActionScript to Dynamically Add Columns to and Remove Columns from a Chart   624
21.9   Overlap Multiple ChartSeries   628
21.10   Drag and Drop Items in a Chart   629
21.11   Create an Editable Line Chart   631

22. Unit Testing with FlexUnit **635**
22.1   Create an Application That Uses the FlexUnit Framework   636
22.2   Create an Application to Run FlexUnit Tests   636
22.3   Create a FlexUnit Test Case   639
22.4   Run Code Before and After Every Test   642
22.5   Share Test Data Between Test Cases   645
22.6   Handle Events in a Test Case   647
22.7   Test Visual Components with FlexUnit   649
22.8   Create Mock Objects for Testing   659
22.9   Use Complex Assertions in a Test Case   662

23. Compiling, Debugging, and Deploying **665**
23.1   Use trace Statements Without Flash Builder   665
23.2   Use the Component Compiler   667
23.3   Install the Flex Ant Tasks   668
23.4   Use mxmlc and Ant to Compile Flex Applications   670
23.5   Use Ant to Compile and Deploy Flex Applications That Use RSLs   672
23.6   Use Rake to Compile Flex Applications   674
23.7   Create and Monitor Expressions in the Flash Builder Debugger   675
23.8   Install the Ant View in the Standalone Version of Flash Builder   678

23.9 Use ASDoc and Ant to Generate Documentation   679
23.10 Use Express Install for Your Application   680
23.11 Use Memory Profiling with Flash Builder to View
      Memory Snapshots   682
23.12 Check the Performance of Specific Methods   684

24. Internationalization, Accessibility, and Printing **687**
24.1 Add an International Character Set to an Application   687
24.2 Use a Resource Bundle to Localize an Application   690
24.3 Use the ResourceManager for Localization   694
24.4 Use Resource Modules for Localization   695
24.5 Support Input Method Editor (IME) Devices   698
24.6 Detect a Screen Reader   700
24.7 Create a Tabbing Reading Order for Accessibility   701
24.8 Print Selected Items in an Application   702
24.9 Format Application Content for Printing   704
24.10 Control Printing of Unknown-Length Content over Multiple Pages 705
24.11 Add a Header and a Footer When Printing   707

Index **711**

Preface

Flex 4 is a powerful framework that provides enterprise-level components for the Flash Player platform in a markup language format recognizable to anyone with HTML or XML development experience. The Flex Framework provides components for visual layout, visual effects, data grids, server communication, charts, and much more.

To put a blunt point on it, the Flex Framework is massive, and any book attempting to cover the entire Framework in any depth will without question fail in some respect or another. With this in mind, we've made an attempt to cover the topics that most vex developers working with Flex 4. Along the way, we'll illuminate how the Framework is structured, as well as helping developers familiar with earlier versions of Flex to start working with the new components and styling functionality in Flex 4. The official Flex documentation is quite good at explaining in depth how particular methods or classes behave, so our focus instead is on how to tackle common tasks within the Flex Framework, how to get different components to work together, and how Flex can partner with other technologies to create Rich Internet Applications (RIA) and more. With the help of Adobe AIR, for example, you can use the tools of Flex and the Flash Player to create deployable desktop applications. This complements the expansion of open source and commercial tools for Java, .NET, and PHP development, among others, making Flex a powerful solution for an ever-wider range of development needs and challenges.

Who This Book Is For

Flex 4 Cookbook is for developers who want to understand the Flex Framework more thoroughly, who need a reference to consult to solve particular problems, or who are looking to understand new additions to the Flex Framework. As such, this book assumes that you have some previous experience with Flex and ActionScript 3. The code samples and explanations are geared toward intermediate developers familiar with the relationship between MXML and ActionScript, with at least some of the components that make up the Flex Framework, and with basic Flex development strategies.

We have made a very deliberate decision to ensure that all the recipes contain usable components and functional, tested implementations of those components. This was not done with the intention of swelling the book unreasonably, but to ensure that this book is suitable for intermediate and advanced developers who simply need to see a small code snippet to understand a technique, as well as readers who are still learning how the Flex Framework can be used and the best practices for working with it.

Who This Book Is Not For

If you need to learn the Flex Framework from scratch, consult *Programming Flex 3* by Joey Lott and Chafic Kazoun (O'Reilly) or *Hello! Flex* by Peter Armstrong (Manning) to gain an understanding of the core concepts of Flex development before reading any further here. With a grounding in Flex and ActionScript basics, you'll be better prepared to take advantage of the techniques in this book. If you need a refresher course in ActionScript development or are looking to learn techniques focused on core Flash ActionScript programming, try *ActionScript 3.0 Cookbook* by Joey Lott, Darron Schall, and Keith Peters (O'Reilly). Although *Flex 4 Cookbook* covers some areas of overlap between the Flex Framework and core Flash ActionScript classes, this book is very much focused on Flex development.

How This Book Is Organized

As its name implies, *Flex 4 Cookbook* is stuffed full with recipes intended to teach you techniques that will help you get more from your Flex applications. To help you find the solutions you need faster, the recipes are organized by theme. Generally, within each chapter, the recipes progress from simpler to more complex topics.

This book was not intended to be read from cover to cover, but rather to be used as a reference for particular problems, and to provide insight into particular aspects of the Flex Framework. The recipes also include complete component implementations to show you how to implement the concepts that are discussed. You should be able to use the demonstrated code in your own applications or, at the very minimum, adapt relevant portions of the code to your needs.

Conventions Used in This Book

The following typographical conventions are used in this book:

Italic

    Indicates new terms, URLs, filenames, and file extensions. Also used for emphasis.

Constant width

> Used for program listings, as well as within paragraphs to refer to program elements such as variable or function names, tags and components, data types, environment variables, statements, and keywords.

Constant width bold

> Shows commands or other text that should be typed literally by the user. Also used for emphasis in code listings.

Constant width italic

> Shows text that should be replaced with user-supplied values or by values determined by context.

> This icon signifies a tip, suggestion, or general note.

> This icon indicates a warning or caution.

Using Code Examples

This book is here to help you get your job done. In general, you may use the code in this book in your programs and documentation. You do not need to contact us for permission unless you're reproducing a significant portion of the code. For example, writing a program that uses several chunks of code from this book does not require permission. Selling or distributing a CD-ROM of examples from O'Reilly books does require permission. Answering a question by citing this book and quoting example code does not require permission. Incorporating a significant amount of example code from this book into your product's documentation does require permission.

We appreciate, but do not require, attribution. An attribution usually includes the title, author, publisher, and ISBN. For example: "*Flex 4 Cookbook* by Joshua Noble, Todd Anderson, Garth Braithwaite, Marco Casario, and Rich Tretola. Copyright 2010 O'Reilly Media, Inc., 978-0-596-80561-6."

If you feel your use of code examples falls outside fair use or the permission given above, feel free to contact us at *permissions@oreilly.com*.

How to Use This Book

Think of this book as a friend and a counselor. Don't put it on a shelf. Keep it on your desk where you can consult it often. When you are uncertain as to how something works or how to approach a specific programming issue, pick up the book and flip to the relevant recipe(s). We have written this book in a format so that you can get answers to specific questions quickly. And since it's a book, you don't ever have to worry that it will laugh at you for asking questions. No question is too big or too small.

Although you can read the book from cover to cover, we encourage you to use this book when you need an answer. Rather than teaching you a bunch of theory, this book intends to help you solve problems and accomplish tasks. This book is meant for field-work, not the research lab.

O'Reilly Cookbooks

Looking for the right ingredients to solve a programming problem? Look no further than O'Reilly Cookbooks. Each cookbook contains hundreds of programming recipes and includes hundreds of scripts, programs, and command sequences you can use to solve specific problems.

The recipes you'll find in an O'Reilly Cookbook follow a simple formula:

Problem
> Each Problem addressed in an O'Reilly Cookbook is clearly stated, specific, and practical.

Solution
> The Solution is easy to understand and implement.

Discussion
> The Discussion clarifies and explains the context of the Problem and the Solution. It also contains sample code to show you how to get the job done. Best of all, all of the sample code you see in this O'Reilly Cookbook can be downloaded from the book's website, at *http://www.oreilly.com/catalog/9780596805616*.

See Also
> The See Also section directs you to additional information related to the topic covered in the recipe. You'll find pointers to other recipes in the book, to other books (including non-O'Reilly titles), websites, and more.

To learn more about the O'Reilly Cookbook series, or to find other Cookbooks that are up your alley, visit the website at *http://cookbooks.oreilly.com*.

Safari® Books Online

Safari Books Online is an on-demand digital library that lets you easily search over 7,500 technology and creative reference books and videos to find the answers you need quickly.

With a subscription, you can read any page and watch any video from our library online. Read books on your cell phone and mobile devices. Access new titles before they are available for print, get exclusive access to manuscripts in development, and post feedback for the authors. Copy and paste code samples, organize your favorites, download chapters, bookmark key sections, create notes, print out pages, and benefit from tons of other time-saving features.

O'Reilly Media has uploaded this book to the Safari Books Online service. To have full digital access to this book and others on similar topics from O'Reilly and other publishers, sign up for free at *http://my.safaribooksonline.com*.

How to Contact Us

Please address comments and questions concerning this book to the publisher:

O'Reilly Media, Inc.
1005 Gravenstein Highway North
Sebastopol, CA 95472
800-998-9938 (in the United States or Canada)
707-829-0515 (international or local)
707-829-0104 (fax)

We have a web page for this book, where we list errata, examples, and any additional information. You can access this page at:

http://www.oreilly.com/catalog/9780596805616

To comment or ask technical questions about this book, send email to:

bookquestions@oreilly.com

For more information about our books, conferences, Resource Centers, and the O'Reilly Network, see our website at:

http://www.oreilly.com

Acknowledgments

This book truly does represent a product of the Flex community. Thanks are due to many developers and the community relations managers at Adobe, to Matt Chotin, Ely Greenfield, and Alex Harui in particular, as well as to the developers who work with Adobe products, and have contributed to the Flex Cookbook site or blogged about what they've discovered. Without all of them, this book would not have been conceivable.

Many, many thanks are also due to the many people at O'Reilly who made this book possible. Many special thanks go to Steve Weiss, Mary Treseler, Linda LaFlamme, and Michele Filshie for their hard work, flexibility, and patience throughout the writing and editing of this book.

The quality of the technical information within this book is not simply due to the knowledge of its many authors. The technical reviewers for this book—Jodie O'Rourke, Ed Mansouri, Kevin Suttle, Mykola Bilokonsky, Chuck Freedman, Russ Ferguson, and Sean Moore—not only provided help debugging, correcting, and clarifying the code for this book, but also provided fantastic insight into ways to clarify explanations, structure chapters, alter recipes, and help the readers' understanding.

From Joshua

First and foremost, I need to thank Joey Lott and Steve Weiss for so graciously helping me get the opportunity to write my first book so many years ago and for all the wonderful opportunities that has provided me since. To my co-authors, Todd Anderson and Garth Braithwaite, and also the writers of the *Adobe AIR 1.5 Cookbook*, Rich Tretola and Marco Casario, this book would have been absolutely impossible without you. The same goes for everyone who has participated in the Adobe Cookbook site and on forums like FlexCoders, making a vibrant, helpful community that helps us all.

I'd also like to thank my friends whom I've known from jobs and from life for providing me with so much help, advice, support, and humor. Finally, I'd like to thank my brother, my father, and in particular my mother, for always providing me with encouragement, support, wisdom, and humor.

From Todd

I would first like to thank Josh Noble for asking me to participate in this book and for providing knowledge, patience, and humor throughout. I'd also like to thank Joey Lott for his huge encouragement and belief in people's abilities. I'd like to thank my friends and the Flash community for offering advice, a few laughs, and expertise. And finally to my family, I cannot thank you enough for the huge love and support.

From Rich

I would like to thank my wife and best friend Kim, who has always been there for me and has been supportive of my many ventures. I would also like to thank my daughters Skye, Coral, and Trinity. I love you all very much! Also, thanks for the hard work of all of my co-authors.

From Garth

I was only able to be part of this project because of Steve Weiss, Josh Noble, and Todd Anderson; I thank them for the opportunity. Additionally, I thank my father for my love of programming, and Dr. Paul Merril for teaching the courses that led to my profession. I'd like to thank my RIA Radio co-hosts for being a part of my weekly fanboy fest: Leif Wells, Zach Stepek, and Stacey Mulcahy. I also need to thank the Adobe community, and particularly Rachel Luxemburg, Edward Sullivan, and Greg Hamer, for their encouragement. Finally, I am nothing without the support of my wife, daughters, mom, and family.

From Marco

Special thanks to my fantastic co-authors for the quality and the amount of work they put into this book. I would also like to thank my colleagues at Comtaste—without their hard work on our internal projects, I would never have achieved what I have done. My sincere and deep thanks to the crew at O'Reilly for their patience, persistent assistance, and professionalism throughout the entire process.

I welcome conversation and comment on this book—email me at *m.casario@ comtaste.com*, or leave a comment on my blogs at *http://blog.comtaste.com* or *http:// casario.blogs.com*.

CHAPTER 1

Flex and ActionScript Basics

A Flex application consists primarily of code written in two different languages: ActionScript and MXML. In its 3.0 incarnation, *ActionScript* went from a prototype-based scripting language to a fully object-oriented, strictly typed language. *MXML* is a markup language that will feel comfortable to anyone who has spent time working with Hypertext Markup Language (HTML), Extensible Markup Language (XML), or a host of newer markup-based languages.

Many newcomers to Flex wonder how MXML and ActionScript relate to one another. The MXML compiler (*mxmlc*), after parsing through the different idioms, translates them into the same objects, so that this:

```
<s:Button id="btn" label="My Button" height="100"/>
```

and this:

```
var btn:Button = new Button();
btn.label = "My Button";
btn.height = 100;
```

produce the same object. The major difference is that while creating that object in ActionScript (the second example) creates the button and nothing else, creating the object in MXML adds the button to whatever component contains the MXML code. The Flex Framework handles calling the constructor of the object described in MXML and either adding it to the parent or setting it as a property of the parent.

MXML files can include ActionScript within a `<fx:Script>` tag, but ActionScript files cannot include MXML. Although it's tempting to think of MXML as describing the appearance and components that make up your application and of ActionScript as describing the event handlers and custom logic your application requires, this is not always true. A far better way to think of their relationship is that both languages ultimately describe the same objects via different syntax. Certain aspects of the Flash platform cannot be accessed without using ActionScript loops, function declarations, and conditional statements, among many other features. Consequently, the use of ActionScript, and the integration between MXML and ActionScript, is necessary for all but the very simplest applications.

This chapter discusses many aspects of integrating MXML and ActionScript: creating components in MXML, creating classes in ActionScript, adding event listeners, creating code-behind files by using ActionScript and MXML, and creating function declarations. Although it doesn't contain all the answers, it will get you started with the basics of ActionScript and MXML.

1.1 Create a Flex Project in Flash Builder

Problem

You want to create a project in Flash Builder.

Solution

Use the Create New Project wizard.

Discussion

Flash Builder is built on top of Eclipse, the venerable and well-respected integrated development environment (IDE) most strongly associated with Java development. Although Flash Builder certainly is not necessary for Flex development, it is the premier tool for creating Flex applications and as such, provides a wealth of features to help you design and develop applications more effectively. You can use Flash Builder either as a standalone application or as a plug-in to an existing installation of Eclipse.

The first thing to do as a Flex developer is to create a new Flex project. A Flex project is different from the other types of projects in Flash Builder because it includes the Flex library SWC (unlike an ActionScript project) and is compiled to a SWF file that can be viewed in the Flash Player (unlike a Flex Library project). To create a project, right-click or Ctrl-click (Mac) in Flash Builder's project navigator to display the contextual menu (Figure 1-1), or use the File menu at the top of the application. From either, choose New→Flex Project. A dialog box will appear to guide you through creating a project.

When prompted to specify how the project will get its data, choose Basic, which brings you to the New Flex Project dialog box (Figure 1-2).

Enter an application name and, below, a location where the files will be stored on your system. The default location is *C:/Documents and Settings/Username/Documents/ workspace/Projectname* on a Windows machine, and *Users/Username/Documents/ workspace/Projectname* on a Mac. You can, of course, uncheck Use Default Location and store your files wherever you like. The name of the project must be unique. The Application Type section lets you select whether you are making an Adobe Integrated Runtime (AIR) application or an application that will run in a browser via the Flash Player plug-in. Finally, the Server Technology settings let you indicate whether the

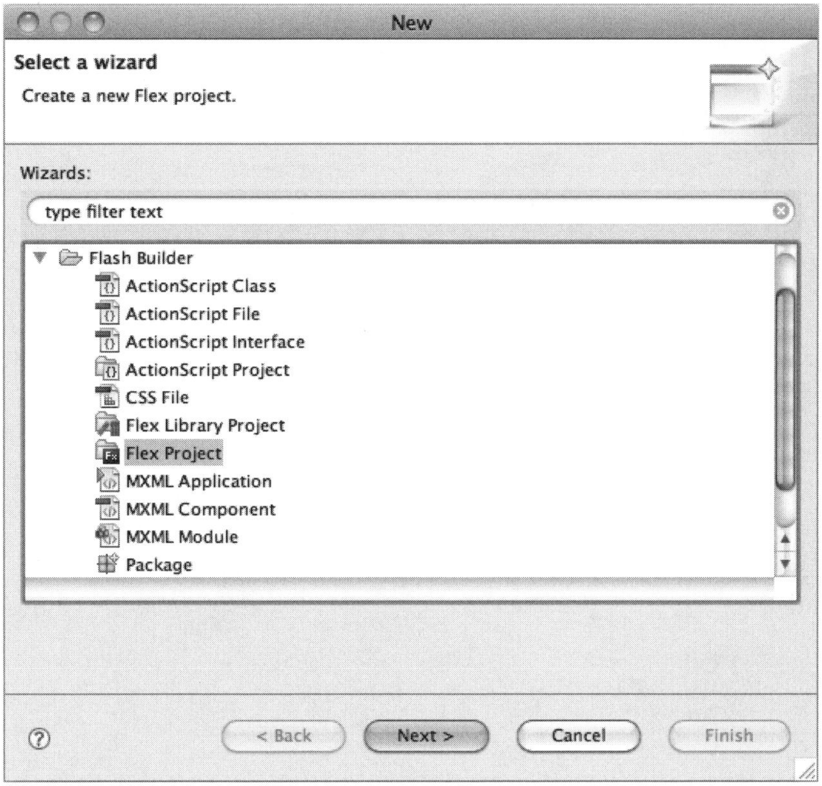

Figure 1-1. Creating a new Flex project

application will be connecting to a server, and if so, what server type and separate configuration type are needed.

If you have nothing more to add, click Finish. To change the location where the compiled SWF file will be placed, click Next to reach the screen shown in Figure 1-3.

Once you've set the location for the generated SWF, you can either click Finish or add source folders or SWC files to the project. To add another folder or set of folders, click the Source Path tab (Figure 1-4). To add SWC files to the project, click the Library Path tab (Figure 1-5). On this screen, you can also change the main MXML application file, which by default has the same name as the project.

With all paths and names specified, click Finish. Your project is now configured, and you are ready to begin development.

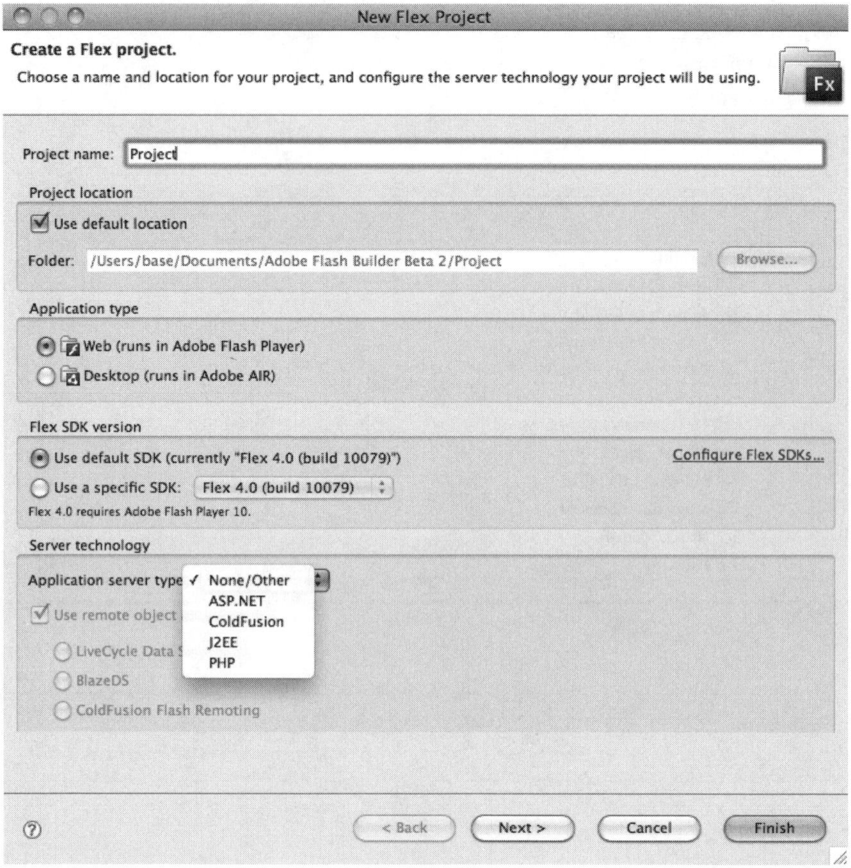

Figure 1-2. Creating a new project in Flash Builder

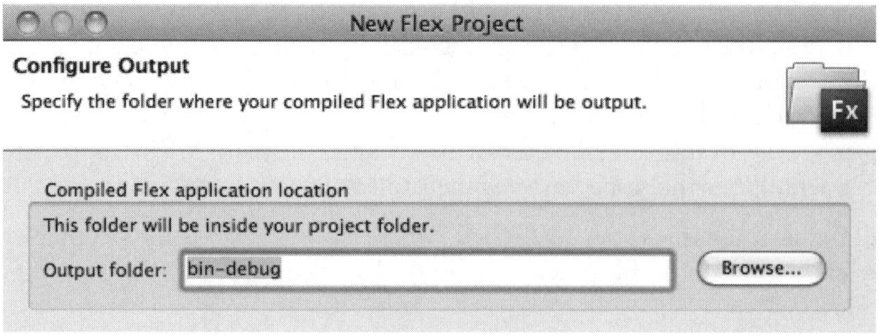

Figure 1-3. Setting the location where the compiled SWF will be placed

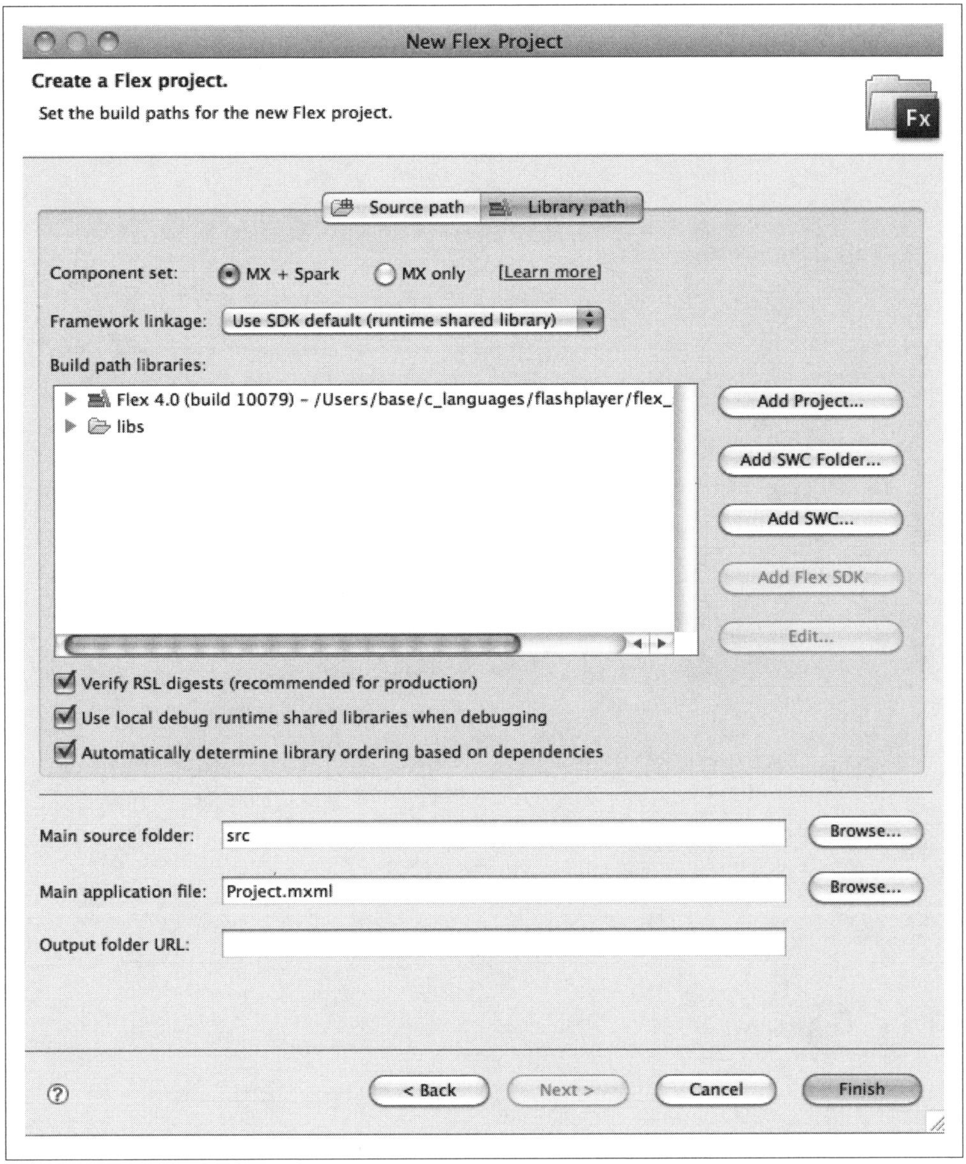

Figure 1-4. Setting the source folder and main application file

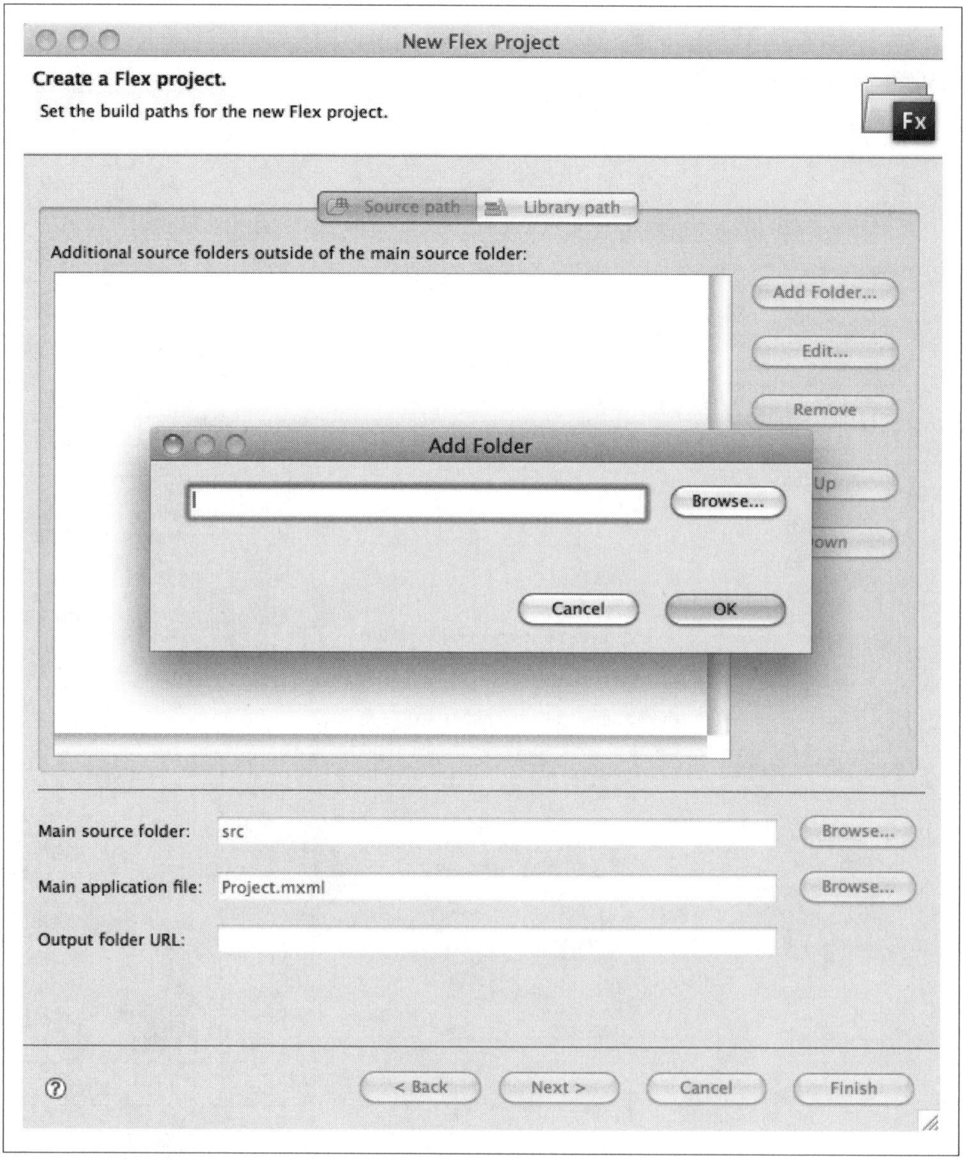

Figure 1-5. Setting any additional source paths for a Flex project

1.2 Create a Flex Library Project in Flash Builder

Problem

You need to create a Flex Library project.

Solution

From the Flex Navigator, choose New Flex Library Project to access the Create New Project wizard.

Discussion

A Flex Library project does not have a main MXML file that is compiled into a SWF. Instead, the project files are compiled into a SWC file that can be used in other applications or as the source for a runtime shared library (usually referred to as an *RSL*). The classes within the library are used to create a group of assets that can be reused in multiple projects at either compile time or runtime. To create a Flex Library project, right-click or Ctrl-click (Mac) in the Flash Builder's project navigator to open the contextual menu (Figure 1-6), or use the File menu. In either case, then choose New→Flex Library Project.

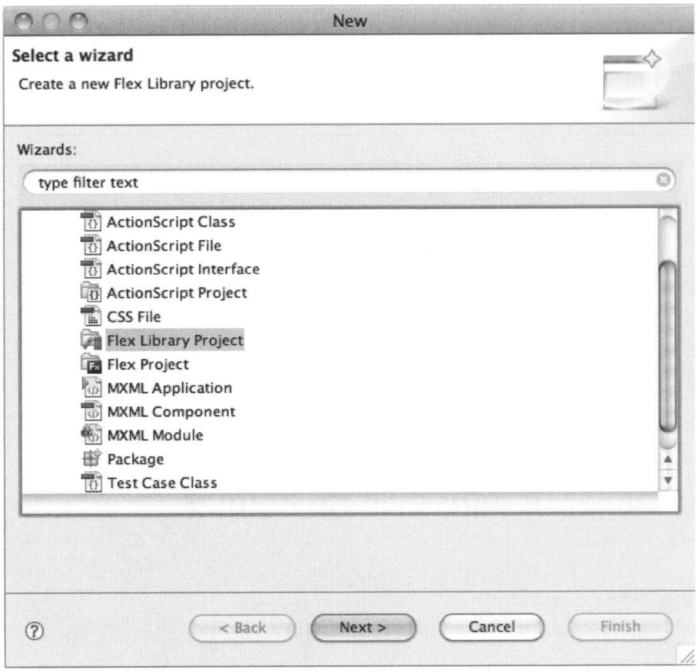

Figure 1-6. Creating a Flex Library Project

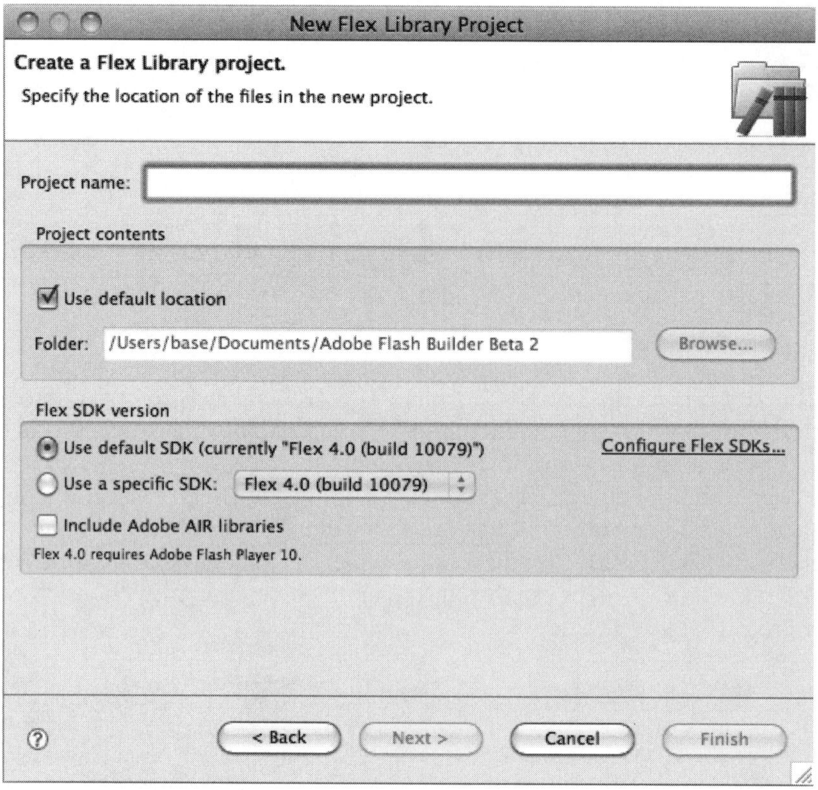

Figure 1-7. Setting the project location and SDK for the compiler

In the resulting dialog box (Figure 1-7), specify a name for your project as well as its location.

If you have nothing more to add, click Finish now. If you need to include files, assets, or other SWC files, including the Adobe AIR libraries, click Next and select them from the resulting screen. To set the path to assets or classes that you would like to add to the library, first browse to a source path you would like to include and then specify the classes or graphical assets to compile into the library. Click Finish to create the project.

1.3 Set Compiler Options in Flash Builder

Problem

You need to set specific compiler options for the MXML compiler.

Solution

Set the options for the compiler arguments in the Flex Compiler screen of the Project Properties dialog box.

Discussion

The *MXML compiler*, also called *mxmlc*, is the application that compiles ActionScript and MXML files into a SWF file that can be viewed in the Flash Player. When you run or debug a Flex application in Flash Builder, the MXML compiler is invoked and the files are passed to the compiler as an argument to the application. When you debug the player, an argument to create a debug SWF is passed to the MXML compiler. Flash Builder lets you pass other arguments to the compiler, as well; for example, you can pass arguments to specify the location of an external library path, allow the SWF to access local files, or set the color of the background.

To change the compiler settings for a project, right-click or Ctrl-click (Mac) on the project and select Properties from the contextual menu (Figure 1-8), or choose Project→Properties from the menu bar.

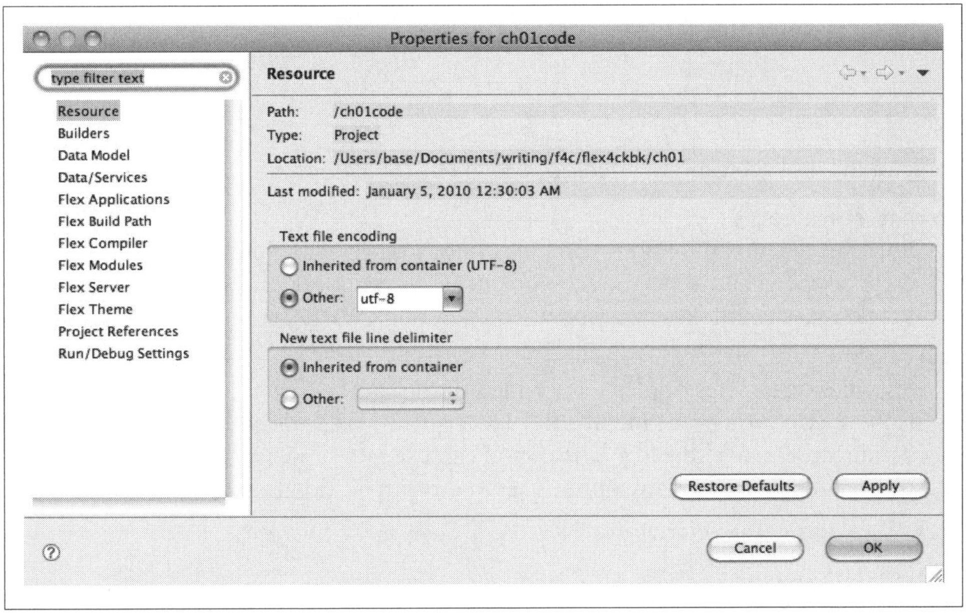

Figure 1-8. Changing the properties of a project

In the resulting Project Properties dialog box (Figure 1-9), select Flex Compiler. Here you have several options to control how the SWF file is compiled. In the input field labeled Additional Compiler Arguments, you can add multiple options; simply type a hyphen (-) in front of each option and separate the options with spaces.

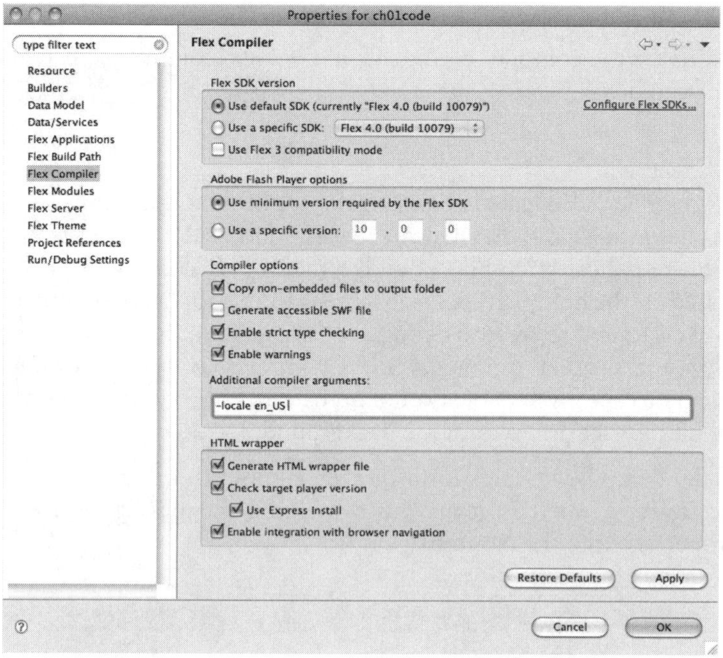

Figure 1-9. Setting compiler options

Some of the most commonly used options are as follows:

`verbose-stacktraces`
Specifies whether the SWF will include line numbers and filenames when a runtime error occurs. This makes the generated SWF larger. Note that a SWF with **verbose-stacktraces** enabled is not the same as a debug SWF.

`source-path path-element`
Specifies directories or files to be added to the source path that contain MXML or ActionScript you want included. You can use wildcards to include all files and subdirectories of a directory. Also, you can use += to append the new argument to the default options or any options set in a configuration file. For example:

```
-source-path+=/Users/base/Project
```

`include-libraries`
Specifies a SWC file to be compiled into the application and links all the classes and assets in the library into the SWF. This option is useful if the application will load in other modules that may need access to the classes in a SWC that the SWF will not be using.

`library-path`
Similar to the `include-libraries` option but includes only classes and assets that are used in the SWF. This lets you keep the size of the SWF file manageable.

---

locale

> Specifies a locale to be associated with a SWF file. For example, you can use
> `-locale=es_ES` to specify that the SWF is localized for Spanish.

use-network

> Indicates whether the SWF will have access to the local filesystem and is intended
> for use on a local machine, or whether the standard Flash Player security will apply.
> For example, use `-use-network=false` to specify that the SWF will have local file-
> system access but will not be able to use any network services. The default value
> is `true`.

frames.frame

> Enables you to add asset factories that stream in after the application and then
> publish their interfaces with the `ModuleManager` class. The advantage of doing this
> is that the application starts faster than it would have if the assets had been included
> in the code, but it does not require moving the assets to a external SWF file.

keep-all-type-selectors

> Ensures that all style information, even if it is not used in the application, is
> compiled into the SWF. This is important if the application will be loading other
> components that require style information. The default value is `false`, which means
> that style information not used in the application is not compiled into the SWF.

After setting the options for the compiler, click the Apply button to save the options
for that project.

1.4 Compile a Flex Project Without Flash Builder

Problem

You are not using Flash Builder for your Flex project, and you need to compile your
project.

Solution

Use a terminal window or command prompt to invoke the MXML compiler.

Discussion

Although Flash Builder is a powerful tool for Flex development, it is certainly not a
requirement for creating Flex applications. The MXML compiler (*mxmlc*) is free to
anyone and can be downloaded from the Adobe website. To compile a Flex application
outside of Flash Builder, open a command prompt (Windows) or a terminal window
(Mac OS X), invoke the MXML compiler, and pass the file containing the application
as an argument, using a command such as the following:

```
home:base$. /Users/base/Flex SDK 4/bin/mxmlc ~/Documents/FlexTest/FlexTest.mxml
```

This will compile the MXML file into a SWF that by default resides in the folder where the MXML file is located. Any warnings or errors from the compiler will be displayed in the terminal or command-prompt window. To add further options to the MXML compiler, you append arguments to the call to the compiler. For example, this command:

```
home:base$ ./mxmlc ~/Documents/FlexTest/FlexTest.mxml
-output=/Users/base/test/generated/Index.swf -library-path+=/Users/lib/MyLib.swc
```

generates a SWF file named *Index.swf*, places it in the directory at */Users/base/test/generated/*, and includes the SWC library */Users/lib/MyLib.swc*.

To invoke the MXML compiler directly from the command line without providing the full path to your SDK installation (which in this example is *C:\flex_sdk_4*), you will need to add the */bin* directory the compiler resides into the `Path` systems variable. On a Windows machine, do the following:

1. Open System from the Control Panel.
2. Select the Advanced tab.
3. Click Environment Variables.
4. Within the System variables grid, navigate to and double-click Path.
5. In the Variable Value field, if the last character is not set to a semicolon (;), enter a semicolon and then the path to the */bin* folder within your Flex SDK installation directory.
6. With the path to the MXML compiler directory set, open a command prompt, navigate to your project directory, and enter the following command:

   ```
   C:\Documents\FlexTest> mxmlc FlexTest.mxml
   ```

   This generates the *FlexTest.swf* file within *C:\Documents\FlexTest*, just as the first command presented in this section does. Setting the path to the */bin* directory of the Flex 4 SDK installation lets you invoke the compiler from any directory, including, in this example, your current project directory.

7. If step 6 results in the following error message:

   ```
   Error: could not find JVM
   ```

   you must manually enter the path to the directory in which the Java Runtime Environment (JRE) is installed on your machine. To manually enter the path, navigate to the */bin* directory of your Flex 4 SDK installation, open the *jvm.config* file in a text editor, and append the path to your JRE installation directory to the variable `java.home`. Assuming the Java installation is on the root of your drive, you would enter the following:

   ```
   java.home=C:/Java/jre
   ```

On a Linux or Mac box, you would do the following:

1. Open your *.bash_profile* file (if you are using Bash) and edit the PATH variable, adding the location of the MXML compiler. Your *.bash_profile* file should look something like this:

```
PATH="${PATH}:~/flex4SDK/bin"
export PATH
```

The *.bash_profile* file will be located in your home directory (which you can always access via a command line by typing cd ~). If you are using *tsch*, the path to the MXML compiler should be added to the *.profile* file.

2. If the Java runtime is not set properly, set the following PATH variable in your terminal shell:

```
PATH="${PATH}:~/flex4SDK/bin"
export PATH
```

Now that you've set the path to the Flex compiler, you're ready to compile your Flex applications from the command line.

1.5 Add an Event Listener in MXML

Problem

You need to add an event listener in MXML that will listen for any events dispatched by children within the MXML file.

Solution

Pass a method name to the **event** property of the component either with or without an **event** object.

Discussion

Flex components dispatch events whenever an action occurs, such as a user clicking a button, the selected item in a combo box changing, or data loading. To listen to these events being broadcast, simply add a reference to a function that will handle the events. For example:

```
<s:Application xmlns:fx="http://ns.adobe.com/mxml/2009"
               xmlns:s="library://ns.adobe.com/flex/spark">
    <fx:Script>
        <![CDATA[

            private function buttonClick():void {
                trace(" Button has been clicked ");
            }
```

```
    ]]>
    </fx:Script>
    <s:Button click="buttonClick()" label="Click Me"/>
</s:Application>
```

Adding click="buttonClick()" invokes the function buttonClick() whenever the button dispatches a click event.

You can also pass the event object itself to the function. Every time a component dispatches an event, the component sends an object of type Event that any object listening to the event can receive. For example:

```
<s:SkinnableComponent xmlns:fx="http://ns.adobe.com/mxml/2009"
                      xmlns:s="library://ns.adobe.com/flex/spark">

    <fx:Script>
        <![CDATA[
            private function buttonClick(event:Event):void {
                trace(event.target.id);
                if(event.target.id == "buttonOne") {
                    trace(" button one was clicked")
                } else {
                    trace(" button two was clicked");
                }
            }
        ]]>
    </fx:Script>
    <s:Button click="buttonClick(event)"
              label="Click Me One" id="buttonOne"/>
    <s:Button click="buttonClick(event)"
              label="Click Me Two" id="buttonTwo"/>

</s:SkinnableComponent>
```

By telling the event listener to listen for an object of type Event, you can have a child component send the event to the event listener method and then respond to that event in different ways depending on the type of event, where the event originated, or data included with the event. In this example, the response depends on where the event originated.

The event object and the event dispatching system in Flex are some of the most important things to understand. All events have a type that is used when those events are being listened for; if an event is of type click, for example, the event-listening method will be added to the click event of the child:

```
<mx:Button click="trace('I was clicked')"/>
```

Notifications about user interactions, messages sent to an application from a server, and timers are all sent via events. The event object defines several properties that you can access in any listening function:

bubbles

Indicates whether an event is a bubbling event; that is, whether it will be redispatched from the object that has received it to any listeners further up the event chain.

cancelable

Indicates whether the behavior associated with the event can be prevented.

currentTarget

Identifies the object that is actively processing the event object with an event listener.

eventPhase

Identifies the current phase in the event flow.

Target

Specifies the event target, which is the object that has dispatched the event.

Type

Indicates the type of event.

You can also write event handlers in the MXML itself by using the binding tags {} to indicate that the code inside of the braces should be executed when the event is fired. For example:

```
<s:Button click="{textComponent.text = 'You clicked the button'}" label="Click Me"/>
<s:Text id="textComponent"/>
```

When it compiles this code, the Flex compiler creates a function and then sets this:

```
textComponent.text = 'You clicked the button'
```

as the body of that function. It may look different from the previous method, but the end result of this function is the same: it listens for the event and executes its code. There's nothing inherently wrong with this approach, but for anything more complex than setting a single property, you should use a defined function to make your code easier to read and understand.

1.6 Create Typed Vectors

Problem

You want to store arrays of typed objects to avoid the need for casting when retrieving elements from the arrays.

Solution

Create a Vector and pass the type of object that it will contain in the declaration and constructor.

Discussion

ActionScript 3 introduced the Vector type with Flash Player 10. The Vector allows you
to create a typed array of elements that only accepts variables of its declared type and
returns variables of its declared type for any operation that returns a value. Because you
don't need to cast an object from a Vector to a type when you access it, you can speed
up your applications substantially by using Vectors wherever you're storing arrays of a
single type of object. To create a Vector containing int variables, for example, you
would do the following:

```
var vec:Vector.<int>;
vec = new Vector.<int>();
vec.push(1, 2, 3, 4);
```

Now any operations involving the vec instance will be compiled as though they were
of the type passed to it when it was declared, as shown here:

```
var newVariable:int = vec[1] + vec[2]; // no need to cast
var anotherVariable:int = vec.pop();   // again no need to cast
```

You can also pass an Interface to the Vector, as shown here:

```
var interfaceVector:Vector.<IUIComponent>;
```

However, you cannot pass a Class variable to a Vector:

```
var clazz:Class = SomeCustomClass;
var classVector:Vector.<clazz>;        // won't compile
```

The type passed to a Vector must be known at compile time.

1.7 Use Event Bubbling

Problem

You want to listen for events passed up from child components to parent components
without adding a long chain of event listeners.

Solution

Use the event-bubbling mechanism in the Flash Player to listen for events passed up
from children.

Discussion

Understanding bubbled events requires looking at several classes. Several types of
events can be bubbled up: mouse-down events, click events, and keyboard events,
among others. The term *bubbling up* refers to the event working its way up through the
display list to the application container, like a bubble rising to the surface through
water. When the user clicks on any component, that event is passed up through the

hierarchy. This means that the parent of a component can listen on that component for a click event, and if one is dispatched, the parent will be notified. To listen for all events of a certain type within a child component, the parent simply needs to add an event listener to that child to receive all bubbled-up events.

Consider this class, defined in *BubblingComponent.mxml*:

```
<mx:HBox xmlns:mx="http://www.adobe.com/2006/mxml" width="400" height="200">
    <mx:Script>
        <![CDATA[
            private function sendClick():void {
                trace(" BubblingComponent:: click ");
            }
        ]]>
    </mx:Script>
    <mx:Button click="sendClick()"/>
</mx:HBox>
```

This component contains a button that will dispatch a click event up the display list to any component that contains an instance of BubblingComponent. To listen to this event, use the click handler in a component that contains BubblingComponent:

```
<cookbook:BubblingComponent click="handleClick()" id="bubbler"/>
```

A BubblingHolder that contains a BubblingComponent could be defined as shown in the following code snippet:

```
<mx:Canvas xmlns:mx="http://www.adobe.com/2006/mxml"
            width="400" height="300" xmlns:cookbook="oreilly.cookbook.*"
            creationComplete="complete()">
    <mx:Script>
        <![CDATA[
            private function handleClick():void {
                trace(" BubblingComponentHolder:: click ");
            }
        ]]>
    </mx:Script>
    <cookbook:BubblingComponent click="handleClick()" id="bubbler"/>
</mx:Canvas>
```

This component will dispatch an event up to any component listening. When you add the BubblingHolder to the main application file:

```
<mx:Application xmlns:mx="http://www.adobe.com/2006/mxml"
                layout="vertical" xmlns:cookbook="oreilly.cookbook.*">
    <mx:Script>
        <![CDATA[
            public function createName():void {
                name = "Flex Cookbook";
            }
        ]]>
    </mx:Script>
    <cookbook:BubblingComponentHolder click="createName()"/>
</mx:Application>
```

the click event from *BubblingComponent.mxml* will be broadcast all the way up to the application level.

The sequence of events in a MouseEvent sends information about the event, such as a click and its location, up the display list through all the children, to the child that should receive the event, and then back down the display list to the stage.

The stage detects the MouseEvent and passes it down the display list until it finds the target of the event—that is, the last component that the user's mouse was interacting with. This is called the *capturing phase*. Next, the event handlers within the target of the event are triggered. This is called the *targeting phase*, when the event is given an actual target. Finally, the *bubbling phase* occurs, sending the event back up the display list to any interested listeners, all the way back to the stage.

1.8 Use Custom Events and Dispatch Data with Events

Problem

You want to dispatch data with an event by using a custom event class.

Solution

Create a class that extends the flash.events.Event class and create a property for the data that you would like to be available from the event.

Discussion

At times, you may need to dispatch data objects with events, enabling listeners to access that data without accessing the objects that dispatched the events. Renderers or deeply nested objects that are dispatching events up through multiple components to listeners will frequently want to send data without requiring the listening component to find the object and access a property. As a solution, create an event type and add any data types that you need to include with the event to the constructor of the event. Remember to call the super() method of the Event class so that the Event object is properly instantiated. For example:

```
package oreilly.cookbook {
    import flash.events.Event;

    public class CustomPersonEvent extends Event {

        public var person:Person;
        public var timeChanged:String;

        public function CustomPersonEvent(type:String, bubbles:Boolean=false,
                                          cancelable:Boolean=false,
                                          personValue:Person=null,
                                          timeValue:String="") {
            super(type, bubbles, cancelable);
```

```
            person = personValue;
            timeChanged = timeValue;
        }

        override public function clone():Event {
            return new CustomPersonEvent(type, bubbles, cancelable, personValue,
                                        timeValue);
        }
    }
}
```

In this custom Event class, the inherited Event.clone() method is overridden so that the CustomPersonEvent can duplicate itself. If an event listener attempts to redispatch this custom event, as shown here:

```
private function customPersonHandler(event:CustomPersonEvent):void {
    dispatchEvent(event);
}
```

the event that is dispatched will not be the event that is received; instead, it will be a copy of the CustomPersonEvent created using the clone() method. This is done inside the flash.events.EventDispatcher class. If the clone() method is not overridden to ensure that all properties of the CustomPersonEvent are carried into a clone of itself, the event returned from the clone will be of type flash.events.Event and will not have any properties of the CustomPersonEvent.

1.9 Listen for a Keyboard Event

Problem

You need to listen for the user pressing a key, determine which key was pressed, and handle the event accordingly.

Solution

Add an event listener for the keyDown event either on the component or on the stage of the application and read the KeyboardEvents keyCode property.

Discussion

To listen for a KeyboardEvent, use the keyDown event handler, which all classes that extend UIComponent possess. The KeyboardEvent class defines a keyCode property that contains the code for the key that the user pressed. That keyCode property is the ASCII representation of the character (ASCII is a standard that defines a mapping of characters to integers). For example:

```
<mx:HBox xmlns:mx="http://www.adobe.com/2006/mxml"
        width="400" height="300" keyDown="keyHandler(event)"
        backgroundColor="#0000ff">
    <mx:Script>
```

```
            <![CDATA[

                import flash.events.KeyboardEvent;

                private function keyHandler(event:KeyboardEvent):void {
                    switch(event.keyCode) {
                        case 13:
                            trace(" Enter pressed ");
                        break;
                        case 32:
                            trace(" Space Bar pressed ");
                        break;
                        case 16:
                            trace(" Shift Key pressed ");
                        break;
                        case 112:
                            trace(" F1 pressed ");
                        break;
                        case 8:
                            trace(" Delete pressed ");
                        break;
                    }
                }

            ]]>
        </mx:Script>
        <mx:Button label="One"/>
    </mx:HBox>
```

A note about this component: it will listen only for events that occur while the button has focus. If you remove the button from this component, there is nothing left that can have focus, and the keyHandler() function will never be called. To catch every Key Event that occurs in the application, whether or not the component has focus, add the following to the opening tag of the component:

```
addedToStage="stage.addEventListener(KeyboardEvent.KEY_DOWN, keyHandler)"
```

This ensures that the keyHandler() method will handle each KeyEvent that the stage catches—i.e., all of them.

1.10 Define Optional Parameters for Methods

Problem

You want to define methods for a parameter that have default values or null values so that those values do not always need to be passed.

Solution

Specify default values or null values in the method declaration by setting the parameter equal to a default value or equal to null.

Discussion

To define one or more optional parameters for a method, simply set the default value of an object to `null` in the signature of the event. The ActionScript primitives `String`, `Number`, `int`, and `Boolean` cannot be null values, however; you must supply default values for these. For example:

```
public function optionalArgumentFunction(value:Object, string:String,
        count:int = 0, otherValue:Object = null):void {
    if(count != 0) {
        // if the count is not the default value, handle the value the
        // call passes in
    }
    if(otherValue != null) {
        // if the otherValue is not null, handle the value the call
        // passes in
    }
}
```

Another strategy for providing not only optional parameters to the method but also an indeterminate number of arguments is to use the `...` or `rest` operator in front of a variable name. For instance, to pass an undefined number of arguments to a method, you would define the method as shown here:

```
public function restMethod(...rest):void {
    trace(" here is the number of arguments passed "+rest.length);
}
```

To use the `rest` operator with defined parameters, simply put the defined parameters first and the `rest` operator after, as shown here:

```
public function restMethod(number:int, name:string, ...rest):void {
    trace(" here is the number of arguments passed "+rest.length);
}
```

1.11 Define and Implement an Interface

Problem

You need to create an interface and then create a component that implements that interface.

Solution

Create an ActionScript file, declare that file as an `Interface`, and define any methods you would like the interface to require. To implement the interface, use the `implements` keyword in the class declaration of the component that will use the interface.

Discussion

Interfaces are powerful tools that let you describe a contract that an object must fulfill. The interface must contain a specified set of methods with a certain scope, name, parameters, and return type; components using the object, in turn, will expect this set of methods to be present. This lets you create lightweight descriptions of a class without actually creating a new class that clutters your inheritance trees. Classes that implement an interface are considered to be of that interface type. This can be used to set the types for parameters of methods or to set the return types of methods, as shown here:

```
public function pay(payment:IPaymentType):IReceipt
```

This method can accept any object that implements `IPaymentType` and will return an object that implements the `IReceipt` interface.

The interface cannot define the method body, nor can it define any variable. In the following code snippet, `IDataInterface` is declared and defines five methods that any object that implements the interface must also possess and define:

```
package oreilly.cookbook {
    public interface IDataInterface {
        function set dataType(value:Object):void;
        function get dataType():Object;
        function update():Boolean;
        function write():Boolean;
        function readData():Object;
    }
}
```

To implement the interface, declare the class and add the `implements` marker to the class declaration. All methods defined in an `Interface` must be implemented by the class. In the following code snippet, all the methods of the preceding interface are included and are given function bodies:

```
package oreilly.cookbook {
    import flash.events.EventDispatcher;
    import flash.events.IEventDispatcher;

    public class ClientData extends EventDispatcher implements IDataInterface {

        private var _dataType:Object;

        public function ClientData(target:IEventDispatcher=null) {
            super(target);
        }

        public function set dataType(value:Object):void {
            _dataType = value;
        }

        public function get dataType():Object {
            return _dataType;
        }
```

```
public function update():Boolean {
    // do the actual updating
    var updateSuccessful:Boolean;
    if(updateSuccessful) {
        return true;
    } else {
        return false;
    }
}

public function write():Boolean {
    var writeSuccess:Boolean;
    if(writeSuccess) {
        return true;
    } else {
        return false;
    }
}

public function readData():Object {
    var data:Object;
    // get all the data we need
    return data;
}
    }
}
```

To implement an interface in MXML, use `implements` in the top-level tag for the component. For example:

```
<mx:HBox xmlns:mx="http://www.adobe.com/2006/mxml"
        width="400" height="300" implements= "IDataInterface">
```

1.12 Access the Parent of a Flex Component

Problem

You want to access either the immediate parent of a component or the parent application of a component.

Solution

Use the `parentDocument` property of the `UIComponent` to access the parent of a component, the `parentApplication` property to access the first `Application` that a component is contained within, and `FlexGlobals.topLevelApplication` to access the top-level application in the hierarchy of a Flex application.

Discussion

A Flex component can be nested within many different parent components, and also within multiple applications. In previous versions of Flex, developers would often access the parent application by using `Application.application` to return a reference to the main application. In Flex 4, you should use either the `parentApplication` property that all `UIComponent`s define to access the application that a particular component is loaded into, or the `FlexGlobals.topLevelApplication` to access the top-most application.

Figure 1-10 shows how a `Button` could access the various parent components within which it is nested.

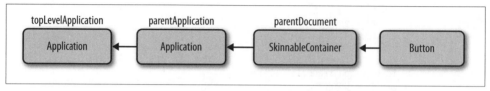

Figure 1-10. Accessing parent documents and applications from a component

Note that the `parentDocument` and the parent of a `UIComponent` are different. For instance, a `Button` within a list may have a `SkinnableContainer` as its parent, but a `List` as its `parentDocument`. It's generally better practice to dispatch a custom event to the parent than to attempt to access it using a reference. This ensures that components you're building will be portable to multiple parent types and reduces dependencies throughout your application.

CHAPTER 2

Containers

The Flex Framework provides two sets of containers: MX and Spark. The introduction of the Spark architecture to the Flex 4 SDK offers a level of abstraction between containers and layouts not available in the MX architecture. An MX container internally manages the size and position of its children based on specified properties and styles. To modify the layout rules of a MX container, you often create a subclass of a similar container or the base `mx.core.Container` class and override methods such as `updateDisplayList()` and `measure()`. In contrast, Spark containers are separated from layout management and allow for a developer to specify layouts available in the `spark.layouts` package or create custom `LayoutBase`-based layouts to manage the size and position of child elements. The separation of responsibilities for Spark containers provides enhanced runtime performance in rendering because layout is handled through delegation.

Included in the Spark layout container architecture are two base classes, `GroupBase` and `SkinnableContainerBase`. Both handle visual elements, but only the latter provides skinning capabilities for the container. The `spark.components.Group` and `spark.compo nents.DataGroup` classes are extensions of `GroupBase`; both are non-skinnable containers, but they differ in how child elements are declared and represented on their display lists. A `Group` container holds children that are implementations of `IVisualElement` and that are added either through MXML markup or through methods of the content API. A `DataGroup` container uses item rendering for visual elements represented as data items, which are provided as `IList` implementations. `DataGroup` also supports virtualization through a layout delegate, which can reduce the rendering time of its visual elements at runtime. `spark.components.SkinnableContainer` (of which `Application` is a subclass) and `spark.components.SkinnableDataContainer` are equivalent to the `GroupBase`-based containers yet support skinning for the visual makeup of the container itself.

Layout containers—those that handle the size and position of their child elements— have equal parity between the MX and Spark container sets. Though using Spark layout containers is recommended because of their improved performance and level of abstraction, there are no Spark equivalents of the MX navigational containers (such as `Accordion` and `ViewStack`). If application requirements dictate the use of navigational containers, the Flex Framework allows for intermixing of MX and Spark containers in the same application. Note, however, that a Spark container cannot be added directly as a child to a MX navigator container. To add a Spark layout container to a MX navigator container, you must wrap the Spark container in a `spark.components.Navigator Content` container instance.

2.1 Position Children Within a Container

Problem

You want to position child elements of a container using a specified layout.

Solution

Assign a layout from the `spark.layouts` package to the `layout` property of the target container and apply constraints on the layout and container as necessary.

Discussion

Spark layout containers, such as `spark.components.Group` and `spark.components.Data Group`, delegate the sizing and positioning of their child elements to `LayoutBase`-based layouts. As child elements are added to a container, whether declaratively in MXML or programmatically, the management of the display list is handed over to the layout, which renders child elements accordingly. Common layouts, such as those for positioning children vertically or horizontally, are provided in the Flex 4 SDK in the `spark.layouts` package. Due to the separation of responsibilities between Spark containers and layouts, custom `LayoutBase`-based layouts can also easily be applied to containers.

The default layout of the base Spark containers is `spark.layouts.BasicLayout`. When the default `BasicLayout` is applied to a container, child elements are displayed based on their individual properties, without regard to the size and position of other children:

```
<s:Group width="300" height="300">

    <s:Button label="button (1)" x="10" y="10" />
    <s:Button label="button (2)" x="10" y="40" />

</s:Group>
```

Using `BasicLayout` affords developers fine-grained control over the layout of child elements by enabling them to specify each element's size and position. Additional constraint properties can be applied to the container as well, to uniformly offset child positions. The child elements of the `s:Group` container in the following example are displayed exactly as in the previous example, yet the `top`, `left`, `right`, and `bottom` constraint properties are used:

```
<s:Group width="300" height="300"
        top="10" left="10" right="10" bottom="10">

    <s:Button label="button (1)" />
    <s:Button label="button (2)" y="30" />

</s:Group>
```

The `HorizontalLayout`, `VerticalLayout`, and `TileLayout` classes are available to display children sequentially and can be applied using the `layout` property:

```
<s:Group width="300" height="300"
        top="10" left="10" right="10" bottom="10">

    <s:layout>
        <s:VerticalLayout gap="10" />
    </s:layout>

    <s:Button label="button (1)" />
    <s:Button label="button (2)" />

</s:Group>
```

Similar to using constraint properties on a container, distances between the border of the container and the child elements can be specified using the `paddingTop`, `paddingLeft`, `paddingRight`, and `paddingBottom` properties of the sequential layout classes of the SDK:

```
<s:Group width="300" height="300">

    <s:layout>
        <s:VerticalLayout gap="10" paddingTop="10" paddingLeft="10"
                          paddingRight="10" paddingBottom="10" />
    </s:layout>

    <s:Button label="button (1)" />
    <s:Button label="button (2)" />

</s:Group>
```

Some convenience classes are available in the Flex 4 SDK to declare containers with predefined layouts. For example, the children of `spark.components.HGroup`, `spark.components.VGroup`, and `spark.components.TileGroup` containers are laid out sequentially in a predetermined manner. You declare these containers just as you would any other, but the `layout` property is attributed as read-only:

```
<s:VGroup width="300" height="300" gap="10"
        paddingTop="10" paddingLeft="10"
        paddingRight="10" paddingBottom="10">

    <s:Button label="button (1)" />
    <s:Button label="button (2)" />

</s:VGroup>
```

There are many different ways to achieve a desired layout. For instance, all the examples in this recipe will display the same way, although they differ in approach. It is important to remember that containers and layout within the Spark architecture are decoupled, affording you more freedom as to how child elements are visually presented.

2.2 Dynamically Add and Remove Children

Problem

You want to add child elements to and remove child elements from a container at runtime.

Solution

Use the `addElement()`, `addElementAt()`, `removeElement()`, and `removeElementAt()` methods of an `IVisualElementContainer` implementation.

Discussion

A layout assigned to a Spark container attributes its children as instances of `IVisualElement` when managing their size and position. Visual components from both the Spark and MX packages are implementations of `mx.core.IVisualElement`, so you can add MX controls that do not have a Spark equivalent to a Spark layout container. `GraphicElement`-based elements also implement `IVisualElement` and afford you a rich set of visual elements to display within a container.

Along with declaring child elements in markup, you can programmatically add children to a container using the `addElement()` and `addElementAt()` methods of an `IVisual ElementContainer` implementation. The `addElement()` method adds a child element to the content layer at an elemental index one higher than any previously assigned. Using `addElementAt()`, you can set the exact elemental location within the display list. When you add an element using the content API's add methods, the element's position depends on the layout delegate specified for the container. The `spark.components.Group` and `spark.components.SkinnableContainer` (of which the Spark `Application` container is a subclass) containers are implementations of `IVisualElementContainer`.

To add a child at the next available elemental index within the display, use the `addElement()` method as shown here:

```
<s:Button label="add" click="{myContent.addElement( new Button() );}" />

<s:Group id="myContent">
    <s:layout>
        <s:VerticalLayout />
    </s:layout>
</s:Group>
```

The click event of the s:Button control triggers the addition of a new Button child element to the targeted container. Depending on the layout applied to a container, the addition and removal of child elements may or may not affect the position of other child elements. In this example, as each new child element is added, it is offset vertically from the last child element. If BasicLayout were assigned to the container, each additional child element would be presented at a higher z-order within the display.

Using the addElementAt() method, you can set the desired position for the new child within the display list:

```
<s:Button label="add" click="{myContent.addElementAt( new Button(), 0 );}" />

<s:Group id="myContent">
    <s:layout>
        <s:VerticalLayout />
    </s:layout>
</s:Group>
```

In this example, as each new Button is added to the container, the control is placed at the elemental index 0. Because VerticalLayout is assigned to the container, each new child added will be placed at the top of the content display, pushing the y-positions of any other child elements downward.

To remove a child element at a specific index, use the removeElementAt() method:

```
myContent.removeElementAt(0);
```

Children can also be removed using the removeElement() method, which takes the reference name of a child element as its argument:

```
myContent.removeElement(myElement);
```

If the reference name is not available, you can use the getElementAt() method of the content API and specify the index of the child element you wish to remove. The following example uses the getElementAt() method to remove the first element from the container's display list:

```
myContent.removeElement( myContent.getElementAt( 0 ) );
```

The Group and SkinnableContainer layout container classes also support the removal of all child elements using the removeAllElements() method.

As children are added to and removed from a container, the numChildren property of the container is updated. This can help in effectively using the methods of the content API exposed by implementations of IVisualElementContainer.

The following example demonstrates the possible ways to programmatically add child elements to and remove them from a container:

```
<s:Application xmlns:fx="http://ns.adobe.com/mxml/2009"
               xmlns:s="library://ns.adobe.com/flex/spark"
               xmlns:mx="library://ns.adobe.com/flex/mx">
```

```
<fx:Script>
    <![CDATA[
        import mx.core.IVisualElement;
        import spark.components.Button;

        private function getNewElement():IVisualElement
        {
            var btn:spark.components.Button = new spark.components.Button();
            btn.label = "button " + myContent.numElements;
            return btn;
        }

        private function addFirstElement():void
        {
            myContent.addElementAt( getNewElement(), 0 );
        }

        private function addLastElement():void
        {
            myContent.addElement( getNewElement() );
        }

        private function removeFirstElement():void
        {
            if( myContent.numElements > 0 )
                myContent.removeElement( myContent.getElementAt( 0 ) );
        }

        private function removeLastElement():void
        {
            if( myContent.numElements > 0 )
                myContent.removeElementAt( myContent.numElements - 1 );
        }

    ]]>
</fx:Script>

<s:layout>
    <s:VerticalLayout />
</s:layout>

<s:Button label="addFirst" click="addFirstElement();" />
<s:Button label="addLast" click="addLastElement();" />
<s:Button label="removeFirst" click="removeFirstElement()" />
<s:Button label="removeLast" click="removeLastElement()" />
<s:Button label="removeAll" click="myContent.removeAllElements()" />

<s:Group id="myContent">
    <s:layout>
        <s:VerticalLayout />
    </s:layout>
</s:Group>

</s:Application>
```

2.3 Reorder Child Elements of a Container

Problem

You want to dynamically reorder the index positions of child elements within a container at runtime.

Solution

Use the `setElementIndex()` method to change the elemental index of an individual child element, or use the `swapElements()` and `swapElementsAt()` methods to transpose the index positions of two children in an `IVisualElementContainer` implementation, such as a `Group` or `SkinnableContainer`. The elemental index corresponds to the order in which a child element is rendered in a layout.

Discussion

As child elements are added to a container, whether programmatically or declaratively in MXML, references to those elements are stored within an **Array**. The container's layout delegate uses that **Array** to display children. A child element can be accessed from this display list using its elemental index, and the order in which the children are displayed can be manipulated by changing these indexes.

In the following example, a child element at the lowest index within the display list is promoted to the highest index using the `setElementIndex()` method of an `IVisual ElementContainer` implementation, consequentially updating the layout of the other children in the `HorizontalLayout`:

```
<s:Application xmlns:fx="http://ns.adobe.com/mxml/2009"
               xmlns:s="library://ns.adobe.com/flex/spark"
               xmlns:mx="library://ns.adobe.com/flex/mx">

    <fx:Script>
        <![CDATA[
            private function reorder():void
            {
                myContent.setElementIndex( myContent.getElementAt(0),
                                            myContent.numElements - 1 );
            }
        ]]>
    </fx:Script>

    <s:layout>
        <s:VerticalLayout />
    </s:layout>

    <s:Group id="myContent">
        <s:layout>
            <s:HorizontalLayout />
        </s:layout>
```

```
        <s:Button id="btn1" label="button 1" />
        <s:DropDownList />
        <s:Button id="btn2" label="button 2" />

    </s:Group>

    <s:Button label="reorder" click="reorder();" />

</s:Application>
```

The reference to the first element within the display list of the s:Group is accessed using the getElementAt() method of the content API. The child element is moved from the front of the list to the end, and the order in which all child elements are rendered is updated on the layout.

The rendering order can also be manipulated at runtime using the swapElements() method, which takes two references to IVisualElement implementations:

```
    myContent.swapElements( btn1, btn2 );
```

The swapElementsAt() method swaps the indexes of two elements of a visual container based on the specified index positions:

```
    myContent.swapElements( 0, 2 );
```

Although a layout will render children sequentially from the list, do not confuse the elemental index of a child with its depth property when considering display. The depth property of an IVisualElement implementation represents the layer position of the child within the layout. Its value is not tied to the length of the child display list, and multiple children can share the same depth. Manipulating the depths therefore differs from manipulating the indexes of children within the display list, in that assigning an index that has already been assigned or is out of the current range (from 0 to the highest assigned index + 1) will throw a runtime exception.

The elemental index and the depth property of a child element may not visually affect the layout of children when using sequential layouts, such as HorizontalLayout and VerticalLayout, but it's important to understand the concepts of rendering order and layer depth when using BasicLayout or a custom layout. To help you understand how the depth property of an element affects the layout, the following example displays the first declared s:Button control on a layer above the second declared s:Button:

```
    <s:Group id="myContent">

        <s:Button depth="100" label="button 1" />
        <s:Button label="button 2" />

    </s:Group>
```

Although the elemental index of the second s:Button control in the display list is greater than that of the first, the first s:Button is rendered before the second and placed on a

---

higher layer within the default `BasicLayout` due to the assigned `depth` property value. The default value of the `depth` property is 0.

2.4 Display Children Using Data Items

Problem

You want to supply to a container an array of data items to be visually represented using item renderers.

Solution

Use the `DataGroup` container, and set the `dataProvider` property to an `IList` implementation and the `itemRenderer` property to the qualified class name of an `IDataRenderer` implementation.

Discussion

The `DataGroup` layout container utilizes item rendering for visual elements represented as data items. Unlike with the `Group` container, which handles visual elements declared directly in MXML or through methods of the content API, an `IList` implementation (`mx.collections.ArrayCollection` or `mx.collections.XMLListCollection`, for example) is supplied to a `DataGroup` container, and an item renderer handles the visual representation of each data item in the collection. Included in the Flex 4 SDK are two convenient item renderer classes that can be used to easily present data items visually: `spark.skins.DefaultItemRenderer` presents data textually, while `spark.skins.Default ComplexItemRenderer` renders data items that are implementations of `IVisualElement`, such as the components from the Spark and MX sets.

In the following example, an array of textual data is supplied to a `DataGroup` and rendered using the `DefaultItemRenderer`:

```
<fx:Declarations>
    <fx:String id="txt">
        Lorem ipsum dolor sit amet consectetur adipisicing elit.
    </fx:String>
</fx:Declarations>

<s:DataGroup itemRenderer="spark.skins.spark.DefaultItemRenderer">

    <s:layout>
        <s:HorizontalLayout />
    </s:layout>

    <s:dataProvider>
        <s:ArrayCollection source="{txt.split(' ')}" />
    </s:dataProvider>

</s:DataGroup>
```

The data items in the `dataProvider` of the `DataGroup` are positioned horizontally from left to right and rendered using the supplied `itemRenderer`. The value of the `itemRenderer` property, a qualified class name, is used internally by the `DataGroup` container to create a new instance of the specified class for each data item in the collection. If the class is an `IDataRenderer` implementation, the `data` property of the implementation is updated with the item within the collection at the time of instantiation.

The `DefaultComplexItemRenderer` class can also be used to easily render `IVisualEle` ment data within a `DataGroup` container:

```
<fx:Declarations>
    <fx:String id="txt">
        Lorem ipsum dolor sit amet consectetur adipisicing elit.
    </fx:String>
</fx:Declarations>

<s:DataGroup itemRenderer="spark.skins.spark.DefaultComplexItemRenderer">

    <s:layout>
        <s:VerticalLayout />
    </s:layout>

    <s:dataProvider>
        <s:ArrayCollection>
            <s:Label text="Using DefaultComplexItemRenderer." />
            <s:Button label="button 1" />
            <s:DropDownList dataProvider="{new ArrayCollection(txt.split(' '))}" />
            <s:CheckBox selected="true" />
            <mx:Button label="button 2" />
        </s:ArrayCollection>
    </s:dataProvider>

</s:DataGroup>
```

When the `itemRenderer` property is set to the `DefaultComplexItemRenderer` class, the `DataGroup` internally determines each data item to be an `IVisualElement` implementation and renders the items directly on the display.

Unlike from a `Group` container, child elements cannot be accessed directly from a `Data Group` container. Although the child elements of both a `Group` and a `DataGroup` are `IVisualElement` implementations, the `Group` class exposes a content API through its implementation of the `IVisualElementContainer` interface that enables you to dynamically add, remove, and set the indexes of elements directly in the container. The display list of a `DataGroup` can be altered using the `IList` instance set as the `dataProvider` property value for the container. Because the `dataProvider` property supports binding, the collection can be affected directly at runtime to update the display of visual elements dynamically.

As item renderers are added to and removed from the display list of a `DataGroup` container, `RendererExistenceEvent` objects are dispatched. The properties of a `RendererExistenceEvent` instance correspond to the item renderer instance, the data supplied to the item renderer, and the elemental index within the display list at which it resides.

The following example demonstrates how to dynamically change the display list of a DataGroup container and listen for the addition and removal of item renderer instances:

```
<s:Application xmlns:fx="http://ns.adobe.com/mxml/2009"
               xmlns:s="library://ns.adobe.com/flex/spark"
               xmlns:mx="library://ns.adobe.com/flex/mx">
    <fx:Script>
        <![CDATA[
            import spark.events.RendererExistenceEvent;
            import mx.collections.ArrayCollection;

            private function itemAdded( evt:RendererExistenceEvent ):void
            {
                trace( "Item Added: " + evt.index + " : " + evt.data +
                    " : " + evt.renderer );
            }
            private function itemRemoved( evt:RendererExistenceEvent ):void
            {
                trace( "Item Removed: " + evt.index + " : " + evt.data +
                    " : " + evt.renderer );
            }

            private function addItem():void
            {
                if( collection.length > 0 )
                    myContent.dataProvider.addItem( collection.removeItemAt(0) );
            }
            private function removeItem():void
            {
                if( myContent.dataProvider.length > 0 )
                {
                    var item:Object = myContent.dataProvider.removeItemAt(
                        myContent.dataProvider.length - 1 );
                    collection.addItem( item );
                }
            }
        ]]>
    </fx:Script>

    <fx:Declarations>
        <fx:String id="txt">
            Lorem ipsum dolor sit amet consectetur adipisicing elit.
        </fx:String>
        <s:ArrayCollection id="collection">
            <s:Label text="Using DefaultComplexItemRenderer." />
            <s:Button label="button 1" />
            <s:DropDownList dataProvider="{new ArrayCollection(txt.split(' '))}" />
            <s:CheckBox selected="true" />
            <mx:Button label="button 2" />
        </s:ArrayCollection>
    </fx:Declarations>
```

```
<s:layout>
    <s:VerticalLayout />
</s:layout>

<s:DataGroup id="myContent"
            rendererAdd="itemAdded(event);"
            rendererRemove="itemRemoved(event);"
            itemRenderer="spark.skins.spark.DefaultComplexItemRenderer">

    <s:layout>
        <s:HorizontalLayout />
    </s:layout>

    <s:dataProvider>
        <s:ArrayCollection />
    </s:dataProvider>

</s:DataGroup>

<s:Button label="add" click="addItem();" />
<s:Button label="remove" click="removeItem();" />

</s:Application>
```

2.5 Use a Custom Item Renderer in a DataGroup

Problem

You want to use a custom item renderer to render data items visually within a DataGroup.

Solution

Create a custom component that implements the IVisualElement and IDataRenderer interfaces and supply the class as the itemRenderer property value for a DataGroup container.

Discussion

The DataGroup container handles making visual representations of data items. In order to properly render visual elements in the display list of a DataGroup and for its layout delegate to handle the size and position of those children, item renderers need to implement at least two interfaces: IVisualElement and IDataRenderer. The layout delegate of a container attributes the visual elements as IVisualElement implementations. The implementation type is also attributed when dispatching RendererExistenceEvents. Implementing the IDataRenderer interface for a custom item renderer exposes the data property, which is used internally by the DataGroup to supply data items to the renderer.

Along with the convenient `DefaultItemRenderer` and `DefaultComplexItemRenderer` classes provided in the Flex 4 SDK, Adobe provides a convenience base class for item renderers to be used with `DataGroup` containers. The item renderer base class—aptly named `ItemRenderer`—is an extension of `spark.components.DataRenderer`, which is a `Group` container that exposes a `data` property, fulfilling the contract of an item renderer being an implementation of `IVisualElement` and `IDataRenderer`. In addition, `spark.components.supportClasses.ItemRenderer` also provides extra support for styling, states, and event handling and is a good jumping-off point for creating a custom item renderer.

The following custom item renderer is an extension of `ItemRenderer` and displays the `firstName` and `lastName` property values of the supplied data item:

```
<s:ItemRenderer xmlns:fx="http://ns.adobe.com/mxml/2009"
                xmlns:s="library://ns.adobe.com/flex/spark"
                xmlns:mx="library://ns.adobe.com/flex/mx"
                width="100%" height="24">

    <s:states>
        <s:State name="normal" />
        <s:State name="hovered" />
    </s:states>

    <s:Rect width="100%" height="100%">
        <s:fill>
            <s:SolidColor color="0xDDDDDD" color.hovered="0xDDDDFF" />
        </s:fill>
    </s:Rect>

    <s:Group width="100%" height="100%">

        <s:layout>
            <s:HorizontalLayout verticalAlign="middle" />
        </s:layout>

        <s:Label text="{data.lastName}," />
        <s:Label text="{data.firstName}" />

    </s:Group>

</s:ItemRenderer>
```

Because `ItemRenderer` is an extension of `Group`, visual elements can be declared directly on the display for visual representation. In this example, two `s:Label` components are laid out horizontally and placed above a background `s:Rect` graphic element that updates its `color` property based on state. When creating a custom item renderer by extending the `ItemRenderer` class, remember that the item renderer manages its current state internally. You can override the `getCurrentRendererState()` method to specify how the current state is determined, but in general the extending class will need to at least declare a `normal` state.

In this example, the background color is updated in response to the current state using dot notation for color property values inline. The CustomItemRenderer created in the previous example is applied to a DataGroup using the itemRenderer property to present visual representations of data from an IList collection:

```
<s:Application xmlns:fx="http://ns.adobe.com/mxml/2009"
               xmlns:s="library://ns.adobe.com/flex/spark"
               xmlns:mx="library://ns.adobe.com/flex/mx"
               xmlns:f4cb="com.oreilly.f4cb.*">

    <fx:Script>
        <![CDATA[
            private var authors:XML =
                    <authors>
                        <author>
                            <firstName>Josh</firstName>
                            <lastName>Noble</lastName>
                        </author>
                        <author>
                            <firstName>Garth</firstName>
                            <lastName>Braithwaite</lastName>
                        </author>
                        <author>
                            <firstName>Todd</firstName>
                            <lastName>Anderson</lastName>
                        </author>
                    </authors>;
        ]]>
    </fx:Script>

    <s:DataGroup width="200"
                itemRenderer="com.oreilly.f4cb.CustomItemRenderer">

        <s:layout>
            <s:VerticalLayout />
        </s:layout>

        <s:dataProvider>
            <s:XMLListCollection source="{authors..author}" />
        </s:dataProvider>

    </s:DataGroup>

</s:Application>
```

As the collection of XML data is iterated through, a new instance of CustomItem Renderer is created and its data property is attributed to the current data item in the iteration.

If a namespace is declared for the package where a custom item renderer resides, the itemRenderer property of the DataGroup container can also be set using MXML markup, as in the following example:

```
<s:DataGroup width="200">

    <s:layout>
        <s:VerticalLayout />
    </s:layout>

    <s:dataProvider>
        <s:XMLListCollection source="{authors..author}" />
    </s:dataProvider>

    <s:itemRenderer>
        <fx:Component>
            <f4cb:CustomItemRenderer />
        </fx:Component>
    </s:itemRenderer>

</s:DataGroup>
```

2.6 Use Multiple Item Renderers in a DataGroup

Problem

You want to use more than one type of item renderer for a collection of data items in a DataGroup container.

Solution

Use the itemRendererFunction property to specify a callback method that will return an item renderer based on the data item.

Discussion

When working with a collection of data items in a DataGroup container, the itemRenderer and itemRendererFunction properties are used to specify the visual representation of elements. Using the itemRenderer property, instances of a single item renderer class are created and optionally recycled when rendering data elements. Assigning a factory method to the itemRendererFunction property of the DataGroup affords more control over the type of item renderer used for a data element.

The return type of the method specified for the itemRendererFunction property is IFactory. As item renderers are created for data elements internally within the DataGroup, item renderers are instantiated using the newInstance() method of the IFactory implementation that is returned. The following is an example of a method attributed as an itemRendererFunction for a DataGroup container:

```
private function getItemRenderer( item:Object ):IFactory
{
    var clazz:Class;
    switch( item.type )
    {
```

```
            case "normal":
                clazz = NormalRenderer;
                break;
            case "special":
                clazz = SpecialRenderer;
                break;
        }
        return new ClassFactory( clazz );
    }
```

Depending on the type of data element provided to the `itemRendererFunction`, a specific item renderer is returned. Any method specified as an `itemRendererFunction` must adhere to the method signature shown in this example. The single argument, of type `Object`, is the current data element within the collection being iterated through and is attributed as the `dataProvider` property of the `DataGroup`. The return type, as mentioned previously, is of type `IFactory`. The `ClassFactory` class is an implementation of `IFactory`, and class declarations are passed to its constructor and used to instantiate new instances of the class when the `newInstance()` method is invoked.

The following example demonstrates setting a method delegate for the `itemRenderer Function` property of a `DataGroup` container:

```
<s:Application xmlns:fx="http://ns.adobe.com/mxml/2009"
               xmlns:s="library://ns.adobe.com/flex/spark"
               xmlns:mx="library://ns.adobe.com/flex/mx">

    <fx:Declarations>
        <s:ArrayCollection id="animalList">
            <fx:Object type="dog" name="Walter" />
            <fx:Object type="cat" name="Zoe" />
            <fx:Object type="dog" name="Cayuga" />
            <fx:Object type="dog" name="Pepper" />
        </s:ArrayCollection>
    </fx:Declarations>

    <fx:Script>
        <![CDATA[
            import com.oreilly.f4cb.DogItemRenderer;
            import com.oreilly.f4cb.CatItemRenderer;
            import spark.skins.spark.DefaultItemRenderer;

            private function getItemRenderer( item:Object ):IFactory
            {
                var clazz:Class;
                switch( item.type )
                {
                    case "dog":
                        clazz = DogItemRenderer;
                        break;
                    case "cat":
                        clazz = CatItemRenderer;
                        break;
```

```
                    default:
                        clazz = DefaultItemRenderer;
                        break;
                }
                return new ClassFactory( clazz );
            }
        ]]>
    </fx:Script>

    <s:DataGroup width="200" height="150"
                dataProvider="{animalList}"
                itemRendererFunction="getItemRenderer">

        <s:layout>
            <s:VerticalLayout paddingTop="5" paddingBottom="5"
                            paddingLeft="5" paddingRight="5" />
        </s:layout>

    </s:DataGroup>

    <s:Rect width="200" height="150">
        <s:stroke>
            <s:SolidColorStroke color="#000000" />
        </s:stroke>
    </s:Rect>

</s:Application>
```

As the items of the `dataProvider` collection are iterated through, the `getItemRenderer()` factory method is invoked and, based on the `type` property of the passed-in data item, a custom item renderer is returned. If the data type is not found, the `spark.skins.spark.DefaultItemRenderer` class of the Flex 4 SDK is returned.

It is important to note that, though a `DataGroup` can support virtualization through its layout delegate, an item renderer returned using `itemRendererFunction` is instantiated each time the delegate method is invoked and not inherently recycled as elements are added to and removed from the display list.

See Also

Recipe 2.5

2.7 Enable Scrolling in a Container

Problem

You want to add scrolling capabilities to a container whose child elements are positioned outside of the defined viewport bounds.

Solution

Wrap a `Group` or `DataGroup` container in an instance of `spark.components.Scroller` and define the dimensions and `clipAndEnableScrolling` property of the container, or assign a container as the `viewport` property of a `spark.components.ScrollBar` instance.

Discussion

Unlike MX containers, which support scrolling internally, the separation of responsibilities within the Spark architecture provides more lightweight containers and affords more control over delegating tasks. Within the new Spark paradigm, you can assign specific controls that handle navigating within a container. The `spark.components.supportClasses.GroupBase` class, which both `DataGroup` and `Group` extend, is an implementation of the `IViewport` interface. By default, the `clipAndEnableScrolling` property of a `GroupBase`-based container is set to `false` and the container renders child elements outside of any specified bounds. Setting the `clipAndEnableScrolling` property to `true` and wrapping the `IViewport` instance in a `Scroller` component renders child elements within a defined area and updates the read-only `contentWidth` and `contentHeight` properties of the container to the specified dimensions.

To enable scrolling for an `IViewport`, the container can be wrapped in a `Scroller` instance with the declared child container attributed as the `viewport` property value:

```
<fx:Declarations>
    <fx:String id="txt">
        Lorem ipsum dolor sit amet consectetur adipisicing elit.
    </fx:String>
</fx:Declarations>

<s:Scroller>

    <s:DataGroup width="100" height="100"
                 clipAndEnableScrolling="true"
                 itemRenderer="spark.skins.spark.DefaultItemRenderer">

        <s:layout>
            <s:VerticalLayout />
        </s:layout>

        <s:dataProvider>
            <s:ArrayCollection source="{txt.split(' ')}" />
        </s:dataProvider>

    </s:DataGroup>

</s:Scroller>
```

Any data elements that are rendered outside of the viewport bounds of a container explicitly set using the `width` and `height` properties are displayed based on the scrolling properties of the `s:Scroller` component. Based on the positions of the child elements within the container viewport, a `VScrollBar` control and a `HScrollBar` control are added to the display. The scroll bars are positioned at the viewport's `width` and `height` property values, unless you specify custom values for the `Scroller` instance's `width` and `height` properties.

Containers that support skinning, such as `BorderContainer`, `SkinnableContainer`, and `SkinnableDataContainer`, do not implement the `IViewport` interface. However, the content layer to which child elements are added for each skinnable container is attributed as an `IViewport` implementation. As such, you have a couple of options for enabling scrolling of child content in a skinnable container.

The skin part that serves as the content layer for a `BorderContainer` and a `Skinnable Container` is the `contentGroup`. When children are declared for a skinnable container directly in MXML markup, the child elements are added and laid out within the content layer. One way to enable scrolling of the content is to declare an `IViewport` implementation wrapped in a `Scroller` component as the only child of the skinnable container, as in the following example:

```
<s:BorderContainer width="120" height="100" backgroundColor="#FFFFFF">
    <s:Scroller width="100%" height="100%">
        <s:Group>
            <s:layout>
                <s:VerticalLayout horizontalAlign="justify"
                                  clipAndEnableScrolling="true" />
            </s:layout>
            <s:Button label="button (1)" />
            <s:Button label="button (2)" />
            <s:Button label="button (3)" />
            <s:Button label="button (4)" />
            <s:Button label="button (5)" />
            <s:Button label="button (6)" />
        </s:Group>
    </s:Scroller>
</s:BorderContainer>
```

The `Scroller`-wrapped `Group` declared as the only child for the `BorderContainer` is added as the only child within the `contentGroup` for the container. Scrolling is not applied to the `contentGroup` layer specifically, but because its only child element is a `Group` container wrapped in a `Scroller` whose dimensions are updated to equal the dimensions of the skinnable container, it appears as if the content for the `BorderContainer` is made scrollable.

Another approach to providing scrolling for the content of a skinnable container is to apply a custom skin to the container that wraps its content-layer skin part in a `Scroller`. This is a custom skin for a `SkinnableDataContainer`:

```
<s:Skin xmlns:fx="http://ns.adobe.com/mxml/2009"
        xmlns:s="library://ns.adobe.com/flex/spark"
        name="CustomScrollableSkin">

    <fx:Metadata>
        <![CDATA[
            [HostComponent("spark.components.SkinnableDataContainer")]
```

```
            ]]>
        </fx:Metadata>

        <s:states>
            <s:State name="normal" />
            <s:State name="disabled" />
        </s:states>

        <s:Rect width="100%" height="100%">
            <s:stroke>
                <s:SolidColorStroke color="#000000" />
            </s:stroke>
            <s:fill>
                <s:SolidColor color="#FFFFFF" />
            </s:fill>
        </s:Rect>

        <s:Scroller width="100%" height="100%"
            left="2" right="2" top="2" bottom="2">
            <s:DataGroup id="dataGroup"
                        left="0" right="0" top="0" bottom="0"
                        minWidth="0" minHeight="0" />
        </s:Scroller>

    </s:Skin>
```

The `CustomScrollableSkin` fulfills a contract to serve as a skin to a `Skinnable` `DataContainer` by declaring the [HostComponent] metadata and required states. Also declared is the required skin part, `dataGroup`, which is the content layer for item renderers and is wrapped in a `s:Scroller` component to enable scrolling within the container.

The custom skin is supplied to the skinnable container as a qualified class name attributed to the `skinClass` property, as in the following example:

```
    <fx:Declarations>
        <fx:String id="txt">
            Lorem ipsum dolor sit amet consectetur adipisicing elit.
        </fx:String>
    </fx:Declarations>

    <s:SkinnableDataContainer width="120" height="100"
                            itemRenderer="spark.skins.spark.DefaultItemRenderer"
                            skinClass="com.oreilly.f4cb.CustomScrollableSkin">
        <s:layout>
            <s:VerticalLayout />
        </s:layout>

        <s:dataProvider>
            <s:ArrayCollection source="{txt.split(' ')}" />
        </s:dataProvider>
    </s:SkinnableDataContainer>
```

The ability to use a `Scroller` to enable scrolling of content within containers is a major convenience. The skin layout of a `Scroller` component is a private implementation, however, and the skin parts for the scroll bars are considered read-only. To have more control over the layout and the relationship between a viewport and scroll bars, add a `ScrollBar`-based control to the display list directly and assign an instance of a target container as the `viewport` property value:

```
<s:Application xmlns:fx="http://ns.adobe.com/mxml/2009"
               xmlns:s="library://ns.adobe.com/flex/spark"
               xmlns:mx="library://ns.adobe.com/flex/mx">

    <fx:Declarations>
        <fx:String id="txt">
            Lorem ipsum dolor sit amet consectetur adipisicing elit.
        </fx:String>
    </fx:Declarations>

    <s:layout>
        <s:HorizontalLayout />
    </s:layout>

    <s:DataGroup id="group" width="100" height="100"
                 clipAndEnableScrolling="true"
                 itemRenderer="spark.skins.spark.DefaultItemRenderer">

        <s:layout>
            <s:VerticalLayout />
        </s:layout>

        <s:dataProvider>
            <s:ArrayCollection source="{txt.split(' ')}" />
        </s:dataProvider>

    </s:DataGroup>

    <s:VScrollBar viewport="{group}" height="100" />

</s:Application>
```

In this example, a `DataGroup` is attributed as the `IViewport` implementation instance of a `s:VScrollBar` control. The thumb size of the scroll bar is based on the `height` of the scroll bar and the `contentHeight` value of the target container. As the scroll position changes on the scroll bar, the `verticalScrollPosition` value is passed down to the `IViewport` implementation and handed to the layout delegate for the container.

While wrapping a container with a `Scroller` internally detects the need for scroll bars based on the content of the container and dimensions of its viewport, with this approach you have less control over the layout with relation to the target viewport. Targeting a container using scroll bars declared directly on the display list allows more control over the layout, but its visibility is not inherently set based on the content Width and `contentHeight` of a viewport. The visibility of a scroll bar control can, however, be determined based on the container's dimensions and its `viewport` counterpart value, as in the following example for updating the visibility of a `s:VScrollBar` control:

```
<s:VScrollBar viewport="{group}" height="100"
              visible="{group.height &lt; group.contentHeight}" />
```

When the `clipAndEnableScrolling` property of an `IViewport` implementation is set to `true`, the read-only `contentWidth` and `contentHeight` properties are set based on the bounds of the container's display list. By comparing the defined `height` property of the viewport with the `contentHeight`, the visibility and necessity of the `VScrollBar` control in this example can be determined.

See Also

Recipe 3.13

2.8 Scale Children of a Container

Problem

You want to resize, scale, and lay out the child elements of a container based on the dimensions of the container.

Solution

Use the `resizeMode` property of a `GroupBase`-based container.

Discussion

Layout delegates applied to `Group` and `DataGroup` containers have properties that modify the layout and size of child elements directly or through transformations. Additionally, the layout of children can be modified based on the `resizeMode` property value of `GroupBase`-based containers that take the size of the container into consideration. The default value of the `resizeMode` property is `noScale`, which specifies that the container resizes itself and children are subsequently resized based on the properties of the layout delegate. The child content of a container can be scaled uniformly by setting the `resizeMode` property value to `scale`, which bases the layout of its children on the measured size of the container.

The following example demonstrates switching between the two resize modes within a `Group` container:

```
<s:Application xmlns:fx="http://ns.adobe.com/mxml/2009"
               xmlns:s="library://ns.adobe.com/flex/spark"
               xmlns:mx="library://ns.adobe.com/flex/mx">

    <fx:Script>
        <![CDATA[
            import mx.events.SliderEvent;
```

```
                import spark.components.ResizeMode;

                private function toggleResizeMode():void
                {
                    group.resizeMode = ( group.resizeMode == ResizeMode.NO_SCALE )
                                    ? group.resizeMode = ResizeMode.SCALE
                                    : group.resizeMode = ResizeMode.NO_SCALE;
                }
            ]]>
        </fx:Script>

        <s:layout>
            <s:VerticalLayout />
        </s:layout>

        <s:Group id="group"
                 width="{slider.value}" height="{slider.value}"
                 resizeMode="{ResizeMode.NO_SCALE}">

            <s:layout>
                <s:TileLayout orientation="columns" />
            </s:layout>

            <s:Button label="button" />
            <s:Rect width="100" height="100">
                <s:fill>
                    <s:SolidColor color="#DDDDDD" />
                </s:fill>
            </s:Rect>
            <s:DropDownList />
            <s:Ellipse>
                <s:fill>
                    <s:SolidColor color="#FF5500" />
                </s:fill>
            </s:Ellipse>

        </s:Group>

        <s:HSlider id="slider"
                   width="120"
                   minimum="100" maximum="300"
                   value="300"
                   liveDragging="true" />

        <s:Button label="toggle resize" click="toggleResizeMode();" />

    </s:Application>
```

As the value of the s:HSlider control changes, the dimensions of the container are
reflected through binding. The resizeMode is changed when a click event is received
from the s:Button control, swapping between the scale and noScale modes enumerated
in the ResizeMode class.

The TileLayout delegate applied to the Group container has an orientation property
value specifying that children should be laid out in columns based on the dimensions

of the container. As the width and height of the container change, the layout is based on the amount of space available within the container to display children within a grid of columns and rows. With the resizeMode set to noScale, children are sized based on their defined or inherited properties within the layout. When the resizeMode property is set to scale, the child elements are scaled to fill the dimensions of the container, while still adhering to the column/row rules of the layout delegate.

2.9 Apply Skins to a Container

Problem

You want to customize the look and feel of a container that holds visual elements or data items.

Solution

Use either a SkinnableContainer or a BorderContainer as a container for visual child elements and a SkinnableDataContainer as a container for data items, and modify the available style properties.

Discussion

The Group and DataGroup containers are considered lightweight containers and as such do not support skinning or expose style properties. To customize the look of a container, the Flex 4 SDK offers the SkinnableContainer, BorderContainer, and Skinnable DataContainer classes. Which you use depends on the type of content provided to the container. The SkinnableContainer and BorderContainer take instances of IVisual Element as child elements; think of them as Group containers that support skinning. The SkinnableDataContainer can be considered a DataGroup container that supports skinning and uses item renderers to display visual representations of data items.

BorderContainer is actually a subclass of SkinnableContainer and is a convenient container to use if you want to apply border and background styles directly without applying a custom skin. You can set border styles (such as cornerRadius and border Color) inline within the MXML declaration for the container, or through Cascading Style Sheet (CSS) style declarations. The following example demonstrates setting the border styles of a BorderContainer for IVisualElement children:

```
<s:BorderContainer width="200" height="200"
                cornerRadius="10" borderColor="#000000"
                borderWeight="2" borderStyle="inset">

    <s:layout>
        <s:VerticalLayout paddingLeft="5" paddingTop="5" paddingBottom="5"
                        paddingRight="5" horizontalAlign="justify" />
    </s:layout>
```

```
    <s:Label text="Lorem ipsum dolor sit amet consectetur adipisicing elit." />
    <s:Button label="click me" />

</s:BorderContainer>
```

Alternatively, you can supply an `IStroke` instance for the `borderStroke` property of a `BorderContainer`. The following example sets a `borderStroke` on a `BorderContainer` through MXML markup:

```
<s:BorderContainer width="200" height="200"
                   cornerRadius="10" borderStyle="inset">

    <s:layout>
        <s:VerticalLayout paddingLeft="5" paddingTop="5" paddingBottom="5"
                          paddingRight="5" horizontalAlign="justify" />
    </s:layout>

    <s:Label text="Lorem ipsum dolor sit amet consectetur adipisicing elit." />
    <s:Button label="click me" />

    <s:borderStroke>
        <s:SolidColorStroke color="#0000" weight="2" />
    </s:borderStroke>

</s:BorderContainer>
```

The `s:SolidColorStroke` element supplied as the `borderStroke` for the `BorderCon tainer` overrides any previously declared color or weight style properties. However, because the `IStroke` interface does not expose a `cornerRadius` or `borderStyle` property, some border style properties need to be provided directly to the `BorderContainer` if they are desired. Because `BorderContainer` is an extension of `SkinnableContainer`, skinning is also supported along with the border convenience styles.

Custom skin classes are set on the `SkinnableContainerBase`-based containers (such as `BorderContainer`) through the `skinClass` property, whose value can be set either inline using MXML markup or via CSS, because `skinClass` is considered a style property. When you create a custom skin for a container, the skin is entering into a contract with the container to provide the necessary skin parts and states for the host. These skin parts are referenced using an agreed-upon `id` property value and, depending on the type of skinnable container, relate to content layers for visual elements.

To create a custom skin for a skinnable container, extend the `spark.skins.SparkSkin` class and declare the `HostComponent` metadata and necessary state and skin part elements. The following is an example of a custom skin fulfilling a contract to be applied to a `SkinnableContainer`:

```
<s:SparkSkin name="CustomGroupSkin"
             xmlns:fx="http://ns.adobe.com/mxml/2009"
             xmlns:s="library://ns.adobe.com/flex/spark"
             xmlns:mx="library://ns.adobe.com/flex/mx">
```

```
<fx:Metadata>
    [HostComponent("spark.components.SkinnableContainer")]
</fx:Metadata>

<s:states>
    <s:State name="normal" />
    <s:State name="disabled" />
</s:states>

<s:Rect width="100%" height="100%">
    <s:fill>
        <s:LinearGradient>
            <s:entries>
                <s:GradientEntry color="0xFF0000" />
                <s:GradientEntry color="0x00FF00" />
                <s:GradientEntry color="0x0000FF" />
            </s:entries>
        </s:LinearGradient>
    </s:fill>
    <s:fill.disabled>
        <s:RadialGradient>
            <s:entries>
                <s:GradientEntry color="0xFF0000" />
                <s:GradientEntry color="0x00FF00" />
                <s:GradientEntry color="0x0000FF" />
            </s:entries>
        </s:RadialGradient>
    </s:fill.disabled>
</s:Rect>

<s:Group id="contentGroup"
         width="100%" height="100%"
         left="10" right="10" top="10" bottom="10">

    <s:layout>
        <s:VerticalLayout horizontalAlign="justify" />
    </s:layout>

</s:Group>

</s:SparkSkin>
```

The CustomGroupSkin declares the type of container component that the skin will be applied to within the [HostComponent] metatag. In this example the host component is a SkinnableContainer, and as such contains a Group container with the id property value of contentGroup. The contentGroup property of SkinnableContainer is considered a skin part and represents the content layer on which visual child elements are drawn. Along with the host component and contentGroup, contractual states are declared to represent the enabled and disabled visual states of the container. You can declare additional states as needed, but at a minimum, normal and disabled need to be added to the available states to support the enabled property of the container. Styles can be applied to elements based on these states, as is shown using inline dot notation for the `fill` type of the `s:Rect` element.

To apply the custom skin to a `SkinnableContainer` instance, set the `skinClass` style property to a `Class` reference either inline or using CSS. The following example applies the `CustomGroupSkin` skin inline using a fully qualified class name:

```
<s:Application xmlns:fx="http://ns.adobe.com/mxml/2009"
               xmlns:s="library://ns.adobe.com/flex/spark"
               xmlns:mx="library://ns.adobe.com/flex/mx">

    <s:layout>
        <s:VerticalLayout />
    </s:layout>

    <s:SkinnableContainer id="container"
                          width="200" height="200"
                          skinClass="com.oreilly.f4cb.CustomGroupSkin">

        <s:Label text="Lorem ipsum dolor sit amet consectetur adipisicing elit." />
        <s:Button label="button (1)" />
        <s:DropDownList />

    </s:SkinnableContainer>

    <s:Button label="enable container"
              click="{container.enabled=!container.enabled}" />

</s:Application>
```

When applying a custom skin, the layout can be set within the skin class (as in this example). It should be noted, however, that if a layout is applied to a container directly in MXML markup, that layout will override any layout supplied to the content layer declared in the skin.

Creating a custom skin for a `SkinnableDataContainer` that uses data elements to represent children is similar to creating a custom skin for a `SkinnableContainer` instance. The difference between the two involves the type of host component declaration and skin part reference. The following custom skin declares the host component references as the `SkinnableDataContainer` class and contains a `DataGroup` container with the reference `id` of `dataGroup`:

```
<s:SparkSkin name="CustomDataGroupSkin"
             xmlns:fx="http://ns.adobe.com/mxml/2009"
             xmlns:s="library://ns.adobe.com/flex/spark"
             xmlns:mx="library://ns.adobe.com/flex/mx">

    <fx:Metadata>
        [HostComponent("spark.components.SkinnableDataContainer")]
    </fx:Metadata>
```

```
        <s:states>
            <s:State name="normal" />
            <s:State name="disabled" />
        </s:states>

        <s:Rect width="100%" height="100%">
            <s:fill>
                <s:LinearGradient>
                    <s:entries>
                        <s:GradientEntry color="0xFF0000" />
                        <s:GradientEntry color="0x00FF00" />
                        <s:GradientEntry color="0x0000FF" />
                    </s:entries>
                </s:LinearGradient>
            </s:fill>
            <s:fill.disabled>
                <s:RadialGradient>
                    <s:entries>
                        <s:GradientEntry color="0xFF0000" />
                        <s:GradientEntry color="0x00FF00" />
                        <s:GradientEntry color="0x0000FF" />
                    </s:entries>
                </s:RadialGradient>
            </s:fill.disabled>
        </s:Rect>

        <s:Scroller width="100%" height="100%">
            <s:DataGroup id="dataGroup"
                        width="100%" height="100%">

                <s:layout>
                    <s:VerticalLayout paddingLeft="10" paddingRight="10"
                                      paddingTop="10" paddingBottom="10" />
                </s:layout>

            </s:DataGroup>
        </s:Scroller>

    </s:SparkSkin>
```

The `CustomDataGroupSkin` fulfills a contract with `SkinnableDataContainer` to provide a `DataGroup` instance as the content layer for data elements supplied to the skinnable container. With the host component metatag and necessary states declared, the custom skin is applied to a `SkinnableDataContainer` through the `skinClass` style property:

```
<s:Application xmlns:fx="http://ns.adobe.com/mxml/2009"
               xmlns:s="library://ns.adobe.com/flex/spark"
               xmlns:mx="library://ns.adobe.com/flex/mx">

    <fx:Declarations>
        <fx:String id="txt">
            Lorem ipsum dolor sit amet consectetur adipisicing elit.
        </fx:String>
    </fx:Declarations>
```

```
        <s:layout>
            <s:VerticalLayout />
        </s:layout>

        <s:SkinnableDataContainer id="container" width="200" height="200"
                                  itemRenderer="spark.skins.spark.DefaultItemRenderer"
                                  skinClass="com.oreilly.fcb4.CustomDataGroupSkin">

            <s:dataProvider>
                <s:ArrayCollection
                id="collection" source="{txt.split(' ')}" />
            </s:dataProvider>

        </s:SkinnableDataContainer>

        <s:Button label="enable container"
                click="{container.enabled=!container.enabled}" />

    </s:Application>
```

The full extent of skinning and styling possibilities that the Flex 4 SDK provides is discussed in Chapter 6, but these examples demonstrate the basic contractual agreement that custom skins must fulfill when working with `SkinnableContainerBase`-based containers.

2.10 Set the Background Image of a BorderContainer

Problem

You want to set the background image of a `BorderContainer` and control how the graphic is applied as a fill.

Solution

Use either the background image style properties of the `BorderContainer` or the `backgroundFill` property to apply a `BitmapFill` directly.

Discussion

The `BorderContainer` is a convenience container for `IVisualElement` child elements that exposes style properties pertaining to the border and background displays of a container not found directly on its superclass, the `SkinnableContainer`. When using a `SkinnableContainer`, border and background styles are handled by a skin class applied to the container. The `BorderContainer` class provides style properties for the border and background that can be set inline in MXML markup or through CSS; it also provides two properties, `borderStroke` and `backgroundImage`, that allow you to apply styles using graphic elements.

The following example demonstrates setting the style properties for a background image inline on a `BorderContainer`:

```
<s:BorderContainer width="200" height="200"
                   cornerRadius="10" borderStyle="inset"
                   backgroundImage="@Embed(source='background.jpg')"
                   backgroundImageFillMode="{BitmapFillMode.REPEAT}">

    <s:layout>
        <s:VerticalLayout paddingLeft="5" paddingTop="5" paddingBottom="5"
                          paddingRight="5" horizontalAlign="justify" />
    </s:layout>

    <s:Label text="Lorem ipsum dolor sit amet consectetur adipisicing elit." />
    <s:Button label="click me" />

</s:BorderContainer>
```

Alternatively, the style properties of a `BorderContainer` can be applied using CSS and set using the `styleName` property:

```
<fx:Style>
    @namespace s "library://ns.adobe.com/flex/spark";
    @namespace mx "library://ns.adobe.com/flex/mx";

    .imageBorder {
        backgroundImage: Embed(source='background.jpg');
        backgroundImageFillMode: repeat;
    }
</fx:Style>

<s:BorderContainer width="200" height="200"
                   cornerRadius="10" borderStyle="inset"
                   styleName="imageBorder">

    <s:layout>
        <s:VerticalLayout paddingLeft="5" paddingTop="5" paddingBottom="5"
                          paddingRight="5" horizontalAlign="justify" />
    </s:layout>

    <s:Label text="Lorem ipsum dolor sit amet consectetur adipisicing elit." />
    <s:Button label="click me" />

</s:BorderContainer>
```

In the previous examples, an image from the local resource is embedded and supplied as the `backgroundImage` style property value. The fill mode for the image is set using the `backgroundImageFillMode` style property, which can take three values—`clip`, `scale`, and `repeat`—all of which are enumerated properties of the `BitmapFillMode` class. When a background image is styled with clipping, the image is rendered at its original dimensions within the container. A background image with a `scale` value for the fill mode is scaled to the dimensions of the container, and the `repeat` value repeats the image in a grid to fill the container region. Each background image fill mode also takes into account the container display when the `cornerRadius` style property is set.

Background image styles can also be applied using the `backgroundFill` property of a `BorderContainer`. The `backgroundFill` property takes an implementation of the `IFill` interface and will override any background style properties that have been set. You can assign to the `backgroundFill` property a `BitmapFill` instance that exposes a `fillMode` property that you can use to apply the same styling you might do with the style properties of a `BorderContainer`:

```
<s:BorderContainer width="200" height="200"
                   cornerRadius="10" borderStyle="inset">

    <s:layout>
        <s:VerticalLayout paddingLeft="5" paddingTop="5" paddingBottom="5"
                          paddingRight="5" horizontalAlign="justify" />
    </s:layout>

    <s:Label text="Lorem ipsum dolor sit amet consectetur adipisicing elit." />
    <s:Button label="click me" />

    <s:backgroundFill>
        <s:BitmapFill source="@Embed('background.jpg')"
                      fillMode="{BitmapFillMode.REPEAT}" />
    </s:backgroundFill>

</s:BorderContainer>
```

2.11 Use a Control Bar

Problem

You want to add a control bar to an `Application` or `Panel` container.

Solution

Use `controlBarContent` to add visual elements to a control bar group, and use `control BarLayout` to define the layout for the control bar group.

Discussion

Both the `Application` and `Panel` containers support the addition of a control bar group by declaring an array of `IVisualElement` instances as the value of the `control BarContent` property. The `contentBarGroup` property is a `Group` container whose default property value for child elements is the `controlBarContent` property. Visual elements declared in MXML markup are added to the group to display a control bar, as in the following example:

```
<s:Application xmlns:fx="http://ns.adobe.com/mxml/2009"
               xmlns:s="library://ns.adobe.com/flex/spark"
               xmlns:mx="library://ns.adobe.com/flex/mx">

    <fx:Declarations>
        <s:ArrayCollection
                id="authors" source="{['Josh Noble',
                'Garth Braithwaite', 'Todd Anderson']}" />
    </fx:Declarations>

    <s:Panel title="Control Bar Example" width="300" height="120">

        <s:controlBarContent>
            <s:DropDownList id="authorCB" width="120" dataProvider="{authors}" />
            <s:Button label="select"
                      click="{printField.text=authorCB.selectedItem}" />
        </s:controlBarContent>

        <s:Group width="100%" height="100%">
            <s:Label id="printField" horizontalCenter="0" verticalCenter="0" />
        </s:Group>

    </s:Panel>

</s:Application>
```

The s:DropDownList and s:Button controls are displayed in a control bar on the bottom region of the Panel container, and upon the receipt of a click event from the Button, the selected item from the DropDownList is printed in the s:Label component of the content group for the Panel.

Panel and Application each have a default layout for the optional control bar when it is added to the display list that has predefined constraints and displays child elements in a horizontal sequence. The layout of the control bar can be modified using the controlBarLayout property:

```
<s:controlBarLayout>
    <s:VerticalLayout horizontalAlign="justify" />
</s:controlBarLayout>
```

Any LayoutBase-based layout can be attributed as a controlBarLayout. In this example, all IVisualElement instances from the controlBarContent list will be added to the control bar group in a vertical sequence and resized to the elemental region width-wise within the group.

When a control bar is added to an Application, it resides by default in the upper region of the Application container. The contentBarGroup property is considered a skin part, allowing for the location and style of the control bar to be modified by setting a custom skin.

2.12 Modify Layout of Content Elements in a Panel

Problem

You want to modify the default layout of the content elements in the display list of a `Panel` container.

Solution

Create a custom skin class that fulfills the contract of a skin for a `Panel` component and set it as the `skinClass` property value. Within the custom skin, modify the layout and declaration of skin parts to change the display of the control bar and content.

Discussion

By default, the `layout` property of a `Panel` is applied to the `contentGroup` skin part, which is the group of visual elements that are displayed between the title bar and optional control bar of the container. The `Panel`'s default skin class handles the layout of the title bar, content group, and control bar, ordering them in a top-down fashion. You can modify the position and size of each of these content elements by providing a custom skin class to the `Panel` using the `skinClass` property.

When creating a custom skin, you must ensure that the skin adheres to a contractual agreement with the target host component and declares any required states and content references, referred to as *skin parts*. The `titleDisplay` and `contentGroup` skin parts refer to the title bar and main content display regions of a panel. The optional `content BarGroup` skin part refers to the control bar. When creating a custom skin class for a `Panel` container that supports a control bar, you must declare all three skin parts as well as the corresponding states of `normal`, `disabled`, `normalWithControlBar`, and `disabled WithControlBar`, as in the following example:

```
<s:SparkSkin name="CustomPanelSkin"
             xmlns:fx="http://ns.adobe.com/mxml/2009"
             xmlns:s="library://ns.adobe.com/flex/spark"
             xmlns:mx="library://ns.adobe.com/flex/mx">

    <s:states>
        <s:State name="normal" />
        <s:State name="normalWithControlBar" />
        <s:State name="disabled" />
        <s:State name="disabledWithControlBar" />
    </s:states>

    <fx:Metadata>
        [HostComponent("spark.components.Panel")]
    </fx:Metadata>

    <s:RectangularDropShadow id="shadow" alpha="0" />

    <!-- Border -->
```

```
<s:Rect left="0" right="0" top="0" bottom="0">
    <s:stroke>
        <s:SolidColorStroke color="0" alpha="0.5" weight="1" />
    </s:stroke>
</s:Rect>

<!-- Background -->
<s:Rect id="background" left="1" top="1" right="1" bottom="1">
    <s:fill>
        <s:SolidColor color="0xFFFFFF" />
    </s:fill>
</s:Rect>

<!-- Content -->
<s:Group width="100%" height="100%" top="1" left="1" right="1" bottom="1">

    <s:layout>
        <s:VerticalLayout gap="0" horizontalAlign="justify" />
    </s:layout>

    <!-- Control Bar -->
    <s:Group>
        <s:Rect width="100%" height="30">
            <s:fill>
                <s:SolidColor color="0xCCCCCC" />
            </s:fill>
        </s:Rect>
        <s:Group id="controlBarGroup"
                left="5" right="5" top="5" bottom="5"
                minWidth="0" minHeight="0" height="30">
            <s:layout>
                <s:HorizontalLayout />
            </s:layout>
        </s:Group>
    </s:Group>

    <!-- Content -->
    <s:Scroller width="100%" height="100%" >
        <s:Group id="contentGroup" />
    </s:Scroller>

    <!-- Title Bar -->
    <s:Group>
        <s:Rect width="100%" height="30">
            <s:fill>
                <s:SolidColor color="0xEEEEEE" />
            </s:fill>
        </s:Rect>
        <s:Label id="titleDisplay" lineBreak="toFit"
            left="10" height="30" verticalAlign="middle"
            fontWeight="bold" />
    </s:Group>
```

```
        </s:Group>

    </s:SparkSkin>
```

CustomPanelSkin is an extension of spark.skins.SparkSkin. It enters into a contract with spark.components.Panel (the host component declared in the [HostComponent] metatag) to expose the content elements for the title, content group, and control bar and any necessary elements for display. The default layout of the target panel in this example is changed by positioning the control bar at the top and the title bar at the bottom. These content elements are declared as controlBarGroup and titleDisplay, respectively, within a Group container with a VerticalLayout.

Visual elements provided in the controlBarContent property of a panel are added to the controlBarGroup skin part, and visual elements added directly to the panel are displayed in the contentGroup skin part. The title property value of the Panel container is printed out in the titleDisplay component. To apply a custom skin to a Panel, set the skin Class property value to the fully qualified name of the custom skin class, as in the following example:

```
<s:Application xmlns:fx="http://ns.adobe.com/mxml/2009"
               xmlns:s="library://ns.adobe.com/flex/spark"
               xmlns:mx="library://ns.adobe.com/flex/mx">

    <fx:Declarations>
        <s:ArrayCollection
                id="authors" source="{['Josh Noble',
                'Garth Braithwaite', 'Todd Anderson']}" />
    </fx:Declarations>

    <s:Panel title="Control Bar Example"
             width="300" height="120"
             skinClass="com.oreilly.f4cb.CustomPanelSkin">

        <s:controlBarContent>
            <s:DropDownList id="authorCB" width="120" dataProvider="{authors}" />
            <s:Button label="select"
                      click="{printField.text=authorCB.selectedItem}" />
        </s:controlBarContent>

        <s:Group width="100%" height="100%">
            <s:Label id="printField" verticalCenter="0" horizontalCenter="0" />
        </s:Group>

    </s:Panel>

</s:Application>
```

The full extent of skinning and style possibilities available in the Flex 4 SDK is discussed in Chapter 6, but the examples presented here demonstrate the basic contractual agreement that a custom skin class must adhere to in order to modify the look and feel of a panel containing an optional control bar group display.

2.13 Track Mouse Position Within a Container

Problem

You want to keep track of the mouse position within a container for visual elements.

Solution

Add an event handler for a mouse gesture event and use the `contentMouseX` and `contentMouseY` properties to retrieve the mouse position within the container, regardless of the position of the interactive element that dispatched the event.

Discussion

When an event handler for a mouse gesture is declared for an event on a container, a `MouseEvent` object is passed to the method with the `localX` and `localY` properties attributed to the mouse position within the interactive element that originally dispatched the event. `UIComponent`-based elements have `contentMouseX` and `content MouseY` read-only properties that relate to the mouse position within those elements, regardless of its position within any child elements. Because the properties are read-only, their values cannot be bound to. You can retrieve these values within an event handler for a mouse gesture, as in the following example:

```
<s:Application xmlns:fx="http://ns.adobe.com/mxml/2009"
               xmlns:s="library://ns.adobe.com/flex/spark"
               xmlns:mx="library://ns.adobe.com/flex/mx">

    <fx:Library>
        <fx:Definition name="RadialBox">
            <s:Rect width="100" height="100">
                <s:fill>
                    <s:LinearGradient>
                        <s:entries>
                            <s:GradientEntry color="0xFF0000" />
                            <s:GradientEntry color="0x00FF00" />
                            <s:GradientEntry color="0x0000FF" />
                        </s:entries>
                    </s:LinearGradient>
                </s:fill>
            </s:Rect>
        </fx:Definition>
        <fx:Definition name="LinearBox">
            <s:Rect width="100" height="100">
                <s:fill>
                    <s:RadialGradient>
                        <s:entries>
                            <s:GradientEntry color="0xFF0000" />
                            <s:GradientEntry color="0x00FF00" />
                            <s:GradientEntry color="0x0000FF" />
                        </s:entries>
                    </s:RadialGradient>
```

```
                    </s:fill>
                </s:Rect>
            </fx:Definition>
        </fx:Library>

        <fx:Script>
            <![CDATA[
                import mx.graphics.SolidColor;
                private var bmd:BitmapData;

                private function handleGroupCreation():void
                {
                    bmd = new BitmapData(group.contentWidth, group.contentHeight);
                    bmd.draw( group );
                }
                private function handleMouseMove( evt:MouseEvent ):void
                {
                    var xpos:int = group.contentMouseX;
                    var ypos:int = group.contentMouseY;
                    var rectColor:SolidColor = new SolidColor(bmd.getPixel(xpos,
                                                                          ypos));

                    chip.fill = rectColor;

                    contentLocalPoint.text = "Content Local: " + xpos + " : " + ypos;
                    mouseLocalPoint.text = "Mouse Local: " + evt.localX + " : "
                                            + evt.localY;
                }

            ]]>
        </fx:Script>

        <s:layout>
            <s:VerticalLayout />
        </s:layout>

        <s:Group id="group"
                 creationComplete="handleGroupCreation();"
                 mouseMove="handleMouseMove(event);">

            <s:layout>
                <s:HorizontalLayout gap="2" verticalAlign="middle" />
            </s:layout>

            <fx:RadialBox />
            <s:Button label="button (1)" />
            <fx:LinearBox />

        </s:Group>

        <s:Label id="contentLocalPoint" />
        <s:Label id="mouseLocalPoint" />

        <s:Rect id="chip" width="30" height="30">
            <s:stroke>
                <s:SolidColorStroke color="0x000000" />
```

```
        </s:stroke>
      </s:Rect>

   </s:Application>
```

As each mouseMove event is received in the Group container, the handleMouseMove() method is invoked and the fill color value for the s:Rect graphic element is updated based on the pixel color under the mouse cursor using the contentMouseX and content MouseY properties. Two s:Label components print out the mouse position in its relation to the container and the interactive element, such as the s:Button control, that first dispatched the event. Because graphic elements are not considered interactive (and thus do not dispatch mouse events), the local mouse positions printed out will be the same as the content mouse positions when the cursor is over a graphic element.

The contentMouseX and contentMouseY properties represent the mouse position within the target UIComponent-based element, including regions that are only accessible through scrolling. The global mouse position with regards to any layout constraints applied to the container itself can be retrieved using the contentToGlobal() method:

```
   var pt:Point = group.contentToGlobal( new Point( group.contentMouseX,
                                                     group.contentMouseY ) );
   globalPoint.text = "Global Point: " + pt.x + " : " + pt.y;
```

Likewise, any global point can be converted to content-local coordinates using the globalToContent() method of a UIComponent-based component.

2.14 Drag and Drop Between Visual Containers

Problem

You want to enable drag-and-drop capabilities so you can move visual elements between containers.

Solution

Enable any interactive visual element as a drag initiator by assigning a mouseDown event handler to the element and enable any container as a drag recipient by assigning it drag-and-drop event handlers. Upon invocation of the mouseDown handler, assign the relevant data to a DragSource instance to be handed to the DragManager. When entering a dragEnter event for the drop target, determine the acceptance of a drop operation on the container based on the appropriate data. Once a drop container has accepted a dragDrop event, remove the dragged visual element from its owner and add it to the target drop container.

Discussion

Drag-and-drop support can be added to any element that extends mx.core.UICompo nent. Within a drag-and-drop operation there is an initiator and a receiver. Any instance of `UIComponent` can receive the series of operations initiated by a drag gesture and dispatch events accordingly; these events include `dragEnter`, `dragExit`, `dragOver`, `dragDrop`, and `dragComplete`.

To initialize a drag-and-drop gesture, add data relevant to the drag-and-drop operation to a `DragSource` object within a `mouseDown` event handler. The `DragSource` object is given to the `DragManager` through the static `doDrag()` method. The `DragSource` object held by the `DragManager` is used to determine the acceptance of a drop event on a target container and is handled in the `dragDrop` event handler to perform the appropriate action.

The following example demonstrates moving children from one visual element container to another:

```
<s:Application xmlns:fx="http://ns.adobe.com/mxml/2009"
               xmlns:s="library://ns.adobe.com/flex/spark"
               xmlns:mx="library://ns.adobe.com/flex/mx">

    <fx:Script>
        <![CDATA[
            import mx.core.IUIComponent;
            import mx.managers.DragManager;
            import mx.core.DragSource;
            import spark.components.SkinnableContainer;
            import mx.events.DragEvent;
            import mx.core.IVisualElement;

            private function handleStartDrag( evt:MouseEvent ):void
            {
                // grab the item renderer and relevant data
                var dragItem:IUIComponent = evt.target as IUIComponent;
                var dragSource:DragSource = new DragSource();
                dragSource.addData( dragItem, "item" );
                DragManager.doDrag( dragItem, dragSource, evt );
            }

            protected function handleDragEnter( evt:DragEvent ):void
            {
                if( evt.dragSource.hasFormat( "item" ) )
                    DragManager.acceptDragDrop( evt.target as IUIComponent );
            }

            protected function handleDragDrop( evt:DragEvent ):void
            {
                var dragItem:Object = evt.dragSource.dataForFormat( "item" );
                var dragItemOwner:SkinnableContainer = ( dragItem.owner as
                                                        SkinnableContainer );
                dragItemOwner.removeElement( dragItem as IVisualElement );

                var targetOwner:SkinnableContainer = ( evt.target as
                                                       SkinnableContainer );
                targetOwner.addElement( dragItem as IVisualElement );
            }
        ]]>
    </fx:Script>
```

```
<s:SkinnableContainer width="200" height="180"
                      dragEnter="handleDragEnter(event);"
                      dragDrop="handleDragDrop(event);"
                      skinClass="com.oreilly.f4cb.CustomBorderSkin">
    <s:layout>
        <s:HorizontalLayout />
    </s:layout>
    <s:Button label="drag me (1)" mouseDown="handleStartDrag(event);" />
    <s:Button label="drag me (2)" mouseDown="handleStartDrag(event);" />
    <s:Button label="drag me (3)" mouseDown="handleStartDrag(event);" />
</s:SkinnableContainer>

<s:SkinnableContainer x="210" width="200" height="180"
                      dragEnter="handleDragEnter(event);"
                      dragDrop="handleDragDrop(event);"
                      skinClass="com.oreilly.f4cb.CustomBorderSkin">
    <s:layout>
        <s:VerticalLayout />
    </s:layout>
    <s:Button label="drag me (4)" mouseDown="handleStartDrag(event);" />
    <s:Button label="drag me (5)" mouseDown="handleStartDrag(event);" />
    <s:Button label="drag me (6)" mouseDown="handleStartDrag(event);" />
</s:SkinnableContainer>

</s:Application>
```

When a s:Button control in the display list of either of the SkinnableContainers dispatches a mouseDown event, the handleStartDrag() method is invoked and a Drag Source object is added to the DragManager. The static doDrag() method of the DragManager initiates a drag-and-drop gesture. It requires at least three arguments: the drag initiator item reference, a DragSource object, and the initiating MouseEvent. The image rendered during a drag operation is a rectangle with alpha transparency, by default. The dragged image (referred to as a *drag proxy*) can be changed through the dragImage and imageAlpha arguments of the doDrag() method.

Assigning event handlers for dragEnter and dragDrop events identifies the containers as targets for the drag-and-drop actions initiated by the Button controls. Within the handleDragEnter() method, the data format is evaluated to see whether the target container accepts drop actions. The static acceptDragDrop() method of the DragManager registers the container as a drop target. Once a container is accepted as a receiver for drag-and-drop actions, any subsequent actions associated with the gesture are passed to the container and the appropriate events are dispatched. Within the dragDrop event handler, the drag initiator held on the DragSource object of the operation is used to remove that object from its current owner container and add it to the target drop container.

Though the previous example demonstrates using the default operation of moving an element from one container to another, it is possible to implement a copy operation. The following example demonstrates copying a visual element from one container to another without allowing the initiating owner to receive a drop operation:

```
<s:Application xmlns:fx="http://ns.adobe.com/mxml/2009"
               xmlns:s="library://ns.adobe.com/flex/spark"
               xmlns:mx="library://ns.adobe.com/flex/mx">

    <fx:Script>
        <![CDATA[
            import spark.components.Button;
            import mx.managers.DragManager;
            import mx.core.DragSource;
            import spark.components.SkinnableContainer;
            import mx.events.DragEvent;
            import mx.core.IVisualElement;
            import mx.core.IUIComponent;

            private function handleStartDrag( evt:MouseEvent ):void
            {
                // grab the item renderer and relevant data
                var dragItem:Button = evt.target as Button;
                var transferObject:Object = {label:dragItem.label,
                                             owner:dragItem.owner};
                var dragSource:DragSource = new DragSource();
                dragSource.addData( transferObject, "item" );
                DragManager.doDrag( dragItem, dragSource, evt, null, 0, 0, 0.5,
                                    false );
            }

            protected function handleDragEnter( evt:DragEvent ):void
            {
                if( evt.dragSource.hasFormat( "item" ) )
                {
                    var targetOwner:SkinnableContainer = ( evt.target as
                                                           SkinnableContainer );
                    var transferObject:Object = evt.dragSource.dataForFormat(
                                                                "item" );
                    if( targetOwner != transferObject.owner )
                    {
                        DragManager.acceptDragDrop( evt.target as IUIComponent );
                    }
                }
            }

            protected function handleDragDrop( evt:DragEvent ):void
            {
                var transferObject:Object = evt.dragSource.dataForFormat( "item" );
                var dragItem:Button = new Button();
                dragItem.label = transferObject.label;

                var targetOwner:SkinnableContainer = ( evt.target as
                                                       SkinnableContainer );
                targetOwner.addElement( dragItem as IVisualElement );
            }
        ]]>
    </fx:Script>

    <s:SkinnableContainer width="200" height="180"
```

```
                    dragEnter="handleDragEnter(event);"
                    dragDrop="handleDragDrop(event);"
                    skinClass="com.oreilly.f4cb.CustomBorderSkin">
        <s:layout>
            <s:HorizontalLayout />
        </s:layout>
        <s:Button label="drag me (1)" mouseDown="handleStartDrag(event);" />
        <s:Button label="drag me (2)" mouseDown="handleStartDrag(event);" />
        <s:Button label="drag me (3)" mouseDown="handleStartDrag(event);" />
    </s:SkinnableContainer>

    <s:SkinnableContainer x="210" width="200" height="180"
                    dragEnter="handleDragEnter(event);"
                    dragDrop="handleDragDrop(event);"
                    skinClass="com.oreilly.f4cb.CustomBorderSkin">
        <s:layout>
            <s:VerticalLayout />
        </s:layout>
        <s:Button label="drag me (4)" mouseDown="handleStartDrag(event);" />
        <s:Button label="drag me (5)" mouseDown="handleStartDrag(event);" />
        <s:Button label="drag me (6)" mouseDown="handleStartDrag(event);" />
    </s:SkinnableContainer>

</s:Application>
```

When the mouseDown event handler is invoked, a generic object representing the initiating s:Button (with any appropriate property values preserved) is created and passed as the data transfer object of the DragSource instance. The handleDragEnter event handler is used not only to determine the validity of the drag initiator, but also to see if the source and target of the operation are the same. If so, no further drag-and-drop operations are allowed on the container that dispatched the dragEnter event. If the target container is a valid receiver for the drag-and-drop action, the handleDragDrop() method is invoked and a new Button control is created based on the generic object of the DragSource and is added to the target container.

Using the DragManager is a convenient way to move and copy visual elements from one container to another. If you need more control over the drag-and-drop operation, however, you can transfer elements from one container to another using mouse event handlers and methods of the content API, such as addElement() and removeElement().

2.15 Drag and Drop Between Data Containers

Problem

You want to enable drag-and-drop capabilities between multiple DataGroup containers so you can easily add and remove data items.

Solution

Assign a `mouseDown` event handler to item renderers as they are added to a `DataGroup` container and assign drag-and-drop event handlers to any receiving data containers. Upon receipt of the `mouseDown` event, assign the data held on the target item renderer as the `DataSource` handled by the `DragManager` to initiate the drag-and-drop operation. Use the data from the `DataSource` object to determine the acceptance of a drop gesture for the target container as drag events are dispatched and, when the `dragDrop` event is received, remove the dragged data from the collection of the initiating container and add the data to the collection of the target drop container.

Discussion

Within a drag-and-drop operation, there is an initiator and a receiver. The initiator begins the drag-and-drop operation by invoking the static `doDrag()` method of the `DragManager`, typically in response to a user gesture such as a `mouseDown` event. Any `UIComponent`-based element can be a receiver of drag-and-drop gestures and dispatch events accordingly. Some list-based components in the Flex SDK, such as `List`, have built-in support for managing drag-and-drop operations to help automate the process of moving data from one container to another or within a container itself. `DataGroup` and `SkinnableDataContainer` do not have built-in support, but they can be enabled to receive drag-and-drop operations as they are extensions of `UIComponent`.

The example for this recipe is split up into two parts, a view and a controller, to better demonstrate how to programmatically move data from one data container's collection to another. The view is an extension of an ActionScript-based controller and is made up of two scroll-enabled `s:SkinnableDataContainer` containers with their own specified data collections and `itemRenderer` instances:

```
<ApplicationViewController xmlns="*"
                           xmlns:fx="http://ns.adobe.com/mxml/2009"
                           xmlns:s="library://ns.adobe.com/flex/spark"
                           xmlns:mx="library://ns.adobe.com/flex/mx">
    <fx:Script>
        <![CDATA[
            import com.oreilly.f4cb.CustomScrollableSkin;
        ]]>
    </fx:Script>

    <fx:Declarations>
        <s:ArrayCollection id="collectionOne">
            <s:Button label="button (1)" />
            <s:Button label="button (2)" />
            <s:Button label="button (3)" />
        </s:ArrayCollection>
        <s:ArrayCollection id="collectionTwo">
            <s:Button label="button (4)" />
            <s:Button label="button (5)" />
            <s:Button label="button (6)" />
        </s:ArrayCollection>
```

```
        </fx:Declarations>

        <layout>
            <s:HorizontalLayout />
        </layout>

        <s:SkinnableDataContainer width="160" height="140"
                                  rendererAdd="handleRendererAdd(event)"
                                  dataProvider="{collectionOne}"
                                  dragEnter="handleDragEnter(event);"
                                  dragDrop="handleDragDrop(event);"
                                  itemRenderer="spark.skins.spark.
                                                 DefaultComplexItemRenderer"
                                  skinClass="com.oreilly.f4cb.CustomScrollableSkin">
            <s:layout>
                <s:VerticalLayout paddingLeft="5" paddingRight="5"
                                  paddingTop="5" paddingBottom="5" />
            </s:layout>
        </s:SkinnableDataContainer>

        <s:SkinnableDataContainer width="160" height="140"
                                  rendererAdd="handleRendererAdd(event)"
                                  dataProvider="{collectionTwo}"
                                  dragEnter="handleDragEnter(event);"
                                  dragDrop="handleDragDrop(event);"
                                  itemRenderer="spark.skins.spark.DefaultItemRenderer"
                                  skinClass="com.oreilly.f4cb.CustomScrollableSkin">
            <s:layout>
                <s:HorizontalLayout paddingLeft="5" paddingRight="5"
                                    paddingTop="5" paddingBottom="5" />
            </s:layout>
        </s:SkinnableDataContainer>

    </ApplicationViewController>
```

The collection for each `SkinnableDataContainer` container is a set of `s:Button` controls. The containers' `itemRenderer` instances differ in how they render data on the content layer: the first declared container renders each button with its skin intact by assigning the `DefaultCompleteItemRenderer` class as the item renderer, while the second declared container renders only the label assigned to the button control by assigning the `DefaultItemRenderer` class as the item renderer.

The `handleRendererAdd()` method is assigned as an event handler for `rendererAdd`. Similar to the `elementAdd` and `elementRemove` events of the content API, `DataGroup` and `SkinnableDataContainer` dispatch `rendererAdd` and `rendererRemove` events whenever an element representing a data object from the collection is added to or removed from the content layer of the container, respectively. Event handlers for the `dragEnter` and `drag` `Drop` events are assigned to each container in order to handle those specific operations during a drag-and-drop operation:

```
package
{
    import flash.display.DisplayObjectContainer;
    import flash.events.MouseEvent;

    import mx.collections.IList;
    import mx.core.DragSource;
    import mx.core.IUIComponent;
    import mx.core.IVisualElement;
    import mx.events.DragEvent;
    import mx.managers.DragManager;

    import spark.components.Application;
    import spark.components.Group;
    import spark.components.SkinnableDataContainer;
    import spark.components.supportClasses.ItemRenderer;
    import spark.events.RendererExistenceEvent;

    public class ApplicationViewController extends Application
    {
        private var dragItem:Group;

        protected function handleRendererAdd( evt:RendererExistenceEvent ):void
        {
            // assign weak reference listener to visual item renderer
            var item:IVisualElement = evt.renderer;
            ( item as DisplayObjectContainer ).mouseChildren = false;
            item.addEventListener( MouseEvent.MOUSE_DOWN, handleStartDrag, false,
                                   0, true );
        }

        private function handleStartDrag( evt:MouseEvent ):void
        {
            // grab the item renderer and relevant data
            var target:UIComponent = evt.target as UIComponent;
            var dragItem:Object = {owner:target.owner,
                                   data:( target as
                                   IDataRenderer ).data};
            var dragSource:DragSource = new DragSource();
            dragSource.addData( dragItem, "itemRenderer" );
            DragManager.doDrag( target, dragSource, evt );
        }

        protected function handleDragEnter( evt:DragEvent ):void
        {
            if( evt.dragSource.hasFormat( "itemRenderer" ) )
                DragManager.acceptDragDrop( evt.target as IUIComponent );
        }

        protected function handleDragDrop( evt:DragEvent ):void
        {
            var dragItem:Object = evt.dragSource.dataForFormat( "itemRenderer" );
            var ownerCollection:IList = ( dragItem.owner as
                                          SkinnableDataContainer ).dataProvider;
            ownerCollection.removeItemAt( ownerCollection.getItemIndex(
```

```
                                      dragItem.data ) );

            var targetCollection:IList = ( evt.target as
                                    SkinnableDataContainer ).dataProvider;
            targetCollection.addItem( dragItem.data );
        }
    }
}
```

The event object for a `rendererAdd` event dispatched from a `DataGroup` or a `Skinnable DataContainer` is a `RendererExistenceEvent`. The item renderer that dispatched the event can be referenced using the `renderer` property of the event object and is attributed as an `IVisualElement`. In this example, a weak-referenced `mouseDown` event handler is assigned to the item renderer upon receipt of a `rendererAdd` event by the `Application ViewController` and is attributed as the `handleStartDrag()` method.

When the `mouseDown` event handler is invoked, the initiating element is attributed as a `UIComponent` instance and a generic `Object` is created to hold the `data` property assigned to the element during instantiation. The generic `Object` is assigned as the drag data on a `DragSource` object, which is passed into the `DragManager` to initiate a drag-and-drop operation. When the dragged item enters the content layer of a container, the `dragEnter` event handler assigned to that container is invoked and is used to determine whether the data being dragged is acceptable for the container, using the static `accept DragDrop()` method of `DragManager`. If the container is accepted as a receiver, the `drag Drop` event handler is invoked upon a drop operation. Upon an accepted drop operation, the generic `Object` handled by the `DragSource` is used to remove the dragged data from the collection of its original container and add it to the collection of the drop target container.

Using the `DragManager` is a convenient way to move data items from one container to another. However, if more control over the operation is needed, data items can be transferred between containers or within a single container using the mouse event handlers and methods of the collections API, such as `addItem()`, `addItemAt()`, and `removeItem()`.

2.16 Add a Spark Layout Container to a MX Navigation Container

Problem

You want to add visual components from the Spark set to a MX navigation container.

Solution

Add a Spark `NavigatorContent` container as a child of the desired MX navigation container. Elements from both the Spark and MX component sets can be added as children to the `NavigatorContent` container.

Discussion

Although it is recommended to use Spark containers in preference to MX containers because of their improved runtime performance and separation of responsibilities, the two sets do not have identical navigation containers in the Flex 4 SDK. Consequently, depending on development requirements, use of MX navigation containers may be necessary. Containers and components from the Spark set cannot be declared directly as content for Halo containers, however, because child containers are attributed as implementations of `INavigatorContent`.

To add Spark elements to a MX container, they must be added to a `NavigatorContent` container as in the following example:

```
<s:Application xmlns:fx="http://ns.adobe.com/mxml/2009"
               xmlns:s="library://ns.adobe.com/flex/spark"
               xmlns:mx="library://ns.adobe.com/flex/mx">

    <mx:Accordion width="300" height="300" headerHeight="50">
        <s:NavigatorContent label="Container 1"
                            width="100%" height="100%">
            <s:layout>
                <s:VerticalLayout />
            </s:layout>
            <s:Button />
            <s:Ellipse width="100" height="100">
                <s:fill>
                    <s:SolidColor color="0xFFCCFF" />
                </s:fill>
            </s:Ellipse>
            <s:DropDownList />
        </s:NavigatorContent>
        <s:NavigatorContent label="Container 2"
                            width="100%" height="100%">
            <s:layout>
                <s:HorizontalLayout />
            </s:layout>
            <s:CheckBox />
            <s:Rect width="100" height="100">
                <s:fill>
                    <s:SolidColor color="0xCCFFCC" />
                </s:fill>
            </s:Rect>
            <s:HSlider />
        </s:NavigatorContent>
    </mx:Accordion>

</s:Application>
```

NavigatorContent is an extension of SkinnableContainer and implements the INaviga
torContent interface. The INavigatorContent interface exposes common properties,
such as label and icon, for child content of MX navigation containers and extends
IDeferredContentOwner. The IDeferredContentOwner interface is an extension of
IUIComponent. It fulfills a contract for NavigatorContent, being a valid child of a navigation container from the MX set, and also allows for deferred instantiation of the
container. Because Spark containers support children from both the Spark and MX
component sets, elements from both architectures (including GraphicElement-based
elements) can be added to a NavigatorContent container.

2.17 Create a Spark-Based ViewStack

Problem

You want to create a container that holds multiple child containers that are lazily
instantiated upon request.

Solution

Create a custom GroupBase-based container and assign an Array-based property to the
[DefaultProperty] metatag for the container that represents the declared MXML children. Expose selectedIndex and selectedChild properties to represent the currently
displayed child container, and override the protected commitProperties() method to
add the appropriate child to the display list of the view stack.

Discussion

The Spark container set does not provide equal parity to the navigational containers in
the MX container set (such as Accordion and ViewStack). You can create Spark equivalents to these MX navigational containers, however, using the content API, as well as
state management and the new skinning capabilities of the Spark architecture.

The ViewStack container from the MX component set acts as a navigation container for
multiple child containers within a single display. As the selected container is changed,
the current container is removed from the display list of the ViewStack and replaced
with the requested container. Optionally, child containers can be lazily created using
what is referred to as *deferred instantiation*. Although the Spark container set does not
offer such a container, you can create a similar one, as shown in the following example:

```
package com.oreilly.f4cb
{
    import mx.core.IVisualElement;

    import spark.components.BorderContainer;
    import spark.events.IndexChangeEvent;

    [Event(name="change", type="spark.events.IndexChangeEvent")]
```

```
[DefaultProperty("content")]
public class CustomViewStack extends BorderContainer
{
    [ArrayElementType("mx.core.IVisualElement")]
    protected var _content:Array;
    protected var _selectedIndex:int = -1;
    protected var _selectedChild:IVisualElement
    protected var _pendingSelectedIndex:int = -1;

    override protected function commitProperties() : void
    {
        super.commitProperties();
        // if pending change to selectedIndex property
        if( _pendingSelectedIndex != -1 )
        {
            // commit the change
            updateSelectedIndex( _pendingSelectedIndex );
            // set pending back to default
            _pendingSelectedIndex = -1;
        }
    }

    protected function updateSelectedIndex( index:int ):void
    {
        // store old for event
        var oldIndex:int = _selectedIndex;
        // set new
        _selectedIndex = index;

        // remove old element
        if( numElements > 0 )
            removeElementAt( 0 );

        // add new element
        selectedChild = _content[_selectedIndex];
        addElement( _selectedChild );

        // dispatch index change
        var event:IndexChangeEvent = new IndexChangeEvent(
                            IndexChangeEvent.CHANGE,
                            false, false,
                            oldIndex, _selectedIndex );
        dispatchEvent( event );
    }

    private function getElementIndexFromContent( element:IVisualElement ):int
    {
        if( _content == null ) return -1;

        var i:int = _content.length;
        var contentElement:IVisualElement;
        while( --i > -1 )
        {
            contentElement = _content[i] as IVisualElement;
```

```
        if( contentElement == element )
        {
            break;
        }
    }
    return i;
}

[Bindable]
[ArrayElementType("mx.core.IVisualElement")]
public function get content():Array /*IVisualElement*/
{
    return _content;
}
public function set content( value:Array /*IVisualElement*/ ):void
{
    _content = value;
    // update selected index based on pending operations
    selectedIndex = _pendingSelectedIndex == -1 ? 0 :
                    _pendingSelectedIndex;
}

[Bindable]
public function get selectedIndex():int
{
    return selectedIndex = _pendingIndex == -1"
                "? 0"
                ": _pendingIndex
}
public function set selectedIndex( value:int ):void
{
    if( _selectedIndex == value ) return;

    _pendingSelectedIndex = value;
    invalidateProperties();
}

[Bindable]
public function get selectedChild():IVisualElement
{
    return _selectedChild;
}
public function set selectedChild( value:IVisualElement ):void
{
    if( _selectedChild == value ) return;

    // if not pending operation on selectedIndex, induce
    if( _pendingSelectedIndex == -1 )
    {
        var proposedIndex:int = getElementIndexFromContent( value );
        selectedIndex = proposedIndex;
    }
```

```
                // else just hold a reference for binding update
                else _selectedChild = value;
            }
        }
    }
```

The `content` property of the `CustomViewStack` in this example is an array of `IVisual Element`-based objects and is declared as the `[DefaultProperty]` value for the class. Consequently, any child elements declared within the MXML markup for a `Custom ViewStack` instance are considered elements of the array, and the view stack manages how those child elements are instantiated.

The `selectedIndex` and `selectedChild` properties are publicly exposed to represent the requested child to display within the custom view stack. Lazy creation of the child containers is accomplished by deferring instantiation of children to the first request to add a child to the display list using the `addElement()` method of the content API.

The `CustomViewStack` container can be added to an application in MXML markup just like any other container, as long as the namespace for the package in which it resides is defined:

```
<s:Application xmlns:fx="http://ns.adobe.com/mxml/2009"
               xmlns:s="library://ns.adobe.com/flex/spark"
               xmlns:mx="library://ns.adobe.com/flex/mx"
               xmlns:f4cb="com.oreilly.f4cb.*">

    <fx:Declarations>
        <fx:String id="lorem">
            Lorem ipsum dolor sit amet consectetur adipisicing elit.
        </fx:String>
    </fx:Declarations>

    <fx:Script>
        <![CDATA[
            private function changeIndex():void
            {
                var index:int = viewstack.selectedIndex;
                index = ( index + 1 > viewstack.content.length - 1 )
                        ? 0 :
                        index + 1;
                viewstack.selectedIndex = index;
            }
        ]]>
    </fx:Script>

    <s:layout>
        <s:VerticalLayout />
    </s:layout>

    <f4cb:CustomViewStack id="viewstack" width="300" height="300"
                        skinClass="com.oreilly.f4cb.CustomBorderSkin">
        <s:Group id="child1"
                width="800" height="100%"
                clipAndEnableScrolling="true">
```

```
            <s:layout>
                <s:VerticalLayout horizontalAlign="justify" />
            </s:layout>
            <s:Button label="top" />
            <s:Button label="bottom" bottom="0" />
        </s:Group>
        <s:Panel id="child2"
                width="100%" height="200"
                title="Child 2">
            <s:Scroller>
                <s:Group width="100%" height="100%">
                    <s:layout>
                        <s:VerticalLayout horizontalAlign="center" />
                    </s:layout>
                    <s:Button label="panel button 1" />
                    <s:Button label="panel button 2" />
                </s:Group>
            </s:Scroller>
        </s:Panel>
        <s:DataGroup id="child3"
                    width="100%" height="100%"
                    itemRenderer="spark.skins.spark.DefaultItemRenderer">
            <s:layout>
                <s:VerticalLayout />
            </s:layout>
            <s:dataProvider>
                <s:ArrayCollection source="{lorem.split(' ')}" />
            </s:dataProvider>
        </s:DataGroup>
    </f4cb:CustomViewStack>

    <s:Button label="switch index" click="changeIndex();" />

    <s:HGroup>
        <s:Button label="select child 1"
                enabled="{viewstack.selectedChild != child1}"
                click="{viewstack.selectedChild = child1}" />
        <s:Button label="select child 2"
                enabled="{viewstack.selectedChild != child2}"
                click="{viewstack.selectedChild = child2}" />
        <s:Button label="select child 3"
                enabled="{viewstack.selectedChild != child3}"
                click="{viewstack.selectedChild = child3}" />
    </s:HGroup>

</s:Application>
```

Children of the CustomViewStack are declared in markup, but they are added to the
defined [DefaultProperty] metatag and are not initially added to the display list of
the view stack. Instead, it is deferred to the container to create children as they are
requested using the selectedIndex and selectedChild properties. The selectedIndex
and selectedChild properties are bindable and allow for visual and functional updates
to the s:Button controls in the Application container for this example.

To enable scrolling within the view stack, a custom skin is applied that fulfills the contract for a `BorderContainer`-based container. A `Group` container with a reference `id` of `contentGroup` is declared and wrapped within a `Scroller` component, as in the following example:

```
<s:Skin xmlns:fx="http://ns.adobe.com/mxml/2009"
        xmlns:s="library://ns.adobe.com/flex/spark">

    <fx:Metadata>
        <![CDATA[
            [HostComponent("spark.components.BorderContainer")]
        ]]>
    </fx:Metadata>

    <s:states>
        <s:State name="normal" />
        <s:State name="disabled" />
    </s:states>

    <s:Rect width="100%" height="100%">
        <s:stroke>
            <s:SolidColorStroke color="#000000" />
        </s:stroke>
        <s:fill>
            <s:SolidColor color="#FFFFFF" />
        </s:fill>
    </s:Rect>

    <s:Scroller width="100%" height="100%"
            left="2" right="2" top="2" bottom="2">
        <s:Group id="contentGroup"
            left="0" right="0" top="0" bottom="0"
            minWidth="0" minHeight="0" />
    </s:Scroller>

</s:Skin>
```

This example demonstrates a technique for accomplishing deferred instantiation of child elements of a Spark-based navigation container that can be applied to creating equivalents of navigation containers from the MX set within the Flex 4 SDK.

CHAPTER 3

Layout

Visual elements of an application are sized and positioned within a parent container based on rules provided to and by a managing layout. The Flex Framework provides two sets of containers for layout: MX and Spark. The MX containers reside in the `mx.containers` package of the Flex Framework, while the Spark containers reside in the `spark.components` package. Though both container sets inherit from `UIComponent`, they differ in how they lay out and manage the children in their display lists.

Within a MX container (such as `Box`), the size and position of the children are managed by the container's layout rules and constraints, which are internally defined and based on specified properties and styles. In contrast, the Spark set provides a level of abstraction between the container and the layout and allows you to define the layout separately from the skin and style. The separation of the layout from the container not only provides greater flexibility in terms of runtime modifications but also cuts down on the rendering cycle for a container, as the style properties of a container may not be directly related to the layout. A Spark layout manages the size and positioning of the target container's child elements and is commonly referred to as the container's *layout delegate*. Commonly used layout classes for Spark containers, such as `VerticalLayout`, can be found in the `spark.layouts` package of the Flex Framework and are extensions of the base `LayoutBase` class.

When you provide a layout delegate to a Spark container, the `target` property of the layout is attributed as the targeted container and considered to be a `GroupBase`-based element. The containers available in the Spark set, such as `Group` and `DataGroup`, are extensions of `GroupBase` and provide a set of methods and properties for accessing their child elements. This set is commonly referred to as the *content API*. Containers that handle visual elements directly, such as `Group` and `SkinnableContainer`, expose methods and attributes of the content API by implementing the `IVisualElementContainer` interface. Containers that handle data items that are presented based on item renderers, such as `DataGroup` and `SkinnableDataContainer`, provide the same methods and attributes directly on their extensions of `GroupBase`. The layout delegate of a container uses the content API to access and manage that container's child elements.

Child elements accessed from the content API are attributed as implementations of the IVisualElement interface. This interface exposes implicit properties that allow you to access and modify common properties that relate to how the element is laid out and displayed in a container. IVisualElement is an extension of the ILayoutElement interface, which exposes constraint properties and accessor methods that layout delegates use to size and position children within a target container. With UIComponent implementing the IVisualElement interface, you can add elements from both the MX and Spark component sets to the display list of a Spark container and manage them using a layout delegate.

3.1 Position Children Linearly

Problem

You want to control the layout of children in a container, positioning them either horizontally or vertically.

Solution

Assign either HorizontalLayout or VerticalLayout to the layout property of the container, and set the desired alignment properties to the children along the axis of the specified layout.

Discussion

The HorizontalLayout and VerticalLayout classes are extensions of the spark.layout. LayoutBase class and lay out the child elements of a container in a horizontal or vertical sequence, respectively. Spark layouts handle only the size and position of child elements. Attributes related to dimension and positioning constraints are not available on Spark layouts; these are properties of the targeted Spark container.

You can define distances between child elements using the gap property of the HorizontalLayout and VerticalLayout classes. For example:

```
<s:Group>

    <s:layout>
        <s:VerticalLayout gap="10" />
    </s:layout>

    <s:TextInput text="hello world" />
    <s:Button label="click me" />

</s:Group>
```

The <s:Group> tag defines the parent Spark container, whose layout manager is specified as a VerticalLayout instance. This example lays out the child elements of the Group container vertically and distanced from each other by 10 pixels.

To position child elements relative to the container boundaries, assign values to the paddingLeft, paddingRight, paddingTop, and paddingBottom properties of the layout container, as shown here:

```
<s:Group>

    <s:layout>
        <s:HorizontalLayout gap="5"
                            paddingLeft="10" paddingRight="10"
                            paddingTop="10" paddingBottom="10" />
    </s:layout>

    <s:TextInput text="hello world" />
    <s:Button label="click me" />

</s:Group>
```

If you define a fixed or relative (using percent values) size for the container, the verti calAlign and horizontalAlign properties of HorizontalLayout and VerticalLayout, respectively, are used by the layout to position each of the container's child elements with respect to each other and the container boundaries:

```
<s:Group width="300">

    <s:layout>
        <s:VerticalLayout horizontalAlign="center" />
    </s:layout>

    <s:TextInput text="hello world" />
    <s:Button label="click me" />

</s:Group>
```

3.2 Switch Layout Management at Runtime

Problem

You want to change the layout sequence of child elements at runtime.

Solution

Update the declared layout property of a Spark container at runtime in response to an event.

Discussion

The layout property of a Spark container defines the layout management delegate for child elements in the container's display list. The default layout instance for a Spark container is spark.layouts.BasicLayout, which places children using absolute positioning. When the default layout is specified for a container, child elements are stacked upon each other based on their declared depths and the position of each element within the declared display list. You can instead supply sequenced-based layouts from the `spark.layouts` package or create custom layouts to manage the size and positioning of child elements.

The layout implementation for a Spark container can also be switched at runtime, as in the following example:

```
<s:Application xmlns:fx="http://ns.adobe.com/mxml/2009"
               xmlns:s="library://ns.adobe.com/flex/spark"
               creationComplete="handleCreationComplete();">

    <fx:Declarations>
        <s:VerticalLayout id="vLayout" gap="5" />
        <s:HorizontalLayout id="hLayout" gap="5" />
    </fx:Declarations>

    <fx:Script>
        <![CDATA[
            import spark.layouts.VerticalLayout;

            private function handleCreationComplete():void
            {
                layout = vLayout;
            }
            private function toggleLayout():void
            {
                layout = ( layout is VerticalLayout ) ? hLayout : vLayout;
            }
        ]]>
    </fx:Script>

    <s:TextInput text="hello world" />
    <s:Button label="click me" click="toggleLayout();" />

</s:Application>
```

In this example, the target container for the layout is the `Application` container. Two separate layout managers are declared in the `<fx:Declarations>` tag, and the designated layout is updated based on a click of the `Button` control, changing from `Vertical Layout` to `HorizontalLayout`.

The next example shows how to switch between these two layouts in a MX container:

```
<s:Application xmlns:fx="http://ns.adobe.com/mxml/2009"
               xmlns:s="library://ns.adobe.com/flex/spark"
               xmlns:mx="library://ns.adobe.com/flex/mx">

    <fx:Script>
        <![CDATA[
            import mx.containers.BoxDirection;

            private function toggleLayout():void
            {
```

```
                container.direction =
                        ( container.direction == BoxDirection.VERTICAL )
                        ? BoxDirection.HORIZONTAL
                        : BoxDirection.VERTICAL;
            }
        ]]>
    </fx:Script>

    <mx:Box id="container" direction="vertical">

        <s:TextInput text="hello world" />
        <s:Button label="click me" click="toggleLayout();" />

    </mx:Box>

</s:Application>
```

With respect to layout management, the main difference between Spark and MX controls has to do with the separation of responsibilities for the parent container. Within the Spark architecture, you specify a layout delegate for a target container. This allows you to easily create multiple layout classes that manage the container's child elements differently. Within the context of the MX architecture, any modifications to the layout of children within a container are confined to properties available on the container. Instead of easily changing layout delegates at runtime as you can do in Spark, one or more properties need to be updated, which invokes a re-rendering of the display.

This ability to switch layout implementations easily is a good example of the advantages of the separation of layout and containers within the Spark architecture of the Flex 4 SDK, and the runtime optimizations it enables.

3.3 Align and Size Children Within a Layout

Problem

You want to define the alignment of child elements within a container.

Solution

Use the `verticalAlign` and `horizontalAlign` properties of a sequenced-based layout.

Discussion

Using `HorizontalLayout`, `VerticalLayout`, and `TileLayout`, you can uniformly align the child elements of a container. To define the alignment along the x-axis, use the `verticalAlign` property of the `HorizontalLayout` class; along the y-axis, use the `horizontalAlign` property of the `VerticalLayout` class. `TileLayout` supports both the `verticalAlign` and `horizontalAlign` properties; it lays out the child elements of a container in rows and columns.

The available property values for horizontalAlign and verticalAlign are enumerated in the spark.layouts.HorizontalAlign and spark.layouts.VerticalAlign classes, respectively, and correspond to the axis on which child elements are added to the container.

The following example demonstrates dynamically changing the alignment of child elements along the *y*-axis:

```
<s:Application xmlns:fx="http://ns.adobe.com/mxml/2009"
               xmlns:s="library://ns.adobe.com/flex/spark"
               xmlns:mx="library://ns.adobe.com/flex/mx">

    <fx:Script>
        <![CDATA[
            import spark.layouts.HorizontalAlign;
            private function changeAlignment():void
            {
                vLayout.horizontalAlign =
                    (vLayout.horizontalAlign == HorizontalAlign.LEFT)
                    ? HorizontalAlign.RIGHT
                    : HorizontalAlign.LEFT;
            }
        ]]>
    </fx:Script>

    <s:Panel title="Alignment Example" width="300">

        <s:layout>
            <s:VerticalLayout id="vLayout"
                              horizontalAlign="{HorizontalAlign.LEFT}" />
        </s:layout>

        <s:DropDownList />
        <s:HSlider />
        <s:Button label="button" click="changeAlignment();" />

    </s:Panel>

</s:Application>
```

When the s:Button control is clicked, the child elements are changed from being left-aligned to being right-aligned within a vertical layout of the s:Panel container.

To align children along the *x*-axis, specify HorizontalLayout as the layout property of the container and set the verticalAlign property value to any of the enumerated properties of the VerticalAlign class. To align the child elements in the center of a container along a specified axis, use HorizontalAlign.CENTER or VerticalAlign.MIDDLE as the property value for verticalAlign or horizontalAlign, respectively, as in the following example:

```
<s:Panel height="300">

    <s:layout>
        <s:HorizontalLayout id="hLayout" verticalAlign="{VerticalAlign.MIDDLE}" />
```

```
            </s:layout>

            <s:DropDownList />
            <s:HSlider />
            <s:Button label="button" click="changeAlignment();" />

    </s:Panel>
```

Alignment properties can also be used to uniformly size all child elements within a layout. The two property values that are available on both HorizontalAlign and VerticalAlign are justify and contentJustify. Setting the justify property value for verticalAlign on a HorizontalLayout or TileLayout will size each child to the height of the target container. Setting the justify property value for horizontalAlign on a VerticalLayout or TileLayout will size each child to the width of the target container. Setting the contentJustify property value sizes children similarly, but sets the appropriate dimension of each child element based on the content height of the target container. The content height of a container is relative to the largest child, unless all children are smaller than the container (in which case it is relative to the height of the container). Both the justify and contentJustify property values uniformly set the corresponding size dimension on all child elements based on the specified layout axes and the target container; any width or height property values defined for the child elements are disregarded.

The following example switches between the center and justify values for the hori zontalAlign property of a VerticalLayout to demonstrate how dimension properties of child elements are ignored when laying out children uniformly based on size:

```
<s:Application xmlns:fx="http://ns.adobe.com/mxml/2009"
               xmlns:s="library://ns.adobe.com/flex/spark"
               xmlns:mx="library://ns.adobe.com/flex/mx">

    <fx:Script>
        <![CDATA[
            import spark.layouts.HorizontalAlign;
            private function changeAlignment():void
            {
                vLayout.horizontalAlign =
                        (vLayout.horizontalAlign == HorizontalAlign.JUSTIFY)
                        ? HorizontalAlign.CENTER
                        : HorizontalAlign.JUSTIFY;
            }
        ]]>
    </fx:Script>

    <s:Panel width="300">

        <s:layout>
            <s:VerticalLayout id="vLayout"
                              horizontalAlign="{HorizontalAlign.JUSTIFY}" />
        </s:layout>

        <s:DropDownList width="200" />
```

```
        <s:HSlider />
        <s:Button label="button" click="changeAlignment();" />

    </s:Panel>

</s:Application>
```

3.4 Lay Out Children Using Rows and Columns

Problem

You want to display child elements in a sequence of rows and columns.

Solution

Assign TileLayout to the layout property of a Spark container to dynamically place its child elements in a grid.

Discussion

TileLayout adds children to the display list in both a horizontal and vertical fashion, positioning them in a series of rows and columns. It displays the child elements in a grid based on the dimensions of the target Spark container, as the following example demonstrates:

```
<s:Application xmlns:fx="http://ns.adobe.com/mxml/2009"
               xmlns:s="library://ns.adobe.com/flex/spark">

    <fx:Declarations>
        <fx:String id="txt">
            Lorem ipsum dolor sit amet consectetur adipisicing elit.
        </fx:String>
    </fx:Declarations>

    <s:layout>
        <s:VerticalLayout />
    </s:layout>

    <s:HSlider id="slider" minimum="100" maximum="400" value="250" />

    <s:DataGroup width="{slider.value}"
                 itemRenderer="spark.skins.spark.DefaultItemRenderer">

        <s:layout>
            <s:TileLayout />
        </s:layout>

        <s:dataProvider>
            <s:ArrayCollection source="{txt.split(' ')}" />
        </s:dataProvider>
```

```
            </s:DataGroup>

        </s:Application>
```

In this example, the width of the parent container for the layout delegate is updated in response to a change to the `value` property of the `HSlider` control. As the width dimension changes, columns are added or removed and child elements of the target `Data Group` container are repositioned accordingly.

By default, the sequence in which child elements are added to the layout is based on rows. Children are added along the horizontal axis in columns until the boundary of the container is reached, at which point a new row is created to continue adding child elements. If desired, you can change this sequence rule using the `orientation` property of `TileLayout`, which takes a value of either `rows` or `columns`. The following example changes the default layout sequence from rows to columns, adding each child vertically in a row until the lower boundary of the container is reached, at which point a new column is created to take the next child element:

```
<s:DataGroup width="{slider.value}"
            itemRenderer="spark.skins.spark.DefaultItemRenderer">

    <s:layout>
        <s:TileLayout orientation="rows" />
    </s:layout>

    <s:dataProvider>
        <s:ArrayCollection source="{txt.split(' ')}" />
    </s:dataProvider>

</s:DataGroup>
```

You can restrict the number of rows and columns to be used in the display by specifying values for the `requestedRowCount` and `requestedColumnCount` properties, respectively, of a `TileLayout`. The default value for these properties is `-1`, which specifies that there is no limit to the number of children that can be added to the display in a row or column. By modifying the default values, you control how many child elements can be added to a row/column (rather than allowing this to be determined by the specified dimensions of the target container).

When you specify a nondefault value for the `requestedRowCount` or `requestedColumn Count` property of a `TileLayout`, the target container is measured as children are added to the display. If a width and height have not been assigned to the target container directly, the dimensions of the container are determined by the placement and size of the child elements laid out in rows and columns by the `TileLayout`, as in the following example:

```
<s:Application xmlns:fx="http://ns.adobe.com/mxml/2009"
            xmlns:s="library://ns.adobe.com/flex/spark">
```

```
<fx:Declarations>
    <fx:String id="txt">
        Lorem ipsum dolor sit amet consectetur adipisicing elit.
    </fx:String>
</fx:Declarations>

<s:layout>
    <s:VerticalLayout />
</s:layout>

<s:Group>

    <s:Scroller>
        <s:DataGroup width="100%"
                     itemRenderer="spark.skins.spark.DefaultItemRenderer">

            <s:layout>
                <s:TileLayout requestedRowCount="2" requestedColumnCount="3"
                              clipAndEnableScrolling="true" />
            </s:layout>

            <s:dataProvider>
                <s:ArrayCollection source="{txt.split(' ')}" />
            </s:dataProvider>

        </s:DataGroup>
    </s:Scroller>

    <s:Rect width="100%" height="100%">
        <s:stroke>
            <s:SolidColorStroke />
        </s:stroke>
    </s:Rect>

</s:Group>

</s:Application>
```

In this example, the TileLayout target container and a Rect graphic element are wrapped in a Group to show how the Group is resized to reflect the child element positioning provided by the layout.

Because the TileLayout disregards the target container's dimensions when strictly positioning child elements in a grid based on the requestedRowCount and requestedColumn Count property values, unless scrolling is enabled children may be visible outside of the calculated row and column sizes. Consequently, in this example the target DataGroup container is wrapped in a Scroller component and the clipAndEnableScrolling property is set to true on the TileLayout.

3.5 Size Children Uniformly

Problem

You want all children within a container to be the same size.

Solution

To restrict the size of the child elements within a target container, use the `columnHeight` and `rowHeight` properties of `HorizontalLayout` and `VerticalLayout`, respectively. To dynamically size and position all children of a target container based on the dimensions of a single child element, use the `typicalLayoutElement` property.

Discussion

By default, the `variableRowHeight` and `variableColumnHeight` properties of `Horizontal Layout` and `VerticalLayout`, respectively, are set to a value of `true`. This default setting ensures that all child elements are displayed based on their individually measured dimensions. This can be beneficial when presenting elements that vary in size, but the rendering costs may prove to be a performance burden at runtime. To speed up rendering time, Spark layouts have properties for setting static values to ensure that all child elements are sized uniformly.

The following example sets the `rowHeight` and `variableRowHeight` property values to constrain the height of child elements in a target container using a vertical layout:

```
<s:Group>

    <s:layout>
        <s:VerticalLayout variableRowHeight="false" rowHeight="50" />
    </s:layout>

    <s:Button id="btn1" label="(1) button" />
    <s:Button id="txt2" label="(2) button" height="10" />
    <s:Button id="txt3" label="(3) button" height="30" />
    <s:Button id="txt4" label="(4) button" />

</s:Group>
```

In this example, the `height` property value assigned to any declared `Button` control is disregarded and all the children are set to the same height as they are positioned vertically without respect to the variable measure calculated by properties of each child.

To apply size constraints in a horizontal layout, use the `columnWidth` and `variable ColumnWidth` properties, as in the following example:

```
<s:Group>

    <s:layout>
        <s:HorizontalLayout variableColumnWidth="false" columnWidth="80" />
    </s:layout>
```

```
<s:Button id="btn1" label="(1) button" />
<s:Button id="btn2" label="(2) button" height="50" />
<s:Button id="btn3" label="(3) button" height="30" />
<s:Button id="btn4" label="(4) button" />

</s:Group>
```

The previous two examples show how to specify static values for the dimensions of all child elements of a target container with regard to the specified layout control. Alternatively, child dimensions and subsequent positions can be determined by supplying an ILayoutElement instance as the value for a layout control's typicalLayoutElement property. In this case, the target container's children are sized and positioned based on the width or height, respectively, of the supplied target instance.

The following example supplies a child target to be used in sizing and positioning all children of a target container with a vertical layout:

```
<s:Application xmlns:fx="http://ns.adobe.com/mxml/2009"
               xmlns:s="library://ns.adobe.com/flex/spark">

    <s:Group>

        <s:layout>
            <s:VerticalLayout variableRowHeight="false"
                              typicalLayoutElement="{btn3}" />
        </s:layout>

        <s:Button id="btn1" label="(1) button" />
        <s:Button id="btn2" label="(2) button" height="50" />
        <s:Button id="btn3" label="(3) button" height="30" />
        <s:Button id="btn4" label="(4) button" />

    </s:Group>

</s:Application>
```

In this example, each Button control is rendered at the height attributed to the assigned typicalLayoutElement; any previously assigned height property values are disregarded.

3.6 Lazily Create and Recycle Children

Problem

You want to improve runtime performance by creating and rendering children of a container as needed.

Solution

Use the useVirtualLayout property of a HorizontalLayout, VerticalLayout, or TileLayout whose target container is a DataGroup.

Discussion

Virtualization improves runtime performance by creating and recycling item renderers and rendering children only as they come into the visible content area of a display container. Layout classes that extend `spark.layouts.LayoutBase`, such as `VerticalLay out`, expose the `useVirtualLayout` property. Attributed as a Boolean value, `useVirtual Layout` is used to determine whether to recycle item renderers in a data element container that supports virtualization, such as `DataGroup`. When employing virtualization, access to data elements using methods of the content API (such as `getElementAt()`) is limited to elements visible within the content area of the container.

The following demonstrates enabling the use of virtualization on the layout delegate of a `DataGroup` container:

```
<fx:Declarations>
    <fx:String id="txt">
        Lorem ipsum dolor sit amet consectetur adipisicing elit.
    </fx:String>
</fx:Declarations>

<s:Scroller>

    <s:DataGroup width="150" height="120"
                 itemRenderer="spark.skins.spark.DefaultItemRenderer">

        <s:layout>
            <s:VerticalLayout useVirtualLayout="true" />
        </s:layout>

        <s:dataProvider>
            <mx:ArrayCollection source="{txt.split(' ')}" />
        </s:dataProvider>

    </s:DataGroup>

</s:Scroller>
```

In this example, the size of the `DataGroup` container is restricted to show approximately four child elements at a time based on the specified item renderer and supplied data. As new child elements are scrolled into view, previously created item renderer instances that have been scrolled out of view are reused to render the new data.

When a layout delegate is provided to a container, the `target` property of the layout is attributed to the target container of type `spark.components.subclasses.GroupBase`. When creating and reusing elements, the layout delegate uses methods of the content API exposed by a `GroupBase` that supports virtualization. At the time of this writing, `DataGroup` is the only container in the Flex 4 SDK that supports virtualization. You can, however, create custom containers that create, recycle, and validate child elements accordingly by extending `GroupBase` and overriding the `getVirtualElementAt()` method.

To demonstrate how virtual and nonvirtual children are treated within a `GroupBase`, the following example loops through the child elements of a container and traces out the virtual elements:

```
<s:Application xmlns:fx="http://ns.adobe.com/mxml/2009"
               xmlns:s="library://ns.adobe.com/flex/spark"
               xmlns:mx="library://ns.adobe.com/flex/mx"
               creationComplete="handleCreationComplete()">

    <fx:Library>
        <fx:Definition name="CustomRect">
            <s:Rect width="100">
                <s:fill>
                    <mx:SolidColor color="#000000" />
                </s:fill>
            </s:Rect>
        </fx:Definition>
    </fx:Library>

    <fx:Script>
        <![CDATA[
            import spark.components.supportClasses.GroupBase;
            private function handleCreationComplete():void
            {
                scroller.verticalScrollBar.addEventListener(Event.CHANGE,
                    inspectVirtualChildren);
            }

            private function inspectVirtualChildren( evt:Event ):void
            {
                var target:GroupBase = vLayout.target;
                for( var i:int = 0; i < target.numElements; i++ )
                {
                    trace( target.getElementAt( i ) );
                }
            }
        ]]>
    </fx:Script>

    <s:Scroller id="scroller">

        <s:DataGroup width="150" height="120"
                     itemRenderer="spark.skins.spark.DefaultComplexItemRenderer"
                     creationComplete="inspectVirtualChildren(event);">

            <s:layout>
                <s:VerticalLayout id="vLayout" useVirtualLayout="true" />
            </s:layout>

            <s:dataProvider>
                <mx:ArrayCollection>
                    <fx:CustomRect height="20" />
                    <s:Button height="100" />
                    <s:DropDownList height="40" />
                    <fx:CustomRect height="60" />
```

```
                        </mx:ArrayCollection>
                    </s:dataProvider>

                </s:DataGroup>

            </s:Scroller>

        </s:Application>
```

As the scroll position of the targeted `DataGroup` container changes, any child elements accessed using the `getElementAt()` method that are not in view are attributed as `null`. When you create a custom layout that respects virtualization of data elements, use the `getVirtualElementAt()` method of the `GroupBase` target with the `getScrollRect()` method to anticipate which elements will be visible in the content area of the container.

The `DefaultComplexItemRenderer` is used as the item renderer for the `DataGroup` container to show that virtualization also works with child elements of differing sizes.

When working with a relatively small data set, such as in this example, using virtualization to improve rendering performance may seem trivial. The true power of using lazy creation and recycling children through virtualization really becomes evident when using large data sets, such as a group of records returned from a service.

3.7 Create a Custom Layout

Problem

You want to create a custom layout for a container to use to display its child elements.

Solution

Create a custom layout by extending the `com.layouts.supportClasses.LayoutBase` class and override the `updateDisplayList()` method to position and size the children accordingly.

Discussion

What if a project comes along in which the desired layout is not available from the layout classes provided by the Flex 4 SDK? You can easily create and apply a custom layout for a container by extending the `LayoutBase` class, thanks to the separation of responsibilities in the Spark component architecture. Child elements of a targeted container are positioned and sized within the `updateDisplayList()` method of a `Layout Base` subclass, such as `HorizontalLayout` or `VerticalLayout`. By overriding the `update DisplayList()` method in a custom layout, you can manipulate the display list of a targeted `GroupBase`-based container.

Each child of a `GroupBase` container is attributed as an `ILayoutElement` instance. Methods are available on the `ILayoutElement` interface that relate to how the child element is drawn on screen with regard to size and position. To create a custom layout for a targeted container's child elements, loop through those children and apply any desired transformations:

```
package com.oreilly.f4cb
{
    import mx.core.ILayoutElement;

    import spark.components.supportClasses.GroupBase;
    import spark.layouts.supportClasses.LayoutBase;

    public class CustomLayout extends LayoutBase
    {

        override public function updateDisplayList(width:Number, height:Number)
                : void
        {
            super.updateDisplayList( width, height );

            var layoutTarget:GroupBase = target;
            var w:Number = width / 2;
            var h:Number = height / 2;
            var angle:Number = 360 / layoutTarget.numElements;
            var radius:Number = w;
            var radians:Number;
            var xpos:Number;
            var ypos:Number;
            var element:ILayoutElement;

            for( var i:int = 0; i < layoutTarget.numElements; i++ )
            {
                element = layoutTarget.getElementAt( i );
                radians = ( ( angle * -i ) + 180 ) * ( Math.PI / 180 );
                xpos = w + ( Math.sin(radians) * radius );
                ypos = h + ( Math.cos(radians) * radius );

                element.setLayoutBoundsSize( NaN, NaN );
                element.setLayoutBoundsPosition( xpos, ypos );
            }
        }
    }
}
```

The CustomLayout class in this example displays the child elements uniformly radiating from the center of a target container in a clockwise manner. As the child elements of the container are accessed within the for loop, each ILayoutElement instance is accessed using the getElementAt() method of the content API and is given a new position based on the additive angle using the setLayoutBoundsPosition() method. The size of each ILayoutElement is determined by a call to the setLayoutBoundsSize() method. Supplying a value of NaN for the width or height argument ensures that the size of the element is determined by the rendered content of the element itself.

A custom layout is set on a container by using the `layout` property of the container:

```
<s:Application xmlns:fx="http://ns.adobe.com/mxml/2009"
               xmlns:s="library://ns.adobe.com/flex/spark"
               xmlns:mx="library://ns.adobe.com/flex/mx"
               xmlns:f4cb="com.oreilly.f4cb.*">

    <fx:Declarations>
        <fx:String id="txt">
            Lorem ipsum dolor sit amet consectetur adipisicing elit.
        </fx:String>
    </fx:Declarations>

    <s:layout>
        <s:VerticalLayout horizontalAlign="center" />
    </s:layout>

    <s:HSlider id="slider" minimum="200" maximum="400" value="300" />

    <s:DataGroup width="{slider.value}" height="{slider.value}"
                 itemRenderer="spark.skins.spark.DefaultItemRenderer">

        <s:layout>
            <f4cb:CustomLayout />
        </s:layout>

        <s:dataProvider>
            <mx:ArrayCollection source="{txt.split(' ')}" />
        </s:dataProvider>

    </s:DataGroup>

</s:Application>
```

When the `updateDisplayList()` method of the layout is invoked, as happens in response to a change in the container size or the addition of an element on the content layer, the children are laid out using the rules specified in the `CustomLayout` class. Generally speaking, it is good practice to also override the `measure()` method when creating a custom layout class extending `LayoutBase`. The `measure()` method handles resizing the target container accordingly based on its child elements and constraint properties. However, because the custom layout created in this example positions children based on the bounds set upon the target container, this is not necessary.

3.8 Measure and Alter the Container Size

Problem

You want to set the size of a target container based on the dimensions of the child elements in the layout.

Solution

Create a LayoutBase-based custom layout and override the measure() method to access the desired bounds for the container based on the dimensions of its child elements.

Discussion

When explicit dimensions are not specified for the target container, control over its size is handed over to the layout. When width and height values are applied to a container, the explicitWidth and explicitHeight properties (respectively) are updated, and their values determine whether to invoke the layout's measure() method. If values for these properties are not set (equated as a value of NaN), the container's layout delegate determines the target dimensions and updates the container's measuredWidth and measuredHeight property values accordingly.

To alter how the dimensions of a target container are determined, create a custom layout and override the measure() method:

```
package com.oreilly.f4cb
{
    import mx.core.IVisualElement;

    import spark.components.supportClasses.GroupBase;
    import spark.layouts.VerticalLayout;

    public class CustomLayout extends VerticalLayout
    {
        override public function measure() : void
        {
            var layoutTarget:GroupBase = target;
            var count:int = layoutTarget.numElements;
            var w:Number = 0;
            var h:Number = 0;
            var element:IVisualElement;
            for( var i:int = 0; i < count; i++ )
            {
                element = layoutTarget.getElementAt( i );
                w = Math.max( w, element.getPreferredBoundsWidth() );
                h += element.getPreferredBoundsHeight();
            }

            var gap:Number = gap * (count - 1 );
            layoutTarget.measuredWidth = w + paddingLeft + paddingRight;
            layoutTarget.measuredHeight = h + paddingTop + paddingBottom + gap;
        }
    }
}
```

The CustomLayout class in this example sets the measuredWidth and measuredHeight properties of the target container based on the largest width and the cumulative height of all child elements, taking into account the padding and gap values of the layout.

When the measure() method is overridden in a custom layout, it is important to set any desired measure properties of the target container. These properties include measured Width, measuredHeight, measuredMinWidth, and measuredMinHeight. These properties correspond to the size of the target container and are used when updating the display during a pass in invalidation of the container.

To apply a custom layout to a container, use the layout property:

```
<s:Application xmlns:fx="http://ns.adobe.com/mxml/2009"
               xmlns:s="library://ns.adobe.com/flex/spark"
               xmlns:mx="library://ns.adobe.com/flex/mx"
               xmlns:f4cb="com.oreilly.f4cb.*">

    <fx:Script>
        <![CDATA[
            import mx.graphics.SolidColor;
            import spark.primitives.Rect;
            private function addRect():void
            {
                var rect:Rect = new Rect();
                rect.width = Math.random() * 300;
                rect.height = Math.random() * 30;
                rect.fill = new SolidColor( 0xCCFFCC );
                group.addElement( rect );
            }
        ]]>
    </fx:Script>

    <s:layout>
        <s:VerticalLayout horizontalAlign="center" paddingTop="30" />
    </s:layout>

    <s:Group>
        <!-- Content group -->
        <s:Group id="group">
            <s:layout>
                <f4cb:CustomLayout paddingTop="5" paddingBottom="5"
                                   paddingLeft="5" paddingRight="5"
                                   horizontalAlign="center" />
            </s:layout>
        </s:Group>
        <!-- Simple border -->
        <s:Rect width="100%" height="100%">
            <s:stroke>
                <mx:SolidColorStroke color="#000000" />
            </s:stroke>
        </s:Rect>
    </s:Group>

    <s:Button label="add rect" click="addRect();" />

</s:Application>
```

When the s:Button control is clicked, a new, randomly sized s:Rect instance is added to the nested <s:Group> container that contains the custom layout. As each new child element is added to the container, the measure() method of the CustomLayout is invoked and the target container is resized. The updated size of the nested container is then reflected in the Rect border applied to the outer container. Although this example demonstrates resizing a Group container based on visual child elements, the same technique can be applied to a DataGroup container whose children are item renderers representing data items.

Layouts that support virtualization from the Flex 4 SDK invoke the private methods measureVirtual() or measureReal(), depending on whether the useVirtualLayout property is set to true or false, respectively, on the layout. Because the custom layout from our example does not use virtualization, child elements of the target container are accessed using the getElementAt() method of GroupBase. If virtualization is used, child elements are accessed using the getVirtualElementAt() method of GroupBase.

3.9 Dynamically Change the Child Depth in the Layout

Problem

You want to change the depth of children in a layout programmatically at runtime.

Solution

Use the depth property of child elements that implement mx.core.IVisualElement.

Discussion

You can access child elements of a GroupBase-based container via methods of the content API such as getElementAt(). When you work with the content API, each element is attributed as an implementation of ILayoutElement, which exposes attributes pertaining to constraints and methods used in determining the size and position of the element within the layout of a target container. The IVisualElement interface is an extension of ILayoutElement and is implemented by UIComponent and GraphicElement. Implementations of IVisualElement expose explicit properties for size and position, as well as attributes related to the owner and parent of the element. Visual elements from the Spark and MX component sets are extensions of UIComponent. This means elements from both architectures can be added to a Spark container, which attributes children as implementations of ILayoutElement.

To use the depth property of an element within a container, access the child using the getElementAt() method of the content API and cast the element as an IVisualElement:

```
<s:Application xmlns:fx="http://ns.adobe.com/mxml/2009"
               xmlns:s="library://ns.adobe.com/flex/spark"
               xmlns:mx="library://ns.adobe.com/flex/mx">
```

```
<fx:Script>
    <![CDATA[
        import mx.core.IVisualElement;
        import spark.components.supportClasses.GroupBase;

        private var currentIndex:int = 0;
        private function swapDepths():void
        {
            var layoutTarget:GroupBase = bLayout.target;
            var element:IVisualElement;
            for( var i:int = 0; i < layoutTarget.numElements; i++ )
            {
                element = layoutTarget.getElementAt( i ) as IVisualElement;
                if( i == currentIndex )
                {
                    element.depth = layoutTarget.numElements - 1;
                }
                else if( i > currentIndex )
                {
                    element.depth = i - 1;
                }
            }
            if( ++currentIndex > layoutTarget.numElements - 1 )
                currentIndex = 0;
        }
    ]]>
</fx:Script>

<s:layout>
    <s:VerticalLayout />
</s:layout>

<s:Group>

    <s:layout>
        <s:BasicLayout id="bLayout" />
    </s:layout>

    <s:Button x="0" label="(1) button" />
    <s:Button x="30" label="(2) button" />
    <s:Rect x="60" width="100" height="30">
        <s:fill>
            <mx:SolidColor color="0x000000" />
        </s:fill>
    </s:Rect>
    <s:Button x="90" label="(3) button" />

</s:Group>

<s:Button label="swapDepths" click="swapDepths();" />

</s:Application>
```

In this example, the child element at the lowest depth is brought to the top of the display stack within the container when a Button control is clicked. Initially, the children of the

Group container are provided depth values relative to the positions at which they are declared, with the first declared s:Button control having a depth value of 0 and the last declared s:Button control having a depth value of 3. Upon each click of the Button control, the IVisualElement residing on the lowest layer is brought to the highest layer by giving that element a depth property value of the highest child index within the container. To keep the highest depth property value within the range of the number of children, the depth values of all the other child elements are decremented.

3.10 Use Matrix3D to Apply Transformations Within a Layout

Problem

You want to apply 2D and 3D transformations to child elements of a layout.

Solution

To apply transformations that affect all children within a layout, set the individual transformation properties (such as rotationX, scaleX, and transformX) that are directly available on instances of UIComponent and GraphicElement, or supply a Matrix3D object to the layoutMatrix3D property of UIComponent-based children.

Discussion

The Flex 4 SDK offers several approaches for applying transformations to child elements of a layout. Before you apply transformations, however, you must consider how (or whether) those transformations should affect all the other child elements of the same layout. For example, setting the transformation properties for rotation, scale, and translation that are available on UIComponent-based and GraphicElement-based child elements will also affect the size and position of all other children within your layout:

```
<s:Button rotationZ="90" scaleY="0.5" transformX="50" />
```

On instances of UIComponent and GraphicElement, the rotation, scale, and transform attributes each expose properties that relate to axes in a 3D coordinate space. These properties are also bindable, so direct reapplication is not necessary when their values are modified at runtime.

Alternatively, you can use the layoutMatrix3D property to apply transformations to UIComponent-based elements; again, all children within the layout will be affected. UIComponent-based elements include visual elements from both the MX and Spark component sets. Using the layoutMatrix3D property, you can supply a flash.geom. Matrix3D object that applies all the 2D and 3D transformations to a visual element. Keep in mind, however, that the layoutMatrix3D property is write-only, so any changes you make to the Matrix3D object to which it is set will not be automatically applied to the target element. You will need to reassign the object in order to apply modifications.

The following example shows how to apply transformations within a layout using the transformation properties and the `layoutMatrix3D` property, which subsequently affects other children in the layout of a target container:

```
<s:Application xmlns:fx="http://ns.adobe.com/mxml/2009"
               xmlns:s="library://ns.adobe.com/flex/spark"
               xmlns:mx="library://ns.adobe.com/flex/mx">

    <fx:Script>
        <![CDATA[
            import mx.core.UIComponent;
            [Bindable] private var rot:Number = 90;
            private function rotate():void
            {
                var matrix:Matrix3D = button.getLayoutMatrix3D();
                matrix.appendRotation( 90, Vector3D.Z_AXIS );
                button.layoutMatrix3D = matrix;

                rot += 90;
            }
        ]]>
    </fx:Script>

    <s:Group>

        <s:Group width="120">

            <s:layout>
                <s:VerticalLayout paddingLeft="5" paddingRight="5"
                                  paddingTop="5" paddingBottom="5" />
            </s:layout>

            <s:Button id="button" label="push over" click="rotate();" />
            <s:Rect id="rect" rotationZ="{rot}"
                    width="110" height="50">
                <s:fill>
                    <s:SolidColor color="#000000" />
                </s:fill>
            </s:Rect>

        </s:Group>

        <s:Rect width="100%" height="100%">
            <s:stroke>
                <mx:SolidColorStroke color="#000000" />
            </s:stroke>
        </s:Rect>

    </s:Group>

</s:Application>
```

When the `click` event is received from the `s:Button` control, the `rotate()` method is invoked. Within the `rotate()` method, the bindable `rot` property is updated and the rotation value along the *z*-axis is updated on the `GraphicElement`-based `Rect` element.

Likewise, rotation along the *z*-axis is updated and reapplied to the `layoutMatrix3D` property of the `Button` control. As mentioned earlier, the `layoutMatrix3D` property is write-only and prevents any modifications to the `Matrix3D` object applied from being bound to an element. As such, the `Matrix3D` object can be retrieved using the `getLayout Matrix3D()` method and transformations can be prepended or appended using methods available on the `Matrix3D` class and reapplied directly to an element.

3.11 Use TransformOffsets to Apply Transformations Within a Layout

Problem

You want to apply 2D and 3D transformations to child elements of a layout without affecting other children within the layout.

Solution

Supply a `TransformOffsets` object to the `postLayoutTransformOffsets` property of instances of `UIComponent` and `GraphicElement`, or use the `transformAround()` method of `UIComponent`-based children.

Discussion

Along with the `Matrix3D` object, which affects all children within a layout, `TransformOffsets` can be used to apply transformations to specific children. When you apply transformations to a `UIComponent` or `GraphicElement` instance by supplying a `TransformOffsets` object as the value of the `postLayoutTransformOffsets` property, the layout does not automatically update the positioning and size of the other child elements within the target container. Like the `Matrix3D` object, `TransformOffsets` is a matrix of 2D and 3D values, but it differs in that it exposes those values as read/write properties. The `TransformOffsets` object supports event dispatching, allowing updates to properties to be applied to a child element without reapplication through binding.

To apply transformations using a `TransformationOffsets` object, set the `postLayout TransformOffsets` property of the target element:

```
<s:Button label="above">
    <s:offsets>
        <mx:TransformOffsets rotationZ="90" />
    </s:offsets>
</s:Button>
<s:Button label="below" />
```

In contrast to how other child elements are affected when applying transformations to an element of a layout using the `layoutMatrix3D` property, when the `s:Button` control in this example is rotated 90 degrees along the z-axis, the position of the second declared `s:Button` control in the layout is not updated in response to the transformation.

When applying transformations to child elements, it is important to keep in mind how you want the application of the transformation to impact the layout, as this will affect whether you choose to use the `layoutMatrix3D` or `postLayoutTransformOffsets` property. If your transformations need to be applied over time and you do not want them to affect the other child elements of the layout, the `postLayoutTransformOffsets` property can be used in conjunction with an `AnimateTransform`-based effect:

```
<s:Application xmlns:fx="http://ns.adobe.com/mxml/2009"
               xmlns:s="library://ns.adobe.com/flex/spark"
               xmlns:mx="library://ns.adobe.com/flex/mx">

    <fx:Declarations>
        <s:Rotate3D id="rotator1" autoCenterTransform="true" target="{btn1}"
                    angleXFrom="0" angleXTo="360" />
        <s:Rotate3D id="rotator2" autoCenterTransform="true" target="{btn2}"
                    angleYFrom="360" angleYTo="0" />
    </fx:Declarations>

    <s:Group width="300" height="300">

        <s:Group width="100%" height="100%">

            <s:layout>
                <s:VerticalLayout paddingLeft="5" paddingRight="5"
                                  paddingTop="5" paddingBottom="5"
                                  horizontalAlign="center" />
            </s:layout>

            <s:Button id="btn1" label="(0) button" click="{rotator1.play();}" />
            <s:Button id="btn2" label="(1) button" click="{rotator2.play();}" />

        </s:Group>

        <s:Rect width="100%" height="100%">
            <s:stroke>
                <mx:SolidColorStroke color="#000000" />
            </s:stroke>
        </s:Rect>

    </s:Group>

</s:Application>
```

In this example, two `s:Rotate3D` effects are declared to apply transformations to targeted child elements over a period of time. By default, `AnimateTransform`-based effects apply transformations using the `postLayoutTransformOffsets` property of a target element, so updates to the transformation values do not affect the size and position of other child elements of the layout. This is a good strategy to use when some visual indication is needed to notify the user of an action, and you do not want to cause any unnecessary confusion by affecting the position and size of other children. If the desired effect is to apply transformations to other child elements of a layout while an animation is active, you can change the value of the `applyChangesPostLayout` property of the `AnimateTransform` class from the default of `true` to `false`.

As an alternative to using the transformation properties for rotation, scale, and translation or the `layoutMatrix3D` property, transformations can be applied to `UIComponent`-based elements using the `transformAround()` method. The `transformAround()` method has arguments for applying transformations to an element that will affect the position and size of other children within the layout, and arguments for applying transformations post-layout without affecting the other child elements.

The following example uses the `transformAround()` method to apply rotations around the *z*-axis to two elements, one that affects the layout of other children and one that does not:

```
<s:Application xmlns:fx="http://ns.adobe.com/mxml/2009"
               xmlns:s="library://ns.adobe.com/flex/spark"
               xmlns:mx="library://ns.adobe.com/flex/mx">

    <fx:Script>
        <![CDATA[
            import mx.core.UIComponent;

            private var newAngle:Number = 0;
            private function pushOver( evt:MouseEvent ):void
            {
                var angle:Number = btn1.rotationZ + 90;
                btn1.transformAround( new Vector3D( btn1.width, btn1.height / 2 ),
                                      null, new Vector3D( 0, 0, angle ) );
            }

            private function pushAround( evt:MouseEvent ):void
            {
                newAngle += 90;
                btn2.transformAround( new Vector3D( btn2.width / 2,
                                      btn2.height / 2 ),
                                      null, null, null,
                                      null, new Vector3D( 0, 0, newAngle ) );
            }
        ]]>
    </fx:Script>

    <s:Group>

        <s:Group id="group" width="120">

            <s:layout>
                <s:VerticalLayout paddingLeft="5" paddingRight="5"
                                  paddingTop="5" paddingBottom="5" />
            </s:layout>

            <s:Button id="btn1" label="push over" click="pushOver(event);" />
            <s:Button id="btn2" label="push around" click="pushAround(event);" />
```

```
        </s:Group>

        <s:Rect width="100%" height="100%">
            <s:stroke>
                <mx:SolidColorStroke color="#000000" />
            </s:stroke>
        </s:Rect>

    </s:Group>

</s:Application>
```

Each parameter of the `transformAround()` method takes a `Vector3D` object and all are optional aside from the first argument, which pertains to the center point for transformations. In this example, the first `s:Button` declared in the markup rotates in response to a `click` event and affects the position of the second `s:Button` declared. As the rotation for the first `Button` element is set using a `Vector3D` object on the rotation parameter of `transformAround()`, the `rotationZ` property of the element is updated. Within the `push Around()` method, a post-layout transformation is applied to the second `Button` by setting the `Vector3D` object to the `postLayoutRotation` argument of `transformAround()`. When post-layout transformations are applied, the explicit transformation properties of the element (such as `rotationZ`) are not updated, and as a consequence the layout of the other children is not affected.

Though transformations can play a powerful part in notifying users of actions to be taken or that have been taken, you must consider how other children of a layout will be affected in response to those transformations.

3.12 Create a Custom 3D Layout

Problem

You want to create a custom layout that applies 3D transformations to all children of a target container.

Solution

Create a custom layout by extending `com.layouts.supportClasses.LayoutBase` and override the `updateDisplayList()` method to apply transformations to child elements accordingly.

Discussion

Along with the layout classes available in the Flex 4 SDK, you can assign custom layouts that extend `LayoutBase` to containers using the `layout` property. When the display of a target container is changed, the `updateDisplayList()` method of the container is invoked, which in turn invokes the `updateDisplayList()` method of the layout delegate.

By overriding `updateDisplayList()` within a custom layout, you can apply transformations such as rotation, scaling, and translation to the child elements of a `GroupBase`-based container.

Each child element of a `GroupBase` container is attributed as an `ILayoutElement` instance, which has methods to apply 3D transformations, such as `setLayoutMatrix3D()` and `transformAround()`. To apply transformations using the utility methods of an `ILayoutElement` instance, access the element using the content API, as in the following example:

```
package com.oreilly.f4cb
{
    import flash.geom.Vector3D;

    import mx.core.IVisualElement;
    import mx.core.UIComponent;

    import spark.components.supportClasses.GroupBase;
    import spark.layouts.supportClasses.LayoutBase;

    public class Custom3DLayout extends LayoutBase
    {
        private var _focalLength:Number = 500;
        private var _scrollPosition:Number = 0;

        override public function updateDisplayList(width:Number,
                                                   height:Number) : void
        {
            super.updateDisplayList( width, height );

            var layoutTarget:GroupBase = target;
            var w:Number = width / 2;
            var h:Number = height / 2;
            var angle:Number = 360 / layoutTarget.numElements;
            var radius:Number = w;
            var radians:Number;
            var scale:Number
            var dist:Number;
            var xpos:Number = w;
            var ypos:Number;
            var element:IVisualElement;

            for( var i:int = 0; i < layoutTarget.numElements; i++ )
            {
                element = layoutTarget.getElementAt( i ) as IVisualElement;
                radians = ( ( angle * i ) + _scrollPosition ) * ( Math.PI / 180 );
                dist = w + ( Math.sin(radians) * radius );
                scale = _focalLength / ( _focalLength + dist );
                ypos = h + ( Math.cos(radians) * radius ) * scale;

                element.depth = scale;
                element.setLayoutBoundsSize( NaN, NaN );
                element.transformAround( new Vector3D((element.width / 2),
                                         (element.height / 2) ),
```

```
                                    null, null, null,
                                    new Vector3D( scale, scale, 0 ),
                                    null,
                                    new Vector3D( xpos, ypos, 0 ));
            }
        }

        public function get scrollPosition():Number
        {
            return _scrollPosition;
        }
        public function set scrollPosition( value:Number ):void
        {
            _scrollPosition = value;
            target.invalidateDisplayList();
        }
    }
}
```

The `Custom3DLayout` class in this example displays the child elements of a target container within a vertical carousel with 3D perspective. As the child elements of the container are accessed within the `for` loop, each instance is cast as an `IVisualElement` implementation (an extension of `ILayoutElement`) in order to set the appropriate `depth` value based on the derived distance from the viewer. As well, the explicit `width` and `height` properties are used to properly apply 3D translations using the `transform Around()` method. The first argument of the `transformAround()` method is a `Vector3D` object representing the center around which to apply transformations to the element. The following three optional arguments are `Vector3D` objects representing transformations that can be applied to an element that affect other children of the same layout, which in this example are attributed as a value of `null`. The last three arguments (also optional) are `Vector3D` objects representing transformations to be applied post-layout. Post-layout scale and translation transformations applied to an element do not affect the position and size of other children.

A `scrollPosition` property has been added to `Custom3DLayout` to allow for scrolling through the carousel of elements. As the `scrollPosition` value changes, the `invalidateDisplayList()` method of the target container is invoked, which in turn invokes the `updateDisplayList()` method of the custom layout delegate.

The following example applies the `Custom3DLayout` to a `DataGroup` container:

```
<s:Application xmlns:fx="http://ns.adobe.com/mxml/2009"
               xmlns:s="library://ns.adobe.com/flex/spark"
               xmlns:mx="library://ns.adobe.com/flex/mx"
               xmlns:f4cb="com.oreilly.f4cb.*">

    <s:layout>
        <s:HorizontalLayout paddingTop="10" paddingLeft="10" />
    </s:layout>

    <s:Group width="300" height="300">
```

```
<s:DataGroup width="100%" height="100%"
             itemRenderer="spark.skins.spark.DefaultComplexItemRenderer">

    <s:layout>
        <f4cb:Custom3DLayout scrollPosition="{slider.value}" />
    </s:layout>

    <s:dataProvider>
        <s:ArrayCollection>
            <s:Button label="Lorem" />
            <s:Button label="ipsum" />
            <s:Button label="dolar" />
            <s:Button label="sit" />
            <s:Button label="amet" />
            <s:Button label="consectetur" />
        </s:ArrayCollection>
    </s:dataProvider>

</s:DataGroup>

<s:Rect width="100%" height="100%">
    <s:stroke>
        <s:SolidColorStroke color="#000000" />
    </s:stroke>
</s:Rect>

</s:Group>

<s:VSlider id="slider" height="300" liveDragging="true"
           minimum="0" maximum="360" />

</s:Application>
```

As the value of the s:VSlider control changes, the scrollPosition of the custom layout
delegate is modified and the transformations on child elements are updated to show a
smooth scrolling carousel with perspective.

3.13 Programmatically Scroll Within a Layout

Problem

You want to programmatically set the scroll position within a container.

Solution

Use the horizontalScrollPosition and verticalScrollPosition properties of a Layout
Base-based layout.

Discussion

When a fixed size is applied to a container and the `clipAndEnableScrolling` property is set to a value of `true`, the rendering of child elements is confined to the dimensions of the container. If the position of a child element is determined as being outside of the parent container's bounds, the layout does not display that child within the container. Containers that implement the `IViewport` interface—as `GroupBase`-based containers do—can be wrapped in a `Scroller` component, and scroll bars will automatically be displayed based on the `contentWidth` and `contentHeight` of the viewport.

Because, unlike MX containers, Spark containers do not inherently support adding scroll bars to their display, programmatically scrolling the content of a viewport is supported by updating the `horizontalScrollPosition` and `verticalScrollPosition` properties of a layout. In fact, that is how a container internally determines its scroll position: by requesting the scroll values of its layout.

As shown in the following example, a container viewport can be scrolled programmatically by using another value-based component:

```
<s:Application xmlns:fx="http://ns.adobe.com/mxml/2009"
               xmlns:s="library://ns.adobe.com/flex/spark"
               xmlns:mx="library://ns.adobe.com/flex/mx">

    <fx:Declarations>
        <fx:String id="txt">
            Lorem ipsum dolor sit amet consectetur adipisicing elit.
        </fx:String>
    </fx:Declarations>

    <s:layout>
        <s:VerticalLayout horizontalAlign="center" />
    </s:layout>

    <s:HSlider id="slider"
               minimum="0"
               maximum="{group.contentHeight - group.height}"
               liveDragging="true" />

    <s:DataGroup id="group" width="100" height="100"
        clipAndEnableScrolling="true"
        itemRenderer="spark.skins.spark.DefaultItemRenderer">

        <s:layout>
            <s:VerticalLayout id="vLayout"
                              verticalScrollPosition="{slider.value}" />
        </s:layout>

        <s:dataProvider>
            <mx:ArrayCollection source="{txt.split(' ')}" />
        </s:dataProvider>
```

```
        </s:DataGroup>

    </s:Application>
```

The maximum scroll value for the s:HSlider control is determined by subtracting the value of the container's height property from its contentHeight property value. The contentHeight property is an attribute of the IViewport interface, which all GroupBase-based containers implement. The verticalScrollPosition of the container's layout delegate is bound to the value of the HSlider control, in turn updating the rendered view within the viewport of the container. As the value increases, child elements that previously resided below the viewport are rendered in the layout. As the value decreases, child elements that previously resided above the viewport are rendered.

Because the scroll position in the previous example is updated prior to the rendering of child elements, the layout can employ virtualization easily. However, determining the scroll position of a virtualized layout based on the size of child elements involves accessing the virtual child elements of a container directly.

The following example demonstrates how to programmatically use virtualized elemental scrolling:

```
<s:Application xmlns:fx="http://ns.adobe.com/mxml/2009"
               xmlns:s="library://ns.adobe.com/flex/spark"
               xmlns:mx="library://ns.adobe.com/flex/mx">

    <fx:Library>
        <fx:Definition name="MyRect">
            <s:Rect width="100">
                <s:fill>
                    <mx:SolidColor color="#000000" />
                </s:fill>
            </s:Rect>
        </fx:Definition>
    </fx:Library>

    <fx:Script>
        <![CDATA[
            import mx.core.IVisualElement;
            import spark.core.NavigationUnit;

            private var elementHeight:Vector.<Number> = new Vector.<Number>();
            private var currentIndex:int;
            private function handleScroll( unit:uint ):void
            {
                currentIndex = (unit == NavigationUnit.UP)
                            ? currentIndex - 1
                            : currentIndex + 1;
                currentIndex = Math.max( 0, Math.min( currentIndex,
                            group.numElements - 1 ) );
                var element:IVisualElement;
                var ypos:Number = 0;
                for( var i:int = 0; i < currentIndex; i++ )
```

```
                  {
                      element = group.getVirtualElementAt( i );
                      if( element != null )
                      {
                          elementHeight[i] = element.getPreferredBoundsHeight();
                      }
                      ypos += elementHeight[i];
                  }
                  ypos += vLayout.paddingTop;
                  ypos += vLayout.gap * currentIndex;
                  vLayout.verticalScrollPosition = ypos;
              }
          ]]>
    </fx:Script>

    <s:layout>
        <s:VerticalLayout horizontalAlign="center" />
    </s:layout>

    <s:DataGroup id="group" width="100" height="100"
                 clipAndEnableScrolling="true"
                 itemRenderer="spark.skins.spark.DefaultComplexItemRenderer">

        <s:layout>
            <s:VerticalLayout id="vLayout" useVirtualLayout="true" />
        </s:layout>

        <s:dataProvider>
            <mx:ArrayCollection>
                <fx:MyRect height="30" />
                <s:DropDownList height="20" />
                <fx:MyRect height="50" />
                <s:Button height="80" />
                <fx:MyRect height="40" />
            </mx:ArrayCollection>
        </s:dataProvider>

    </s:DataGroup>

    <s:Button label="up" click="handleScroll(NavigationUnit.UP)" />
    <s:Button label="down" click="handleScroll(NavigationUnit.DOWN)" />

</s:Application>
```

The elemental index on which to base the vertical scroll position of the container viewport is determined by a `click` event dispatched from either of the two declared `s:Button` controls. As the `currentIndex` value is updated, the position is determined by the stored `height` values of child elements retrieved from the `getVirtualElementAt()` method of the `GroupBase` target container.

See Also

Recipe 2.7

3.14 Determine the Visibility of Elements in a Sequence-Based Layout

Problem

You want to determine the visibility of an element within a container with a sequence-based layout delegate and possibly scroll the element into view.

Solution

Use the `fractionOfElementInView()` method of a sequence-based layout such as `VerticalLayout` or `HorizontalLayout` to determine the visibility percentage value of an element within the container's viewport and set the container's scroll position based on the corresponding coordinate offset value returned from the `getScrollPositionDeltaToElement()` method of a `LayoutBase`-based layout.

Discussion

Sequence-based layouts available in the Flex 4 SDK, such as `VerticalLayout` and `HorizontalLayout`, have convenience properties and methods for determining the visibility of an element within the viewport of its parent container. The `fractionOfElementInView()` method returns a percentage value related to the visibility of an element within a range of 0 to 1. A value of `0` means the element is not present in the view, while a value of `1` means the element is completely in view. The argument value for the `fractionOfElementInView()` method is the elemental index of an element in the container's display list. This index is used, along with the `firstIndexInView` and `lastIndexInView` convenience properties, to determine the visibility of the element; you can also use it to determine whether to update a container's scroll position and if so, by how much.

If it is determined that the element needs to be scrolled into view, the scroll position of the container viewport can be updated programmatically using the `verticalScrollPosition` and `horizontalScrollPosition` properties, as in the following example:

```
<s:Application xmlns:fx="http://ns.adobe.com/mxml/2009"
            xmlns:s="library://ns.adobe.com/flex/spark"
            xmlns:mx="library://ns.adobe.com/flex/mx">

    <fx:Script>
        <![CDATA[
            import spark.layouts.VerticalLayout;
            import mx.core.IVisualElement;

            private function scrollTo( index:int ):void
            {
                var amt:Number = (group.layout as
                            VerticalLayout).fractionOfElementInView(index);
                if( amt < 1.0 )
```

```
                    {
                        var pt:Point = group.layout.getScrollPositionDeltaToElement(
                                    index );
                        if( pt != null ) group.verticalScrollPosition += pt.y;
                        // else already in view
                    }
                    // else already fully in view
                }

                private function getRandomInRange( min:int, max:int ):int
                {
                    return ( Math.floor( Math.random() * (max - min + 1) ) + min );
                }

                private function handleClick( evt:MouseEvent ):void
                {
                    var item:IVisualElement = evt.target as IVisualElement;
                    var index:Number = group.getElementIndex( item );
                    scrollTo( index );
                }

                private function handleRandomScroll():void
                {
                    var index:int = getRandomInRange( 0, 9 );
                    scrollTo( index );
                    scrollToField.text = (index+1).toString();
                }
            ]]>
        </fx:Script>

        <s:layout>
            <s:VerticalLayout />
        </s:layout>

        <s:Scroller width="200" height="100">
            <s:VGroup id="group" horizontalAlign="justify">
                <s:Button label="button (1)" click="handleClick(event)" />
                <s:Button label="button (2)" click="handleClick(event)" />
                <s:Button label="button (3)" click="handleClick(event)" />
                <s:Button label="button (4)" click="handleClick(event)" />
                <s:Button label="button (5)" click="handleClick(event)" />
                <s:Button label="button (6)" click="handleClick(event)" />
                <s:Button label="button (7)" click="handleClick(event)" />
                <s:Button label="button (8)" click="handleClick(event)" />
                <s:Button label="button (9)" click="handleClick(event)" />
                <s:Button label="button (10)" click="handleClick(event)" />
            </s:VGroup>
        </s:Scroller>

        <s:HGroup verticalAlign="middle">
            <s:Button label="random scroll to:" click="handleRandomScroll()" />
            <s:Label id="scrollToField" text="1" />
        </s:HGroup>

    </s:Application>
```

Each element in the layout of the `<s:VGroup>` container is assigned a handler for a `click` event, which determines the elemental index of that item using the `getElementIndex()` method of the content API. This example also provides the ability to randomly scroll to an element within the container using the `handleRandom Scroll()` method, which (similar to the `handleClick()` event handler) hands an elemental index to the `scrollTo()` method to determine the visibility percentage of that element within the container viewport. If the element is not fully in view, it is scrolled into view using the `getScrollPositionDeltaToElement()` method of a `LayoutBase`-based layout. This method returns a `Point` object with position values that indicate the element's offset from the container viewport (i.e., how far to scroll to make it completely visible). If the return value is `null`, either the elemental index lies outside of the display list or the element at that index is already fully in view.

The display list indexes of the elements visible in the container viewport can also be determined using the `firstIndexInView` and `lastIndexInView` convenience properties of a sequence-based layout, as in the following snippet:

```
private function scrollTo( index:int ):void
{
    var amt:Number = ( group.layout as VerticalLayout ).fractionOfElementInView(
                  index );
    if( amt < 1.0 )
    {
        var pt:Point = group.layout.getScrollPositionDeltaToElement( index );
        if( pt != null ) group.verticalScrollPosition += pt.y;
        // else already in view
    }
    // else already fully in view
    trace( "firstIndex: " + ( group.layout as VerticalLayout ).firstIndexInView );
    trace( "lastIndex: " + ( group.layout as VerticalLayout ).lastIndexInView );
}
```

Upon a change to the scroll position of the layout delegate assigned to a container, the read-only `firstIndexInView` and `lastIndexInView` properties of a sequence-based layout are updated and a bindable `indexInViewChanged` event is dispatched.

CHAPTER 4

Graphics

With the introduction of the Spark architecture in the Flex 4 SDK, graphics have become first-class citizens and can be sized and positioned within a layout along with the other elements in the container's display list. As in previous versions of the SDK, vector graphics are rendered using the drawing API of a read-only `flash.display.Graphics` object held on the lowest layer of a `Sprite`-based element. Yet for Flex 4, the concept has been given an overhaul. Now display objects are created and held internally by `GraphicElement`-based elements to render graphics, providing a level of abstraction that allows for graphics to be treated the same as any other visual element within a layout.

Along with this new graphical rendering concept, Flex 4 incorporates the Flash XML Graphics (referred to as *FXG*) format, which is a readable vector graphics format that is interchangeable between multiple software tools and does not require knowledge of the ActionScript language or MXML markup.

A FXG *fragment* is a grouping of graphical elements, such as shapes, text, and raster images, along with optional masking and filters that can be contained inline in MXML or within a FXG document with the *.fxg* file extension. FXG is a subset of MXML and does not include the ability to reference external classes or respond to runtime events, such as data binding and state changes. However, FXG fragments can be declared inline in MXML to take advantage of such features, which most skin classes in the Spark architecture employ.

The declaration of FXG fragments within FXG and MXML documents is similar, although the namespace scope and the available and required attributes of the graphic elements differ. The root node of a FXG document must be declared as a `Graphic` type with the required `version` and `xmlns` attributes. The following snippet is an example of a FXG 2.0 document (the current version at the time of this writing):

```
<Graphic version="2.0" xmlns="http://ns.adobe.com/fxg/2008">
    <Group>
        <Rect width="100" height="100">
            <fill>
                <SolidColor color="#DDDDDD" />
            </fill>
```

```
        </Rect>
        <RichText>
            <content>Hello World!</content>
        </RichText>
    </Group>
</Graphic>
```

With the namespace properly scoped, graphic elements can be added to the document singularly or wrapped in a `<Group>` element. The declared node names for graphic elements in a FXG document, such as `Rect` and `BitmapImage`, are the same as those available in the Flex 4 SDK's `spark.primitives` package. A `RichText` element is also available for FXG; it can be found in the `spark.components` package of the SDK.

A FXG document fragment can be added to the display list of a MXML container similarly to any other component, either through markup with the proper namespace scope or using the content API in ActionScript. However, there is no API available in the Flex 4 SDK to load a FXG document with the *.fxg* file extension and add it to the display list at runtime. When a FXG document fragment is declared in an application, the graphical data is compiled into the application and wrapped in a `spark.core.SpriteVisualElement` instance so it can be handled like any other visual element by the layout delegate of the target container.

FXG fragments can also be declared directly in MXML in an application with the Spark namespace declared. Scoped to the Spark namespace, `GraphicElement`-based elements from the `spark.primitives` package and the `spark.components.RichText` element of the Flex 4 SDK can be added in markup along with other visual elements, as in the following:

```
<s:Graphic>
    <s:Rect width="100" height="100">
        <s:fill>
            <s:SolidColor color="#DDDDDD" />
        </s:fill>
    </s:Rect>
    <s:RichText text="Hello FXG!" />
</s:Graphic>
```

Graphic elements declared in MXML have more properties than elements declared in FXG documents and can take advantage of MXML concepts available to other visual elements, such as data binding and runtime styling. Although runtime access of elements and properties of a FXG fragment declared in MXML markup can prove to be a valuable asset in some applications, it should be noted that this approach does add more overhead than using a FXG document that is compiled in and rasterized as a graphic element.

The following recipes will show you how these new elements work for both FXG and MXML documents.

4.1 Size and Position a Graphic Element

Problem

You want to control the size and position of a grouping of graphical elements.

Solution

Add graphic elements to a `Graphic` display element and modify the `viewWidth` and `viewHeight` properties along with the inherited size and translation properties.

Discussion

The `Graphic` display element is an extension of `Group` and serves as a wrapper to contain graphic elements. When you create a FXG document with a *.fxg* file extension, the `Graphic` element must be the root tag of the document. When declaring a `<Graphic>` element in MXML markup, the element can be placed in a container as long as it is scoped to the proper namespace.

Aside from the inability to specify a layout delegate, most inherited properties of `Group` can be applied to a `Graphic` instance, which also exposes a few specific properties of its own: `version`, `viewWidth`, and `viewHeight`. The `version` property specifies the target FXG version for the `Graphic`. This property is not required when declaring the `<Graphic>` element in MXML, but it is necessary when creating a FXG document.

The `viewWidth` and `viewHeight` properties specify the size at which to render the element within the container's layout. Just as with setting the viewport bounds of a `Group`, specifying `viewWidth` and `viewHeight` values for a `Graphic` element does not inherently clip the visible area of the element. If you want parts of the graphic that extend beyond the bounds of the view to be visible, you must also wrap the `Graphic` element in a `Scroller` instance, as in the following snippet:

```
<s:Scroller>
    <s:Graphic viewWidth="100" viewHeight="100">
        <s:Rect width="500" height="500">
            <s:fill>
                <s:SolidColor color="0x333333" />
            </s:fill>
        </s:Rect>
    </s:Graphic>
</s:Scroller>>
```

In this example, although the `Rect` graphic element is larger than the view size specified by the `Graphic` container, only a portion of the graphic (the top-left corner, extending 100 pixels along the *x* and *y* axes) is visible. However, because the `Graphic` element, which is considered an implementation of `IViewport`, has been wrapped by a `Scroller` instance to enable scrolling, it's possible to view the rest of the graphic.

The `viewWidth` and `viewHeight` properties differ from the `width` and `height` properties inherited from `Group`; when they are set, `width` and `height` scale the graphics in the `Graphic` control as opposed to modifying the viewport. To demonstrate how the graphic element grouping is scaled when the `width` and `height` properties are specified, the following example contains a `RichText` element as well as the `Rect`:

```
<s:Graphic width="100" height="100">
    <s:Rect width="300" height="300">
        <s:fill>
            <s:SolidColor color="0x333333" />
        </s:fill>
    </s:Rect>
    <s:RichText color="#FFFFFF"
                horizontalCenter="0" verticalCenter="0">
        <s:span>Graphic Example</s:span>
    </s:RichText>
</s:Graphic>
```

When rendered in the layout, the graphic is scaled down and contained in a view bound to 50 pixels along the *x* and *y* axes. By setting a `noScale` value for the `resizeMode` property, you can override the default scaling applied to a `Graphic` object when `width` and `height` property values are specified. Doing so will, in essence, use the `width` and `height` property values similarly to how the `viewWidth` and `viewHeight` properties are used within a layout.

4.2 Use Path to Draw a Shape with Stroke and Fill

Problem

You want to draw a custom complex shape with a fill and a stroke.

Solution

Use the `Path` element and modify the `data` property to specify the path segments denoted by space-delimited command and parameter value pairs. Supply valid `IFill` and `IStroke` implementations to the `fill` and `stroke` properties, respectively, to fill and apply a stroke to the element.

Discussion

The `Path` element is a graphic element that supports fill and stroke and is used to create vector graphics more complex than those available in the Flex 4 SDK. The shape of the vector is constructed from a series of segments, which are supplied as a space-delimited string of commands to the `data` property of the `Path` element. The syntax for defining a shape typically starts with first positioning the pen at a point in the coordinate plane and then using `Line`, `CubicBezier`, and `QuadraticBezier` segments to draw the graphic. The commands for drawing these segments are denoted by characters when assembling the drawing data for a path. The parameter values for the segment commands vary, though they are related to coordinate points and, in the case of Bezier segments, may also include control points.

The following is a list of the available commands and their usage. Specifying the uppercase version of a command causes the drawing procedure to treat the parameter values as absolute, while specifying the lowercase version causes it to consider them as relative:

M/m
> Moves the pen to the specified position to begin drawing

L/l
> Draws a line segment from the current position to the specified coordinate

C/c
> Draws a curve segment to the specified coordinate based on supplied control points

Q/q
> Draws a curve segment to the specified coordinate based on a single control point

H/h
> Draws a horizontal line

V/v
> Draws a vertical line

Z/z
> Closes the path

The following is an example of drawing a simple polygon using line segments:

```
<s:Path data="M 0 0
              L 100 0
              L 100 100
              L 0 100
              Z">
    <s:stroke>
        <s:SolidColorStroke color="#333333" caps="square" joints="miter" />
    </s:stroke>
    <s:fill>
        <s:SolidColor color="#00CCFF" />
    </s:fill>
</s:Path>
```

First the pen is moved to 0,0 along the coordinate plane using the M command. It is then moved using Line segments to draw a polygon with a width and height of 100 pixels and closed using the Z command. Because Path is an extension of Filled Element, a stroke and a fill can be applied to the element.

A polygon can also be created using the H and V commands to move the pen along the x and y axes, respectively, as in the following example:

```
<s:Path data="M 0 0
            H 100
            V 100
            H 0
            Z">
    <s:stroke>
        <s:SolidColorStroke color="#333333" caps="square" joints="miter" />
    </s:stroke>
    <s:fill>
        <s:SolidColor color="#00CCFF" />
    </s:fill>
</s:Path>
```

It is important to note that using the uppercase H and V drawing commands treats the parameter values as absolute. That is, if the pen is originally moved to a coordinate other than 0,0, the line segments will still be drawn to 100 pixels along the *x* and *y* axes starting from 0,0, not from the point specified in the M command. To have the line segments treated as relative, use lowercase commands, as in the following example:

```
<s:Path data="M 20 20
            h 100
            v 100
            h -100
            z">
    <s:stroke>
        <s:SolidColorStroke color="#333333" caps="square" joints="miter" />
    </s:stroke>
    <s:fill>
        <s:SolidColor color="#00CCFF" />
    </s:fill>
</s:Path>
```

In this example, a series of 100-pixel line segments are drawn starting from the 20,20 origin specified in the M command. The result is a polygon with a width and height of 100 pixels.

The Path element also exposes a winding property, which allows you to specify the fill rule for the vector graphic with respect to intersecting or overlapping path segments. By default the winding value is evenOdd, which will render the intersection of multiple path segments as a knockout. Let's look at an example:

```
<s:Graphic x="10" y="10">
    <s:Path winding="{GraphicsPathWinding.EVEN_ODD}"
            data="M 0 0
                L 100 0
                L 100 100
                L 0 100
                Z
                M 50 50
                L 150 50
                L 150 150
                L 50 150
                Z">
        <s:stroke>
```

```
                <s:SolidColorStroke color="#333333" caps="square" joints="miter" />
            </s:stroke>
            <s:fill>
                <s:SolidColor color="#00CCFF" />
            </s:fill>
        </s:Path>
    </s:Graphic>
```

Here, two overlapping polygons are drawn within a Path element: first a shape is drawn at 0,0, then the pen is moved to 50,50 and another shape is drawn. The intersection of the two polygons at 50,50 and extended to 100 pixels along the *x*-axis and 100 pixels along the *y*-axis is not rendered because of the specified evenOdd winding rule. Because each path segment in this example is drawn in a clockwise direction, the winding property value can be changed to nonZero in order to fill the intersection if needed. However, if the drawing sequence for each polygon is different—as in the following example, which draws the first polygon using a clockwise path and the second using a counterclockwise path—the winding property value is negated:

```
    <s:Path winding="{GraphicsPathWinding.NON_ZERO}"
            data="M 0 0
                L 100 0
                L 100 100
                L 0 100
                Z
                M 50 50
                L 50 150
                L 150 150
                L 150 50
                Z">
        <s:stroke>
            <s:SolidColorStroke color="#333333" caps="square" joints="miter" />
        </s:stroke>
        <s:fill>
            <s:SolidColor color="#00CCFF" />
        </s:fill>
    </s:Path>
```

Drawing paths using evenOdd winding or overlapping counterclockwise and clockwise paths might look like Figure 4-1.

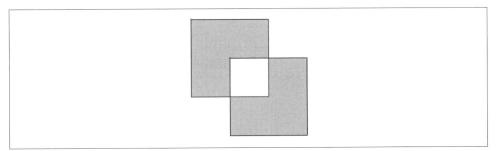

Figure 4-1. An example of a knockout within a Path element

4.3 Display Text in a Graphic Element

Problem

You want to render textual content within a graphic element.

Solution

Use the `RichText` element and either supply formatted text as the `content` property value or specify a `TextFlow` instance that manages textual content to be rendered within a FXG fragment.

Discussion

Included in the 2.0 version of the FXG specification is a `RichText` element that can be used to render rich-formatted textual content as a vector graphic. The `RichText` element makes use of the Text Layout Framework (TLF)—discussed in more detail in Chapter 7—to offer better support for typography and layout of text, although the resulting text is noninteractive and does not allow for scrolling or selection.

Unlike the other representations of graphic elements in the Flex 4 SDK, such as shape paths and raster images, `RichText` is not a `GraphicElement`-based object; rather, it is an extension of `TextBase`. `TextBase` is a `UIComponent`-based element that exposes a few properties related to the display of text and supports applying CSS styles for formatting. `RichText` utilizes the TLF API in order to render styled and formatted textual content in a `TextFlow` element. The value supplied to the `content` property of `RichText` is managed by an instance of `flashx.textLayout.elements.TextFlow`, which treats formatted text as a hierarchical tree of elements. As such, `RichText` supports many tags for properly rendering the textual content of a story, such as `<div>`, `<p>`, `<span>`, and `<img>`.

When using the `RichText` element in a FXG document, the `content` property is used to supply rich-formatted text, as in the following example:

```
<Graphic version="2.0" xmlns="http://ns.adobe.com/fxg/2008">
    <RichText width="400" height="60"
              columnCount="4"
              fontFamily="Helvetica">
        <content>
            <div>
                <img source='assets/icon.png' width='20' height='20' />
                <p>Lorem ipsum dolor sit amet, consectetuer adipiscing elit,
                <span fontWeight="bold">sed diam nonummy nibh euismod tincidunt ut
                laoreet dolore</span>
                magna aliquam erat volutpat.
                </p>
            </div>
        </content>
    </RichText>
</Graphic>
```

In this example, an image from a local resource is loaded and rendered alongside textual content that is represented using the glyph information of the Helvetica font. An image can be rendered within the content of a `RichText` element in a FXG document only at compile time. Consequently, the image path must point to a location on the local disk from which the application is compiled and cannot be a URL.

With `width` and `height` property values specified for the element, a `columnCount` style property—along with `columnGap` and `columnWidth`—can be applied to render text using multiple lines across multiple columns.

Along with enabling you to take advantage of runtime concepts such as data binding and changes to state, defining a `RichText` graphic in MXML allows you to specify a `TextFlow` instance to use in rendering the textual content. The `TextFlow` object is the root element of a tree of textual elements, such as spans and paragraphs. A richly formatted string using element tags is converted into a tree structure of elements from the `flashx.textLayout.elements` package, which contains the core classes used to represent textual content in TLF. Typically, the `spark.utils.TextFlowUtil` class is used to retrieve an instance of `TextFlow` from the static `importFromString()` and `importFromXML()` methods, as in the following example:

```
<s:Application xmlns:fx="http://ns.adobe.com/mxml/2009"
               xmlns:s="library://ns.adobe.com/flex/spark"
               xmlns:mx="library://ns.adobe.com/flex/mx">

    <fx:Script>
        <![CDATA[
            import spark.utils.TextFlowUtil;

            [Bindable]
            public var txt:String = "<div>" +
            "<img source='assets/icon.png' width='20' height='20' />" +
            "<p>Lorem ipsum dolor sit amet, consectetuer adipiscing elit," +
            "<span fontWeight='bold'>sed diam nonummy nibh euismod tincidunt ut" +
            "laoreet dolore</span>" +
            "magna aliquam erat volutpat.</p></div>";
        ]]>
    </fx:Script>
    <s:Graphic x="10" y="10">
        <s:RichText width="400" height="60"
                    columnCount="4"
                    fontFamily="Helvetica"
                    textFlow="{TextFlowUtil.importFromString(txt)}"/>
    </s:Graphic>

</s:Application>
```

The string value of the `txt` property is rendered within a `TextFlow` object returned from the static `importFromString()` method of `TextFlowUtil`. An instance of `TextFlow` can also be created and assigned to the `textFlow` property of a `RichText` object in ActionScript. Doing so, however, generally requires more fine-grained configuration of how the textual content is contained for layout, and elements from the `flashx.textLayout`

`.elements` package are added directly using the `addChild()` method, as opposed to supplying a rich-formatted string in the static convenience method of the `TextFlowUtil` class.

The Flash Text Engine (FTE) in Flash Player 10 and the ancillary classes and libraries included in the Flex 4 SDK that manage the rendering of textual content (such as TLF) are too complex to discuss in a single recipe and are covered in more detail in Chapter 7. The examples in this recipe, however, should serve as a starting point for providing richly formatted text in graphics.

4.4 Display Bitmap Data in a Graphic Element

Problem

You want to display a raster image within a graphic element.

Solution

Use the `BitmapImage` element or supply a `BitmapFill` to a `FilledElement`-based element and set the `source` property to a value of a valid representation of a bitmap. Optionally, set the `fillMode` of the graphic to clip, scale, or repeat the image data within the element.

Discussion

Bitmap information from an image source can be rendered within a graphic element in a FXG fragment. The `BitmapImage` element can be used to define a rectangular region in which to render the source bitmap data, or any `FilledElement`-based element can be assigned a `BitmapFill` to render the data within a custom filled path. `fillMode` is a property of both `BitmapImage` and `BitmapFill` that defines how the bitmap data should be rendered within the element. The values available for `fillMode` are enumerated in the `BitmapFillMode` class and allow for clipping, scaling, and repeating the bitmap data within the defined bounds of the element. By default, the `fillMode` property is set to a value of `scale`, which fills the display area of an element with the source bitmap data.

The following example demonstrates using both the `BitmapImage` element and `Bitmap Fill` within a MXML fragment to display bitmap information:

```
<s:Application xmlns:fx="http://ns.adobe.com/mxml/2009"
               xmlns:s="library://ns.adobe.com/flex/spark"
               xmlns:mx="library://ns.adobe.com/flex/mx">

    <fx:Script>
        <![CDATA[
            import mx.graphics.BitmapFillMode;
        ]]>
    </fx:Script>
```

```
<s:Graphic>
    <s:Group>
        <s:layout>
            <s:HorizontalLayout />
        </s:layout>
        <s:BitmapImage id="img" width="450" height="400"
                    source="@Embed('assets/icon.png')" />
        <s:Ellipse id="imgEllipse" width="450" height="400">
            <s:fill>
                <s:BitmapFill id="imgFill"
                            fillMode="{BitmapFillMode.REPEAT}"
                            source="@Embed('assets/icon.png')" />
            </s:fill>
        </s:Ellipse>
    </s:Group>
</s:Graphic>

</s:Application>
```

The `source` property of a `BitmapImage` element or the `BitmapFill` of an element, when declared in MXML, can point to various graphic resources. The source could be a `Bitmap` object, a `BitmapData` object, any instance or class reference of a `DisplayObject`-based element, or an image file specified using the `@Embed` directive. If a file reference is used, the image file path must be relative as it is compiled in; there is no support for runtime loading of an image when using FXG elements in MXML markup.

Figure 4-2 shows a few examples of effects you can achieve using the various graphic elements and fill modes. On the left, an image is loaded and resized to fill a rectangle shape. On the right, the same image is loaded into an ellipse shape and repeated at its original size to fill the shape.

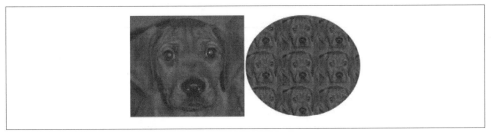

Figure 4-2. Examples of rendering a raster image in a graphic

The `source` property value for an element rendering bitmap data in a FXG document can point either to a relative file path for an image resource, or to a URL. Bitmap information is compiled into the graphic element within the FXG document, and such runtime concepts as updating the source based on loaded graphic information are not applicable.

The following is an example of supplying a URL to the `source` property of a `Bitmap Image` element within a FXG document:

```
<!-- MyBitmapGraphic.fxg -->
<Graphic version="2.0" xmlns="http://ns.adobe.com/fxg/2008">
    <BitmapImage width="600" height="150" fillMode="repeat"
                 source="http://covers.oreilly.com/images/9780596529857/bkt.gif"
/>
</Graphic>
```

Supplying a URL for the bitmap fill of an element is not permitted in a FXG fragment within MXML markup. However, graphics declared in MXML take advantage of various runtime concepts, including responding to state changes, data binding, and (with regard to displaying bitmap information) loading graphic resources and updating the source of a bitmap element at runtime. The following example demonstrates setting the source property of a BitmapImage to a Bitmap instance at runtime alongside rendering the graphic element of a FXG document:

```
<s:Application xmlns:fx="http://ns.adobe.com/mxml/2009"
               xmlns:s="library://ns.adobe.com/flex/spark"
               xmlns:mx="library://ns.adobe.com/flex/mx"
               xmlns:f4cb="com.oreilly.f4cb.*"
               creationComplete="handleCreationComplete();">

    <fx:Script>
        <![CDATA[
            import mx.graphics.BitmapFillMode;

            private function handleCreationComplete():void
            {
                var loader:Loader = new Loader();
                loader.contentLoaderInfo.addEventListener(Event.COMPLETE,
                                                          handleLoadComplete);
                loader.load( new URLRequest(
                    'http://covers.oreilly.com/images/9780596529857/bkt.gif' ) );
            }

            private function handleLoadComplete( evt:Event ):void
            {
                var bmp:Bitmap = ( evt.target as LoaderInfo ).content as Bitmap;
                img.source = bmp;
            }
        ]]>
    </fx:Script>

    <s:layout>
        <s:VerticalLayout />
    </s:layout>

    <s:Graphic>
        <s:Group>
            <s:layout>
                <s:HorizontalLayout />
            </s:layout>
            <s:BitmapImage id="img"
                           width="450" height="400"
                           fillMode="{BitmapFillMode.SCALE}" />
```

```
            <f4cb:MyBitmapGraphic />
        </s:Group>
    </s:Graphic>

</s:Application>
```

4.5 Display Gradient Text

Problem

You want to render textual content using a gradient color.

Solution

Apply a gradient fill to a `FilledElement`-based element and apply a `RichText` element as the mask for a graphic.

Discussion

The `color` style property of the `RichText` element takes a single color component and does not support multiple gradient entries. You can, however, render noninteractive text in a linear or radial gradient by using the text graphic as a mask applied to a filled path.

The following is an example of applying a `RichText` element as a mask for a graphic element that renders a rectangular gradient, shown in Figure 4-3:

```
<s:Graphic maskType="alpha">
    <s:Rect width="{textMask.width}" height="{textMask.height}">
        <s:fill>
            <s:LinearGradient rotation="90">
                <s:entries>
                    <s:GradientEntry color="#000000" />
                    <s:GradientEntry color="#DDDDDD" />
                </s:entries>
            </s:LinearGradient>
        </s:fill>
    </s:Rect>
    <s:mask>
        <s:RichText id="textMask" fontFamily="Arial" fontSize="20">
            <s:content>Hello World!</s:content>
        </s:RichText>
    </s:mask>
</s:Graphic>
```

Hello World!

Figure 4-3. Example of gradient text using a RichText element as a mask

With the `maskType` property of the `Graphic` element set to `alpha`, the `RichText` element renders using the gradient values of the child `s:Rect` element based on the glyph information of the text. Binding the dimensions of the `RichText` instance to the `width` and `height` properties of the `Rect` element ensures the rendering of the full gradient when the textual content is applied to the graphic, even though it is a mask.

4.6 Apply Bitmap Data to a Graphic Element as a Mask

Problem

You want to take advantage of the alpha transparency or luminosity of a bitmap when applying a mask to a graphic element.

Solution

Apply an `Image` element or a `Group`-wrapped `BitmapImage` to a `Graphic` as the mask source and set the desired `maskType` property value. Depending on the `maskType` property value, optionally set the `luminosityClip` and `luminosityInvert` properties of the `Graphic` element as well.

Discussion

The `mask` property of `Graphic`, which is inherited from its extension of `Group`, is typed as a `DisplayObject` instance. You cannot, therefore, directly apply a `GraphicElement`-based element (such as `Rect` or `BitmapImage`) as a mask for a `GroupBase`-based element. You can, however, wrap graphic elements in a `Group` object and apply them as a mask. Likewise, any `DisplayObject`-based element, including the visual elements from the MX set, can be applied as a mask source for a `Graphic` element.

By default, masking of content within a `GroupBase`-based element is performed using clipping. With the `maskType` property value set to `clip`, the content is rendered based on the area of the mask source. Along with `clip`, there are two other valid values for the `maskType` property of a `GroupBase`-based element when applying a mask: `alpha` and `luminosity`. When you assign an `alpha` mask type, the alpha values of the mask source are used to determine the alpha and color values of the masked content. Assigning a luminosity mask is similar in that the content's and mask source's alpha values are used to render the masked pixels, as well as their RGB values.

The following example applies all three valid `maskType` property values to a `Graphic` element that is masked using an image containing some alpha transparency:

```
<s:Application xmlns:fx="http://ns.adobe.com/mxml/2009"
               xmlns:s="library://ns.adobe.com/flex/spark"
               xmlns:mx="library://ns.adobe.com/flex/mx"
               creationComplete="handleCreationComplete();">
```

```
<fx:Script>
    <![CDATA[
        import mx.collections.ArrayCollection;
        import spark.core.MaskType;

        [Bindable] public var masks:ArrayCollection;
        private function handleCreationComplete():void
        {
            masks = new ArrayCollection( [ MaskType.CLIP,
                                          MaskType.ALPHA,
                                          MaskType.LUMINOSITY ] );
            maskList.selectedIndex = 0;
        }
    ]]>
</fx:Script>

<s:layout>
    <s:VerticalLayout />
</s:layout>

<s:DropDownList id="maskList" dataProvider="{masks}" />

<s:Graphic id="group" maskType="{maskList.selectedItem}">
    <s:Rect width="320" height="320">
        <s:fill>
            <s:LinearGradient>
                <s:entries>
                    <s:GradientEntry color="#000000" />
                    <s:GradientEntry color="#DDDDDD" />
                </s:entries>
            </s:LinearGradient>
        </s:fill>
    </s:Rect>
    <s:mask>
        <s:Group>
            <s:BitmapImage source="@Embed('/assets/alpha_bitmap.png')" />
        </s:Group>
    </s:mask>
</s:Graphic>

<s:Group enabled="{maskList.selectedItem==MaskType.LUMINOSITY}">
    <s:layout>
        <s:HorizontalLayout />
    </s:layout>
    <s:CheckBox selected="@{group.luminosityInvert}" label="invert" />
    <s:CheckBox selected="@{group.luminosityClip}" label="clip" />
</s:Group>

</s:Application>
```

With the maskType property of the Graphic element set to clip, the gradient-filled Rect is clipped to the rectangular bounds of the embedded image. With the maskType set to alpha, the alpha values of the bitmap are used to render the masked pixels. When luminosity is selected as the maskType, two s:CheckBox controls are enabled, allowing you to set the `luminosityInvert` and `luminosityClip` properties of the `Graphic` element. If you are using an image that supports alpha transparency you might see something similar to Figure 4-4, which allows you to play with the different types of masks.

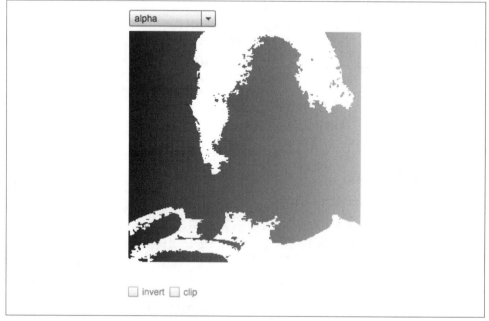

Figure 4-4. Example of applying an image with alpha transparency to a graphic element as a mask

The `luminosityInvert` and `luminosityClip` properties are only used when the `mask Type` is set to `luminosity`. With both property values set to `false` (the default), the pixels of the content source and the mask are clipped to the bounds of the image area and are blended. A `true` value for `luminosityInvert` inverts and multiplies the RGB color values of the source, and a `true` value for `luminosityClip` clips the masked content based on the opacity values of the mask source.

4.7 Create a Custom Shape Element

Problem

You want to create a custom graphic element and modify the drawing rules based on specific properties.

Solution

Extend `FilledElement`, override the `draw()` method to render the custom vector graphic, and optionally override the `measuredWidth` and `measuredHeight` accessors in order to properly lay out the element.

Discussion

The `spark.primitives.supportClasses.GraphicElement` class is a base class for all graphic elements, including raster images, text, and shapes. `GraphicElement` exposes the necessary properties to size and position elements within a layout delegate, and essentially manages the display object that graphics are drawn into, and onto which transformations and filters are applied. `StrokedElement` is a subclass of `Graphic Element` that exposes the ability to apply a stroke to a vector shape. `FilledElement` is a subclass of `StrokedElement` that provides the ability to apply a fill to a vector shape and can be extended to customize the drawing paths of a custom shape.

The stroke and fill applied to a `FilledElement` are implementations of `IStroke` and `IFill`, respectively, and standard classes to apply to a shape as strokes and fills can be found in the `mx.graphics` package. Typically, the initiation and completion of rendering the stroke and fill of a shape are handled in the protected `beginDraw()` and `endDraw()` methods. When extending the `FilledElement` class to create a custom shape element, the protected `draw()` method is overridden in order to apply drawing paths to a `Graphics` object using the drawing API, as in the following example:

```
package com.oreilly.f4cb
{
    import flash.display.Graphics;
    import spark.primitives.supportClasses.FilledElement;

    public class StarburstElement extends FilledElement
    {
        private var _points:int = 5;
        private var _innerRadius:Number = 50;
        private var _outerRadius:Number = 100;

        override public function get measuredWidth():Number
        {
            return _outerRadius * 2;
        }
        override public function get measuredHeight():Number
        {
            return _outerRadius * 2;
        }

        override protected function draw( g:Graphics ):void
        {
            var start:Number = ( Math.PI / 2 );
            var step:Number = Math.PI * 2 / _points;

            var rad:Number = outerRadius;
            var inRad:Number = innerRadius;
            var angle:Number = start;
            var sangle:Number = angle - step / 2;
            var x:Number = rad * Math.cos( sangle ) + rad;
            var y:Number = rad * Math.sin( sangle ) + rad;
            g.moveTo( x,y );
            x = inRad * Math.cos( angle ) + rad;
```

```
                y = inRad * Math.sin( angle ) + rad;
                g.lineTo( x, y );
                for( var i:int = 1; i < points; i++ )
                {
                    angle = start + ( i * step );
                    sangle = angle - step / 2;
                    g.lineTo( rad * Math.cos( sangle ) + rad,
                              rad * Math.sin( sangle ) + rad );
                    g.lineTo( inRad * Math.cos( angle ) + rad,
                              inRad * Math.sin( angle ) + rad );
                }
            }

            [Bindable]
            public function get points():int
            {
                return _points;
            }
            public function set points( value:int ):void
            {
                _points = value;
                invalidateSize();
                invalidateDisplayList();
                invalidateParentSizeAndDisplayList();
            }

            [Bindable]
            public function get innerRadius():Number
            {
                return _innerRadius;
            }
            public function set innerRadius( value:Number ):void
            {
                _innerRadius = value;
                invalidateSize();
                invalidateDisplayList();
                invalidateParentSizeAndDisplayList();
            }

            [Bindable]
            public function get outerRadius():Number
            {
                return _outerRadius;
            }
            public function set outerRadius( value:Number ):void
            {
                _outerRadius = value;
                invalidateSize();
                invalidateDisplayList();
                invalidateParentSizeAndDisplayList();
            }
        }
    }
```

The `StarburstElement` created in this example is an extension of `FilledElement` and overrides the `draw()` method in order to render a starburst shape in the supplied `Graphics` object. `draw()`, along with `beginDraw()` and `endDraw()`, is invoked upon each request to update the display list. The line segments to be drawn are determined using the `points`, `innerRadius`, and `outerRadius` properties of `StarburstElement`, which each invoke internal methods to update the size and display list of the element and its parent element. Doing so ensures that the element is properly laid out in a container. The `measuredWidth` and `measuredHeight` accessors are also overridden to return an accurate size for the element used by the layout.

The following example demonstrates adding the custom `StarburstElement` element to the display list and provides `HSlider` controls to modify the properties of the element at runtime:

```
<s:Application xmlns:fx="http://ns.adobe.com/mxml/2009"
               xmlns:s="library://ns.adobe.com/flex/spark"
               xmlns:mx="library://ns.adobe.com/flex/mx"
               xmlns:f4cb="com.oreilly.f4cb.*">

    <s:layout>
        <s:VerticalLayout />
    </s:layout>

    <f4cb:StarburstElement id="star">
        <f4cb:fill>
            <s:SolidColor color="#333333" />
        </f4cb:fill>
        <f4cb:stroke>
            <s:SolidColorStroke color="#FF00FF" />
        </f4cb:stroke>
    </f4cb:StarburstElement>

    <s:HSlider id="ptSlider"
               minimum="3" maximum="20"
               value="{star.points}"
               change="star.points=ptSlider.value" />
    <s:HSlider id="inSlider"
               minimum="5" maximum="50"
               value="{star.innerRadius}"
               change="{star.innerRadius=inSlider.value}" />
    <s:HSlider id="outSlider"
               minimum="55" maximum="100"
               value="{star.outerRadius}"
               change="{star.outerRadius=outSlider.value}" />

</s:Application>
```

Figure 4-5 shows the end result.

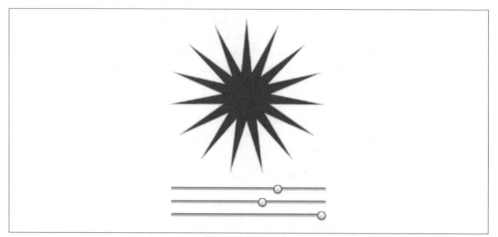

Figure 4-5. Example of a custom graphic element with attributes available for modification at runtime

4.8 Create a Custom Standalone Graphic Component

Problem

You want to create a graphic component that can be used throughout multiple applications.

Solution

Create a FXG fragment within a root `<Graphic>` node and save it as a standalone FXG or MXML document with the required document attributes declared.

Discussion

The structure and availability of elements is similar when creating graphics within a FXG or a MXML document. In some cases, such as with declaring library definitions wrapped in a `<Group>` element within a FXG document, the node structure may vary, yet both types of documents contain a fragment of graphical information declared in a root `<Graphic>` node and can be added to an application at compile time or at runtime.

The required attributes for the root `<Graphic>` node of a FXG document (with the *.fxg* extension) are `version` and `xmlns`, as shown in the following snippet:

```
<Graphic version="2.0" xmlns="http://ns.adobe.com/fxg/2008">
```

A `Graphic` element is similar to a `Group` element, in that children are defined declaratively to make up the visual representation of the FXG fragment. Along with the declaration of a mask and a library of reusable symbols, any valid graphic element (`Rect`, `Bitmap Graphic`, `RichText`, etc.) can be declared, either wrapped in a `Group` element or as a standalone element. The following is an example of the markup of a FXG document:

```
<Graphic version="2.0" xmlns="http://ns.adobe.com/fxg/2008">

    <Rect width="100" height="100">
        <fill>
            <RadialGradient>
                <GradientEntry color="#FFFFFF" />
                <GradientEntry color="#000000" />
            </RadialGradient>
        </fill>
        <stroke>
            <SolidColorStroke color="#333333" />
        </stroke>
    </Rect>

</Graphic>
```

A `Graphic` object declared in MXML, whether as a standalone graphic or an inline fragment within a document, must be scoped to the Spark namespace declared within the document. The following is an example of a standalone graphic component declared as a MXML document:

```
<s:Graphic name="CustomMXMLGraphic"
        xmlns:fx="http://ns.adobe.com/mxml/2009"
        xmlns:s="library://ns.adobe.com/flex/spark"
        xmlns:mx="library://ns.adobe.com/flex/mx">

    <s:Rect width="100" height="100">
        <s:fill>
            <s:LinearGradient rotation="90">
                <s:GradientEntry color="#FFFFFF" />
                <s:GradientEntry color="#000000" />
            </s:LinearGradient>
        </s:fill>
        <s:stroke>
            <s:SolidColorStroke color="#333333" />
        </s:stroke>
    </s:Rect>

</s:Graphic>
```

Standalone graphic elements saved as FXG and MXML documents are added to the display list in the same manner, by declaring the element scoped to the namespace representing the package directory in which the document resides. The following example demonstrates adding the previous two examples, saved as *CustomFXG Graphic.fxg* and *CustomMXMLGraphic.mxml*, respectively, to a MXML document:

```
<s:Application xmlns:fx="http://ns.adobe.com/mxml/2009"
            xmlns:s="library://ns.adobe.com/flex/spark"
            xmlns:mx="library://ns.adobe.com/flex/mx"
            xmlns:f4cb="com.oreilly.f4cb.*">

    <s:layout>
        <s:VerticalLayout />
    </s:layout>
```

```
<f4cb:CustomMXMLGraphic />
<f4cb:CustomFXGGraphic />

</s:Application>
```

Though the two graphical fragments are saved with different file extensions, they are declared similarly to each other and to other component declarations in MXML mark-up, and are scoped to the f4cb namespace, which points to a directory relative to the root of the Application document.

The decision to use a graphic element scoped to the FXG namespace, as in the first example, or scoped to the Spark namespace, as in the second, depends on the role of the graphic element within the lifespan of the application in which it is used. Because FXG is a subset of MXML, graphic elements scoped to the FXG namespace and saved as *.fxg* documents have a limited property list and cannot take full advantage of features available to graphic fragments in MXML markup. Graphic elements declared in MXML can be treated the same as any other elements within the document markup and can reference external classes, respond to changes of state and data binding at runtime, and have their properties modified by transitions. Although using FXG fragments in MXML has its benefits, more memory is used to store references that may be accessed at runtime.

4.9 Define and Reuse Graphic Symbols

Problem

You want to create a library of common graphic symbols that can be used multiple times within an application.

Solution

Declare symbols as Definition instances within a Library tag and assign a unique name property value to each Definition to be used as the element type in a FXG fragment.

Discussion

Symbol definitions are held in the Library tag of a FXG or MXML document, which must be declared as the first child of the root tag. Singular and grouped graphic elements can be created as symbol definitions and can be reused multiple times throughout the document in which the containing Library is declared. Usage of symbol definitions in a FXG document is limited to the fragment markup, while symbol definitions within a MXML document can be added to the display list through markup or by using the new operator in ActionScript.

When declared in a `Library` within a FXG document, symbol definitions are considered groupings of graphic elements regardless of the number of elements declared and must always be wrapped within a `Group` tag, as in the following example:

```
<!-- com.oreilly.f4cb.CustomFXGCircle.fxg -->
<Graphic version="2.0" xmlns="http://ns.adobe.com/fxg/2008">

    <Library>
        <Definition name="Circle">
            <Group>
                <Ellipse width="100" height="100">
                    <fill>
                        <SolidColor color="#FFCC00" />
                    </fill>
                </Ellipse>
            </Group>
        </Definition>
    </Library>

    <Circle />
    <Circle x="100">
        <filters>
            <DropShadowFilter />
        </filters>
    </Circle>

</Graphic>
```

The `Library` element is declared as the first child of the document and is scoped to the FXG namespace defined in the root `<Graphic>` tag. The `name` attribute value of a symbol definition is used to declare new instances of the symbol within the document. Several properties are available for the instance declarations, and transformations and filters can be applied separately from the definition in a FXG document.

Symbol definitions declared within a library of a MXML document differ from definition declarations in a FXG document in that a symbol with a single graphic element does not need to be wrapped in a `<Group>` tag:

```
<fx:Library>
    <fx:Definition name="MXMLCircle">
        <s:Ellipse width="100" height="100">
            <s:fill>
                <s:SolidColor color="#00FFCC" />
            </s:fill>
        </s:Ellipse>
    </fx:Definition>
</fx:Library>
```

If, however, more than one graphic element makes up the symbol definition, the elements must be wrapped in a `<Group>` tag. The `name` attribute of the symbol definition is used, just as in a FXG document, to declare instances of the symbol within MXML markup:

```
<s:Application xmlns:fx="http://ns.adobe.com/mxml/2009"
              xmlns:s="library://ns.adobe.com/flex/spark"
              xmlns:mx="library://ns.adobe.com/flex/mx">

    <fx:Library>
        <fx:Definition name="MXMLCircle">
            <s:Ellipse width="100" height="100">
                <s:fill>
                    <s:SolidColor color="#00FFCC" />
                </s:fill>
            </s:Ellipse>
        </fx:Definition>
    </fx:Library>

    <s:layout>
        <s:VerticalLayout />
    </s:layout>

    <fx:MXMLCircle />
    <fx:MXMLCircle x="100">
        <fx:filters>
            <fx:Array>
                <s:DropShadowFilter />
            </fx:Array>
        </fx:filters>
    </fx:MXMLCircle>

</s:Application>
```

Upon declaration of a symbol within the document, properties (such as those related to transformations and filters) can be reset from any values attributed in the definition for the symbol.

Libraries and definitions are a convenient way to declare graphic symbols that you can then reference and use multiple instances of within a FXG document. Symbol definitions can even be used in other symbol definitions declared in a Library. As mentioned earlier, by using the name property of a symbol definition along with the new operator, new instances of the graphic symbol can also be instantiated at runtime using Action-Script, as in the following example:

```
private function addSymbolFromLibrary():void
{
    var mySymbol:IVisualElement = new FXGCircle() as IVisualElement;
    addElement( mySymbol );
}
```

CHAPTER 5

Components

The Flex 4 SDK provides a set of classes and user interface (UI) components to facilitate rapid and standardized development. The fourth iteration of the SDK has been designed to enable the use of Flex 3 (Halo) components as well as Flex 4 (Spark) components based on the new architecture. By default, the Spark and Halo components are differentiated by the s and mx namespaces, respectively. For example:

```
<s:Button id="sparkButton"/>
<mx:Button id="haloButton"/>
```

This use of XML namespaces enables developers to switch between the new *Spark* components and the legacy *Halo* components. Additionally, it improves the readability of the code. Although many Spark components have Halo counterparts and the two can often be used interchangeably, it is recommended that you use the Spark versions when possible as they are most likely to be supported by future iterations of the Flex SDK.

5.1 Handle a Button's Click Event

Problem

You need to perform a task in response to user interaction, such as outputting a list of names to the console when the user clicks a button.

Solution

Use the click event attribute of the s:Button tag to assign a handler for the event in MXML. Alternatively, in ActionScript, use the addEventListener() method on the button instance to assign a listener for the click event.

Discussion

The following code shows how to listen for a button click by using MXML to assign a handler for the `click` event attribute of the `s:Button` tag:

```
<s:Application xmlns:fx="http://ns.adobe.com/mxml/2009"
               xmlns:s="library://ns.adobe.com/flex/spark"
               xmlns:mx="library://ns.adobe.com/flex/mx">
    <fx:Script>
        <![CDATA[
            protected var names:Array = ['Leif','Zach','Stacey'];
            protected function btn_clickHandler(event:MouseEvent):void
            {
                trace(names.toString());
            }
        ]]>
    </fx:Script>
    <s:layout>
        <s:VerticalLayout/>
    </s:layout>
    <s:Button id="btn" label="Show Names" click="btn_clickHandler(event)"/>
</s:Application>
```

The code creates an application that contains an instance of the button control `btn`. So that the application will output a list of names to the console when the `btn` instance is clicked, the `click` event attribute of the `btn` instance is wired to the method `showNames()`:

```
<s:Button id="btn" label="Show Names" click="btn_clickHandler(event)"/>
```

Every time a user clicks the button, the Flex Framework dispatches an event of type `MouseEvent.CLICK`. The preceding line of code assigns the method `btn_clickHandler()` to be invoked every time the button dispatches the `click` event. Within the `btn_click Handler()` method, an array of names is created and output to the console. Notice that an event object of type `MouseEvent` is automatically passed into the handler function. Depending on the event being dispatched, this object can be queried for detailed information about the event itself. Run the application in debug mode (F11 in Eclipse), and you'll see the following output in the console window:

```
Leif,Zach,Stacey
```

Event listeners can also be assigned using ActionScript:

```
<?xml version="1.0" encoding="utf-8"?>
<s:Application xmlns:fx="http://ns.adobe.com/mxml/2009"
               xmlns:s="library://ns.adobe.com/flex/spark"
               xmlns:mx="library://ns.adobe.com/flex/mx"
               creationComplete="app_creationCompleteHandler(event)">

    <fx:Script>
        <![CDATA[
            import mx.events.FlexEvent;
            protected var names:Array = ['Leif','Zach','Stacey','Seth','Leonard'];
```

```
                  protected var titles:Array = ['Evangelist','Director',
                                                'Information Architect','Director',
                                                'Creative Director'];


                  protected function app_creationCompleteHandler(event:FlexEvent):void
                  {
                      btn.addEventListener(MouseEvent.CLICK, showNames);
                      btn.addEventListener(MouseEvent.CLICK, showtitles);
                  }
                  protected function showNames(event:MouseEvent):void
                  {
                      trace(names.toString());
                  }
                  protected function showtitles(event:MouseEvent):void
                  {
                      trace(titles.toString());
                  }
              ]]>
          </fx:Script>
          <s:layout>
              <s:VerticalLayout/>
          </s:layout>
          <s:Button id="btn" label="Show Names and Titles"/>
      </s:Application>
```

Note here that the handler of the application's `creationComplete` event is used to wire up the button's `click` event to two listeners, `showNames` and `showTitles`:

```
          protected function app_creationCompleteHandler(event:FlexEvent):void
          {
              btn.addEventListener(MouseEvent.CLICK, showNames);
              btn.addEventListener(MouseEvent.CLICK, showtitles);
          }
```

Running this application in debug mode generates the following output in the console window:

```
Leif,Zach,Stacey,Seth,Leonard
Evangelist,Director,Information Architect,Director,Creative Director
```

The listeners are called in the same order as they are registered. Because `showNames` was registered before `showTitles`, the list of names is generated before the list of titles. To change the order of execution, either change the order in which the listeners are registered with the button, or set their `priority` values while registering them with the button, as shown here:

```
protected function app_creationCompleteHandler(event:FlexEvent):void
{
    /* Note that the third parameter, useCapture, in the addEventListener() method
    is already set to false by default and is manually set to false in this
    example to access the fourth parameter: priority. */
    btn.addEventListener(MouseEvent.CLICK, showNames, false, 0);
```

```
        btn.addEventListener(MouseEvent.CLICK, showtitles, false, 1);
    }
```

Running the application in debug mode, with the modified code, displays the following:

```
Evangelist,Director,Information Architect,Director,Creative Director
Leif,Zach,Stacey,Seth,Leonard
```

Listeners registered with larger priority values will be called earlier than those with smaller priority values. If more than one listener has the same priority value, the order of execution will be based on the order of registration.

5.2 Create a Button Bar

Problem

You need to present the user with a set of buttons that allow a single option to be selected at a time.

Solution

Use the `s:ButtonBar` control and an `ArrayCollection` to create the series of buttons.

Discussion

To build a series of buttons, create an application with an instance of the `s:Button Bar` control. This control defines a group of buttons that maintain their selected or deselected state. Here's one approach:

```
<?xml version="1.0" encoding="utf-8"?>
<s:Application xmlns:fx="http://ns.adobe.com/mxml/2009"
               xmlns:s="library://ns.adobe.com/flex/spark"
               xmlns:mx="library://ns.adobe.com/flex/mx">
    <fx:Script>
        <![CDATA[
            import spark.events.IndexChangeEvent;

            protected function btnBar_changeHandler(event:IndexChangeEvent):void {
                var selectedItem:Object = btnBarData.getItemAt(event.newIndex);
                switch(selectedItem.mode) {
                    case "labels":
                        trace('Leif, Zach, Stacey');
                        break;
                    case "titles":
                        trace('Evangelist, Director, Information Architect');
                        break;
                    default:
                        break;
                }
            }
        ]]>
    </fx:Script>
```

```
<fx:Declarations>
    <s:ArrayCollection id="btnBarData">
        <fx:Object label="Show Labels" mode="labels"/>
        <fx:Object label="Show Titles" mode="titles"/>
    </s:ArrayCollection>
</fx:Declarations>

<s:ButtonBar id="btnBar"
            dataProvider="{btnBarData}"
            change="btnBar_changeHandler(event)"/>

</s:Application>
```

The application contains only one component that is visible to the user: an instance of s:ButtonBar with its id property set to btnBar. Bound to the dataProvider property of btnBar is an s:ArrayCollection with an id of btnBarData. Because btnBarData is a nonvisual MXML element, it is declared in <fx:Declarations>.

By default, the label property values of the items in the ArrayCollection show up as the labels of the buttons in the <s:ButtonBar> instance. To set any other property (for example, mode) to be used as the button's label, use the labelField property of the s:ButtonBar as follows:

```
<s:ButtonBar id="btnBar"
            dataProvider="{btnBarData}"
            labelField="mode"
            change="btnBar_changeHandler(event)"/>
```

The change event of the s:ButtonBar instance is set to call the method btnBar_change Handler() when the selectedIndex property of btnBar is changed. Note that this event will fire regardless of whether the value is changed by the user clicking a different button than the current selected item, or programmatically. When the change event calls the btnBar_changeHandler() method, it passes an instance of IndexChangeEvent through as the event. Using the newIndex property of event, the handler can determine the index of the button the user selected and trace the corresponding string.

Although this is an effective method for creating a set of buttons, the practice of declaring the dataProvider in MXML is really only effective when the instance of s:ButtonBar will be mainly static. In most cases, it is beneficial to bind the dataProvider property of s:ButtonBar to an ArrayCollection declared in ActionScript. This will enable the dataProvider, and in turn the s:ButtonBar, to be updated more easily:

```
<?xml version="1.0" encoding="utf-8"?>
<s:Application xmlns:fx="http://ns.adobe.com/mxml/2009"
            xmlns:s="library://ns.adobe.com/flex/spark"
            xmlns:mx="library://ns.adobe.com/flex/mx">
    <fx:Script>
        <![CDATA[
            import mx.collections.ArrayCollection;
            import spark.events.IndexChangeEvent;

            [Bindable]
            protected var btnBarData:ArrayCollection = new ArrayCollection(
```

```
                    [
                        {label: 'Show Labels', mode: 'labels'},
                        {label: 'Show Titles', mode: 'titles'}
                    ]
                );

                protected function btnBar_changeHandler(event:IndexChangeEvent):void {
                    var selectedItem:Object = btnBarData.getItemAt(event.newIndex)
                        as Object;
                    switch(selectedItem.mode) {
                        case "labels":
                            trace('Leif, Zach, Stacey');
                            break;
                        case "titles":
                            trace('Evangelist, Director, Information Architect');
                            break;
                        default:
                            break;
                    }
                }
            ]]>
        </fx:Script>

        <s:ButtonBar id="btnBar"
                    dataProvider="{btnBarData}"
                    change="btnBar_changeHandler(event)"/>

    </s:Application>
```

5.3 Load a External SWF

Problem

You want to load external SWFs created either with Flash Builder or Flash Professional into the current Flex application at runtime.

Solution

Use the SWFLoader component to load external SWFs at runtime and track the download progress.

Discussion

To load external SWFs at runtime, use the SWFLoader component. The example code shown here loads a external SWF and traces the bytes that have been loaded and the total bytes of the SWF. The ProgressEvent provides the ability to create a visual indicator enabling the end user to monitor the download progress of large SWFs and images. Despite its name, SWFLoader can load .swf, .gif, .jpeg, .png, or .svg files:

```
<?xml version="1.0" encoding="utf-8"?>
<s:Application xmlns:fx="http://ns.adobe.com/mxml/2009"
               xmlns:s="library://ns.adobe.com/flex/spark"
               xmlns:mx="library://ns.adobe.com/flex/mx ">

    <fx:Script>
        <![CDATA[
            protected function sampleOpenHandler(event:Event):void {
                trace('open');
            }

            protected function sampleProgressHandler(event:ProgressEvent):void {
                trace(event.bytesLoaded+' of '+event.bytesTotal+' loaded');
            }

            protected function sampleCompleteHandler(event:Event):void {
                trace('complete');
            }
        ]]>
    </fx:Script>
    <mx:SWFLoader id="sampleSWFLoader" source="assets/sample.swf"
                  open="sampleOpenHandler(event)"
                  progress="sampleProgressHandler(event)"
                  complete="sampleCompleteHandler(event)"/>

</s:Application>
```

This application will output the following to the console:

```
open
0 of 29730 bytes loaded
16384 of 29730 bytes loaded
16384 of 29730 bytes loaded
29730 of 29730 bytes loaded
complete
```

The `SWFLoader` component can also load SWFs that are embedded in the Flex application. Use the `Embed` directive for this. In the following example, *sample.swf* will be compiled into the main application:

```
<mx:SWFLoader source="@Embed('assets/sample.swf')"/>
```

For simple bitmap images that do not need loading event listeners, it is more efficient to use an instance of `s:BitmapImage`:

```
<s:BitmapImage source="@Embed('assets/sample.swf')"/>
```

5.4 Use a Calendar Date Input

Problem

You want to allow the user to select a date from a range using a calendar-like control.

Solution

Use the `DateField` control or the `DateChooser` control to provide the user with a convenient calendar-like control to pick dates.

Discussion

The Flex Framework provides two controls for calendar-like functionality: the `Date Field` control and the `DateChooser` control. The `DateField` control provides a `Text Input` control with a calendar icon that, when clicked, opens a pop-up calendar. The `DateChooser`, on the other hand, provides a persistent calendar to the user. The following example is a simple trip calculator that illustrates both types of controls. The user selects a start date using `DateField` and an end date using `DateChooser`. The program then calculates the duration of the trip on the `change` event of the controls in the `startChangeHandler()` and `endChangeHandler()` event handlers. The `selectedDate` property of each control returns a `Date` object representing the user's selection. Both controls have a `selectableDateRange` property that is bound to an `Object` that defines a `rangeStart` and `rangeEnd`. With these properties applied, the end user can only select dates within the specified range. In the following example, the `rangeStart` is today's date and the `rangeEnd` is a year from today:

```
<?xml version="1.0" encoding="utf-8"?>
<s:Application xmlns:fx="http://ns.adobe.com/mxml/2009"
               xmlns:s="library://ns.adobe.com/flex/spark"
               xmlns:mx="library://ns.adobe.com/flex/mx">

    <fx:Script>
        <![CDATA[
            import mx.events.CalendarLayoutChangeEvent;
            private var today:Date = new Date();
            private var nextYear:Date = new Date(today.fullYear + 1, today.month,
                                                 today.date);
            [Bindable]
            protected var displayText:String = 'Please select a Start and End
                                                Date';
            [Bindable]
            protected var startDateRange:Object = {
                rangeStart: today,
                rangeEnd: nextYear
            };
            [Bindable]
            protected var endDateRange:Object = {
                rangeStart: today,
                rangeEnd: nextYear
            };

            protected function startChangeHandler(event:CalendarLayoutChangeEvent):
                    void {
                endDateRange = {
                    rangeStart: event.newDate,
                    rangeEnd: nextYear
```

```
            };
            if(endDate.selectedDate && endDate.selectedDate <= event.newDate) {
                endDate.selectedDate = null;
            }
            updateDateRange();
        }

        protected function endChangeHandler(event:CalendarLayoutChangeEvent):
                void {
            updateDateRange();
        }

        protected function updateDateRange():void {
            if(startDate.selectedDate && endDate.selectedDate) {
                var startTime:Number = startDate.selectedDate.getTime();
                var endTime:Number = endDate.selectedDate.getTime();
                var dayDifference:int = int((endTime - startTime)/86400000);
                displayText = dayDifference.toString();
            } else {
                displayText = 'Please select a Start and End Date';
            }
        }

    ]]>
    </fx:Script>

    <mx:Form>
        <mx:FormHeading label="Trip Calculator"/>
        <mx:FormItem label="Start Date">
            <mx:DateField id="startDate" change="startChangeHandler(event)"
                          selectableRange="{startDateRange}"/>
        </mx:FormItem>
        <mx:FormItem label="End Date">
            <mx:DateChooser id="endDate" change="endChangeHandler(event)"
                            selectableRange="{endDateRange}"/>
        </mx:FormItem>
        <mx:FormItem label="Trip Duration (days)">
            <mx:Label text="{displayText}"/>
        </mx:FormItem>
    </mx:Form>
</s:Application>
```

To ensure that the user cannot select an end date that occurs before the start date, the startChangeHandler() method updates the endDateRange so that its rangeStart property is equal to the selected start date. If a start date and end date have already been selected and the user updates the start date to occur after the end date, the startChangeHandler() clears the selected end date by setting it equal to null. Both startChangeHandler() and endChangeHandler() call the updateDateRange() method, which first checks that two dates have been selected and then calculates the difference between them to update the Label that is displayed to the user, as shown in Figure 5-1.

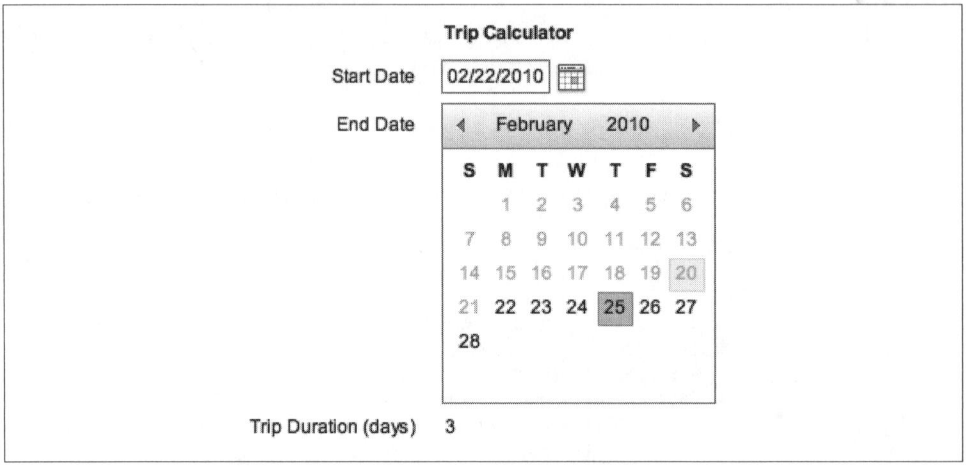

Figure 5-1. A trip calculator created using the date components

5.5 Create Event Handlers for Menu-Based Controls

Problem

You need to act in response to user interaction with the menu bar.

Solution

Add event listeners for the `itemClick` event of the `MenuBar` control.

Discussion

To respond to menu bar interaction, assign a listener function, `handleMenuClick()`, to the `itemClick` event attribute of the `MenuBar` control. The `itemClick` event is dispatched whenever a user selects a menu item. The listener function receives as an argument an instance of `MenuEvent` containing information about the menu item from which the event was dispatched. The `item` property of the `MenuEvent` object contains a reference to the item in the `dataProvider` that is associated with that particular menu item. Here is an example `MenuBar` implementation:

```
<?xml version="1.0" encoding="utf-8"?>
<s:Application xmlns:fx="http://ns.adobe.com/mxml/2009"
               xmlns:s="library://ns.adobe.com/flex/spark"
               xmlns:mx="library://ns.adobe.com/flex/mx">
    <fx:Declarations>
        <fx:XMLList id="dataProvider" xmlns="">
            <menuitem label="File">
                <menuitem label="New"/>
                <menuitem label="Open"/>
                <menuitem label="Close" enabled="false"/>
            </menuitem>
            <menuitem label="Edit"/>
```

```
                <menuitem label="Source"/>
                <menuitem label="View">
                    <menuitem label="50%" type="radio" groupName="one"/>
                    <menuitem label="100%" type="radio" groupName="one"
                            selected="true"/>
                    <menuitem label="150%" type="radio" groupName="one"/>
                </menuitem>
            </fx:XMLList>
        </fx:Declarations>
        <fx:Script>
            <![CDATA[
                import mx.events.MenuEvent;

                private function handleMenuClick(event:MenuEvent):void {
                    subItemDisplayLabel.text = event.item.@label + " was selected";
                }
            ]]>
        </fx:Script>
        <s:VGroup>
            <mx:MenuBar labelField="@label"
                        itemClick="handleMenuClick(event)"
                        dataProvider="{dataProvider}"/>
            <s:Label id="subItemDisplayLabel"/>
        </s:VGroup>
    </s:Application>
```

Notice in this example that when an item is clicked on the instance of `mx:MenuBar`, the `itemClick` event is handled by the method `handleMenuClick()`, which in turn updates the `text` property of the instance of `s:Label` with the selected item's label, as shown in Figure 5-2.

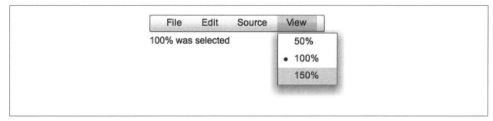

Figure 5-2. A drop-down menu created using <mx:MenuBar>

5.6 Display an Alert in an Application

Problem

You want to show a modal message to the user and optionally present the user with action choices.

Solution

Use the `Alert` control to display a message to the user.

Discussion

The `Alert` control provides a modal dialog box with buttons that the user can click to respond to a message in the dialog box. This component is a pop up and is placed on top of and obscures content in the application.

The `Alert` control cannot be created using MXML. You need to use ActionScript instead. For example:

```
<?xml version="1.0" encoding="utf-8"?>
<s:Application xmlns:fx="http://ns.adobe.com/mxml/2009"
               xmlns:s="library://ns.adobe.com/flex/spark"
               xmlns:mx="library://ns.adobe.com/flex/mx">
    <s:layout>
        <s:VerticalLayout/>
    </s:layout>
    <mx:Button id="showAlertButton" click="showAlert(event)" label="Alert"/>
    <mx:Label id="displaySelectionLabel"/>
    <fx:Script>
        <![CDATA[
            import mx.events.CloseEvent;
            import mx.controls.Alert;
            import mx.events.MenuEvent;

            private function showAlert(evt:MouseEvent):void {
                var alert:Alert = Alert.show("Button was clicked",
                                        "Alert Window Title", Alert.OK |
                                        Alert.CANCEL | Alert.NO | Alert.YES,
                                        this, onAlertClose);
            }

            private function onAlertClose(evt:CloseEvent):void {
                switch (evt.detail) {
                    case Alert.OK:
                        displaySelectionLabel.text = "OK Clicked";
                        break;
                    case Alert.CANCEL:
                        displaySelectionLabel.text = "CANCEL Clicked";
                        break;
                    case Alert.NO:
                        displaySelectionLabel.text = "NO Clicked";
                        break;
                    case Alert.YES:
                        displaySelectionLabel.text = "YES Clicked";
                        break;
                }
            }
        ]]>
```

```
        </fx:Script>
    </s:Application>
```

When the user clicks the btn button, the example code creates an Alert control by using the static method show() on the Alert class. The show() method accepts the following arguments to configure the alert:

text
> The message to display to the user.

title
> The title of the Alert box.

flags
> The buttons to be shown on the Alert. Valid values are Alert.OK, Alert.CANCEL, Alert.NO, and Alert.Yes. More than one button can be shown by using the bitwise OR operator, as in Alert.OK | Alert.CANCEL.

parent
> The display object on which to center the Alert.

closeHandler
> The event handler to be called when any button on the Alert control is pressed.

iconClass
> The asset class of the icon to be placed to the left of the display message on the Alert.

defaultButtonFlag
> The button to be used as the default on the Alert control. Pressing the Enter key activates the default button. Valid values are Alert.OK, Alert.CANCEL, Alert.NO, or Alert.Yes.

In the previous example, the onAlertClose() method is set as the closeHandler for the Alert. This method receives a CloseEvent object as an argument, and uses the detail property of the CloseEvent to determine which button was clicked on the Alert control.

5.7 Display a Custom Pop Up in a Custom Component

Problem

You want a custom pop-up component to appear when a user clicks on a button.

Solution

Wrap the pop-up component in a PopUpAnchor control.

Discussion

The s:PopUpAnchor displays a component as a pop up; it also specifies the location where the pop up will appear. By default, the pop up will shift its location to ensure that it appears within the application stage. The s:PopUpAnchor is used in the s:DropDown List and s:VolumeBar controls.

In the following example, the s:Application contains two instances of a custom component called CustomPopUp that extends <s:Group>:

```
<?xml version="1.0" encoding="utf-8"?>
<s:Application xmlns:fx="http://ns.adobe.com/mxml/2009"
               xmlns:s="library://ns.adobe.com/flex/spark"
               xmlns:mx="library://ns.adobe.com/flex/mx"
               xmlns:local="*">
    <local:CustomPopUp message="You have clicked the Top button"
                       top="10" left="10"/>
    <local:CustomPopUp message="You have clicked the Bottom button"
                       bottom=" 10" left="10"/>
</s:Application>
```

The CustomPopUp consists of a button with an id of openButton and a s:PopUpAnchor control with an id of panelPopUp that contains a s:Panel control. The s:Panel control contains a message to display to the user and a button to close the pop up:

```
<?xml version="1.0" encoding="utf-8"?>
<s:Group xmlns:fx="http://ns.adobe.com/mxml/2009"
         xmlns:s="library://ns.adobe.com/flex/spark"
         xmlns:mx="library://ns.adobe.com/flex/mx">
    <fx:Script>
        <![CDATA[

            [Bindable]
            public var title:String = 'Custom PopUp';

            [Bindable]
            public var message:String;

            public function openPopUp():void {
                panelPopUp.displayPopUp = true;
            }

            public function closePopUp():void {
                panelPopUp.displayPopUp = false;
            }
        ]]>
    </fx:Script>
    <s:Button id="openButton" label="Click Me" click="openPopUp()"/>
    <s:PopUpAnchor id="panelPopUp">
        <s:Panel title="{title}">
            <s:RichText text="{message}" width="50"
                        top="5" left="5" right="5" bottom="30"/>
            <s:Button id="closeButton" label="Close Me"
                      click="closePopUp()" right="5" bottom="5"/>
        </s:Panel>
```

```
                </s:PopUpAnchor>
        </s:Group>
```

When the button with an `id` of `openButton` is clicked it calls the `openPopUp()` method, which sets the `displayPopUp` property of `panelPopUp` equal to `true`. This causes the panel to be displayed as a pop up. When `closeButton` is clicked it calls `closePopUp()`, which closes the panel again.

5.8 Detect a Mouse Click Outside a Pop Up to Close It

Problem

You want your pop up to close if the user clicks outside of it.

Solution

Listen for the `mouseDownOutside` event on your pop-up control.

Discussion

The `mouseDownOutside` event provides a simple way to detect when the user clicks away from a component. The `FlexMouseEvent` that is passed through as a parameter provides a property called `relatedObject` to check what the user did click on.

The following example has a `s:ToggleButton` control and a `s:PopUpAnchor` control that contains a `s:Panel` with an `id` of `myPanel`:

```xml
<?xml version="1.0" encoding="utf-8"?>
<s:Application xmlns:fx="http://ns.adobe.com/mxml/2009"
               xmlns:s="library://ns.adobe.com/flex/spark"
               xmlns:mx="library://ns.adobe.com/flex/mx">
    <fx:Script>
        <![CDATA[
            import mx.events.FlexMouseEvent;
            [Bindable]
            protected var displayMyPanelFlag:Boolean; // initialized as false

            protected function mouseDownOutsideHandler(event:FlexMouseEvent):void {
                if (event.relatedObject != myToggle) {
                    displayMyPanelFlag = false;
                }
            }
        ]]>
    </fx:Script>
    <s:ToggleButton id="myToggle" label="Toggle!"
                    x="5" y="5" selected="@{displayMyPanelFlag}"/>
    <s:PopUpAnchor top="115" right="302" displayPopUp="{displayMyPanelFlag}">
        <s:Panel id="myPanel"
                 mouseDownOutside="mouseDownOutsideHandler(event)"/>
    </s:PopUpAnchor>
</s:Application>
```

The s:ToggleButton control has an id of myToggle and a selected property that is two-way bound, indicated by the "@" syntax, to a Boolean called displayMyPanelFlag. This Boolean is also bound to the displayPopUp property of the s:PopUpAnchor instance causing myPanel to be displayed when myToggle is selected.

When the user clicks outside of myPanel, it is handled by mouseDownOutsideHandler(). This handler sets displayMyPanelFlag equal to false after verifying that the user did not click on myToggle. This ensures the action is not duplicated.

5.9 Using s:Scroller to Create a Scrollable Container

Problem

You have more content than you have viewable area available.

Solution

Wrap any component that implements the IViewport interface with a s:Scroller component.

Discussion

One of the goals of the new Spark architecture is to provide a more divisible set of resources and provide a pay-as-you-go system. In previous versions of the Flex SDK, scroll bar policies were accessible to containers by default. To use resources more efficiently in Flex 4, however, this functionality was separated into a s:Scroller control to be used on an a as-needed basis.

The s:Scroller control is simple to use—it can only contain one scrollable component that implements the IViewport interface:

```
<?xml version="1.0" encoding="utf-8"?>
<s:Application xmlns:fx="http://ns.adobe.com/mxml/2009"
               xmlns:s="library://ns.adobe.com/flex/spark"
               xmlns:mx="library://ns.adobe.com/flex/mx">
    <fx:Declarations>
        <s:LinearGradient id="gradient" rotation="45">
            <s:GradientEntry color="#000000" ratio="0"/>
            <s:GradientEntry color="#FFFFFF" ratio="1"/>
        </s:LinearGradient>
    </fx:Declarations>
    <s:Scroller width="100%" height="100%"
                horizontalScrollPolicy="off" verticalScrollPolicy="on">
        <s:Group>
            <s:Rect height="3000" width="400" fill="{gradient}"/>
            <s:Scroller left="500" top="500" width="500" height="600">
                <s:Group>
                    <s:Rect height="600" width="800" fill="{gradient}"/>
                </s:Group>
            </s:Scroller>
```

```
            </s:Group>
        </s:Scroller>
    </s:Application>
```

This example has one scrollable area for the whole application area with a smaller nested scrollable area within it. The s:Scroller component has horizontalScroll Policy and verticalScrollPolicy properties that control whether the scroll bars are visible by default by setting them to "on" or "off", or are shown as needed by setting them to "auto".

5.10 Handle focusIn and focusOut Events

Problem

You want to display a description of a s:TextInput control to the user while it has focus and hide it again when the focus changes.

Solution

Use the focusIn and focusOut events (available to all instances of classes inheriting from the InteractiveObject class) to change the displayPopUp property of an instance of s:PopUpAnchor.

Discussion

The focusIn and focusOut events allow events to be fired when focus is given or taken away from a component. The focus can be changed by the user clicking on another InteractiveObject or hitting the Tab key.

In this example, when the instance of s:TextInput, which has an id of text, has focus, a s:Panel pops up displaying a more in-depth description of what is expected to be entered in the field:

```
<?xml version="1.0" encoding="utf-8"?>
<s:Application xmlns:fx="http://ns.adobe.com/mxml/2009"
               xmlns:s="library://ns.adobe.com/flex/spark"
               xmlns:mx="library://ns.adobe.com/flex/mx">
    <s:layout>
        <s:VerticalLayout/>
    </s:layout>
    <fx:Script>
        <![CDATA[
            protected function text_focusOutHandler(event:FocusEvent):void {
                customPopUp.displayPopUp = false;
            }
            protected function text_focusInHandler(event:FocusEvent):void {
                customPopUp.displayPopUp = true;
            }
        ]]>
    </fx:Script>
```

```
<s:HGroup>
    <s:TextInput id="text" focusIn="text_focusInHandler(event)"
                 focusOut="text_focusOutHandler(event)"/>
    <s:PopUpAnchor id="customPopUp">
        <s:Panel id="myPanel" title="Some Description Here">
            <s:Label text="This is the description for the TextInput"/>
        </s:Panel>
    </s:PopUpAnchor>
</s:HGroup>
<s:Button label="Click to Switch Focus"/>
</s:Application>
```

The event handlers text_focusOutHandler() and text_focusInHandler() display and hide myPanel by changing the displayPopUp property of customPopUp when called. These handlers expect an instance of FocusEvent to be passed as a parameter. Not only does the FocusEvent allow the handler to know when focus is changed, but it also points to the component that has had or will have the focus through its property relatedObject.

5.11 Open a DropDownList with a Keyboard Shortcut

Problem

You would like to open an instance of s:DropDownList when the user presses a specific key combination.

Solution

Use the keyDown event to listen for specific keys being pressed.

Discussion

Components that inherit from InteractiveObject have keyDown and keyUp events that are triggered when a user presses and releases a key, respectively. An instance of KeyboardEvent is passed to the handler as a parameter that has properties such as charCode and keyCode to identify which key was pressed.

In the following example the s:Application contains an instance of s:TextInput with an id of textInput and an instance of s:DropDownList with an id of seasonDropDown. Added to textInput is a keyDown event listener that will call the keyPressHandler() method any time a key is pressed while textInput has focus. If the character code of the key pressed is equal to 83, which corresponds to the letter "s," and the Alt key was pressed at the same time (signaled by the altKey event attribute), the seasonDropDown drop-down menu will be opened, as shown in Figure 5-3. Here's the code:

```
<?xml version="1.0" encoding="utf-8"?>
<s:Application xmlns:fx="http://ns.adobe.com/mxml/2009"
               xmlns:s="library://ns.adobe.com/flex/spark"
               xmlns:mx="library://ns.adobe.com/flex/mx">

    <s:layout>
        <s:VerticalLayout/>
    </s:layout>

    <fx:Script>
        <![CDATA[
            import mx.events.FlexEvent;

            import spark.events.IndexChangeEvent;
            [Bindable]
            protected var seasonLabel:String;

            protected function buttonClickHandler(event:MouseEvent):void {
                seasonDropDown.openDropDown();
            }

            protected function seasonChangeHandler(event:IndexChangeEvent):void {
                seasonLabel = seasonsData.getItemAt(event.newIndex).label as
                            String;
            }

            protected function keyPressHandler(event:KeyboardEvent):void {
                if(event.keyCode == 83 && event.altKey) {
                    seasonDropDown.setFocus();
                    seasonDropDown.openDropDown();
                }

            }

        ]]>
    </fx:Script>

    <fx:Declarations>
        <s:ArrayCollection id="seasonsData">
            <fx:Object label="Winter"/>
            <fx:Object label="Spring"/>
            <fx:Object label="Summer"/>
            <fx:Object label="Fall"/>
        </s:ArrayCollection>
    </fx:Declarations>
    <s:TextInput id="textInput" keyDown="keyPressHandler(event)"/>
    <s:DropDownList id="seasonDropDown" dataProvider="{seasonsData}"
                    change="seasonChangeHandler(event)"/>
    <s:Label text="{seasonLabel}"/>
</s:Application>
```

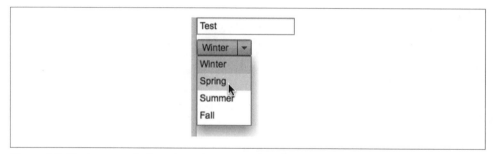

Figure 5-3. The instance of s:DropDownList opens when the user presses the "s" and Alt keys together while the instance of s:TextInput has focus

5.12 Grouping Radio Buttons

Problem

You want to use a set of radio buttons and determine when one is selected.

Solution

Use the `groupName` and `group` properties to group a set of radio buttons and listen for selection changes.

Discussion

Using `s:RadioButton` can be a useful alternative to `s:DropDownList`, as it provides a simple solution to display all options to the user. Because radio buttons require an instance of `s:RadioButton` per option, it is important to group a set of them together. Another consequence of having multiple instances of the component is that it is slightly more complicated to listen to selection changes and access the currently selected option.

In the following example, the instances of `s:RadioButton` are grouped together in a set using the `groupName` property, which is typed as a `String`. All instances of `s:RadioButton` with the same `groupName` value are grouped together, and no two radio buttons of the same group can be selected simultaneously:

```
<?xml version="1.0" encoding="utf-8"?>
<s:Application xmlns:fx="http://ns.adobe.com/mxml/2009"
               xmlns:s="library://ns.adobe.com/flex/spark"
               xmlns:mx="library://ns.adobe.com/flex/mx">
    <s:layout>
        <s:VerticalLayout/>
    </s:layout>
    <fx:Script>
        <![CDATA[
            protected function radioChangeHandler(event:Event):void {
```

```
                        label.text = 'Selected: ';
                        label.text += RadioButton(event.target).label;
                    }
                ]]>
            </fx:Script>
        <mx:FormItem label="Code Style">
            <s:RadioButton label="Cairngorm" groupName="microarchitecture"
                        change="radioChangeHandler(event)"/>
            <s:RadioButton label="PureMVC" groupName="microarchitecture"
                        change="radioChangeHandler(event)"/>
            <s:RadioButton label="robotlegs" groupName="microarchitecture"
                        change="radioChangeHandler(event)"/>
            <s:RadioButton label="Mate" groupName="microarchitecture"
                        change="radioChangeHandler(event)"/>
            <s:RadioButton label="Parsley" groupName="microarchitecture"
                        change="radioChangeHandler(event)"/>
            <s:RadioButton label="Swiz" groupName="microarchitecture"
                        change="radioChangeHandler(event)"/>
        </mx:FormItem>
        <s:Label id="label" text="Make a Selection"/>
    </s:Application>
```

In this example, all the instances of s:RadioButton are grouped using groupName and use the same event handler, radioChangeHandler(), to handle the change event. This method updates the text property of an instance of s:Label to indicate to the user which selection has been made.

Although this is a functional solution, the s:RadioButtonGroup component can provide the same functionality in a slightly more efficient fashion. Similar to grouping radio buttons with the groupName property, all s:RadioButton instances with the same instance of s:RadioButtonGroup assigned to their group property will be grouped together. The added benefit to using s:RadioButtonGroup is that it dispatches a change event when any instance of s:RadioButton in its set is selected, as shown in the following example:

```
<fx:Script>
    <![CDATA[
        protected function groupChangeHandler(event:Event):void {
            label.text = "Looks like you are a code ";
            label.text += codeStyleRadioGroup.selectedValue;
            label.text += ". Good Choice.";
        }
    ]]>
</fx:Script>
<fx:Declarations>
    <s:RadioButtonGroup id="codeStyleRadioGroup"
                        change="groupChangeHandler(event)"/>
</fx:Declarations>
<mx:FormItem label="Code Style">
    <s:RadioButton label="Ninja" group="{codeStyleRadioGroup}"
                value="ninja"/>
    <s:RadioButton label="Pirate" group="{codeStyleRadioGroup}"
                value="pirate"/>
</mx:FormItem>
<s:Label id="label" text="Make a Selection"/>
```

In this example, the change event handler is applied to the instance of s:RadioBut
tonGroup, not to the individual radio buttons, as in the previous example. Also notice
that the instance of s:RadioButtonGroup is nested in a fx:Declarations tag because it is
a nonvisual element.

5.13 Submit a Flex Form to a Server-Side Script

Problem

You want to submit data from a Flex form to a server-side script (e.g., a PHP script)
using *post*, as you might do with a HTML form.

Solution

Use an instance of URLVariables and the sendToURL() method to send data from a Flex
form to a server.

Discussion

It is fairly simple to submit data to a server-side script using ActionScript. Variable data
can be gathered into an instance of URLVariables and submitted to a URL via *post* or
get by passing an instance of URLRequest, along with the variables, as a parameter to the
sendToURL() method.

The following example is a sample email contact form containing instances of
s:TextInput for the name, email, and subject fields, and an instance of s:TextArea for
the message field. Also, the example contains an instance of s:Spinner that allows the
user to scroll through values from an ArrayCollection containing reasons for the email.

The s:Spinner component is a simple control that allows the user to step between
numeric values. Its minimum and maximum properties determine the range the user can
step through, and it also contains an allowValueWrap property that enables the user to
loop back to the first value if he continues past the last allowed value. It is important
to note that the s:Spinner component does not display the selected value; rather, it
consists of increment and decrement buttons. To display a numeric value with similar
functionality, it is simpler to use s:NumericStepper. The following example uses an
instance of s:Label to display the String that corresponds to the selected value of the
s:Spinner:

```
<?xml version="1.0" encoding="utf-8"?>
<s:Application xmlns:fx="http://ns.adobe.com/mxml/2009"
               xmlns:s="library://ns.adobe.com/flex/spark"
               xmlns:mx="library://ns.adobe.com/flex/mx">
    <s:layout>
        <s:VerticalLayout/>
    </s:layout>
    <fx:Script>
        <![CDATA[
```

```
            import flash.net.sendToURL;
            protected function submit():void {
                var variables:URLVariables = new URLVariables();
                variables.name = nameText.text;
                variables.email = emailText.text;
                variables.subject = subjectText.text;
                variables.message = subjectText.text;
                variables.reason = reason.text;

                var url:String = 'http://www.example.com/script.php';
                var request:URLRequest = new URLRequest(url);
                request.data = variables;
                request.method = URLRequestMethod.POST;
                sendToURL(request);
            }
        ]]>
    </fx:Script>
    <fx:Declarations>
        <s:ArrayCollection id="reasonArrayCollection">
            <fx:String>Complement</fx:String>
            <fx:String>Comment</fx:String>
            <fx:String>Complaint</fx:String>
        </s:ArrayCollection>
    </fx:Declarations>
    <mx:Form>
        <mx:FormItem label="Name">
            <s:TextInput id="nameText"/>
        </mx:FormItem>
        <mx:FormItem label="Email">
            <s:TextInput id="emailText"/>
        </mx:FormItem>
        <mx:FormItem label="Subject">
            <s:TextInput id="subjectText"/>
        </mx:FormItem>
        <mx:FormItem label="Message">
            <s:TextArea id="messageText"/>
        </mx:FormItem>
        <mx:FormItem label="Reason">
            <s:HGroup verticalAlign="middle">
                <s:Label id="reason"
                        text="{reasonArrayCollection.getItemAt(
                            reasonSpinner.value )}"/>
                <s:Spinner id="reasonSpinner" minimum="0"
                        maximum="{reasonArrayCollection.length -1}"
                        allowValueWrap="true"/>
            </s:HGroup>
        </mx:FormItem>
        <s:Button label="Submit" click="submit()"/>
    </mx:Form>
</s:Application>
```

The click event for the submit button calls the submit() method, which gathers the values from the form and sends the data to a URL using the sendToUrl() method. If you wished to add validation logic to the form, it would be simple to add it to the submit() method. Flex Validators will be discussed in Chapter 14.

CHAPTER 6

Skinning and Styles

The previous chapter discussed Flex Framework components that encourage standard and efficient development. However, when using a framework of components you often lose a certain degree of visual customization, and the resulting applications have a "cookie-cutter" appearance. To offset this side effect, the Flex 4 Spark components are equipped with a new and improved skinning architecture.

In Flex 4, a *skin* is a class, usually defined in MXML, that extends `s:Skin` and determines the visual appearance of a Spark component. The Spark component that is being skinned, also referred to as the *host component*, can declare and access parts in the `Skin` class. This new skinning architecture creates a greater separation between functionality (in the host component) and design (in the skin component). This separation allows skins and Spark components to be easily reused and updated with a minimal amount of code refactoring.

Styles are property settings—color, sizing, or font instructions—that modify the appearance of components and can be customized programmatically at both compile time and runtime. Style properties can be defined in multiple ways: by setting them inline within a component declaration, by using the `setStyle()` method to apply them, or by using Cascading Style Sheets (CSS). You can use CSS to define styles locally in a MXML file or in an external file.

For the sake of simplicity, the examples in the following recipes use a basic wire-frame design in their custom skins and styles. However, it is important to note that the principles used as a basis for these examples provide the developer (or designer) with a powerful set of tools capable of drastically redesigning components.

6.1 Create a Skin for s:Button

Problem

The standard `s:ButtonSkin` does not match your design.

Solution

Extend `s:SparkSkin` with MXML to create a reusable custom button skin.

Discussion

Although the new skinning architecture is designed to enhance the separation between functional logic and design, there are three things that correspond to properties declared in the host component that should be included in the skin component:

`HostComponent` *metadata*

> The component that is being skinned can be referenced in the skin component using the `HostComponent` metadata tag. The following example would be included in a skin intended for an instance of `s:Button`:

```
<fx:Metadata>
    <![CDATA[
        [HostComponent("spark.components.Button")]
    ]]>
</fx:Metadata>
```

States

> In the host component, skin states are referenced using the `SkinState` metadata tag. For example, if the `s:ButtonBase` class contains the following:

```
[SkinState("up")]
```

> the skin should have the corresponding state, as follows:

```
<s:states>
    <s:State name="up"/>
```

Skin parts

> Properties in the host component can be defined as required or optional skin parts using the `SkinPart` metadata tag; the optional `required` parameter of the `Skin Part` metadata tag is set to `false` by default. If the `s:ButtonBase` class contains the following property:

```
[SkinPart(required="false")]
public var labelDisplay:TextBase;
```

> the skin component should contain the following corresponding element:

```
<s:Label id="labelDisplay"/>
```

It is important to note that the `id` property of the element in the skin component must match the property name in the host component. Also, in this example the `labelDisplay` element is allowed to be an instance of `s:Label` because it extends `s:TextBase`.

In the following example the application consists of a single instance of `s:Button` with its `skinClass property` set to `skins.WireButtonSkin`, which points to the *WireButtonSkin.mxml* file in the *skins* folder:

```
<?xml version="1.0" encoding="utf-8"?>
<s:Application xmlns:fx="http://ns.adobe.com/mxml/2009"
               xmlns:s="library://ns.adobe.com/flex/spark"
               xmlns:mx="library://ns.adobe.com/flex/mx">
    <s:Button skinClass="skins.WireButtonSkin"
              label="Click Me!"
              top="50" left="50"/>
</s:Application>
```

`WireButtonSkin` extends `s:SparkSkin`, and it contains all the essential elements just mentioned. The only `SkinPart` included in this skin is an instance of `s:Label` with its id set to `labelDisplay`:

```
<?xml version="1.0" encoding="utf-8"?>
<s:SparkSkin xmlns:fx="http://ns.adobe.com/mxml/2009"
             xmlns:s="library://ns.adobe.com/flex/spark"
             alpha.disabled="0.5">
    <fx:Metadata>
        <![CDATA[
            [HostComponent("spark.components.Button")]
        ]]>
    </fx:Metadata>

    <fx:Declarations>
        <s:SolidColor id="fillColor" color="#FFFFFF"
                      color.over="#DDDDDD"/>
        <s:SolidColorStroke id="strokeColor" color="#333333"
                            color.over="#111111" weight="2"/>
    </fx:Declarations>

    <s:states>
        <s:State name="up"/>
        <s:State name="over"/>
        <s:State name="down"/>
        <s:State name="disabled"/>
    </s:states>

    <s:Rect top="0" left="0" bottom="0" right="0"
            radiusX="15" radiusY="15" fill="{fillColor}"
            stroke="{strokeColor}"/>
    <s:Label id="labelDisplay" left="25" right="25" top="9"
             bottom="6" color="{strokeColor.color}"
             fontWeight="bold">
    </s:Label>
</s:SparkSkin>
```

The instance of `s:Rect` in this example creates a rounded rectangle around the button's label. For more information on MXML graphics, see Chapter 4.

6.2 Apply a Repeating Background Image to an Application

Problem

You want to apply a skin to your main application class that includes a repeating background image.

Solution

Extend `s:Application` using MXML and include an instance of `s:Rect` with a repeating bitmap fill.

Discussion

The requirements are the same when creating a skin for `s:Application` as for any other skin component. The following application contains a single instance of `s:Button`, to make sure the content is displayed, and its `skinClass` property points to the *skins/AppSkin.mxml* file:

```
<?xml version="1.0" encoding="utf-8"?>
<s:Application xmlns:fx="http://ns.adobe.com/mxml/2009"
               xmlns:s="library://ns.adobe.com/flex/spark"
               xmlns:mx="library://ns.adobe.com/flex/mx"
               skinClass="skins.AppSkin">
    <s:Button left="20" right="20" label="test"/>
</s:Application>
```

The following skin component, *skins/AppSkin.mxml*, contains an instance of s:Data Group with its `id` set to `contentGroup` to correspond with the `skinPart` in `s:Application`. It also contains an instance of `s:Rect` with a `s:BitmapFill` that repeats the source image across the background of the entire application:

```
<?xml version="1.0" encoding="utf-8"?>
<s:Skin xmlns:fx="http://ns.adobe.com/mxml/2009"
        xmlns:s="library://ns.adobe.com/flex/spark"
        xmlns:fb="http://ns.adobe.com/flashbuilder/2009">

    <fx:Metadata>
        <![CDATA[
            [HostComponent("spark.components.Application")]
        ]]>
    </fx:Metadata>

    <s:states>
        <s:State name="normal"/>
        <s:State name="disabled"/>
        <s:State name="normalWithControlBar"/>
        <s:State name="disabledWithControlBar"/>
    </s:states>

    <s:Rect id="backgroundRect" left="0" right="0"
            top="0" bottom="0">
```

```
        <s:fill>
            <s:BitmapFill source="@Embed('assets/pattern.png')" />
        </s:fill>
    </s:Rect>
    <s:Group id="contentGroup"
            left="0" right="0"
            top="0" bottom="0"/>
</s:Skin>
```

6.3 Create a Skin for s:ButtonBar and s:ButtonBarButton

Problem

You want to create a custom skin for s:ButtonBar and any nested buttons, including distinct skins for the first and last buttons.

Solution

Extend s:Skin with MXML to create a reusable skin for s:ButtonBar, and additional skins for the first, middle, and last instances of s:ButtonBarButton within that component.

Discussion

Because s:ButtonBar is a complex component with nested buttons, it is necessary to create skins for the nested buttons as well as the button bar itself.

The following application contains an instance of s:ButtonBar with its dataProvider bound to an ArrayCollection of strings (navArrayCollection). The result is a horizontal bar of buttons, one for each element in navArrayCollection, with the strings themselves assigned to the label property of each button:

```
<?xml version="1.0" encoding="utf-8"?>
<s:Application xmlns:fx="http://ns.adobe.com/mxml/2009"
               xmlns:s="library://ns.adobe.com/flex/spark"
               xmlns:mx="library://ns.adobe.com/flex/mx"
               minWidth="955" minHeight="600">
    <fx:Declarations>
        <s:ArrayCollection id="navArrayCollection">
            <fx:String>Home</fx:String>
            <fx:String>About</fx:String>
            <fx:String>Gallery</fx:String>
            <fx:String>Contact</fx:String>
        </s:ArrayCollection>
    </fx:Declarations>
    <s:ButtonBar top="10" left="10"
                 requireSelection="true"
                 skinClass="skins.WireButtonBarSkin"
                 dataProvider="{navArrayCollection}"/>
</s:Application>
```

The skin for the s:ButtonBar, located at *skins/WireButtonBarSkin.mxml*, extends s:Skin and contains an instance of s:DataGroup with an id of dataGroup. This s:Data Group creates each instance of the buttons required by the dataProvider in the HostComponent. The buttons that make up the bar are included in a fx:Declarations tag and the host component manages the buttons included in the itemRenderer of data Group.

s:ButtonBar expects three types of buttons as skin parts: firstButton, middleButton, and lastButton. middleButton is the only one of the three that is required and will be used for all the buttons if the others are not included in the skin:

```
<?xml version="1.0" encoding="utf-8"?>
<s:Skin xmlns:fx="http://ns.adobe.com/mxml/2009"
        xmlns:s="library://ns.adobe.com/flex/spark"
        alpha.disabled="0.5">

    <fx:Metadata>
        <![CDATA[
            [HostComponent("spark.components.ButtonBar")]
        ]]>
    </fx:Metadata>

    <s:states>
        <s:State name="normal"/>
        <s:State name="disabled"/>
    </s:states>

    <fx:Declarations>
        <fx:Component id="firstButton">
            <s:ButtonBarButton skinClass="skins.WireFirstButtonSkin"/>
        </fx:Component>
        <fx:Component id="middleButton">
            <s:ButtonBarButton skinClass="skins.WireMiddleButtonSkin"/>
        </fx:Component>
        <fx:Component id="lastButton">
            <s:ButtonBarButton skinClass="skins.WireLastButtonSkin"/>
        </fx:Component>
    </fx:Declarations>

    <s:DataGroup id="dataGroup" width="100%" height="100%">
        <s:layout>
            <s:ButtonBarHorizontalLayout gap="0"/>
        </s:layout>
    </s:DataGroup>

</s:Skin>
```

Notice in this skin declaration that the only difference between the three button declarations is the skinClass property. Here is an example of a first button skin, located at *skins/WireFirstButtonSkin.mxml*. The difference between this skin and the last and middle button skins is that it has rounded corners on the left side, while the last button skin has rounded corners on the right and the middle has neither:

```xml
<?xml version="1.0" encoding="utf-8"?>
<s:SparkSkin xmlns:fx="http://ns.adobe.com/mxml/2009"
             xmlns:s="library://ns.adobe.com/flex/spark"
             minWidth="21" minHeight="21"
             alpha.disabledStates="0.5">
    <fx:Metadata>
        <![CDATA[
            [HostComponent("spark.components.ButtonBarButton")]
        ]]>
    </fx:Metadata>

    <s:states>
        <s:State name="up"/>
        <s:State name="over" stateGroups="overStates"/>
        <s:State name="down" stateGroups="downStates"/>
        <s:State name="disabled"
                stateGroups="disabledStates"/>
        <s:State name="upAndSelected"
                stateGroups="selectedStates, selectedUpStates"/>
        <s:State name="overAndSelected"
                stateGroups="overStates, selectedStates"/>
        <s:State name="downAndSelected"
                stateGroups="downStates, selectedStates"/>
        <s:State name="disabledAndSelected"
                stateGroups="selectedUpStates, disabledStates, selectedStates"/>
    </s:states>

    <fx:Declarations>
        <s:SolidColor id="fillColor" color="#FFFFFF"
                    color.selectedStates="#DDDDDD"/>
        <s:SolidColorStroke id="strokeColor" color="#333333"
                            color.selectedStates="#111111"
                            weight="2"/>
    </fx:Declarations>

    <s:Rect top="0" left="0" bottom="0" right="0"
            topLeftRadiusX="15" topLeftRadiusY="15"
            bottomLeftRadiusX="15" bottomLeftRadiusY="15"
            fill="{fillColor}" stroke="{strokeColor}"/>
    <s:Label id="labelDisplay" left="25" right="25" top="9"
            bottom="6" color="{strokeColor.color}"
            fontWeight="bold">
    </s:Label>

</s:SparkSkin>
```

6.4 Skin an s:DropDownList

Problem

You want to create a skin for a complex component such as s:DropDownList.

Solution

Extend s:Skin to create a skin for s:DropDownList with its several nested skin parts.

Discussion

Similar to the previous recipe, the following application contains an ArrayCollection of strings. However, this example contains an instance of s:DropDownList that shows the user only the currently selected item and uses a pop up to display a list of all the items:

```
<?xml version="1.0" encoding="utf-8"?>
<s:Application xmlns:fx="http://ns.adobe.com/mxml/2009"
               xmlns:s="library://ns.adobe.com/flex/spark"
               xmlns:mx="library://ns.adobe.com/flex/mx"
               minWidth="955" minHeight="600">
    <fx:Declarations>
        <s:ArrayCollection id="stylesArrayCollection">
            <fx:String>Ninja</fx:String>
            <fx:String>Pirate</fx:String>
            <fx:String>Jedi</fx:String>
            <fx:String>Rockstar</fx:String>
        </s:ArrayCollection>
    </fx:Declarations>
    <s:DropDownList dataProvider="{stylesArrayCollection}"
                    top="10" left="10"
                    requireSelection="true"
                    skinClass="skins.DropDownListSkin"/>
</s:Application>
```

The following skin for s:DropDownList has an instance of s:PopUpAnchor that displays and hides the drop-down portion of the component and overlays it on top of the application. It also contains four skin parts, defined by the host component (s:DropDown List) and its parent classes, with corresponding id properties:

dropDown
: The instance of s:DisplayObject that is shown when open; a mouse click outside of dropDown closes the s:DropDownList (in the following example, dropDown is an instance of s:Group, which extends s:DisplayObject).

openButton
: The button that opens the host component.

dataGroup
: The instance of s:DataGroup that manages the options in the s:DropDownList dictated by the dataProvider.

labelDisplay
: The instance of s:Label that displays the current selection.

Another common skin part not shown in this recipe is scroller, an instance of s:Scroller, which manages the scroll bars for the dataGroup.

The following skin file is located at *skins/DropDownListSkin.mxml* and is referenced by the `skinClass` property of the instance of `s:DropDownList` in the preceding code:

```
<?xml version="1.0" encoding="utf-8"?>
<s:SparkSkin xmlns:fx="http://ns.adobe.com/mxml/2009"
             xmlns:s="library://ns.adobe.com/flex/spark"
             alpha.disabled=".5">
    <fx:Script>
        <![CDATA[
            import spark.skins.spark.DropDownListSkin
        ]]>
    </fx:Script>
    <fx:Metadata>
        <![CDATA[
            [HostComponent("spark.components.DropDownList")]
        ]]>
    </fx:Metadata>

    <s:states>
        <s:State name="normal"/>
        <s:State name="open"/>
        <s:State name="disabled"/>
    </s:states>

    <s:PopUpAnchor displayPopUp.normal="false"
                   displayPopUp.open="true" includeIn="open"
                   left="0" right="0" top="0" bottom="0"
                   itemDestructionPolicy="auto"
                   popUpPosition="right"
                   popUpWidthMatchesAnchorWidth="false">

        <s:Group id="dropDown">

            <s:Rect id="border" left="0" right="0" top="0"
                    bottom="0" radiusX="5" radiusY="5">
                <s:fill>
                    <s:SolidColor color="#FFFFFF"/>
                </s:fill>
                <s:stroke>
                    <s:SolidColorStroke id="borderStroke" weight="1"/>
                </s:stroke>
                <s:filters>
                    <s:DropShadowFilter blurX="3"
                                        blurY="3"
                                        alpha="0.5"
                                        distance="1"
                                        angle="90"
                                        color="#000000"/>
                </s:filters>
            </s:Rect>

            <s:DataGroup id="dataGroup"
                         itemRenderer="ItemRenderers.DropDownItemRenderer"
                         left="1" right="1" top="1"
                         bottom="1">
```

```
                <s:layout>
                    <s:TileLayout orientation="rows"
                                  requestedColumnCount="2"
                                  verticalGap="0"
                                  horizontalGap="0" columnWidth="70"/>
                </s:layout>
            </s:DataGroup>
        </s:Group>
    </s:PopUpAnchor>

    <s:Button id="openButton" width="25" height="25"
            right="0" verticalCenter="0"
            focusEnabled="false"
            skinClass="skins.DropDownButtonSkin"/>

    <s:Label id="labelDisplay" maxDisplayedLines="1"
            fontWeight="bold" mouseEnabled="false"
            mouseChildren="false" right="32" minWidth="75"
            verticalCenter="2"/>
</s:SparkSkin>
```

The skin for openButton is not detailed here, but it is similar to the skin for the button shown at the beginning of this chapter. Additionally the itemRenderer property for dataGroup is not detailed in this recipe; for further information on custom item renderers, see Chapter 8.

6.5 Skin a Spark Container

Problem

You want to create a custom design for s:SkinnableContainer.

Solution

Extend s:Skin and include the required skin part: contentGroup.

Discussion

Skinning a Spark container is similar to skinning other Spark components, with the exception that the skin needs to be equipped to handle nested items. The following application contains an instance of s:SkinnableContainer, the simplest Spark container, which contains an instance of s:Label as a nested item:

```
<?xml version="1.0" encoding="utf-8"?>
<s:Application xmlns:fx="http://ns.adobe.com/mxml/2009"
               xmlns:s="library://ns.adobe.com/flex/spark"
               xmlns:mx="library://ns.adobe.com/flex/mx"
               minWidth="955" minHeight="600">
    <s:SkinnableContainer left="0" right="0" bottom="0"
                          skinClass="skins.FooterSkin">
```

```
        <s:Label horizontalCenter="0" bottom="20" top="40"
                     text="© 2010 Wireframe, Inc"/>
    </s:SkinnableContainer>
</s:Application>
```

Spark containers also require an instance of `s:Group` with an `id` of `contentGroup`. Note that although it is possible to set the layout for the `contentGroup`, the property will be overridden if it is set in the instance of the host component.

The following skin component, located at *skins/FooterSkin.mxml*, contains a rectangle with a simple gradient:

```
<?xml version="1.0" encoding="utf-8"?>
<s:Skin xmlns:fx="http://ns.adobe.com/mxml/2009"
        xmlns:s="library://ns.adobe.com/flex/spark"
        xmlns:fb="http://ns.adobe.com/flashbuilder/2009"
        alpha.disabled="0.5">

    <fx:Metadata>
        <![CDATA[
            [HostComponent("spark.components.SkinnableContainer")]
        ]]>
    </fx:Metadata>


    <s:states>
        <s:State name="normal"/>
        <s:State name="disabled"/>
    </s:states>

    <s:Rect id="background" left="0" right="0" top="0"
            bottom="0">
        <s:fill>
            <s:LinearGradient rotation="-90">
                <s:GradientEntry color="#CCCCCC"/>
                <s:GradientEntry color="#999999"/>
            </s:LinearGradient>
        </s:fill>
    </s:Rect>

    <s:Group id="contentGroup" left="0" right="0" top="0"
            bottom="0" minWidth="0" minHeight="0">
        <s:layout>
            <s:BasicLayout/>
        </s:layout>
    </s:Group>

</s:Skin>
```

6.6 Change the Appearance of Components Using Styles

Problem

You want to stylize text displayed in your application.

Solution

Declare new styles and properties using stylesheets.

Discussion

There are two parts to declaring styles in Cascading Style Sheets (CSS): the *selector*, which defines which elements of the application are being styled, and the *style properties* that are being applied.

There are four types of simple selectors:

- Type
- Universal
- Class
- ID

A *type* selector matches instances of a component by local name. The following example matches every instance of `s:Button` and assigns the label text to be white:

```
s|Button{ color: #FFFFFF; }
```

Notice the selector syntax; because Flex 4 uses multiple namespaces, it is required to include the namespace in all type selectors. Also notice that in CSS, the namespace separator is a pipe character (|) because the colon syntax is reserved for property declarations and pseudoselectors.

The following is the corresponding namespace, declared at the top of the stylesheet or `fx:Style` tag:

```
@namespace s "library://ns.adobe.com/flex/spark";
```

Similarly to namespaces in MXML, CSS namespaces for custom components must declare the file path. For example:

```
@namespace skins "skins.*";
```

The *universal* selector is the asterisk (*); it matches every instance of any component. The following style declaration sets all font weights to bold:

```
* { fontWeight: bold; }
```

A *class* selector matches instances of any component with a corresponding `styleName` property assigned to it. Class selectors are type-agnostic and begin with a period (.).

The following example has a style declaration that matches the `styleName` properties of instances of `s:Panel` and `s:Button`:

```
<fx:Style>
    @namespace s "library://ns.adobe.com/flex/spark";
    @namespace mx "library://ns.adobe.com/flex/mx";
    .rounded {
        cornerRadius: 10;
    }
</fx:Style>
<s:Panel styleName="rounded" title="Here be a Panel">
    <s:Button styleName="rounded" label="Here be a Button"/>
</s:Panel>
```

An *ID* selector is similar to a class selector with the exception that it matches the `id` property of an instance of a component. Because the `id` property must be unique within each component, an ID selector can only match one instance per component. ID selectors are type-agnostic and begin with a hash sign (#). The following selector matches any instance of any component with its `id` set to `header`:

```
#header{ backgroundColor: #FF0000; }
```

You can combine simple selectors to create a selector with a more narrow scope using *descendant selectors*. A descendant selector matches components depending on their relationship to ancestor components in the document. That is, it allows you to match components based on whether they descend from (i.e., are children, grandchildren, great-grandchildren, etc. of) particular types of components. The following selector matches every instance of `s:Button` that descends from a component instance with its `styleName` property set to `main`:

```
.main s|Button{ fontSize: 15; }
```

A *pseudoselector* matches a state of an instance. The following selector changes the text color to green for any component instance with its `currentState` property set to `over`:

```
*:over{ color: #00FF00; }
```

6.7 Apply Skins and Properties to Spark and MX Components with CSS

Problem

You want to apply skins using CSS selectors.

Solution

Use CSS to apply skins to components throughout your application.

Discussion

Styles can be declared in an external CSS file, referenced by a `fx:Style` tag, or declared in the `fx:Style` tag itself. There are several style properties that can alter the appearance of a component, including `skinClass` for Spark components. Check the Flex documentation or component source code from the Flex 4 SDK to find a list of style properties for a component.

The following application contains an instance of `s:Button`, an instance of a custom component, `components:IconButton`, and an instance of `mx:BarChart`. It also references *main.css*, which is shown in the next listing:

```
<?xml version="1.0" encoding="utf-8"?>
<s:Application xmlns:fx="http://ns.adobe.com/mxml/2009"
               xmlns:s="library://ns.adobe.com/flex/spark"
               xmlns:mx="library://ns.adobe.com/flex/mx"
               minWidth="955" minHeight="600"
               xmlns:components="components.*">
    <fx:Style source="main.css"/>
    <fx:Script>
        <![CDATA[
            import mx.collections.ArrayCollection;
            [Bindable]
            public var sales:ArrayCollection = new ArrayCollection([
                {Sales: "Q1", Amount: 500},
                {Sales: "Q2", Amount: 1100},
                {Sales: "Q3", Amount: 100},
                {Sales: "Q4", Amount: 800}
            ]);
        ]]>
    </fx:Script>
    <s:Button label="Button One" top="10" left="10"/>
    <components:IconButton source="assets/images/close.png"
                           label="close" top="40" left="10"/>
    <mx:BarChart id="myChart" dataProvider="{sales}"
                 verticalCenter="0" horizontalCenter="0"
                 showDataTips="true">
        <mx:verticalAxis>
            <mx:CategoryAxis dataProvider="{sales}"
                             categoryField="Sales"/>
        </mx:verticalAxis>
        <mx:series>
            <mx:BarSeries xField="Amount" displayName="Amount"/>
        </mx:series>
    </mx:BarChart>

</s:Application>
```

The stylesheet *main.css*, shown next, changes the `color`, `fontWeight`, and `corner Radius` for all `s:Button` instances; the `fill` color for all `mx:BarChart` instances; and the `skinClass` for all instances of `comp:IconButton`. Because the `skinClass` property refers to a class, it is necessary to use `ClassReference` in the property declaration:

```
@namespace s "library://ns.adobe.com/flex/spark";
@namespace mx "library://ns.adobe.com/flex/mx";
@namespace comp "components.*";
s|Button {
    color: #00003C;
    fontWeight: bold;
    cornerRadius: 8px;
}
mx|BarChart {
    fill: #DDDDDD;
}
comp|IconButton {
    skinClass: ClassReference("skins.WireIconButtonSkin");
}
```

Because skinClass is defined using a type selector, it will apply the skin to all instances of comp:IconButton unless explicitly overridden in the individual instances.

6.8 Create a Button Component with an Icon

Problem

You want to extend s:Button and add a property for an icon that is available as a skin part.

Solution

Extend s:Button with an ActionScript class and add the necessary properties and skin parts.

Discussion

Skin parts are referenced in a component using the [SkinPart] metadata tag. This tag has an optional required property that specifies whether the skin part is optional and is set to true by default.

The following component extends s:Button using ActionScript and adds two additional properties: icon, which is an instance of mx:Image, and source, a String.

icon is defined as an optional skin part and will be added to the skin class further on in the recipe. Because, in the lifecycle of the component, the source property can be defined before icon has been added to the displayList of the button, getter and setter functions are used for the source property and the value is only assigned to icon if it is defined.

The protected function `partAdded()` is also overridden to assign the `source` property to `icon` when it is added to the `displayList`. Here's the code:

```
package components {
    import mx.controls.Image;

    import spark.components.Button;

    public class IconButton extends Button {

        protected var _source:String;

        [SkinPart(required="false")]
        public var icon:Image;

        [Bindable("sourceChanged")]
        [Inspectable(category="General", defaultValue="", format="File")]
        public function get source():String {
            return _source;
        }

        public function set source(val:String):void {
            _source = val;
            if (icon) {
                icon.source = val;
            }
        }

        override protected function partAdded(partName:String,
                                            instance:Object):void {
            super.partAdded(partName, instance);
            if (instance == icon) {
                if (source !== null)
                    icon.source = source;
            }
        }
    }
}
```

The skin class contains a simple rectangle, an instance of `s:Label`, and an instance of `mx:Image` with an `id` of `icon`. It is important to remember that the property names of the skin parts declared in the host component must match the `id`s of the corresponding components in the skin class:

```
<?xml version="1.0" encoding="utf-8"?>
<s:SparkSkin xmlns:fx="http://ns.adobe.com/mxml/2009"
            xmlns:s="library://ns.adobe.com/flex/spark"
            xmlns:fb="http://ns.adobe.com/flashbuilder/2009"
            minWidth="21" minHeight="30"
            alpha.disabled="0.5"
            xmlns:mx="library://ns.adobe.com/flex/mx">
    <fx:Metadata>[HostComponent("components.IconButton")]</fx:Metadata>
```

```
<s:states>
    <s:State name="up"/>
    <s:State name="over"/>
    <s:State name="down"/>
    <s:State name="disabled"/>
</s:states>

<fx:Declarations>
    <s:SolidColor id="fillColor" color="#FFFFFF"
                  color.over="#DDDDDD"/>
    <s:SolidColorStroke id="strokeColor" color="#333333"
                        color.over="#111111" weight="2"/>
</fx:Declarations>

<s:Rect top="0" left="0" bottom="0" right="0"
        radiusX="15" radiusY="15" fill="{fillColor}"
        stroke="{strokeColor}"/>
<s:Group left="8" right="25" top="2" bottom="2">
    <s:layout>
        <s:HorizontalLayout verticalAlign="middle" gap="8"/>
    </s:layout>

    <mx:Image id="icon" maxHeight="24"/>
    <s:Label id="labelDisplay" left="25" right="25"
             top="9" bottom="6"
             color="{strokeColor.color}"
             fontWeight="bold"/>
</s:Group>

</s:SparkSkin>
```

6.9 Add Custom Style Properties

Problem

You want to define a custom style property that can be assigned using CSS and is accessible in the skin class.

Solution

Use the [Style] metadata tag to add any style name and property that is needed.

Discussion

The [Style] metadata tag can be applied to a class declaration to add style properties to a class. The following component extends s:SkinnableContainer and adds two style properties: cornerRadii, which is expected to be an array of numbers, and bgColor, which should be a color in the form of a number (hexadecimal). These properties do not affect the class itself but will be accessible to the corresponding skin class:

```
package components {
    import spark.components.SkinnableContainer;

    [Style(name="cornerRadii", type="Array", format="Number", inherit="no")]
    [Style(name="bgColor", type="Number", format="Color", inherit="no")]
    public class BoxContainer extends SkinnableContainer {
        public function BoxContainer() {
            super();
        }


    }
}
```

The styles declared in the host component can be retrieved in the skin component using the method getStyle(). Although it is not shown here, it is usually best to define default values in case the style is not set. In the following example, the cornerRadii and bgColor properties are retrieved using the getStyle() method and are used to change the individual corner radii and the background color of the container:

```
<?xml version="1.0" encoding="utf-8"?>
<s:Skin xmlns:fx="http://ns.adobe.com/mxml/2009"
        xmlns:s="library://ns.adobe.com/flex/spark"
        alpha.disabled="0.5">
    <fx:Metadata>
        <![CDATA[
            [HostComponent("components.BoxContainer")]
        ]]>
    </fx:Metadata>
    <fx:Script>
        <![CDATA[
            override protected function updateDisplayList(unscaledWidth:Number,
                        unscaledHeight:Number):void {

                var corners:Array = hostComponent.getStyle('cornerRadii');
                var color:uint = hostComponent.getStyle('bgColor');
                bgRect.topLeftRadiusX = corners[0];
                bgRect.topLeftRadiusY = corners[0];
                bgRect.topRightRadiusX = corners[1];
                bgRect.topRightRadiusY = corners[1];
                bgRect.bottomRightRadiusX = corners[2];
                bgRect.bottomRightRadiusY = corners[2];
                bgRect.bottomLeftRadiusX = corners[3];
                bgRect.bottomLeftRadiusY = corners[3];
                bgColor.color = color;

                super.updateDisplayList(unscaledWidth, unscaledHeight);
            }
        ]]>
    </fx:Script>

    <s:states>
        <s:State name="normal"/>
        <s:State name="disabled"/>
    </s:states>
```

```
<fx:Declarations>
    <s:SolidColor id="bgColor" color="#FFFFFF"/>
    <s:SolidColorStroke id="strokeColor" color="#333333" weight="2"/>
</fx:Declarations>

<s:Rect id="bgRect" top="0" left="0" bottom="0" right="0"
        fill="{bgColor}" stroke="{strokeColor}"/>

<s:Group id="contentGroup" left="10" right="10" top="10" bottom="10">
    <s:layout>
        <s:BasicLayout/>
    </s:layout>
</s:Group>

</s:Skin>
```

Notice in the previous example that the instance of the host component is accessed using the `hostComponent` property that is set in the skin component automatically.

The following is an example of an instance of `components:BoxContainer` and its corresponding style properties:

```
<fx:Style>
    @namespace comp "components.*";
    comp|BoxContainer {
        cornerRadii: 0, 20, 0, 20;
        bgColor: #CCCCCC;
        skinClass: ClassReference("skins.BoxContainerSkin");
    }
</fx:Style>
<components:BoxContainer width="250" height="150" left="10" top="10"/>
```

6.10 Partially Embed Fonts with CSS

Problem

You want to use a font that may not be available on the end users' computers.

Solution

Use the `@font-face` declaration in CSS and include the needed font files.

Discussion

Embedding fonts is a powerful design feature for Flex, and has been improved in Flex 4. This feature allows you to include fonts that the end user may not have installed, and provides a more consistent experience across browsers and operating systems.

The downside to embedding fonts is the added size to the final SWF file. To minimize this increase in size, it is possible to assign a character range.

In the following example the OpenType font Fertigo Pro is embedded and used where fontFamily is set to Fertigo. The unicodeRange style property restricts the embedded character set to letters, the period (.), and numbers 0 through 4:

```
<fx:Style>
    @namespace s "library://ns.adobe.com/flex/spark";
    @namespace mx "library://ns.adobe.com/flex/mx";
    @font-face {
        src: url("assets/fonts/Fertigo_PRO.otf");
        fontFamily: Fertigo;
        fontStyle: normal;
        fontWeight: normal;
        advancedAntiAliasing: true;
        unicodeRange:
            U+0041-005A, /* Upper-Case [A..Z] */
            U+0061-007A, /* Lower-Case a-z */
            U+0030-0034, /* Numbers [0..4] */
            U+002E-002E; /* Period [. ] */
    }
    s|Label {
        fontFamily: Fertigo;
    }
</fx:Style>
```

CHAPTER 7

Text and TextFlows

The text components in Flex 4 have been updated to take advantage of the new text-rendering engine in Flash Player 10, referred to as the *Flash Text Engine*. To work with text in a Flex application, you'll want to use the new components that utilize the Text Layout Framework: `TextArea`, `RichText`, and `RichEditableText`. Each of these components provides different functionality in a Flex application. The `Label` component provides simple, lightweight, basic text functionality. `Label` supports all of the properties of the `GraphicElement`, as well as bidirectional text and a limited subset of text formatting, but it doesn't support hypertext or inline graphics. The `RichText` control supports HTML and, unlike `Label`, uses the `TextFlow` object model. It supports multiple formats and paragraphs but not scrolling, selection, or editing. Lastly, `RichEditable Text` supports scrolling, selection, editing, and hyperlinks, as well as supporting all the functionality of the `Label` and `RichText` components. `Label` does not use the Text Layout Framework, relying solely on the Flash Text Engine, while the other two components leverage the Text Layout Framework built into Flex 4.

The Text Layout Framework also introduces the `TextFlow` class, which is an XML document of `FlowElement`s that can be written using tags or using `FlowElement` classes. For instance, a paragraph within a `TextFlow` can be created using a `<p>` tag in a Text Flow XML document or by attaching a `ParagraphElement` directly to a `TextFlow` instance, because the `<p>` tag is converted to a `ParagraphElement` when the content of the Text Flow is rendered. The Text Layout Framework's core functionality is to create, render, manipulate, and edit `TextFlow` objects.

Within a `TextFlow`, you can display plain text and HTML. You can also apply text formatting and CSS styles to control the font, text size, and spacing of text or properties of graphical objects using universal selectors, classes (the `.` operator), or IDs (the `#` operator). When using the subset of HTML that is supported by the Flash Player, you can load images and other SWF files into the player. Text formatting—that is, controlling the font size and color—can be done using CSS if you use the correct `IFormatResolver` and `TextLayoutFormat` objects.

7.1 Create a TextFlow Object

Problem

You want to create a `TextFlow` object.

Solution

You can create a `TextFlow` object either in ActionScript or in MXML.

Discussion

When creating a `TextFlow` object in ActionScript, there is a very particular hierarchy to which the elements must adhere (see Figure 7-1).

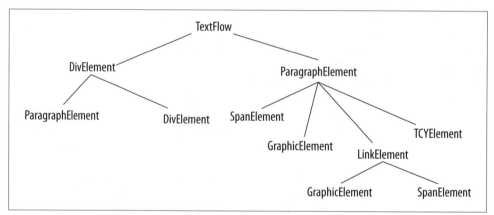

Figure 7-1. The elements of a TextFlow

The root of the `TextFlow` element can have only `ParagraphElements` or `DivElements` added to it. A `DivElement` can only have other `DivElements` or `ParagraphElements` added to it, while a `ParagraphElement` can have any element added to it. The following example illustrates how to create a `TextFlow` object in ActionScript:

```
private function create():TextFlow {

    var textFlow:TextFlow = new TextFlow();

    var paragraph:ParagraphElement = new ParagraphElement();
    var span:SpanElement = new SpanElement();
    span.text = "An image";

    paragraph.addChild(span);
    textFlow.addChild(paragraph);

    return textFlow;
}
```

You can also create a `TextFlow` object in MXML by declaring a `TextFlow` within the `<fx:Declarations>` tag of your application, as shown here:

```
<fx:Declarations>
    <s:TextFlow id="tf1">
        <s:p>
            <s:span>
                Hello World
            </s:span>
            <s:br/>
            <s:a href="http://www.oreilly.com">
                <s:span>
                    A link.
                </s:span>
            </s:a>
        </s:p>
    </s:TextFlow>
</fx:Declarations>
```

Note that you use the same hierarchy when you declare a `TextFlow` in MXML.

7.2 Generate a TextFlow Object from Another Source

Problem

You need to create a `TextFlow` object from HTML.

Solution

Use the `TextConverter` class to generate the `TextFlow` object, passing the object to use as the source for the `TextFlow` object and the type of object that is being used as the source to the `TextConverter.importToFlow()` method.

Discussion

The `TextConverter` class has methods to help you generate new `TextFlow` objects from existing source objects or to export `TextFlow` objects to another type of object. To generate a `TextFlow` object, use the `importToFlow()` method. This has the following signature:

```
importToFlow(source:Object, format:String,
            config:IConfiguration = null):flashx.textLayout.elements:TextFlow
```

The method takes three parameters: `source:Object`, `format:String`, and `config:ICon figuration`. The first, `source:Object`, specifies the source content, which can be a string, an `Object`, or an XML object. The second, `format:String`, specifies the format of source content. There are three self-explanatory options: `HTML_FORMAT`, `PLAIN_TEXT_FORMAT`, and `TEXT_LAYOUT_FORMAT`. Finally, `config:IConfiguration` indicates the configuration to use when creating new `TextFlow` objects. By default this parameter is null, but if you want to pass custom formats for links or include other custom formats within your

TextFlow, you'll want to pass in a Configuration object or an instance of an object that extends the IConfiguration interface when you create the TextFlow.

This simple example shows how to create all three types of objects that the Text Converter class supports:

```
<s:Application xmlns:fx="http://ns.adobe.com/mxml/2009"
               xmlns:s="library://ns.adobe.com/flex/spark"
               xmlns:mx="library://ns.adobe.com/flex/halo" minWidth="1024"
               minHeight="768">

    <s:layout><s:HorizontalLayout/></s:layout>

    <fx:Declarations>
        <fx:String id="plainText">Here's some plain text</fx:String>
    </fx:Declarations>


    <fx:Script>
        <![CDATA[
            import flashx.textLayout.conversion.TextConverter;

            import spark.events.IndexChangeEvent;

            private var tlfMarkup:String = "<TextFlow
                    xmlns='http://ns.adobe.com/textLayout/2008'><p>" +
                    "<span>Here's some Text " +
                    "Layout Format markup</span></p></TextFlow>";

            private var htmlText:String = "Here's <b>some</b> text in some
                    <a href=\"www.w3c.org\">HTML</a>";

            private function convertPlainText():void {
                tArea.textFlow = TextConverter.importToFlow(plainText,
                            TextConverter.PLAIN_TEXT_FORMAT);
            }

            private function convertHTMLText():void {
                tArea.textFlow = TextConverter.importToFlow(htmlText,
                            TextConverter.TEXT_FIELD_HTML_FORMAT);
            }

            private function convertTextFlow():void {
                tArea.textFlow = TextConverter.importToFlow(tlfMarkup,
                            TextConverter.TEXT_LAYOUT_FORMAT);
            }


            protected function buttonbarChangeHandler(event:IndexChangeEvent):void
            {
                switch (buttonBar.selectedItem) {
                    case "Plain Text":
                        convertPlainText();
                    break;
                    case "HTML Text":
```

```
                    convertHTMLText();
                break;
                case "TLF Markup":
                    convertTextFlow();
                break;
            }
        }

        ]]>
    </fx:Script>
    <s:ButtonBar id="buttonBar" change="buttonbarChangeHandler(event)">
        <s:dataProvider>
            <s:ArrayList>
                <fx:String>Plain Text</fx:String>
                <fx:String>HTML Text</fx:String>
                <fx:String>TLF Markup</fx:String>
            </s:ArrayList>
        </s:dataProvider>
    </s:ButtonBar>
    <s:TextArea id="tArea"/>
</s:Application>
```

You can pass a string or HTML to the `text` property of the `TextArea`, `RichEditable Text`, or `RichText` component, and that control will convert the object to a `TextFlow` for you.

7.3 Create Links in a TextFlow

Problem

You need to create hyperlinks in a `TextFlow` document.

Solution

Use the `<a>` tag with an `href` attribute in a TextFlow XML document, declare a `Link Element` object and add it to a `TextFlow`, or use the `TextConverter.importToFlow()` method to import HTML.

Discussion

There are a few ways to create links in a `TextFlow`. One option is to create an HTML document and import it by using the `TextConverter.importToFlow()` method with the second parameter set to `TextConverter.TEXT_FIELD_HTML_FORMAT`. For example, say you want to import the following string of HTML:

```
private var htmlText:String = "Here's <b>some</b> text in some
        <a href=\"www.w3c.org\">HTML</a>";
```

You can create a TextFlow XML document with an `<a>` tag within it and import it using the `TextConverter.importToFlow()` method with the second parameter set to `TextConverter.TEXT_LAYOUT_FORMAT`:

```
private var tlfMarkup:XML = <TextFlow xmlns="http://ns.adobe.com/textLayout/2008">
    <p>Here's some <a target="_blank" href="http://www.adobe.com">Text Layout
    Format</a> markup</p></TextFlow>;
```

You can also create a `LinkElement` in ActionScript and add it to a `TextFlow`. The `LinkElement` does not have a text property. To create the text for the link (which is what the user will see as the link), use a `SpanElement`. Another important thing to note is that, as demonstrated in Recipe 7.1, the `TextFlow` can have only `ParagraphElement` objects added to it. Thus, you'll have to add the `LinkElement` to a `ParagraphElement`:

```
var paragraph:ParagraphElement = new ParagraphElement();

var span:SpanElement = new SpanElement();
span.text = "A link to Adobe";

var linkElement:LinkElement = new LinkElement();
linkElement.href = "http://www.adobe.com";
linkElement.addChild(span);

paragraph.addChild(linkElement);

tArea.textFlow.addChild(paragraph);
```

You can also set `rollOut()` or `rollOver()` methods on the link by adding `rollOut` or `rollOver` attributes to the `link` tag within a Text Layout Document:

```
<a rollOut="showRollOut(event)" rollOver="showRollOver(event)"
    target="_blank" href="http://www.adobe.com">Text Layout Format</a>
```

These events dispatch instances of the `FlowElementMouseEvent` class, which contain references to the object that was rolled over (in this case, the actual `LinkElement` that has been rolled over):

```
private function showRollOut(event:FlowElementMouseEvent):void {
    event.flowElement.color = 0x000000;
}

private function showRollOver(event:FlowElementMouseEvent):void {
    event.flowElement.color = 0xFFFF00;
}
```

7.4 Add Graphic Elements to a TextFlow

Problem

You want to add an external SWF file, another `DisplayObject`, or a JPG file to a `TextFlow`.

Solution

Create an `InlineGraphicElement` object in ActionScript or in MXML.

Discussion

The `InlineGraphicElement` allows you to load image files (in JPG, PNG, or other file formats) or SWF files, or use a `Sprite`, `BitmapAsset`, or `MovieClip` instance within a `TextFlow`:

```
var tf:TextFlow = new TextFlow();
var pgElement:ParagraphElement = new ParagraphElement();
tf.addChild(pgElement);
```

In this example, the graphic is created from a loaded JPG file:

```
var gElement:InlineGraphicElement = new InlineGraphicElement();
```

Here, the source property is set to the URL of an image:

```
gElement.source = "sample.jpg";
gElement.width = 60;
gElement.height = 60;
pgElement.addChild(gElement);

var sprite:Sprite = new Sprite();
sprite.graphics.beginFill(0x0000ff);
sprite.graphics.drawRect(0, 0, 75, 75);
sprite.graphics.endFill();

var span:SpanElement = new SpanElement();
span.text = "Some text to fill in";
pgElement.addChild(span);
```

Here, the graphic is created from another `DisplayObject` by using the `addChild()` method of the `InlineGraphicElement`:

```
var gElement2:InlineGraphicElement = new InlineGraphicElement();
gElement2.source = sprite;
gElement2.width = 60;
gElement2.height = 60;
pgElement.addChild(gElement2);
```

`InlineGraphicElements` can also be declared in MXML using the `<img>` tag, as shown here:

```
<s:TextFlow id="tFlow">
    <s:p>
        <s:span>
            Here's a graphic.
        </s:span>
        <s:img width="60" height="60" source="sample.jpg"/>
    </s:p>
</s:TextFlow>
```

If the source is set to a string, the InlineGraphicElement will load the image or SWF and update the TextFlow when the image has loaded.

7.5 Bind a Value to a s:TextInput Control

Problem

You need to bind the value of a user's input in a s:TextInput control to another control.

Solution

Use binding tags to bind the text of the s:TextInput component to the Text component that will display the input.

Discussion

The s:TextInput control here is used to provide the text that a s:TextArea will display. As the amount of text is increased, you can use the Flex Framework's binding mechanism to increase the width of the s:TextArea:

```
<s:TextArea text="{tiInstance.text}"/>
<s:TextInput id="tiInstance"/>
```

You can also bind the s:TextArea to a s:RichEditableText component where a user will be entering HTML. For example:

```
<s:TextArea textFlow="{TextConverter.importToFlow(retInstance.text,
                        TextConverter.TEXT_FIELD_HTML_FORMAT)}"/>
<s:RichEditableText id="retInstance" height="200" width="200"/>
```

The handler for the change event simply needs to get the s:RichEditableText component within the s:TextInput:

```
private function selectChangeHandler(event:Event):void {
    var richText:RichEditableText = (event.currentTarget as TextInput).textDisplay;
    var flow:TextFlow = richText.textFlow;
    tArea.text = selectionTI.text.substring( flow.interactionManager.absoluteStart,
                                flow.interactionManager.absoluteEnd );
}
```

The two components would be set up as follows:

```
<s:TextArea id="tArea"/>
<s:TextInput id="selectionTI" selectionChange="selectChangeHandler(event)"
            creationComplete="initTI(event)" text="Some Textual Prompt"/>
```

Text will flow around InlineGraphicElements that are added to the same Paragraph Element or DivElement objects.

7.6 Create a Custom Selection Style

Problem

You want to create a custom style that can be applied to any object within a `TextFlow` using that object's `id`.

Solution

You can assign a style for any element that has an `id` property, or you can create a style for particular elements by using the `tlf` namespace for the style.

Discussion

You can apply styles listed in a `<fx:Style>` tag or in an external CSS file to a `TextFlow` using `TextLayoutFormat` objects if you set the `s:formatResolver` property of the Text Flow to be a `CSSFormatResolver`. If you do not create an instance of `CSSFormatResolver` and pass it to the `TextFlow`, styles that you attempt to apply to the `TextFlow` will not change its appearance. You can also create `s:TextLayoutFormat` objects and use those to style the `TextFlow`. Both techniques are shown in the following samples:

```
<s:TextLayoutFormat id="bgTLF" backgroundColor="#333333" color="#ffffff"/>
<s:TextLayoutFormat id="largerTLF" fontSize="16"/>
<s:TextFlow id="flow">
    <s:formatResolver>
        <local:CSSFormatResolver/>
    </s:formatResolver>
    <s:p>
```

Here, an instance of the `TextLayoutFormat` object is used to set the properties of the `<span>`:

```
<s:span format="{largerTLF}">
    Some Larger Text.
</s:span>
```

Both a `selector` and a `TextLayoutFormat` can be used together to style an object:

```
<s:span id="smaller" format="{bgTLF}">
    Some Smaller Text.
</s:span>
```

The `styleName` attribute of the `span` also can be used to style the object:

```
<s:span styleName="header">
    Some styled Text.
</s:span>
    </s:p>
</s:TextFlow>
```

Here are some styles that have been created locally and will be applied to the TextFlow:

```
<fx:Style>
    @namespace s "library://ns.adobe.com/flex/spark";
    @namespace mx "library://ns.adobe.com/flex/halo";

    global {
        fontFamily: "Verdana"
    }

    .header {
        fontSize:"30";
    }

    #smaller {
        fontSize:"11";
    }

</fx:Style>
```

You can also compile a CSS file to a SWF and load that using the `StyleManager.load StyleDeclarations()` method. For instance, the following CSS file could be compiled to a SWF called *SimpleCSS.swf*:

```
@namespace tlf "flashx.textLayout.elements.*";

.linkStyle {
    fontSize:        "18";
    color:"0xff0000";
}

.italic
{
    fontStyle:        "italic";
    color:            "0xff0000";
    fontFamily:        "Helvetica";
}

.center
{
    textAlign:        "center";
}

#bold
{
    fontWeight:        "bold";
}
```

Once the SWF is compiled, you can load it into the application and update the styles of the elements within the TextFlow by calling the `invalidateAllFormats()` method on the TextFlow and then calling `flowComposer.updateAllControllers()` on the TextFlow. This ensures that all the newly loaded styles are read into the TextFlow:

```
private function loadCSS():void {
    var dispatcher:IEventDispatcher =
```

```
            StyleManager.loadStyleDeclarations("SimpleCSS.swf");
        dispatcher.addEventListener(StyleEvent.COMPLETE,styleEventComplete);
    }

    private function styleEventComplete(e:StyleEvent):void {
        textArea.textFlow.invalidateAllFormats();
        textArea.textFlow.flowComposer.updateAllControllers();
    }
```

7.7 Style Links Within a TextFlow

Problem

You want to style the `LinkElement` instances contained within a `TextFlow`.

Solution

Set the `linkActiveFormat`, `linkHoverFormat`, and `linkNormalFormat` properties of the `TextFlow` to instances of `TextLayoutFormat`.

Discussion

A `TextFlow` has three different properties that control the way a link appears: `linkActiveFormat`, `linkHoverFormat`, and `linkNormalFormat`. You can set these properties for all the elements in a `TextFlow` or on an individual element, as shown here:

```
<s:TextLayoutFormat id="bg" backgroundColor="#333333" color="#ffffff"/>
<s:TextLayoutFormat id="larger" fontSize="16"/>
<s:TextLayoutFormat id="red" color="#ff0000"/>
<s:TextFlow id="flow" linkActiveFormat="{red}" linkHoverFormat="{red}"
            linkNormalFormat="{red}">
    <s:p>
        <s:a href="http://www.adobe.com">A link.</s:a>
    </s:p>
    <s:a href="http://www.adobe.com"
        linkActiveFormat="{bg}"
        linkHoverFormat="{bg}"
        linkNormalFormat="{bg}">
        Another link.
    </s:a>
</s:TextFlow>
```

You can also set these properties using ActionScript at runtime:

```
private function setLinkStyles():void {

    var p:ParagraphElement = new ParagraphElement();
    var link:LinkElement = new LinkElement();
```

When doing this, you can set the link formats either by using the `TextLayoutFormat` or by using key/value pairs:

```
link.linkActiveFormat = {"color":0xff00ff};
link.linkHoverFormat = {"color":0xff00ff};
link.linkNormalFormat = {"color":0xff00ff};

var span:SpanElement = new SpanElement();
span.text = "Some Text";

link.addChild(span);
p.addChild(link);
textArea.textFlow.addChild(p);

textArea.textFlow.invalidateAllFormats();
textArea.textFlow.flowComposer.updateAllControllers();
}
```

The calls to the `invalidateAllFormats()` method and the `FlowComposer.updateAll Controllers()` methods are necessary so that the `TextFlow` will reflect the changes made to it.

7.8 Locate Elements Within a TextFlow

Problem

You want to locate particular elements within a `TextFlow`.

Solution

Retrieve the elements by their `id` attributes, by their style names, or by walking the structure of the `TextFlow` itself.

Discussion

The `TextFlow` defines two methods for retrieving `FlowElement` objects within it. The first method, `FlowElement getElementByID(idName:String)`, returns an element whose `id` property matches the `idName` parameter. The second, `Array getElementsByStyleName (styleNameValue:String)`, returns an array of all elements whose `styleName` property is set to `styleNameValue`.

The following code snippets show a style called "bold" being defined. That style will be used to retrieve all elements whose `styleName` attribute is set to `bold`. One of the `SpanElement` objects has its `id` set to `spark`, and this ID is used to retrieve it:

```
<fx:Style>
    @namespace s "library://ns.adobe.com/flex/spark";
    @namespace mx "library://ns.adobe.com/flex/halo";
    @namespace tlf "flashx.textLayout.elements.*";

    .bold { fontWeight:"bold"; }

</fx:Style>
```

```
private var tfXML:XML = <TextFlow xmlns="http://ns.adobe.com/textLayout/2008"
                                  fontSize="16">
                        <p>The <span styleName="bold">Label</span>,
                            <span styleName="bold">RichText</span>, and
                            <span styleName="bold">RichEditableText</span>
                            <span id="spark">Spark</span>
                            text controls are used in the skins of skinnable
                            components.
                        </p>
                        </TextFlow>;

private var tflow:TextFlow;

private function createTextFlow():void {
    tflow = new TextFlow();
    tflow.formatResolver = new CSSFormatResolver();
    var pElement:ParagraphElement = new ParagraphElement();
    tflow.addChild(pElement);
    var span:SpanElement = new SpanElement();
    span.text = "Some Text";
```

If you create a TextFlow in ActionScript and then set the styleName and id properties:

```
    span.styleName = "bold";
    span.id = "spark";
    pElement.addChild(span);
    tArea.textFlow = tflow;
}
```

you can retrieve all the FlowElement objects by styleName and id:

```
    var styleArray:Array = tArea.textFlow.getElementsByStyleName("bold");
    var sparkElement:FlowElement = tArea.textFlow.getElementByID("spark");
```

You can also get the children of any node within a TextFlow using the hierarchical structure of the TextFlow. All the FlowElements define the getNextSibling() and getPreviousSibling() methods. getNextSibling() returns the next FlowElement in the TextFlow hierarchy. For example, if three SpanElement objects are nested within a ParagraphElement, calling getNextSibling() on the first one will return the second one. FlowElement getPreviousSibling() returns the previous FlowElement in the TextFlow hierarchy, so if there are three SpanElement objects nested within a ParagraphElement, calling getNextSibling() on the first one will return the second one.

If the element is a FlowLeafElement, which both the InlineGraphicElement and Span Element objects are, it has two other methods available as well. FlowLeafElement getFirstLeaf() returns the first FlowLeafElement descendant of the group, so if you have four SpanElement objects within a group, this method will return the first one within the group. Similarly, FlowLeafElement getLastLeaf() returns the last FlowLeaf Element descendant of the group, so if you have four SpanElement objects within a group, this method will return the last one within the group.

7.9 Determine All Fonts Installed on a User's Computer

Problem

You want to determine all the fonts installed on a user's computer and let the user set which of those fonts the Text component will display.

Solution

Use the enumerateFonts() method defined in the Font class and set the fontFamily style of the Text component with the fontName property of the selected font.

Discussion

The Font class defines a static method called enumerateFonts() that returns all the system fonts on the user's computer as an array of **flash.text.Font** objects. These objects define three properties:

fontName
> The name of the font as reported by the system. In some cases, such as with Japanese, Korean, or Arabic characters, the Flash Player may not render the font correctly.

fontStyle
> The style of the font: Regular, Bold, Italic, or BoldItalic.

fontType
> Either Device, meaning that the font is installed on the user's computer, or Embedded, meaning the font is embedded in the SWF file.

In the following example, the fonts are passed to a ComboBox from which the user can select the font type for the Text area. The call to setStyle sets the actual font in the Text component, using the fontName property of the Font object selected in the ComboBox:

```
text.setStyle("fontFamily", (cb.selectedItem as Font).fontName);
```

Here is a complete code listing:

```
<?xml version="1.0" encoding="utf-8"?>
<s:SkinnableContainer xmlns:fx="http://ns.adobe.com/mxml/2009"
                      xmlns:s="library://ns.adobe.com/flex/spark"
                      xmlns:mx="library://ns.adobe.com/flex/halo"
                      width="400" height="300"
                      creationComplete="findAllFonts()">
    <s:layout><s:HorizontalLayout/></s:layout>
    <fx:Declarations>
        <!-- Place nonvisual elements (e.g., services, value objects) here -->
    </fx:Declarations>
```

```
<fx:Script>
    <![CDATA[
        import mx.collections.ArrayList;

        private var style:StyleSheet;

        [Bindable]
        private var arr:Array;

        private function findAllFonts():void {
            arr = Font.enumerateFonts(true);
            arr.sortOn("fontName", Array.CASEINSENSITIVE);
        }

        private function setFont():void {
            text.setStyle("fontFamily", (cb.selectedItem as Font).fontName);
        }

    ]]>
</fx:Script>
<s:ComboBox id="cb" dataProvider="{new ArrayList(arr)}" change="setFont()"
        labelField="fontName"/>
<s:TextArea text="Sample Text" id="text" fontSize="16"/>
</s:SkinnableContainer>
```

7.10 Display Vertical Text in a TextArea

Problem

You want to display vertical text, such as Chinese characters.

Solution

Set either the FlowElement object's textRotation property to change the orientation of individual characters, or its blockProgression property to change the way in which the lines of text are arranged. You can also set these properties on the TextArea or Rich Text components.

Discussion

In previous recipes you've seen how to style a FlowElement using styles or configuration objects. Both of these are actually properties of the TextLayoutFormat object, so you can create a new TextLayoutFormat object and set the hostLayout format of the TextFlow, or set that property directly on the TextFlow:

```
<s:Group xmlns:fx="http://ns.adobe.com/mxml/2009"
        xmlns:s="library://ns.adobe.com/flex/spark"
        xmlns:mx="library://ns.adobe.com/flex/halo"
        width="500" height="300">
```

```
<fx:Script>
    <![CDATA[

        import flash.text.engine.TextRotation;
        import flashx.textLayout.formats.BlockProgression;
        import flashx.textLayout.formats.VerticalAlign;

        import mx.collections.ArrayList;
        import spark.events.IndexChangeEvent;

        protected function rotateText(event:IndexChangeEvent):void {
            var target:String = event.target.selectedItem;
            switch(target) {
                case "0":
```

Here, the textRotation for each character in the TextFlow is changed:

```
                    tArea.textFlow.textRotation = TextRotation.ROTATE_0;
                break;
                case "90":
                    tArea.textFlow.textRotation = TextRotation.ROTATE_90;
                break;
                case "180":
                    tArea.textFlow.textRotation = TextRotation.ROTATE_180;
                break;
                case "270":
                    tArea.textFlow.textRotation = TextRotation.ROTATE_270;
                break;
            }

            tArea.textFlow.invalidateAllFormats();
            tArea.textFlow.flowComposer.updateAllControllers();
        }

    ]]>
</fx:Script>

<s:ComboBox change="rotateText(event)" x="400"
            dataProvider="{new ArrayList(['0', '90', '180', '270'])}"/>

<s:RichText id="tArea" width="300" id="tArea" fontSize="20" paddingTop="10">
    <s:textFlow>
        <s:TextFlow>
            <s:p>
                邓小平出身于中国四川省广安县协兴乡牌坊村的一个客家家庭
            </s:p>
            <s:p>
                Vertical alignment or justification (adopts default value if
                undefined during cascade). Determines how TextFlow elements
                align within the container.
            </s:p>
        </s:TextFlow>
    </s:textFlow>
</s:RichText>
</s:Group>
```

To change the direction of the lines of text themselves, you can use the `blockProgression` property of the `TextFlow`. There are two possible values: `BlockProgression.RL`, which lays out each line right to left, as in Chinese, or `BlockProgression.TB`, which lays them out top to bottom, as in English. Figure 7-2 shows the different `BlockProgression` values in use by the following code:

```
protected function rotateBlock(e:IndexChangeEvent):void {

    var target:String = e.target.selectedItem;
    switch(target) {
        case "Vertical":
            tArea.textFlow.blockProgression = BlockProgression.RL;
            tArea.textFlow.verticalAlign = VerticalAlign.BOTTOM;
        break;
        case "Horizontal":
            tArea.textFlow.blockProgression = BlockProgression.TB;
            tArea.textFlow.verticalAlign = VerticalAlign.TOP;
        break;
    }
    tArea.textFlow.invalidateAllFormats();
    tArea.textFlow.flowComposer.updateAllControllers();
}
```

In addition to setting the `textRotation` on a `TextFlow`, you can set it on any `FlowElement`, like a `ParagraphElement` or `SpanElement`. You can also set the `textRotation` on a `RichText` or `TextArea` component. However, you can only set the `blockProgression` on a `TextFlow`; setting it on a `ParagraphElement` or `SpanElement` will not have any effect.

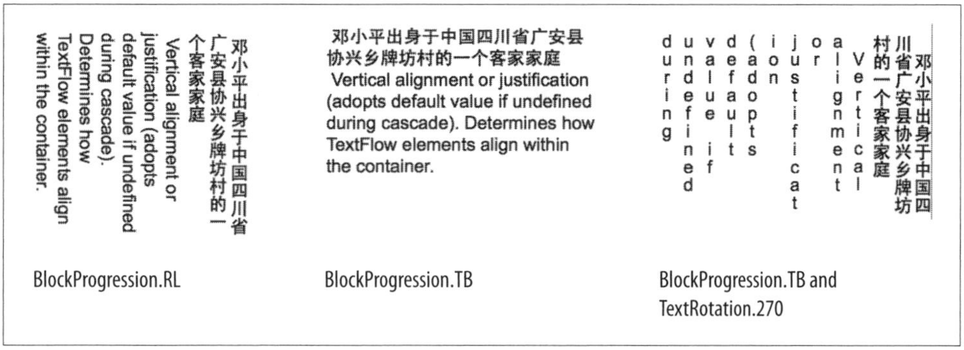

Figure 7-2. Setting the textRotation and blockProgression properties of a TextFlow

7.11 Set the Selection in a TextArea

Problem

You want to create a `TextArea` in which a user can search, and you want to highlight text the user enters in a `TextInput`.

Solution

Use the `spark.components.TextArea` object and set the `alwaysShowSelection` property to `true`. Then use the `setSelection()` method to set the index and length of the selected text.

Discussion

Setting the `selectionHighlighting` property to `always` ensures that the `TextArea` will show a selection whether or not it has focus. Now when the `setSelection()` method is called, the `TextField` within the `TextArea` component will display and the `TextArea` will automatically scroll correctly to show the selection:

```
<mx:Canvas xmlns:mx="http://www.adobe.com/2006/mxml" width="1000" height="800"
           xmlns:cookbook="oreilly.cookbook.*">
<s:Application xmlns:fx="http://ns.adobe.com/mxml/2009"
               xmlns:s="library://ns.adobe.com/flex/spark"
               xmlns:mx="library://ns.adobe.com/flex/halo"
               minWidth="1024" minHeight="768">
    <s:layout>
        <s:HorizontalLayout/>
    </s:layout>
    <fx:Script>
        <![CDATA[

            private var text_string:String = "Aenean quis nunc id purus pharetra" +
            "pharetra. Cras a felis sit amet ipsum ornare luctus. Nullam" +
            "scelerisque placerat velit. Pellentesque ut arcu congue risus" +
            "facilisis pellentesque. Duis in enim. Mauris eget est. Quisque" +
            "tortor.";

            private function searchText():void {
                var index:int = masterText.text.indexOf(input.text);
                masterText.scrollToRange(0);
                if(index != -1) {
                    masterText.selectRange(index, index+input.text.length);
                    masterText.scrollToRange(index);
                }
            }

        ]]>
    </fx:Script>
    <s:TextInput id="input" change="searchText()"/>
    <s:TextArea editable="false" id="masterText" text="{text_string}"
                selectionHighlighting="always"
                fontSize="20" width="600" height="200" x="200"/>

</s:Application>
```

7.12 Control the Appearance of the Selected Text

Problem

You want to change the appearance of the selected text in a s:TextArea control.

Solution

Set the unfocusedTextSelectionColor, inactiveTextSelectionColor, and focusedText
SelectionColor properties.

Discussion

The following TextArea has its text selection color properties set in MXML. The unfocused
TextSelectionColor property sets the color of text when the TextArea does not have
focus, the focusedTextSelectionColor when it does have focus, and the inactiveText
SelectionColor when the TextArea has its enabled property set to false:

```
<s:TextArea id="tArea" fontSize="20" paddingTop="10"
        unfocusedTextSelectionColor="0xFF7777"
        focusedTextSelectionColor="0x7777FF"
        inactiveTextSelectionColor="0x777777"
        selectionHighlighting="always" textFlow="{generateTextFlow()}"/>
```

Because these are styles, you can also set them in CSS:

```
<fx:Style>
    @namespace s "library://ns.adobe.com/flex/spark";
    @namespace mx "library://ns.adobe.com/flex/halo";

    s|TextArea {
        unfocusedTextSelectionColor:"0xFF7777";
        focusedTextSelectionColor:"0x7777FF";
        disabledTextSelectionColor:"0x777777";
    }

</fx:Style>
```

If you want the highlighting within the TextArea to show even when the TextArea does
not have focus, you'll need to also set the selectionHighlighting property to always.

Only the s:TextArea and s:RichEditableText components support these styles. The
Spark Label component can be made selectable, but it doesn't support selection colors,
and the RichText component does not support selection at all. Generally, you should
use the lightest-weight component that fits your needs.

7.13 Copy a Character as a Bitmap

Problem

You want to copy the pixels of a character within a TextFlow to use as BitmapData somewhere else in your application (e.g., the character that a user has selected).

Solution

Listen for a SelectionEvent to be dispatched by the TextFlow and find the TextLine from which you want to copy the data. Then create a BitmapData object and draw the Text Line into it using a matrix to transform the position of the drawing operation.

Discussion

This recipe uses the BitmapData draw() operation and one of the components in the underlying Flash Text Engine: TextLine. The TextLine is the base element of the Text Flow's IFlowComposer instance. When the IFlowComposer that the TextFlow is using updates, it creates TextLine instances and adds them to the container that holds the TextFlow. The TextLine is the DisplayObjectContainer that the graphics and characters are actually added to, so to read the pixel data of a character, you simply copy the pixel data of the TextLine, using a matrix to correctly position the area of the TextLine that you want to copy.

The TextLine also defines a getAtomGraphic() method that you can use to retrieve the DisplayObject of a bitmap, SWF file, or other graphical object that has been created within the TextLine. For the purposes of this recipe, though, that method won't work because getAtomGraphic() returns null if the atom is a character.

The key to knowing when the selection has changed is the SelectionEvent dispatched by the TextFlow when the user changes the cursor position in the TextFlow or selects new text in the TextFlow. Create a listener for this event, as shown here:

```
<s:TextArea id="textAreaInst" fontSize="16">
    <s:TextFlow>
        <s:TextFlow selectionChange="selectionChanged(event)">
```

Once the event is captured, you can access the flowComposer property of the TextFlow that dispatched it and begin locating the character the user has selected:

```
<?xml version="1.0" encoding="utf-8"?>
<s:Application xmlns:fx="http://ns.adobe.com/mxml/2009"
               xmlns:s="library://ns.adobe.com/flex/spark"
               xmlns:mx="library://ns.adobe.com/flex/halo"
               minWidth="1024" minHeight="768">

    <s:layout><s:HorizontalLayout paddingLeft="10"/></s:layout>
```

```
<fx:Declarations>
    <!-- Place nonvisual elements (e.g., services, value objects) here -->
</fx:Declarations>

<fx:Script>
    <![CDATA[
        import flash.text.engine.TextLine;

        import flashx.textLayout.compose.IFlowComposer;
        import flashx.textLayout.compose.TextFlowLine;
        import flashx.textLayout.edit.SelectionState;
        import flashx.textLayout.events.SelectionEvent;

        [Bindable]
        private var bitmapData:BitmapData;

        private function selectionChanged(event:SelectionEvent):void {
```

The SelectionEvent contains a SelectionState object that defines two properties of interest. The first, int anchorPosition, gives the position of the line within the Text Flow where the selection has occurred. The second, int absoluteStart, gives the absolute position of the start of the selection in the TextFlow. This means that if your TextFlow is 400 characters long and the user selects the 380th character, the absoluteStart will be 379. Let's continue our example:

```
if(event.selectionState) {
    var state:SelectionState = event.selectionState;
    var composer:IFlowComposer =
            textAreaInst.textFlow.flowComposer;
```

Here, anchorPosition is used to find the correct TextFlowLine:

```
var tfline:TextFlowLine =
        composer.findLineAtPosition(state.anchorPosition);
var tline:TextLine = tfline.getTextLine();

if(tline) {
```

To determine the relative position of the atom *from the beginning of the line*, use the TextLine.absoluteStart property to find out how far into the line the atom is located. The getAtomBounds() method returns a Rectangle that contains the *x* and *y* positions, height, and width of the atom you want:

```
var rect:Rectangle =
        tline.getAtomBounds(state.absoluteStart -
                            tfline.absoluteStart);
```

Now, re-create the BitmapData using the same font size used in the TextLine so that the pixel data will be scaled appropriately. You can access the font size with the Text Line.textBlock.baselineFontSize property. If your TextLines are going to contain many different sizes of text this approach may not work quite right, but for this example, assuming some simplicity, it works fine:

```
                            bitmapData = new
                                BitmapData(tline.textBlock.baselineFontSize + 3,
                                tline.textBlock.baselineFontSize + 3, false,
                                0xf6f6f6);
```

Now, position the drawing operation using the *x* and *y* positions of the Rectangle object that the getAtomBounds() method returned:

```
                    var scaleMatrix:Matrix = new Matrix(0.9, 0, 0, 0.9,
                                        0.9 * rect.x * -1,
                                        rect.y * -1);
```

Finally, draw the TextLine to the BitmapData, using the Matrix to alter the drawing operation and set the source of the BitmapImage to be the pixel data that was captured in the BitmapData.draw() operation:

```
                    bitmapData.draw(tline, scaleMatrix);
                    img.source = bitmapData;


                }
            }
        }


    ]]>
</fx:Script>

<s:BitmapImage id="img" width="200" height="200" source="{bitmapData}"/>

<s:TextArea id="textAreaInst" fontSize="16">
    <s:textFlow>
        <s:TextFlow selectionChange="selectionChanged(event)">
            <s:p>
                <s:span>
                    The TextFlow class is responsible for managing all the text
                    content of a story.
                </s:span>
                <s:span>
                    In TextLayout, text is stored in a hierarchical tree of
                    elements.
                </s:span>
            </s:p>
        </s:TextFlow>
    </s:textFlow>
</s:TextArea>

</s:Application>
```

There are many other complex operations that you can perform by accessing the IFlow Composer of a TextFlow: for instance, controlling precisely which containers will be updated for a TextFlow, finding the locations of changes to a TextFlow, determining the number of lines in a TextFlow, or setting the focus in a TextFlow to a particular container.

7.14 Create Linked Containers in a TextFlow

Problem

You want to display text in multiple columns, each with their own independent height, width, and position.

Solution

Create a `TextFlow` and add a `ContainerController` to it using the `TextFlow.addControl`
`ler()` method for each object that the text will be spread across.

Discussion

Linked containers are multiple containers that contain a single `TextFlow`. They share selection attributes and as the `TextFlow` changes the text will flow across all the containers; however, scrolling is not reflected across all containers. To add a container to a `TextFlow`, first create a new instance of the `ContainerController` class. The `Container` `Controller` sets how a `TextFlow` and the container inside it interact with one another, measuring the container and laying out the lines in the `TextFlow` accordingly. You create the `ContainerController` as shown here:

```
ContainerController(container:Sprite, compositionWidth:Number = 100,
                    compositionHeight:Number = 100)
```

Next, access the `IFlowComposer` instance within the `TextFlow` and use the `addController()` method. For example, `addController(controller:ContainerController):void` adds a controller to this `IFlowComposer` instance.

Any `TextFlow` can have multiple containers defining its size and layout. In the following example, a single `TextFlow` is spread across two containers:

```
<s:Application xmlns:fx="http://ns.adobe.com/mxml/2009"
               xmlns:s="library://ns.adobe.com/flex/spark"
               xmlns:mx="library://ns.adobe.com/flex/halo"
               minWidth="1024" minHeight="768"
               creationComplete="init()">

    <fx:Script>
        <![CDATA[
            import flash.text.engine.FontLookup;

            import flashx.textLayout.container.ContainerController;
            import flashx.textLayout.conversion.TextConverter;
            import flashx.textLayout.edit.EditManager;
            import flashx.textLayout.elements.TextFlow;
            import flashx.undo.UndoManager;

            import mx.collections.ArrayList;
            import mx.core.UIComponent;
```

```
import spark.utils.TextFlowUtil;
private var textFlow:TextFlow;

private var textXML:XML = <TextFlow
        xmlns="http://ns.adobe.com/textLayout/2008"
        fontSize="30" color="0x000000">
        <p>You do not typically add skins or chrome to the Spark text
        controls.</p>

        </TextFlow>;

private function init():void {

        XML.ignoreWhitespace = false;
        textFlow = TextConverter.importToFlow(textXML,
                TextConverter.TEXT_LAYOUT_FORMAT);
```

Here, the `ContainerController` is created and added to the `TextFlow`. After calling `updateAllControllers()`, the text of the `TextFlow` will flow across the containers:

```
        textFlow.flowComposer.addController(new
                ContainerController(this.topText, 500, 400));
        textFlow.flowComposer.addController(new
                ContainerController(this.bottomText, 500, 400));

        textFlow.interactionManager = new EditManager(new UndoManager());
        textFlow.flowComposer.updateAllControllers();
        invalidateDisplayList();
}

private function setFontSize():void {
        textFlow.setStyle('fontSize', comboBox.selectedItem);
        textFlow.flowComposer.updateAllControllers();
}

    ]]>
</fx:Script>

<s:RichEditableText y="20" id="tSprite"/>
<s:RichEditableText x="500" y="400" id="bSprite"/>
<s:ComboBox id="comboBox" dataProvider="{new ArrayList([10, 12, 16, 20, 24])}"
        change="setFontSize()"/>

</s:Application>
```

7.15 Use a Custom Format Resolver

Problem

You want to create custom style elements or format properties.

Solution

Create a custom format resolver class that implements the `IFormatResolver` interface.

Discussion

The primary job of a format resolver is to create an `ITextLayoutFormat` object for each node in the `TextFlow`, examine each node and any additional properties, and return the correct format for that object. Reading CSS styles and converting them into the correct types is a common usage for format resolvers. The `IFormatResolver` declares five methods:

`getResolverForNewFlow(oldFlow:TextFlow,newFlow:TextFlow):IFormatResolver`
Returns a new copy of the format resolver when a `TextFlow` is copied.

`invalidate(target:Object):void`
Invalidates cached formatting information for this element because, for example, the parent has changed, or the `id` or the `styleName` has changed.

`invalidateAll(textFlow:TextFlow):void`
Invalidates all the cached formatting information for a `TextFlow` so that its formatting must be recomputed.

`resolveFormat(target:Object):ITextLayoutFormat`
Given a `FlowElement` or `ContainerController` object, returns any format settings for it.

`resolveUserFormat(target:Object, userFormat:String):*`
Given a `FlowElement` or `ContainerController` object and the name of a format property, returns the user format value or undefined if the value is not found. For example, this is called when the `getStyles()` method is called on an object.

Suppose you need to be able to read in data that will load a SWF file and pass it a type of media that the SWF file will load, and the name of a file to load and play, as shown here. First, create an `InlineGraphicsElement` with the `<img>` tag:

```
<img type="mp3" source="player.swf" file="song.mp3" height="30" width="400"/>
```

The simple `IFormatResolver` looks like this. The only method that the `CustomFormat Resolver` needs to define is `resolveFormat()`:

```
package oreilly.cookbook.flex4 {
    import flash.display.Loader;
    import flash.display.MovieClip;
    import flash.utils.Dictionary;

    import flashx.textLayout.elements.FlowElement;
    import flashx.textLayout.elements.FlowGroupElement;
    import flashx.textLayout.elements.IFormatResolver;
    import flashx.textLayout.elements.InlineGraphicElement;
    import flashx.textLayout.elements.TextFlow;
    import flashx.textLayout.events.StatusChangeEvent;
    import flashx.textLayout.events.TextLayoutEvent;
```

```
import flashx.textLayout.formats.ITextLayoutFormat;
import flashx.textLayout.formats.TextLayoutFormat;
import flashx.textLayout.tlf_internal;

import mx.styles.CSSStyleDeclaration;
import mx.styles.StyleManager;

use namespace tlf_internal;

public class CustomFormatResolver implements IFormatResolver {

    private var fmtDictionary:Dictionary = new Dictionary(true);

    public function CustomFormatResolver() {
        // cache results
    }

    public function invalidateAll(textFlow:TextFlow):void {
        fmtDictionary = new Dictionary(true);
    }

    public function invalidate(target:Object):void {
        // nothing in this instance
        delete fmtDictionary[target];
        var blockElem:FlowGroupElement = target as FlowGroupElement;
        if (blockElem) {
            for (var idx:int = 0; idx < blockElem.numChildren; idx++)
                invalidate(blockElem.getChildAt(idx));
        }
    }
}
```

The resolveFormat() method reads the type property of the <img> tag. An event listener
is then attached to the parent text flow so that when the InlineGraphicElement loads
the SWF, the file property will be used to set the *.mp3* file that the SWF should load:

```
public function resolveFormat(target:Object):ITextLayoutFormat {
    var format:TextLayoutFormat = new TextLayoutFormat();

    if(target is InlineGraphicElement) {
        var ige:InlineGraphicElement = target as InlineGraphicElement;
        var type:String = ige.getStyle("type");
        if(type == "mp3" || type == "video") {
            var fileStr:String = ige.getStyle("file");
            if(!ige.getTextFlow().hasEventListener(
                    StatusChangeEvent.INLINE_GRAPHIC_STATUS_CHANGE)) {
                ige.getTextFlow().addEventListener(
                        StatusChangeEvent.INLINE_GRAPHIC_STATUS_CHANGE,
                        statusChangeHandler);
            }
            if(fmtDictionary[type]) {
                return fmtDictionary[type];
            }
            else {
                format.paddingLeft = 5;
                format.paddingRight = 5;
```

```
                    fmtDictionary[target] = format;
                }
            }
        }
        return format;
    }

    public function resolveUserFormat(target:Object, userFormat:String):* {
        return null;
    }

    public function getResolverForNewFlow(oldFlow:TextFlow,
            newFlow:TextFlow):IFormatResolver {
        return this;
    }
```

The statusChangeHandler() method handles the events from any InlineGraphic
Element that has its type property set to video or mp3:

```
    private static function statusChangeHandler(event:StatusChangeEvent):void {

        var elem:InlineGraphicElement = event.element as InlineGraphicElement;
        var type:String = elem.getStyle("type");
        if(type == "mp3" || type == "video") {
            var fileStr:String = elem.getStyle("file");
            var loader:Loader = (elem.graphic as Loader);
            if(loader.content) {
                (loader.content as MovieClip).song = fileStr;
            }
        }

    }
}

import flashx.textLayout.elements.TextFlow;
import flashx.textLayout.conversion.TextConverter;

protected var tfString:String = '<TextFlow
        xmlns="http://ns.adobe.com/textLayout/2008">' +
        '<p>' +
        '<span>Hi there</span>' +
        '<img type="mp3" source="player.swf" file="song.mp3" height="30"
            width="400"/>' +
        '</p>' +
        '</TextFlow>';

protected function createTextFlow():void {
    var tf:TextFlow = TextConverter.importToFlow(tfString,
                    TextConverter.TEXT_LAYOUT_FORMAT);
    tf.formatResolver = new CustomFormatResolver();
    area.textFlow = tf;
}
```

7.16 Skin the TextArea Control

Problem

You want to skin the `TextArea` control to show custom graphics in the background.

Solution

The `TextArea` extends the `SkinnableContainer` class, so it can have a `spark.skins.Spark Skin` assigned to its `skinClass` property.

Discussion

The `TextArea` has two required `SkinPart` objects: a `Scroller` with the `id` set to `scroller` and a `RichEditableText` with the `id` set to `textDisplay`. The following `Spark Skin` class creates a very simple skin that will draw a gradient behind the displayed text:

```
<s:SparkSkin xmlns:fx="http://ns.adobe.com/mxml/2009"
             xmlns:s="library://ns.adobe.com/flex/spark"
             xmlns:mx="library://ns.adobe.com/flex/halo"
             xmlns:flex4="oreilly.cookbook.flex4.*">

    <fx:Metadata>
        [HostComponent("spark.components.TextArea")]
    </fx:Metadata>

    <fx:Script>
        <![CDATA[
            import spark.components.TextArea;
        ]]>
    </fx:Script>

    <s:states>
        <s:State name="normal"/>
        <s:State name="disabled"/>
    </s:states>


    <s:Rect width="{width}" height="{height}">
        <s:fill>
            <s:LinearGradient>
                <s:GradientEntry color="0xFFFFFF" ratio="0.0"/>
                <s:GradientEntry color="0xFF0000" ratio="0.5"/>
                <s:GradientEntry color="0x0000FF" ratio="1.0"/>
            </s:LinearGradient>
        </s:fill>
    </s:Rect>
```

The `Scroller` creates a scroll bar on the side of the `TextArea` and allows the user to scroll through the text:

```
<s:Scroller width="{hostComponent.width}"
            height="{hostComponent.height}"
```

```
                    id="scroller" verticalScrollPolicy="auto">
            <s:RichEditableText id="textDisplay" />
        </s:Scroller>

    </s:SparkSkin>
```

You can provide an additional class for the Scroller if you need to by setting its skin Class property to a SparkSkin class that has all the requisite SkinPart instances.

7.17 Create Multiple Text Columns

Problem

You want to use multiple columns within a TextFlow displayed by a TextArea control.

Solution

Create a TextLayoutFormat object and set its columnCount property. Then set the host Format of the TextFlow.

Discussion

A TextFlow will calculate the width of each column and how to flow the text across the columns based on the number of columns passed to the columnCount property. The following code snippet sets the columnCount of a TextFlow using a ComboBox populated with the numbers 1 through 4:

```
    <fx:Script>
        <![CDATA[
            import flashx.textLayout.formats.TextLayoutFormat;
            import mx.collections.ArrayList;
            import spark.events.IndexChangeEvent;

            protected function changeHandler(event:IndexChangeEvent):void {
                var hostFormat:TextLayoutFormat = new TextLayoutFormat();
                hostFormat.columnCount = event.target.selectedItem;
                hostFormat.fontSize = 20;
                tArea.textFlow.hostFormat = hostFormat;
```

Remember to call the invalidateAllFormats() method and then the flowComposer. updateAllControllers() method after setting the new TextLayoutFormat so that the formatting changes will be reflected:

```
                tArea.textFlow.invalidateAllFormats();
                tArea.textFlow.flowComposer.updateAllControllers();
            }

        ]]>
    </fx:Script>
    <s:ComboBox dataProvider="{new ArrayList([1, 2, 3, 4])}"
            change="changeHandler(event)"/>
```

7.18 Highlight the Last Character in a TextFlow

Problem

You want to find the last displayed character in a `TextArea` component.

Solution

Locate the last `TextLine` instance in the `TextFlow` and use the `atomCount` property to retrieve the bounds of the last atom in the `TextFlow`.

Discussion

Each `TextFlow` is, at the core, comprised of multiple `TextLine` instances into which the actual characters are drawn. Each `TextLine` provides information about the position and size of the individual characters or graphics contained within it via an instance of the `flash.geom.Rectangle` class returned from the `getAtomBounds()` method. This `Rectangle` can be used to position another graphic as a highlight. Here is the code for the full example:

```
<s:Application xmlns:fx="http://ns.adobe.com/mxml/2009"
               xmlns:s="library://ns.adobe.com/flex/spark"
               xmlns:mx="library://ns.adobe.com/flex/halo"
               minWidth="1024" minHeight="768">
    <s:layout>
        <s:BasicLayout/>
    </s:layout>
    <fx:Declarations>
        <fx:String id="string">
            "Lorem ipsum dolor sit amet, consectetuer adipiscing elit, sed diam
             nonummy"
        </fx:String>
    </fx:Declarations>

    <fx:Script>
        <![CDATA[
            import flash.text.engine.TextLine;

            import flashx.textLayout.compose.StandardFlowComposer;
            import flashx.textLayout.compose.TextFlowLine;
            import flashx.textLayout.container.TextContainerManager;
            import flashx.textLayout.elements.TextFlow;

            protected function highlightLastAtom(event:Event):void {

                var flow:TextFlow = tArea.textFlow;
                var composer:StandardFlowComposer = (flow.flowComposer as
                                                     StandardFlowComposer);
```

The IFlowComposer instance contains the number of lines in the TextFlow. Here, that is used to access the last line and retrieve the TextLine:

```
var tfline:TextFlowLine = composer.getLineAt(composer.numLines-1);
var line:TextLine = tfline.getTextLine();
```

Next, you get the bounds of the last atom in the TextLine:

```
var rect:Rectangle = line.getAtomBounds(line.atomCount-1);
```

and finally position the graphics:

```
                graphicsRect.x = rect.x;
                graphicsRect.y = tfline.y;
                graphicsRect.width = rect.width+2;
                graphicsRect.height = tfline.height;

            }
        ]]>
    </fx:Script>

    <s:TextArea height="600" width="400" id="tArea" content="{string}"
            editable="true" updateComplete="highlightLastAtom(event)"/>

    <s:Rect id="graphicsRect">
        <s:fill>
            <s:SolidColor color="#ff0000" alpha="0.4"/>
        </s:fill>
    </s:Rect>

</s:Application>
```

CHAPTER 8

Lists and ItemRenderers

In this chapter, as in some of the other chapters in this book, many of the recipes will need to address both Spark components and MX components. The three MX components covered (`List`, `Tile`, and `Tree`) all extend the `mx.controls.listclasses.List Base` class.

On the Spark side, you'll see how to create renderers for the `List` component, apply styles, and create layouts for `List` and other data-driven controls. The Spark `List` component, along with the Spark `ButtonBar` component, extends the `spark.compo nents.SkinnableDataContainer` class. The `SkinnableDataContainer` enables you to create controls whose children are generated by a data provider, and allows for sorting, filtering, reordering, and the setting of visual components to act as item renderers and item editors. Like the Halo `List` that you may be familiar with, the Spark `List` component recycles all the item renderers it creates. This means that if you create 1000 items but only 20 are visible at a given time, only 20 item renderers will be created, and each one's data will be refreshed as the list is scrolled so that the correct values are displayed. All of these controls also allow for dragging and dropping in slightly different ways, as you'll learn.

The topics covered in this chapter do not begin to exhaust the possibilities for working with these `ListBase` controls or with the Spark `List` and layouts. For recipes on working with skinning, see Chapter 6. For recipes on working with Spark `Group`s, see Chapter 2.

8.1 Create an Item Renderer for a Spark List

Problem

You need to create a custom item renderer for a Spark `List` component.

Solution

Extend the `spark.components.supportClasses.ItemRenderer` class and assign that component to the `itemRenderer` property of the `List` using the fully qualified class name or the `<fx:Component>` tag.

Discussion

The `itemRenderer` property of the `List` allows you to create a custom component that will be rendered for each item in the data provider that is passed to the `List`. The first way to create the item renderer is to use the `<fx:Component>` tag, as shown here:

```
<fx:Script>
    <![CDATA[

        [Bindable]
        public var provider:ArrayCollection;

        public function init():void {
            provider = new ArrayCollection(["one", "two", "three", "four", "five",
                                            "six"]);
        }

    ]]>
</fx:Script>

<s:List id="list" dataProvider="{provider}" selectedIndex="0">
    <s:itemRenderer>
        <fx:Component>
            <s:ItemRenderer>
                <s:states>
                    <s:State name="normal" />
                    <s:State name="hovered" />
                    <s:State name="selected" />
                </s:states>

                <s:Rect left="0" right="0" top="0" bottom="0">
                    <s:fill>
                        <s:SolidColor color="0x000088" alpha="0.6"/>
                    </s:fill>
                </s:Rect>
```

```
        <s:Rect left="0" right="0" top="0" bottom="0">
            <s:fill>
                <s:SolidColor color="0x008800" alpha="0.6"/>
            </s:fill>
        </s:Rect>

        <s:Label text="{data}"/>
    </s:ItemRenderer>
  </fx:Component>
 </s:itemRenderer>
</s:List>
```

The second method is to define a class in a separate file and reference it using the fully
qualified class name:

```
<s:List id="list" dataProvider="{provider}"
        itemRenderer="oreilly.cookbook.flex4.SampleRenderer"/>
```

Here, the `SampleRenderer` needs to extend the `ItemRenderer` class and define three states:

normal

> Displayed when the item is not hovered over or selected

hovered

> Displayed when the user hovers over the item renderer

selected

> Displayed when the user selects the item renderer by clicking on it or using the
> keyboard

8.2 Create an Editable List

Problem

You need to create a Spark `List` in which all the items are editable.

Solution

Create an item renderer with a selected state and include a `TextInput` or other control
in that state.

Discussion

The Spark `List`, unlike the Halo `List`, does not have an `itemEditor` property. You can,
however, easily extend the `spark.components.supportClasses.ItemRenderer` class to use
the `selected` state to add a `TextInput` or other control to set the data passed to the item.
Here's how:

```
<?xml version="1.0" encoding="utf-8"?>
<s:ItemRenderer xmlns:fx="http://ns.adobe.com/mxml/2009"
                xmlns:s="library://ns.adobe.com/flex/spark"
                xmlns:mx="library://ns.adobe.com/flex/halo">
```

```
<fx:Metadata>
    [HostComponent("spark.components.List")]
</fx:Metadata>
<fx:Script>
    <![CDATA[
        import mx.events.FlexEvent;
        import spark.components.List;
```

When the enter event is dispatched from the TextInput control, set the data to the text inside that control and then set the currentState property to normal to hide the TextInput control and show the Label control:

```
        protected function dataChangeHandler():void {
            this.data = textInput.text;
            currentState = "normal";
        }

    ]]>
</fx:Script>

<s:states>
    <s:State name="normal" />
    <s:State name="hovered" />
```

Make sure that you set the focus to the TextInput when the item renderer is selected so that the user can enter text right away:

```
    <s:State name="selected" enterState="textInput.setFocus()"/>
</s:states>

<s:Rect height="{height}" width="{hostComponent.width}">
    <s:fill>
        <s:SolidColor color="0xeeffff"
                        alpha="0" alpha.hovered="0.1" alpha.selected="0.4" />
    </s:fill>
</s:Rect>

<s:Label text="{data}" includeIn="hovered, normal"/>

<s:TextInput includeIn="selected" id="textInput" text="{data}"
            enter="dataChangeHandler()" width="100"/>

</s:ItemRenderer>
```

To ensure that the user's keystrokes do not trigger list navigation, the following List has the findKey() method disabled (an alternative would be to examine each of the ItemRenderer instances to determine if any of them is in the selected state and then disable the findKey() method):

```
<s:List xmlns:fx="http://ns.adobe.com/mxml/2009"
        xmlns:s="library://ns.adobe.com/flex/spark"
        xmlns:mx="library://ns.adobe.com/flex/halo">
```

```
<fx:Script>
    <![CDATA[

        override protected function findKey(eventCode:int) : Boolean {
            return false;
        }

    ]]>
</fx:Script>

</s:List>
```

To implement the `List` and the item renderer, simply create an instance of the `KeyNav DisabledList` and set its `itemRenderer` property to `oreilly.cookbook.flex4.ItemEditor`:

```
<flex4:KeyNavDisabledList itemRenderer="oreilly.cookbook.flex4.ItemEditor"
                          dataProvider="{provider}"/>
```

8.3 Scroll to an Item in a Spark List

Problem

You want to scroll to a certain index within your data provider in a Spark `List`.

Solution

Use the `ensureIndexIsVisible()` method of the Spark `List`.

Discussion

Any Spark `List` can scroll to any `ItemRenderer` by its index using the `ensureIndexIsVisible()` method, which has the following signature:

```
ensureIndexIsVisible(index:int):void
```

This method uses the `getScrollPositionDeltaToElement()` method of the `LayoutBase` contained by the `DataGroup`, which means that whether your `List` (or any `DataCon tainer`, for that matter) is using a horizontal, vertical, or tiled layout, the scroll will make the index visible, regardless of whether the scrolling required is vertical, horizontal, or a combination of the two.

8.4 Change the Layout of a Spark List

Problem

You want to create a Spark `List` that lays itself out horizontally or in a grid.

Solution

Create a `Skin` class that has a `DataGroup` with a `TileLayout`, and assign it to the `List`.

Discussion

Any `List` can have a `Skin` class created for it that changes the `layout` property. Simply create a `DataGroup` with an `id` of `dataGroup` and change its layout type. This sets the `DataGroup` `skinPart` of the `List`, replacing the default vertical layout:

```
<s:Skin xmlns:fx="http://ns.adobe.com/mxml/2009"
        xmlns:s="library://ns.adobe.com/flex/spark"
        xmlns:mx="library://ns.adobe.com/flex/halo">
    <fx:Metadata>
        [HostComponent("spark.components.List")]
    </fx:Metadata>

    <fx:Script>
        <![CDATA[
            import spark.components.List;
        ]]>
    </fx:Script>

    <s:states>
        <s:State name="normal"/>
        <s:State name="disabled"/>
        <s:State name="selected"/>
    </s:states>

    <s:DataGroup id="dataGroup" height="{hostComponent.height}"
                 width="{hostComponent.width}">
        <s:layout><s:TileLayout clipAndEnableScrolling="true"/></s:layout>
    </s:DataGroup>
</s:Skin>
```

For more information on skinning, see Chapter 6.

8.5 Create a Nested List

Problem

You want to be able to nest multiple `List` objects within a single parent list.

Solution

Create an `ItemRenderer` that contains a `List` and listen for a `SelectionEvent` on the nested `List` instance.

Discussion

The component that holds the List listens for a selectionEvent dispatched from the item renderers within the List. In that event handler, the parent component looks through each ItemRenderer and sets its state to normal.

When the List adds or removes an ItemRenderer, it dispatches a RendererExistence Event that contains the data held by the ItemRenderer, the index of the renderer, and a reference to the renderer itself. In this example, that event is used to keep track of the item renderers that the List contains:

```
<fx:Script>
    <![CDATA[
        import spark.events.RendererExistenceEvent;
        import mx.collections.ArrayCollection;

        private var rendererArray:Array = [];

        [Bindable]
        private var arr:ArrayCollection;

        private function init():void {
            arr = new ArrayCollection([
                    new ArrayCollection(["one", "two", "three", "four", "five"]),
                    new ArrayCollection(["uno", "dos", "tres", "quatro",
"cinco"]),
                    new ArrayCollection(["un", "deux", "trois", "quatre",
"cinq"]),
                    new ArrayCollection(["一", "二", "三","四","五"])]);
        }
```

When an ItemRenderer is added to the List, you should also add the event listener for the selectionEvent that each ItemRenderer instance will dispatch:

```
private function handleRendererAdd(event:RendererExistenceEvent):void {
    rendererArray.push(event.renderer);
    event.renderer.addEventListener("selectionEvent", selected);
}
```

When an ItemRenderer is removed from the List, remove the event listener for the selectionEvent:

```
private function handleRendererRemove(event:RendererExistenceEvent):
        void {
    rendererArray.splice(rendererArray.indexOf(event.renderer), 1);
    event.renderer.removeEventListener("selectionEvent", selected);
}
```

On the event, loop through each ItemRenderer and, if it isn't the one that dispatched the event, set its currentState to normal:

```
        private function selected(event:Event):void {
            for(var i:int = 0; i < rendererArray.length; i++) {
                if(event.target != rendererArray[i]) {
                    rendererArray[i].currentState = "normal";
                }
            }
        }

    ]]>
</fx:Script>

<s:List itemRenderer="oreilly.cookbook.flex4.NestedRenderer" id="list"
        dataProvider="{arr}" rendererAdd="handleRendererAdd(event)"
        rendererRemove="handleRendererRemove(event)"/>
```

The NestedRenderer class that extends ItemRenderer listens for the mouseDown event and dispatches an Event with the name property set to selectionEvent:

```
<s:ItemRenderer xmlns:fx="http://ns.adobe.com/mxml/2009"
                xmlns:s="library://ns.adobe.com/flex/spark"
                xmlns:mx="library://ns.adobe.com/flex/halo"
                height="15" mouseDown="mouseDownHandler(event)">

    <fx:Metadata>
        [Event( name="selectionEvent", type="flash.events.Event" )]
    </fx:Metadata>

    <fx:Script>
        <![CDATA[

            public function mouseDownHandler(event:MouseEvent):void {
                if(currentState != "selected") {
                    currentState = "selected";
                    dispatchEvent(new Event("selectionEvent"));
                }
            }
```

The currentState() method sets the height of the itemRenderer to be the height of the List within the item renderer:

```
            override public function set currentState(value:String) : void {
                switch(value) {
                    case "selected":
                        this.height = innerList.height;
                    break;
                    case "hovered":
                        this.height = 20;
                    break;
                    case "normal":
                        this.height = 20;
                        innerList.selectedItem = null;
                    break;
                }
                super.currentState = value;
            }
```

```
        ]]>
    </fx:Script>

    <s:states>
        <s:State name="normal" />
        <s:State name="hovered" />
        <s:State name="selected" />
    </s:states>

    <s:layout>
        <s:BasicLayout/>
    </s:layout>

    <!-- hover/select highlight -->
    <s:Rect left="0" right="0" top="0" bottom="0">
        <s:fill>
            <s:SolidColor color="0x000000"
                          alpha="0" alpha.hovered="0.1" alpha.selected="0.4" />
        </s:fill>
    </s:Rect>
```

This inner `List` shows the `ArrayList` or collection passed to the `ItemRenderer`:

```
        <s:List id="innerList" dataProvider="{data}"/>
    </s:ItemRenderer>
```

8.6 Set XML Data for a Spark List

Problem

You want to display complex XML data in a Spark `List`.

Solution

Create a `XMLListCollection` from the XML data and use that to set the data for the `List` instance.

Discussion

The `dataProvider` of the `List` can be set to anything that extends the `IList` interface. For example, `ArrayList`, `AsyncListView`, `ListCollectionView`, and `XMLListCollection` all implement the `IList` interface. To display XML data, create a `XMLListCollection` from each node in the XML that contains multiple items. To determine whether a node has complex content, you'll use the `hasComplexContent()` method on the `XML` object:

```
<s:Application xmlns:fx="http://ns.adobe.com/mxml/2009"
               xmlns:s="library://ns.adobe.com/flex/spark"
               xmlns:mx="library://ns.adobe.com/flex/halo"
               minWidth="1024" minHeight="768" creationComplete="init()">
    <fx:Declarations>
```

Here's the XML data that the `List` will display:

```
<fx:XML xmlns="" id="sampleXML">
    <data label="2004">
        <result label="Jan-04">
            <product label="apple">81156</product>
            <product label="orange">58883</product>
            <product label="grape">49280</product>
        </result>
        <result label="Feb-04">
            <product label="apple">81156</product>
            <product label="orange">58883</product>
            <product label="grape">49280</product>
        </result>
        <result label="March-04">
            <product label="apple">81156</product>
            <product label="orange">58883</product>
            <product label="grape">49280</product>
        </result>
    </data>

</fx:XML>
</fx:Declarations>

<fx:Style>
    @namespace s "library://ns.adobe.com/flex/spark";
    @namespace mx "library://ns.adobe.com/flex/halo";

    s|List {
        borderStyle:"none";
        borderAlpha:"0";
    }

</fx:Style>

<fx:Script>
    <![CDATA[
        import mx.collections.XMLListCollection;

        [Bindable]
        private var xmlList:XMLListCollection;
```

Here, the XMLListCollection is created and used to set the dataProvider of the List. Note that the collection is instantiated from a XMLList:

```
        private function init():void {
            xmlList = new XMLListCollection(new XMLList(sampleXML.result));
        }

    ]]>
</fx:Script>
<s:List left="10" dataProvider="{xmlList}"
        itemRenderer="oreilly.cookbook.flex4.XMLItemRenderer"/>
</s:Application>
```

Here's the XMLItemRenderer that the List will use. It contains a List instance and it uses the same renderer, allowing the List to display complex nested data:

```
<?xml version="1.0" encoding="utf-8"?>
<s:ItemRenderer xmlns:fx="http://ns.adobe.com/mxml/2009"
                xmlns:s="library://ns.adobe.com/flex/spark"
                xmlns:mx="library://ns.adobe.com/flex/halo">

    <fx:Script>
        <![CDATA[

            import mx.collections.XMLListCollection;
```

If the XML object has complex content, create another XMLListCollection and use it to set the dataProvider of the List:

```
            override public function set data(value:Object) : void {

                if(value is XML && (value as XML).hasComplexContent()) {

                    simpleDataLabel.text = String(value.@label);

                    list.visible = true;
                    list.includeInLayout = true;

                    list.dataProvider = new XMLListCollection(new
                            XMLList(value.product));

                } else {
```

If the data does not contain complex data, it is a leaf of the XML and can be displayed without the list, simply using the label attribute of the node:

```
                    list.visible = false;
                    list.includeInLayout = false;

                    simpleDataLabel.text = String(value)+" "+String(value.@label);
                }
            }

        ]]>
    </fx:Script>
```

Like all ItemRenderer instances, this one must define the normal, hovered, and selected states:

```
    <s:states>
        <s:State name="normal" />
        <s:State name="hovered" />
        <s:State name="selected" />
    </s:states>

    <s:Rect height="20" width="180">
        <s:fill>
            <s:SolidColor color="0xf0f0ff" alpha="0.2" alpha.hovered="1.0" />
        </s:fill>
    </s:Rect>

    <s:Label id="simpleDataLabel" top="5" left="10" />
```

```
        <s:List left="25" top="25" id="list"
                itemRenderer="oreilly.cookbook.flex4.XMLItemRenderer" />

    </s:ItemRenderer>
```

8.7 Allow Only Certain Items in a Spark List to Be Selectable

Problem

You want to parse the `dataProvider` of a list to ensure that certain items are not selectable by the user.

Solution

Create a `filterFunction` property that can be set on a subclass of the `List` component. Use `mouseEventToItemRenderer()` and `finishKeySelection()` to check the user's selection via the `filter()` function and allow or disallow the selection.

Discussion

To control the user's selection of certain items in a list, you need to control the items that the user can select with the mouse and the keyboard. Mouse selection is slightly easier to deal with: simply override the `mouseEventToItemRenderer()` method and return `null` if the `ItemRenderer` contains data you want to be unselectable. The keyboard event handling is more complex because you want to send users to the next selectable item in the list if they try to navigate to an unselectable item by using the up or down arrow keys:

```
<s:ItemRenderer xmlns:fx="http://ns.adobe.com/mxml/2009"
                xmlns:s="library://ns.adobe.com/flex/spark"
                xmlns:mx="library://ns.adobe.com/flex/halo"
                selectionColor="#ff0000">
    <fx:Script>
        <![CDATA[

            private var __fun:Function;

            public function set selectableFunction(fun:Function):void {
                __fun = fun;
            }
```

Call the function instances passed to `selectableFunction()` to determine whether the `ItemRenderer` should be enabled or not:

```
            override public function set data(value:Object) : void {
                if(value && __fun(value)) {
                    mouseEnabled = true;
                    enabled = true;
```

```
                    } else {
                        mouseEnabled = false;
                        enabled = false;
                    }
                    super.data = value;
                }

            ]]>
        </fx:Script>

        <s:states>
            <s:State name="normal" />
            <s:State name="hovered" />
            <s:State name="selected" />
        </s:states>

        <!-- hover/select highlight -->
        <s:Rect left="0" right="0" top="0" bottom="0">
            <s:fill>
                <s:SolidColor color="0x000088"
                              alpha="0" alpha.hovered="0.1" alpha.selected="0.4" />
            </s:fill>
        </s:Rect>
        <s:Label text="{data}" />
    </s:ItemRenderer>
```

Here is the `Application` with a `List` utilizing the `ItemRenderer` just defined:

```
<s:Application xmlns:fx="http://ns.adobe.com/mxml/2009"
               xmlns:s="library://ns.adobe.com/flex/spark"
               xmlns:mx="library://ns.adobe.com/flex/halo"
               creationComplete="init()"
               xmlns:flex4="oreilly.cookbook.flex4.*">

    <fx:Script>
        <![CDATA[
            import oreilly.cookbook.flex4.SelectionRestrictedRenderer;
            import mx.collections.ArrayCollection;

            [Bindable]
            public var provider:ArrayCollection;

            public function init():void {
                provider = new ArrayCollection([12, 13, 4, 5, 16, 19, 400]);
            }
```

Here, the `ClassFactory` instance, which assigns the `selectionAllowFunction()` method to the `ItemRenderers` created by that factory, is created. This allows all the `Item Renderer` instances created to call that method without needing to refer to the `parent Document` or calling a method on the parent component:

```
        public function customItemRendererFunction(item:*):IFactory {

            var factory:ClassFactory = new ClassFactory(
                                    SelectionRestrictedRenderer );
```

```
            factory.properties = {"selectableFunction":selectionAllowFunction};
            return factory;
        }

        public function selectionAllowFunction(value:*):Boolean {
            if(value < Number(textInput.text)) {
                return false;
            } else {
                return true;
            }
        }

        public function updateList():void {
            list.executeBindings();
        }
    ]]>
</fx:Script>

<s:layout><s:HorizontalLayout/></s:layout>
<s:TextInput id="textInput" change="updateList()" />
```

Note that the `itemRendererFunction` is used to return the `ClassFactory` instead of using the `itemRenderer` property to pass the name of a `Class` that implements `IFactory`:

```
<s:List id="list" itemRendererFunction="{customItemRendererFunction}"
        dataProvider="{provider}"/>
```

```
</s:Application>
```

8.8 Format and Validate Data Added in a Spark List Item Editor

Problem

You need to validate any data that the user enters in an item editor before committing the value to the list.

Solution

On the `itemEditEnd` event, retrieve the text from the item editor by using the `itemEditorInstance` property of the `ListBase` class and parse the results.

Discussion

The Halo `List` by default dispatches events to indicate when the user has begun and finished editing an item in an item editor. However, in a Spark `List` you'll need to add the event dispatching explicitly in your item renderer. In this recipe the Spark `List` will be made to mimic a Halo `List`, dispatching the same events when the item editor is edited:

```
<s:List xmlns:fx="http://ns.adobe.com/mxml/2009"
        xmlns:s="library://ns.adobe.com/flex/spark"
        xmlns:mx="library://ns.adobe.com/flex/halo"
```

```
        itemRenderer="oreilly.cookbook.flex4.renderers.ValidationEditor"
        initialize="initializeHandler()">

<fx:Script>
    <![CDATA[
        import oreilly.cookbook.flex4.renderers.ValidationEditor;

        protected var _isEditing:Boolean;

        public function get isEditing():Boolean { return _isEditing; }
```

When a new `ItemRenderer` instance is created in the Spark `List`, the `RendererExistenceEvent.`
`RENDERER_ADD` event is dispatched. Listen for that event to add event listeners to the
`ItemRenderer` instance itself:

```
        protected function initializeHandler():void {
            this.addEventListener(RendererExistenceEvent.RENDERER_ADD,
                    rendererAdded);
            this.addEventListener(RendererExistenceEvent.RENDERER_REMOVE,
                    rendererRemoved);
        }

        protected function rendererAdded(event:RendererExistenceEvent):void {
            event.renderer.addEventListener(ValidationEditor.EDIT_BEGIN,
                    rendererEventHandler);
            event.renderer.addEventListener(ValidationEditor.EDIT_COMPLETE,
                    rendererEventHandler);
            event.renderer.addEventListener(ValidationEditor.EDIT_CANCEL,
                    rendererEventHandler);
        }

        protected function rendererRemoved(event:RendererExistenceEvent):void {
            event.renderer.removeEventListener(ValidationEditor.EDIT_COMPLETE,
                    rendererEventHandler);
            event.renderer.removeEventListener(ValidationEditor.EDIT_BEGIN,
                    rendererEventHandler);
            event.renderer.removeEventListener(ValidationEditor.EDIT_CANCEL,
                    rendererEventHandler);
        }

        // We have to override this to ignore events while editing or
        // the user's keystrokes will select other items in the data.
        override protected function keyDownHandler(event:KeyboardEvent) {
            if(!isEditing) {
                super.keyDownHandler(event);
            }
        }
```

Overriding the `selectedIndex()` setter enables you to forbid the `List` to set the
`selectedIndex` if an item editor is currently being edited:

```
        override public function set selectedIndex(value:int) : void {
            if(!isEditing) {
                super.selectedIndex= value;
            }
        }
```

This example uses event bubbling to ensure that the parent receives these events:

```
protected function rendererEventHandler(event:EditEvent):void {

    if(event.type == ValidationEditor.EDIT_COMPLETE || event.type ==
        ValidationEditor.EDIT_CANCEL)
        _isEditing = false;

    if(event.type == ValidationEditor.EDIT_BEGIN)
        _isEditing = true;
}

        ]]>
    </fx:Script>
</s:List>
```

Here is the ItemRenderer that allows the user to double-click to change the value and then ensures that the name the user entered is correct:

```
<s:ItemRenderer xmlns:fx="http://ns.adobe.com/mxml/2009"
                xmlns:s="library://ns.adobe.com/flex/spark"
                xmlns:mx="library://ns.adobe.com/flex/halo"
                mouseDownOutside="editHandler(event)"
                focusOut="editHandler(event)"
                doubleClick="beginEdit()"
                doubleClickEnabled="true">
    <fx:Script>
        <![CDATA[

            import mx.events.FlexMouseEvent;
            import oreilly.cookbook.flex4.EditEvent;
            import oreilly.cookbook.flex4.EditableList;

            public static const EDIT_BEGIN:String = "editBegin";
            public static const EDIT_COMPLETE:String = "editComplete";
            public static const EDIT_CANCEL:String = "editCancel";

            private const CANCELLED:int = 0;
            private const CHANGED:int = 1;

            // Flag for expanded state.
            protected var isEditing:Boolean = false;
```

In the beginEdit() method, the parent list is checked to see whether another Item Renderer is being edited. If not, this instance sets its currentState property to editing and dispatches an event to the owner to notify it that no other ItemRenderers should be edited until this one has either completed or cancelled its edit operation:

```
protected function beginEdit():void {

    if((owner as EditableList).isEditing)
        return;

    isEditing = true;
    currentState = "editing";
    input.setFocus();
```

```
            dispatchEvent(new EditEvent(EDIT_BEGIN, null, null));
        }
```

The editHandler() method is triggered in three different scenarios: when the user clicks outside of the ItemRenderer, the user presses the Enter or Escape key, or the Item Renderer loses focus in some other way. The value within the TextInput is then checked to confirm that it is valid, and if it is, an EditEvent of type EDIT_COMPLETE is dispatched. If the value is not valid, the errorString of the TextInput is set and the user is prevented from selecting other ItemRenderers within the List:

```
protected function editHandler(evt:Event):void {

    var reason:int;

    if(evt is KeyboardEvent) {
        if( (evt as KeyboardEvent).keyCode == Keyboard.ESCAPE) {
            reason = CANCELLED;
        } else if ((evt as KeyboardEvent).keyCode == Keyboard.ENTER) {
            reason = CHANGED;
        } else {
            return;
        }
    }
    if(evt is FlexMouseEvent) {
        if((evt as FlexMouseEvent).type ==
                FlexMouseEvent.MOUSE_DOWN_OUTSIDE) {
            reason = CHANGED;
        } else {
            return;
        }
    }
    if(evt is FocusEvent) {
        reason = CHANGED;
    }

    var previousValue:Object = data.name;
    if(reason == CHANGED) {
        // Get the new data value from the editor.
        var newData:String = input.text;
        // Determine if the new value is an empty String.
        var reg:RegExp = /\d/;
        if(newData == "" || reg.test(newData)) {
            // Prevent the user from removing focus,
            // and leave the cell editor open.
            // Use the errorString to inform the user that
            // something is wrong.
            input.setStyle("borderColor", 0xff0000);
            input.errorString = "Enter a valid string.";
            return;
        }
        // Test for FirstName LastName format.
        reg = /\w+.\s.\w+/
        if(!reg.test(newData)) {
            input.setStyle( "borderColor", 0xff0000);
            input.errorString = "Enter first name and last name";
```

```
                    return;
                } else {

                    // Make sure the name is properly formatted.
                    var firstName:String = newData.substring(0,
                            newData.indexOf(" "));
                    var lastName:String = newData.substring(newData.indexOf(
                            " ")+1);
                    firstName = firstName.charAt(0).toUpperCase() +
                            firstName.substr(1);
                    lastName = lastName.charAt(0).toUpperCase() +
                            lastName.substr(1);
                    input.text = firstName+" "+lastName;
                    data.name = newData.charAt(0).toLocaleUpperCase() +
                            newData.substring( 1, newData.indexOf(" ")) +
                            newData.charAt(newData.indexOf(" ")+1) +
                            newData.substring(newData.indexOf(" ")+2);
                }
                var editEvent:EditEvent = new EditEvent(EDIT_COMPLETE,
                        previousValue, input.text);
                dispatchEvent(editEvent);

                isEditing = false;
                currentState = getCurrentRendererState();

            } else if (reason == CANCELLED) {
                var editEvent:EditEvent = new EditEvent(EDIT_CANCEL, null,
                                                        null);
                dispatchEvent(editEvent);

                isEditing = false;
                currentState = getCurrentRendererState();
            }
        }

        override protected function getCurrentRendererState():String {
            var skinState:String;
            if (isEditing) {
                skinState = "editing";
            } else {
                skinState = super.getCurrentRendererState();
            }
            return skinState;
        }


    ]]>
</fx:Script>

<s:states>
    <s:State name="normal" />
    <s:State name="hovered" />
    <s:State name="selected" />
```

The extra `editing` state is to hide and show the `TextInput`:

```
        <s:State name="editing" />
    </s:states>
```

One final thing to note: because the `ItemRenderer` needs to allow mouse events to be dispatched from the children, you should add a `doubleClick` listener to the `Label` as well so that double-clicking on either the background of the `ItemRenderer` or the `Label` will trigger the `beginEdit()` event handler:

```
    <s:Label text="{data.name}" id="display" excludeFrom="editing"
            left="20" top="3" right="10" bottom="3" width="100"
            doubleClickEnabled="true" doubleClick="beginEdit()"
            mouseChildren="false" />
    <s:TextInput text="{data.name}" id="input" keyDown="editHandler(event)"
                includeIn="editing" />

</s:ItemRenderer>
```

8.9 Create a Right-Click Menu for a Spark List

Problem

You need to create a custom context menu to display when the user right-clicks or Ctrl-clicks on a specific item.

Solution

Create `ContextMenu` and `ContextMenuItem` objects and assign those to the renderer that will be assigned to the list as the `itemRenderer`.

Discussion

The context menu is what appears when a user right-clicks or Ctrl-clicks on your Flex application. By default, this menu shows Loop, Play, Print, Quality, Rewind, Save, and Zoom controls, as well as a link to an info screen about Flash Player 10. You can easily customize this menu for your users, however, by creating a new `ContextMenu` object. Simply call the constructor for the `ContextMenu` class and set the `contextMenu` property of any display object to be the object just created, as shown here:

```
    var menu:ContextMenu = new ContextMenu();
    this.contextMenu = menu;
```

This code needs to be run within a `DisplayObject`; that is, any object with a visual display. The custom context menu created here will appear only if the user has right- or Ctrl-clicked the `DisplayObject` or a component with the `contextMenu` property set.

To add new items to a context menu, use the `customItems` array defined by the `Context Menu` object. Instantiate new `ContextMenuItem` objects and add them to the array by using the `push()` method.

The constructor for the `ContextMenuItem` object has the following signature:

```
ContextMenuItem(caption:String, separatorBefore:Boolean = false,
                enabled:Boolean = true, visible:Boolean = true)
```

The `caption` property determines the title of the menu item—for example, Look Up Employees. The `separatorBefore` property determines whether a thin bar will appear above the `ContextMenuItem` to divide it from the items above it in the menu. Finally, the `visible` and `enabled` properties control whether the item is visible to and able to be selected by the user, respectively.

The `ContextMenuItem` dispatches a `ContextMenuEvent` event of type `SELECT` when the user selects the item.

The example that follows creates a renderer for a `List` control that will create custom context menus based on the data type passed in from the `List`:

```
<s:ItemRenderer xmlns:fx="http://ns.adobe.com/mxml/2009"
                xmlns:s="library://ns.adobe.com/flex/spark"
                xmlns:mx="library://ns.adobe.com/flex/halo"
                width="150" height="80">
    <fx:Script>
        <![CDATA[

            import flash.display.*;

            override public function set data(value:Object):void {
                if(value is Name) {
                    text1.text = value.firstName;
                    text2.text = value.lastName;
                    var personMenu:ContextMenu = new ContextMenu();
                    var lookupRecord:ContextMenuItem = new
                            ContextMenuItem("Look Up Record");
                    var lookupPicture:ContextMenuItem = new
                            ContextMenuItem("Look Up Picture");
                    personMenu.customItems.push(lookupRecord);
                    personMenu.customItems.push(lookupPicture);
                    this.contextMenu = personMenu;
                }
                else if(value is Office) {
                    text1.text = value.officeAddress;
                    text2.text = value.officeName;
                    var officeMenu:ContextMenu = new ContextMenu();
                    var lookupMap:ContextMenuItem = new
                            ContextMenuItem("Look Up  Map");
                    lookupMap.addEventListener(ContextMenuEvent.MENU_ITEM_SELECT,
                            showMap);
                    var lookupEmployees:ContextMenuItem = new
                            ContextMenuItem("Look Up Employees");
                        lookupEmployees.addEventListener(
                            ContextMenuEvent.MENU_ITEM_SELECT, showEmployees );
```

```
                            officeMenu.customItems.push(lookupEmployees);
                            officeMenu.customItems.push(lookupMap);
                            this.contextMenu = officeMenu;
                        }
                    }

                    private function showMap(event:ContextMenuEvent):void {
                        // do something with the map
                    }

                    private function showEmployees(event:ContextMenuEvent):void {
                        // do something to look up all the employees
                    }

                ]]>
        </fx:Script>
        <s:Label id="text1" />
        <s:Label id="text2" />
    </s:ItemRenderer>
```

8.10 Enable Dragging in a Spark List

Problem

You want to enable dragging in a Spark `List` component.

Solution

Create handlers for the `mouseDown`, `dragEnter`, and `dragDrop` events that the `List` dispatches, and call the `DragManager.doDrag()` and `DragManager.acceptDragDrop()` methods to start the dragging operation and accept the dragged item. On the `drag Drop` event, update the data provider of the `List` with the new item.

Discussion

The `DragManager` defines several key operations that you'll use in creating a drag-enabled `List`. The `doDrag()` method allows you to pass the component that initiated the drag, a `DragSource` containing data, and several other optional properties to start the drag operation.

The `acceptDragDrop()` method is called by a component that will accept the data in a drag operation. Usually this is done by inspecting the format of the data and ensuring that it can be displayed properly or meets other requirements, using the `Drag Source.dataForFormat()` method. For example:

```
<s:Application xmlns:fx="http://ns.adobe.com/mxml/2009"
               xmlns:s="library://ns.adobe.com/flex/spark"
               xmlns:mx="library://ns.adobe.com/flex/halo"
               minWidth="1024" minHeight="768">
```

```
<s:layout>
    <s:HorizontalLayout/>
</s:layout>

<fx:Declarations>
    <s:AnimateFilter id="glowFilter" target="{listTwo}"
                     bitmapFilter="{filter}"/>
    <s:GlowFilter id="filter"/>

</fx:Declarations>

<fx:Script>
    <![CDATA[
        import mx.core.DragSource;
        import mx.core.IDataRenderer;
        import mx.core.IUIComponent;
        import mx.events.DragEvent;
        import mx.managers.DragManager;
```

If the drag event was initiated by another component, you must call the `acceptDrag Drop()` method. In addition, you can allow components to drag within themselves (e.g., a `List` that reorders itself by dragging items around). The goal of this recipe's example, however, is to allow users to drag items between multiple lists:

```
private function dragEnterHandler(event:DragEvent):void {
    if(event.target != event.dragInitiator && event.target !=
            event.dragInitiator.owner) {
        DragManager.acceptDragDrop(event.target as IUIComponent);
        DragManager.showFeedback(DragManager.MOVE);
    } else {
        DragManager.showFeedback(DragManager.NONE);
    }
}

private function dragDropHandler(event:DragEvent):void {
    var val:Object = event.dragSource.dataForFormat("listData");
    (event.target as List).dataProvider.addItem(val);
    glowFilter.play();
}
```

You begin a drag operation by calling the `doDrag()` method:

```
private function dragBegin(event:MouseEvent):void {
    var target:IUIComponent = event.target as IUIComponent;
    target.addEventListener(DragEvent.DRAG_COMPLETE,
                            dragCompleteHandler);
    var source:DragSource = new DragSource();
    source.addData((target as IDataRenderer).data, "listData");
    DragManager.doDrag(target, source, event);
}

private function dragCompleteHandler(event:DragEvent):void {
    if(event.action != DragManager.NONE) {
        event.target.removeEventListener(DragEvent.DRAG_COMPLETE,
            dragCompleteHandler);
```

```
                        var list:List = (event.target.owner as List);
                        var data:Object = event.dragSource.dataForFormat("listData");
                        list.dataProvider.removeItemAt(
                                list.dataProvider.getItemIndex(data) );
                    }

                }

            ]]>
        </fx:Script>
```

Using the `mouseDown` event, you can get access to the value being dragged after the user selects an item in the list. This means you can get the selected item without a lot of extra work:

```
        <s:List id="listOne"
                itemRenderer="oreilly.cookbook.flex4.DragDropRenderer"
                mouseDown="dragBegin(event)"
                dragEnter="dragEnterHandler(event)"
                dragDrop="dragDropHandler(event)">
            <s:dataProvider>
                <s:ArrayList source="['one', 'two', 'three', 'four', 'five']"/>
            </s:dataProvider>
        </s:List>

        <s:List id="listTwo"
                itemRenderer="oreilly.cookbook.flex4.DragDropRenderer"
                mouseDown="dragBegin(event)"
                dragEnter="dragEnterHandler(event)"
                dragDrop="dragDropHandler(event)">
            <s:dataProvider>
                <!-- empty arraylist -->
                <s:ArrayList/>
            </s:dataProvider>
        </s:List>

    </s:Application>
```

Here is the `ItemRenderer`:

```
    <s:ItemRenderer xmlns:fx="http://ns.adobe.com/mxml/2009"
                    xmlns:s="library://ns.adobe.com/flex/spark"
                    xmlns:mx="library://ns.adobe.com/flex/halo"
                    width="400" height="300">
        <s:states>
            <s:State name="normal" />
            <s:State name="hovered" />
            <s:State name="selected" />
        </s:states>

        <s:Rect left="0" right="0" top="0" bottom="0" includeIn=" hovered ">
            <s:fill>
                <s:SolidColor color="0x000088" alpha="0.6" alpha.selected="1.0"/>
            </s:fill>
        </s:Rect>
```

Make sure to set the `mouseEnabled` and `mouseChildren` properties to `false` for the `Label`:

```
    <s:Label mouseEnabled="false" mouseChildren="false" text="{data}"/>
</s:ItemRenderer>
```

8.11 Customize the Drop Indicator of a Spark List

Problem

You want to customize the graphic display of the drop indicator shown in a `List` control during drag-and-drop operations.

Solution

Create a custom skin class that extends `spark.skins.Skin` and assign it to the `List` control.

Discussion

This recipe is a rather lengthy one: it includes the three distinct code listings required to show a custom graphic when a user drags an item into a `List`. The first listing is for the `ItemRenderer` that will be used within the `List`. Notice that the `mouseChildren` property is set to `false`, and `Label` is not `mouseEnabled` either. This ensures that only the `ItemRenderer` itself is dispatching mouse events for the parent `List` to listen for. The `ItemRenderer` implements an `Interface`, but it is an empty `Interface` used only for type safety:

```
    <s:ItemRenderer xmlns:fx="http://ns.adobe.com/mxml/2009"
                    xmlns:s="library://ns.adobe.com/flex/spark"
                    xmlns:mx="library://ns.adobe.com/flex/halo"
                    mouseChildren="false"
                    implements="oreilly.cookbook.flex4.IFlexCookbookRenderer">
        <mx:Label text="{data}" mouseEnabled="false"/>
    </s:ItemRenderer>
```

Next is the `Skin` for the `List`. The `spark.components.List` has two optional parts: a `DataGroup` with the `id` of `dataGroup` and a `Scroller` with the `id` of `scroller`. This `Skin` also defines two `Fade` instances, one that will be triggered when the `List` accepts a drag operation and one for when a drag operation is completed:

```
    <s:Skin xmlns:fx="http://ns.adobe.com/mxml/2009"
            xmlns:s="library://ns.adobe.com/flex/spark"
            xmlns:mx="library://ns.adobe.com/flex/halo">
        <fx:Declarations>
            <s:Fade id="showAccept" target="{glowFill}" duration="500" alphaFrom="0.0"
                alphaTo="1.0"/>

            <s:Fade id="showDrop" target="{glowFill}" duration="500" alphaFrom="1.0"
                alphaTo="0.0" effectEnd="{currentState = 'normal'}"/>
        </fx:Declarations>
```

```
<fx:Metadata>
    [HostComponent("spark.components.List")]
</fx:Metadata>
```

The first two State objects are required by the List, and the second two states are used by the parent List on the DragEvent.DRAG_DROP event and the DragEvent.DRAG_ENTER event:

```
<s:states>
    <s:State name="normal"/>
    <s:State name="disabled"/>
    <s:State name="dragEnterState" enterState="{showAccept.play()}"/>
    <s:State name="dropState" enterState="{showDrop.play()}"/>
</s:states>

<s:Rect height="{hostComponent.height}" width="{hostComponent.width}">
    <s:fill>
        <s:SolidColor id="glowFill" color="0xccccff" alpha="0.0"/>
    </s:fill>
</s:Rect>
```

The DataGroup is where the item renderers are actually displayed, so you'll want to ensure that any background fill objects are behind the DataGroup:

```
<s:DataGroup id="dataGroup">
    <s:layout><s:VerticalLayout/></s:layout>
</s:DataGroup>
```

```
</s:Skin>
```

This example is quite simple, but you can do much more complex drawing in the Skin instance.

Finally, you must create the List itself, which shows a menu that the user can access after dropping an Item in the List. Although this is not actually a good user experience, it does demonstrate how to perform drawing routines triggered by drag operations. First, set up the handlers for the drag events:

```
<s:List xmlns:fx="http://ns.adobe.com/mxml/2009"
        xmlns:s="library://ns.adobe.com/flex/spark"
        xmlns:mx="library://ns.adobe.com/flex/halo"
        dragEnter="dragEnterHandler(event)"
        dragDrop="dragDropHandler(event)"
        dragComplete="dragCompleteHandler(event)"
        mouseMove="dragBegin(event)"
        itemRenderer="oreilly.cookbook.flex4.MouseChildrenDisabledRenderer"
        width="400" height="300">

    <fx:Script>
        <![CDATA[

            import mx.core.DragSource;
            import mx.core.IDataRenderer;
            import mx.core.IUIComponent;
            import mx.events.DragEvent;
```

```
import mx.managers.DragManager;
import spark.components.Button;
import spark.components.Group;
import spark.layouts.HorizontalLayout;
```

Next, specify the variables that store the data, the List instance that created the DragEvent.DRAG_DROP event, and the stage coordinates at which the DragEvent occurred:

```
private var lastDroppedData:Object;
private var selectMenu:Group;
private var lastPoint:Point;

private function createSelectMenu():Group {
    if(!selectMenu) {
        selectMenu = new Group();
        selectMenu.layout = new HorizontalLayout();
        var beginningButton:Button = new Button();
        beginningButton.name = "beginning";
        beginningButton.addEventListener(MouseEvent.CLICK,
                                         clickHandler);
        beginningButton.label = "Beginning";
        selectMenu.addElement(beginningButton);
        var endButton:Button = new Button();
        endButton.name = "end";
        endButton.addEventListener(MouseEvent.CLICK, clickHandler);
        endButton.label = "End";
        selectMenu.addElement(endButton);
        var positionButton:Button = new Button();
        positionButton.name = "position";
        positionButton.addEventListener(MouseEvent.CLICK,
                                        clickHandler);
        positionButton.label = "Where I Dropped It";
        selectMenu.addElement(positionButton);
    }
    return selectMenu;
}
```

Once the user has clicked on the menu, place the dragged item correctly, either at the beginning or end of the dataProvider, or at the location where the user has dropped the item (in a production application, you might want to abstract this logic out into a separate class):

```
protected function clickHandler(event:MouseEvent):void {
    if(event.target.name == "beginning") {
        dataProvider.addItemAt(lastDroppedData, 0);
    } else if(event.target.name == "position") {
        var currentIndex:int;
        var arr:Array = getObjectsUnderPoint(lastPoint);
        for(var i:int = 0; i<arr.length; i++) {
            if(arr[i] is IFlexCookbookRenderer) {
                break;
            }
        }
```

```
        dataProvider.addItemAt(lastDroppedData, i);
    } else {
        dataProvider.addItemAt(lastDroppedData, dataProvider.length);
    }
    this.skin.removeElement(selectMenu);
}
```

Finally, you need the three drag event handlers, which are very similar to the event handlers used in Recipe 8.10. The dragEnterHandler() method is called when the user drags the mouse over the component and shows the user visual feedback to indicate whether the drag operation will be accepted or not. The dragDropHandler() method stores the properties from the drag operation so that they can be used once the user selects one of the options from the menu. The dragBegin() method uses the IFlexCook bookRenderer Interface to determine if the MouseEvent is originating from one of the ItemRenderers or from the Skin or Scrollbar of the List:

```
protected function dragEnterHandler(event:DragEvent):void {
    if(event.target != event.dragInitiator && event.target !=
            event.dragInitiator.owner) {
        DragManager.acceptDragDrop(event.target as IUIComponent);
        DragManager.showFeedback(DragManager.MOVE);
    } else {
        DragManager.showFeedback(DragManager.NONE);
    }
}

protected function dragDropHandler(event:DragEvent):void {
    lastDroppedData = event.dragSource.dataForFormat("listData");
    lastPoint = new Point(event.stageX, event.stageY);
    this.skin.addElement(createSelectMenu());
}

protected function dragBegin(event:MouseEvent):void {
    var target:IUIComponent = (event.target as IUIComponent);

    var str:String = getQualifiedClassName(itemRenderer)

    if(!(target is IFlexCookbookRenderer))
        return;

    target.addEventListener(DragEvent.DRAG_COMPLETE,
                            dragCompleteHandler);
    var source:DragSource = new DragSource();
    source.addData((target as IDataRenderer).data, "listData");
    DragManager.doDrag(target, source, event);
}

protected function dragCompleteHandler(event:DragEvent):void
{
    if(event.action != DragManager.NONE) {
        event.target.removeEventListener(DragEvent.DRAG_COMPLETE,
                dragCompleteHandler);
```

```
                    var list:List = (event.target.owner as List);
                    var data:Object = event.dragSource.dataForFormat("listData");
                    list.dataProvider.removeItemAt(
                            list.dataProvider.getItemIndex(data) );
                }
            }
        ]]>
    </fx:Script>
</s:List>
```

8.12 Display Asynchronously Loaded Data in a Spark List

Problem

You want to display data that may be loaded asynchronously when it is requested by the List.

Solution

Create an AsyncListView object and use it as the data provider for the List.

Discussion

The AsyncListView object is one of the new components in Flex 4 that enables you to easily display data that may be pending from a server or other process or that may fail in loading. The AsyncListView implements IList, which means that it uses many of the same methods you use with ArrayCollection, ArrayList, and other collections:

- addItem()
- addItemAt()
- getItemAt()
- getItemIndex()
- removeAll()
- removeItemAt()
- setItemAt()

It does, however, define an additional method specifically designed to aid you in handling asynchronously loaded data:

```
itemUpdated(item:Object, property:Object = null, oldValue:Object = null,
        newValue:Object = null):void
```

You can use the itemUpdated() method to notify the collection that an item has been updated (when it has loaded, for instance).

The AsyncListView extends the Spark List and defines two other properties to help you work with asynchronous data providers:

createPendingItemFunction : Function

    This function is called when an item that was requested by the List throws an ItemPending error, indicating that the item is still being loaded.

createFailedItemFunction : Function

    This function is called when an item that was being loaded fails.

The following example component uses these methods when the AsyncListView is set to use a collection that loads paged data from a service. Chapter 12 covers how to use paged data, so this recipe focuses on making the ItemRenderer display asynchronous data properly. This example supposes that you're loading multiple data objects that each possess a very large data object as one of their properties:

```
package oreilly.cookbook.flex4 {
    import flash.events.EventDispatcher;

    [Bindable]
    public class LargeRemoteDataObj extends EventDispatcher implements IAsyncDO {
        public var id:int;
        public var name:String;
        public var largeObject:Object;

        private var _isPending:Boolean;

        public function get isPending():Boolean {
            return _isPending;
        }

        public function set isPending(value:Boolean):void {
            _isPending = value;
        }
    }
}
```

The component to render this data object using an AsyncListView might look something like this:

```
<s:Group xmlns:fx="http://ns.adobe.com/mxml/2009"
        xmlns:s="library://ns.adobe.com/flex/spark"
        xmlns:mx="library://ns.adobe.com/flex/halo" width="400" height="300"
        creationComplete="init()">

    <fx:Script>
        <![CDATA[
            import mx.collections.ArrayList;
            import mx.collections.AsyncListView;
            import mx.collections.errors.ItemPendingError;

            [Bindable]
            private var list:AsyncListView;

            private var timer:Timer;

            protected function init():void {
```

Make sure that the `AsyncListView` is passed an `ArrayCollection` or `ArrayList` when it is created:

```
list = new AsyncListView(new ArrayList([]));
```

Then, set the two functions for the `AsyncListView` to call:

```
        list.createFailedItemFunction = fetchFailedFunction;
        list.createPendingItemFunction = fetchPendingFunction;

    }
```

If the item fails, remove it from the collection:

```
    private function fetchFailedFunction(index:int, info:Object):Object {
        list.removeItemAt(index);
        return {hasFailed:true};
    }
```

For the purposes of this recipe, assume that a class implementing an interface called `IAsyncDataObject` can be created and passed to an `ItemRenderer` when a call to a server-side method does not return immediately. When the server operation doesn't return, call the `fetchPendingFunction()` method and create a temporary object that will be passed to the `ItemRenderer`. This allows the `ItemRenderer` to display a graphical notification informing the user that the item has not been loaded yet:

```
    private function fetchPendingFunction(index:int,
            ipe:ItemPendingError):Object {
        var employee:IAsyncDataObjectImpl= new IAsyncDataObjectImpl();
        employee.isPending = true;
        return employee;
    }

        ]]>
    </fx:Script>

    <s:List dataProvider="{list}"
            itemRenderer="oreilly.cookbook.flex4.AsyncItemRenderer"/>
    </s:Group>
```

Finally, the `ItemRenderer` needs to allow both an item that is complete and one that has its `isPending` property set to `true`:

```
<s:ItemRenderer xmlns:fx="http://ns.adobe.com/mxml/2009"
                xmlns:s="library://ns.adobe.com/flex/spark"
                xmlns:mx="library://ns.adobe.com/flex/halo">

    <fx:Script>
        <![CDATA[

            import mx.binding.utils.ChangeWatcher;

            private var _data:IAsyncDataObject;
```

Specify the `ChangeWatcher` to be notified when the item is updated and its `isPending` property is set to `false`, meaning that it has been loaded:

```
private var loadPendingChangeWatcher:ChangeWatcher;

override public function set data(value:Object) : void {
```

The `IAsyncDataObject` interface is used so that if the object has not been loaded yet the `ItemRenderer` can still display something indicating that the item will be loaded. The `ChangeWatcher` listens for the `isPending` property to change and then, when it does, notifies the `ItemRenderer` so that it can update its graphics to show the downloaded item:

```
    if(value is IAsyncDataObject) {
        if(loadFailedChangeWatcher) {
            loadPendingChangeWatcher.unwatch();
        }
        _data = ( value as IAsyncDataObject);
        if(_data.isPending) {
            loadPendingChangeWatcher = ChangeWatcher.watch(_data,
                    ["isPending"], loadComplete, false, true);
        }
    }
}

private function loadComplete(event:Event):void {
    // show graphics for completed load
}
]]>
</fx:Script>
</s:ItemRenderer>
```

CHAPTER 9

DataGrid

The `DataGrid` control is a list-based control optimized to display large data sets in a multicolumn layout. It features resizable columns, customizable item renderers, and sorting capabilities, among other features. As of the writing of this book, the `Data Grid` component only has a Halo or `mx`-prefixed version. The Spark component is still forthcoming, so all of the recipes in this chapter will use Halo components. Some recipes, however, do show how to use the Spark `ItemRenderer` or other Spark components within a Flex `DataGrid`.

The `DataGrid` control (and its sister `AdvancedDataGrid`, included in the Data Visualization package for Flex 4) is typically used to display arrays or collections of data objects with similar types. The `DataGrid` control can also display `HierarchicalData` objects, show the parent/child relationships among complex data objects, and allow for the creation of specialized groupings of data, although, as you'll see, this is easier to do with `AdvancedDataGrid`.

9.1 Create Custom Columns for a DataGrid

Problem

You need to specify custom columns for a `DataGrid` and explicitly control the display.

Solution

Use the `DataGridColumn` tag to specify custom properties for columns in a `DataGrid`.

Discussion

This recipe adds three `DataGridColumn` tags to the `columns` property of a `DataGrid`. It uses a data file titled *homesforsale.xml*, although the data that you use could have any name and represent any array of information. The `DataGridColumn` tags specify the order in which to display the properties of the objects in the `dataProvider` and the titles to use for the column headers. The `dataField` property of the `DataGridColumn` specifies the property of the object to be displayed in the cells of that column. In this example, the object's range property is not displayed in the DataGrid control because there is no DataGridColumn with a dataField associated to the range property:

```
<s:Application xmlns:fx="http://ns.adobe.com/mxml/2009"
              xmlns:s="library://ns.adobe.com/flex/spark"
              xmlns:mx="library://ns.adobe.com/flex/halo"
              creationComplete="initApp()">
    <fx:Declarations>
        <mx:HTTPService id="srv" url="assets/homesforsale.xml"
                        resultFormat="object" result="onResult(event)"/>
    </fx:Declarations>

    <fx:Script>
        <![CDATA[
            import mx.collections.ArrayCollection;
            import mx.rpc.events.ResultEvent;

            [Bindable]
            private var homesForSale:ArrayCollection;

            private function initApp():void {
                this.srv.send();
            }

            private function onResult(evt:ResultEvent):void {
                this.homesForSale = evt.result.data.region;
            }

        ]]>
    </fx:Script>

    <mx:DataGrid id="grid"
                 width="100%"
                 height="100%"
                 dataProvider="{homesForSale}">
        <mx:columns>
            <mx:DataGridColumn headerText="Total No." dataField="total"/>
            <mx:DataGridColumn headerText="City" dataField="city"/>
            <mx:DataGridColumn headerText="State" dataField="state"/>
        </mx:columns>
    </mx:DataGrid>
</s:Application>
```

The DataGridColumn supports further customization of the display through the use of itemRenderers. The following code sample adds a new DataGridColumn that uses a custom renderer, RangeRenderer, to render the range property in a more meaningful way. The range property contains three values that indicate the percentage of houses for sale based on their price ranges (range1 contains the percentage of houses on sale for under $350,000, range2 is the percentage of houses on sale for between $350,000 and $600,000, and range3 contains the houses going for over $600,000):

```
<s:Application xmlns:fx="http://ns.adobe.com/mxml/2009"
               xmlns:s="library://ns.adobe.com/flex/spark"
               xmlns:mx="library://ns.adobe.com/flex/halo"
               creationComplete="initApp()">

    <fx:Declarations>
        <mx:HTTPService id="srv" url="assets/homesforsale.xml"
                        resultFormat="object" result="onResult(event)"/>
    </fx:Declarations>

    <mx:DataGrid id="grid"
                 width="100%"
                 height="100%"
                 dataProvider="{homesForSale}">
        <mx:columns>
            <mx:DataGridColumn headerText="Total No." dataField="total"/>
                <mx:DataGridColumn headerText="City" dataField="city"/>
                <mx:DataGridColumn headerText="State" dataField="state"/>
                <mx:DataGridColumn headerText="Price Ranges" dataField="range"
                    itemRenderer="oreilly.cookbook.flex4.RangeRenderer"/>
        </mx:columns>
    </mx:DataGrid>
    <fx:Script>
        <![CDATA[
            import mx.collections.ArrayCollection;
            import mx.rpc.events.ResultEvent;

            [Bindable]
            private var homesForSale:ArrayCollection;

            private function initApp():void {
                this.srv.send();
            }

            private function onResult(evt:ResultEvent):void {
                this.homesForSale = evt.result.data.region;
            }

        ]]>
    </fx:Script>
</s:Application>
```

The RangeRenderer shown in the following code uses the range percentage values to draw color-coded bars that indicate the values of each range. This is done by overriding the updateDisplayList() method to draw the colored bars using the drawing API:

```
package {
    import flash.display.Graphics;

    import mx.containers.Canvas;

    public class RangeRenderer extends Canvas {
        override public function set data(value:Object):void {
            super.data = value;
            if(value!= null && value.range != null) {
```

```
            this.invalidateDisplayList();
        }
    }

    override protected function updateDisplayList(unscaledWidth:Number,
            unscaledHeight:Number):void {
        var g:Graphics = this.graphics;

        if(this.data) {
            var w1:Number = (this.data.range.range1 * unscaledWidth)/100;
            var w2:Number = (this.data.range.range2 * unscaledWidth)/100;
            var w3:Number = (this.data.range.range3 * unscaledWidth)/100;

            var x1:Number = 0;
            var x2:Number = w1;
            var x3:Number = w1 + w2;

            g.beginFill(0x0000ff);
            g.drawRect(x1,0,w1,unscaledHeight);
            g.beginFill(0x00ff00);
            g.drawRect(x2,0,w2,unscaledHeight);
            g.beginFill(0xff0000);
            g.drawRect(x3,0,w3,unscaledHeight);
        }
    }
}
}
```

If you want to take advantage of the Spark `ItemRenderer`, note that you can also use
that within the `DataGrid` by implementing the `IListItemRenderer` interface, as shown
here:

```
<s:ItemRenderer xmlns:fx="http://ns.adobe.com/mxml/2009"
                xmlns:s="library://ns.adobe.com/flex/spark"
                xmlns:mx="library://ns.adobe.com/flex/halo" width="400"
                        height="300"
                        implements="mx.controls.listClasses.IListItemRenderer">
    <fx:Script>
        <![CDATA[
            import mx.controls.listClasses.IListItemRenderer;
            // include layout logic here

        ]]>
    </fx:Script>
    <s:states>
        <s:State name="normal"/>
        <s:State name="disabled"/>
    </s:states>
</s:ItemRenderer>
```

However, be aware that if you use the Spark `ItemRenderer`, not all of the state functionality may work in the same way as it does in the Spark `List`.

See Also

Recipe 9.2

9.2 Specify Sort Functions for DataGrid Columns

Problem

You want to use custom sorting logic to sort complex objects within a `DataGrid`.

Solution

Use the `sortCompareFunction` property of the `DataGridColumn` tag to assign a reference to a function that performs the custom sorting logic.

Discussion

You can modify the `DataGrid` used in the previous recipe to add a custom sorting function. This example uses a custom `itemRenderer` called `RangeRenderer` to add the sorting function `sortRanges()` to the `DataGridColumn` that displays the `range` property:

```
<s:Application xmlns:fx="http://ns.adobe.com/mxml/2009"
               xmlns:s="library://ns.adobe.com/flex/spark"
               xmlns:mx="library://ns.adobe.com/flex/halo"
                       creationComplete="initApp()">
    <fx:Declarations>
        <mx:HTTPService id="srv" url="assets/homesforsale.xml"
                        resultFormat="object" result="onResult(event)"/>
    </fx:Declarations>

    <s:layout><s:VerticalLayout/></s:layout>

    <mx:DataGrid id="grid" width="!00%" height="600"
                dataProvider="{homesForSale}">
        <mx:columns>
            <mx:DataGridColumn headerText="Total No." dataField="total"/>
            <mx:DataGridColumn headerText="City" dataField="city"/>
            <mx:DataGridColumn headerText="State" dataField="state"/>
            <mx:DataGridColumn headerText="Price Ranges [&lt;350K] [350K -600K]
                               [&gt;600K]" dataField="range"
                               itemRenderer="oreilly.cookbook.flex4.RangeRenderer"
                               sortCompareFunction="sortRanges"/>
        </mx:columns>
    </mx:DataGrid>
    <fx:Script>
        <![CDATA[
            import mx.collections.ArrayCollection;
            import mx.rpc.events.ResultEvent;

            [Bindable]
            private var homesForSale:ArrayCollection;
```

```
                private function initApp():void {
                    this.srv.send();
                }

                private function onResult(evt:ResultEvent):void {
                    this.homesForSale = evt.result.data.region;
                }

                private function sortRanges(obj1:Object, obj2:Object):int {
                    var value1:Number = obj1.range.range1;
                    var value2:Number = obj2.range.range1;

                    if(value1 < value2) {
                        return -1;
                    }
                    else if(value1 > value2) {
                        return 1;
                    }
                    else {
                        return 0;
                    }
                }

            ]]>
        </fx:Script>
    </s:Application>
```

Here, the sortCompareFunction property of the fourth DataGridColumn is assigned to sortRanges(), which implements the custom logic to sort the ranges. This property expects a function with the following signature:

```
    sortCompareFunction(obj1:Object, obj2:Object):int
```

The function accepts two parameters that correspond to two objects in the dataProvider being sorted at any given time, and it returns an integer value of -1, 1, or 0 that indicates the order in which the two objects were placed after the sort. When the user clicks the header for the DataGridColumn, the DataGrid runs this function for each item in the dataProvider and uses the return value to figure out how to order the items. The sortRanges() function looks at the nested range1 property of each dataProvider item to calculate the sort order. Thus, when the user clicks the header of the Price Ranges column, the items are sorted based on their range1 values.

See Also

Recipe 9.1

9.3 Filter Items in a DataGrid

Problem

You need to provide "live" client-side filtering for a data set displayed in a DataGrid.

Solution

Use the `filterFunction` property of the `ArrayCollection` to assign a reference to a custom function that performs the filter matching.

Discussion

To demonstrate implementing client-side filtering, the following example adds a city-filtering feature to Recipe 9.2. The UI features a `TextInput` field that enables the user to type city names and filter out the records in the `DataGrid` that match the input. When the user types an entry into the `cityFilter TextInput` control, it dispatches a `change` event that is handled by the `applyFilter()` method. The `applyFilter()` method assigns a function reference to the `filterFunction` property of the `homesForSale` `ArrayCollection` instance, if it hasn't already been assigned, and calls the `refresh()` method on the `ArrayCollection`. The `filterCities()` method implements a simple check for a lowercase string match between the `city` property of the `dataProvider` item and the input text:

```
<s:Application xmlns:fx="http://ns.adobe.com/mxml/2009"
               xmlns:s="library://ns.adobe.com/flex/spark"
               xmlns:mx="library://ns.adobe.com/flex/halo"
               creationComplete="initApp()">

    <s:layout><s:VerticalLayout/></s:layout>

    <fx:Declarations>
        <mx:HTTPService id="srv" url="assets/example.xml" resultFormat="object"
                    result="onResult(event)"/>
    </fx:Declarations>

    <s:TextInput id="cityFilter" change="applyFilter()"/>

    <mx:DataGrid id="grid" width="100%" height="100%"
            dataProvider="{homesForSale}">
        <mx:columns>
            <mx:DataGridColumn headerText="Total No." dataField="total"/>
            <mx:DataGridColumn headerText="City" dataField="city"/>
            <mx:DataGridColumn headerText="State" dataField="state"/>
            <mx:DataGridColumn headerText="Price Ranges [&lt;350K]
                            [350K -600K] [&gt;600K]" dataField="range"
                            itemRenderer="oreilly.cookbook.flex4.RangeRenderer"
                            sortCompareFunction="sortRanges"/>
        </mx:columns>
    </mx:DataGrid>
    <fx:Script>
        <![CDATA[
            import mx.events.FlexEvent;
            import mx.collections.ArrayCollection;
            import mx.rpc.events.ResultEvent;

            [Bindable]
            private var homesForSale:ArrayCollection;
```

```
private function initApp():void {
    this.srv.send();
}

private function onResult(evt:ResultEvent):void {
    this.homesForSale = evt.result.data.region;
}

private function sortRanges(obj1:Object, obj2:Object):int {
    var value1:Number = obj1.range.range1;
    var value2:Number = obj2.range.range1;

    if(value1 < value2) {
        return -1;
    } else if(value1 > value2) {
        return 1;
    } else {
        return 0;
    }
}
```

Here, the filter function is applied to the `dataProvider` of the `DataGrid`, and the `refresh()` method is called to ensure that the grid will redraw all of its renderers:

```
private function applyFilter():void {
    if(this.homesForSale.filterFunction == null) {
        this.homesForSale.filterFunction = this.filterCities;
    }
    this.homesForSale.refresh();
}
```

The filter method used simply returns `true` if the item should be included in the filtered array, and `false` if it should not:

```
private function filterCities(item:Object):Boolean {
    var match:Boolean = true;

    if(cityFilter.text != "") {
        var city:String = item["city"];
        var filter:String = this.cityFilter.text;
        if(!city ||
                city.toLowerCase().indexOf(filter.toLowerCase()) < 0) {
            match = false;
        }
    }

    return match;
}
            ]]>
        </fx:Script>
    </s:Application>
```

See Also

Recipe 9.2

9.4 Create Custom Headers for a DataGrid

Problem

You want to customize the header for a `DataGrid` by adding a `CheckBox`.

Solution

Extend the `DataGridHeaderRenderer` class by overriding the `createChildren()` and `updateDisplayList()` methods to add a `CheckBox`.

Discussion

This recipe builds on Recipe 9.3 by specifying a custom header renderer for the `city` `DataGridColumn`. Creating a custom header renderer is similar to creating a custom item renderer or item editor. A class reference that implements the `IFactory` interface is passed to the `headerRenderer` property of the `DataGridColumn`, and the column takes care of instantiating the object. This example uses a renderer class called `Check BoxHeaderRenderer` to create a header with a `CheckBox` contained within it:

```
<s:Application xmlns:fx="http://ns.adobe.com/mxml/2009"
               xmlns:s="library://ns.adobe.com/flex/spark"
               xmlns:mx="library://ns.adobe.com/flex/halo"
               creationComplete="initApp()">

    <s:layout><s:VerticalLayout/></s:layout>

    <fx:Declarations>
        <mx:HTTPService id="srv" url="assets/example.xml" resultFormat="object"
                        result="onResult(event)"/>
    </fx:Declarations>

    <s:TextInput id="cityFilter" change="applyFilter()"/>

    <mx:DataGrid id="grid" width="100%" height="100%"
                 dataProvider="{homesForSale}">
        <mx:columns>
            <mx:DataGridColumn headerText="Total No." dataField="total"/>
```

Because the custom header renderer should be set for this particular column and not the others, you set the `headerRenderer` property on the `DataGrid` column to the class name that will be used to create the headers:

```
            <mx:DataGridColumn headerText="City" dataField="city"
                headerRenderer="oreilly.cookbook.flex4.CheckBoxHeaderRenderer"/>
            <mx:DataGridColumn headerText="State" dataField="state"/>
            <mx:DataGridColumn headerText="Price Ranges [&lt;350K]
                               [350K -600K] [&gt;600K]" dataField="range"
                               itemRenderer="oreilly.cookbook.flex4.RangeRenderer"
                               sortCompareFunction="sortRanges"/>
        </mx:columns>
    </mx:DataGrid>
```

```
<fx:Script>
    <![CDATA[
        import mx.events.FlexEvent;
        import mx.collections.ArrayCollection;
        import mx.rpc.events.ResultEvent;

        [Bindable]
        private var homesForSale:ArrayCollection;

        private function initApp():void {
            this.srv.send();
        }

        private function onResult(evt:ResultEvent):void {
            this.homesForSale = evt.result.data.region;
        }

        private function sortRanges(obj1:Object, obj2:Object):int {
            var value1:Number = obj1.range.range1;
            var value2:Number = obj2.range.range1;

            if(value1 < value2) {
                return -1;
            } else if(value1 > value2) {
                return 1;
            } else {
                return 0;
            }
        }

        private function applyFilter():void {
            if(this.homesForSale.filterFunction == null) {
                this.homesForSale.filterFunction = this.filterCities;
            }
            this.homesForSale.refresh();
        }

        private function filterCities(item:Object):Boolean {
            var match:Boolean = true;

            if(cityFilter.text != "") {
                var city:String = item["city"];
                var filter:String = this.cityFilter.text;
                if(!city || city.toLowerCase().indexOf(filter.toLowerCase())
                        < 0) {
                    match = false;
                }
            }
            return match;
        }

    ]]>
    </fx:Script>
</s:Application>
```

The code for the custom header renderer class `CheckBoxHeaderRenderer` follows. Note that it overrides the `createChildren()` method of the `UIComponent` class to create a new `CheckBox` and add it to the display list. The `updateDisplayList()` method forces the `CheckBox` to resize itself to its default size:

```
package oreilly.cookbook.flex4 {

    import flash.events.Event;
    import mx.containers.Canvas;
    import mx.controls.CheckBox;
    import mx.controls.listClasses.IListItemRenderer;
    import mx.events.DataGridEvent;

    public class CheckBoxHeaderRenderer extends Canvas implements IListItemRenderer
    {

        private var selector:CheckBox;

        override public function set data(value:Object):void {

        }
        override public function get data():Object { return null; }

        override protected function createChildren():void {
            super.createChildren();
            this.selector = new CheckBox();
            this.selector.x = 5;
            this.addChild(this.selector);
        }

        override protected function updateDisplayList(unscaledWidth:Number,
                unscaledHeight:Number):void {
            super.updateDisplayList(unscaledWidth, unscaledHeight);
            this.selector.setActualSize(this.selector.getExplicitOrMeasuredWidth(),
                    this.selector.getExplicitOrMeasuredHeight());
        }
    }
}
```

Recipe 9.5 explains how to dispatch events from the custom renderer and handle them.

You can also use a Spark component to render the header of a `DataGrid` column by extending the `IListItemRenderer` interface, as shown in Recipe 9.1.

See Also

Recipes 9.1 and 9.5

9.5 Handle Events from a DataGrid

Problem

You need to manage events dispatched by the DataGrid and its item renderers.

Solution

Use the owner property inside the item renderer to dispatch an event from the parent DataGrid.

Discussion

In the previous recipe, a custom header renderer was created for a DataGridColumn by passing a class reference to the headerRenderer property of the column. In this recipe, the header renderer class used in Recipe 9.4 will be extended. When the CheckBox in the header renderer is clicked, the class will dispatch an event up to the DataGrid that owns the column in which the headerRenderer is used:

```
<s:Application xmlns:fx="http://ns.adobe.com/mxml/2009"
               xmlns:s="library://ns.adobe.com/flex/spark"
               xmlns:mx="library://ns.adobe.com/flex/halo"
               xmlns:mx="http://www.adobe.com/2006/mxml"
               creationComplete="initApp()">
    <s:layout><s:VerticalLayout/></s:layout>

    <fx:Declarations>
        <mx:HTTPService id="srv" url="assets/homesassets.xml"
                        resultFormat="object" result="onResult(event)"/>
    </fx:Declarations>

    <mx:Form>
        <mx:FormItem label="City">
            <mx:TextInput id="cityFilter" change="applyFilter()"/>
        </mx:FormItem>
    </mx:Form>

    <mx:DataGrid id="grid" width="100%" height="100%" dataProvider="{homesForSale}"
                 creationComplete="assignListeners()">
        <mx:columns>
            <mx:DataGridColumn headerText="Total No." dataField="total"/>
            <mx:DataGridColumn headerText="City" sortable="false"
                               headerRenderer="CheckBoxHeaderRenderer2"
                               dataField="city"/>
            <mx:DataGridColumn headerText="State" dataField="state"/>
            <mx:DataGridColumn headerText="Price Ranges [&lt;350K] [350K -600K]
                               [&gt;600K]" dataField="range"
                               itemRenderer="oreilly.cookbook.flex4.RangeRenderer"
                               sortCompareFunction="sortRanges"/>
        </mx:columns>
    </mx:DataGrid>
```

```
<fx:Script>
    <![CDATA[
        import mx.events.FlexEvent;
        import mx.collections.ArrayCollection;
        import mx.rpc.events.ResultEvent;

        [Bindable]
        private var homesForSale:ArrayCollection;

        private function initApp():void {
            this.srv.send();
        }

        private function onResult(evt:ResultEvent):void {
            this.homesForSale = evt.result.data.region;
        }

        private function sortRanges(obj1:Object, obj2:Object):int{
            var value1:Number = obj1.range.range1;
            var value2:Number = obj2.range.range1;

            if(value1 < value2) {
                return -1;
            }
            else if(value1 > value2) {
                return 1;
            }
            else {
                return 0;
            }
        }

        private function applyFilter():void {
            if(this.homesForSale.filterFunction == null) {
                this.homesForSale.filterFunction = this.filterCities;
            }
            this.homesForSale.refresh();
        }

        private function filterCities(item:Object):Boolean {
            var match:Boolean = true;

            if(cityFilter.text != "") {
                var city:String = item["city"];
                var filter:String = this.cityFilter.text;
                if(!city ||
                    city.toLowerCase().indexOf(filter.toLowerCase()) < 0) {
                    match = false;
                }
            }

            return match;
        }
```

Because the event bubbles up from the `DataGridColumn` to the parent `DataGrid`, you can simply add an event listener to the `DataGrid` itself to capture the event. The `onColumn Select()` method will receive a custom event of type `ColumnSelectedEvent` that will contain information about the column in which the header renderer is used:

```
private function assignListeners():void {
    this.grid.addEventListener(ColumnSelectedEvent.COLUMN_SELECTED,
                                onColumnSelect);
}

private function onColumnSelect(evt:ColumnSelectedEvent):void {
    trace("column selected = " + evt.colIdx);
}

    ]]>
  </fx:Script>
</s:Application>
```

This example code builds on the previous recipe by adding a new header renderer, `CheckBoxHeaderRenderer2`, for the city column of the `DataGrid`. The code also assigns a listener to the `ColumnSelectedEvent`, which is a custom event dispatched by the `Data Grid`. The listener function `onColumnSelected()` merely traces out the selected column index to the console for display purposes.

The component that renders the header of the `DataGrid` will implement the `IDropIn ListItemRenderer` interface, which gives the renderer not only access to the data that has been passed into it via the `owner` property of the `BaseListData` type, but also access to the `List` or `DataGridColumn` that the renderer belongs to. The `BaseListData` type defines the following properties:

columnIndex : int
> The index of the column of the `List`-based control relative to the currently visible columns of the control, where the first column is at an index of 1.

owner : IUIComponent
> The `List` or `DataGridColumn` object that owns this renderer.

rowIndex : int
> The index of the row of the `DataGrid`, `List`, or `Tree` control relative to the currently visible rows of the control, where the first row is at an index of 1.

uid : String
> The unique identifier for this item. Each item in an `itemRenderer` is given a unique id so that even if the data is the same for two or more `itemRenderer`s, the `List Base` component will still be able to identify them.

Here is the `CheckBoxHeaderRenderer2` class:

```
package oreilly.cookbook.flex4 {
    import flash.events.MouseEvent;

    import mx.containers.Canvas;
    import mx.controls.CheckBox;
```

```
import mx.controls.DataGrid;
import mx.controls.listClasses.BaseListData;
import mx.controls.listClasses.IDropInListItemRenderer;
import mx.controls.listClasses.IListItemRenderer;

public class CheckBoxHeaderRenderer2 extends Canvas implements
        IDropInListItemRenderer, IListItemRenderer {

    protected var selector:CheckBox;
    protected var _listData:BaseListData;

    override protected function createChildren():void {
        super.createChildren();
        this.selector = new CheckBox();
        this.selector.x = 5;
        this.addChild(this.selector);
        this.selector.addEventListener(MouseEvent.CLICK,
                                       dispatchColumnSelected);
    }
```

The IDropInListItemRenderer interface defines a getter and setter for listData that
allows the parent DataGrid to pass in additional information about the data for that
particular item that includes a reference to the parent DataGrid itself (this will come in
useful later, when you'll determine where the item renderer is located within the Data
Grid):

```
[Bindable("dataChange")]
public function get listData():BaseListData {
    return _listData;
}

public function set listData(value:BaseListData):void {
    _listData = value;
}

override public function set data(data:Object):void { }

override public function get data():Object { return null; }

override protected function updateDisplayList(unscaledWidth:Number,
        unscaledHeight:Number):void {
    super.updateDisplayList(unscaledWidth, unscaledHeight);

    this.selector.setActualSize(this.selector.getExplicitOrMeasuredWidth(),
            this.selector.getExplicitOrMeasuredHeight());
}

private function dispatchColumnSelected(evt:MouseEvent):void {
    var event:ColumnSelectedEvent = new ColumnSelectedEvent(
            ColumnSelectedEvent.COLUMN_SELECTED, listData.columnIndex,
            selector.selected );
    DataGrid(listData.owner).dispatchEvent(event);
}
    }
}
```

Note that although the DataGrid dispatches the ColumnSelectedEvent, the event originates from the header renderer instance when the checkbox is selected. The dispatchColumnSelected() method of the CheckBoxHeaderRenderer2 class uses the list Data.owner property to get a reference to the parent DataGrid and subsequently dispatches the event from the "owner":

```
DataGrid(listData.owner).dispatchEvent(event);
```

Finally, let's take a look at the code for the custom event class CustomSelectedEvent. This simply extends the Event class with two properties, colIdx to store the column index and isSelected to indicate whether the column is selected:

```
package {
    import flash.events.Event;

    public class ColumnSelectedEvent extends Event {

        public var colIdx:int;
        public var isSelected:Boolean;

        public static const COLUMN_SELECTED:String = "columnSelected";

        public function ColumnSelectedEvent(type:String, colIdx:Int,
                isSelected:Boolean) {
            super(type);

            // set the new property
            this.colIdx = colIdx;
            this.isSelected = isSelected;
        }

        override public function clone():Event {
            return new ColumnSelectedEvent(type, colIdx,isSelected);
        }
    }
}
```

9.6 Enable Drag and Drop in a DataGrid

Problem

You want to make items in a DataGrid drag-and-drop enabled, so that users can drag them from one grid to another.

Solution

Set the dragEnabled property to true on the source DataGrid and the dropEnabled property to true on the destination DataGrid.

Discussion

Enabling drag-and-drop in list-based controls such as `DataGrid` is often as simple as setting the appropriate properties to `true`, because the Flex Framework takes care of all the underlying work to support dragging and dropping. For example, the following example sets the `dragEnabled` property of the `DataGrid` to `true`, which essentially enables the functionality to drag items outside this control. Notice that the `dropEnabled` property on the `DataGrid` is also set to `true`, which enables the functionality for this control to accept items dropped inside it:

```
<s:Application xmlns:fx="http://ns.adobe.com/mxml/2009"
               xmlns:s="library://ns.adobe.com/flex/spark"
               xmlns:mx="library://ns.adobe.com/flex/halo"
               xmlns:mx="http://www.adobe.com/2006/mxml"
               layout="horizontal" creationComplete="initApp()">
    <fx:Declarations>
        <mx:HTTPService id="srv" url="assets/homesforsale.xml"
                        resultFormat="object" result="onResult(event)"/>
    </fx:Declarations>
    <mx:DataGrid id="grid" width="100%" height="100%" sortableColumns="false"
            dragEnabled="true" dataProvider="{homesForSale}">
        <mx:columns>
            <mx:DataGridColumn headerText="Total No." dataField="total"/>
            <mx:DataGridColumn headerText="City" sortable="false"
                            dataField="city"/>
            <mx:DataGridColumn headerText="State" dataField="state"/>
        </mx:columns>
    </mx:DataGrid>

    <mx:DataGrid width="100%" height="100%" dropEnabled="true">
        <mx:columns>
            <mx:DataGridColumn headerText="Total No." dataField="total"/>
            <mx:DataGridColumn headerText="City" sortable="false"
                            dataField="city"/>
            <mx:DataGridColumn headerText="State" dataField="state"/>
        </mx:columns>
    </mx:DataGrid>

    <fx:Script>
        <![CDATA[
            import mx.events.FlexEvent;
            import mx.collections.ArrayCollection;
            import mx.rpc.events.ResultEvent;

            [Bindable]
            private var homesForSale:ArrayCollection;

            private function initApp():void {
                this.srv.send();
            }

            private function onResult(evt:ResultEvent):void {
                this.homesForSale = evt.result.data.region;
            }
```

```
                                    ]]>
                            </fx:Script>
                    </s:Application>
```

An additional property that affects drag-and-drop behavior is the `dragMoveEnabled`
property on the source `DataGrid`. This property dictates whether items are moved out
of the source or simply copied to the destination. The default value is `false`, which
results in an item being copied to the destination.

9.7 Edit Items in a DataGrid

Problem

You need to make items in a `DataGrid` editable.

Solution

Set the `editable` property of the `DataGrid` to `true`.

Discussion

In this example, two `DataGrid` controls are bound to the same `dataProvider`. The `edit`
`able` property of each grid is set to `true`, enabling editing of each cell within the grid.
Because both controls are bound to the same source `dataProvider`, editing a cell in one
grid propagates the change to the second grid:

```
<s:Application xmlns:fx="http://ns.adobe.com/mxml/2009"
               xmlns:s="library://ns.adobe.com/flex/spark"
               xmlns:mx="library://ns.adobe.com/flex/halo"
               xmlns:mx="http://www.adobe.com/2006/mxml"
               creationComplete="initApp()">

    <fx:Declarations>
        <mx:HTTPService id="srv" url="assets/homesforsale.xml"
                        resultFormat="object" result="onResult(event)"/>
    </fx:Declations>

    <mx:DataGrid id="grid" width="100%" height="100%" sortableColumns="false"
                 editable="true" dataProvider="{homesForSale}">
        <mx:columns>
            <mx:DataGridColumn headerText="Total No." dataField="total"/>
            <mx:DataGridColumn headerText="City" sortable="false"
                               dataField="city"/>
            <mx:DataGridColumn headerText="State" dataField="state"/>
        </mx:columns>
    </mx:DataGrid>

    <mx:DataGrid width="100%" height="100%"
                 editable="true" dataProvider="{homesForSale}">
        <mx:columns>
            <mx:DataGridColumn headerText="Total No." dataField="total"/>
```

```
                    <mx:DataGridColumn headerText="City" sortable="false"
                                       dataField="city"/>
                    <mx:DataGridColumn headerText="State" dataField="state"/>
                </mx:columns>
            </mx:DataGrid>

            <fx:Script>
                <![CDATA[
                    import mx.events.FlexEvent;
                    import mx.collections.ArrayCollection;
                    import mx.rpc.events.ResultEvent;

                    [Bindable]
                    private var homesForSale:ArrayCollection;

                    private function initApp():void {
                        this.srv.send();
                    }

                    private function onResult(evt:ResultEvent):void {
                        this.homesForSale = evt.result.data.region;
                    }
                ]]>
            </fx:Script>
        </s:Application>
```

9.8 Search Within a DataGrid and Autoscroll to the Match

Problem

You want to search for an item in a DataGrid and scroll to the match.

Solution

Use the findFirst() method of an IViewCursor on an ArrayCollection to search for an item. Use the scrollToIndex() method of the DataGrid to scroll to the index of the matching item.

Discussion

The keys to this technique are a DataGrid and a simple form that provides the user with a TextInput control to enter the search terms (in this example, a city name), as well as a button to start the search process. When the user clicks the button (search_btn), the DataGrid's dataProvider is searched for an exact match, and the corresponding row is selected and scrolled into view if not already visible.

The two main aspects of this solution are finding the matching item and positioning it in the DataGrid appropriately. To find the matching item, use an IViewCursor, which is an interface that specifies properties and methods to enumerate a collection view. All Flex collection objects support a createCursor() method that returns an instance of a concrete IViewCursor class that works with that particular collection. In this example, the following lines create a cursor for the ArrayCollection instance that acts as the dataProvider for the DataGrid:

```
private function onResult(evt:ResultEvent):void {
    var sort:Sort = new Sort();
    sort.fields = [ new SortField("city",true) ];
    this.homesForSale = evt.result.data.region;
    this.homesForSale.sort = sort;
    this.homesForSale.refresh();
    this.cursor = this.homesForSale.createCursor();
}
```

Note that you also assign a Sort object to the ArrayCollection that uses the city property of the dataProvider's items as a sortable field. This is because findFirst() and the other find methods of the IViewCursor can be invoked only on sorted views.

After a cursor has been created, it can be used to navigate through and query the associated view. The searchCity() method that follows is invoked when the user clicks the Search City button:

```
private function searchCity():void {
    if(search_ti.text != "") {
        if(this.cursor.findFirst({city:search_ti.text})) {
            var idx:int = this.homesForSale.getItemIndex(this.cursor.
                                                            current);
            this.grid.scrollToIndex(idx);
            this.grid.selectedItem = this.cursor.current;
        }
    }
}
```

In this method, the user's entry for the city is used as a search parameter for the find First() method of the IViewCursor. This method returns true for the first occurrence of the match found within the ArrayCollection and updates the current property of the cursor object to reference the matching item. After a matching item is found, the getItemIndex() method of the ArrayCollection is used to figure out the index of that item within the dataProvider. Finally, the DataGrid display is updated by using the scrollToIndex() method to scroll to the matching index, and the selectedItem property of the grid is set to the matching item.

The complete listing follows:

```
<s:Application xmlns:fx="http://ns.adobe.com/mxml/2009"
                xmlns:s="library://ns.adobe.com/flex/spark"
                xmlns:mx="library://ns.adobe.com/flex/halo"
                creationComplete="initApp()">

    <fx:Declarations>
        <mx:HTTPService id="srv" url="assets/homesforsale.xml"
                        resultFormat="object" result="onResult(event)"/>
    </fx:Declarations>

    <s:Group>
```

```
            <s:layout><s:HorizontalLayout/></s:layout>
            <s:Label text="Search">
            <s:TextInput id="search_ti"/>
            <s:Button label="Search City" click="searchCity()"/>
        </s:Group>

        <mx:DataGrid id="grid" width="300" height="150" editable="true"
                    dataProvider="{homesForSale}">
            <mx:columns>
                <mx:DataGridColumn headerText="Total No."dataField="total"/>
                <mx:DataGridColumn headerText="City" dataField="city"/>
                <mx:DataGridColumn headerText="State" dataField="state"/>
            </mx:columns>
        </mx:DataGrid>

        <fx:Script>
            <![CDATA[
                import mx.collections.SortField;
                import mx.collections.Sort;
                import mx.collections.IViewCursor;
                import mx.events.FlexEvent;
                import mx.collections.ArrayCollection;
                import mx.rpc.events.ResultEvent;

                [Bindable]
                private var homesForSale:ArrayCollection;
                private var cursor:IViewCursor;

                private function initApp():void {
                    this.srv.send();
                }

                private function onResult(evt:ResultEvent):void {
                    var sort:Sort = new Sort();
                    sort.fields = [ new SortField("city",true) ];
                    this.homesForSale = evt.result.data.region;
                    this.homesForSale.sort = sort;
                    this.homesForSale.refresh();
                    this.cursor = this.homesForSale.createCursor();
                }

                private function searchCity():void {
                    if(search_ti.text != "") {
                        if(this.cursor.findFirst({city:search_ti.text})) {
                            var idx:int = this.homesForSale.getItemIndex(this.cursor.
                                                                current);
                            this.grid.scrollToIndex(idx);
                            this.grid.selectedItem = this.cursor.current;
                        }
                    }
                }

            ]]>
        </fx:Script>
</s:Application>
```

9.9 Generate a Summary for Flat Data by Using a Grouping Collection

Contributed by Sreenivas Ramaswamy (*http://flexpearls.blogspot.com*)

Problem

You need to generate summary values for flat data in a grid.

Solution

Use `GroupingCollection2` to generate summary values for flat data and configure the `AdvancedDataGrid` such that it looks like you have a summary for the data.

Discussion

This recipe and the next one make use of the `AdvancedDataGrid` control, which is included with the Data Visualization package for Flash Builder. Though you can replicate this functionality without using the `AdvancedDataGrid`, it is much easier to implement using this control, which is why we've decided to include these two recipes in this book.

To generate a summary for flat data, use the `GroupingCollection2` class and configure the `AdvancedDataGrid` to display it as a flat data summary. When generating the summary, you don't want to sort and group on any existing `dataField` because you want to display data from the flat data. Instead, the example code generates a dummy group using an invalid grouping field (specifically, the code uses `fieldNameNotPresent` as the `dataField` value for `GroupingField`). You can then specify the summary you want using the `SummaryRow` and `SummaryField2` objects.

With the summary ready, you can take up the second task. When a `GroupingCollection2` instance is fed to the `dataProvider`, the data provider will try to display the collection in a tree view, as `GroupingCollection2` implements `IHierarchicalData`. Internally, it is converted into a `HierarchicalCollectionView` and the `dataProvider` returns a `HierarchicalCollectionView` instance. (This is similar to feeding an array to the `dataProvider`, which gets converted to an `ArrayCollection` internally.) You can control the display of the root node by using `HierarchicalCollectionView`'s `showRoot` property. By setting it to `false`, you can prevent the dummy group from being displayed.

By default, the `AdvancedDataGrid` control uses the `DataGridGroupItemRenderer` to display hierarchical data. This `itemRenderer` displays the folder and disclosure icons for parent items. By specifying the default `DataGridItemRenderer` as `AdvancedDataGrid.groupItemRenderer`, you can prevent the group icons from being displayed. The `DataGrid` also defines a `groupLabelFunction` property that defines the method the grid will use to determine the label to be displayed for any parent node with its `dataProvider`.

The complete listing follows:

```
<s:Application xmlns:fx="http://ns.adobe.com/mxml/2009"
               xmlns:s="library://ns.adobe.com/flex/spark"
               xmlns:mx="library://ns.adobe.com/flex/halo"
               width="460" height="428">

    <fx:Script>
        <![CDATA[
            import mx.controls.DataGridClasses.DataGridItemRenderer;
            import mx.collections.IGroupingCollection;
            import mx.controls.dataGridClasses.AdvancedDataGridColumn;
            import mx.collections.GroupingField;
            import mx.collections.Grouping;
            import mx.collections.ArrayCollection;
            import mx.collections.GroupingCollection2;
            var flatData:ArrayCollection = new ArrayCollection(
                    [{ Region:"Southwest", Territory:"Arizona",
                       Territory_Rep:"Barbara Jennings", Estimate:40000,
                       Actual:38865 },
                     { Region:"Southwest", Territory:"Arizona",
                       Territory_Rep:"Dana Binn", Estimate:30000, Actual:29885 },
                     { Region:"Southwest", Territory:"Central California",
                       Territory_Rep:"Joe Schmoe", Estimate:30000, Actual:29134 },
                     { Region:"Southwest", Territory:"Northern California",
                       Territory_Rep:"Lauren Ipsum", Estimate:40000,
                       Actual:38805 },
                     { Region:"Southwest", Territory:"Northern California",
                       Territory_Rep:"T.R. Smith", Estimate:40000, Actual:55498 },
                     { Region:"Southwest", Territory:"Southern California",
                       Territory_Rep:"Jane Grove", Estimate:45000, Actual:44913 },
                     { Region:"Southwest", Territory:"Southern California",
                       Territory_Rep:"Alice Treu", Estimate:45000, Actual:44985 },
                     { Region:"Southwest", Territory:"Nevada",
                       Territory_Rep:"Bethany Pittman", Estimate:45000,
                       Actual:52888 }

                    ]);
```

Here, the `styleFunction` property of the `DataGrid` is used to format the `itemRenderers` that possess the `summary` property within their data object:

```
            private function formatSummary(data:Object, col:DataGridColumn):
                    Object {
                if (data.hasOwnProperty("summary")) {
                    return { color:0xFF0000, fontWeight:"bold", fontSize:12 };
                }

                return {};
            }

            private function flatSummaryObject():Object {
                return { Territory_Rep:"Total", summary:true };
            }

        ]]>
    </fx:Script>
```

The `DataGridItemRenderer` is used here as the `groupItemRenderer` to avoid displaying the icons in the first column. The `groupItemRenderer` property specifies the renderer to be used for branch nodes in the navigation tree. A branch node is a graphical representation of a parent node—that is, a node with children—in the `dataProvider`:

```
<mx:AdvancedDataGrid id="adg"
                    creationComplete="groupedData.refresh();
                            adg.dataProvider.showRoot=false"
                    groupItemRenderer="mx.controls.dataGridClasses.
                            AdvancedDataGridItemRenderer"
                    x="30" y="30" wid mth="400" height="377"
                    styleFunction="formatSummary">
    <mx:dataProvider>
        <mx:GroupingCollection2 id="groupedData" source="{flatData}">
            <mx:Grouping>
                <!-- use some dummy field and set showRoot=false for the ADG
                dataProvider -->
                <mx:GroupingField name="fieldNameNotPresent">
                    <mx:summaries>
                        <!-- use the summaryObjectFunction to return a custom
                        object that can then be used in the format function to
                        detect a summary row -->
                        <mx:SummaryRow summaryPlacement="last"
                                summaryObjectFunction="flatSummaryObject">
                            <mx:fields>
                                <mx:SummaryField2 dataField="Estimate" />
                                <mx:SummaryField2 dataField="Actual" />
                            </mx:fields>
                        </mx:SummaryRow>
                    </mx:summaries>
                </mx:GroupingField>
            </mx:Grouping>
        </mx:GroupingCollection2>

    </mx:dataProvider>

    <mx:groupedColumns>
        <mx:DataGridColumn headerText = "Territory Rep"
                        dataField="Territory_Rep" />

        <mx:DataGridColumn Group headerText="Sales Figures" textAlign="center">
            <mx:DataGridColumn headerText = "Estimate" textAlign="center"
                            dataField="Estimate" width="100" />

            <mx:DataGridColumn headerText = "Actual" textAlign="center"
                            dataField="Actual" width="100" />
        </mx:DataGridColumn Group>
    </mx:groupedColumns>
</mx:AdvancedDataGrid>
</s:Application>
```

9.10 Create an Async Refresh for a Grouping Collection

Contributed by Sreenivas Ramaswamy (*http://flexpearls.blogspot.com*)

Problem

You want to asynchronously refresh the contents of a very large `GroupingCollection2`'s grid so that it redraws only when called.

Solution

Use `GroupingCollection.refresh(async:Boolean)` with the `async` flag set to `true`.

Discussion

The `GroupingCollection.refresh()` method takes a flag to indicate whether the grouping needs to be carried out synchronously or asynchronously. When the number of input rows is large, this flag can be set to `true` in the call to refresh the grouping result displayed earlier. This can also be used to avoid the Flash Player timing out when a `GroupingCollection.refresh()` call is taking a long time.

This asynchronous generation of groups also helps in scenarios when users want to group items interactively. `GroupingCollection.cancelRefresh()` can be used to stop an ongoing grouping and start a fresh grouping based on new user inputs.

In the following example, clicking the `Button` labeled "Populate ADG" generates random data and displays it in a `DataGrid`. You can modify the number of data rows by using the numeric stepper. Clicking the Group button starts the asynchronous refresh, and the `DataGrid` starts displaying the results immediately. The user can cancel grouping at any time by clicking the `Button` labeled "Cancel Grouping." Here's the code:

```
<s:Application xmlns:fx="http://ns.adobe.com/mxml/2009"
              xmlns:s="library://ns.adobe.com/flex/spark"
              xmlns:mx="library://ns.adobe.com/flex/halo"
              width="520" height="440">

    <fx:Script>
        <![CDATA[
            import mx.controls.Alert;
            import mx.collections.IGroupingCollection;
            import mx.collections.GroupingField;
            import mx.collections.Grouping;
            import mx.collections.GroupingCollection2;

            [Bindable]
            private var generatedData:Array = [];

            private var companyNames:Array = ["Adobe", "BEA", "Cosmos", "Dogma",
                    "Enigma", "Fury", "Gama", "Hima", "Indian", "Jaadu", "Karish",
                    "Linovo", "Micro", "Novice", "Oyster", "Puple", "Quag",
                    "Rendi", "Scrup", "Tempt",  "Ubiqut", "Verna", "Wision",
```

```
                    "Xeno", "Yoga", "Zeal" ];

        private var products:Array = [ "Infuse", "MaxVis", "Fusion", "Horizon",
                "Apex", "Zeeta", "Maza", "Orion", "Omega", "Zoota", "Quata",
                "Morion" ];

        private var countries:Array = [ "India", "USA", "Canada", "China",
                "Japan", "France", "Germany", "UK", "Brazil", "Italy", "Chile",
                "Bhutan", "Sri Lanka" ];

        private var years:Array = ["2000", "2001", "2002", "2003", "2004",
                "2005", "2006", "2007", "2008", "2009", "2010", "2011", "2012",
                "2013", "2014", "2015", "2016","2017", "2018", "2019", "2020",
                "2021", "2022", "2023", "2024" ];
        private var quarters:Array = ["Q1", "Q2", "Q3", "Q4"];
        private var months:Array = ["Jan", "Feb", "Mar", "Apr", "May", "Jun",
                "Jul", "Aug", "Sep", "Oct", "Nov", "Dec" ];

        private var sales:Array = [ 1, 2, 3, 4, 5, 6, 7, 8, 9, 10] ;

        private var costs:Array = [ 1, 2, 3, 4, 5, 6, 7, 8, 9, 10] ;

        private var dimNameMatch:Object = { Company:companyNames,
                Product:products, Country:countries, Year:years,
                Quarter:quarters, Month:months, Sales:sales, Cost:costs};
```

The preceding arrays are randomly selected from to create a **dataProvider** with the correct number of rows:

```
        private function generateData():void {
            generatedData = [];
            var length:int = numRows.value;
            var dimNameMap:Object = dimNameMatch;
            for (var index:int = 0; index < length; ++index) {
                var newObj:Object = {};
                for (var prop:String in dimNameMap) {
                    var input:Array = dimNameMap[prop];
                    var inputIndex:int = Math.random()*input.length;
                    newObj[prop] = input[inputIndex];
                }
                generatedData.push(newObj);
            }
        }

        private function populateADG():void {
            if (generatedData.length != numRows.value)
                generateData();
            adg.dataProvider = generatedData;
        }

        [Bindable]
        private var gc:GroupingCollection2;
        private function groupData():void {
            var fields:Array = [];
            if (company.selected)
                fields.push(new GroupingField("Company"));
```

```
            if (product.selected)
                fields.push(new GroupingField("Product"));

            if (year.selected)
                fields.push(new GroupingField("Year"));

            if (fields.length == 0) {
                Alert.show("Select at least one of the items to group on");
                return;
            }

            gc = new GroupingCollection2();
            gc.source = generatedData;

            gc.grouping = new Grouping();

            gc.grouping.fields = fields;

            // use async refresh so that we get to see the results early
            gc.refresh(true);

            adg.dataProvider = gc;
        }

        private function handleOptionChange():void {
            // user has not started grouping yet
            if (!gc)
                return;

            // stop any refresh that might be going on
            gc.cancelRefresh();

            var fields:Array = [];
            if (company.selected)
                fields.push(new GroupingField("Company"));

            if (product.selected)
                fields.push(new GroupingField("Product"));

            if (year.selected)
                fields.push(new GroupingField("Year"));

            // user might have checked off everything
            if (fields.length == 0) {
                return;
            }

            gc.grouping.fields = fields;

            gc.refresh(true);
        }
    ]]>
</fx:Script>
```

```
<s:HGroup>
    <s:NumericStepper id="numRows" stepSize="1000" minimum="1000"
                        maximum="10000" />
    <s:Button label="Populate ADG" click="populateADG()"
                id="populateADGButton"/>
</s:HGroup >
<s:VGroup>
    <s:HGroup>
        <mx:AdvancedDataGrid id="adg" width="100%" height="260" >
            <mx:columns>
                <mx:DataGridColumn dataField="Company" />
                <mx:DataGridColumn dataField="Product" />
                <mx:DataGridColumn dataField="Year" />
                <mx:DataGridColumn dataField="Sales" />
            </mx:columns>
        </mx:AdvancedDataGrid>
    </s:HGroup>
    <s:HGroup>
```

This allows the user to select the grouping fields:

```
<s:Label text="Grouping fields:" />

<!-- We can use cancelRefresh() to stop the refresh and immediately
call refresh(true) in the change handler -->
<s:CheckBox id="company" label="Company" selected="true"
            click="handleOptionChange()"/>
<s:CheckBox id="product" label="Product" click="handleOptionChange()"/>
<s:CheckBox id="year" label="Year" click="handleOptionChange()"/>
</s:HGroup>
<s:HGroup>
    <mx:Button label="Group" click="groupData()" />
```

Here, the cancelRefresh() method of the GroupingCollection2 class is invoked:

```
<s:Button label="Cancel Grouping" click="gc.cancelRefresh()"
            enabled="{gc != null}"/>
        </s:HGroup>
    </s:VGroup>
</s:Application>
```

The three checkboxes allow different combinations of groupings to be performed. Users can change the grouping choice while a refresh is going on. The cancel Refresh() method is used to stop the DataGrid from creating and displaying the new grouping.

CHAPTER 10

Video

With a high level of adoption and good codec support, the Flash Player is a powerful platform for creating video players. Customizing these video players has never been easier, thanks to the Flex 4 SDK's improved video support and the new Spark skinning architecture. The `s:VideoPlayer` component contains skin parts for the individual video controls, including a play/pause button, video scrub bar, volume control, and full screen button. This chapter covers the basics of setting, using, and skinning the video players provided in the SDK.

This chapter looks at the *Open Source Media Framework* (OSMF) for displaying video within a Flex application. The OSMF is an ActionScript 3-based extensible media framework designed to facilitate video monetization through advertising and standard player development. As the name implies, it is an open source project; it was created by Adobe (*http://opensource.adobe.com*), and although it is not dependent on any Flex classes, it is included in the SDK. The fact that it is not dependent on the Flex framework allows the OSMF to facilitate standard video player development across Flex and ActionScript-only projects.

10.1 Create a Basic Video Player

Problem

You need to display video in your Flex application.

Solution

Use `s:VideoDisplay` to create a basic chromeless video player.

Discussion

The `s:VideoDisplay` component is a simple way to display video. Because the component is chromeless, it does not contain any controls. You must, therefore, control the video by external components via ActionScript, which is discussed in the next recipe.

This application contains an instance of `s:VideoDisplay` with its `source` property pointing to a video file located at *assets/video/sample.flv*:

```
<?xml version="1.0" encoding="utf-8"?>
<s:Application xmlns:fx="http://ns.adobe.com/mxml/2009"
               xmlns:s="library://ns.adobe.com/flex/spark">
    <s:layout>
        <s:VerticalLayout/>
    </s:layout>
    <s:VideoDisplay id="videoDisplay" autoPlay="true"
                    autoRewind="true" source="assets/video/sample.flv"/>

</s:Application>
```

The `s:VideoDisplay` instance's `autoPlay` property is set to `true`, which causes the video to play automatically once enough of the video file is downloaded. Because this example is only using an instance of `s:VideoDisplay` without any playback controls, this is the simplest way to view the video.

See Also

Recipe 10.2

10.2 Display Video Playback Progress

Problem

You need to display the playback progress of a video.

Solution

Add event listeners to the `currentTimeChange` and `durationChange` events dispatched by `s:VideoDisplay`.

Discussion

The following example renders a simple video player, as in the previous recipe, but it adds the functionality of a play/pause toggle button. Also, through an instance of `s:Label`, it displays the current playback position and total playback time to the user:

```
<?xml version="1.0" encoding="utf-8"?>
<s:Application xmlns:fx="http://ns.adobe.com/mxml/2009"
               xmlns:s="library://ns.adobe.com/flex/spark">
    <fx:Script>
        <![CDATA[
            import org.osmf.events.TimeEvent;

            [Bindable]
            private var currentTime:String = '0';
```

```
            [Bindable]
            private var duration:String = '0';

            protected function toggleChangeHandler(event:Event):void {
                if (ToggleButton(event.target).selected) {
                    videoDisplay.play();
                    ToggleButton(event.target).label = 'Pause';
                } else {
                    videoDisplay.pause();
                    ToggleButton(event.target).label = 'Play';
                }
            }

            protected function videoCompleteHandler(event:TimeEvent):void {
                playButton.selected = false;
            }

            protected function videoTimeChangeHandler(event:TimeEvent):void {
                currentTime = event.time.toString();
            }

            protected function videoDurationChangeHandler(event:TimeEvent):void {
                duration = event.time.toString();
            }
        ]]>
    </fx:Script>
    <s:layout>
        <s:VerticalLayout/>
    </s:layout>
    <s:VideoDisplay id="videoDisplay" autoPlay="false"
                    complete="videoCompleteHandler(event)" autoRewind="true"
                    currentTimeChange="videoTimeChangeHandler(event)"
                    durationChange="videoDurationChangeHandler(event)"
                    source="assets/video/sample.flv"/>

    <s:ToggleButton id="playButton" label="Play/Pause"
                    change="toggleChangeHandler(event)"/>
    <s:Label id="playPosition" text="Time: {currentTime+' / '+duration}"/>

</s:Application>
```

In this example, the s:VideoDisplay instance, which has an id of videoDisplay, features event listeners on its complete, currentTimeChange, and durationChange events. The complete event is dispatched when the video reaches the end of its total duration. The associated event handler, videoCompleteHandler(), deselects the play/pause toggle button because the video automatically stops. The currentTimeChange event is dispatched when the current playback position is changed, either programmatically or while the video is playing. Its handler, videoTimeChangeHandler(), updates a String, current Time, which is bound to an instance of s:Label to show the end user the current playback position. Similarly, the durationChange event is dispatched when the total duration of the video changes; its handler, videoDurationChangeHandler(), updates the text property of the s:Label instance displayed to the user to reflect the new duration.

Notice that while both the currentTimeChange and durationChange events are instances of TimeEvent and contain the property time, the property represents different values for each: for currentTimeChange, time represents the video's current time, while for duration Change it specifies the video's total duration.

10.3 Create a Skinned Video Player

Problem

You want to display video with custom controls in your Flex application.

Solution

Use s:VideoPlayer to create a skinnable video player with its associated controls.

Discussion

The s:VideoPlayer component is a skinnable Spark video player that contains a wide range of skin parts and functionality for its associated controls. Although it contains more skin parts and states than most Spark components, s:VideoPlayer is simple to use, as demonstrated in the following application:

```
<?xml version="1.0" encoding="utf-8"?>
<s:Application xmlns:fx="http://ns.adobe.com/mxml/2009"
               xmlns:s="library://ns.adobe.com/flex/spark"
               xmlns:mx="library://ns.adobe.com/flex/mx">
    <fx:Style>
        @namespace s "library://ns.adobe.com/flex/spark";
        @namespace mx "library://ns.adobe.com/flex/mx";
        s|VideoPlayer {
            skinClass: ClassReference('skins.WireVideoPlayerSkin');
        }
    </fx:Style>
    <s:VideoPlayer source="assets/video/sample.flv"/>
</s:Application>
```

This application contains an instance of s:VideoPlayer that has its skin set to the component file *skins/WireVideoPlayerSkin.mxml* using CSS.

The s:VideoPlayer contains 12 skin parts, which are nested components defined in the host component. Of the 12 parts, the only one required in the associated skin file is videoDisplay; an instance of s:VideoDisplay is used to actually show the video. The remainder of the skin parts are optional controls that can be used to provide a wide range of customization. Another consequence of the complexity of controlling video is a significant number of states; s:VideoDisplay contains 16 states, and the default Spark skin contains 10 state groups.

The following skin file, *skins/WireVideoPlayerSkin.mxml*, is a MXML component that extends s:Skin and includes a play/pause button, play head and track bar, volume control, and full screen button:

```
<?xml version="1.0" encoding="utf-8"?>
<s:Skin xmlns:fx="http://ns.adobe.com/mxml/2009"
        xmlns:s="library://ns.adobe.com/flex/spark"
        alpha.disabledStates="0.5">
    <fx:Metadata>
        [HostComponent("spark.components.VideoPlayer")]
    </fx:Metadata>

    <!-- states -->
    <s:states>
        <s:State name="uninitialized"
                 stateGroups="uninitializedStates, normalStates"/>
        <s:State name="loading" stateGroups="loadingStates, normalStates"/>
        <s:State name="ready" stateGroups="readyStates, normalStates"/>
        <s:State name="playing" stateGroups="playingStates, normalStates"/>
        <s:State name="paused" stateGroups="pausedStates, normalStates"/>
        <s:State name="buffering" stateGroups="bufferingStates, normalStates"/>
        <s:State name="playbackError"
                 stateGroups="playbackErrorStates, normalStates"/>
        <s:State name="disabled" stateGroups="disabledStates, normalStates"/>
        <s:State name="uninitializedAndFullScreen"
                 stateGroups="uninitializedStates, fullScreenStates"/>
        <s:State name="loadingAndFullScreen"
                 stateGroups="loadingStates, fullScreenStates"/>
        <s:State name="readyAndFullScreen"
                 stateGroups="readyStates, fullScreenStates"/>
        <s:State name="playingAndFullScreen"
                 stateGroups="playingStates, fullScreenStates"/>
        <s:State name="pausedAndFullScreen"
                 stateGroups="pausedStates, fullScreenStates"/>
        <s:State name="bufferingAndFullScreen"
                 stateGroups="bufferingStates, fullScreenStates"/>
        <s:State name="playbackErrorAndFullScreen"
                 stateGroups="playbackErrorStates, fullScreenStates"/>
        <s:State name="disabledAndFullScreen"
                 stateGroups="disabledStates, fullScreenStates"/>
    </s:states>

    <fx:Declarations>
        <s:SolidColor id="wireFill" color="#FFFFFF"/>
        <s:SolidColorStroke id="wireStroke" color="#000000"/>
    </fx:Declarations>

    <s:Group minWidth="263" minHeight="184" left="0" right="0" top="0"
             bottom="0">
        <s:Rect bottom="1" left="1" right="1" top="1"
                bottom.fullScreenStates="0" left.fullScreenStates="0"
                right.fullScreenStates="0" top.fullScreenStates="0"
                fill="{wireFill}" stroke="{wireStroke}"/>
```

```
<s:VideoDisplay id="videoDisplay" bottom="24" left="1" right="1" top="1"
                bottom.fullScreenStates="0" left.fullScreenStates="0"
                right.fullScreenStates="0" top.fullScreenStates="0"/>
<s:Group left="0" right="0" height="24" bottom="0"
         bottom.fullScreenStates="150">
    <s:Group bottom="0" horizontalCenter="0" left="0" right="0"
             maxWidth.fullScreenStates="755" id="playerControls">
        <s:ToggleButton id="playPauseButton" left="0" bottom="0"
                        skinClass="skins.WirePlayPauseButtonSkin"
                        focusIn="event.target.depth=1"
                        focusOut="event.target.depth=0"/>
        <s:Group left="39" right="75" top="0" bottom="0">
            <s:Rect left="0" right="0" top="0" bottom="0"
                    fill="{wireFill}" stroke="{wireStroke}"/>
            <s:Rect left="1" right="1" top="1" height="11" alpha="0.3"
                    excludeFrom="fullScreenStates" fill="{wireFill}"
                    stroke="{wireStroke}"/>
            <s:Rect left="-1" right="0" top="0" bottom="0"
                    alpha.fullScreenStates="0.66" fill="{wireFill}"
                    stroke="{wireStroke}"/>
            <s:Group left="0" right="0" height="23" bottom="0">
                <s:layout>
                    <s:HorizontalLayout verticalAlign="middle" gap="1"/>
                </s:layout>
                <s:ScrubBar id="scrubBar" width="100%"
                            liveDragging="true"
                            skinClass="skins.WireScrubBarSkin"/>
                <s:Label id="currentTimeDisplay"
                         color.fullScreenStates="0xFFFFFF"/>
                <s:Label id="timeDivider" text="/"
                         color.fullScreenStates="0xFFFFFF"/>
                <s:Label id="durationDisplay"
                         color.fullScreenStates="0xFFFFFF"/>
            </s:Group>
        </s:Group>
        <s:VolumeBar id="volumeBar" snapInterval=".01" stepSize=".01"
                     liveDragging="true" right="37" bottom="0"
                     skinClass="skins.WireVolueBarSkin"
                     focusIn="event.target.depth=1"
                     focusOut="event.target.depth=0"/>
        <s:Button id="fullScreenButton" right="0" bottom="0"
                  label="Fullscreen"
                  skinClass="skins.WireFullScreenButtonSkin"
                  focusIn="event.target.depth=1"
                  focusOut="event.target.depth=0"/>
    </s:Group>
</s:Group>
</s:Group>
</s:Skin>
```

Because the s:VideoPlayer has nested skin parts that can be individually skinned, like
the instances of s:VolumeBar and the various buttons, if you want to create a completely
custom player you have to create individual skins for those components as well. The
code for the skins referenced in the preceding example (skins.WirePlayPauseButton

Skin, `skins.WireScrubBarSkin`, `skins.WireVolumeBarSkin`, and `skins.WireFullScreen`
`ButtonSkin`) is not shown here, but the skins are similar to those shown in Chapter 6.

10.4 Display Streaming Video

Problem

You need to display a streaming video in your Flex application.

Solution

Use the `s:VideoPlayer` or `s:VideoDisplay` component to display streaming video.

Discussion

The Flash Player can access video by:

- Embedding the video in a SWF file
- Progressive download
- Streaming the video from a server

Video files are often too large to be embedded in a SWF, so the most common way to deliver video from a server is through progressive download or streaming.

When the `source` property of a Flex video component is set to an external video file on a basic web server (IIS, Apache, etc.), the application will begin downloading the file and displaying the video even before finishing the download; this is called a *progressive download*. Besides usually being the simplest solution, this method has the benefit of not adding to the developer's software costs. One of the main downsides is that the file is downloaded from beginning to end, so the user must wait until a given portion has been loaded before she can skip to it.

Flash Media Server (FMS) is a server-side solution that can stream video over the *Real Time Media Protocol* (RTMP), which is Adobe's proprietary protocol for streaming audio, video, and data to the Flash Player. A few of the benefits of video streaming using FMS include:

- The video often can begin playing faster.
- It is slightly more difficult for a user to save the streamed content because it is not stored in the cache.
- The video can be streamed from any point, allowing the user to seek to a playback position that has not already been buffered.
- Live video can be delivered.

Depending on the size and scope of the project, however, FMS can be an expensive solution. An alternative is to take advantage of a hosted solution, such as the services provided by Influxis (*http://influxis.com*) or an open source server solution like Red5 (*http://osflash.org/red5*).

The following is an example of `s:VideoPlayer` displaying a streaming video. The instance of `s:VideoPlayer` contains a `source` property set to an instance of `s:DynamicStreamingVideoSource`. Notice in the example that the `host` property only points to a folder on the server, and the file itself is referenced in the nested instance of `s:DynamicStreamingVideoItem`:

```
<?xml version="1.0" encoding="utf-8"?>
<s:Application xmlns:fx="http://ns.adobe.com/mxml/2009"
               xmlns:s="library://ns.adobe.com/flex/spark"
               xmlns:mx="library://ns.adobe.com/flex/mx">
    <s:VideoPlayer>
        <s:source>
            <s:DynamicStreamingVideoSource host="rtmp://fmsexamples.adobe.com/vod/"
                                           streamType="recorded">
                <s:DynamicStreamingVideoItem streamName="mp4:_cs4promo_1000.f4v"/>
            </s:DynamicStreamingVideoSource>
        </s:source>
    </s:VideoPlayer>
</s:Application>
```

10.5 Display the Bytes Loaded of a Video

Problem

You want to make sure your users can see the percentage of a progressively downloaded video that has been loaded.

Solution

Use event listeners to capture events dispatched by `s:VideoDisplay` or `s:VideoPlayer` when the number of bytes loaded changes.

Discussion

As bytes of a video file are downloaded and displayed in an instance of `s:Video Display` (or `s:VideoPlayer`), the component periodically dispatches `LoadEvent` instances that contain a `bytesLoaded` property specifying the number of bytes loaded so far. In the following example, the application listens for this event and then calculates the percentage loaded by comparing the bytes loaded to the total bytes in the file:

```
<?xml version="1.0" encoding="utf-8"?>
<s:Application xmlns:fx="http://ns.adobe.com/mxml/2009"
               xmlns:s="library://ns.adobe.com/flex/spark">
    <s:layout>
        <s:VerticalLayout/>
    </s:layout>
```

```
<fx:Script>
    <![CDATA[
        import org.osmf.events.LoadEvent;

        [Bindable]
        private var percent:String = '0';

        protected function bytesLoadedChangeHandler(event:LoadEvent):void {
            var bytesLoaded:Number = event.bytes;
            var totalBytes:Number = event.currentTarget.bytesTotal;
            if (totalBytes > 0) {
                percent = Math.floor(100 * (bytesLoaded /
                                         totalBytes)).toString();
            }

        }
    ]]>
</fx:Script>
<s:VideoDisplay id="videoDisplay" autoPlay="true" autoRewind="true"
                source="http://helpexamples.com/flash/video/cuepoints.flv"
                bytesLoadedChange="bytesLoadedChangeHandler(event)"/>

<s:Label id="downloadProgressLabel" text="Loaded: {percent}%"/>

</s:Application>
```

Note that the LoadEvent is not dispatched every time a byte is loaded, but is updated
frequently enough to provide a useful progress dialog for the user.

10.6 Create a Basic Video Player Using the Open Source Media Framework

Problem

You want to leverage the Open Source Media Framework (OSMF) in your application
to display video.

Solution

Use the MediaPlayer class from the OSMF to create a video player.

Discussion

As mentioned earlier, the Open Source Media Framework is an ActionScript 3 library
that you can use with or without the Flex Framework. You cannot, however, add it to
a Flex application using only MXML, because it does not extend mx:UIComponent. There
are several ways around this, but one of the simplest is to add an instance of mx:UI

Component using MXML and, using the method `addChild()`, attach an instance of `Media Player` to it, as demonstrated in the following example:

```
<?xml version="1.0" encoding="utf-8"?>
<s:Application xmlns:fx="http://ns.adobe.com/mxml/2009"
               xmlns:s="library://ns.adobe.com/flex/spark"
               xmlns:mx="library://ns.adobe.com/flex/mx" xmlns:local="*"
               creationComplete="application1_creationCompleteHandler(event)">
    <fx:Script>
        <![CDATA[
            import mx.core.UIComponent;
            import mx.events.FlexEvent;

            import org.osmf.media.MediaPlayer;
            import org.osmf.media.URLResource;
            import org.osmf.net.NetLoader;
            import org.osmf.utils.URL;
            import org.osmf.video.VideoElement;

            private var source:String =
                    "http://helpexamples.com/flash/video/cuepoints.flv";

            protected function application1_creationCompleteHandler(
                    event:FlexEvent ):void {
                var playerSprite:MediaPlayer = new MediaPlayer();
                var resource:URLResource = new URLResource(new URL(source));
                var video:VideoElement = new VideoElement(new NetLoader,
    resource);

                playerSprite.media = video;
                helloWorldUIComponent.addChild(playerSprite.displayObject);
            }
        ]]>
    </fx:Script>
    <mx:UIComponent left="20" top="20" id="helloWorldUIComponent"/>
</s:Application>
```

10.7 Access and Display Cue Points Embedded in a Video File

Problem

You wish to display the cue points embedded in a video file's metadata.

Solution

Use the Open Source Media Framework (OSMF) to access and display cue points stored in the metadata of a video.

Discussion

Flash video (*.flv*) files can contain cue points as metadata. These cue points can include names, their temporal locations within the video file, and even such custom data as screenshots. Using the OSMF, you can display a list of the cue points, seek to individual cue points in the video, and display the current cue point.

In the following example an instance of `MediaPlayer` is added to an instance of `mx:UICom ponent`, as in the previous recipe. The instance of `VideoElement` added as the `media` property of the player contains a `metadata` property that dispatches an instance of `MetadataEvent` when the metadata of the video file has been read. This event instance contains a property called `facet` that is set to an instance of `TemporalFacet`. This class manages the temporal metadata from the video file and dispatches an instance of `TemporalFacetEvent` when a cue point has been reached in the video. In the example, the handler of this event instance (`onCuePoint()`) accesses the current cue point and displays its name to the user. Also, the handler for the `MetadataEvent` (`onFacetAdd()`) loops through each cue point and adds it to an instance of `ArrayCollection` named `_cuePoints`, which is displayed through an instance of `s:List`:

```
<?xml version="1.0" encoding="utf-8"?>
<s:Application xmlns:fx="http://ns.adobe.com/mxml/2009"
               xmlns:s="library://ns.adobe.com/flex/spark"
               xmlns:mx="library://ns.adobe.com/flex/mx" xmlns:local="*"
               creationComplete="init(event)">
    <fx:Script>
        <![CDATA[
            import mx.collections.ArrayCollection;
            import mx.core.UIComponent;
            import mx.events.FlexEvent;

            import org.osmf.events.MetadataEvent;
            import org.osmf.media.MediaPlayer;
            import org.osmf.media.URLResource;
            import org.osmf.metadata.MetadataNamespaces;
            import org.osmf.metadata.TemporalFacet;
            import org.osmf.metadata.TemporalFacetEvent;
            import org.osmf.net.NetLoader;
            import org.osmf.utils.URL;
            import org.osmf.video.CuePoint;
            import org.osmf.video.CuePointType;
            import org.osmf.video.VideoElement;

            import spark.events.IndexChangeEvent;

            [Bindable]
            private var _cuePointsCollection:ArrayCollection;
            [Bindable]
            private var currentCue:String;
            private var player:MediaPlayer = new MediaPlayer();

            protected function init(event:FlexEvent):void {
                var resource:URLResource = new URLResource(new
                        URL("http://helpexamples.com/flash/video/cuepoints.flv"));
                var video:VideoElement = new VideoElement(new NetLoader, resource);
                video.metadata.addEventListener(MetadataEvent.FACET_ADD,
                        onFacetAdd);
                player.media = video;
```

```
            helloWorldUIComponent.addChild(player.displayObject);
        }

        private function onFacetAdd(event:MetadataEvent):void {
            var facet:TemporalFacet = event.facet as TemporalFacet;
            if (facet) {
                facet.addEventListener(TemporalFacetEvent.POSITION_REACHED,
                                    onCuePoint);
                if (_cuePointsCollection == null && facet.namespaceURL.rawUrl
                    == MetadataNamespaces.TEMPORAL_METADATA_DYNAMIC.rawUrl) {
                    this._cuePointsCollection = new ArrayCollection();
                    for (var i:int = 0; i < facet.numValues; i++) {
                        this._cuePointsCollection.addItem(facet.getValueAt(i));
                    }
                }
            }

        }

        private function onCuePoint(event:TemporalFacetEvent):void {
            var cue:CuePoint = event.value as CuePoint;
            currentCue = cue.name;
        }

    }
        ]]>
    </fx:Script>
    <mx:UIComponent left="20" top="20" id="helloWorldUIComponent"/>
    <s:Label text="Cue Point: {currentCue}" left="20" top="280"/>
    <s:List dataProvider="{_cuePointsCollection}" left="20" top="300"
            itemRenderer="CuePointItemRenderer">
        <s:layout>
            <s:VerticalLayout/>
        </s:layout>
    </s:List>
</s:Application>
```

The instance of `s:List` uses the following item renderer, located at *CuePointItem Renderer.mxml*:

```
<?xml version="1.0" encoding="utf-8"?>
<s:ItemRenderer xmlns:fx="http://ns.adobe.com/mxml/2009"
                xmlns:s="library://ns.adobe.com/flex/spark"
                autoDrawBackground="true">
    <s:Label text="{data.name}"/>
</s:ItemRenderer>
```

To allow the user to seek to each individual cue point, set up an event listener for the change event on the instance of `s:List`, as follows:

```
<s:List dataProvider="{_cuePointsCollection}" left="20" top="300"
        change="cueSelecetedHandler(event)" allowMultipleSelection="false"
        itemRenderer="CuePointItemRenderer">
    <s:layout>
        <s:VerticalLayout/>
    </s:layout>
</s:List>
```

Also set up the event handler, `cueSelectedHandler()`, in the `fx:Script` tag in the application. The event handler seeks the video to the selected point:

```
protected function cueSelecetedHandler(event:IndexChangeEvent):void {
    var cuePoint:CuePoint = event.currentTarget.selectedItem as CuePoint;
    if (cuePoint.type == CuePointType.NAVIGATION) {
        player.seek(cuePoint.time);
    }
}
```

10.8 Create a Wrapper for the Open Source Media Framework

Problem

You want to more easily use the Open Source Media Framework with MXML.

Solution

Create a wrapper that extends `mx:UIComponent` to more easily access the OSMF.

Discussion

The following example is a simple ActionScript class that extends `mx:UIComponent`. This class acts like a wrapper for the `MediaPlayer` class in the Open Source Media Framework. It also contains a property called **source** with associated getter and setter functions; when set or changed, the set function updates the instance of `VideoElement` nested in the `MediaPlayer`, making it easier to set the URL of the video being played. The following component is located at *org/osmf/wrapper.as*:

```
package org.osmf.wrapper {
    import flash.events.Event;

    import mx.core.UIComponent;

    import org.osmf.events.LoadEvent;
    import org.osmf.media.MediaPlayer;
    import org.osmf.media.URLResource;
    import org.osmf.net.NetLoader;
    import org.osmf.traits.LoadState;
    import org.osmf.utils.URL;
    import org.osmf.video.VideoElement;

    public class MediaPlayerWrapper extends UIComponent {

        private var _player:MediaPlayer = new MediaPlayer();
        private var _source:String;

        public function MediaPlayerWrapper() {
        }
```

```
            public function get source():String {
                return _source;
            }

            public function set source(value:String):void {
                _source = value;
                if (_player) {

                    var resource:URLResource = new URLResource(new URL(value));
                    var video:VideoElement = new VideoElement(new NetLoader, resource);
                    _player.media = video;
                }
            }

            override protected function createChildren():void {
                super.createChildren();
                addChild(_player.displayObject);
                dispatchEvent(new Event("mediaPlayerChange"));

            }
        }
    }
```

The wrapper class can then be easily accessed in MXML:

```
<?xml version="1.0" encoding="utf-8"?>
<s:Application xmlns:fx="http://ns.adobe.com/mxml/2009"
               xmlns:s="library://ns.adobe.com/flex/spark"
               xmlns:mx="library://ns.adobe.com/flex/mx"
               xmlns:samples="org.osmf.wrapper.*">
    <samples:MediaPlayerWrapper
            source="http://helpexamples.com/flash/video/cuepoints.flv"/>
</s:Application>
```

10.9 Display Captions with the Open Source Media Framework

Problem

You would like to parse and display captioning with your video.

Solution

Use the Open Source Media Framework's captioning plug-in.

Discussion

The OSMF can use custom plug-ins developed to display certain forms of media or to parse and display associated metadata. Captions are similar to the cue points discussed in Recipe 10.7 because they are *temporal metadata*, meaning metadata connected to a certain point in time in the associated media.

To keep multiple temporal metadata types separate (such as cue points and captions), they are divided into distinct *facets* with separate namespaces, similar to namespaces in MXML. This is explained clearly on *http://opensource.adobe.com*:

> All metadata is organized by Namespaces, which are instances of the URL class. A metadata collection consists of a set of Metadata organized first by Namespace, and then by facet type. Each metadata has a facet type and a namespace. The facet type/namespace pair act as a key into the collection of metadata. Metadata can be quickly accessed this way, while guaranteeing the interface of the given metadata. This helps reduce collisions of metadata, while maintaining an easy to use API.

The captioning plug-in is included in the version of OSMF that you download from the website (*http://opensourcemediaframework.com*), but it is not included in the Flex 4 SDK. The plug-in also contains one example. The following application uses the same principles, but is substantially simpler:

```
<?xml version="1.0" encoding="utf-8"?>
<s:Application xmlns:fx="http://ns.adobe.com/mxml/2009"
               xmlns:s="library://ns.adobe.com/flex/spark"
               xmlns:mx="library://ns.adobe.com/flex/mx"
               backgroundColor="#000000" xmlns:samples="org.osmf.samples.*"
               applicationComplete="init()">
    <s:layout>
        <s:VerticalLayout/>
    </s:layout>
    <fx:Script>
        <![CDATA[
            import org.osmf.captioning.CaptioningPluginInfo;
            import org.osmf.captioning.model.Caption;
            import org.osmf.display.MediaPlayerSprite;
            import org.osmf.events.MetadataEvent;
            import org.osmf.media.MediaElement;
            import org.osmf.media.MediaFactory;
            import org.osmf.media.MediaInfo;
            import org.osmf.media.MediaResourceBase;
            import org.osmf.media.URLResource;
            import org.osmf.metadata.KeyValueFacet;
            import org.osmf.metadata.ObjectIdentifier;
            import org.osmf.metadata.TemporalFacet;
            import org.osmf.metadata.TemporalFacetEvent;
            import org.osmf.net.NetLoader;
            import org.osmf.plugin.PluginInfoResource;
            import org.osmf.plugin.PluginManager;
            import org.osmf.utils.FMSURL;
            import org.osmf.utils.URL;
            import org.osmf.video.VideoElement;

            import spark.utils.TextFlowUtil;

            private static const STREAM_URL:String =
                    "rtmp://cp67126.edgefcs.net/ondemand/mediapm/osmf/content/
                    test/akamai_10_year_f8_512K";
```

```
private static const CAPTION_URL:String =
        "http://mediapm.edgesuite.net/osmf/content/test/captioning/
        akamai_sample_caption.xml";

private static const DEFAULT_PROGRESS_DELAY:uint = 100;
private static const MAX_VIDEO_WIDTH:int = 480;
private static const MAX_VIDEO_HEIGHT:int = 270;

private var pluginManager:PluginManager;
private var mediaFactory:MediaFactory;
private var temporalFacet:TemporalFacet;

private var player:MediaPlayerSprite = new MediaPlayerSprite();

private function init():void {

    mediaFactory = new MediaFactory();
    pluginManager = new PluginManager(mediaFactory);
    loadPlugin("org.osmf.captioning.CaptioningPluginInfo");
    loadMedia(STREAM_URL);
}

private function loadMedia(url:String):void {

    var resource:URLResource = new URLResource( new FMSURL(url) );
    var kvFacet:KeyValueFacet = new KeyValueFacet(
            CaptioningPluginInfo.CAPTIONING_METADATA_NAMESPACE );
    kvFacet.addValue(new ObjectIdentifier(
            CaptioningPluginInfo.CAPTIONING_METADATA_KEY_URI ),
            CAPTION_URL);
    resource.metadata.addFacet(kvFacet);
    var netLoader:NetLoader = new NetLoader();
    mediaFactory.addMediaInfo(new MediaInfo("org.osmf.video",
            netLoader, createVideoElement));
    var mediaElement:MediaElement =
            mediaFactory.createMediaElement(resource);

    mediaElement.metadata.addEventListener(MetadataEvent.FACET_ADD,
            onFacetAdd);

    player.mediaElement = mediaElement;
    helloWorldUIComponent.addChild(player);
}

private function createVideoElement():MediaElement {
    return new VideoElement(new NetLoader());
}

private function loadPlugin(source:String, load:Boolean = true):void {
    var pluginResource:MediaResourceBase;
    if (source.substr(0, 4) == "http" || source.substr(0, 4) == "file")
    {
        pluginResource = new URLResource(new URL(source));
```

```
        } else {
            var pluginInfoRef:Class =
                    flash.utils.getDefinitionByName(source) as Class;
            pluginResource = new PluginInfoResource(new pluginInfoRef);
        }
        loadPluginFromResource(pluginResource);

    }

    private function
            loadPluginFromResource(pluginResource:MediaResourceBase):void {
        pluginManager.loadPlugin(pluginResource);
    }

    private function onFacetAdd(event:MetadataEvent):void {
        var facet:TemporalFacet = event.facet as TemporalFacet;
        if (facet) {
            temporalFacet = facet;
            temporalFacet.addEventListener(
                    TemporalFacetEvent.POSITION_REACHED, onShowCaption);
        }
    }

    private function onShowCaption(event:TemporalFacetEvent):void {

        var caption:Caption = event.value as Caption;
        var ns:URL = (event.currentTarget as TemporalFacet).namespaceURL;
        this.captionLabel.textFlow =
                TextFlowUtil.importFromString(caption.text);
        this.captionLabel.validateNow();

    }
    ]]>
</fx:Script>
<mx:UIComponent id="helloWorldUIComponent" width="480" height="270"/>
<s:TextArea id="captionLabel" color="#000000" width="480" height="44"/>
</s:Application>
```

To use the plug-in, you must first load it by calling the loadPlugin() method. Although
in this example the plug-in is embedded in the application and can be accessed directly,
it is best to use the loadPlugin() method in case this or any other plug-ins are loaded
at runtime. The loadPlugin() method loads the plug-in using an instance of
MediaResourceBase:

```
var source: String = "org.osmf.captioning.CaptioningPluginInfo";
var pluginResource:MediaResourceBase;
var pluginInfoRef:Class = flash.utils.getDefinitionByName(source) as Class;
pluginResource = new PluginInfoResource(new pluginInfoRef);
pluginManager.loadPlugin(pluginResource);
```

Before the video is loaded, a new facet is added with a namespace for captioning in the loadMedia() method:

```
var kvFacet:KeyValueFacet = new
        KeyValueFacet(CaptioningPluginInfo.CAPTIONING_METADATA_NAMESPACE);
kvFacet.addValue(new ObjectIdentifier(
        CaptioningPluginInfo.CAPTIONING_METADATA_KEY_URI ), CAPTION_URL);
resource.metadata.addFacet(kvFacet);
```

Once the facet is set up correctly and the plug-in is loaded, the captions are displayed similarly to cue points as the temporal metadata points are reached while the video is playing.

See Also

Recipe 10.7

CHAPTER 11

Animations and Effects

Effects, transitions, and animations are important elements of Flex applications, and important contributors to the "Rich" in the popular moniker Rich Internet Application (RIA). Understanding effects and the effect framework in Flex is important not only so you can design and implement element effects that users will see, but also so you can avoid users seeing things they shouldn't—those artifacts of incorrectly implemented effects, application lags, and inefficient garbage collection. To help you, Flex 4 offers a new way of creating what were previously called Tweens: the `Animate` class.

At the core of the way Flex creates animations is a system of timers and callbacks that are not all that different conceptually from this:

```
var timer:Timer = new Timer(100, 0);
timer.addEventListener(TimerEvent.TIMER, performEffect);
timer.start();

private function performEffect(event:Event):void {
    // effect implementation
}
```

Of course, in reality there's more to the effect framework than simply allowing the developer to create an instance of an `Animation` class and call a `play()` method on it. An effect has two distinct elements: the `EffectInstance` or `AnimateInstance` class (which contains information about the effect, what it should do, and what elements it will affect), and the `Animate` or `Effect` class (which acts as a factory, generating the effect, starting it, and deleting it when it has finished).

The playing of an effect consists of four distinct actions. First, the `Animate` class creates an instance of the `AnimateInstance` class for each target component of the effect. That means that an effect that will affect four targets will result in the creation of four `AnimateInstance` objects. Second, the framework copies all the configuration information from the factory object to each instance; the duration, number of repetitions, delay time, and so on are all set as properties of the new instance. Third, the effect is played on the target using the instance object created for it. Finally, the framework (specifically, the `EffectManager` class) deletes the instance object when the effect completes.

Usually when working with effects, you deal only with the factory class that handles generating the effect. However, when you begin creating custom effects, you'll create both an `Animate` object that will act as the factory for that effect type and an `AnimateInstance` object that will actually play on the target. Using an effect, whether you're aware of it or not, consists of creating a factory that will generate your instance objects. Any configuration that you create is setting up the factory object, which will then pass those values on to the generated instance object. Look in the framework source, and you'll notice a `Glow` class and a `GlowInstance` class, for example. To create your own effects, you'll create a similar pair of classes.

Both the Halo package effects stored in the `mx.effects` package and the Spark effects stored in the `spark.effects` package extend the base class `mx.effects.Effect`. The Spark effects package contains several classes for creating effects: *property* effects animate properties of the target, *transform* effects animate changes in transform-related properties of the target (scale, rotation, and position), *pixel-shader* effects animate changes from one bitmap image to another, *filter* effects change the properties of the filter, and *3D* effects change the 3D transform properties of the target.

11.1 Dynamically Set a Filter for a Component

Problem

You want to dynamically add effects to or remove them from a component at runtime.

Solution

Create a new `Array`, copying in any filters currently applied to the component that you want to keep (and adding new ones if desired), and reset the `filters` property of the component to that `Array`

Discussion

Every `UIComponent` defines a `filters` property that contains all the filters applied to that component. To update those filters, you need to set the `filters` property to a new `Array`. To begin, you need code similar to this:

```
<?xml version="1.0" encoding="utf-8"?>
<s:Group xmlns:fx="http://ns.adobe.com/mxml/2009"
        xmlns:s="library://ns.adobe.com/flex/spark"
        xmlns:mx="library://ns.adobe.com/flex/halo" width="400" height="300">
    <fx:Declarations>
        <!-- Place nonvisual elements (e.g., services, value objects) here -->
    </fx:Declarations>

    <s:layout>
        <s:HorizontalLayout/>
    </s:layout>
```

```
<fx:Script>
    <![CDATA[

        import flash.filters.*;

        protected const BLUR:Class = flash.filters.BlurFilter;
        protected const GLOW:Class = flash.filters.GlowFilter;
        protected const SHADOW:Class = flash.filters.DropShadowFilter;

        protected function addFilter(value:Class):void {
```

Copy all the filters that have already been applied to the component into a new Array, and add the new one (if you didn't copy over the existing filters, only the most recently created filter would be applied to the component). Then set the `filters` property to the new Array:

```
            var arr:Array = this.filters.concat();
            var fil:BitmapFilter = new value() as BitmapFilter;
            arr.push(fil);
            filters = arr;
        }

    ]]>
</fx:Script>

<s:Button click="addFilter(BLUR)" label="Blur"/>
<s:Button click="addFilter(GLOW)" label="Glow"/>
<s:Button click="addFilter(SHADOW)" label="Shadow"/>

</s: Group>
```

To set filters for a component in MXML, simply create `BitmapFilter` instances within the component's `<s:filters>` tag:

```
<s:filters>
    <s:BlurFilter/>
    <s:GlowFilter/>
</s:filters>
```

11.2 Call an Animation in MXML and in ActionScript

Problem

You want to create and call an `Animate` instance in your application.

Solution

To define an effect in MXML, add the `Animation` tag as a top-level tag within your component's `<fx:Declarations>`. To define an effect in ActionScript, import the correct effect class, instantiate an instance of it, assign a `UIComponent` as its target, and call the `play()` method to play the effect.

Discussion

The `Effect` class requires a target `UIComponent` to be set. When instantiating an `Animation` in ActionScript, the target can be passed into the `Animation` through the constructor:

```
var blur:Blur = new Blur(component);
```

You can also set the target once the `Animation` has been instantiated by using the `target` property of the `Animation` class. The target is the `UIComponent` that the `Animation` will affect when the `play()` method of the `Animation` is called. When an `Animation` is defined in MXML, a target `UIComponent` must be passed:

```
<s:Glow id="glowEffect" duration="1000" color="#ff0f0f" target="{glowingTI}"/>
```

In the following example, the `Glow` effect in MXML will be instantiated when the button is clicked:

```
<s:Button click="glowEffect.play()"/>
```

In the next example, a `Blur` effect in the `applyBlur()` method assigns the `glowingTI` object as its target through the constructor. After the relevant properties of the `Effect` are set, the `play()` method is called:

```
<s:Group xmlns:fx="http://ns.adobe.com/mxml/2009"
        xmlns:s="library://ns.adobe.com/flex/spark"
        xmlns:mx="library://ns.adobe.com/flex/halo"
        width="400" height="600">
    <s:layout>
        <s:VerticalLayout/>
    </s:layout>
    <fx:Script>
        <![CDATA[
            import mx.effects.Blur;
            private var blur:Blur;
            private function applyBlur():void {
                blur = new Blur(glowingTI);
                blur.blurXFrom = 0;
                blur.blurXTo = 20; // the amount of blur in pixels
                blur.blurYFrom = 0;
                blur.blurYTo = 20; // the amount of blur in pixels
                blur.duration = 1000;
                blur.play();
            }
        ]]>
    </fx:Script>
    <!-- the properties of the Glow effect set here are the color of the Glow and
         the length of time that the Glow will be displayed -->
    <fx:Declarations>
        <mx:Glow id="glowEffect" duration="1000" color="#ff0f0f"
                target="{glowingTI}"/>
    </fx:Declarations>
```

```
    <s:TextInput id="glowingTI"/>
    <s:Button click="applyBlur()"id="glowToggle" label="Play the BlurEffect"/>
    <s:Button click="glowEffect.play()" label="Play the Glow Effect"/>
</s: Group>
```

11.3 Create Show and Hide Effects for a Component

Problem

You want to create an effect that will play when a component is shown or hidden or in response to any other event.

Solution

Set the showEffect and hideEffect properties of the component to instances of an effect.

Discussion

The UIComponent class defines several properties that can be set to play in response to different actions, as shown in Table 11-1.

Table 11-1. UIComponent properties

Property	Event
addedEffect	The component is added as a child to a container.
creationCompleteEffect	The component is created.
focusInEffect	The component gains keyboard focus.
focusOutEffect	The component loses keyboard focus.
hideEffect	The component becomes invisible.
mouseDownEffect	The user presses the mouse button while over the component.
mouseUpEffect	The user releases the mouse button while over the component.
moveEffect	The component is moved.
removedEffect	The component is removed from a container.
resizeEffect	The component is resized.
rollOutEffect	The user rolls the mouse so it is no longer over the component.
rollOverEffect	The user rolls the mouse over the component.
showEffect	The component becomes visible.

To set an effect to be triggered by any of the events in Table 11-1, you can bind the event handler to a reference to an effect, define the effect inline, or set a style of the UIComponent. The following three code snippets demonstrate these techniques. The first uses binding:

```
<s:Group xmlns:fx="http://ns.adobe.com/mxml/2009"
         xmlns:s="library://ns.adobe.com/flex/spark"
         xmlns:mx="library://ns.adobe.com/flex/halo"
         width="400" height="300"
         showEffect="{componentShowEffect}"
         hideEffect="{componentHideEffect}">
    <fx:Declarations>
        <s:Scale scaleXFrom="0" scaleXTo="1.0" duration="500"
                 id="componentShowEffect"/>
        <s:Scale scaleXFrom="1.0" scaleXTo="0.0" duration="500"
                 id="componentHideEffect"/>
    </fx:Declarations>
</s:Group>
```

You can also define the effects inline using MXML, as shown here:

```
<s:Group xmlns:fx="http://ns.adobe.com/mxml/2009"
         xmlns:s="library://ns.adobe.com/flex/spark"
         xmlns:mx="library://ns.adobe.com/flex/halo"
         width="400" height="300">
    <s:showEffect>
        <s:Scale scaleXFrom="0" scaleXTo="1.0" duration="500"
                 id="componentShowEffect"/>
    </s:showEffect>
    <s:hideEffect
        <s:Scale scaleXFrom="1.0" scaleXTo="0.0" duration="500"
                 id="componentHideEffect"/>
    </s:hideEffect>
</s:Group>
```

Or you can use a Style declaration to set the effect. Note, however, that this is being done in a parent container or at the Application level here. You cannot define a Style for a component within that component:

```
<s:Application xmlns:fx="http://ns.adobe.com/mxml/2009"
               xmlns:s="library://ns.adobe.com/flex/spark"
               xmlns:mx="library://ns.adobe.com/flex/halo"
               minWidth="1024" minHeight="768"
               xmlns:flex4="oreilly.cookbook.flex4.*">
    <fx:Style>
        @namespace s "library://ns.adobe.com/flex/spark";
        @namespace mx "library://ns.adobe.com/flex/halo";
        @namespace flex4 "oreilly.cookbook.flex4.*";
        flex4|TriggerExample {
            showEffect: componentShowEffect;
            hideEffect: componentHideEffect;
            }

    </fx:Style>

    <fx:Declarations>
        <s:Scale scaleXFrom="0" scaleXTo="1.0" duration="500"
                 id="componentShowEffect"/>
        <s:Scale scaleXFrom="1.0" scaleXTo="0.0" duration="500"
                 id="componentHideEffect"/>
```

```
        </fx:Declarations>
    </s:Application>
```

This can also be done by creating an instance of the Scale effect in ActionScript and using the setStyle() method:

```
var someComponent:UIComponent = new UIComponent();
someComponent.setStyle("showEffect", componentShowEffect);
someComponent.setStyle("hideEffect", componentHideEffect);
```

11.4 Define Keyframes for an Animation

Problem

You want to define a series of keyframes for an effect so you have control over what values the animation will interpolate between.

Solution

Create a SimpleMotionPath or MotionPath and pass a Vector of Keyframe objects to the keyframes property. Then pass the MotionPath or SimpleMotionPath to an instance of Animate.

Discussion

The Keyframe class allows you to set points for an animation, much like the keyframes of an animation, that will be interpolated between as the animation plays. For instance, you might want to set an initial value at 0, a second value for when the animation has played for 1 second, and a third value for when the animation has played for 2 seconds:

```
<s:Keyframe time="0" value="0"/>
<s:Keyframe time="2000" value="20.0"/>
<s:Keyframe time="4000" value="0"/>
```

This would be added to a Vector set in the keyframes property of a MotionPath, which is then passed to an Animate instance:

```
<s:Animate duration="3000" target="{blurFilter}">
    <s:motionPaths>
        <fx:Vector type="spark.effects.animation.MotionPath">
            <s:MotionPath property="blurX">
                <s:keyframes>
                    <fx:Vector type="spark.effects.animation.Keyframe">
                        <s:Keyframe time="0" value="0"/>
                        <s:Keyframe time="2000" value="20.0"/>
                        <s:Keyframe time="4000" value="0"/>
                    </fx:Vector>
                </s:keyframes>
            </s:MotionPath>
        </fx:Vector>
    </s:motionPaths>
</s: Animate>
```

Here's an example of how this would be done in ActionScript:

```
<fx:Declarations>
    <s:Animate id="animateInstance"/>
</fx:Declarations>

<fx:Script>
    <![CDATA[
        import spark.effects.animation.Keyframe;
        import spark.effects.animation.MotionPath;

        private var motionPathsVector:Vector.<MotionPath>;

        protected function creationCompleteHandler():void {

            motionPathsVector = new Vector.<MotionPath>();

            // pass the property that this motion path will affect to the
            // constructor
            var xMotionPath:MotionPath = new MotionPath("x");
            var yMotionPath:MotionPath = new MotionPath("y");

            // now create keyframes for each of these motion paths to use
            var keyframes:Vector.<Keyframe> = new Vector.<Keyframe>();

            keyframes.push(new Keyframe(0, 0));
            keyframes.push(new Keyframe(0, 40));
            keyframes.push(new Keyframe(0, 0));

            // now set the keyframes property on the motionPath
            xMotionPath.keyframes = keyframes;
            yMotionPath.keyframes = keyframes;

            // now add the MotionPath instances to a motionPathsVector
            motionPathsVector.push(xMotionPath, yMotionPath);
            // now set the motionPaths on the instance of Animate
            animateInstance.motionPaths = motionPathsVector;
        }

    ]]>
</fx:Script>
```

11.5 Create Parallel Series or Sequences of Effects

Problem

You want to create multiple effects that either play in parallel (at the same time) or play one after another.

Solution

Use the `Parallel` tag to wrap multiple effects that will play at the same time, or use the `Sequence` tag to wrap multiple effects that will play one after another.

Discussion

The `Sequence` tag plays the next effect in the sequence when the previous `Effect` object fires its `effectComplete` event:

```
<s:Sequence id=" sequencee" target="{this}">
    <s:Rotate3D targets="{[bar, foo]}" duration="4000" angleYFrom="0"
              angleYTo="360"/>
    <s:Glow duration="3000" color="#ffff00"/>
</s:Sequence>
```

Sequences can, of course, consist of multiple `Parallel` effect tags, because a `Parallel` tag is treated the same as an `Effect` and possesses the `play()` method that the `Sequence` will call when the previous `Effect` or `Parallel` has finished playing.

The `Parallel` tag works by passing all the target objects to each `Effect` or `Sequence` in the `Parallel` declaration, and calling the `play()` method on each `Effect` that it wraps:

```
<fx:Declarations>

    <s:BlurFilter id="blur" blurX="0" blurY="0"/>

    <s:Parallel id="parallel">
        <s:Rotate3D targets="{[bar, foo]}" duration="4000" angleYFrom="0"
                  angleYTo="360"/>
        <s:Animate target="{blur}">
            <s:motionPaths>
                <fx:Vector type="spark.effects.animation.MotionPath">
                    <s:MotionPath property="blurX">
                        <s:keyframes>
                            <fx:Vector type="spark.effects.animation.Keyframe">
                                <s:Keyframe time="0" value="0"/>
                                <s:Keyframe time="2000" value="50.0"/>
                                <s:Keyframe time="4000" value="0"/>
                            </fx:Vector>
                        </s:keyframes>
                    </s:MotionPath>
                </fx:Vector>
            </s:motionPaths>
        </s:Animate>
    </s:Parallel>

</fx:Declarations>
```

11.6 Pause, Reverse, and Restart an Effect

Problem

You need to be able to pause an effect while it is running, and then restart the effect either from its current position or from the beginning.

Solution

Use the pause() or stop() method to stop the effect so that it can be restarted. If paused, use the resume() method to resume the effect from the location where it was stopped.

Discussion

The stop() method of the Effect class produces the same behavior as the pause() method: they both stop the effect as it is playing. The stop() method, however, resets the underlying timer of the effect so the effect cannot be resumed. The pause() method simply pauses the timer, and hence the effect, enabling you to restart it from the exact point where it paused. An effect can be reversed while it is paused, but it cannot be reversed when it is stopped.

You can pause and resume a set of effects wrapped in a Parallel or Sequence tag as well:

```
<s:Group xmlns:fx="http://ns.adobe.com/mxml/2009"
        xmlns:s="library://ns.adobe.com/flex/spark"
        xmlns:mx="library://ns.adobe.com/flex/halo"
        width="400" height="300" filters="{[blurFilter]}">

    <s:layout><s:VerticalLayout/></s:layout>

    <fx:Script>
        <![CDATA[
            import spark.effects.animation.Keyframe;
            import spark.effects.animation.MotionPath;
        ]]>
    </fx:Script>
    <fx:Declarations>

        <s:BlurFilter id="blurFilter" blurX="0" blurY="0"/>

        <s:Parallel id="parallel" >
            <s:Animate duration="3000" target="{blurFilter}">
                <s:motionPaths>
                    <fx:Vector type="spark.effects.animation.MotionPath">
                        <s:MotionPath property="blurX">
                            <s:keyframes>
                                <fx:Vector
type="spark.effects.animation.Keyframe">
                                    <s:Keyframe time="0" value="0"/>
                                    <s:Keyframe time="2000" value="20.0"/>
                                    <s:Keyframe time="4000" value="0"/>
                                </fx:Vector>
```

```
                </s:keyframes>
            </s:MotionPath>
            <s:MotionPath property="blurY">
                <s:keyframes>
                    <fx:Vector
  type="spark.effects.animation.Keyframe">
                        <s:Keyframe time="0" value="0"/>
                        <s:Keyframe time="2000" value="20.0"/>
                        <s:Keyframe time="4000" value="0"/>
                    </fx:Vector>
                </s:keyframes>
            </s:MotionPath>
        </fx:Vector>
      </s:motionPaths>
    </s:Animate>
  </s:Parallel>
</fx:Declarations>

<s:Button click="parallel.play();" label="play()"/>
<s:Button click="parallel.pause();" label="pause()"/>
<s:Button click="parallel.reverse()" label="reverse()"/>
<s:Button click="parallel.resume()" label="resume ()"/>
</s:Group>
```

If the reverse() method is called on the Sequence, Parallel, or Effect after the pause() method has been called, the resume() method will need to be called before the effect will begin playing in reverse.

11.7 Set Effects for Adding a Component to or Removing One from a Parent Component

Problem

You want to create effects that are played when a component is added to or removed from a parent component.

Solution

Use instances of the spark.effects.AddAction and spark.effects.RemoveAction classes.

Discussion

An AddAction instance is called when a component is added during a Transition. For instance, if a TextArea has the includeIn property set on it, as shown here:

```
<s:TextArea includeIn="addedChild" id="addedTextField" width="200" height="25"/>
```

a Transition can be created that will be triggered when that State is entered:

```
<s:Transition fromState="*" toState="addedChild">
```

Within that `Transition` you can use an `AddAction` component to control when the `TextArea` will be added and its position within the parent component:

```
<s:SkinnableContainer xmlns:fx="http://ns.adobe.com/mxml/2009"
                      xmlns:s="library://ns.adobe.com/flex/spark"
                      xmlns:mx="library://ns.adobe.com/flex/halo"
                      width="500" height="30" currentState="base"
                      skinClass="oreilly.cookbook.flex4.SimpleSkin">

    <s:layout>
        <s:HorizontalLayout/>
    </s:layout>

    <s:transitions>
        <s:Transition id="toAddedChild" fromState="*" toState="addedChild">
            <s:Sequence id="t1" target="{this}">
                <s:AnimateColor colorFrom="0xffffff" colorTo="0xffff00"
                                target="{this.skin}" duration="1000"/>
```

In the following example, the `AddAction` instance controls when the target component will actually be added to the stage. Setting the `startDelay` property ensures that the component will not be added until the `AnimateColor` effect is finished playing:

```
                <s:AddAction startDelay="1000" target="{addedTextField}"/>
                <s:AnimateColor colorFrom="0xffff00" colorTo="0xffffff"
                                target="{this.skin}" duration="1000"/>
            </s:Sequence>
        </s:Transition>

        <s:Transition id="toRemoveChild" fromState="*" toState="removedChild">
            <s:Sequence id="t2" target="{this}">
                <s:AnimateColor colorFrom="0xffffff" colorTo="0xff0000"
                                target="{this.skin}" duration="500"/>
```

The `RemoveAction` instance controls when the target component will actually be removed from the stage. As with the `AddAction` instance, the `startDelay` property ensures that the component will not be added until the `AnimateColor` effect is finished playing:

```
                <s:RemoveAction startDelay="500" target="{addedTextField}"/>
                <s:AnimateColor colorFrom="0xff0000" colorTo="0xffffff"
                                target="{this.skin}" duration="500"/>
            </s:Sequence>
        </s:Transition>
    </s:transitions>

    <s:states>
        <s:State name="base">
        </s:State>
        <s:State name="addedChild">
        </s:State>
        <s:State name="removedChild">
        </s:State>
    </s:states>
```

```
        <s:Button click="{currentState = 'addedChild'}" label="add"/>
        <s:Button click="{currentState = 'removedChild'}" label="remove"/>

        <s:TextArea includeIn="addedChild" id="addedTextField" width="200"
                    height="25"/>

    </s:SkinnableContainer>
```

The SkinnableComponent shown in the previous code snippet uses the following simple Skin class. It allows the color of the fill to be set by the AnimateColor instances in that component by creating getter and setter methods called color():

```
<?xml version="1.0" encoding="utf-8"?>
<s:Skin xmlns:fx="http://ns.adobe.com/mxml/2009"
        xmlns:s="library://ns.adobe.com/flex/spark"
        xmlns:mx="library://ns.adobe.com/flex/halo">

    <fx:Script>
        <![CDATA[

            public function set color(value:uint):void {
                solidFill.color = value;
            }

            public function get color():uint {
                return solidFill.color;
            }

        ]]>
    </fx:Script>

    <s:states>
        <s:State name="normal" />
        <s:State name="disabled" />
    </s:states>

    <!-- Background -->
    <s:Rect left="0" right="0" top="0" bottom="0" radiusX="5" radiusY="5" >
        <s:fill>
            <s:SolidColor color="#ffffff" id="solidFill"/>
        </s:fill>
    </s:Rect>

    <!-- Content area -->
    <s:Group id="contentGroup" left="0" right="0" top="0" bottom="0">
        <s:layout>
            <s:BasicLayout/>
        </s:layout>
    </s:Group>
</s:Skin>
```

11.8 Create Custom Animation Effects

Problem

You want to create a custom animation effect that slowly changes its properties over a specified duration.

Solution

Make a class that extends the `Animate` class and have that class create instances of the `AnimateInstance` class.

Discussion

Tweening and animated effects in Flex 4 are handled using the `Animate` object. The notable difference between `Effect` and `Animate` is that an `Animate` instance takes place over time. The beginning values and ending values of the `Animate` are passed into `AnimateInstance`, which then uses those values over time either to generate the new filter instances that will be added to the target or to alter properties of the `target`. These changing values are generated over the duration of the effect by using either a `spark.effects.animation.MotionPath` or a `spark.effects.animation.SimpleMotionPath` object passed to the `Animate` class.

The example that follows demonstrates how to build a simple tween effect that slowly fades out the alpha channel of its target over the duration assigned to the `Animate` instance. An `Animate` instance is built from two classes: in this case, a factory `Tween` `Effect` class to generate the `TweenInstance`s for each target passed to the `TweenEffect`, and the `TweenInstance` that will create the `Tween` object and use the values that the `Tween` object generates over the duration of the effect.

First, let's take a look at the `TweenEffect`:

```
package oreilly.cookbook {
    import mx.effects.TweenEffect;
    public class CustomTweenEffect extends Animate {
        public var finalAlpha:Number = 1.0;
        public function CustomTweenEffect (target:Object=null) {
            super(target);
        }
        public function CustomDisplacementEffect(target:Object=null) {
            super(target);
            this.instanceClass = CustomTweenInstance;
        }
        // create our new instance
        override protected function initInstance(instance:IEffectInstance):void {
            super.initInstance(instance);
            // now that the instance is created, set its properties
            CustomTweenInstance(instance).finalAlpha = this.finalAlpha;
```

```
    }
    override public function getAffectedProperties():Array {
        trace(" return all the target properties ");
        return [];
    }
  }
}
```

The `finalAlpha` property of each `CustomTweenInstance` object passed into the `initInstance` method is set when the `TweenInstance` is instantiated.

The `CustomTweenInstance` class extends the `TweenEffectInstance` class and overrides the `play()` and `onTweenUpdate()` methods of that class. The overridden `play()` method contains the logic for instantiating the `Tween` object that generates the changing values over the duration of the `TweenEffect`:

```
override public function play():void {
    super.play();
    this.tween = new Tween(this, 0, finalAlpha, duration);
    (target as DisplayObject).alpha = 0;
}
```

The `finalAlpha` property and the `duration` property are passed in from the Custom `TweenEffect`, and `mx.effects.Tween` generates a value for each frame of the SWF file that moves smoothly from the initial value (in this case, 0) to the final value (in this case, the `finalAlpha` variable). Multiple values can be passed to the `Tween` object in an array if needed, as long as the array of initial values and the array of final values have the same number of elements. The `play()` method of the `TweenEffectInstance` object, called here by `super.play()`, adds an event listener to the `Tween` for the `onTween` `Update()` method. By overriding this method, you can add any custom logic you like to the `TweenEffectInstance`:

```
override public function onTweenUpdate(value:Object):void {
    (target as DisplayObject).alpha = value as Number;
}
```

Here, the `alpha` property of the target is set to the value returned by the `Tween` instance, slowly bringing the `alpha` property of the `target` to the value of the `finalValue` variable:

```
package oreilly.cookbook {
    import flash.display.DisplayObject;
    import mx.effects.effectClasses.TweenEffectInstance;
    public class CustomTweenInstance extends TweenEffectInstance {
        public var finalAlpha:Number;
        public function NewTweenInstance(target:Object) {
            super(target);
        }
        override public function play():void {
            super.play();
            this.tween = new Tween(this, 0, finalAlpha, duration);
            (target as DisplayObject).alpha = 0;
```

```
        }
        override public function onTweenUpdate(value:Object):void {
            (target as DisplayObject).alpha = value as Number;
        }
    }
}
```

Each time the onTweenUpdate() method is called, the value of alpha is recalculated and updated for the target.

11.9 Use the DisplacementMapFilter Filter in a Flex Effect

Problem

You want to create a tween effect that causes one image to transform into another.

Solution

Extend both the Animate and AnimateInstance classes, creating an Animate instance that can have final displacement values passed into each instance of the AnimateInstance class that it creates. Within the custom AnimateInstance class, create a Displacement MapFilter object and use the Flex Framework's tweening engine to reach the desired displacement values by generating new filters on each animateUpdate event.

Discussion

The DisplacementMapFilter object displaces or deforms the pixels of one image by using the pixels of another image to determine the location and amount of the deformation. This technique is often used to create the impression of an image being underneath another image.

The location and amount of displacement applied to a given pixel is determined by the color value of the displacement map image. The DisplacementMapFilter constructor looks like this:

```
public function DisplacementMapFilter(mapBitmap:BitmapData = null,
        mapPoint:Point = null, componentX:uint = 0, componentY:uint = 0,
        scaleX:Number = 0.0, scaleY:Number = 0.0, mode:String = "wrap",
        color:uint = 0, alpha:Number = 0.0)
```

Understanding such a long line of code is often easier when it's broken down piece by piece:

BitmapData *(default* = null*)*

   This is the BitmapData object that will be used to displace the image or component to which the filter is applied.

mapPoint

> This is the location on the filtered image where the top-left corner of the displacement filter will be applied. You can use this if you want to apply the filter to only part of an image.

componentX

> This specifies which color channel of the map image affects the *x* position of pixels. The `BitmapDataChannel` class defines all the valid options as constants with the values `BitmapDataChannel.BLUE` or `4`, `BitmapDataChannel.RED` or `1`, `BitmapDataChannel.GREEN` or `2`, or `BitmapDataChannel.ALPHA` or `8`.

componentY

> This specifies which color channel of the map image affects the *y* position of pixels. The possible values are the same as the `componentX` values.

scaleX

> This multiplier value specifies how strong the *x*-axis displacement is.

scaleY

> This multiplier value specifies how strong the *y*-axis displacement is.

mode

> This is a string that determines what should be done in any empty spaces created by pixels being shifted away. The options, defined as constants in the `DisplacementMapFilterMode` class, are to display the original pixels (`mode = IGNORE`), wrap the pixels around from the other side of the image (`mode = WRAP`, which is the default), use the nearest shifted pixel (`mode = CLAMP`), or fill in the spaces with a color (`mode = COLOR`).

The `CustomDisplacementEffect` instance instantiates a `CustomDisplacementInstance`. It's shown here:

```
package oreilly.cookbook.flex4 {
    import mx.effects.IEffectInstance;
    import mx.events.EffectEvent;

    import spark.effects.Animate;

    public class DisplacementMapAnimate extends Animate {

        public var image:Class;
        public var yToDisplace:Number;
        public var xToDisplace:Number;

        public function DisplacementMapAnimate(target:Object=null) {
            super(target);
```

Here, you set the `instanceClass` property of the `Animate` instance so that when the `DisplacementMapAnimate` creates a new `EffectInstance` object, it uses the `DisplacementMapAnimateInstance` class to create it:

```
            this.instanceClass = DisplacementMapAnimateInstance;
        }
        override protected function initInstance(instance:IEffectInstance):void {
            trace(" instance initialized ");
            super.initInstance(instance);
            // now that we've instantiated our instance, we can set its properties
            DisplacementMapAnimateInstance(instance).image = image;
            DisplacementMapAnimateInstance(instance).xToDisplace =
                    this.xToDisplace;
            DisplacementMapAnimateInstance(instance).yToDisplace =
                    this.yToDisplace;
        }
        override public function getAffectedProperties():Array {
            return [];
        }
    }
}
```

DisplacementMapAnimateInstance handles actually creating the DisplacementEffect object that will be applied to the target. The bitmap object, the filter used in DisplacementEffect, and the *x* and *y* displacement amounts of CustomDisplacementTween are applied to the instance and passed into DisplacementEffect.

As mentioned earlier in this recipe, DisplacementMapAnimate generates instances of DisplacementMapAnimateInstance, as shown here:

```
package oreilly.cookbook.flex4 {

    import flash.display.BitmapData;
    import flash.display.BitmapDataChannel;
    import flash.display.DisplayObject;
    import flash.filters.DisplacementMapFilter;
    import flash.filters.DisplacementMapFilterMode;
    import flash.geom.Point;

    import spark.effects.animation.Animation;
    import spark.effects.supportClasses.AnimateInstance;

    public class DisplacementMapAnimateInstance extends AnimateInstance {

        public var image:Class;
        public var xToDisplace:Number;
        public var yToDisplace:Number;
        public var filterMode:String = DisplacementMapFilterMode.WRAP;

        private var filter:DisplacementMapFilter;
        private var img:DisplayObject;
        private var bmd:BitmapData;

        public function DisplacementMapAnimateInstance(target:Object) {
            super(target);
        }

        override public function play():void {
            super.play();
```

```
// make our embedded image accessible to use
img = new image();
bmd = new BitmapData(img.width, img.height, true);
// draw the actual byte data into the image
bmd.draw(img);
```

First you create the new filter, setting all the values to the beginning state:

```
filter = new DisplacementMapFilter(bmd, new
        Point(DisplayObject(target).width/2 - (img.width/2),
        DisplayObject(target).height/2 - (img.height/2))),
        BitmapDataChannel.RED, BitmapDataChannel.RED, 0, 0,
        filterMode, 0.0, 1.0);
```

Now you copy any filters already existing on the target so that you don't lose them when you add your new filter:

```
var targetFilters:Array = (target as DisplayObject).filters;
targetFilters.push(filter);
// set the actual filter onto the target
(target as DisplayObject).filters = targetFilters;
// create a tween that will begin to generate the next values of each
// frame of our effect
this.tween = new Tween(this, [0, 0], [xToDisplace, yToDisplace],
            duration);

    }
```

Much of the heavy work for this class is done in the setDisplacementFilter() method. Because filters are cumulative (they are applied one atop the other), any previous DisplacementMapFilter instances must be removed. This is done by looping through the filters array of the target:

```
private function setDisplacementFilter(displacement:Object):void {
    var filters:Array = target.filters;
    // remove any existing displacement filters to ensure that ours is the
    // only one
    var n:int = filters.length;
    for (var i:int = 0; i < n; i++) {
        if (filters[i] is DisplacementMapFilter)
            filters.splice(i, 1);
    }
```

Now a new filter is created using the values passed in from Animate, and the filter is applied to the target. Note that for the filter to be displayed properly, the filter's Array must be reset. Adding the filter to the Array by using the Array.push() method will not cause the target DisplayObject to be redrawn with the new filter:

```
filter = new DisplacementMapFilter(bmd, new Point(0, 0),
        BitmapDataChannel.RED, BitmapDataChannel.RED,
        displacement.xToDisplace as Number, displacement.yToDisplace
        as Number, filterMode, 0.0, 0);
// add the filter to the filters on the target
filters.push(filter);
target.filters = filters;
```

```
        }

        // each time we're ready to update, re-create the displacement map filter
        override public function animationUpdate(animation:Animation):void
        {
            setDisplacementFilter(animation.currentValue);
        }

        // set the filter one last time and then dispatch the tween end event
        override public function animationStop(animation:Animation) : void
        {
            setDisplacementFilter(animation.currentValue);
            super.animationStop(animation);
        }

    }
}
```

When the tween is finished, the final values of the `DisplacementMapFilter` are used to set the final appearance of the target `DisplayObject`, and the `animationStop()` method of the `AnimateInstance` instance is called.

11.10 Use the Convolution Filter to Create an Animation

Problem

You want to create an `Animation` to use on a MXML component that uses a `ConvolutionFilter`.

Solution

Create an `AnimationInstance` class that instantiates new `ConvolutionFilter` instances in the `animationUpdate()` event handler and then assign those `ConvolutionFilter` instances to the target `DisplayObject` filters array.

Discussion

A `ConvolutionFilter` alters its target `DisplayObject` or `BitmapImage` in a very flexible manner, allowing the creation of effects such as blurring, edge detection, sharpening, embossing, and beveling. Each pixel in the source image is altered according to the values of its surrounding pixels. The alteration to each pixel is determined by the `Matrix` array passed into a `ConvolutionFilter` in its constructor. The `Convolution Filter` constructor has the following signature:

```
public function ConvolutionFilter(matrixX:Number = 0, matrixY:Number = 0,
    matrix:Array = null, divisor:Number = 1.0, bias:Number = 0.0,
    preserveAlpha:Boolean = true,
    clamp:Boolean = true, color:uint = 0, alpha:Number = 0.0)
```

Take a closer look piece by piece:

matrixX:Number *(default = 0)*
This is the number of columns in the matrix.

matrixY:Number *(default = 0)*
This specifies the number of rows in the matrix.

matrix:Array *(default = null)*
This is the array of values used to determine how each pixel will be transformed. The number of items in the array needs to be the same value as matrixX * matrixY.

divisor:Number *(default = 1.0)*
This specifies the divisor used during the matrix transformation and determines how evenly the ConvolutionFilter applies the matrix calculations. If you sum the matrix values, the total will be the divisor value that evenly distributes the color intensity.

bias:Number *(default = 0.0)*
This is the bias to add to the result of the matrix transformation.

preserveAlpha:Boolean *(default = true)*
A value of false indicates that the alpha value is not preserved and that the convolution applies to all channels, including the alpha channel. A value of true indicates that the convolution applies only to the color channels.

clamp:Boolean *(default = true)*
A value of true indicates that, for pixels that are off the source image, the input image should be extended along each of its borders as necessary by duplicating the color values at the given edge of the input image. A value of false indicates that another color should be used, as specified in the color and alpha properties. The default is true.

color:uint *(default = 0)*
This is the hexadecimal color to substitute for pixels that are off the source image.

alpha:Number *(default = 0.0)*
This is the alpha of the substitute color.

The Animate class creates AnimateInstance objects, which in turn create Convolution Filters:

```
package oreilly.cookbook.flex4 {
    import mx.effects.IEffectInstance;

    import spark.effects.Animate;

    public class ConvolutionTween extends Animate {
```

The values that will be passed to the each new Effect instance created are set here:

```
        public var alpha:Number = 1.0;
        public var color:uint = 0xffffff;
        public var matrix:Array = [5, 5, 5, 5, 0, 5, 5, 5, 5];
```

```
public var divisor:Number = 1.0;
public var bias:Number = 0.0;

public function ConvolutionTween(target:Object=null) {
    super(target);
    this.instanceClass = ConvolutionTweenInstance;
}
```

Each newly created instance of the `ConvolutionTweenInstance` class has its properties set as shown here:

```
override protected function initInstance(instance:IEffectInstance):void {
    trace(" instance initialized ");
    super.initInstance(instance);
    // now that we've instantiated our instance, we can set its properties
    ConvolutionTweenInstance(instance).alpha = alpha;
    ConvolutionTweenInstance(instance).color = color;
    ConvolutionTweenInstance(instance).divisor = divisor;
    ConvolutionTweenInstance(instance).matrix = matrix;
    ConvolutionTweenInstance(instance).bias = bias;

}

override public function getAffectedProperties():Array {
    trace(" return all the target properties ");
    return [];
}
    }
}
```

The `ConvolutionTweenInstance` receives its `target` object and values from the `ConvolutionTweenEffect` factory class:

```
package oreilly.cookbook.flex4 {
    import flash.filters.ConvolutionFilter;

    import spark.effects.animation.Animation;
    import spark.effects.supportClasses.AnimateInstance;

    public class ConvolutionTweenInstance extends AnimateInstance {

        private var convolutionFilter:ConvolutionFilter;

        public var alpha:Number;
        public var color:uint;
        public var matrixX:Number;
        public var matrixY:Number;
```

Here is the `Array` that is used to create the `ConvolutionFilter` and alter its effects over time. Later in this recipe you'll see how this is used when creating an instance of the `ConvolutionTween` class:

```
public var matrix:Array;
public var divisor:Number;
public var bias:Number;
```

```
public function ConvolutionTweenInstance(target:Object) {
    super(target);
}
```

In the overridden play() method, the ConvolutionTweenInstance uses the initial values from the ConvolutionTween class to create a ConvolutionFilter:

```
override public function play():void {
    super.play();
    convolutionFilter = new ConvolutionFilter(matrixX, matrixY,
            matrix, 1.0, 0, true, true, alpha, color);
}
```

Each new value from the parent Animate class is passed into the animationUpdate() method as an Animation object. Within this object, all the current values are stored by their property names, as you saw in Recipe 11.9. Because ConvolutionFilter requires an array, each value in the array is altered using a MultiValueInterpolator object (you'll see this later in this recipe) and then passed into a new array for the matrix parameter of ConvolutionFilter:

```
override public function animationUpdate(animation:Animation) : void {

    // get the filters from the target
    var filters:Array = target.filters;
```

Now, remove any existing convolution filters to ensure that the one currently added is the only one being applied to the target:

```
    var n:int = filters.length;
    for (var i:int = 0; i < n; i++) {
        if (filters[i] is ConvolutionFilter)
            filters.splice(i, 1);
    }

    var currValues:Object = animation.currentValue;
    trace((currValues.matrix as Array).join(", "));
    // create the new filter
    convolutionFilter = new ConvolutionFilter(3, 3,
            [currValues.matrix[0], currValues.matrix[1],
            currValues.matrix[2], currValues.matrix[3],
            currValues.matrix[4], currValues.matrix[5],
            currValues.matrix[6], currValues.matrix[7],
            currValues.matrix[8]], 1.0);
    // add the filter to the target
    filters.push(convolutionFilter);
    target.filters = filters;

}
```

In the animationStop() method, you set the filter one last time and then, by calling the super.animationStop() method, clean up the AnimationInstance:

```
override public function animationStop(animation:Animation) : void {
    // get the filters from the target
    var filters:Array = target.filters;
```

```
            var currValues:Object = animation.currentValue;

            // create the new filter
            convolutionFilter = new ConvolutionFilter(3, 3,
                    [currValues.matrix[0], currValues.matrix[1],
                    currValues.matrix[2], currValues.matrix[3],
                    currValues.matrix[4], currValues.matrix[5],
                    currValues.matrix[6], currValues.matrix[7]], 1.0);
            // add the filter to the target
            filters.push(convolutionFilter);
            target.filters = filters;
            super.animationStop(animation);
        }
    }
}
```

Now that you've seen the `Animate` and `AnimateInstance` classes, the next part to look at is instantiating a `ConvolutionTween`:

```
<s:SkinnableContainer xmlns:fx="http://ns.adobe.com/mxml/2009"
                      xmlns:s="library://ns.adobe.com/flex/spark"
                      xmlns:mx="library://ns.adobe.com/flex/halo"
                      width="400" height="300"
                      xmlns:flex4="oreilly.cookbook.flex4.*"
                      skinClass="oreilly.cookbook.flex4.SimpleSkin"
                      click="convolutionTween.play()">
    <fx:Declarations>
        <flex4:ConvolutionTween target="{this}" id="convolutionTween"
                                duration="4000">
```

Since `ConvolutionTween` is going to change the matrix `Array` property of `Convolution Filter`, a `SimpleMotion` path is not going to be able to properly interpolate the values of the matrix. To interpolate the values of the array, you'll want to create a `Motion Path` instance with keyframes containing the values of the array that will be used to create the tween for the `ConvolutionFilter` within the `ConvolutionTweenInstance`. The `property` of `MotionPath` is set to `matrix` so that the matrix property of the `ConvolutionTw een` will be altered by each keyframe:

```
<flex4:motionPaths>
    <fx:Vector type="spark.effects.animation.MotionPath">
        <s:MotionPath property="matrix">
            <s:keyframes>
                <fx:Vector type="Vector">
                    <s:Keyframe value="{[0, -1, 0, -1, 5, -1, 0, -1,
                                        0]}" time="0"/>
                    <s:Keyframe value="{[-30, 30, 0, -30, 30, 0, -30,
                                        30, 0]}" time="2000"/>
                    <s:Keyframe value="{[0, -1, 0, -1, 5, -1, 0, -1,
                                        0]}" time="4000"/>
                </fx:Vector>
            </s:keyframes>
```

Since the property being tweened to is an array, a `MultiValueInterpolator` is used to interpolate the values in the array:

```
                    <s:interpolator>
                        <s:MultiValueInterpolator />
                    </s:interpolator>
                </s:MotionPath>
            </fx:Vector>
        </flex4:motionPaths>
    </flex4:ConvolutionTween>
</fx:Declarations>

<fx:Script>
    <![CDATA[
        import spark.effects.animation.MotionPath;

    ]]>
</fx:Script>

</s:SkinnableContainer>
```

As you've seen in the last two recipes, any `BitmapFilter` can be used to create a custom effect by extending the `Animate` and `AnimateInstance` classes.

11.11 Use Pixel Bender to Create a Transition

Problem

You want to use a Pixel Bender filter to create a transition effect.

Solution

Use the `AnimateTransitionShader` object to apply a Pixel Bender filter to bitmaps in your application.

Discussion

Although not part of the Flex SDK, the Pixel Bender Toolkit is freely downloadable from the Adobe website. With it, you can create complex effects that use per-pixel processing to read and manipulate each pixel of a graphic much more quickly than would be possible using plain ActionScript. This recipe uses a simple radial wipe filter to demonstrate the Pixel Bender Toolkit.

 Before continuing with the recipe, download the toolkit from *http://labs .adobe.com/technologies/pixelbender/*.

The following should be saved as *RadialWipe.pbj*:

```
<languageVersion : 1.0;>

kernel RadialWipe
<   namespace : "flex";
    vendor : "thefactoryfactory";
    version : 1;
    description : "Super sweet radial crossfade between two images, for use with
            Flex effects"; >
{
```

For a Pixel Bender filter to be usable in a Spark effect, you need to give it three images marked with the `input` flag, as well as `progress`, `width`, and `height` variables marked with the `parameter` flag:

```
parameter float progress;
parameter float width;
parameter float height;

// first parameter is unused in the AnimateTransitionShader effect
input image4 src0;
input image4 from;
input image4 to;
output pixel4 dst;
```

The filter's `evaluatePixel()` method determines what the value of each filter will be. Because the example filter is a simple radial wipe, it estimates a circle and uses the Pythagorean theorem to determine whether a pixel is inside the circle or not. There are two bitmaps: the bitmap that is being wiped to and the bitmap that is being wiped from. If the location passed to the `evaluatePixel()` method is within the calculated circle, the method returns the appropriate pixel from the bitmap being wiped to. Otherwise, it returns the appropriate pixel from the bitmap being wiped from:

```
void evaluatePixel()
{
    // acquire the pixel values from both images at the current location
    float2 coord = outCoord();
    float4 color0 = sampleNearest(src0, coord);
    float4 fromPixel = sampleNearest(from, coord);
    float4 toPixel = sampleNearest(to, coord);

    float circleRad = width * progress; // progress is 0.0 to 1.0
    float deltaX;
    float deltaY;
    float deltaR;

    deltaX = coord.x - width/2.0;
    deltaY = coord.y - height/2.0;
    deltaR = sqrt(deltaX*deltaX+(deltaY*deltaY));
    if(deltaR <= circleRad || deltaR < 0.0) {
        dst = toPixel;
    } else {
        dst = fromPixel;
```

```
        }

        // workaround for Flash filter bug that replicates last column/row
        if (coord.x >= width || coord.y >= height)
            dst.a = 0.0;
    }
}
```

To use it, you need to compile the filter into a *.pbj* file using the Pixel Bender Toolkit's Pixel Bender utility and give it a name; the example file is called *RadialWipe.pbj*. You can then use the Pixel Bender filter in a Flex application by creating an instance of the `AnimateTransitionShader` object and passing your compiled filter to its `shaderByte Code` property. You can pass either a `Class` or a `ByteArray` storing an instance of a class to the `shaderByteCode`. For example:

```
<?xml version="1.0" encoding="utf-8"?>
<s:Application xmlns:fx="http://ns.adobe.com/mxml/2009"
               xmlns:s="library://ns.adobe.com/flex/spark"
               xmlns:mx="library://ns.adobe.com/flex/halo"
               minWidth="1024" minHeight="768"
               >
    <s:layout>
        <s:HorizontalLayout/>
    </s:layout>
```

The declaration of the `AnimateTransitionShader` instance is shown next. Its `target` property is bound to the image that it will be updating. The `effectEnd` event sets the `source` property of the bitmap image because once the effect is finished the source will revert to the original source. In order to show the bitmap data that is being transitioned to after the effect is finished, you need to change the `source` property of the image or update whatever `UIComponent` you're using accordingly. The `shaderByteCode` property is set to the class that is used to store the embedded data:

```
<fx:Declarations>
    <s:AnimateTransitionShader target="{img}" id="shadeAnim"
                               shaderByteCode="{ RadialWipeClass }"
                               effectEnd="setBitmap()" duration="1000" />
</fx:Declarations>
<fx:Script>
    <![CDATA[
        import mx.core.BitmapAsset;
```

Next, the *.pbj* file is embedded so that it can be accessed. If the *.pbj* file is large, you can instead load it at runtime. Note that the `mimeType` is declared as `application/octet-stream` to load the Pixel Bender properly:

```
[Embed(source="assets/RadialWipe.pbj",
        mimeType="application/octet-stream")]
private static var RadialWipeClass:Class;

[Bindable]
private static var radialWipeCode:ByteArray = new RadialWipeClass();
```

The two `BitmapAsset` instances that will be used to create the transition are shown here:

```
[Embed(source='assets/first.jpg')]
public var first:Class;
[Bindable]
public var firstBitmap:BitmapAsset = new first();

[Embed(source='assets/second.jpg')]
public var second:Class;
[Bindable]
public var secondBitmap:BitmapAsset = new second();
```

Note that the effect doesn't actually change the source of the bitmap, so you must set it when the effect is finished to make the changes stay after the effect has finished running:

```
private function setBitmap():void {
    img.source = secondBitmap;
}

private function playEffect():void {
    shadeAnim.bitmapFrom = firstBitmap.bitmapData;
    shadeAnim.bitmapTo = secondBitmap.bitmapData;
    shadeAnim.play(); // call the play() method
}

    ]]>
</fx:Script>
```

As you can see here, `BitmapImage` is the target of the `AnimateTransitionShader` instance, and will show the transition as it runs:

```
<s:BitmapImage id="img" source="{firstBitmap}"/>
<s:Button click="{playEffect()}" label="Start Animation"/>
</s:Application>
```

CHAPTER 12

Collections

Collections are powerful extensions to ActionScript's indexed array component, the core ActionScript `Array`. Collections add functionality for sorting the contents of an array, maintaining a read position within an array, and creating views that can show a sorted version of the array. Collections also can notify event listeners that the data they contain has been changed, as well as performing custom logic on items added to the source array. It is this capability of the collection to notify listeners of data changes that allows data binding, and it is the collection's capability to sort its content that allows `ListBase`-based components to sort and filter their contents. Collections are an integral part of working with both data-driven controls and server-side services returned from a database.

The three most commonly used types of collections are `ArrayCollection`, `ArrayList`, and `XMLListCollection`. `ArrayCollection` and `ArrayList` both wrap an `Array` element and provide convenient methods for adding and removing items by implementing the `IList` interface. By extending the `ListCollectionView` class, which implements the `ICollectionView` interface, `ArrayCollection` also provides the ability to create a cursor enabling the last read position in the `Array` to be stored easily. The `XMLListCollec tion` wraps an XML object and provides similar functionality: access to objects via an index, convenience methods for adding new objects, and cursor functionality. The `XMLListCollection` is particularly powerful when dealing with arrays of XML objects and frequently removes the need for parsing XML into arrays of data objects.

12.1 Add, Remove, or Retrieve Data from an ArrayList

Problem

You need to push new data into an `ArrayList` and remove and retrieve certain items from the same `ArrayList`.

Solution

Declare an `ArrayList` and use the `addItemAt()` or `addItem()` method to insert objects into it. Use the `removeItem()` and `removeItemAt()` methods to remove items and the `getItemAt()` and `getItemIndex()` methods to retrieve items from an `ArrayList`.

Discussion

The `ArrayList` class is a wrapper for a source `Array` object and provides for lightweight access and manipulation of items by implementing the `IList` interface. An `ArrayList` can be declared in MXML markup, as in the following example, within the `<fx:Decla rations>` tag of a document:

```
<fx:Declarations>
    <s:ArrayList id="list">
        <fx:String>Josh Noble</fx:String>
        <fx:String>Garth Braithwaite</fx:String>
        <fx:String>Todd Anderson</fx:String>
        <fx:String>Marco Casario</fx:String>
        <fx:String>Rich Tretola</fx:String>
    </s:ArrayList>
</fx:Declarations>
```

To add an item to the end of the `ArrayList`, use the `addItem()` method. To insert an item at a specific elemental index within the `ArrayList`, use the `addItemAt()` method, specifying the index at which to place the item:

```
list.addItemAt( "Martin Foo", 2 );
```

When inserting an item using the `addItemAt()` method, any items within the `Array List` that are held past the supplied index are moved out by one. The index argument specified must lie within the `length` value of the `ArrayList`, or a `RangeError` will be thrown at runtime.

An item within the `ArrayList` can also be replaced using the `setItemAt()` method, by specifying a new item and the index within the source `Array` at which it should reside:

```
list.setItemAt( "Martin Foo", 2 );
```

To remove an item from the `ArrayList`, use the `removeItem()` method to specify the object to be removed or the `removeItemAt()` method to specify the index at which the item resides in the source `Array` object:

```
list.removeItemAt( 2 );
list.removeItem( list.getItemAt( 2 ) );
```

The `getItemAt()` method is used to retrieve an item at a specified index from the `Array List`. To retrieve the index at which an item resides in the `ArrayList`, use the `getItemIndex()` method:

```
trace( "index: " + list.getItemIndex( "Josh Noble" ) );
```

12.2 Retrieve and Sort Data from an ArrayCollection

Problem

You need to retrieve certain items from the same `ArrayCollection`.

Solution

Use the `getItemIndex()` or `contains()` method to determine whether an item exists in the `ArrayCollection`, and provide a `Sort` object to the `sort` property of the `ArrayCollec``tion` to sort the collection on a certain field and retrieve the first and last items.

Discussion

To see how the various methods of retrieving and sorting the items in an `ArrayCollec``tion` work, you first need a collection. Declare an `ArrayCollection` within the `<fx:Dec`­`larations>` tag of an MXML document:

```
<fx:Declarations>
    <s:ArrayCollection id="collection">
        <fx:Object name="Martin Foo" age="25" />
        <fx:Object name="Joe Bar" age="15" />
        <fx:Object name="Joe Baz" age="23" />
    </s:ArrayCollection>
</fx:Declarations>
```

To determine whether a complex object is present in the `ArrayCollection`, you need to compare the objects' property values. It might be tempting to try something like this:

```
private function checkExistence():void
{
    trace(collection.contains({name:nameTI.text, age:Number(ageTI.text)}));
    trace(collection.getItemIndex({name:nameTI.text, age:ageTI.text}));
    // traces -1 if not present
}
```

However, this will not work, because the `contains()` and `getItemIndex()` methods compare the pointers of the objects, not their actual property values. Because the comparison is between two distinct objects—that is, two distinct locations in memory with unique identifiers—the Flash Player does not recognize them as being equal. Consequently, the `getItemIndex()` method will not return the index of the item or confirm that the `ArrayCollection` contains a match. To determine whether an item with the same values exists within the collection, you must compare each item in the source `Array` of the collection. To do so, use a function similar to this:

```
private function checkExistence():int
{
    var arr:Array = collection.source;
    var i:int = arr.length;
    while( --i > -1 )
```

```
        {
            if(arr[i].name == nameTI.text && arr[i].age == Number(ageTI.text))
            {
                break;
            }
        }
    }
    return i;
}
```

The Sort object provides a findItem() method that performs a similar and more flexible search through all the objects of an ArrayCollection, via the source property of the ArrayCollection. The findItem() method has the following signature:

```
public function findItem(items:Array, values:Object, mode:String,
        returnInsertionIndex:Boolean = false, compareFunction:Function = null):int
```

The values parameter can be any object that contains all the properties and required values. The mode argument value can be Sort.ANY_INDEX_MODE, if you want the index of any instance; Sort.FIRST_INDEX_MODE, if you want the index of the first instance; or Sort.LAST_INDEX_MODE, if you want the index of the last instance. The returnInsertionIndex parameter indicates whether the findItem() function should return the position in the sorted array where the item would be placed if no object matching the values parameter is found. The compareFunction parameter specifies the function that the Sort object should use to determine whether two items are similar.

To replace the preceding method, you can use the findItem() method of the Sort object as follows:

```
private function checkExistence():int
{
    var sort:Sort = new Sort();
    return sort.findItem( collection.source,
                        {name:nameTI.text, age:Number(ageTI.text)},
                        Sort.ANY_INDEX_MODE );
}
```

To sort the ArrayCollection, create a Sort object and pass it an array of SortField objects. These SortField objects contain a string representing the property within each object contained by the ArrayCollection that should be used to determine the sort order. To sort on the age property of each object in the collection, create a Sort object and pass it a SortField with its field set to age:

```
private function getOldest():void
{
    var sort:Sort = new Sort();
    sort.fields = [new SortField("age", false, true)];
    collection.sort = sort;
    collection.refresh();
    trace( collection.getItemAt(0).age + " " + collection.getItemAt(0).name );
}
```

This function sorts the `ArrayCollection` based on the `age` value of each item, in descending order.

See Also

Recipe 12.1

12.3 Filter an ArrayCollection

Problem

You need to filter an `ArrayCollection`, removing any results that don't match the criteria set in the filter.

Solution

Pass a filter function with the signature `function(item:Object):Boolean` to the `filter` property of the `ArrayCollection`. The filter function will return a value of `true` if the item should stay in the `ArrayCollection`, and `false` if the item should be removed.

Discussion

The `filterFunction` property is defined on the `ICollectionView` interface and implemented by the `ListCollectionView` class, which the `ArrayCollection` class extends. After a `filterFunction` is passed to any class that extends the `ListCollectionView`—in this case, an instance of `ArrayCollection`—the `refresh()` method must be called in order for the filter to be applied to the `ArrayCollection`:

```
<s:Application xmlns:fx="http://ns.adobe.com/mxml/2009"
               xmlns:s="library://ns.adobe.com/flex/spark"
               xmlns:mx="library://ns.adobe.com/flex/mx">

    <fx:Declarations>
        <s:ArrayCollection id="collection">
            <fx:Object name="Martin Foo" age="25" />
            <fx:Object name="Joe Bar" age="15" />
            <fx:Object name="Joe Baz" age="23" />
        </s:ArrayCollection>
    </fx:Declarations>

    <fx:Script>
        <![CDATA[

            private function applyFilter():void
            {
                collection.filterFunction = filterFunc;
                collection.refresh();
            }
```

```
        private function filterFunc(value:Object):Object
        {
            return (Number(value.age) > 21);
        }

    ]]>
</fx:Script>

<s:layout>
    <s:VerticalLayout />
</s:layout>

<s:DropDownList labelField="name" dataProvider="{collection}" />
<s:Button label="set filter" click="applyFilter();" />

</s:Application>
```

It is important to note that the source array of the ArrayCollection is not altered by the filterFunction. That is, in the preceding example, after the refresh() method is called, the source array will remain at a length of three elements. Because the source array always remains the same, multiple instances of filterFunction can be passed, and each one will remove the previous filter and filter the original source array.

See Also

Recipe 12.2

12.4 Determine When an Item Within an ArrayCollection Is Modified

Problem

You need to determine when an item has been added to or removed from an ArrayCollection by an out-of-scope process.

Solution

Listen for an event of type collectionChange or CollectionEvent.COLLECTION_CHANGE dispatched by the ArrayCollection class, which extends EventDispatcher.

Discussion

Any time an object is added to or removed from an ArrayCollection, a CollectionEvent of type collectionChange is dispatched. When a control is bound to a collection, the binding is notified that the collection has changed through this event. Adding an event listener to the collection to listen for the COLLECTION_CHANGE event lets you write logic to handle any changes to the collection:

```
private var coll:ArrayCollection = new ArrayCollection();
coll.addEventListener(CollectionEvent.COLLECTION_CHANGE, collChangeHandler);
```

The CollectionEvent class defines the following additional properties:

items:Array
> When the event is dispatched in response to items being added to the ArrayCollec
> tion, the items property is an array of added items. If items have been removed
> from the collection, the items array contains all the removed items.

kind:String
> This is a string that indicates the kind of event that occurred. Possible values are
> add, remove, replace, or move.

location:int
> This property is the zero-based index in the collection of the item(s) specified in
> the items property.

oldLocation:int
> When the kind value is move, this property is the zero-based index in the target
> collection of the previous location of the item(s) specified by the items property.

Using the CollectionEvent, the state of the ArrayCollection or XMLListCollection
before and after a change can be inferred. This is very useful when you need to ensure
that any changes in the Flex application are updated on a server.

See Also

Recipe 12.2

12.5 Create a GroupingCollection

Problem

You need to create distinct groups based on certain properties of the items contained
in a collection.

Solution

Pass an Array to the constructor of the GroupingCollection2 or set the source property
of an already instantiated GroupingCollection2 object.

Discussion

Any GroupingCollection2 can be passed an instance of Grouping containing an array of
GroupingField objects that define the properties of the data objects that will be used to
generate the group. Thus, you can use a GroupingCollection2 to group data objects by
a property that they all share. For instance, to populate a GroupingCollection2 with

data objects that all possess `city`, `state`, and `region` properties, you could specify the following within the `<fx:Declaration>` tag of an MXML document:

```
<fx:Declarations>
    <mx:GroupingCollection2 id="groupingCollection">
        <mx:source>
            <fx:Object city="Columbus" state="Ohio" region="East" />
            <fx:Object city="Cleveland" state="Ohio" region="East" />
            <fx:Object city="Sacramento" state="California" region="West" />
            <fx:Object city="Atlanta" state="Georgia" region="South" />
        </mx:source>
    </mx:GroupingCollection2>
</fx:Declarations>
```

To group the objects by their `state` properties—that is, to create groupings of all objects that are within the same state—create and assign a `Grouping` instance to the `grouping` property of the `GroupingCollection2` instance and pass it an array of `GroupingField` objects:

```
<fx:Declarations>
    <mx:GroupingCollection2 id="groupingCollection">
        <mx:source>
            <fx:Object city="Columbus" state="Ohio" region="East" />
            <fx:Object city="Cleveland" state="Ohio" region="East" />
            <fx:Object city="Sacramento" state="California" region="West" />
            <fx:Object city="Atlanta" state="Georgia" region="South" />
        </mx:source>
        <mx:grouping>
            <mx:Grouping>
                <mx:GroupingField name="state" />
            </mx:Grouping>
        </mx:grouping>
    </mx:GroupingCollection2>
</fx:Declarations>
```

The `GroupingCollection2` instance can be assigned to the `dataProvider` of an `Advanced DataGrid` component through binding, as follows:

```
<mx:AdvancedDataGrid id="grid" dataProvider="{groupingCollection}">
    <mx:columns>
        <mx:AdvancedDataGridColumn dataField="city" />
        <mx:AdvancedDataGridColumn dataField="state" />
        <mx:AdvancedDataGridColumn dataField="region" />
    </mx:columns>
</mx:AdvancedDataGrid>
```

The `Grouping` object assigned to a `GroupingCollection2` instance can be changed at runtime. When a new `Grouping` is provided, the `refresh()` method is called in order for the bound collection to update the target view. In the following example, the `create Grouping()` method is used to update the grouped collection within an `AdvancedData Grid`:

```
<s:Application xmlns:fx="http://ns.adobe.com/mxml/2009"
               xmlns:s="library://ns.adobe.com/flex/spark"
```

```
                xmlns:mx="library://ns.adobe.com/flex/mx"
                creationComplete="handleCreationComplete();">

    <fx:Declarations>
        <mx:GroupingCollection2 id="groupingCollection">
            <mx:source>
                <fx:Object city="Columbus" state="Ohio" region="East" />
                <fx:Object city="Cleveland" state="Ohio" region="East" />
                <fx:Object city="Sacramento" state="California" region="West" />
                <fx:Object city="Atlanta" state="Georgia" region="South" />
            </mx:source>
            <mx:grouping>
                <mx:Grouping>
                    <mx:GroupingField name="state" />
                </mx:Grouping>
            </mx:grouping>
        </mx:GroupingCollection2>
    </fx:Declarations>

    <fx:Script>
        <![CDATA[
            import mx.collections.Grouping;
            import mx.collections.GroupingField;

            private function handleCreationComplete():void
            {
                groupingCollection.refresh();
            }

            private function createGrouping( field:String ):void
            {
                var groupingInst:Grouping = new Grouping();
                groupingInst.fields = [new GroupingField( field )];
                groupingCollection.grouping = groupingInst;
                groupingCollection.refresh(false);
            }

        ]]>
    </fx:Script>

    <s:layout>
        <s:VerticalLayout />
    </s:layout>

    <mx:AdvancedDataGrid id="grid" dataProvider="{groupingCollection}">
        <mx:columns>
            <mx:AdvancedDataGridColumn dataField="city" />
            <mx:AdvancedDataGridColumn dataField="state" />
            <mx:AdvancedDataGridColumn dataField="region" />
        </mx:columns>
    </mx:AdvancedDataGrid>
    <s:Button label="region group" click="{createGrouping('region')}" />

</s:Application>
```

To pass multiple groupings, provide multiple `GroupingField` objects to the `fields` property of the `Grouping` object:

```
groupingInst.fields = [new GroupingField("region"), new GroupingField("state")];
```

This will group all the data objects first by region and then by state. Thus, for the data set shown in this example, Columbus and Cleveland will be grouped together twice, by region (East) and by state (Ohio).

See Also

Recipe 12.10

12.6 Create a Hierarchical Data Provider for a Control

Problem

You want to use a *flat object* (an object without parent-to-child relationships) that represents hierarchical data as the `dataProvider` for a `DataGrid`.

Solution

Create a custom data class that implements the `IHierarchicalData` interface and create methods to determine whether a node or object in the data has parent nodes and whether it has child nodes.

Discussion

The `IHierarchicalData` interface defines all the methods that the `DataGrid` and `AdvancedDataGrid` components need to display hierarchical data. The term *hierarchical data* refers to data that describes a series of parent/child relationships. For example, imagine a representation of different types of vehicles—cars, trucks, boats—each of which can be subdivided into more specific kinds of vehicles. The hierarchy from sedans to the top might look like Figure 12-1.

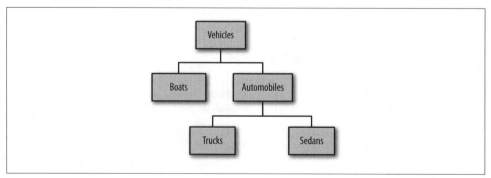

Figure 12-1. An object hierarchy

One way to represent this data is the following:

```
private var data:Object = [{name:"Vehicles", id:1, parentId:0, type:"parent"},
      {name:"Automobiles", id:2, parentId:1, type:"parent"},
      {name:"Boats", id:3, parentId:0, type:"parent"},
      {name:"Trucks", id:4, parentId:1, type:"parent"},
      {name:"Sedans", id:5, parentId:2, type:"parent"}];
```

Here, you assign each node an id and a parentId that defines the parent of that node. This type of data structure can quickly grow unwieldy and is typically quite difficult to represent. An alternative is to use the IHierarchicalData interface; with this approach, the AdvancedDataGrid can display the data as grouped data, or the Tree control can display it as a data tree. The IHierarchicalData interface requires that the following methods be defined:

canHaveChildren(node:Object):Boolean
> Determines whether any given node has children

dispatchEvent(event:Event):Boolean
> Dispatches an event

getChildren(node:Object):Object
> Returns all the children of a node as an object

getData(node:Object):Object
> Returns all the data of a node, including children, as an object

getParent(node:Object):*
> Returns the parent of any node

getRoot():Object
> Returns the root of an object with hierarchical data

hasChildren(node:Object):Boolean
> Returns true if a node possesses children, and false if it does not

The ObjectHierarchicalData class detailed next implements each of these methods by using the same hierarchical structure shown in Figure 12-1:

```
package com.oreilly.f4cb
{
    import flash.events.EventDispatcher;

    import mx.collections.IHierarchicalData;

    [DefaultProperty("source")]
    public class ObjectHierarchicalData extends EventDispatcher implements
            IHierarchicalData {
        private var _source:Object;

        public function ObjectHierarchicalData() {}

        /* in our simple system, only parents with their type set to
        'parent' can have children */
        public function canHaveChildren(node:Object):Boolean
```

```
{
    return ( node.type == 'parent' );
}

/* for any given node, determine whether that node has any children by
looking through all the other nodes for that node's ID as a parentTask */
public function hasChildren(node:Object):Boolean
{
    var obj:Object;
    for each( obj in source )
    {
        if( obj.parentTask == node.objId )
            return true;
    }
    return false;
}

/* for any given node, return all the nodes that are children of that
node in an array */
public function getChildren(node:Object):Object
{
    var parentId:String = node.objId;
    var children:Array = [];
    var obj:Object;
    for each( obj in source )
    {
        if( obj.parentTask == parentId )
            children.push( obj );
    }
    return children;
}

public function getData(node:Object):Object
{
    var obj:Object;
    var prop:String;
    for each( obj in source )
    {
        for each( prop in node )
        {
            if( obj[prop] == node[prop] )
                return obj;
            else
                break;
        }
    }
    return null;
}

/* we want to return every obj that is a root object, which
in this case is going to be all nodes that have a parent node
of '0' */
public function getRoot():Object
{
```

```
                    var rootsArr:Array = [];
                    var obj:Object;
                    for each( obj in source )
                    {
                        if( obj.parentTask == "0" )
                        {
                            rootsArr.push( obj );
                        }
                    }
                    return rootsArr;
                }

                public function getParent(node:Object):*
                {
                    var obj:Object;
                    for each( obj in source )
                    {
                        if( obj.parentTask == node.parentTask )
                            return obj;
                    }
                    return null;
                }

                public function get source():Object
                {
                    return _source;
                }
                public function set source( value:Object ):void
                {
                    _source = value;
                }
            }
        }
```

The [DefaultProperty] metadata tag is declared and valued as the source property to allow an instance of ObjectHierarchicalData to be declared and filled using MXML markup. The source object is then used within the method implementations to derive the correct data values needed by the view client.

Now that all the correct methods are in place to determine the relations between the nodes within the data object, you can assign the new hierarchical data class to the dataProvider of an AdvancedDataGrid. This allows the control to display the correct relationships in the hierarchical data. A data object with the relationships between nodes described through the parentTask and id properties can be passed into the new ObjectHierarchicalData object:

```
<s:Application xmlns:fx="http://ns.adobe.com/mxml/2009"
            xmlns:s="library://ns.adobe.com/flex/spark"
            xmlns:mx="library://ns.adobe.com/flex/mx"
            xmlns:f4cb="com.oreilly.f4cb.*">
```

```
<fx:Declarations>
    <f4cb:ObjectHierarchicalData id="ohd">
        <fx:Object objId="1" name="Misc" type="parent" parentTask="0" />
        <fx:Object objId="2" name="Clean The Kitchen" type="parent"
                    parentTask="0" />
        <fx:Object objId="3" name="Pay The Bills" type="parent"
                    parentTask="0" />
        <fx:Object objId="4" name="Paint The Shed" type="parent"
                    parentTask="1" />
        <fx:Object objId="5" name="Get Ready For Party" type="parent"
                    parentTask="1" />
        <fx:Object objId="6" name="Do The Dishes" type="child"
                    parentTask="2" />
        <fx:Object objId="7" name="Take Out The Trash" type="child"
                    parentTask="2" />
        <fx:Object objId="8" name="Gas Bill" type="child" parentTask="3" />
        <fx:Object objId="9" name="Fix The Car" type="parent" parentTask="0" />
        <fx:Object objId="10" name="New Tires" type="child" parentTask="10" />
        <fx:Object objId="11" name="Emission Test" type="child"
                    parentTask="10" />
        <fx:Object objId="12" name="Get New Paint" type="child"
                    parentTask="4" />
        <fx:Object objId="13" name="Buy Brushes" type="child" parentTask="4" />
        <fx:Object objId="14" name="Buy Drinks" type="child" parentTask="5" />
        <fx:Object objId="10" name="Clean Living Room" type="child"
                    parentTask="5" />
        <fx:Object objId="10" name="Finish Invitations" type="child"
                    parentTask="5" />
    </f4cb:ObjectHierarchicalData>
</fx:Declarations>

<mx:AdvancedDataGrid dataProvider="{ohd}" width="300" height="200">
    <mx:columns>
        <!-- all we want to display of the object is the name, the ADG will
        take care of displaying the parent child relationship -->
        <mx:AdvancedDataGridColumn dataField="name" />
    </mx:columns>
</mx:AdvancedDataGrid>

</s:Application>
```

12.7 Navigate a Collection Object and Save Your Position

Problem

You want to navigate a collection bidirectionally and save the location at which you stop progressing.

Solution

Use the `createCursor()` method of the `ListViewCollection` class to create a cursor that can be moved forward and back while maintaining its position in the collection so that it can be used later to determine where progression stopped.

Discussion

You can use a collection's `createCursor()` method to return a view cursor, which you can use to traverse the items in the collection's data view and access and modify data in the collection. A *cursor* is a position indicator; it points to a particular item in the collection. View cursor methods and properties are defined in the `IViewCursor` interface.

By using the `IViewCursor` methods, you can move the cursor backward and forward, seeking items with certain criteria within the collection, getting the item at a certain location, saving the point of last access in the collection, and adding, removing, or changing the values of items.

When you use the standard Flex collection classes, `ArrayCollection` and `XMLList Collection`, you use the `IViewCursor` interface directly, and you do not reference an object instance. For example:

```
<s:Application xmlns:fx="http://ns.adobe.com/mxml/2009"
               xmlns:s="library://ns.adobe.com/flex/spark"
               xmlns:mx="library://ns.adobe.com/flex/mx"
               creationComplete="handleCreationComplete();">

    <fx:Declarations>
        <s:ArrayCollection id="collection">
            <s:source>
                <fx:Object city="Columbus" state="Ohio" region="East" />
                <fx:Object city="Cleveland" state="Ohio" region="East" />
                <fx:Object city="Sacramento" state="California" region="West" />
                <fx:Object city="Atlanta" state="Georgia" region="South" />
            </s:source>
        </s:ArrayCollection>
    </fx:Declarations>

    <fx:Script>
        <![CDATA[
            import mx.collections.IViewCursor;
            import mx.collections.Sort;
            import mx.collections.SortField;

            [Bindable] public var cursor:IViewCursor;

            private function handleCreationComplete():void
            {
                cursor = collection.createCursor();
            }
```

In the following example, the `findFirst()` method of the `IViewCursor` object is used to locate the first object in the collection that contains any property matching the input entered by the user into the `TextInput` control:

```
private function findRegion():void
{
    var sort:Sort = new Sort();
    sort.fields = [new SortField("region")];
    collection.sort = sort;
    collection.refresh();
    cursor.findFirst( {region:regionInput.text} );
}

private function findState():void
{
    var sort:Sort = new Sort();
    sort.fields = [new SortField("state")];
    collection.sort = sort;
    collection.refresh();
    cursor.findFirst( {state:stateInput.text} );
}
    }
]]>
</fx:Script>

<s:layout>
    <s:VerticalLayout />
</s:layout>

<s:Label text="{cursor.current.city}" />
<s:Button label="next" click="{cursor.moveNext()}" />
<s:Button label="previous" click="{cursor.movePrevious()}" />
<s:HGroup>
    <s:TextInput id="regionInput" />
    <s:Button label="find region" click="findRegion();" />
</s:HGroup>
<s:HGroup>
    <s:TextInput id="stateInput" />
    <s:Button label="find state" click="findState();" />
</s:HGroup>

</s:Application>
```

The `IViewCursor` defines three methods for searching within a collection:

`findFirst(values:Object):Boolean`
This method sets the cursor location to the first item that meets the criteria.

`findLast(values:Object):Boolean`
This method sets the cursor location to the last item that meets the criteria.

`findAny(values:Object):Boolean`
This method sets the cursor location to any item that meets the criteria. This is the quickest method and should be used if the first or last item is not needed.

It is important to note that none of these methods will work on an unsorted `ArrayCollection` or `XMLListCollection`.

12.8 Create a HierarchicalViewCollection Object

Problem

You want to create a collection that will let you work with an `IHierarchicalData` object as a collection.

Solution

Create a class that implements the `IHierarchicalData` interface to determine the parent and child nodes of each node. Create a new `HierarchicalViewCollection` object and pass the `IHierarchicalData` object to the constructor of the `HierarchicalViewCollec` tion class.

Discussion

By default, to work with `HierarchicalData`, the `AdvancedDataGrid` creates a `HierarchicalCollectionView`. This `HierarchicalCollectionView` allows the `Advanced DataGrid` to retrieve an `ArrayCollection` and apply all its methods to that `Hierarchical Data`. This is also helpful when working with custom components that will display hierarchical data. The `ObjectHierarchicalData` class from Recipe 12.6 implements `IHierarchicalData` and provides methods to determine the parent/child relationships between different nodes. The `HierarchicalCollectionView` class uses these methods to visually open and close nodes, as well as to determine whether a data object contains a certain value. This recipe uses `ObjectHierarchicalData` to create an instance of the `HierarchicalCollectionView`.

The methods of the `HierarchicalCollectionView` are as follows:

`addChild(parent:Object, newChild:Object):Boolean`
  Adds a child node to a node of the data.

`addChildAt(parent:Object, newChild:Object, index:int):Boolean`
  Adds a child node to a node at the specified index.

`closeNode(node:Object):void`
  Closes a node to hide its children.

`contains(item:Object):Boolean`
  Checks whether the specified data item exists within the collection. Passing in a complex object with a different location in memory than an object with the same values within the collection won't return `true`.

`createCursor():IViewCursor`
  Returns a new instance of a view iterator to iterate over the items in this view.

```
getParentItem(node:Object):*
```
Returns the parent of a node.

```
openNode(node:Object):void
```
Opens a node to display its children.

```
removeChild(parent:Object, child:Object):Boolean
```
Removes the specified child node from the specified parent node.

```
removeChildAt(parent:Object, index:int):Boolean
```
Removes the specified child node from the node at the specified index.

Determining which node to manipulate relies on a good implementation of the `get Data()` method of the `IHierarchicalData` interface. By allowing an object with a key/value pairing to be passed into the `getData()` method, which then returns the node that contains that same pairing, the `HierarchicalCollectionView` can determine which object in the source data object to manipulate. Here, a large hierarchical data object is defined and passed to a `HierarchicalData` object, and then a `HierarchicalCollection View` is created:

```
<s:Application xmlns:fx="http://ns.adobe.com/mxml/2009"
               xmlns:s="library://ns.adobe.com/flex/spark"
               xmlns:mx="library://ns.adobe.com/flex/mx"
               xmlns:f4cb="com.oreilly.f4cb.*">

    <fx:Declarations>
        <f4cb:ObjectHierarchicalData id="ohd">
            <fx:Object objId="1" name="Misc" type="parent" parentTask="0" />
            <fx:Object objId="2" name="Clean The Kitchen" type="parent"
                       parentTask="0" />
            <fx:Object objId="3" name="Pay The Bills" type="parent"
                       parentTask="0" />
            <fx:Object objId="4" name="Paint The Shed" type="parent"
                       parentTask="1" />
            <fx:Object objId="5" name="Get Ready For Party" type="parent"
                       parentTask="1" />
            <fx:Object objId="6" name="Do The Dishes" type="child"
                       parentTask="2" />
            <fx:Object objId="7" name="Take Out The Trash" type="child"
                       parentTask="2" />
            <fx:Object objId="8" name="Gas Bill" type="child" parentTask="3" />
            <fx:Object objId="9" name="Fix The Car" type="parent" parentTask="0" />
            <fx:Object objId="10" name="New Tires" type="child" parentTask="10" />
            <fx:Object objId="11" name="Emission Test" type="child"
                       parentTask="10" />
            <fx:Object objId="12" name="Get New Paint" type="child"
                       parentTask="4" />
            <fx:Object objId="13" name="Buy Brushes" type="child" parentTask="4" />
            <fx:Object objId="14" name="Buy Drinks" type="child" parentTask="5" />
            <fx:Object objId="10" name="Clean Living Room" type="child"
                       parentTask="5" />
            <fx:Object objId="10" name="Finish Invitations" type="child"
                       parentTask="5" />
```

```
                </f4cb:ObjectHierarchicalData>
            </fx:Declarations>

            <fx:Script>
                <![CDATA[
                    import mx.collections.ArrayCollection;
                    import mx.collections.HierarchicalCollectionView;
                    import mx.collections.ICollectionView;

                    private static const NODE_ID:String = "3";
                    private static const NODE_NAME:String = "Pay The Bills";
                    private function showNode():void
                    {
                        // pass that class to the HierarchicalCollectionView class
                        var hCollectionView:HierarchicalCollectionView =
                                new HierarchicalCollectionView( ohd );
                        hCollectionView.openNode( ohd.source[2] );

                        var arrayCollection:ICollectionView =
                                hCollectionView.getChildren(
                                hCollectionView.source.getData( {objId:NODE_ID } ) );
                        hCollectionView.closeNode( hCollectionView.source.getData(
                                {name:NODE_NAME } ) );
                        grid.dataProvider = arrayCollection;
                    }
                ]]>
            </fx:Script>

            <s:layout>
                <s:VerticalLayout />
            </s:layout>

            <mx:AdvancedDataGrid id="grid" dataProvider="{ohd}" width="300" height="200">
                <mx:columns>
                    <!-- all we want to display of the object is the name, the ADG will
                    take care of displaying the parent/child relationship -->
                    <mx:AdvancedDataGridColumn dataField="name" />
                </mx:columns>
            </mx:AdvancedDataGrid>

            <s:HGroup>
                <s:Button label="showNode" click="showNode();" />
                <s:Button label="showFull" click="{grid.dataProvider=ohd}" />
            </s:HGroup>

        </s:Application>
```

The HierarchicalCollectionView wraps the IHierarchicalData view object, providing methods to create views from the objects within the collection by using the get Children() method.

12.9 Filter and Sort an XMLListCollection

Problem

You need to filter and then sort an XMLListCollection.

Solution

Use the filterFunction and sortFunction properties of the ListViewCollection class that the XMLListCollection class extends, or simply pass a custom Sort object to the sort property of an XMLListCollection instance.

Discussion

An XMLListCollection describes XML data that has multiple nodes contained within its root. For example, a collection of food items contained within a nutrition node will translate into an XMLListCollection that allows the food nodes to be treated as a collection:

```
<nutrition>
    <food>
        <name>Avocado Dip</name>
        <calories>110</calories>
        <total-fat>11</total-fat>
        <saturated-fat>3</saturated-fat>
        <cholesterol>5</cholesterol>
        <sodium>210</sodium>
        <carb>2</carb>
        <fiber>0</fiber>
        <protein>1</protein>
    </food>
    ...
</nutrition>
```

You filter an XMLListCollection in the same way you filter an ArrayCollection: by passing a reference to a function that accepts an object and returns a Boolean value indicating whether or not the object should remain in the filtered view. For example:

```
collection.filterFunction = lowCalFilter;
private function lowCalFilter(value:Object):Boolean
{
    return ( Number(value.calories) < 500 );
}
```

Sorting an XMLListCollection requires a Sort object with its fields array populated with SortField objects:

```
var sort:Sort = new Sort();
sort.fields = [new SortField( "calories", false, false, true )];
collection.sort = sort;
collection.refresh();
```

A complete code listing showing an XMLListCollection being built from a declared XML object, sorted, and then filtered is shown here:

```
<s:Application xmlns:fx="http://ns.adobe.com/mxml/2009"
               xmlns:s="library://ns.adobe.com/flex/spark"
               xmlns:mx="library://ns.adobe.com/flex/mx"
               creationComplete="handleCreationComplete();">

    <fx:Declarations>
        <fx:XML id="nutritionData" source="assets/data.xml" />
    </fx:Declarations>

    <fx:Script>
        <![CDATA[
            import mx.collections.Sort;
            import mx.collections.SortField;
            import mx.collections.XMLListCollection;

            [Bindable] public var collection:XMLListCollection;
            private function handleCreationComplete():void
            {
                collection = new XMLListCollection( nutritionData..food );
                var sort:Sort = new Sort();
                sort.fields = [new SortField( "calories", false, false, true )];
                collection.sort = sort;
                collection.refresh();
            }

            private function applyFilter():void
            {
                collection.filterFunction = lowCalFilter;
                collection.refresh();
            }

            private function lowCalFilter( value:Object ):Boolean
            {
                return ( Number(value.calories) < 500 );
            }

        ]]>
    </fx:Script>

    <s:layout>
        <s:VerticalLayout />
    </s:layout>

    <mx:DataGrid dataProvider="{collection}">
        <mx:columns>
            <mx:DataGridColumn dataField="calories" />
            <mx:DataGridColumn dataField="name" />
        </mx:columns>
    </mx:DataGrid>
```

```
    <s:Button label="filter" click="applyFilter();" />

</s:Application>
```

You can perform complex filtering by using ECMAScript for XML (E4X) statements with various nodes in the XML collection. For example, you can access attributes by using the @ syntax, as shown here:

```
private function lowFatFilter(value:Object):Boolean
{
    return (value.calories(@fat) < Number(value.calories)/5);
}
```

12.10 Sort on Multiple Fields in a Collection

Problem

You need to sort a collection on multiple fields.

Solution

Pass multiple `SortField` objects to a `Sort` object and then assign that object to the `sort` property of the collection.

Discussion

The `field` property of the `Sort` class is of type `Array` and can receive multiple instances of `SortField`. These multiple sorts create a hierarchy in which all objects are sorted into groups that match the first `SortField` object's `field` property, then the second's, and so on. This example code sorts the collection first into regions and then into states:

```
<fx:Declarations>
    <s:ArrayCollection id="collection">
        <s:source>
            <fx:Object city="Columbus" state="Ohio" region="East" />
            <fx:Object city="Cleveland" state="Ohio" region="East" />
            <fx:Object city="Sacramento" state="California" region="West" />
            <fx:Object city="Atlanta" state="Georgia" region="South" />
        </s:source>
        <s:sort>
            <mx:Sort>
                <mx:SortField name="region" />
                <mx:SortField name="state" />
            </mx:Sort>
        </s:sort>
    </s:ArrayCollection>
</fx:Declarations>

<mx:AdvancedDataGrid dataProvider="{collection}">
    <mx:columns>
        <mx:AdvancedDataGridColumn dataField="city" />
```

```
        <mx:AdvancedDataGridColumn dataField="state" />
            <mx:AdvancedDataGridColumn dataField="region" />
        </mx:columns>
    </mx:AdvancedDataGrid>
```

The items in the array collection will now appear as shown in Figure 12-2.

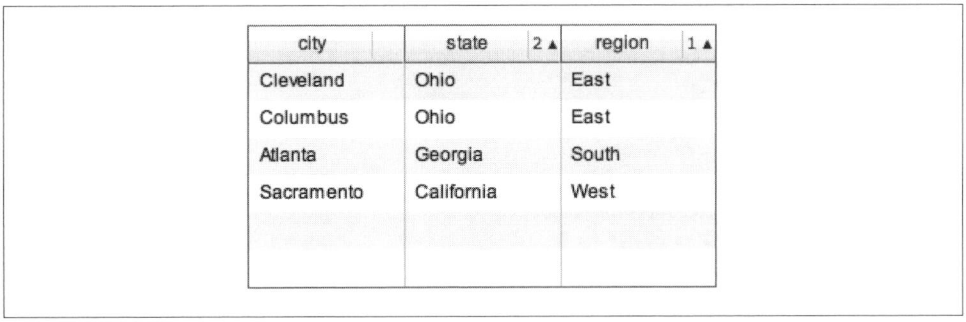

city	state	2 ▲	region	1 ▲
Cleveland	Ohio		East	
Columbus	Ohio		East	
Atlanta	Georgia		South	
Sacramento	California		West	

Figure 12-2. Data sorted on multiple fields

See Also

Recipes 12.2 and 12.5

12.11 Sort on Dates in a Collection

Problem

You need to sort on the date values that are stored as string properties of data objects.

Solution

Create new `Date` objects from each object's `date` property and use the `dateCompare()` method of the `mx.utils.ObjectUtil` class to compare the dates.

Discussion

The `ObjectUtil` class provides a `dateCompare()` method that can determine which of two `Date` objects occurs earlier. You can use this method to sort a collection of `Date` objects by creating a `sortFunction` that returns the result of the `ObjectUtil:date Compare()` method. `dateCompare()`returns 0 if the values are both null or are equal, 1 if the first value is null or is located before the second value in the sort, or -1 if the second value is null or is located before first value in the sort. The following example demonstrates sorting by date:

```
<s:Application xmlns:fx="http://ns.adobe.com/mxml/2009"
               xmlns:s="library://ns.adobe.com/flex/spark"
               xmlns:mx="library://ns.adobe.com/flex/mx">
```

```
<fx:Declarations>
    <s:ArrayCollection id="collection">
        <s:source>
            <fx:Object name="Josh" dob="08/17/1983" />
            <fx:Object name="John" dob="07/30/1946" />
            <fx:Object name="John" dob="07/30/1990" />
            <fx:Object name="Jeff" dob="07/30/1986" />
        </s:source>
    </s:ArrayCollection>
</fx:Declarations>

<fx:Script>
    <![CDATA[
        import mx.collections.Sort;
        import mx.utils.ObjectUtil;

        private function handleSort():void
        {
            var sort:Sort = new Sort();
            sort.compareFunction = sortFunction;
            collection.sort = sort;
            collection.refresh();
        }

        private function sortFunction( a:Object, b:Object,
                fields:Array = null ):Boolean
        {
            var dateA:Date = new Date( Date.parse( a.dob ) );
            var dateB:Date = new Date( Date.parse( b.dob ) );
            return ObjectUtil.dateCompare( dateA, dateB );
        }
    ]]>
</fx:Script>

<s:layout>
    <s:VerticalLayout />
</s:layout>

<mx:DataGrid dataProvider="{collection}">
    <mx:columns>
        <mx:DataGridColumn dataField="name" />
        <mx:DataGridColumn dataField="dob" />
    </mx:columns>
</mx:DataGrid>

<s:Button label="sort" click="handleSort();" />

</s:Application>
```

See Also

Recipe 12.2

12.12 Create a Deep Copy of an ArrayCollection

Problem

You need to copy all the items in an indexed array or an object into a new object.

Solution

Use the `mx.utils.ObjectUtil.copy()` method.

Discussion

As a quick demonstration shows, copying an object simply creates a pointer to the new object, which means that any changes to the values of the first object are reflected in the second object:

```
var objOne:Object = {name:"foo", data:{first:"1", second:"2"}};
var objTwo = objOne;
objOne.data.first = "4";
trace(objTwo.data.first); //traces 4
```

To make a separate and independent copy of the object instead, use the `copy()` method of the `mx.utils.ObjectUtil` class. This method accepts an object and returns a *deep copy* of that object in a new location in memory. Any properties of the original object are copied over to the new one and no longer refer to the same location. The method is used like this:

```
var objTwo = mx.utils.ObjectUtil.copy( objOne );
```

`copy()` works by creating a `ByteArray` from the object passed into it and then writing that `ByteArray` back as a new object, as shown here:

```
var ba:ByteArray = new ByteArray();
ba.writeObject( objToCopy );
ba.position = 0;
var objToCopyInto:Object = ba.readObject();
return objToCopyInto;
```

Now the original example will behave as expected:

```
var objOne:Object = {name:"foo", data:{first:"1", second:"2"}};
var objTwo = objOne;
var objThree = mx.utils.ObjectUtil.copy( objOne );
objOne.data.first = "4";
trace(objTwo.data.first);   //traces 4
trace(objThree.data.first); //traces 1, which is the original value
```

Copying an object of a specific type into a new object of that type presents a special difficulty. The following code will throw an error:

```
var newFoo:Foo = ObjectUtil.copy(oldFoo) as Foo;
```

because the Flash Player will not know how to convert the `ByteArray` into the type requested by the cast. Using `ByteArray` serializes the object into ActionScript Message Format (AMF) binary data, the same way that serialized objects are sent in Flash Remoting. To deserialize the data object, the type must be registered with the Flash Player by using the `flash.net.registerClassAlias()` method. This method registers the class so that any object of the specified type can be deserialized from binary data into an object of that type. The `registerClassAlias()` method requires two parameters:

```
public function registerClassAlias(aliasName:String, classObject:Class):void
```

The first parameter is the fully qualified class name of the class, and the second is an object of type `Class`. The fully qualified class name will be something like `mx.containers.Canvas` or `com.oreilly.f4cb.Foo`. In our example, neither the class name nor the reference to the class will be known when the object is copied. Fortunately, the `flash.utils.getQualifiedClassName()` method returns the fully qualified class name of the object passed to it, and the `flash.utils.getDefinitionByName()` method returns a reference to the class of the object passed into it. By using these two methods, you can register the class of any object:

```
private function copyOverObject(objToCopy:Object, registerAlias:Boolean =
        false):Object
{
        if(registerAlias)
        {
            var className:String = flash.utils.getQualifiedClassName(objToCopy);
            flash.net.registerClassAlias(className,
                    (flash.utils.getDefinitionByName(className) as Class));
        }
        return mx.utils.ObjectUtil.copy(objToCopy);
}
```

Now an `ArrayCollection` of strongly typed objects can be correctly copied over by passing each object in the `ArrayCollection` to the `copyOverObject()` method:

```
private function copyOverArray(arr:Array):Array {

    var newArray:Array = [];
    var i:int;
    for( i; i < arr.length; i++ )
    {
        newArray.push( copyOverObject(arr[i], true) );
    }
    return newArray;
}
var ac:ArrayCollection = new ArrayCollection([{name:'Joseph', id:21}, foo,
                                             {name:'Josef', id:81},
                                             {name:'Jose', id:214}]);

var newAC:ArrayCollection = new ArrayCollection(copyOverArray(ac.source));
```

Note that all the data contained within the objects of the original `ArrayCollection` will be present in the copied `ArrayCollection` if the two `ArrayCollection` instances are simply copied using `mx.utils.ObjectUtil.copy()`. However, the class information about each object will not be present, and any attempt to cast an object from the collection to a type will result in an error or a null value.

12.13 Use Data Objects with Unique IDs

Problem

You have multiple data objects in multiple locations throughout your application, and you need to ensure that all the objects are assigned unique `id` properties that can be used to test equality between objects and determine whether they represent the same pieces of data.

Solution

Have your data objects implement the `IUID` interface and use the `mx.core.UIDUtil.createUID()` method to generate a new application-unique `id` for each object.

Discussion

This situation can be especially important when using messaging, either via Adobe LiveCycle or other services, because objects are compared by reference when testing for simple equality (the == operator) or complex equality (the === operator). Determining whether two objects represent the same data is frequently done by comparing the property values of all of their fields. With large complex objects, this can drag resources down unnecessarily. When you implement the `IUID` interface, however, a class is marked as containing a `uid` property that can be compared to determine whether two objects represent the same data. Even if two objects are deep copies of one another, their `uid` property values will remain the same and the objects will be identifiable as representing the same data.

The `uid` generated by the `createUID()` method of the `UIDUtil` class is a 32-digit hexadecimal number of the following format:

```
E4509FFA-3E61-A17B-E08A-705DA2C25D1C
```

The following example uses the `createUID()` method to create a new instance of a `Message` class that implements `IUID`. The `uid` accessor and mutator methods of the `IUID` interface provide access to the object's generated `id`:

```
package {
    import mx.core.IUID;
    import mx.utils.UIDUtil;

    [Bindable]
    public class Message implements IUID
```

```
{
    public var messageStr:String;
    public var fromID:String;
    private var _uid:String;

    public function Message()
    {
        _uid = UIDUtil.createUID();
    }

    public function get uid():String
    {
        return _uid;
    }

    public function set uid(value:String):void
    {
        // Since we've already created the id, there's
        // nothing to be done here, but the method is
        // required by the IUID interface
    }
}
}
```

CHAPTER 13

Data Binding

The Flex Framework provides a robust structure for architecting component-driven applications. Within this powerful framework is an event-based system in which objects can subscribe to updates of property values on other objects by using *data binding*.

Data binding provides a convenient way to pass data between different layers within an application, by linking a source property to a destination property. Changes to properties on a destination object occur after an event is dispatched by the source object, notifying all destination objects of an update. With the property on a source object marked as bindable, other objects can subscribe to updates by assigning a destination property. To enable data binding on a property, you must define the [Bindable] metadata tag in one of three ways:

Before a class definition:

```
package com.oreilly.f4cb
{
    import flash.events.EventDispatcher;

    [Bindable]
    public class DataObject extends EventDispatcher{}
}
```

Adding a [Bindable] tag prior to a class definition establishes a binding expression for all readable and writable public attributes held on that class. Classes using binding must implement the IEventDispatcher interface because data binding is an event-based notification system for copying source properties to destination properties.

Before a public, protected, or private variable:

```
[Bindable] private var _lastName:String;
[Bindable] protected var _age:Number;
[Bindable] public var firstName:String;
```

Bindable variables marked as **private** are available for binding within that class only. Protected variables are available for binding within the class in which the variable is declared and any subclasses of that class. Public variables are available for binding within that class, any subclasses, and any classes with an instance of that class.

Before the definition of a public, protected, or private attribute using implicit getter/setter methods:

```
private var _lastName:String;
...
[Bindable]
public function get lastName():String
{
    return _lastName;
}
public function set lastName( str:String ):void
{
    _lastName = str;
}
```

When you define implicit getter/setter methods as bindable, by adding the [Binda ble] metadata tag above the getter declaration, the property can be bound to using dot notation syntax. This allows you to use the same syntax you would use to access a nonbound variable (**Owner.property**, for example) to set the source of the data binding.

Setting the [Bindable] metadata tag on a read-only property will result in a compiler warning, because a property must be writable to be bindable. Internally, bindable properties held on objects within the Framework dispatch a **propertyChange** event when their values are updated. The [Bindable] metadata tag accepts an **event** attribute that you can define with a custom event type:

```
[Bindable(event="myValueChanged")]
```

By default, the **event** attribute is set as **propertyChange**. If the **event** attribute's value is left as the default, destination properties are notified using that event type without your having to dispatch the event yourself. If you assign a custom event type to notify objects of updates to a value, you must also dispatch the event explicitly within the class.

Binding through event notification occurs upon initialization of the source object and at any time during the application's run when the source property is modified. The **executeBindings()** method of an **mx.core.UIComponent**-based object allows you to force any data bindings for which the object is considered a destination object.

Data binding provides a layer of data synchronization between multiple objects, facilitating the creation of rich applications. This chapter addresses the various techniques for incorporating data binding into the architecture of an application.

13.1 Bind to a Property

Problem

You want to bind a property of one object to that of another object.

Solution

Use either curly braces ({}) within a MXML component declaration or the `<fx:Bind ing>` tag.

Discussion

When you assign a property of one object (the *destination object*) to be bound to a property of another object (the *source object*), an event from the source object is dispatched to notify the destination object of any update to its value. Internally, the property value of the source is copied to the property value of the destination. To bind properties within a MXML declaration, you can use curly braces ({}) or the `<fx:Bind ing>` tag. To assign a binding within a component declaration, curly braces are used to wrap the source property and evaluate updates to its value. Consider an example:

```
<s:Application xmlns:fx="http://ns.adobe.com/mxml/2009"
               xmlns:s="library://ns.adobe.com/flex/spark"
               xmlns:mx="library://ns.adobe.com/flex/mx">

    <s:Panel title="Data Binding Example"
            width="300" height="300">

        <s:layout>
            <s:VerticalLayout paddingLeft="5" paddingRight="5"
                              paddingTop="5" paddingBottom="5" />
        </s:layout>

        <s:Label text="Enter name:" />
        <s:TextInput id="nameInput" maxChars="20" />
        <s:Label text="You entered:" />
        <s:RichText text="{nameInput.text}" />

    </s:Panel>

</s:Application>
```

In this example, the `text` property of a `RichText` control is bound to the `text` property of the `TextInput` control. As the value of the `text` property held on the `TextInput` instance is updated, so is the value of the `text` property held on the `RichText` instance. Within the curly braces, dot notation syntax is used to evaluate the `text` attribute value held on the `TextInput` instance, which is given the `id` of `nameInput`.

You can also use the `<fx:Binding>` tag within MXML to define a data-binding expression; the result is the same as using curly braces within a component declaration. Which method should you use? The answer is based on the control. In terms of a Model-View-Controller (MVC) architecture, when you define a `<fx:Binding>` tag, you are creating a controller for your view. When using curly braces, you are not afforded the separation of view and controller because the view control acts as the controller.

Though curly braces are easy, quick to develop, and have the same end result, choosing to use the `<fx:Binding>` tag may prove beneficial in your development process because the syntax is easy to read and because it lets you bind more than one source property to the same destination.

To use the `<fx:Binding>` tag, you define a `source` attribute and a `destination` attribute:

```
<fx:Binding source="nameInput.text" destination="nameOutput.text" />

<s:Panel title="Data Binding Example"
        width="300" height="300">

    <s:layout>
        <s:VerticalLayout paddingLeft="5" paddingRight="5"
            paddingTop="5" paddingBottom="5" />
    </s:layout>

    <s:Label text="Enter name:" />
    <s:TextInput id="nameInput" maxChars="20" />
    <s:Label text="You entered:" />
    <s:RichText id="nameOutput" />

</s:Panel>
```

The result is the same as in the previous example, but this example assigns `id` properties to both the `TextInput` and `RichText` controls to be used as the source and destination properties, respectively, in the `<fx:Binding>` declaration.

Notice that curly braces are not needed within the `source` and `destination` attributes, unlike during an inline binding declaration. The reason is that the source and destination attribute values are evaluated as ActionScript expressions. Thus, you can add any extra data needed within the expression. For instance, if you wanted the `RichText` control in this example to display the length of the input text appended with the string `'letters.'`, you could define the `source` attribute value as the following:

```
<mx:Binding source="nameInput.text.length + ' letters.'"
            destination="nameOutput.text" />
```

13.2 Bind to a Function

Problem

You want to use a function as the source for binding to a property value.

Solution

Use curly braces within a component declaration to pass a bound property as an argument to a function or to define a function that is invoked based on a bindable event.

Discussion

Updating a destination property value based on a source property value is a quick and easy way to achieve data syncing. When using just property values, the type of the destination property must be the same as that of the source property. There may come a time, however, when you need the binding property to be of a different type or to display a different but related value—which is where the power of using functions for binding comes into play.

You can use functions for binding in two ways: by passing a bound property as the argument to a function or by defining a function as bound to a property.

The following example passes a bound property of a source object into a function to update the property value on a destination object:

```
<s:Application xmlns:fx="http://ns.adobe.com/mxml/2009"
               xmlns:s="library://ns.adobe.com/flex/spark"
               xmlns:mx="library://ns.adobe.com/flex/mx">

    <fx:Declarations>
        <mx:CurrencyFormatter id="formatter" precision="2" />
    </fx:Declarations>

    <s:layout>
        <s:VerticalLayout />
    </s:layout>

    <s:HGroup verticalAlign="bottom">
        <s:Label text="Enter the withdrawal amount:" />
        <s:TextInput id="amtInput" />
    </s:HGroup>
    <s:HGroup verticalAlign="bottom">
        <s:Label text="Formatted amount:" />
        <s:RichText text="{formatter.format( amtInput.text )}" />
    </s:HGroup>

</s:Application>
```

The text property of the TextInput instance is used in formatting the value to be displayed by the RichText instance. Through binding, the format() method of Currency Formatter is called upon each update of the text property value of amtInput. Passing a bound property as an argument to a function is a convenient way to ensure data synchronization even if there is not a one-to-one correspondence between the source and destination property values.

To bind to a function without passing a bound property as an argument, you can use the event attribute of the [Binding] metadata tag to define the function as being bindable to an event. When the specified event is captured, the function is invoked and enforces an update to any bound properties. Consider an example:

```
<s:Application xmlns:fx="http://ns.adobe.com/mxml/2009"
               xmlns:s="library://ns.adobe.com/flex/spark"
               xmlns:mx="library://ns.adobe.com/flex/mx">

    <fx:Declarations>
        <s:ArrayCollection id="fruitCollection">
            <fx:String>Apple</fx:String>
            <fx:String>Banana</fx:String>
            <fx:String>Orange</fx:String>
        </s:ArrayCollection>
    </fx:Declarations>

    <fx:Script>
        <![CDATA[
            private var _selectedFruit:String;

            [Bindable(event="fruitChanged")]
            private function isOrangeChosen():Boolean
            {
                return _selectedFruit == "Orange";
            }

            public function get selectedFruit():String
            {
                return _selectedFruit;
            }
            public function set selectedFruit( value:String ):void
            {
                _selectedFruit = value;
                dispatchEvent( new Event( "fruitChanged" ) );
            }
        ]]>
    </fx:Script>

    <s:layout>
        <s:VerticalLayout />
    </s:layout>

    <s:Label text="Select a Fruit:" />
    <s:HGroup>
        <s:DropDownList id="fruitCB"
                        dataProvider="{fruitCollection}"
                        change="{selectedFruit = fruitCB.selectedItem}" />
        <s:Button label="eat the orange."
                  enabled="{isOrangeChosen()}" />
    </s:HGroup>

</s:Application>
```

In this example, the `enabled` attribute of the `Button` instance is bound to the Boolean value returned by the `isOrangeChosen()` method. The return value is based on the value of the `_selectedFruit` variable, which is updated when the `DropDownList` selection is changed. Any update to the `selectedFruit` attribute will dispatch the `fruitChanged` event and invoke the `isOrangeChosen()` method, which in turn will enforce an update to the value of the `enabled` attribute of the `Button` instance.

Essentially, the enabling of the button is bound to the label selected in the `DropDown List` control. As this example demonstrates, defining a function for binding is a convenient way to update values on a destination object that may be of a different type than the properties of the source object.

See Also

Recipe 13.1

13.3 Create a Bidirectional Binding

Problem

You want to bind the properties of two controls as the source and destination objects of each other.

Solution

Supply the property of each control as the source in a data-binding expression, or use the shorthand two-way binding syntax of `@{bindable_property}`.

Discussion

The term *bidirectional binding* refers to two components each acting as the source object for the destination properties of the other. The Flex Framework supports bidirectional binding and ensures that the property updates do not result in an infinite loop. Consider an example:

```
<s:VGroup>
    <s:Label text="From Input 2:" />
    <s:TextInput id="input1" text="{input2.text}" />
    <s:Label text="From Input 1:" />
    <s:TextInput id="input2" text="{input1.text}" />
</s:VGroup>
```

Both `TextInput` instances act as source and destination, updating the other's `text` property. As text is entered into one `TextInput`, the value is copied to the other `TextInput` field.

Alternatively, the shorthand @ syntax can be used inline in a MXML declaration to create the same binding logic, as in the following example:

```
<s:VGroup>
    <s:Label text="From Input 2:" />
    <s:TextInput id="input1" text="@{input2.text}" />
    <s:Label text="From Input 1:" />
    <s:TextInput id="input2" />
</s:VGroup>
```

The same expression can be declared using the `<fx:Binding>` tag with the `twoWay` property value defined as `true`:

```
<fx:Binding source="input1.text" destination="input2.text" twoWay="true" />
```

```
<s:VGroup>
    <s:Label text="From Input 2:" />
    <s:TextInput id="input1" />
    <s:Label text="From Input 1:" />
    <s:TextInput id="input2" />
</s:VGroup>
```

See Also

Recipe 13.1

13.4 Bind to Properties by Using ActionScript

Problem

You want to create a data-binding expression by using ActionScript rather than declarative MXML.

Solution

Use the `mx.utils.binding.BindingUtils` class to create `mx.utils.binding.Change Watcher` objects.

Discussion

Creating data-binding expressions using ActionScript affords you more control over when and how destination property values are updated. To establish a binding using ActionScript, you use the `BindingUtils` class to create a `ChangeWatcher` object. There are two static methods of `BindingUtils` that can be used to create a data binding: `bindProperty()` and `bindSetter()`.

Using the `bindProperty()` method of `BindingUtils` is similar to using the `<fx:Bind ing>` tag in MXML, as you define source and destination arguments. But unlike the comparable attributes used by the `<fx:Binding>` tag, which evaluates assignments as ActionScript expressions, the arguments for `BindingUtils.bindProperty()` are separated by defining a *site* and a *host* (destination and source, respectively) and then establishing their properties. For example:

```
var watcher:ChangeWatcher =
        BindingUtils.bindProperty( destination, "property", source, "property" );
```

Using the `BindingUtils.bindSetter()` method, you can assign a function to handle data-binding updates of a source property:

```
var watcher:ChangeWatcher =
        BindingUtils.bindSetter( invalidateProperty, source, "property" );
...
private function invalidateProperty( arg:* ):void
{
    // perform any necessary operations
}
```

It isn't necessary to define a `ChangeWatcher` variable when invoking the static `bindProperty()` and `bindSetter()` methods. However, at times you may want to utilize the returned `ChangeWatcher` object, as it exposes methods you can use at runtime that give you the capability to change the data source, change the destination property, and stop the binding operation.

The following example establishes data binding between the `text` property of a `TextInput` control and the `text` property of a `RichText` control by using the `BindingUtils.bindProperty()` method:

```
<s:Application xmlns:fx="http://ns.adobe.com/mxml/2009"
               xmlns:s="library://ns.adobe.com/flex/spark"
               xmlns:mx="library://ns.adobe.com/flex/mx"
               creationComplete="handleCreationComplete();">

    <fx:Script>
        <![CDATA[
            import mx.binding.utils.BindingUtils;
            import mx.binding.utils.ChangeWatcher;

            private var nameWatcher:ChangeWatcher;

            private function handleCreationComplete():void
            {
                nameWatcher = BindingUtils.bindProperty( nameField, "text",
                                                         nameInput, "text" );
            }
            private function handleClick():void
            {
                if( nameWatcher.isWatching() )
                {
                    nameWatcher.unwatch();
                    btn.label = "watch";
                }
                else
                {
                    nameWatcher.reset( nameInput );
                    btn.label = "unwatch";
                }
            }
        ]]>
```

```
        </fx:Script>

        <s:Panel title="User Entry.">
            <s:layout>
                <s:VerticalLayout paddingLeft="5" paddingRight="5"
                                  paddingTop="5" paddingBottom="5" />
            </s:layout>
            <s:HGroup verticalAlign="bottom">
                <s:Label text="Name:" />
                <s:TextInput id="nameInput" />
            </s:HGroup>
            <s:HGroup verticalAlign="bottom">
                <s:Label text="You Entered:" />
                <s:RichText id="nameField" />
            </s:HGroup>
            <s:Button id="btn"
                      label="unwatch"
                      click="handleClick();" />
        </s:Panel>

    </s:Application>
```

Using the `BindingUtils.bindProperty()` method, data binding is defined as a one-to-one relationship between the source property and the destination property. In this example, any updates made to the `text` property of the `TextInput` control instance are reflected in the `text` property of the `Text` control instance. The lifecycle of the binding expression can be stopped and reset by `ChangeWatcher` on interaction with the `Button` instance.

To have more control over how a destination property value is updated or to update multiple destinations based on a single source, use the `BindingUtils.bindSetter()` method to assign a function to act as the marshal for data binding, as shown here:

```
<s:Application xmlns:fx="http://ns.adobe.com/mxml/2009"
               xmlns:s="library://ns.adobe.com/flex/spark"
               xmlns:mx="library://ns.adobe.com/flex/mx"
               creationComplete="handleCreationComplete();">

    <fx:Script>
        <![CDATA[
            import mx.binding.utils.BindingUtils;
            import mx.binding.utils.ChangeWatcher;

            private var nameWatcher:ChangeWatcher;

            private function handleCreationComplete():void
            {
                nameWatcher = BindingUtils.bindSetter( invalidateName,
                                                       nameInput, "text" );
            }

            private function invalidateName( value:String ):void
            {
```

```
                    if( btn.label == "unwatch" )
                        nameField.text = value;
                }

                private function handleClick():void
                {
                    if( nameWatcher.isWatching() )
                    {
                        nameWatcher.unwatch();
                        btn.label = "watch";
                    }
                    else
                    {
                        nameWatcher.reset( nameInput );
                        btn.label = "unwatch";
                    }
                }
            }
        ]]>
    </fx:Script>

    <s:Panel title="User Entry.">
        <s:layout>
            <s:VerticalLayout paddingLeft="5" paddingRight="5"
                              paddingTop="5" paddingBottom="5" />
        </s:layout>
        <s:HGroup verticalAlign="bottom">
            <s:Label text="Name:" />
            <s:TextInput id="nameInput" />
        </s:HGroup>
        <s:HGroup verticalAlign="bottom">
            <s:Label text="You Entered:" />
            <s:RichText id="nameField" />
        </s:HGroup>
        <s:Button id="btn"
                  label="unwatch"
                  click="handleClick();" />
    </s:Panel>

</s:Application>
```

Updates to any values within the destination are determined by the operations within the setter argument that is passed as the first parameter to the `BindingUtils.bind Setter()` method. This setter method acts as the event handler any time the destination object dispatches an event to notify listeners that its value has changed. In this example, the `text` property is updated based on the `label` property of the `Button` instance.

Although the `invalidateName()` method will be invoked upon any change to the `text` property of the `nameInput` control, updates to the destination property value are dictated by the current activity of the `ChangeWatcher`, which is evaluated in the `if` statement based on the label of the button.

It is important that any ChangeWatcher objects created within an instance be directed to unwatch data-binding expressions in order to be eligible for garbage collection by the Flash Player. When creating a Change Watcher object, as is done in the previous examples using the Binding Utils class, a reference is held in memory for both the source and destination of the binding. To release those references from memory and have an object marked for garbage collection be freed appropriately, you need to remove them by using the unwatch() method.

13.5 Use Bindable Property Chains

Problem

You want to define a source property that is part of a property chain.

Solution

Use dot notation to access the source within a property chain using either the `<fx:Bind ing>` tag or curly braces ({}), or use an array of strings for the chain argument of the static `BindingUtils.bindProperty()` and `BindingUtils.bindSetter()` methods.

Discussion

When a property source is defined in a data-binding expression, changes to all properties leading up to that property are monitored. If you specify a binding to the `text` property of a `TextInput` control, the `TextInput` instance is part of a bindable property chain:

```
<s:TextInput id="myInput" />
<s:Label text="{myInput.text}" />
```

Technically, the class hosting the `myInput` control is also part of this property chain, but the `this` directive is not necessary within the definition of a data-binding expression as it is scoped. Essentially, the value of `myInput` is first evaluated to being not null and the binding moves down the chain to the source: the `text` property of the `TextInput` instance. For updates to be triggered and the source value copied over to the destination object, only the source property has to be bindable.

You access the source property within a property chain of a model just as you would the source property from a control, as seen in the previous example in this recipe. Within MXML, you can define the bindable property chain by using dot notation syntax:

```
<!-- property chain binding using <mx:Binding> -->
<fx:Binding source="usermodel.name.firstName" destination="fNameField.text" />
<s:Label id="fNameField" />
```

```
<!-- property chain binding using curly braces ({}) -->
<s:Label text="{usermodel.name.firstName}" />
```

To define the bindable property chain using ActionScript 3, you specify the chain as an array of string values when you call either the `BindingUtils.bindProperty()` or the `BindingUtils.bindSetter()` method:

```
BindingUtils.bindProperty( nameField, "text",
                           usermodel, ["name", "firstName"] );
BindingUtils.bindSetter( invalidateProperties,
                         this, ["usermodel", "name", "firstName"] );
```

The `chain` argument for each of these methods is an array of strings that defines the bindable property chain relative to the host.

The following example uses curly braces, the `<fx:Binding>` tag, and the `BindingUtils.bindProperty()` method to define data-binding expressions that use property chains:

```
<s:Application xmlns:fx="http://ns.adobe.com/mxml/2009"
               xmlns:s="library://ns.adobe.com/flex/spark"
               xmlns:mx="library://ns.adobe.com/flex/mx"
               creationComplete="handleCreationComplete();">

    <fx:Declarations>
        <fx:Model id="userModel">
            <user>
                <name>
                    <firstName>Ted</firstName>
                    <lastName>Henderson</lastName>
                </name>
                <birth>
                    <date>February 29th, 1967</date>
                </birth>
            </user>
        </fx:Model>
    </fx:Declarations>

    <fx:Script>
        <![CDATA[
            import mx.binding.utils.BindingUtils;

            private function handleCreationComplete():void
            {
                BindingUtils.bindProperty( lastNameField, "text",
                                           userModel, ["name", "lastName"] );
            }
            private function handleClick():void
            {
                userModel.name.firstName = fNameInput.text;
                userModel.name.lastName = lNameInput.text;
                userModel.birth.date = dateInput.text;
            }
        ]]>
    </fx:Script>
```

```
<s:layout>
    <s:VerticalLayout />
</s:layout>

<fx:Binding source="userModel.birth.date" destination="dateField.text" />
<mx:Form borderStyle="solid">
    <mx:FormItem label="First Name:">
        <!-- create data binding using curly braces -->
        <s:RichText text="{userModel.name.firstName}" />
    </mx:FormItem>
    <mx:FormItem label="Last Name:">
        <s:RichText id="lastNameField" />
    </mx:FormItem>
    <mx:FormItem label="Birthday:">
        <s:RichText id="dateField" />
    </mx:FormItem>
</mx:Form>

<mx:Form>
    <mx:FormItem label="First Name:">
        <s:TextInput id="fNameInput" />
    </mx:FormItem>
    <mx:FormItem label="Last Name:">
        <s:TextInput id="lNameInput" />
    </mx:FormItem>
    <mx:FormItem label="Birthday:">
        <s:TextInput id="dateInput" />
    </mx:FormItem>
    <mx:FormItem label="Submit Changes">
        <s:Button label="ok" click="handleClick();" />
    </mx:FormItem>
</mx:Form>

</s:Application>
```

See Also

Recipes 13.1 and 13.3

13.6 Bind to Properties on a XML Source by Using E4X

Problem

You want to bind properties of a destination object to a XML source.

Solution

Use ECMAScript for XML (E4X) when defining a data-binding expression using curly braces or the `<fx:Bindable>` tag.

Discussion

The E4X language in ActionScript 3 is used for filtering data from XML (Extensible Markup Language) via expressions that are similar to the syntax of ActionScript expressions. There is not enough room in this recipe to discuss the finer details of writing an E4X expression, but it is important to note that you can use the language to create bindings between a control and XML.

E4X expressions can be defined by using curly braces within a component declaration and within a `<fx:Binding>` tag. You cannot use E4X with the `BindingUtils` class. To better understand how the E4X technique works, consider an example based on this XML:

```
<item>
    <name>Moe</name>
    <type>The brains.</type>
    <description>Has bowl cut.</description>
</item>
```

You can wrap an E4X expression in an attribute by using curly braces:

```
<s:Label text="{_data..item.(name == 'Moe').description}" />
```

Or you can create the binding by using the `<fx:Binding>` tag:

```
<fx:Binding source="_data..item.(name == 'Moe').description"
    destination="desc.text" />
<s:Label id="desc" />
```

Both of these methods produce the same result. Curly braces are not needed in the source attribute of a `<fx:Binding>` tag, however, because the value is evaluated as an ActionScript expression.

The following example uses E4X to create a binding for the `dataProvider` property of a `List` and a `DataGrid`:

```
<s:Application xmlns:fx="http://ns.adobe.com/mxml/2009"
               xmlns:s="library://ns.adobe.com/flex/spark"
               xmlns:mx="library://ns.adobe.com/flex/mx">

    <fx:Declarations>
        <fx:XML id="itemData" xmlns="">
            <items>
                <item id='1'>
                    <name>Larry</name>
                    <type>The foil.</type>
                    <description>Has curly hair.</description>
                </item>
                <item id='2'>
                    <name>Moe</name>
                    <type>The brains.</type>
                    <description>Has bowl cut.</description>
                </item>
```

```
                    <item id='3'>
                        <name>Curly</name>
                        <type>The brawn.</type>
                        <description>Has bowl cut.</description>
                    </item>
                </items>
            </fx:XML>
        </fx:Declarations>

        <fx:Script>
            <![CDATA[
                import mx.collections.XMLListCollection;
            ]]>
        </fx:Script>

        <s:layout>
            <s:VerticalLayout />
        </s:layout>

        <fx:Binding source="{itemData..item.(@id == '1').name} {itemData..item.(@id ==
                            '1').description.toLowerCase()}" destination="lab.text" />

        <s:Label id="lab" />
        <s:List width="200"
                dataProvider="{new XMLListCollection(itemData..item.name)}" />
        <mx:DataGrid width="200"
                    dataProvider="{new XMLListCollection(itemData..item)}">
            <mx:columns>
                <mx:DataGridColumn dataField="name" />
                <mx:DataGridColumn dataField="type" />
            </mx:columns>
        </mx:DataGrid>
    </s:Application>
```

Upon initialization of the components in the display, binding is executed and property values are updated based on the E4X expressions supplied.

See Also

Recipe 13.1

13.7 Create Customized Bindable Properties

Problem

You want data binding to occur based on a custom event rather than relying on the default propertyChange event.

Solution

Set the event attribute of the [Bindable] metadata tag and dispatch an event by using that event string as the type argument.

Discussion

The data-binding infrastructure of the Flex Framework is an event-based system. The default event type dispatched from a binding is the propertyChange event. Internally, updates to destination property values are made without your having to dispatch this event directly from the source of the binding. You can specify a custom event type to be associated with a data-binding expression by using the event property of the [Bindable] metadata tag. For example:

```
[Bindable(event="myValueChanged")]
```

When you override the default event attribute within a [Bindable] tag definition, you must dispatch the specified event in order for binding to take effect.

The following example uses custom binding events to update destination property values:

```
<s:Application xmlns:fx="http://ns.adobe.com/mxml/2009"
               xmlns:s="library://ns.adobe.com/flex/spark"
               xmlns:mx="library://ns.adobe.com/flex/mx">

    <fx:Script>
        <![CDATA[
            private var _firstName:String;
            private var _lastName:String;
            private static const FN_EVENT_TYPE:String = "fnChanged";
            private static const LN_EVENT_TYPE:String = "lnChanged";

            private function submitHandler():void
            {
                firstName = fnInput.text;
                lastName = lnInput.text;
            }

            [Bindable(event="fnChanged")]
            public function get firstName():String
            {
                return _firstName;
            }
            public function set firstName( value:String ):void
            {
                _firstName = value;
                dispatchEvent( new Event( FN_EVENT_TYPE ) );
            }

            [Bindable(event="lnChanged")]
            public function get lastName():String
```

```
                {
                    return _lastName;
                }
                public function set lastName( value:String ):void
                {
                    _lastName = value;
                    dispatchEvent( new Event( LN_EVENT_TYPE ) );
                }
        ]]>
    </fx:Script>

    <s:layout>
        <s:VerticalLayout />
    </s:layout>

    <s:BorderContainer borderStyle="solid">
        <s:layout>
            <s:VerticalLayout />
        </s:layout>
        <s:HGroup verticalAlign="bottom">
            <s:Label text="First Name:" />
            <s:TextInput id="fnInput" />
        </s:HGroup>
        <s:HGroup verticalAlign="bottom">
            <s:Label text="Last Name:" />
            <s:TextInput id="lnInput" />
        </s:HGroup>
        <s:Button label="submit" click="submitHandler();" />
    </s:BorderContainer>

    <s:VGroup>
        <s:Label text="You Entered-" />
        <s:HGroup>
            <s:Label text="First Name:" />
            <s:RichText text="{firstName}" />
        </s:HGroup>
        <s:HGroup>
            <s:Label text="Last Name:" />
            <s:RichText text="{lastName}" />
        </s:HGroup>
    </s:VGroup>

</s:Application>
```

When a user submits entries for his first and last name, the firstName and lastName properties are updated. Within each respective setter method, the corresponding event defined in the [Bindable] tags is dispatched to invoke updates on all destination properties.

A valuable aspect of creating customized bindable properties is that you can dictate when a destination property within the data-binding expression is updated. Because data binding is based on an event model, using customized binding affords you control over when or if the data binding is triggered.

The following example adds a timer to defer dispatching a bindable property event:

```
<s:Application xmlns:fx="http://ns.adobe.com/mxml/2009"
               xmlns:s="library://ns.adobe.com/flex/spark"
               xmlns:mx="library://ns.adobe.com/flex/mx"
               creationComplete="handleCreationComplete();">

    <fx:Script>
        <![CDATA[
            private var _timer:Timer;
            private var _firstName:String;
            private var _lastName:String;
            private static const FN_EVENT_TYPE:String = "fnChanged";
            private static const LN_EVENT_TYPE:String = "lnChanged";

            private function handleCreationComplete():void
            {
                _timer = new Timer( 2000, 1 );
                _timer.addEventListener( TimerEvent.TIMER_COMPLETE, handleTimer );
            }

            private function handleTimer( evt:TimerEvent ):void
            {
                dispatchEvent( new Event( FN_EVENT_TYPE ) );
            }

            private function submitHandler():void
            {
                firstName = fnInput.text;
                lastName = lnInput.text;
            }

            [Bindable(event="fnChanged")]
            public function get firstName():String
            {
                return _firstName;
            }
            public function set firstName( value:String ):void
            {
                _firstName = value;
                _timer.reset();
                _timer.start();
            }

            [Bindable(event="lnChanged")]
            public function get lastName():String
            {
                return _lastName;
            }
            public function set lastName( value:String ):void
            {
                _lastName = value;
                dispatchEvent( new Event( LN_EVENT_TYPE ) );
            }
        ]]>
    </fx:Script>
```

```
<s:layout>
    <s:VerticalLayout />
</s:layout>

<s:BorderContainer borderStyle="solid">
    <s:layout>
        <s:VerticalLayout />
    </s:layout>
    <s:HGroup verticalAlign="bottom">
        <s:Label text="First Name:" />
        <s:TextInput id="fnInput" />
    </s:HGroup>
    <s:HGroup verticalAlign="bottom">
        <s:Label text="Last Name:" />
        <s:TextInput id="lnInput" />
    </s:HGroup>
    <s:Button label="submit" click="submitHandler();" />
</s:BorderContainer>

<s:VGroup>
    <s:Label text="You Entered-" />
    <s:HGroup>
        <s:Label text="First Name:" />
        <s:RichText text="{firstName}" />
    </s:HGroup>
    <s:HGroup>
        <s:Label text="Last Name:" />
        <s:RichText text="{lastName}" />
    </s:HGroup>
</s:VGroup>

</s:Application>
```

The event type is still defined on the implicit getter for the `firstName` attribute, but dispatching the event is deferred to the completion of a `Timer` instance. If you run this program, data binding to the `lastName` property will happen instantaneously as the custom event is dispatched within the setter method for that attribute. Updates on the binding destination of the `firstName` property, however, are performed after 2 seconds because a `Timer` instance is set to dispatch the custom event `fnChanged`.

See Also

Recipe 13.1

13.8 Bind to a Generic Object

Problem

You want to bind properties by using a top-level `Object` instance as the source.

Solution

Use the `mx.utils.ObjectProxy` class to wrap the `Object` and dispatch binding events.

Discussion

Creating a binding to a generic `Object` directly invokes an update only upon initialization of the destination object. To update properties on the destination object as property values change on the `Object`, use the `ObjectProxy` class. To create an instance of `ObjectProxy`, pass the `Object` in the constructor. For example:

```
var obj:Object = {name:'Tom Waits', album:'Rain Dogs', genre:'Rock'};
var proxy:ObjectProxy = new ObjectProxy( obj );
```

Modifications to the properties of the original object are handled by the `ObjectProxy`, which dispatches a `propertyChange` event when an update has occurred. The `property Change` event is the default event dispatched from a binding. When the default event is dispatched, the source property value is copied over to the specified destination object property. The following example passes a generic object to an instance of the `Object Proxy` class as a constructor argument:

```
<s:Application xmlns:fx="http://ns.adobe.com/mxml/2009"
               xmlns:s="library://ns.adobe.com/flex/spark"
               xmlns:mx="library://ns.adobe.com/flex/mx">

    <fx:Script>
        <![CDATA[
            import mx.utils.ObjectProxy;

            private var obj:Object = {name:'Tom Waits',
                                      album:'Rain Dogs',
                                      genre:'Rock'};

            [Bindable]
            private var proxy:ObjectProxy = new ObjectProxy( obj );

            private function handleClick():void
            {
                proxy.name = nameField.text;
                proxy.album = albumField.text;
                proxy.genre = genreField.text;
            }
        ]]>
    </fx:Script>

    <s:layout>
        <s:VerticalLayout />
    </s:layout>

    <mx:Form borderStyle="solid">
        <mx:FormItem label="Name:">
            <s:TextInput id="nameField" />
        </mx:FormItem>
```

```
            <mx:FormItem label="Album:">
                <s:TextInput id="albumField" />
            </mx:FormItem>
            <mx:FormItem label="Genre:">
                <s:TextInput id="genreField" />
            </mx:FormItem>
            <mx:FormItem label="Submit Changes">
                <s:Button label="ok" click="handleClick();" />
            </mx:FormItem>
        </mx:Form>

        <mx:Form borderStyle="solid">
            <mx:FormItem label="Name:">
                <s:RichText text="{proxy.name}" />
            </mx:FormItem>
            <mx:FormItem label="Album:">
                <s:RichText text="{proxy.album}" />
            </mx:FormItem>
            <mx:FormItem label="Genre:">
                <s:RichText text="{proxy.genre}" />
            </mx:FormItem>
        </mx:Form>

    </s:Application>
```

In this example, when updates are submitted, the properties on the `ObjectProxy` are modified and changes are reflected in the controls that are bound to the proxy. You are not limited to updating only predefined property values on a proxy object; you can define binding expressions for properties that can be assigned to the proxy at any time.

You should create a custom class and expose bindable properties instead of using generic `Object`s. However, when that is not possible within the application architecture, the use of an `ObjectProxy` is beneficial.

See Also

Recipe 13.1

13.9 Bind to Properties on a Dynamic Class

Problem

You want to bind properties on a destination object to properties not explicitly defined on a dynamic class.

Solution

Create a subclass of `mx.utils.Proxy` that implements the `mx.events.IEventDispatcher` interface and dispatch a `propertyChange` event within the `setProperty()` override of the `flash_proxy` namespace.

Discussion

The `Proxy` class lets you access and modify properties by using dot notation. To effectively work with dynamic property references, override the `getProperty()` and `setProperty()` methods of the `flash_proxy` namespace within your subclass implementation. The `flash_proxy` namespace is essentially a custom access specifier, and it is used the same way as the `public`, `private`, and `protected` modifiers when declaring members within that namespace. With custom behaviors defined within `getProp erty()` and `setProperty()` methods marked with the `flash_proxy` modifier, you gain access to properties as if they were exposed directly on that class. However, dynamic property references are not enough to establish binding, because data binding is event-based.

Because bindings are triggered by events, to create a `Proxy` class that is eligible for data binding you must also implement the `IEventDispatcher` interface and its methods. In order for dynamic property references to be made for binding, the class is declared using the `dynamic` keyword and defined using the `[Bindable]` metadata tag, with the `event` attribute set as `propertyChange`:

```
[Bindable(event="propertyChange")]
dynamic public class Properties extends Proxy implements IEventDispatcher {}
```

An excellent example of when you would want to create a custom `Proxy` class is to access data loaded from an external source by establishing behavior rules within the `setProperty()` and `getProperty()` override methods, as opposed to writing a parser that will fill property values on a custom object from that loaded data.

For instance, suppose an application loads the following XML from which element properties can be accessed and modified:

```
<properties>
    <property id="name"><![CDATA[Tom Waits]]></property>
    <property id="album"><![CDATA[Rain Dogs]]></property>
    <property id="genre"><![CDATA[Rock]]></property>
</properties>
```

You can create a subclass of `mx.utils.Proxy` and use E4X in the `setProperty()` and `getProperty()` method overrides, allowing a client to access and modify XML data properties:

```
override flash_proxy function getProperty( name:* ):*
{
    return xml..property.(@id == String( name ) );
}

override flash_proxy function setProperty( name:*, value:* ):void
{
    var index:Number = xml..property.(@id == String( name ) ).childIndex();
    xml.replace( index, '<property id="' + name + '">' + value + '</property>' );
}
```

Data bindings are triggered by an event upon updates to a property value. The setProp erty() override in this example, although it updates a property value, does not dispatch a notification of change. In order for binding to dynamic property references to be invoked, you must dispatch a PropertyChangeEvent from the Proxy subclass:

```
override flash_proxy function setProperty( name:*, value:* ):void
{
    var oldVal:String = xml..property.(@id == String( name ) );
    var index:Number = xml..property.(@id == String( name ) ).childIndex();
    xml.replace( index, '<property id="' + name + '">' + value + '</property>' );
    var evt:Event = PropertyChangeEvent.createUpdateEvent( this, name,
                                                  oldVal, value );
    dispatchEvent( evt );
}
```

The static createUpdateEvent() method of the PropertyChangeEvent class returns an instance of a PropertyChangeEvent with the type property set to propertyChange, which is the default event for bindings and the one assigned in the [Bindable] metadata tag for the class.

The following example is a complete implementation of a Proxy subclass eligible for data binding:

```
package com.oreilly.f4cb
{
    import flash.events.Event;
    import flash.events.EventDispatcher;
    import flash.events.IEventDispatcher;
    import flash.net.URLLoader;
    import flash.net.URLRequest;
    import flash.utils.Proxy;
    import flash.utils.flash_proxy;

    import mx.events.PropertyChangeEvent;

    [Bindable(event="propertyChange")]
    dynamic public class Properties extends Proxy implements IEventDispatcher
    {
        private var _evtDispatcher:EventDispatcher;
        private var _data:XML;

        public function Properties( source:XML )
        {
            _evtDispatcher = new EventDispatcher();
            data = source;
        }

        public function get data():XML
        {
            return _data;
```

```
}
public function set data( xml:XML ):void
{
    _data = xml;
}
// use E4X to return property value held on XML
override flash_proxy function getProperty( name:* ):*
{
    if( _data == null ) return "";
    var attributeValue:String = QName( name ).toString();
    var value:* = _data..property.(@id == attributeValue );
    return value;
}
// use E4X to modify property value on XML, and dispatch 'propertyChange'
override flash_proxy function setProperty( name:*, value:* ):void
{
    var attributeValue:String = QName( name ).toString();
    var oldVal:String = _data..property.(@id == attributeValue );
    var index:Number = _data..property.(@id == attributeValue ).
            childIndex();
    _data.replace( index, <property id={name}>{value}</property> );
    var evt:Event = PropertyChangeEvent.createUpdateEvent( this, name,
                                                   oldVal, value );
    dispatchEvent( evt );
}

// IEventDispatcher implementation
public function addEventListener( type:String,
                                  listener:Function,
                                  useCapture:Boolean = false,
                                  priority:int = 0,
                                  useWeakReference:Boolean = false):void
{
    _evtDispatcher.addEventListener( type, listener, useCapture,
                                     priority, useWeakReference );
}
// IEventDispatcher implementation
public function removeEventListener( type:String,
                                     listener:Function,
                                     useCapture:Boolean = false ):void
{

    _evtDispatcher.removeEventListener( type, listener, useCapture );
}
// IEventDispatcher implementation
public function dispatchEvent( evt:Event ):Boolean
{
    return _evtDispatcher.dispatchEvent( evt );
}
// IEventDispatcher implementation
public function hasEventListener( type:String ):Boolean
```

```
            {
                return _evtDispatcher.hasEventListener( type );
            }
            // IEventDispatcher implementation
            public function willTrigger( type:String ):Boolean
            {
                return _evtDispatcher.willTrigger( type );
            }
        }
    }
```

You can access and modify elements within the loaded XML held on the `Properties` proxy by using dot notation syntax:

```
var myProxy:Properties = new Properties( sourceXML );
...
var name:String = myProxy.name;
myProxy.album = "Blue Valentine";
```

Although you can work with dynamic property references using dot notation, you cannot use that syntax in curly braces or the `<fx:Binding>` tag to create data-binding expressions in MXML. If you were to use dot notation, you would receive a warning when you compiled your application.

Because the XML data is loaded at runtime, it makes sense that you establish binding after it has been loaded. To do so, the `mx.utils.BindingUtils` class is employed to force an update and ensure proper data binding to the proxy.

The following snippet creates an application that uses an instance of the `Properties` proxy class to establish data binding to control properties:

```
<s:Application xmlns:fx="http://ns.adobe.com/mxml/2009"
               xmlns:s="library://ns.adobe.com/flex/spark"
               xmlns:mx="library://ns.adobe.com/flex/mx"
               creationComplete="handleCreationComplete();">

    <fx:Declarations>
        <fx:XML id="propertiesData" source="assets/properties.xml" />
    </fx:Declarations>

    <fx:Script>
        <![CDATA[
            import com.oreilly.f4cb.Properties;
            import mx.binding.utils.BindingUtils;
            private var properties:Properties;

            private function handleCreationComplete():void
            {
                properties = new Properties( propertiesData );
                establishBindings();
            }
```

```
            private function establishBindings():void
            {
                BindingUtils.bindProperty( nameOutput, "text",
                                           properties, "name" );
                BindingUtils.bindProperty( albumOutput, "text",
                                           properties, "album" );
                BindingUtils.bindProperty( genreOutput, "text",
                                           properties, "genre" );
            }

            private function handleSubmit():void
            {
                properties.name = nameInput.text;
                properties.album = albumInput.text;
                properties.genre = genreInput.text;
            }
        ]]>
    </fx:Script>

    <s:layout>
        <s:VerticalLayout />
    </s:layout>

    <mx:Form borderStyle="solid">
        <mx:FormItem label="Name:">
            <s:TextInput id="nameInput" />
        </mx:FormItem>
        <mx:FormItem label="Album:">
            <s:TextInput id="albumInput" />
        </mx:FormItem>
        <mx:FormItem label="Genre:">
            <s:TextInput id="genreInput" />
        </mx:FormItem>
        <mx:FormItem label="Submit Changes">
            <s:Button label="ok" click="handleSubmit();" />
        </mx:FormItem>
    </mx:Form>

    <mx:Form borderStyle="solid">
        <mx:FormItem label="Name:">
            <s:RichText id="nameOutput" />
        </mx:FormItem>
        <mx:FormItem label="Album:">
            <s:RichText id="albumOutput" />
        </mx:FormItem>
        <mx:FormItem label="Genre:">
            <s:RichText id="genreOutput" />
        </mx:FormItem>
    </mx:Form>

</s:Application>
```

Within the `propertiesHandler` event handler, data binding is accomplished by using the `BindingUtils.bindProperty()` method after a successful load of the XML data by the `Properties` instance. The `text` property of each respective `RichText` control from the second `Form` is bound to a corresponding element within the XML based on the `id` attribute. Using E4X in the `getProperty()` override method of the `Properties` class, a binding update is made and the values are copied over.

Changes to property values are made by using dot notation in the `handleSubmit()` event handler, which in turn invokes the `setProperty()` method on the `Properties` instance and dispatches a notification to invoke binding using a `PropertyChangeEvent` object.

See Also

Recipes 13.4, 13.5, and 13.6

CHAPTER 14

Validation, Formatting, and Regular Expressions

Validation, formatting, and regular expressions may seem a somewhat strange grouping at first glance, but they tend to be used for similar things in the everyday experience of developers: parsing the format of strings to detect a certain pattern, altering strings into a certain format if specific patterns are or are not encountered, and returning error messages to users if necessary properties are not encountered. That is, all three are useful for dealing with the sorts of data that we need from third parties or users that may not always be supplied in the format required by our applications—things like phone numbers, capitalized names, currencies, zip codes, and ISBN numbers. The Flex Framework provides two powerful tools to integrate this type of parsing and formatting with the UI elements of the Framework in the `Validator` and `Formatter` classes. Beneath both of these is the *regular expression* or `RegExp` object introduced in ActionScript 3. This is a venerable and powerful programming tool, used by nearly all, and loved and loathed in equal measure for its incredible power and difficult syntax.

The `Validator` is an event dispatcher object that checks a field within any Flex control to ensure that the value submitted falls within its set parameters. These parameters can indicate a certain format, whether a field is required, or the length of a field. Validation can be implemented simply by setting the `source` property of the `Validator` to the control where the user input will occur and indicating the property that the `Validator` should check. If a validation error occurs, the `Validator` will dispatch the error event to the control, and the control will display a custom error message that has been set in the `Validator`. There are many predefined validators in the Flex Framework (e.g., for credit cards, phone numbers, email, and social security numbers), but this chapter focuses primarily on building custom validators and integrating validators and validation events into controls.

The `Formatter` class has a simple but highly important job: accepting any value and altering it to fit a prescribed format. This can mean changing nine sequential digits into a properly formatted phone number such as (555) 555-5555, formatting a date correctly, or formatting zip codes for different countries. The `Formatter` class itself defines a single method of importance to us: `format()`. This is the method that takes the input and returns the proper string.

Both of these classes, at their roots, perform the type of string manipulation that can be done with a regular expression, though they do not tend to use regular expressions in their base classes. Regular expressions are certainly one of the most powerful, elegant, and difficult tools available in most modern programming languages. They let a programmer create complex sets of rules that will be executed on any chosen string. Almost all major programming languages have a built-in regular expression engine that, while varying somewhat in its features, maintains the same syntax, making the regular expression a useful tool to add to your repertoire.

The ActionScript implementation of the regular expression is the `RegExp` class, which defines two primary methods: the `test()` method, which returns a `true` or `false` value depending on whether the `RegExp` is matched anywhere in the string, and the `exec()` method, which returns an array of all matches along with the location in the string where the first match is encountered. A regular expression can also be tested by using the `match()`, `search()`, and `replace()` methods of the `String` class. Of these, I find that the methods in the `String` class tend to be most useful, because they allow manipulation of the characters using the regular expression. Regular expressions are a vast topic, and whole books are devoted to their proper use, so this chapter covers only some of their more specific aspects and provides solutions to common problems, rather than attempting to illustrate a general set of use cases.

14.1 Use Validators and Formatters with TextInput Controls

Problem

You need to validate and then format multiple `TextInput` and `TextArea` controls.

Solution

For each type of input—date, phone number, currency—use a `Validator` to ensure that the input is appropriate and then use a `Formatter` control to format the text of the `TextInput` appropriately.

Discussion

To use validators and formatters together in a component, simply create multiple validators for each of the needed types of validation. When the `focusOut` event occurs on a `TextInput` control, call the `validate()` method on the proper validator. To bind the validator to the correct TextInput, set the TextInput as the source of the validator and the text as the property of the TextInput that we want to validate:

```
<mx:NumberValidator id="numValidator" source="{inputCurrency}" property="text"/>
```

The formatter is called after the data has been validated. The base Formatter class accepts a formatting string consisting of hash marks that will be replaced by the digits or characters of the string that is being formatted. For a phone number, for example, the formatting string is as follows:

```
(###) ###-####
```

You can set up a phone number formatter as shown here:

```
<mx:PhoneFormatter id="phoneFormatter" formatString="(###) ###-####"
                   validPatternChars="#-() "/>
```

To use this formatter, call the format() method and pass the text property of the desired TextInput:

```
inputPhone.text = phoneFormatter.format(inputPhone.text);
```

A complete code listing implementing our validator and formatter follows. In practice, this probably would not be the best user experience, but note that in each of its example methods, if the result is not valid, the application clears the user-entered text and displays an error message:

```
<s:Application xmlns:fx="http://ns.adobe.com/mxml/2009"
               xmlns:s="library://ns.adobe.com/flex/spark"
               xmlns:mx="library://ns.adobe.com/flex/halo"
               minWidth="1024" minHeight="768">
    <fx:Declarations>
        <mx:DateFormatter id="dateFormatter" formatString="day: DD, month: MM,
                          year: YYYY"/>
        <mx:DateValidator id="dateVal" inputFormat="mm/dd/yyyy"/>
        <mx:PhoneNumberValidator id="phoneValidator" property="text"
                                 source="{inputPhone}"/>
        <mx:PhoneFormatter id="phoneFormatter" formatString="(###) ###-####"
                           validPatternChars="#-() "/>
        <mx:CurrencyFormatter id="currencyFormatter" currencySymbol="£"
                              thousandsSeparatorFrom="." decimalSeparatorFrom=","/>
        <mx:NumberValidator id="numValidator" property="text"/>
    </fx:Declarations>

    <fx:Script>
        <![CDATA[

            import mx.events.ValidationResultEvent;
            private var vResult:ValidationResultEvent;
            // event handler to validate and format input
            private function dateFormat():void
            {
                vResult = dateVal.validate(inputDate.text);
                if (vResult.type==ValidationResultEvent.VALID) {
                    inputDate.text = dateFormatter.format(inputDate.text);
```

```
                } else {
                    inputDate.text= "";
                }
            }

            private function phoneFormat():void {
                vResult = phoneValidator.validate();
                if (vResult.type==ValidationResultEvent.VALID) {
                    inputPhone.text = phoneFormatter.format(inputPhone.text);
                } else {
                    inputPhone.text= "";
                }
            }

            private function currencyFormat():void {
                vResult = numValidator.validate(inputCurrency.text);
                if (vResult.type==ValidationResultEvent.VALID) {
                    inputCurrency.text =
                            currencyFormatter.format(inputCurrency.text);
                } else {
                    inputCurrency.text= "";
                }
            }

        ]]>
    </fx:Script>


    <s:VGroup>
        <s:HGroup>
            <s:Label text="Currency Input"/>
            <s:TextInput id="inputCurrency" focusOut="currencyFormat()"
                         width="300"/>
        </s:HGroup>

        <s:HGroup>
            <s:Label text="Phone Number Input"/>
            <s:TextInput id="inputPhone" focusOut="phoneFormat()" width="300"/>
        </s:HGroup>

        <s:HGroup>
            <s:Label text="Date Input"/>
            <s:TextInput id="inputDate" focusOut="dateFormat();" width="300"/>
        </s:HGroup>

    </s:VGroup>
</s:Application>
```

14.2 Create a Custom Formatter

Problem

You want to create a custom formatter that will accept any appropriate string and return it with the correct formatting.

Solution

Extend the `Formatter` class and override the `format()` method.

Discussion

In the `format()` method of the `Formatter`, you'll create a `SwitchSymbolFormatter` instance and pass to its `formatValue()` method a string of hash marks representing the characters you want replaced with your original string. For example, if provided the format `###-###` and the source `123456`, the `formatValue()` method will return `123-456`. You'll then return this value from the `format()` method of your custom formatter.

The `Formatter` class uses a string of hash marks that will be replaced by all the characters in the string passed to the `format()` method. Replacing those characters is simply a matter of looping through the string and, character by character, building out the properly formatted string and then replacing the original:

```
package oreilly.cookbook {
    import mx.formatters.Formatter;
    import mx.formatters.SwitchSymbolFormatter;

    public class ISBNFormatter extends Formatter {

    public var formatString : String = "####-##-####";

        public function ISBNFormatter() {
            super();
        }

        override public function format(value:Object):String {
            // we need to check the length of the string
            // ISBN can be 10 or 13 characters
            if( ! (value.toString().length == 10 ||
                    value.toString().length == 13) ) {
                error="Invalid String Length";
                return ""
            }

            // count the number of hash marks passed into our format string
            var numCharCnt:int = 0;
            for( var i:int = 0; i<formatString.length; i++ ) {
                if( formatString.charAt(i) == "#" ) {
                    numCharCnt++;
                }
            }
```

```
        // if we don't have the right number of items in our format string
        // time to return an error
        if( ! (numCharCnt == 10 || numCharCnt == 13)  ) {
            error="Invalid Format String";
            return ""
        }

        // if the formatString and value are valid, format the number
        var dataFormatter:SwitchSymbolFormatter = new SwitchSymbolFormatter();
        return dataFormatter.formatValue( formatString, value );
    }

  }
}
```

14.3 Use Regular Expressions to Create an International Zip Code Validator

Problem

You need to validate all the South American postal code formats for countries that use them.

Solution

Create a series of regular expressions using groups to represent each country that has a postal code to be validated. Create a custom `Validator` class that can be passed a country value, and based on that value, apply the correct `RegExp` in the `doValidation()` method. If the value passed to the `doValidation()` method matches the `RegExp`, or the country selected doesn't have a `RegExp` for its postal code, return `true`; otherwise, return `false`.

Discussion

Using regular expressions in custom validators lets you create far more versatile validation methods than would be possible without them. Without regular expressions, the `Validator` is restricted to a single string that it can validate. Using more than one regular expression in a validator enables you to create a class that can validate multiple string formats.

This code sample sets up a hash table of different countries' postal codes. When the user selects a country and passes it into the validator, the correct regular expression is chosen from the hash:

```
        private var countryHash:Object = {"Argentina":/[a-zA-Z]\d{4}[a-zA-Z]{3}/,
            "Brazil":/\d{5}-\d{3}/, "Mexico":/\d{5}/, "Bolivia":/\d{4}/,
            "Chile":/\d{7}/,  "Paraguay":/\d{4}/,"Uruguay":/\d{5}/};
```

The country property of the validator is used in the doValidation() method of the Validator class that the example overrides:

```
                // ensure that we have a country set
                if(countryHash[_country] != null) {
                    // read from our hash table and get the correct RegExp
                    var regEx:RegExp = countryHash[_country];
                    if(regEx.test(value as String)) {
                        return results;
                    } else {
                        // if the postal code doesn't validate, return an error
                        var err:ValidationResult = new ValidationResult(true, "",
                                "", "Please Enter A Correct Postal Code");
                        results.push(err);
                    }
                } else {
                    return results;
                }
```

The complete code listing for the validator is shown here:

```
package oreilly.cookbook {
    import mx.validators.ValidationResult;
    import mx.validators.Validator;

    public class SouthAmericanValidator extends Validator {
        // store all of our countries and their postal codes in a hash table
        private var countryHash:Object = {"Argentina":/[a-zA-Z]\d{4}[a-zA-Z]{3}/,
                "Brazil":/\d{5}-\d{3}/, "Mexico":/\d{5}/, "Bolivia":/\d{4}/,
                "Chile":/\d{7}/, "Paraguay":/\d{4}/, "Uruguay":/\d{5}/};

        private var results:Array;
        private var _country:String;

        public function SouthAmericanValidator() {
            super();
        }

        public function set country(str:String):void {
            _country = str;
            trace(_country);
        }

        // define the doValidation() method
        override protected function doValidation(value:Object):Array {
            // clear results Array
            results = [];

            // if we don't have a country set, we return an error
            if(_country == "") {
                var err:ValidationResult = new ValidationResult(true, "", "",
                        "Please Select a Country");
                results.push(err);
                return results;
            } else {
```

```
                    // if it's a country that doesn't have a zip code, we return
                    // w/o an error
                    if(countryHash[_country] != null) {
                        // read from our hash table and get the correct RegExp
                        var regEx:RegExp = countryHash[_country];
                        if(regEx.test(value as String)) {
                            return results;
                        } else {
                            // if the postal code doesn't validate, return an error
                            var err:ValidationResult = new ValidationResult(true, "",
                                    "", "Please Enter  A Correct Postal Code");
                            results.push(err);
                        }
                    } else {
                        return results;
                    }
                }
                return results;
            }

        }
    }
```

To implement the custom validator, ensure that the country property is set before calling its doValidation() method. In this example, a ComboBox component is used to set
the country property of the SouthAmericanValidator object:

```
<s:Group xmlns:fx="http://ns.adobe.com/mxml/2009"
            xmlns:s="library://ns.adobe.com/flex/spark"
            xmlns:mx="library://ns.adobe.com/flex/halo"
            xmlns:cookbook="oreilly.cookbook.*">
    <cookbook:SouthAmericanValidator property="text" source="{zip}" required="true"
                                id="validator" invalid="showInvalid(event)"/>
    <fx:Script>
        <![CDATA[
            import mx.events.ValidationResultEvent;

            private function showInvalid(event:ValidationResultEvent):void {
                trace( " event " + event.message );
                zip.errorString = event.message;
            }

        ]]>
    </fx:Script>
    <s:HGroup>
        <mx:ComboBox dataProvider="{new ArrayList(['Argentina', 'Brazil', 'Mexico',
                                'Bolivia', 'Ecuador', 'Colombia',
                                'Chile','Paraguay','Uruguay'])}"
                    id="cb"
                    change="validator.country = cb.selectedItem as String"/>
        <s:Label text="Enter zip "/>
        <s:TextInput id="zip"/>
    </s:HGroup>
</s:Group>
```

14.4 Validate Combo Boxes and Groups of Radio Buttons

Problem

You need to validate groups of radio buttons and combo boxes to ensure that one of the radio buttons in the group is selected and that the combo box prompt is not selected.

Solution

Use a `NumberValidator` to check the radio buttons, and a custom `Validator` to validate the combo box.

Discussion

To return a `ValidationResultEvent` for a group of radio buttons, use a `NumberValidator` to check that the `selectedIndex` of the `RadioButtonGroup` is not `-1`, which would indicate that no radio button is selected. To validate a combo box, create a custom validator and check that the value of the `ComboBox`'s `selectedItem` property is not null and is not either the custom prompt that was supplied or an invalid value.

The code for the custom `ComboBox` validator is quite straightforward and is commented and shown here:

```
package oreilly.cookbook.flex4 {
    import mx.validators.ValidationResult;
    import mx.validators.Validator;

    public class ComboValidator extends Validator {
        // this is the error message that is returned if an item in the
        // ComboBox is not selected
        public var error:String;
        // if the developer sets a manual prompt, but pushes something into the
        // array of the ComboBox (I've seen it many times for different reasons)
        // we want to check that against what the selected item in the CB is
        public var prompt:String;

        public function ComboValidator() {
            super();
        }
        // here we check for either a null value or the possibility that
        // the developer has added a custom prompt to the ComboBox, in which
        // case we want to return an error
        override protected function doValidation(value:Object):Array {
            var results:Array = [];
            if(value as String == prompt || value == null) {
                var res:ValidationResult = new ValidationResult(true, "", "",
                                                                error);
                results.push(res);
            }
```

```
            return results;
        }
    }
}
```

One strategy for performing multiple validations is to use an array: you add to the array all of the component's validators that need to be called, and then use the public static `Validator.validateAll()` method to validate all the validators in the array. This technique is particularly valuable when multiple fields need to be validated at the same time. If any of the validators return errors, all those errors are joined together and displayed in an `Alert` control. The following example demonstrates performing multiple validations, including validation of a radio button selection:

```
<s:Group xmlns:fx="http://ns.adobe.com/mxml/2009"
        xmlns:s="library://ns.adobe.com/flex/spark"
        xmlns:mx="library://ns.adobe.com/flex/halo"
        width="600" height="400" xmlns:cookbook="oreilly.cookbook.flex4.*"
        creationComplete="init()">

    <fx:Declarations>
        <mx:StringValidator id="rbgValidator" source="{rbg}"
                            property="selectedValue"
                            error="Please Select a Radio Button"/>
        <mx:NumberValidator id="toggleValidator" source="{toggleButton}"
                            property="selected Index" allowNegative="false" />
        <cookbook:ComboValidator id="comboValidator" error="Please Select A State"
                            prompt="{stateCB.prompt}" source="{stateCB}"
                            property="selectedItem"/>

        <mx:RadioButtonGroup id="rbg"/>
    </fx:Declarations>
    <fx:Script>
        <![CDATA[

            import mx.events.ValidationResultEvent;
            import mx.validators.Validator;
            import mx.controls.Alert;

            [Bindable]
            private var validatorArr:Array;
            // make an array of all the validators that we'll check with one
            // method later
            private function init():void {
                validatorArr = new Array();
                // push all the validators into the same array
                validatorArr.push(rbgValidator);
                validatorArr.push(toggleValidator);
                validatorArr.push(comboValidator);
            }
            // validate all the items in the validator array and show an alert
            // if there are any errors
            private function validateForm():void {
                // the validateAll method will validate all the validators
```

```
                // in an array
                // passed to the validateAll method
                var validatorErrorArray:Array =
                        Validator.validateAll(validatorArr);
                var isValidForm:Boolean = validatorErrorArray.length == 0;
                if (!isValidForm) {
                    var err:ValidationResultEvent;
                    var errorMessageArray:Array = [];
                    for each (err in validatorErrorArray) {
                        errorMessageArray.push(err.message);
                    }
                    Alert.show(errorMessageArray.join("\n"), "Invalid form...",
                            Alert.OK);
                }
            }

        ]]>
    </fx:Script>
    <s:VGroup id="form">
        <mx:ComboBox id="stateCB" dataProvider="{someDataProvider}"
                    prompt="Select A State"/>
        <s:HGroup>
            <s:RadioButton group="{rbg}" label="first" id="first"/>
            <s:RadioButton group="{rbg}" id="second" label="second"/>
            <s:RadioButton id="third" label="third" group="{rbg}"/>
        </s:HGroup>
        <s:ButtonBar id="toggleButton">
            <fx:dataProvider>
                <fx:ArrayList>
                    <fx:Number>1</fx:Number>
                    <fx:Number>2</fx:Number>
                    <fx:Number>3</fx:Number>
                </fx:ArrayList>
            </fx:dataProvider>
        </s:ButtonBar>
    </s:VGroup>
    <s:Button label="validate" click="validateForm()"/>
</s:Group>
```

14.5 Show Validation Errors by Using ToolTips in a Form

Problem

You want to create and display multiple validation error results regardless of whether the user has the TextInput or another control in focus.

Solution

Use the ToolTipManager to create a new ToolTip class and position it over the control where the error occurred. Create a Style object and assign it to the ToolTip to give it a red background and an appropriate font color.

Discussion

The error tip that displays when a validator returns an error is simply a `ToolTip` component. You can use a style to represent all the necessary visual information for the `ToolTip`: `backgroundColor`, `fontColor`, `fontType`, and so forth. Use the `setStyle()` method of the `ToolTip` to apply this style to the new tooltips created for each validation error. For example:

```
errorTip.setStyle("styleName", "errorToolTip");
```

To display multiple tooltips, position them by using the stage positions of the relevant controls. For example:

```
var pt:Point = this.stage.getBounds(err.currentTarget.source);
var yPos:Number = pt.y * -1;
var xPos:Number = pt.x * -1;
// now create the error tip
var errorTip:ToolTip = ToolTipManager.createToolTip(err.message,
        xPos + err.currentTarget.source.width, yPos) as ToolTip;
```

When the form validates, all the tooltips are removed using the `ToolTipManager destroy ToolTip()` method, which loops through each `ToolTip` added:

```
<s:VGroup xmlns:fx="http://ns.adobe.com/mxml/2009"
        xmlns:s="library://ns.adobe.com/flex/spark"
        xmlns:mx="library://ns.adobe.com/flex/halo"
        width="500" height="400"
        xmlns:cookbook="oreilly.cookbook.flex4.*"
        creationComplete="init();">
    <fx:Style>
        /* here's the CSS class that we'll use to give our tooltip the appearance
        of an error message */
        .errorToolTip {
            color: #FFFFFF;
            fontSize: 9;
            fontWeight: "bold";
            shadowColor: #000000;
            borderColor: #CE2929;
            borderStyle: "errorTipRight";
            paddingBottom: 4;
            paddingLeft: 4;
            paddingRight: 4;
            paddingTop: 4;
        }

    </fx:Style>
    <fx:Script>
        <![CDATA[
            import mx.controls.ToolTip;
            import mx.managers.ToolTipManager;
            import mx.events.ValidationResultEvent;
            import mx.validators.Validator;
            import mx.controls.Alert;
```

```
[Bindable]
private var validatorArr:Array;

private var allErrorTips:Array;

private function init():void {
    validatorArr = new Array();
    validatorArr.push(comboValidator1);
    validatorArr.push(comboValidator2);
}
```

Here's where the actual validation occurs:

```
private function validateForm():void {
    // if we have error tips already, we want to remove them
    if(!allErrorTips) {
        allErrorTips = new Array();
    } else {
        for(var i:int = 0; i<allErrorTips.length; i++) {
            // remove the tooltip
            ToolTipManager.destroyToolTip(allErrorTips[i]);
        }
        // empty our array
        allErrorTips.length = 0;
    }
    var validatorErrorArray:Array =
            Validator.validateAll(validatorArr);
```

If nothing has been pushed into the validatorErrorArray, you know that no validation errors have been thrown. Otherwise, you'll want to go about creating the error tips and placing them:

```
var isValidForm:Boolean = validatorErrorArray.length == 0;
if (!isValidForm) {
    var err:ValidationResultEvent;
    for each (err in validatorErrorArray) {
        // Use the target's x and y positions to set position
        // of error tip. We want their actual stage positions
        // in case there's some layout management going on, so
        // we use the getBounds() method.
```

Because the ErrorEvent's target property is the control or component that threw the event, use that property to place the error tip:

```
var pt:Rectangle =
        stage.getBounds(err.currentTarget.source);
var yPos:Number = pt.y * -1;
var xPos:Number = pt.x * -1;
// now create the error tip
var errorTip:ToolTip =
        ToolTipManager.createToolTip(err.message,
        xPos + err.currentTarget.source.width, yPos)
        as ToolTip;
// apply the errorTip class selector
errorTip.setStyle("styleName", "errorToolTip");
```

```
                        // store the error tip so we can remove it later when
                        // the user revalidates
                        allErrorTips.push(errorTip);
                    }
                }
            }
        ]]>
    </fx:Script>
    <!-- our two validators -->
    <cookbook:ComboValidator id="comboValidator1"
                             error="Please Select A State"
                             prompt="{stateCB1.prompt}" source="{stateCB1}"
                             property="selectedItem"/>
    <cookbook:ComboValidator id="comboValidator2"
                             error="Please Select A State"
                             prompt="{stateCB2.prompt}" source="{stateCB2}"
                             property="selectedItem"/>
    <s:VGroup id="form">
        <s:ComboBox id="stateCB1" dataProvider="{someDataProvider}"
                    prompt="Select A State"/>
        <s:ComboBox id="stateCB2" dataProvider="{someDataProvider}"
                    prompt="Select A State"/>
    </s:VGroup >
    <s:Button label="validate" click="validateForm()"/>
</s:VGroup>
```

14.6 Use Regular Expressions for Locating Email Addresses

Problem

You need to identify any email addresses entered or encountered in text.

Solution

Create a regular expression to match the *name@host.com* email address format and use
the global flag (**g**) to indicate that the expression can match multiple times.

Discussion

The necessary regular expression looks like this:

```
var reg:RegExp = /\w+?@\w+?\.\w{3}/g;
```

To match all the email addresses in a large block of text, use the `String match()` method,
which returns an array of all matches. The `match()` method accepts either a string or a
regular expression to search for.

14.7 Use Regular Expressions for Matching Credit Card Numbers

Problem

You need a regular expression that will match the major credit card types: Visa, MasterCard, American Express, and Discover.

Solution

Create a regular expression that uses the initial digits of each major credit card type and match the expected number of digits for each type.

Discussion

The numbers of each major credit card type start with the same identifying digits, and you can use this fact to create a single regular expression for determining whether a card number is valid. All MasterCard card numbers start with 5, all Visa card numbers start with 4, all American Express card numbers start with 30, and all Discover card numbers start with 6011. The expression you need is as follows:

```
(5[1-5]\d{14})|(4\d{12}(\d{3})?)|(3[47]\d{13})|(6011\d{14})
```

For MasterCard, the expression (5[1-5]\d{14}) matches only valid numbers without any spaces in them. It's generally a good idea to clear the spaces out of any credit card numbers before sending them on to a processing service. The next segments of the expression match Visa cards, then American Express cards, and finally Discover cards. The alternation flag (|) in between the regular expression's four parts indicates that you can match any one of the four valid card patterns to return a match.

14.8 Use Regular Expressions for Validating ISBNs

Problem

You want to create a regular expression to validate International Standard Book Numbers (ISBNs).

Solution

Create a pattern that allows for the use of hyphens, the possibility that the ISBN number is 10 or 13 digits long, and that the number may or may not end with a X.

Discussion

The regular expression shown here uses the caret (^) and dollar sign ($) markers to indicate that the pattern must be the only item in the string. These symbols could be removed to match all ISBN numbers within a block of text as well:

```
private var isbnReg:RegExp = /^(?=.{13}$)\d{1,5}([- ])\d{1,7}\1\d{1,6}\1(\d|X)$/;
private function testISBN():void {
    var s:String ="ISBN 1-56389-016-X";
    trace(s.match(isbnReg));
}
```

The caret indicates that the pattern must occur at the beginning of a line, and the dollar sign indicates that whatever directly precedes it must be the end of the line. Between these two symbols, you have groups of integers, optionally separated by hyphens (-).

14.9 Create Regular Expressions by Using Explicit Character Classes

Problem

You want to use regular expressions with explicit characters to match patterns in text—for example, words containing only vowels.

Solution

Use brackets ([and]) to hold all the characters that you would like to match the pattern—for example, [aeiou] to match all vowels.

Discussion

To match patterns in a block of text, you can use multiple character flags in a regular expression to signal the various character classes that you may wish to match. Here are a few common flags:

[ ] *(square brackets)*
: Defines a character class, which defines possible matches for a single character; for example, /[aeiou]/ matches any one of the specified characters.

- *(hyphen)*
: Within character classes, use the hyphen to designate a range of characters; for example, /[A-Z0-9]/ matches uppercase A through Z or 0 through 9.

/ *(backslash)*
: Within character classes, insert a backslash to escape the] and - characters; for example, /[+\-]\d+/ matches either + or - before one or more digits. Within character classes, other characters, which are normally metacharacters, are treated as normal characters (not metacharacters), without the need for a backslash: /[$£]/

matches either $ or £. For more information, see the Flex documentation on character classes.

| *(pipe)*

Used for alternation, to match either the part on the left side or the part on the right side; for example, /abc|xyz/ matches either *abc* or *xyz*.

To match only odd numbers, you would write this:

```
var reg:RegExp = /[13579]/;
```

To match only vowels, you would use this:

```
var vowels:RegExp = /[aeiou]/;
```

To not match vowels, you would use this:

```
var notVowels:RegExp = /[^aeiou]/;
```

Note that the caret in the preceding example means *not* only within the square brackets. Outside the square brackets, the caret indicates that the string must occur at the beginning of a line.

14.10 Use Character Types in Regular Expressions

Problem

You want to use regular expressions to match character types (integers, characters, spaces, or the negations of these) in your patterns.

Solution

Use the character type flags.

Discussion

Using the character class is by far the easiest and most efficient way to match characters when creating patterns to test against. To perform those tests, use character type flags. These consist of a backslash to tell the regular expression engine that the following characters are a character type (as opposed to a character to be matched), followed by the desired character class specification. Many of these character types also have negations. Here are some examples:

\d

matches a decimal digit. This is the equivalent of [0-9].

\D

matches any character other than a digit. This is the equivalent of [^0-9].

\b

> matches at the position between a word character and a nonword character. If the first or last character in the string is a word character, \b also matches the start or end of the string.

\B

> matches at the position between two word characters. Also matches the position between two nonword characters.

\f

> matches a form-feed character.

\n

> matches the newline character.

\r

> matches the return character.

\s

> matches any whitespace character (a space, tab, newline, or return character).

\S

> matches any character other than a whitespace character.

\t

> matches the tab character.

\unnnn

> matches the Unicode character with the character code specified by the hexadecimal number *nnnn*. For example, \u263a is the smiley character.

\v

> matches a vertical-feed character.

\w

> matches a word character (A–Z, a–z, 0–9, or _). Note that \w does not match non-English characters, such as é, ñ, or ç.

\W

> matches any character other than a word character.

\xnn

> matches the character with the specified ASCII value, as defined by the hexadecimal number *nn*.

\ (backslash)

> escapes the special metacharacter meaning of special characters.

. (dot)

> matches any single character. A dot matches a newline character (\n) only if the s (dotall) flag is set. For more information, see the s (dotall) flag in the Flex documentation.

A few quick examples show the usage of these metacharacters. To match a 1 followed by two letters, use the following:

```
/1\w\w/;
```

To match a 1 followed by two nonletters, use this:

```
/1\W\W/;
```

To match five consecutive numbers, you could use this:

```
/\d\d\d\d\d/;
```

although a far easier way to do this is shown here:

```
/\d{5}/;
```

To match two numbers separated by a space:

```
/\d\b\d/;
```

To match three numbers separated by any character:

```
/\d.\d.\d/;
```

The metacharacters allow you to create expressions that will match certain patterns of any integer, alphabetic character, or blank space, as well as matching the negation of all of these. This lets you create much more powerful and terse regular expressions.

14.11 Match Valid IP Addresses by Using Subexpressions

Problem

You want to find multiple valid IP addresses in a block of text.

Solution

Use subexpressions to create valid matches for each three-digit number in the IP address.

Discussion

Using what you learned in Recipe 14.10, you can match between one and three numbers of an IP address by using the \d flag:

```
\d{1,3}
```

If you want to match three sets of one and four numbers, use this:

```
(\d{1,4}){3}
```

Just as \d{3} matches 333, when you create a subexpression, you can match that subexpression. The subexpression is a distinct element that can be treated like any other pattern. So for the IP address, you want to match four sets of three numbers separated by periods. Think about this as three sets of three numbers with periods and then one set of three numbers. Doing so leads to a far more efficient expression, such as the following:

    (\d{1,3}\.){3}\d{1,3}

This approach will bring you closer, but it won't work completely because it also matches a string like 838.381.28.999, which is not a valid IP address. What you need is something that takes into account that the maximum value for one of the three-digit numbers in the IP address is 255. Using subexpressions, you can create just such a regular expression:

    ((((\d{1,2})|(1\d{2})|(2[0-4]\d)|(25[0-5]))\.){3}((\d{1,2})|(1\d{2})|
    (2[0-4]\d)|(25[0-5]))

Take a closer look at this section:

    ((((\d{1,2})|(1\d{2})|(2[0-4]\d)|(25[0-5]))\.){3}

Translating this into English, you see two digits that are either 1 or 2, (\d{1,2}), or a 1 followed by two other numbers (1\d{2}), or a 2 followed by two of anything between 0 and 4 (2[0-4]\d), or 2 and 5 followed by anything between 0 and 5 (25[0-5]). Any one of these is then followed by a period.

Finally, you wind up with something like this:

    (((\d{1,2})|(1\d{2})|(2[0-4]\d)|(25[0-5]))

This is exactly the same as the previous pattern, with one exception: the exclusion of the period at the end. An IP address (for example, 192.168.0.1) doesn't contain a final period.

The subexpression syntax functions as follows:

- {n} indicates at least *n* times.
- {n,m} indicates at least *n* but no more than *m* times.

See Also

Recipe 14.10

14.12 Use Regular Expressions for Different Types of Matches

Problem

You want to match a pattern described with a regular expression a certain number of times.

Solution

Use the grouping syntax—either the period (.) expression or the plus (+) expression—to match different groups various numbers of times.

Discussion

As you saw in Recipe 14.11, the braces syntax allows you to indicate the number of times that a subexpression should be matched and whether the results should be returned. Suppose, for example, you want to match all characters between 0 and 4 in two strings:

```
var firstString:String = "12430";
var secondString:String = "603323";
```

Consider all the types of matches that you could execute on these two strings. The modifiers you could use are as follows:

- ?? matches zero or one time only.
- *? matches zero or more times.
- +? matches one or more times.

Remember that matching and returning matches are quite different. If you want to find out whether the two example strings contain only characters between 0 and 4, for example, you can use the RegExp test() method, which returns a Boolean true or false value. If you want to include all characters in the String that match until a non-match is found, use the String match() method. If you want to include all characters in the String that match regardless of any nonmatches, use the global flag on the regular expression (/[0-4]+g/) together with the String match() method.

For example, /[abc]+/ matches *abbbca* or *abba* and returns abc from abcss.

\w+@\w+\.\w+ matches anything resembling an email address. Note that the period is escaped, meaning it is simply a period and not read as part of the regular expression's syntax. The use of the + symbol indicates that any number of characters can be found; these characters must be followed by the at sign (@), which in turn can be followed by any number of additional characters.

This code snippet demonstrates various quantifiers and comments their results:

```
var atLeastOne:RegExp = /[0-4]+/g;
var zeroOrOne:RegExp = /[0-4]*/g;
var atLeastOne2:RegExp = /[0-4]+?/g;
var zeroOrOne2:RegExp = /[0-4]*?/g;
var firstString:String = "12430";
var secondString:String = "663323";

firstString.match(atLeastOne));    // returns "1243"
secondString.match(atLeastOne));   // returns "3323" because we want as many
                                   // characters as will match
firstString.match(zeroOrOne));     // returns "1243" because the first few
                                   // characters match
secondString.match(zeroOrOne));    // returns "" because the first few characters
                                   // don't match, so we stop looking
firstString.match(atLeastOne2));   // returns "1,2,4,3" because all we need is
                                   // one match
secondString.match(atLeastOne2));  // returns "3,3,2,3"
```

```
firstString.match(zeroOrOne2));    // returns ""
secondString.match(zeroOrOne2));   // returns ""
zeroOrOne2.test(firstString));     // returns true
zeroOrOne2.test(secondString));    // returns false
```

14.13 Match Ends or Beginnings of Lines with Regular Expressions

Problem

You want to match patterns that occur only at the beginning or the end of a string, or patterns that exist on the line of a string with either nothing in front of or nothing behind them.

Solution

Use the caret (^) and dollar sign ($) markers in your regular expression.

Discussion

When matching patterns on discrete lines or at a line's start or end, place the caret marker at the beginning of your regular expressions to indicate that your pattern must occur at the beginning of a line, and place the dollar sign at the end of your pattern to indicate that the end of the line must follow your pattern.

For example, to match *.jpg* or *.jpeg* with any length of a filename, but only where the name is encountered on a line with nothing else around it, use the following:

```
/^.+?\.jpe?g$/i
```

To match only words that occur at the end of a line in a text field, use this:

```
/\w+?$/;
```

And to match words that occur only at the beginning of a line, use this:

```
/^\w+?/;
```

14.14 Use Back-References

Problem

You want to match a pattern and then use that match to check the next potential match—for example, matching pairs of HTML tags.

Solution

Use back-references in your regular expression to check each match against the most recent match.

Discussion

The Flash Player regular expression engine can store up to 99 back-references (i.e., a list of the 99 previous matches). The flag \1 always indicates the most recent match, \2 indicates the second most recent match, and so on. Likewise, in the `String` `replace()` method, which uses the matches from another regular expression, the most recent match is indicated by `$1`.

To ensure that pairs of HTML tags match (for example, that <h2> is followed by </h2>), this example uses the back-reference \1 to indicate the most recent match:

```
private var headerBackreference:RegExp = /<H([1-6])>.*?<\/H\1>/g;
private function init():void {
    var s:String = "<BODY> <H2>Valid Chocolate</H2> <H2>Valid Vanilla</H2>
        <H2>This is not valid HTML</H3></BODY>";
    var a:Array = s.match(headerBackreference);
    if(a != null) {
        for(var i:int = 0; i<a.length; i++) {
            trace(a[i]);
        }
    }
}
```

You could also use back-references to wrap all valid URLs with an <a> tag to make hyperlinks. The way of indicating the back-reference here is slightly different. Here's the code:

```
private var domainName:RegExp = /(ftp|http|https|file):\/\/[\S]+(\b|$)/gim;
private function matchDomain():void {
    var s:String = "Hello my domain is http://www.bar.com, but I also like
        http://foo.net as well as www.baz.org";
    var replacedString = (s.replace(domainName, '<a href="$&">$&</a>').
        replace(/([^\/])(www[\S]+(\b|$))/gim,'$1<a href="http://$2">$2</a>'));
}
```

The first match is made by matching a valid URL:

```
/(ftp|http|https|file):\/\/[\S]+(\b|$)/gim;
```

Next, all the valid URLs are wrapped in <a> tags:

```
s.replace(domainName, '<a href="$&">$&</a>')
```

At this point you will have:

```
Hello my domain is <a href="http://www.bar.com">http://www.bar.com</a>,
but I also like <a href="http://foo.net">http://foo.net</a> as well as www.baz.org
```

which is not quite right. Because the original RegExp looked for strings starting with *ftp*, *http*, *https*, or *file*, *www.baz.org* isn't matched. The second `replace()` statement looks through the string for any instance of *www* that is not prefaced by a /, which would have already matched:

```
replace(/([^\/])(www[\S]+(\b|$))/gim,'$1<a href="http://$2">$2</a>'))
```

The $1 and $2 here indicate the first and second matches within the pattern, the second being the actual URL name that you want.

14.15 Use a Look-Ahead or Look-Behind

Problem

You want to match patterns that are not preceded or followed by certain other characters.

Solution

Use a negative look-ahead, (?!) or negative look-behind, (?<!), to indicate any characters that cannot be in front of or behind your match. Use a positive look-ahead (?=) or positive look-behind (?<=) to indicate characters that should be located in front of or behind your match.

Discussion

A positive look-behind indicates a pattern whose presence in front of an expression will be used in determining a match, but that you do *not* want included in the match itself. For example, to match all numbers that follow a dollar sign, but not the dollar sign itself, in the following string:

```
400 boxes at $100 per unit and 300 boxes at $50 per unit.
```

you could use a regular expression with a positive look-behind:

```
/(?<=\$)\d+/
```

If you want to match all characters that do *not* have a dollar sign in front of them, you can instead use a negative look-behind:

```
/\b(?<!\$)\d+\b/
```

Note that the negative look-behind replaces the = of the positive look-behind with a ! symbol to indicate that in order for the string to match, the dollar sign must not be present.

To match only the prices from a string, you can use a positive look-ahead:

```
private var lookBehindPrice:RegExp = /(?<=[\$|¢])[0-9.]+/g;

private function matchPrice():void {
    var s:String = "dfsf24ds: ¢23.45 ds2e4d: $5.31 CFMX1: $899.00 d3923: ¢69";
    trace(s.match(this.lookBehindPrice));
}
```

Similarly, to match variable declarations in a string you can use positive look-aheads as shown here:

```
private var lookBehindVariables:RegExp = /(?<=var )[0-9_a-zA-Z]+/g;
private function matchVars():void {
    var s:String = " private var lookAheadVariables:RegExp = /blah/
            private var str:String = 'foo'";
    trace(s.match(lookBehindVariables));
}
```

If you want, for example, to match all strings with the value *pic* that do not have *.jpg* behind them, you can instead use a negative look-ahead:

```
var reg:RegExp = /pic(?!\.jpg)/;
```

CHAPTER 15

Working with Services and Server-Side Communication

One of the most important aspects of working with Flex is communicating with a server and its exposed service methods. The recipes in this chapter focus mainly on configuring a Flex application to communicate with servers and processing data sent to the application from a server, in one of the three main ways that servers and applications communicate.

Flex provides three classes to communicate with servers: HTTPService, RemoteObject, and WebService. The HTTPService class facilitates communication with a server using the Hypertext Transfer Protocol (HTTP). A Flex application can use GET or POST requests to send data to a server and process the XML or character strings that are returned from the requests. With the HTTPService class, you can communicate with PHP pages, ColdFusion pages, JavaServer Pages (JSP), Java servlets, Ruby on Rails, and Microsoft Active Server Pages (ASP). You can use the RemoteObject class for communicating with a server using ActionScript Message Format (AMF), with Java or ColdFusion remoting gateways, or with .NET and PHP by using open source projects such as AMFPHP, SabreAMF, or WebORB. The WebService class communicates with a web service that defines its interface by using the Web Services Description Language (WSDL) and uses either SOAP-based XML or XML.

To create a service component, you need to configure the service by specifying the URL of the server that will be used to send requests and receive data and providing information about the type of data expected. For the HTTPService object, you need to set the method for passing parameters to the server, either GET or POST, and the result Format. For the WebService component, you must set the URL of the WSDL document for the service, and in the <mx:Operation> tag you can describe each operation that the WebService will use and set result and fault handlers for that operation. For the RemoteObject class, the URL of the service is described in the *services-config.xml* file that is compiled into the SWF file. Each method that the service defines can be listed and its result and fault handlers defined.

After a call is made to a HTTPService, the data returned by the service is placed in a lastResult object contained in the service component. The resultFormat property of the service components is an ActionScript Object by default. All data returned by the service is represented as properties of the Object. Flex transforms any XML data returned by a WebService or a HTTPService into its respective base types, Number, String, Boolean, and Date. If a strongly typed object is needed, a custom data type and then instances of that type must be created and populated by using the objects stored within the lastResult. The WebService and RemoteObject classes use a result event handler function that's called when the result of the service is returned. A fault event handler is used to handle any faults returned by the service. Any data processing done on the results of the service is performed in the body of the result function.

Another important part of working with services is parsing the XML that your service may return. There are a few recipes included in this chapter for parsing, reading, and creating XML documents and files.

15.1 Configure a HTTPService

Problem

You need to create and configure a HTTPService component to allow your application to communicate with HTTP-based services.

Solution

Add a HTTPService component to your application and set its url property to the URL from which the application will request data. If the response from the service will be XML that requires custom processing, set the xmlDecode property to a method that accepts a XML object.

Discussion

The HTTPService object facilitates all communication done over HTTP. This includes any information sent via GET or POST commands, as well as information retrieved from a URL request (even static files). The HTTPService object can have result and fault event handlers assigned to it that accept mx.event.ResultsEvent objects and mx.event.FaultEvent objects, respectively:

```
<mx:HTTPService url="http://192.168.1.101/service.php" id="service"
                result="serviceResult(event)" fault="serviceFault(event)">
```

This lets you process the results of a HTTP request. You can also bind a variable or event handler to the result property of the HTTPService object, using the result property of the HTTPService object:

```
<mx:Image source="{service.lastResult as String}"/>
```

Note that the lastResult of the HTTPService is an object and must be cast as a String.

The HTTPService object can also be used to send information to a script via GET or POST, configuring the request property of the HTTPService object:

```
<mx:HTTPService>
    <mx:request xmlns="">
        <id>{requestedId}</id>
    </mx:request>
</mx:HTTPService>
```

This sends the requestedId property wrapped within an <id> tag to the URL set within the HTTPService object.

In the following example, a HTTPService object loads XML from a PHP script:

```
<?xml version="1.0" encoding="utf-8"?>
<s:Application xmlns:fx="http://ns.adobe.com/mxml/2009"
               xmlns:s="library://ns.adobe.com/flex/spark"
               xmlns:mx="library://ns.adobe.com/flex/halo"
               minWidth="1024" minHeight="768">
    <fx:Declarations>
        <mx:HTTPService url="http://localhost/service.php" id="service"
                        result="serviceResult(event)" fault="serviceFault(event)"
                        method="GET" contentType="application/xml"
                        useProxy="false">
            <mx:request xmlns="">
                <id>{requestedId}</id>
            </mx:request>
        </mx:HTTPService>
    </fx:Declarations>
    <fx:Script>
        <![CDATA[
            import mx.rpc.events.FaultEvent;
            import mx.rpc.events.ResultEvent;

            [Bindable]
            private var requestedId:Number;

            // trace out the result of the service
            private function serviceResult(event:Event):void {
                trace(service.lastResult.name);
            }

            // in the event that the service faults or times out
            private function serviceFault(event:Event):void {
                trace('broken service');
            }

            private function callService():void {
                requestedId = input.text as Number;
                service.send()
            }

        ]]>
    </fx:Script>
```

```
        <s:TextInput id="input"/>
        <s:Button label="get user name" click="callService()"/>
        <s:TextArea text="{service.lastResult.name}"/>
        <s:TextArea text="{service.lastResult.age}"/>
    </s:Application>
```

This is the PHP script that will read from the GET variables sent by the Flex application and return properly formatted XML data:

```
<?php
$id_number = $_GET["id"];
echo('<?xml version="1.0" encoding="utf-8"?>');
echo('<xml><author><id>'.$id_number.
'</id><name>Todd Anderson</name><age>30</age><author><xml>');
?>
```

This is perhaps the easiest way to communicate with a service, though it is somewhat limited by the HTTP methods that the Flash Player allows you to send. In the next recipe, you'll learn how to use HTTP communication more effectively by using libraries that allow you to access all of the available HTTP method headers.

See Also

Recipe 15.2

15.2 Use RESTful Communication Between Flex Applications

Problem

You need to integrate a Flex application with a server that uses RESTful (Representational State Transfer-style) communication, such as Rails or another server.

Solution

Create a HTTPService object to communicate with your server and use the appropriate paths in conjunction with POST and GET methods to call server methods.

Discussion

The term *RESTful* is used to describe a service that uses all four possible HTTP headers: PUT, POST, DELETE, and GET. These four headers are usually mapped to the four basic data-access operations: create, read, update, and delete (commonly referred to with the charming acronym CRUD). In practice, a single overloaded server-side method performs one of the four basic data-access operations, depending on the header sent. In a RESTful application, the method is frequently mapped to a resource, so the four data-access operations allow the creation, deletion, updating, or request of that resource. The resource can be a simple resource, a table in a database, or a complexly modeled object.

The Flash Player is limited to using only GET and POST methods, which means that any communication between a Flex application and a service will need to indicate the DELETE or PUT methods through a different manner, such as by appending them to a GET or POST message.

To send a PUT command to a Rails application, you can do something like the following:

```
var request:URLRequest = new URLRequest();
var loader:URLLoader = new URLLoader();
loader.addEventListener(Event.COMPLETE, resultHandler);
loader.addEventListener(IOErrorEvent.IO_ERROR, errorHandler);
loader.addEventListener(HTTPStatusEvent.HTTP_STATUS,httpStatusHandler);
request.url = "http://rails/view/resource";

// Set the request type as POST and send the DELETE command as
// a variable in the data of the request
request.method = URLRequestMethod.POST;
request.data._method = "DELETE";

loader.load(request);
```

Ruby on Rails allows the _method variable to indicate the desired method even when the correct HTTP method cannot be used. For other types of RESTful services, similar approaches must be used.

To work around this with a HTTPService object, you can use the BlazeDS or Adobe LiveCycle servers. The HTTPService object defines a useProxy property that, if set to true, instructs the Flash Player to communicate only with a server defined in the *services-config.xml* file. A request to build and send a proxied PUT/DELETE/OPTIONS (and so forth) request is sent to the Adobe LiveCycle or BlazeDS server, and the server builds and sends the actual HTTP request and returns the response to the player. The proxy also handles fault responses in the HTTP 500 code range (which represents messages for server errors) and returns them to the player in a form that HTTPService can process usefully, because the Flash Player doesn't handle responses in the 500 range.

After you configure the HTTPService object to use the BlazeDS or LiveCycle proxy, you can use the full range of headers with the HTTPService object by setting the method property of the service:

```
<mx:HTTPService id="proxyService" destination="http://localhost/app/url"/>
<fx:Script>
    <![CDATA[
        private function sendPut():void {
            proxyService.method = "DELETE";
            proxyService.send("id=2");
        }
    ]]>
</fx:Script>
```

Finally, there is a library called *RestfulX* (originally developed by Dima Berastau and hosted at *http://restfulx.github.com*) that aims to make integration with RESTful Web Services as simple as possible. It utilizes a library called *as3httpclient* developed by

Gabriel Handford that uses the binary Flash socket to read the HTTP stream and decode the HTTP response. This allows you to send and read GET, POST, PUT, and DELETE HTTP responses, but it requires that a *crossdomain.xml* file be created that will allow the Flash Player to connect to the server using port 80. While communicating with a server using the Socket is difficult, if you need to communicate with a server that uses RESTful responses and strict HTTP, this library provides a powerful alternative to the standard HTTPService. Used in tandem with RestfulX, it provides an easy way to communicate with a REST-based service.

15.3 Communicate with a Service That Returns JSON-Formatted Data

Problem

You need to be able to send and parse JSON data to communicate with a service.

Solution

Configure a HTTPService object and use the JSON.decode() method from the *as3corelib* open source library.

Discussion

First, you'll want to create and configure a HTTP service. From the Flash Builder Data menu, select "Connect to a HTTPService." You can then use the wizard to create your service, as shown in Figures 15-1, 15-2, and 15-3.

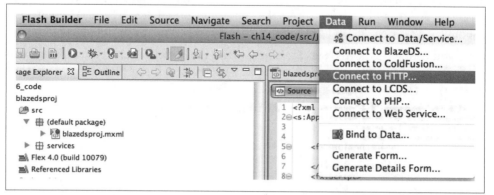

Figure 15-1. Creating a HTTP service

Note the parameters that will be passed to the service (Figure 15-2). Because the service is using the GET method, when the googleSearch() method is called both parameters are expected.

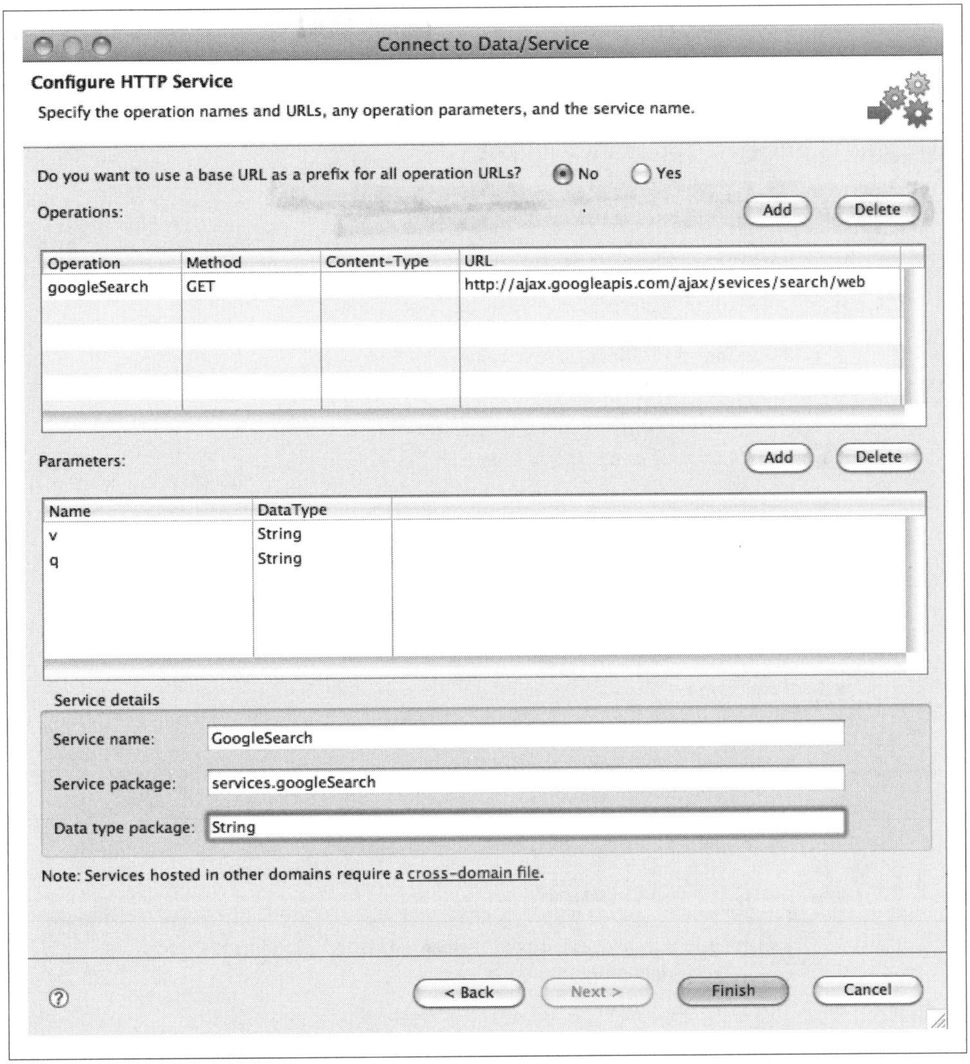

Figure 15-2. Defining methods in the Service configuration wizard

Next, set the return type of your service to `String` so that the JSON string can be parsed more easily (Figure 15-3).

Figure 15-3. Setting the return type of a method

To parse JSON requests you'll need to use the *as3corelib* library, which is available from several sources. Include the *as3corelib.swc* in your *libs* folder, and you're ready to use the JSON.decode() method that the library defines. This method takes a JSON string and returns a complex object with another object or array of data in the response Data.results property. You can use it like so:

```
var obj:Object = JSON.decode(googleSearchResult.lastResult);
var array:Array = (obj.responseData.results as Array);
```

Couldn't be easier, right? Here's the entire application:

```
<s:Application xmlns:fx="http://ns.adobe.com/mxml/2009"
               xmlns:s="library://ns.adobe.com/flex/spark"
               xmlns:mx="library://ns.adobe.com/flex/halo"
               minWidth="1024" minHeight="768"
               xmlns:googleajax="services.googleajax.*">

    <s:layout><s:VerticalLayout/></s:layout>

    <fx:Declarations>
        <s:CallResponder id="googleSearchResult" result="parseJsonResult()"/>
        <googleajax:GoogleAjax id="googleAjax"
                            fault="Alert.show(event.fault.faultString + '\n' +
                                                event.fault.faultDetail)"
                            showBusyCursor="true"/>
        <mx:ArrayList id="resultList"/>
    </fx:Declarations>
    <fx:Script>
        <![CDATA[
            import mx.collections.ArrayList;
            import mx.controls.Alert;
            import com.adobe.serialization.json.JSON;
            import spark.layouts.HorizontalLayout;

            protected function sendRequest():void
            {
                googleSearchResult.token = googleAjax.googleSearch("1.0",
                        queryInput.text);
            }

            protected function parseJsonResult():void {
                var obj:Object = JSON.decode(googleSearchResult.lastResult);
                resultList.source = (obj.responseData.results as Array);
            }

        ]]>
    </fx:Script>
    <s:Group layout="{new HorizontalLayout()}">
        <s:TextInput id="queryInput"/>
        <s:Button click="sendRequest()"/>
    </s:Group>
    <mx:DataGrid dataProvider="{resultList}"/>
</s:Application>
```

If you're not using Flash Builder, you can simply configure a `HTTPService` object as shown here:

```
<mx:HTTPService id="googleService"
                url="http://ajax.googleapis.com/ajax/services/search/web"
                method="GET" result="parseJsonResult(event)"/>
```

and then parse the result of the service like so:

```
protected function parseJsonResult(event:ResultEvent):void {
    var obj:Object = JSON.decode(String(googleService.lastResult));
    resultList.source = (obj.responseData.results as Array);

}
```

15.4 Configure Services for an Application Using BlazeDS

Problem

You need to configure the remoting services that your application will use.

Solution

Create *services-config.xml* and *remoting-config.xml* files and place them in the web root of your project. In your compiler arguments, set the location of the *services-config.xml* file as the value of the **services** parameter.

Discussion

Flex uses two different XML files to link the application to remoting services: *services-config.xml*, which defines the channels that the remote server provides, and *remoting-config.xml*, which defines the adapters and default channels that the server supports. The *web.xml* file needs to be configured so that the `RDSDispatchServlet` is accessible:

```
<?xml version="1.0" encoding="UTF-8"?>

<!DOCTYPE web-app PUBLIC "-//Sun Microsystems, Inc.//DTD Web Application 2.3//EN"
        "http://java.sun.com/dtd/web-app_2_3.dtd">

<web-app>
    <display-name>BlazeDS to Flex</display-name>
    <description>Sample Application</description>

    <!-- HTTP Flex Session attribute and binding listener support -->
    <listener>
        <listener-class>flex.messaging.HttpFlexSession</listener-class>
    </listener>

    <!-- MessageBroker Servlet -->
    <servlet>
        <servlet-name>MessageBrokerServlet</servlet-name>
        <display-name>MessageBrokerServlet</display-name>
```

```
        <servlet-class>flex.messaging.MessageBrokerServlet</servlet-class>
        <init-param>
            <param-name>services.configuration.file</param-name>
            <param-value>/WEB-INF/flex/services-config.xml</param-value>
        </init-param>
        <load-on-startup>1</load-on-startup>
    </servlet>
    <servlet-mapping>
        <servlet-name>MessageBrokerServlet</servlet-name>
        <url-pattern>/messagebroker/*</url-pattern>
    </servlet-mapping>

    <welcome-file-list>
        <welcome-file>index.htm</welcome-file>
    </welcome-file-list>
```

The next part is particularly important if you want to use the data-configuration services available in Flash Builder. Including the RDSDispatchServlet allows Flash Builder to inspect your services and bind components to an available service in the IDE very easily:

```
    <servlet>
        <servlet-name>RDSDispatchServlet</servlet-name>
        <display-name>RDSDispatchServlet</display-name>
        <servlet-class>flex.rds.server.servlet.FrontEndServlet</servlet-class>
        <init-param>
            <param-name>useAppserverSecurity</param-name>
            <param-value>false</param-value>
        </init-param>
        <load-on-startup>10</load-on-startup>
    </servlet>

    <servlet-mapping id="RDS_DISPATCH_MAPPING">
        <servlet-name>RDSDispatchServlet</servlet-name>
        <url-pattern>/CFIDE/main/ide.cfm</url-pattern>
    </servlet-mapping>

</web-app>
```

Next is the *services-config.xml* file. The services node contains the individual data services or references that are the XML files containing the service definitions. Inside the services node is the service-include file-path node. This provides the service file locations. Their paths are relative to the directory containing the *services-config.xml* file. All the definitions can be listed together, but it's convention to separate them out.

The channels node provides all the information needed about data transfer between the server and the clients. The channel-definition node defines the message channel that can be used to transport the data; its id attribute should match the one defined in the service definition and its class attribute should be the fully qualified AS3 class for the message channel, which is AMF in this case. The other options are RTMP, AMF Polling, Secure RTMP, Secure AMF, HTTP, and Secure HTTP. Per the "Configuring message channels" documentation, you can actually pair any type of service with any type of channel. Next, the endpoint node is where the client should begin requesting

---

the service, with its `url` attribute pointing to the URL of the service and its `class` attribute the fully qualified AS3 class for the endpoint.

The code of the *services-config.xml* file is:

```xml
<?xml version="1.0" encoding="UTF-8"?>
<services-config>

    <services>
        <service-include file-path="remoting-config.xml" />
        <service-include file-path="proxy-config.xml" />
        <service-include file-path="messaging-config.xml" />
        <default-channels>
            <channel ref="my-amf"/>
        </default-channels>
    </services>

    <security>
        <security-constraint id="sample-users">
            <auth-method>Custom</auth-method>
            <roles>
                <role>sampleusers</role>
            </roles>
        </security-constraint>
        <!-- You'll want to use something else if you're not using Tomcat -->
        <login-command class="flex.messaging.security.TomcatLoginCommand"
                        server="Tomcat"/>
    </security>

    <!-- Simplest config for channels, only using a single AMF channel -->
    <channels>

        <channel-definition id="my-amf" class="mx.messaging.channels.AMFChannel">
            <endpoint url="http://{server.name}:{server.port}/{context.root}/
                            messagebroker/amf"
                      class="flex.messaging.endpoints.AMFEndpoint"/>
            <properties>
                <polling-enabled>false</polling-enabled>
            </properties>
        </channel-definition>
    </channels>

    <logging>
        <!-- You may also use flex.messaging.log.ServletLogTarget -->
        <target class="flex.messaging.log.ConsoleTarget" level="Error">
            <properties>
                <prefix>[BlazeDS] </prefix>
                <includeDate>false</includeDate>
                <includeTime>false</includeTime>
                <includeLevel>true</includeLevel>
                <includeCategory>false</includeCategory>
            </properties>
            <filters>
                <pattern>Endpoint.*</pattern>
                <pattern>Service.*</pattern>
```

```
              <pattern>Configuration</pattern>
           </filters>
       </target>
   </logging>

   <system>
       <redeploy>
           <enabled>true</enabled>
           <watch-interval>20</watch-interval>
           <watch-file>{context.root}/WEB-INF/flex/services-config.xml
           </watch-file>
           <watch-file>{context.root}/WEB-INF/flex/proxy-config.xml
           </watch-file>
           <watch-file>{context.root}/WEB-INF/flex/remoting-config.xml
           </watch-file>
           <watch-file>{context.root}/WEB-INF/flex/messaging-config.xml
           </watch-file>
           <touch-file>{context.root}/WEB-INF/web.xml</touch-file>
       </redeploy>
   </system>

</services-config>
```

The *remoting-config.xml* file, like the *services-config.xml* file, contains many nodes and attributes. The biggest difference is that *remoting-config.xml* references only RemoteObject calls, whereas *services-config.xml* can reference any kind of service.

The service node defines the type of service. In the following example, the service is a RemotingService, but it can also be a HTTPProxyService, an AuthenticationService, or a MessageService. Each service should have an id and a class defined within the *remoting-config.xml* file. The default-channel corresponds to the channel-definition found in the *services-config.xml* file. The destination node names the remote object that will be available on the service and correlates to a compiled class object on the server. The id attribute is what is referred to in your MXML or ActionScript 3 code when you set the destination of the RemoteObject. The source refers to the fully qualified class name of the object that will return data to your Flex application.

Here's the code for *remoting-config.xml*:

```
<?xml version="1.0" encoding="UTF-8"?>
<service id="remoting-service"
        class="flex.messaging.services.RemotingService">

    <adapters>
        <adapter-definition id="java-object"
                class="flex.messaging.services.remoting.adapters.JavaAdapter"
                default="true"/>
    </adapters>

    <default-channels>
        <channel ref="my-amf"/>
    </default-channels>
```

```
        <destination id="simpleChat">
            <properties>
                <source>flex.samples.runtimeconfig.SimpleChat</source>
            </properties>
        </destination>
    </service>
```

The next recipe will go into greater detail on how to configure and connect to a
RemoteObject.

See Also

Recipe 15.5

15.5 Configure and Connect to a RemoteObject

Problem

You need to configure a RemoteObject for a Flex application to connect to a ColdFusion,
AMFPHP, or Java object that has been exposed for service communication with your
Flex application.

Solution

Create a RemoteObject instance in your application and set an id for your service, as
well as a URL where the service will be accessible.

Discussion

The RemoteObject lets you define methods for communication between your application and actual class objects on a server. This is quite different from the WebService
component (which relies on the WSDL file of a WebService) or the HTTPService component (which simply uses the URL to send and receive HTTP information). The
RemoteObject component can be used to call methods on a ColdFusion CFC component
or Java class that has been exposed for communication. RemoteObjects can also be used
to communicate with objects and resources defined by open source projects like
BlazeDS or AMFPHP, among others. The RemoteObject defines the following configu-
rable properties:

channelSet : ChannelSet
    Provides access to the ChannelSet used by the service.

concurrency : String
    Indicates how to handle multiple calls to the same service.

constructor : Object
    Provides a reference to the class object or constructor function for a given object
    instance.

destination : String

> Specifies the destination of the service.

endpoint : String

> Lets you quickly specify an endpoint for a RemoteObject destination without referring to a services configuration file (*services-config.xml*) at compile time or programmatically creating a ChannelSet.

makeObjectsBindable : Boolean

> Forces returned anonymous objects to bindable objects when true.

operations : Object

> Specifies methods that the service defines; used when defining a RemoteObject in MXML. This tag is not typically used in ActionScript.

requestTimeout : int

> Provides access to the request timeout, in seconds, for sent messages.

showBusyCursor : Boolean

> Displays a busy cursor while a service is executing, if true.

source : String

> Lets you specify a source value on the client; not supported for destinations that use the JavaAdapter to serialize communication between a SWF file and a Java object.

Because RemoteObject methods can return objects that do not need to be processed or deserialized from XML, the result of a RemoteObject call can be cast to an ArrayCollection or a strongly typed value object from the ResultEvent. In the following code snippet, a RemoteObject is configured to use a Java service available at *http://localhost:8400*:

```
<?xml version="1.0" encoding="utf-8"?>
<s:Application xmlns:fx="http://ns.adobe.com/mxml/2009"
               xmlns:s="library://ns.adobe.com/flex/spark"
               xmlns:mx="library://ns.adobe.com/flex/halo"
               minWidth="1024" minHeight="768">
    <fx:Declarations>
        <mx:RemoteObject id="local_service" concurrency="single"
                         destination="http://localhost:8400/app"
                         showBusyCursor="true"
                         source="LocalService.Namespace.Service.ServiceName">
            <mx:method name="getNames" fault="getNamesFault(event)"
                       result="getNamesResult(event)"/>
            <mx:method name="getAges" fault="getAgesFault(event)"
                       result="getAgesResult(event)"/>
        </mx:RemoteObject>
    </fx:Declarations>
    <fx:Script>
        <![CDATA[
            import mx.collections.ArrayCollection;
            import mx.rpc.events.ResultEvent;
            import mx.controls.Alert;
            import mx.rpc.events.FaultEvent;
```

```
            private function getNamesFault(event:FaultEvent):void {

                mx.controls.Alert.show(event.message as String, "Service Error");
            }

            private function getNamesResult(event:ResultEvent):void {

                var namesColl:ArrayCollection = event.result as ArrayCollection;
            }

            private function getAgesFault(event:FaultEvent):void {

                mx.controls.Alert.show(event.message as String, "Service Error");
            }

            private function getAgesResult(event:ResultEvent):void {

                var agesColl:ArrayCollection = event.result as ArrayCollection;
            }

        ]]>
    </fx:Script>

</s:Application>
```

The ResultEvent of each method is bound to a different event-handling method. In ActionScript this would be done by adding an event-listening method to the RemoteObject:

```
import mx.collections.ArrayCollection;
import mx.rpc.events.ResultEvent;
import mx.controls.Alert;
import mx.rpc.events.FaultEvent;
import mx.rpc.AbstractService;
import mx.rpc.AsyncToken;
import mx.rpc.Responder;

private function init():void {

    var responder:Responder = new Responder( getNamesResult, getNamesFault );
    var call:AsyncToken = ( local_service as AbstractService).getNames();
    call.addResponder(responder);

}

private function getNamesFault(event:FaultEvent):void {

    Alert.show(event.message as String, "Service Error");

}

private function getNamesResult(event:ResultEvent):void {

    var namesColl:ArrayCollection = event.result as ArrayCollection;
}
```

In the preceding example, the `mx.rpc.Responder` class is used to store the methods that will handle the result and fault events from the server. This responder is then added to an `AsyncToken` class that will fire when the service returns either a result or a fault.

15.6 Use Publish/Subscribe Messaging for Chat Applications

Problem

You want to notify the client Flex application whenever data has changed on the server side or to broadcast messages to all listeners on a messaging server, as in a chat application.

Solution

Use the `mx.messaging.Producer` and `mx.messaging.Consumer` tags to configure the destination channel that will be used for communication and to set the event handler for the message event. Configuring these correctly requires using either the Adobe Live-Cycle or BlazeDS servers.

Discussion

The Publish/Subscribe model uses two components: `mx.messaging.Producer` and `mx.messaging.Consumer`. The `Producer` sends messages to a location on the server where messages are processed (the *destination*). The `Consumer` subscribes to messages at a destination and processes those messages when they arrive from the destination.

Flex allows *ActionScript Messaging* and *Java Message Service* (JMS) messaging. Action-Script Messaging supports only clients that can speak AMF and support the necessary classes to work properly. JMS messaging allows LiveCycle or BlazeDS servers to participate in the Java Message Service and can interact with any JMS client. Any application that can talk to JMS can be called directly from a Flex client, and any Java application can publish events to Flex.

The `Consumer` receives messages via the `mx.messaging.events.MessageEvent`:

```
private function receiveChatMessage(msgEvent:MessageEvent):void
{
    var msg:AsyncMessage = AsyncMessage(msgEvent.message);
    trace("msg.body "+msg.body);
}
```

The `Producer` sends messages by using the `send()` method, which accepts an instance of `mx.messaging.AsyncMessage` as a parameter. The body of the `AsyncMessage` is the value sent to all subscribers of the channel:

```
var msg:AsyncMessage = new AsyncMessage();
msg.body = "test message";
producer.send(msg);
```

The example that follows uses two different types of `AMFChannel`: `StreamingAMFChannel` and `AMFChannel`. The `StreamingAMFChannel` provides support for messaging and offers a different push model than the base `AMFChannel`. Instead of polling the server, the streaming channel opens a HTTP connection to the server that is held open so that data can be streamed down to the client.

The `AMFChannel` can be configured to poll a server at an interval. You can also use this channel with polling disabled to send RPC messages to remote destinations to invoke their methods. The `AMFChannel` relies on network services that are native to the Flash Player and AIR and are exposed to ActionScript by the `NetConnection` class. The channel creates a new `NetConnection` for each instance. Channels are created within the framework using the `ServerConfig.getChannel()` method and can be constructed directly and assigned to a `ChannelSet` instance. Channels represent a physical connection to a remote endpoint and are shared across destinations by default. This means that a client targeting different destinations may use the same channel to communicate with these destinations.

In polling mode, `AMFChannel` polls the server for new messages at the `pollingInterval` property, 3 seconds by default. To enable polling, the channel must be connected and the `polling-enabled` property in the configuration file must be set to `true`, or the `pollingEnabled` property of the channel must be set to `true`.

The complete code listing is as follows:

```
<?xml version="1.0" encoding="utf-8"?>
<s:Application xmlns:fx="http://ns.adobe.com/mxml/2009"
               xmlns:s="library://ns.adobe.com/flex/spark"
               xmlns:mx="library://ns.adobe.com/flex/halo"
               minWidth="1024" minHeight="768"
               creationComplete=" initializeHandler()">
    <s:layout>
        <s:HorizontalLayout/>
    </s:layout>

    <fx:Script>
        <![CDATA[
            import spark.layouts.HorizontalLayout;
            import spark.layouts.VerticalLayout;
        ]]>
    </fx:Script>
    <fx:Declarations>
        <mx:Producer id="producer"/>
        <mx:Consumer id="consumer" message="messageHandler(event)"/>
        <mx:RemoteObject id="srv" destination="simpleChat" fault="trace('Error')"/>
    </fx:Declarations>

    <fx:Script>
        <![CDATA[
            import mx.messaging.channels.StreamingAMFChannel;
            import mx.messaging.ChannelSet;
            import mx.messaging.channels.AMFChannel;
            import mx.messaging.events.MessageEvent;
```

```
import mx.messaging.messages.AsyncMessage;
import mx.messaging.messages.IMessage;
```

Here, you create the `AMFChannel` and `StreamingAMFChannel` instances that will poll the service for new messages:

```
private function initializeHandler():void
{
    var myStreamingAMF:AMFChannel = new
            StreamingAMFChannel("my-streaming-amf",
            "pathToService/streamingamf");
    var myPollingAMF:AMFChannel = new
            AMFChannel("my-polling-amf", "pathToService/amfpolling");
    myPollingAMF.pollingEnabled = true;
    myPollingAMF.pollingInterval = 1000;
    var channelSet:ChannelSet = new ChannelSet();
    channelSet.addChannel(myStreamingAMF);
    channelSet.addChannel(myPollingAMF);
```

You then use the new `ChannelSet` instance to configure the `Consumer` and `Producer` instances:

```
    consumer.channelSet = channelSet;
    producer.channelSet = channelSet;
}

public function set room(name:String):void
{
    if (!name) return;

    if (consumer && consumer.subscribed)
    {
        chatLogTextArea.text += "Leaving room " +
                consumer.destination + "\n";
        consumer.unsubscribe();
    }
    consumer.destination = name;
    producer.destination = name;
    consumer.subscribe();
    chatLogTextArea.text += "Entering room " + name + "\n";
}

private function send():void
{
    var message:IMessage = new AsyncMessage();
    message.body = msgTextInput.text;
    producer.send(message);
    msgTextInput.text = "";
}

private function messageHandler(event:MessageEvent):void {

    chatLogTextArea.text += event.message.body + "\n";
}
```

Here, the messages are sent via the `Producer` instance:

```
private function sendMsg():void {

    var message:IMessage = new AsyncMessage();
    message.body.chatMessage = msgTextInput.text;
    producer.send(message);
    msgTextInput.text = "";
}
```

```
    ]]>
</fx:Script>

<s:Panel title="Chat Sample" width="100%" height="100%"
        layout="{new VerticalLayout()}">

    <s:Group layout="{new HorizontalLayout()}">
        <s:List id="list" dataProvider="{srv.getRoomList.lastResult}"
                width="100%" height="100%"/>
    </s:Group>

    <s:TextArea id="chatLogTextArea" width="100%" height="100%"/>
    <s:Group>
        <s:layout>
            <s:HorizontalLayout/>
        </s:layout>
        <mx:TextInput id="msgTextInput" width="100%" enter="sendMsg()"/>
        <mx:Button label="Send" click="sendMsg()"/>
    </s:Group>
</s:Panel>

</s:Application>
```

In your *service-config.xml* file, you'll need to define two channels for the service to use
(a `StreamingAMFChannel` and a `PollingAMFChannel`), like so:

```
<channels>

    <channel-definition id="my-streaming-amf"
                        class="mx.messaging.channels.StreamingAMFChannel">
        <endpoint url="http://{server.name}:{server.port}/{context.root}/
                    messagebroker/streamingamf"
                class="flex.messaging.endpoints.StreamingAMFEndpoint"/>
    </channel-definition>

    <channel-definition id="my-polling-amf"
                        class="mx.messaging.channels.AMFChannel">
        <endpoint url="http://{server.name}:{server.port}/{context.root}/
                    messagebroker/amfpolling"
                class="flex.messaging.endpoints.AMFEndpoint"/>
        <properties>
            <polling-enabled>true</polling-enabled>
            <polling-interval-seconds>4</polling-interval-seconds>
        </properties>
    </channel-definition>
</channels>
```

In the *messaging-config.xml* file, note that the default channels have been configured and that the destination is *not* declared. This is because `SimpleChat` will dynamically create destinations to which the messages will be sent:

```
<service id="message-service" class="flex.messaging.services.MessageService">
    <default-channels>
        <channel ref="my-streaming-amf"/>
        <channel ref="my-polling-amf"/>
    </default-channels>
</service>
```

`SimpleChat` defines a `getRooms()` method available over remoting that returns all the rooms that have been created. In a more robust chat application, this method would be implemented using messaging rather than a remoting call so that all clients would be notified when a new room is created.

Here is the code of *remoting-config.xml*:

```
<destination id="simpleChat">
    <properties>
        <source>oreilly.cookbook.flex4.SimpleChat</source>
        <scope>application</scope>
    </properties>
</destination>
```

The following is the code for a simple chat service (*SimpleChat.java*) for the BlazeDS server. You might want to expand this service to allow users to dynamically add and delete chat rooms or create private chat rooms, but for this recipe it suffices to show how rooms can dynamically be created on the fly:

```
package oreilly.cookbook.flex4;

import java.util.ArrayList;
import java.util.Collections;
import java.util.List;
import flex.messaging.MessageBroker;
import flex.messaging.MessageDestination;
import flex.messaging.services.MessageService;

public class SimpleChat {

    private List rooms;

    private final String firstChatRoom = "firstChatRoom";
    private final String secondChatRoom = "secondChatRoom";
    private final String serviceName = "message-service";

    private MessageDestination firstDestination;
    private MessageDestination secondDestination;

    public SimpleChat() {

        rooms = Collections.synchronizedList(new ArrayList());
```

```
        }
        // note: not really the sleekest Java code, but has simplicity + readability
        public List getRoomList() {

            MessageBroker broker = MessageBroker.getMessageBroker(null);
            MessageService service = (MessageService) broker.getService(serviceName);

            if(firstDestination == null)
            {
                firstDestination = (MessageDestination)
                        service.getDestination(firstChatRoom);
                if(service.getDestination(firstChatRoom) == null) {
                    firstDestination = (MessageDestination)
                            service.createDestination(firstChatRoom);
                    if (service.isStarted())
                    {
                        firstDestination.start();
                    }
                }
                rooms.add(firstChatRoom);
            }

            if(secondDestination == null)
            {
                secondDestination = (MessageDestination)
                        service.getDestination(secondChatRoom);
                if(secondDestination == null) {
                    secondDestination = (MessageDestination)
                            service.createDestination(secondChatRoom);
                    if (service.isStarted())
                    {
                        secondDestination.start();
                    }
                }
                rooms.add(secondChatRoom);
            }

            return rooms;
        }
    }
```

You'll also need to make sure that you set the following compiler arguments:

```
-locale en_US -services={$BLAZE_ROOT}/webapps/samples/WEB-INF/flex/services-config.xml
```

To see how to fully configure the *services-config.xml* file, refer back to the two previous recipes.

See Also

Figures 15.4 and 15.5

15.7 Use the IExternalizable Interface for Custom Serialization

Contributed by Peter Farland

Problem

You want to customize which properties are sent over the wire when sending strongly typed data via a `RemoteObject` or `DataService` component.

Solution

Use the ActionScript 3 API `flash.utils.IExternalizable`, which is compatible with Java's `java.io.IExternalizable` API.

Discussion

A common scenario for using externalizable classes is to include read-only properties in serialization. Although there are other approaches to achieve this for server code, there aren't many approaches available for client code. So, for an elegant solution that works for both the client and the server, you can make your classes externalizable for two-way custom serialization.

This approach is relatively straightforward. The client ActionScript class simply implements `flash.utils.IExternalizable`. This API requires two methods, `readExternal()` and `writeExternal()`, which take `flash.utils.IDataInput` and `flash.utils.IDataOutput` streams, respectively. The implementations of these methods mirror the server Java class, which implements `java.io.Externalizable`. `java.io.Externalizable` also has `readExternal()` and `writeExternal()` methods that take `java.io.ObjectInput` and `java.io.ObjectOutput` streams, respectively.

Although the `IDataInput` and `IDataOutput` classes let you design your own protocol and write such fundamental data types as `byte`, `int`, and UTF-8-encoded `String`s, most implementations take advantage of the `readObject()` and `writeObject()` methods, respectively, as these use AMF 3 to efficiently deserialize and serialize ActionScript objects. (Remember that AMF 3 has three advantages. First, you can send objects by reference to avoid redundant instances from being serialized, to retain object relationships, and to handle cyclical references. Second, you can send object traits so that the description of a type is sent only once rather than repeated for each instance. Finally, you can send reoccurring strings by reference to again avoid redundant information being sent.) You may even decide to omit property names altogether in your externalizable classes' custom serialization code and rely on a fixed order to send just the property values.

This example focuses on serializing read-only properties, but there may be many other usages for custom serialization, such as omitting properties, avoiding redundant serialization of information, or including properties from custom namespaces.

Notice how the following Java `writeExternal()` method:

```
public void writeExternal(ObjectOutput out) throws IOException
{
    out.writeObject(id);
    out.writeObject(name);
    out.writeObject(description);
    out.writeInt(price);
}
```

mirrors the client `readExternal()` method in ActionScript:

```
public function readExternal(input:IDataInput):void
{
    _id = input.readObject() as String;
    name = input.readObject() as String;
    description = input.readObject() as String;
    price = input.readInt();
}
```

A similar relationship exists for the reverse situation, sending instances back from the client to the server.

15.8 Track Results from Multiple Simultaneous Service Calls

Contributed by Andrew Alderson

Problem

You need to determine what returned data belongs to which of your multiple simultaneous service calls.

Solution

Use `ASyncToken` to add a variable to each call to identify it.

Discussion

Because `mx.rpc.ASyncToken` is a dynamic class, you can add properties and methods to it at runtime. The Flex documentation states that it is "a place to set additional or token-level data for asynchronous `rpc` operations."

As an example, consider an application with a `DateChooser` control in it. Every time the user scrolls to a new month, you need to retrieve a XML file from the server for that month. Because there is no way to guarantee in what order these files will come back, you need a way to identify them. By using `ASyncToken`, you can add an identifying property to the result event that is returned by the service call. For example:

```
<mx:Application xmlns:mx="http://www.adobe.com/2006/mxml" layout="horizontal">
    <mx:Script>
        <![CDATA[
            import mx.rpc.events.FaultEvent;
            import mx.rpc.events.ResultEvent;
            import mx.rpc.AsyncToken;
            import mx.events.DateChooserEvent;
            private function scrollHandler(event:DateChooserEvent):void {
                var month:int = event.currentTarget.displayedMonth;
                var monthName:String = event.currentTarget.monthNames[month];

                service.url = "xml/"+monthName+".xml";
                var token:AsyncToken = service.send();
                token.resultHandler = onResult;
                token.faultHandler = onFault;
                token.month = monthName;
            }
            private function onResult(event:ResultEvent):void {
                resultText.text = "MonthName: "+event.token.month+"\n\n";

                resultText.text += "Result: "+event.result.data.month;
            }
            private function onFault(event:FaultEvent):void {
                resultText.text = event.fault.faultString;
            }
        ]]>
    </mx:Script>
    <mx:HTTPService id="service" result="event.token.resultHandler(event)"
                    fault="event.token.faultHandler(event)"/>
    <mx:DateChooser id="dateChooser" scroll="scrollHandler(event)"/>
    <mx:TextArea id="resultText" width="300" height="200"/>
</mx:Application>
```

The preceding code calls the `scrollHandler` event to retrieve a XML file from the server. If the user clicks fast enough, you can have multiple requests happening at the same time. In `HTTPService`, the `send()` method returns an `AsyncToken` so you can access the result and add a property to identify the month to which the returned data belongs. You can use the `ResultEvent`'s `token` property to access your `month` property through this in the result handler.

This method can also be used with `WebService` and `RemoteObject` calls. In these calls, the operation or method that is called returns the `AsyncToken`:

```
var token : AsyncToken = service.login( loginVO );
```

15.9 Register a Server-Side Data Type Within a Flex Application

Problem

You need to register a server-side data type in your application so that objects received from a `RemoteObject` can be cast as instances of that remote class within your Flex application.

Solution

Use the `flash.net.registerClassAlias()` method or mark the class as a `RemoteClass` in the class declaration.

Discussion

Before an object can be deserialized from AMF data into a `Class` object, the signature of that class must be registered with the Flash Player. This ensures that the objects will be deserialized into the correct types. For instance, say the following type is defined in C#:

```
using System;
using System.Collections;

namespace oreilly.cookbook.vo
{
    public class RecipeVO {
        public string title;
        public ArrayList ingredients;
        public ArrayList instructions;

        public RecipeVO(){}
    }
}
```

The corresponding ActionScript type could be the following:

```
package oreilly.cookbook.vo
{
    public class RecipeVO

    public var ingredients:Array;
    public var instructions:Array;
    public var title:String;

    public function RecipeVO(){}

}
```

The service that returns the `RecipeVO` object can create a new object in C# and return it:

```
using System;
using System.Web;
using oreilly.cookbook.vo;
```

```
namespace oreilly.cookbook.service
{
    public class RecipeService
    {
        public RecipeService() { }

        public RecipeVO getRecipe() {
            RecipeVO rec = new RecipeVO();
            rec.title = "Apple Pie";
            string[] ingredients = {"flour", "sugar", "apples", "eggs", "water"};
            rec.ingredients = new ArrayList(ingredients);
            string[] instructions = {"instructions are long", "baking is hard",
                                     "maybe I'll just buy it at the store"};
            rec.instruction = new ArrayList(instructions);
            return rec;
        }
    }
}
```

Even though this service and the corresponding value object (in this case, the Recipe
VO) are written in C#, the service and the corresponding serialization would be very
similar in Java and many other server-side languages.

When the service returns, the resulting RecipeVO can be accessed as shown here:

```
<mx:RemoteObject id="recipeService" destination="fluorine"
              source="oreilly.cookbook.FlexService" showBusyCursor="true"
              result="roResult(event)" fault="roFault(event)" />

<mx:Script>
    <![CDATA[

        private function initApp():void {
            // we have to register the object for the result to be able
            // to properly cast as the RecipeVO
            flash.net.registerClassAlias("oreilly.cookbook.vo.RecipeVO",
                                         RecipeVO);
        }

        public function serviceResult(e:ResultEvent):void {
            var rec:RecipeVO = (e.result as RecipeVO)
        }

        public function serviceFault(e:FaultEvent):void {
            trace(" Error :: "+(e.message as String));
        }

    ]]>
</mx:Script>
```

After the class has been registered by using the registerClassAlias() method, objects
with a matching signature that have been sent via remoting can be cast to the
RecipeVO class.

15.10 Communicate with a WebService

Problem

You need to enable your Flex application to communicate with a server via web services that will send WSDL messages to describe their service methods, and then to use that information to call methods on the web service.

Solution

Create a `mx.rpc.WebService` object and set its `wsdl` property to the location of the WSDL document that defines your service.

Discussion

The `WebService` component enables an application to communicate with a web service using a defined Web Services Description Language (WSDL) file. The Flash Player recognizes the following properties within a WSDL file:

binding
> Specifies the protocol that clients, such as Flex applications, use to communicate with a web service. Bindings exist for SOAP, HTTP `GET`, HTTP `POST`, and Multipurpose Internet Mail Extensions (MIME). Flex supports only the SOAP binding.

fault
> Specifies an error value that's returned as a result of a problem processing a message.

input
> Specifies a message that a client, such as a Flex application, sends to a web service.

message
> Defines the data that a web service operation transfers.

operation
> Defines a combination of `input`, `output`, and `fault` tags.

output
> Specifies the message that the web service sends to its client.

port
> Defines a web service endpoint, which specifies an association between a binding and a network address.

portType
> Defines one or more operations that a web service provides.

service
> Defines a collection of `port` tags. Each service maps to one `portType` tag and specifies different ways to access the operations in that tag.

types

Defines the data types that a web service's messages use.

The Flex application inspects the WSDL file to determine all the methods that the service supports and the types of data that it will return. A typical WSDL file defines the name of the service, any types used by the service, and the content of any messages that the service expects and returns.

To create a `WebService` object, set an `id` for the service and specify the location of the WSDL file that defines the service:

```
<mx:WebService id="userRequest" wsdl="http://localhost:8400/service/service?wsdl">
    <mx:operation name="getRecipes" result="getRecipeHandler()"
                fault="mx.controls.Alert.show(event.fault.faultString)"/>
</mx:WebService>
```

The `WebService` dispatches a `LoadEvent` of type `load` or `LoadEvent.LOAD` to indicate that it has loaded and parsed the WSDL file specified in the `wsdl` property and is ready to have methods called on it. The `WebService` object cannot be called before this, so it is recommended that this event be used to indicate that the service can be called. The `WebService` component also defines a `ready` Boolean value that can be checked to confirm that the WSDL file has been loaded and that the `WebService` is ready. In the following example, a method is defined and event handlers are attached to the `result` and `fault` events of the service:

```
<mx:Application xmlns:mx="http://www.adobe.com/2006/mxml" width="400" height="300">
    <mx:WebService id="userRequest"
                wsdl="http://localhost:8500/service/service?wsdl"
                load="callService()">
        <mx:operation name="getRecipes" resultFormat="object"
                    fault="createRecipeFault(event)"
                    result="createRecipeHandler(event)"/>
    </mx:WebService>
    <mx:Script>
        <![CDATA[
            import mx.rpc.events.FaultEvent;
            import mx.collections.ArrayCollection;
            import mx.rpc.events.ResultEvent;
            import mx.controls.Alert;

            private function callService():void {
                userRequest.getRecipes();
            }

            private function createRecipeHandler(event:ResultEvent):void {
                var arrayCol:ArrayCollection = event.result as ArrayCollection;
            }

            private function createRecipeFault(event:FaultEvent):void {
                Alert.show(" error :: "+event.message);
            }
```

```
        ]]>
    </mx:Script>
</mx:Application>
```

15.11 Add a SOAP Header to a Request to a WebService

Problem

You need to send a SOAP header along with a request to a `WebService` component.

Solution

Create a `SOAPHeader` object and pass in the namespace that should be used with the values passed in and the content that should be appended to the header. Then use the `WebService.addHeader()` method to send the header along with the request.

Discussion

SOAP headers are frequently used by web services to receive logins, user information, or other data along with a request. A `SOAPHeader` object is created with a `QName` that will define the qualified namespace of the data contained within it and an object defining the data to be sent in the header in key/value pairs:

```
SOAPHeader(qname:QName, content:Object)
```

Here is an example of creating two `SOAPHeader` objects:

```
// create a QName that can be used with your header
var qname:QName=new QName("http://soapinterop.org/xsd", "CookbookHeaders");
var headerone:SOAPHeader = new SOAPHeader(qname, {string:"header_one",int:"1"});
var headertwo:SOAPHeader = new SOAPHeader(qname, {string:"header_two",int:"2"});
```

To add a header to all requests made through a web service, call the `addHeader()` method on the `WebService` object itself:

```
// call addHeader() on the WebService
service.addHeader(headerone);
```

To add a `SOAPHeader` to only a specific method that the service defines, use the name of the method to assign the `SOAPHeader` to that method:

```
// add the headertwo SOAPHeader to the getRecipes() operation
service.getRecipes.addHeader(headertwo);
```

When the SOAP headers are no longer needed, call the `clearHeaders()` method on any `WebService` or method that has had headers added to it:

```
service.clearHeaders();
service.getRecipes.clearHeaders();
```

15.12 Parse a SOAP Response from a WebService

Problem

You need to parse a SOAP response returned in answer to a request.

Solution

Use the Flash Player's native deserialization of SOAP types to ActionScript types for the SOAP-encoded XML that is returned from a `WebService`.

Discussion

The results of a SOAP response can be parsed using E4X expressions. The most commonly used types are shown in Table 15-1, along with their correct SOAP and Action-Script representations.

Table 15-1. SOAP types and their corresponding ActionScript types

Generic type	SOAP	ActionScript 3
String	`xsd:String`	`String`
Integer	`xsd:int`	`Int`
Float	`xsd:float`	`Number`
Boolean	`xsd:Boolean`	`Boolean`
Date	`xsd:date`	`Date`
Array	`xsd:string[]`, `xsd:int[]`, and so forth	`ArrayCollection`
Object	`Element`	`Object`
Binary	`xsd:Base64Binary`	`flash.utils.ByteArray`
Null	`xsl:Nil`	`Null`

A WSDL file that defines the following return types:

```
<wsdl:types>
    <schema elementFormDefault="qualified"
            targetNamespace="http://cookbook.webservices.com"
            xmlns="http://www.w3.org/2001/XMLSchema">
        <complexType name="Recipe">
            <sequence>
                <element name="title" nillable="true" type="xsd:string"/>
                <element name="ingredients" nillable="true" type="xsd:string[]"/>
                <element name="instructions" nillable="true" type="xsd:string[]"/>
            </sequence>
        </complexType>
    </schema>
</wsdl:types>
```

may have the following response returned from a request to the `WebService`:

```
<soap:Envelope xmlns:soap="http://www.w3.org/2001/12/soap-envelope"
               soap:encodingStyle="http://www.w3.org/2001/12/soap-encoding">
    <soap:Body xmlns:ns="http://cookbook.oreilly.com/service">
        <ns:GetRecipes>
            <ns:Recipe>
                <ns:title>"Blueberry Pie"</ns:title>
                <SOAP-ENC:Array SOAP-ENC:arrayType="xsd:string[3]">
                    <ns:ingredient>"Blueberry"</ns:ingredient>
                    <ns:ingredient>"Sugar"</ns:ingredient>
                    <ns:ingredient>"Crust"</ns:ingredient>
                </SOAP-ENC:Array>
                <SOAP-ENC:Array SOAP-ENC:arrayType="xsd:string[3]">
                    <ns:instruction>"Blueberry"</ns:instruction>
                    <ns:instruction>"Sugar"</ns:instruction>
                    <ns:instruction>"Crust"</ns:instruction>
                </SOAP-ENC:Array>
            </ns:Recipe>
        </ns:GetRecipes>
    </soap:Body>
</soap:Envelope>
```

This response could be parsed easily into the requisite objects by using dot notation, as would be done with any XML object. For more information on the different SOAP types and their ActionScript equivalents, see *http://www.adobe.com/go/kb402005*, which describes all the possible SOAP types.

15.13 Communicate Securely with AMF by Using SecureAMFChannel

Problem

You need to communicate over Flash remoting, using AMF data and the Secure Sockets Layer (SSL).

Solution

Define your channel to be a `SecureAMFChannel` in the *services-config.xml* file that you use when compiling your application.

Discussion

The `SecureAMFChannel` lets you use an `AMFChannel` for communication over SSL, ensuring that any data sent over an `AMFChannel` is secure. To create a new channel that uses the secured versions of the AMF classes, simply create the *services-config.xml* file with a channel that uses the `mx.messaging.channels.SecureAMFChannel` as its class. The endpoint should also be configured to use the `flex.messaging.endpoints.SecureAMFEndpoint` class, as shown here:

```
<channels>
    <channel ref="secure-amf"/>
</channels>

<channel-definition id="secure-amf" class="mx.messaging.channels.SecureAMFChannel">
    <endpoint uri="https://{server.name}:{server.port}/gateway/"
              class="flex.messaging.endpoints.SecureAMFEndpoint"/>
    <properties>
        <add-no-cache-headers>false</add-no-cache-headers>
        <polling-enabled>false</polling-enabled>
        <serialization>
            <instantiate-types>false</instantiate-types>
        </serialization>
    </properties>
</channel-definition>
```

The preceding code snippet will work for ColdFusion, Adobe LiveCycle, and BlazeDS:

```
<mx:Application xmlns:mx="http://www.adobe.com/2006/mxml"
                width="400" height="300"
                creationComplete="init()">
    <mx:RemoteObject id="channelRO"/>
    <mx:Script>
        <![CDATA[

            import mx.messaging.ChannelSet;
            import mx.messaging.channels.SecureAMFChannel;

            private var cs:ChannelSet

            private function init():void {

                cs = new ChannelSet();
                // note that the name of the channel is the same as in the
                // services-config.xml file
                var chan: SecureAMFChannel = new SecureAMFChannel("secure-amf",
                                                                  "gateway")
                chan.pollingEnabled = true;
                chan.pollingInterval = 3000;
                cs.addChannel(chan);
                channelRO.channelSet = cs;

            }

        ]]>
    </mx:Script>
</mx:Application>
```

Now you can use the channel to call through the RemoteObject and make secured AMF polling calls.

15.14 Send and Receive Binary Data via a Binary Socket

Problem

You want to receive binary data and respond in a similar binary format after processing that data.

Solution

Use the `flash.net.Socket` to open a socket connection to the server and pass in the port number on which your application will communicate.

Discussion

The `flash.net.Socket` is the lowest-level tool for communication available in the Flex Framework or in ActionScript 3. It enables you to make socket connections and to read and write raw binary data. The `Socket` lets you send and receive messages in Post Office Protocol Version 3 (POP-3), Simple Mail Transfer Protocol (SMTP), and Internet Message Access Protocol (IMAP), as well as in custom binary formats. The Flash Player can interface with a server by using the binary protocol of that server directly.

To create a new `Socket`, first create the `Socket` instance by using the constructor, and then call the `connect()` method, passing in an IP address or domain name and a port number:

```
var socket:Socket;
// create the new socket and connect to 127.0.0.1 on port 8080
private function init():void {

    socket = new Socket();
    socket.addEventListener(ProgressEvent.SOCKET_DATA, readSocketData);
    socket.connect("127.0.0.1", 8080);

}
// send data to the socket
private function sendSocketData(string:String):void {
    // send the string data and specify the encoding for the string -
    // in this case iso-08859-1, standard Western European encoding
    socket.writeMultiByte(string, "iso-8859-1");
}

// when data is passed to socket, read it into a new ByteArray
private function readSocketData(progressEvent:ProgressEvent):void {

    trace(progressEvent.bytesLoaded);
    var ba:ByteArray = new ByteArray();
    trace(socket.readBytes(bs));

}
```

In the sendSocketData() method, the writeMultiByte() method sends data through the Socket to the connection. This method accepts a string value to send as binary data in the encoding specified by the second parameter. The readSocketData() method reads any data sent to the Socket and reads the bytes of the data into the new ByteArray object. To read data back from the ByteArray, you can use the various methods for reading integers, strings, and arrays. Objects sent over a Socket as binary data can be read by using the ByteArray readObject() method if the class type has been registered via the flash.net.registerClassAlias() method.

To connect a Socket to a port number lower than 1024, you need a *cross-domain.xml* file at the root of the site to explicitly allow access to that port. For instance, to allow the Flash Player to communicate with a web server on port 80, use the following:

```
<?xml version="1.0"?>
<cross-domain-policy>
    <allow-access-from domain="*" to-ports="80" />
</cross-domain-policy>
```

Once the correct *cross-domain.xml* file is in place, the Socket can communicate with the server on the correct port.

15.15 Communicate Using a XMLSocket

Problem

You need to create a connection to a server that will receive XML data without requesting it.

Solution

Use the XMLSocket class to open a connection to a server that will allow the server to send information to the client and have that information be received and handled when it arrives.

Discussion

The XMLSocket class implements client sockets that let a Flash Player or AIR application communicate with a server computer identified by an IP address or domain name. To use the XMLSocket class, the server computer must run a daemon that understands the protocol used by that class. For the protocol:

- XML messages are sent over a full-duplex Transmission Control Protocol/Internet Protocol (TCP/IP) stream socket connection.
- Each XML message is a complete XML document, terminated by a zero (0) byte.

You can send and receive an unlimited number of XML messages over a single XMLSocket connection. To connect to a XMLSocket object, first create a new XMLSocket and then call the connect() method, passing in an IP address or domain name and then a port number:

```
var xmlsock:XMLSocket = new XMLSocket();
xmlsock.connect("127.0.0.1", 8080);
```

The port number is required because the XMLSocket can't communicate on ports lower than 1024. To receive data from the XMLSocket, add an event listener for the DataEvent.DATA event:

```
xmlsock.addEventListener(DataEvent.DATA, onData);
private function onData(event:DataEvent):void
{
    trace("[" + event.type + "] " + XML(event.data));
}
```

The string returned can be cast as XML and parsed using E4X.

15.16 Navigate a XML Document in E4X

Problem

You need to select certain nodes from a XML file based on properties of the attributes.

Solution

Use the E4X syntax's @ operator to access attributes, the [ ] operator (indexed array) to indicate multiple child relationships, and the . operator to indicate named child relationships.

Discussion

An important part of working with services is parsing the XML they return. With E4X, you can navigate a XML file to access a specific child by using the . operator after the child's name. For example, from this file:

```
var xml:XML = <foo>
<bar>Hello World</bar>
</foo>
```

you could access the value of <bar> as shown here:

```
xml.bar
```

A reference to the <foo> node is not needed because it is the root node of the XML object.

To access the attribute of a node from a file such as this:

```
var xml:XML = <foo>
<bar type="salutation">Hello World</bar>
</foo>
```

use the @ operator to indicate that the desired property is an attribute:

```
xml.bar.@type
```

To access multiple child nodes of the same name, use the [ ] operator. From an example such as this:

```
var xml:XML = <foo>
<bar type="salutation">Hello World</bar>
<bar type="salutation">Hola</bar>
<bar type="salutation">Guten Tag</bar>
</foo>
```

you can access the third object in the series of <bar> children like so:

```
xml.bar[2].@type
```

For a simple XML structure defining items on a menu, use a snippet like the following:

```
private var xmlItems:XML =
        <order>
            <item id='1'>
                <menuName>burger</menuName>
                <price>3.95</price>
            </item>
            <item id='2'>
                <menuName>fries</menuName>
                <price>1.45</price>
            </item>
        </order>

private var arr:Array;

private function init():void {
    arr = new Array();
    for each(var xml:XML in xmlItems.item) {
        arr.push(Number(xml.@id));
    }
}
```

To test the value of an attribute or a node, use the equality operator (==):

```
trace(xmlItems.item.(@id == "2").menuName);
```

Any node that meets all the criteria will be traced, and all others will be ignored. The following example will set the text of the Label component to the menuName of the item that has an id of 2:

```
<fx:Script>
    <![CDATA[
        private var xmlItems:XML =
                <order>
                    <item id="1">
                        <menuName>burger</menuName>
                        <price>3.95</price>
                    </item>
                    <item id="2">
                        <menuName>fries</menuName>
```

```
                        <price>1.45</price>
                    </item>
                </order>

        private function init():void {
            xmlLabel.text = xmlItems.item.(@id == "2").menuName;
        }
    ]]>
</fx:Script>

<s:Label id="xmlLabel"/>
```

Both the equality (==) and inequality (!=) operators can be used to test the value of an attribute or a node, as can any string or number method that returns a Boolean value.

15.17 Use Regular Expressions in E4X Queries

Problem

You need to create complex E4X queries by using regular expressions.

Solution

Add a regular expression to the E4X statement as a literal and call the regular expression's `test()` method.

Discussion

When combined, regular expressions and E4X allow very precise filtering of XML nodes. The literal syntax of the regular expression enables you to add a regular expression without a call to a constructor and to use the `test()` method of the regular expression on the attribute or value of the XML node. This line, for example, tests the id attribute of the `item` node:

```
xmlItems.item.(/\d\d\d/.test(@id)).price
```

Any item that possesses a three-digit id property will have the price value of the property returned. Any item that does not possess all of these fields or return `true` from the regular expression's `test()` method will not have its value returned. The following code snippet shows a XML file's nodes each tested against the E4X expression:

```
private var xmlItems:XML =
        <order>
            <item id="1">
                <menuName>burger</menuName>
                <price>3.95</price>
            </item>
            <item id="100">
                <menuName>burger</menuName>
                <price>3.95</price>
            </item>
```

```
            <item id="2000">
                <menuName>fries</menuName>
                <price>1.45</price>
            </item>
        </order>

    private var arr:Array;

    private function init():void {
        arr = new Array();
        for each ( var xml:XML in xmlItems) {
            arr.push(xmlItems.item.(/\d\d\d/.test(@id)).price);
        }
        trace(arr);
    }
```

It is worth noting as well that you can use these E4X queries as properties for data binding within controls.

15.18 Add a XMLList to a XML Object

Problem

You need to append the value of a XMLList object to a node within a XML object.

Solution

Use an E4X expression to locate the node to which the XMLList object should be appended and then call the appendChild() method on that node.

Discussion

You can add a XMLList directly to a XML object or to another XMLList object by using the appendChild() method of the XML class. For example, say you are given this XML object:

```
var xmlNode:XML = <data>
            <item id="1"/>
            <item id="2"/>
            <item id="3"/>
                </data>
```

Calling appendChild with a new node, like so:

```
var newXML:XML = <item id="4"/>
xmlNode.appendChild(newXML);
```

produces the following:

```
var xmlNode:XML = <data>
            <item id="1"/>
            <item id="2"/>
            <item id="3"/>
```

```
        <item id="4"/>
            </data>
```

The new node will be added to the root node of the XML object. You can call the appendChild() method on any node within the XML object as well:

```
var list:XMLList = new XMLList('<characteristic name="cuts through metal"/>
        <characteristic name="never dulls"/><characteristic name="dishwasher
        safe"/><characteristic name="composite handle"/>');
    var node:XMLList = xmlNode.item.(@id == 3);
    node.appendChild(list);

}
```

To add items from one XMLList to another, you could loop through the origin list and assign the indexed value of the origin to the destination XMLList:

```
var newXML:XMLList = new XMLList();
for(var i:int = 0; i<list.length(); i++) {
    newXML[i] = list[i];
}
```

This approach will not work, however, if newXML is of type XML. To loop through a list and add certain or all items from a list, use the appendChild() method:

```
var newXML:XML = <data></data>;
for(var i:int = 0; i<list.length(); i++) {
    newXML.appendChild(list[i]);
}
```

15.19 Handle Namespaces in XML Returned by a Service

Problem

You need to parse XML returned from a web service that contains a custom namespace and extension.

Solution

Declare a namespace variable, set it to the location of the namespace for the returned XML, and then call the use() method with that namespace before doing any XML processing.

Discussion

Parsing XML that contains a custom namespace requires that the namespace be declared before any XML is returned and parsed within that namespace. For example, many web services return XML that contains a namespace declaration such as the following:

```
HTTP/1.1 200 OK
Content-Type: application/soap+xml; charset=utf-8
```

```
Content-Length: nnn

<?xml version="1.0"?>
<soap:Envelope xmlns:soap="http://www.w3.org/2001/12/soap-envelope"
               soap:encodingStyle="http://www.w3.org/2001/12/soap-encoding">

    <soap:Body xmlns:m="http://www.example.org/stock">
        <m:PriceResult>
            <m:Price>34.5</m:Price>
        </m:PriceResult>
    </soap:Body>

</soap:Envelope>
```

The namespace declared in this line:

```
xmlns:soap="http://www.w3.org/2001/12/soap-envelope"
```

must be declared before the XML is processed. This is done as shown here:

```
private namespace w3c = "http://www.w3.org/2001/12/soap-envelope";
use namespace w3c;
// To access the price node of the above SOAP response, use the
// namespace title in the E4X statement as shown here:
// var prices:XMLList = xml.m::PriceResult.m::Price;
```

Using the . operator to access the child of any XML response that uses a qualified namespace requires that the namespace be declared and followed by the :: operator and then the node name. For the following XML object:

```
<m:PriceResult>
    <m:Price>34.5</m:Price>
</m:PriceResult>
```

the price node would be accessed as follows:

```
m::PriceResult.m::Price
```

15.20 Encode an ActionScript Data Object as XML

Problem

You need to convert an ActionScript object into XML.

Solution

Use the SimpleXMLEncoder.encodeValue() method to write an object and all of its properties to a XMLDocument.

Discussion

The `SimpleXMLEncoder` object is very useful when creating XML to send to a web service or to the URL of a server-side method that expects XML. The `SimpleXMLEncoder` object defines an `encodeValue()` method with the following signature:

```
encodeValue(obj:Object, qname:QName, parentNode:XMLNode):XMLNode
```

This method requires that the legacy `XMLDocument` object have the generated XML attached to it, so the generated XML is not only returned by the method, but also attached to the `XMLNode` within the `XMLDocument` object to which the `parentNode` is attached. After the `XMLDocument` has been generated, it can be converted to a `XML` object by calling the constructor of the `XML` object and passing the document as an argument to the constructor:

```
var doc:XMLDocument = new XMLDocument('<data></data>');
var xml:XML = new XML(doc);
```

A complete code listing that will encode an object into a XML document is shown here:

```
<s:Group xmlns:mx="http://www.adobe.com/2006/mxml"
         width="400" height="300"
         creationComplete="init()">
    <fx:Script>
        <![CDATA[
            import mx.rpc.xml.SimpleXMLEncoder;

            private var o:Object = {name:"Josh", description_items:{height:'183cm',
                                    weight:'77k'}};

            private var doc:XMLDocument;

            private function init():void {

                doc = new XMLDocument('<data></data>');
                var simpleEncode:SimpleXMLEncoder = new SimpleXMLEncoder(doc);
                var node:XMLNode = simpleEncode.encodeValue(o, new
                        QName('http://localhost/ns/ws', 'ls'), doc.firstChild);

            }

        ]]>
    </fx:Script>
</s:Canvas>
```

After the `SimpleXMLEncoder.encodeValue()` method is called, the `XMLDocument` object will have the following structure:

```
<data>
    <obj>
        <description_items>
            <height>183cm</height>
            <weight>77k</weight>
        </description_items>
        <name>Josh</name>
    </obj>
</data>
```

15.21 Decode XML from a Web Service into Strongly Typed Objects

Problem

You need to transform a `XML` object or a `XMLList` object into one or more strongly typed objects.

Solution

Use the `SchemaTypeRegistry.registerClass()` method to register the class by using the qualified namespace and the `SimpleXMLDecoder` class to decode the XML into objects.

Discussion

The `SchemaTypeRegistry.registerClass()` method lets you register a class based on a type that will be returned from a web service. The class must be described in the WSDL file, where the web service describes all its methods and types. For example, all properties of an object named `Plant` are defined here:

```
<types>
    <xsd:schema targetNamespace="http://localhost/ns/ws"
                xmlns:SOAP-ENC="http://schemas.xmlsoap.org/soap/encoding/"
                xmlns:wsdl="http://schemas.xmlsoap.org/wsdl/"
                xmlns:xsd="http://www.w3.org/2001/XMLSchema">
        <xsd:complexType name="Plant">
            <xsd:sequence>
                <xsd:element maxOccurs="1" minOccurs="1" name="common"
                             nillable="true" type="xsd:string"/>
                <xsd:element maxOccurs="1" minOccurs="1" name="botanical"
                             nillable="true" type="xsd:string"/>
                <xsd:element maxOccurs="1" minOccurs="1" name="zone"
                             nillable="true" type="xsd:string"/>
                <xsd:element maxOccurs="1" minOccurs="1" name="light"
                             nillable="true" type="xsd:string"/>
                <xsd:element maxOccurs="1" minOccurs="1" name="price"
                             nillable="true" type="xsd:string"/>
                <xsd:element maxOccurs="1" minOccurs="1" name="availability"
                             nillable="true" type="xsd:int"/>
            </xsd:sequence>
```

```
        </xsd:complexType>
    </xsd:schema>
</types>
```

The method that will return the `Plant` object is defined like this:

```
<binding name="PlantService" type="tns:Plant">
    <soap:binding style="rpc"
                  transport="http://schemas.xmlsoap.org/soap/http"/>
    <operation name="getPlants">
        <soap:operation soapAction="getPlants"/>
        <input>
            <soap:body use="encoded"
                       encodingStyle="http://schemas.xmlsoap.org/soap/encoding/"
                       namespace="http://localhost/ns/ws"/>
            <soap:header message="tns:getPlants" part="header" use="literal"/>
        </input>
        <output>
            <soap:body use="encoded"
                       encodingStyle="http://schemas.xmlsoap.org/soap/encoding/"
                       namespace="http://localhost/ns/ws"/>
        </output>
    </operation>
```

Note that the type of the service is defined as `tns:Plant`, indicating that the service will return `Plant` objects as defined in the preceding code. The `SchemaTypeRegistry` uses this declaration to map the web service `Plant` object to an ActionScript representation of the data in that object. The method requires a qualified `Namespace` object and a `Class` object that contains the ActionScript representation of the class.

```
var qname:QName = new QName("http://localhost/ns/ws", "Plant");
mx.rpc.xml.SchemaTypeRegistry.getInstance().registerClass(qname, Plant);
```

The `Plant` class that will be generated is a simple value object with public properties representing the data required for the `Plant` object:

```
package oreilly.cookbook
{
    public class Plant
    {

        public var common:String;
        public var botanical:String;
        public var zone:String;
        public var light:String;
        public var price:String;
        public var availability:String;


    }
}
```

After the type has been registered, the resulting object of the web service will be cast as type Plant, allowing you to work with strongly typed objects without the use of an AMF service:

```
<mx:Canvas xmlns:mx="http://www.adobe.com/2006/mxml"
           width="400" height="300"
           creationComplete="init()">
    <mx:WebService id="ws" wsdl="http://localhost/service.php?wsdl"
                   result="trace(event.result)"/>
    <mx:Script>
        <![CDATA[
            import mx.rpc.events.ResultEvent;
            import mx.rpc.xml.SchemaTypeRegistry;
            import mx.rpc.xml.QualifiedResourceManager;
            import mx.rpc.xml.SimpleXMLDecoder;

            private function init():void {

                var qname:QName = new QName("http://localhost/ns/ws", "Plant");
                mx.rpc.xml.SchemaTypeRegistry.getInstance().registerClass(qname,
                                                            Plant);
            }

        ]]>
    </mx:Script>
</mx:Canvas>
```

CHAPTER 16

Browser Communication

In many cases, you may find it necessary to communicate with the browser that contains your application. Browser communication enables you to build applications that go beyond Flex itself; you can link to existing sites, communicate with other applications via JavaScript, and interact with the browser's history, as a start. The `ExternalInter face` class lets you call out to the browser in which the application is running, get information about the containing HTML page, and call JavaScript methods, as well as letting JavaScript methods call into the Flex application. This chapter focuses on the functionality contained within the core Flex Framework, though there are other tools to assist with integration of the browser and the Flash Player.

16.1 Link to an External URL

Problem

You need to navigate to a separate URL.

Solution

Use the `navigateToURL()` method to navigate the browser to the new URL.

Discussion

The `navigateToURL()` method enables you to navigate the browser to a new URL in either the same window, a new window, or a specific window frame. This is one of the most common communications with the browser from a Flex application. To invoke the `navigateToURL()` method from within your Flex 4 application, use this approach:

```
<s:Application xmlns:fx="http://ns.adobe.com/mxml/2009"
               xmlns:s="library://ns.adobe.com/flex/spark"
               xmlns:mx="library://ns.adobe.com/flex/halo">
```

```
<mx:Script>
    <![CDATA[
        import flash.net.navigateToURL;

        private function goToURL() : void
        {
            navigateToURL( new URLRequest( newUrl.text ),
                    target.selectedItem as String );
        }
    ]]>
</mx:Script>

<mx:TextInput id="newUrl"
            top="10" left="10" right="10"
            text="http://www.oreilly.com/" />

<mx:ComboBox id="target"
            top="40" left="10"
            dataProvider="{ [ '_blank', '_self' ] }" />

<mx:Button label="Go"
            left="10" top="70"
            click="goToURL()" />

</mx:Application>
```

In this example, users can type in any URL and click the Go button to navigate to it. The first parameter of navigateToURL() is a URLRequest object for the desired URL. The second parameter is the target window where that URL should be displayed. This can be any named window in the browser: _blank for a new window, _self for the current page, _top for the topmost frame container, or _parent for the parent of the current frame container.

16.2 Work with FlashVars

Problem

You need to pass data from the containing HTML page to your Flex 4 application.

Solution

Use FlashVars to add parameters directly into the HTML <embed> tag containing your Flex 4 SWF.

Discussion

You can embed data directly into the HTML that contains your Flex 4 application and easily read that data at runtime by using FlashVars variables. There are two ways to get these values into your Flex application.

First, you can modify the JavaScript that is used to embed your Flex application in the HTML page, as shown in the following example. By default, Flash Builder uses the *SWFObject* library developed by Geoff Stearns to create the embed statement. The seventh parameter passed to the constructor method of the `swfObject` class specifies the `flashvars` that the application will be able to access:

```
var swfVersionStr = "10.0.0";
var xiSwfUrlStr = "playerProductInstall.swf";
var flashvars = {};
var params = {};
params.quality = "high";
params.bgcolor = "#ffffff";
params.allowscriptaccess = "sameDomain";
params.allowfullscreen = "true";
var attributes = {};
attributes.id = "main";
attributes.name = "main";
attributes.align = "middle";
swfobject.embedSWF("main.swf", "flashContent",
                   "100%", "100%",
                   swfVersionStr, xiSwfUrlStr,
                   flashvars, params, attributes);
```

To pass four parameters into the application using `flashvars`, you would add the properties and values to the `flashvars` object as shown here:

```
var flashvars = {};
flashvars.param1 = "param1";
flashvars.param2 = "param2";
flashvars.param3 = "param3";
flashvars.param4 = "param4";
```

Alternatively, if you are not using JavaScript to embed your Flex 4-compiled SWF file, you can modify the `<object>` and `<embed>` HTML tags directly:

```
<object classid="clsid:D27CDB6E-AE6D-11cf-96B8-444553540000"
        id="${application}" width="${width}" height="${height}"
        codebase="http://fpdownload.macromedia.com/get/flashplayer/current/
                  swflash.cab">
    <param name="movie" value="${swf}.swf" />
    <param name="quality" value="high" />
    <param name="bgcolor" value="${bgcolor}" />
    <param name="allowScriptAccess" value="sameDomain" />
    <param name="FlashVars" value="param1=one&param2=2&param3=3&param4=four" />
    <embed src="${swf}.swf" quality="high" bgcolor="${bgcolor}"
           width="${width}" height="${height}"
           name="${application}" align="middle"
           play="true"
           loop="false"
           quality="high"
           allowScriptAccess="sameDomain"
           type="application/x-shockwave-flash"
           pluginspage="http://www.adobe.com/go/getflashplayer"
           FlashVars="param1=one&param2=2&param3=3&param4=four" />
</object>
```

In the Flex application, you can access `FlashVars` data any time through the `Application.application.parameters` object. This ActionScript example shows you how to access each of four `FlashVars` parameters as strings, and then display them in a TextArea's text field:

```
private function onCreationComplete() : void
{
    var parameters : Object = Application.application.parameters;
    var param1 : String = parameters.param1;
    var param2 : int = parseInt( parameters.param2 );
    var param3 : int = parseInt( parameters.param3 );
    var param4 : String = parameters.param4;

    output.text = "param1: " + param1 + "\n" +
                  "param2: " + param2 + "\n" +
                  "param3: " + param3 + "\n" +
                  "param4: " + param4;
}
```

16.3 Invoke JavaScript Functions from Flex

Problem

You need to invoke JavaScript functions from your Flex application.

Solution

Use `ExternalInterface` to invoke JavaScript functions from ActionScript.

Discussion

The `ExternalInterface` ActionScript class encapsulates everything that you need to communicate with JavaScript at runtime. You can simply use the `ExternalInter face.call()` method to execute a JavaScript function in the HTML page that contains your Flex application.

To invoke a simple JavaScript function in ActionScript, pass the name of the function to the `call()` method:

```
ExternalInterface.call( "simpleJSFunction" );
```

The basic JavaScript function invoked by this call is shown next. The name of the JavaScript function is passed into the `call()` method as a string value, and a JavaScript alert window appears above your Flex application:

```
function simpleJSFunction()
{
    alert("myJavaScriptFunction invoked");
}
```

You can use this same technique to pass data from ActionScript into JavaScript with function parameters:

```
ExternalInterface.call( "simpleJSFunctionWithParameters", "myParameter" );
```

Using this approach, you can pass multiple parameters, complex value objects, or simple parameters from ActionScript into JavaScript.

In JavaScript, you handle such a call just as you would any other function call that accepts a parameter. When invoked, the preceding function will display the parameter value myParameter in a JavaScript alert above your Flex application:

```
function simpleJSFunctionWithParameters( parameter )
{
    alert( parameter);
}
```

Often, you may find it necessary to invoke a JavaScript function to return a value from JavaScript to your Flex application. You can do this as follows:

```
var result:String = ExternalInterface.call( "simpleJSFunctionWithReturn" );
```

The corresponding JavaScript function returns a string value, which will be stored in the result string instance within the ActionScript class:

```
function simpleJSFunctionWithReturn()
{
    return "this is a sample return value: " + Math.random();
}
```

16.4 Invoke ActionScript Functions from JavaScript

Problem

You need to invoke ActionScript functions from JavaScript in the HTML containing the Flex application.

Solution

Use the ExternalInterface class to set up callbacks from JavaScript to Flex and invoke ActionScript functions from JavaScript.

Discussion

The ExternalInterface ActionScript class not only encapsulates everything you need to communicate with JavaScript at runtime, but also includes everything that you need to invoke ActionScript functions from JavaScript.

Before you can invoke ActionScript functions from JavaScript, you need to register callbacks for the ActionScript functions that you want to expose to JavaScript. The callbacks are registered through the `ExternalInterface` class within ActionScript. Callbacks provide a mapping for JavaScript function calls to actual ActionScript functions.

This example shows you how to register callbacks for three ActionScript functions:

```
private function registerCallbacks() : void
{
    ExternalInterface.addCallback( "function1", callback1 );
    ExternalInterface.addCallback( "function2", callback2 );
    ExternalInterface.addCallback( "function3", callback3 );
}
```

The corresponding ActionScript functions are as follows:

```
private function callback1() : void
{
    Alert.show( "callback1 executed" );
}

private function callback2( parameter : * ) : void
{
    Alert.show( "callback2 executed: " + parameter.toString() );
}

private function callback3() : Number
{
    return Math.random()
}
```

Notice that `callback1()` is a simple ActionScript function that can be invoked. It does not require any parameters and does not return a value. The function `callback2()` accepts a single parameter, and the function `callback3()` returns a randomly generated number.

When you want to invoke these functions from JavaScript, you must call a JavaScript function with the callback alias. The following JavaScript code illustrates how to invoke the ActionScript functions just exposed:

```
function invokeFlexFunctions()
{
    var swf = "mySwf";
    var container;
    if (navigator.appName.indexOf("Microsoft") >= 0)
    {
        container = document;
    }
    else
    {
        container = window;
    }
    container[swf].function1();
    container[swf].function2( "myParameter" );
    var result = container[swf].function3();
    alert( result );
}
```

The variable `swf` contains the name of the Flex application, as it has been embedded within the HTML page (in this case, it is `mySwf`). The first thing this script does is get a reference to the JavaScript DOM, based on the browser type. After the script has the proper browser DOM, it invokes the Flex functions based on the publicly exposed mappings that are specified when registering callbacks.

The ActionScript function `callback1()` gets invoked simply by calling the `function1()` callback on the Flex application instance within the JavaScript DOM, as follows:

```
container[swf].function1();
```

After this function is invoked, an alert message appears within the Flex application.

The ActionScript function `callback2()` gets invoked by calling the `function2()` callback and passing a value into it:

```
container[swf].function2( "myParameter" );
```

When invoked, this function displays an alert window within the Flex application that shows the parameter value specified by the JavaScript invocation.

The following example shows how to return a value from Flex to JavaScript. The `function3()` callback invokes the `callback3()` ActionScript function, which returns a randomly generated number to JavaScript. When `callback3()` is invoked, a random number is generated by Flex and returned to JavaScript. This value is then displayed in a JavaScript alert window:

```
var result = container[swf].function3();
alert( result );
```

16.5 Change the HTML Page Title via BrowserManager

Problem

You need to change the HTML page title for your Flex 4 application.

Solution

Use the `BrowserManager` class instance's `setTitle()` method to change the HTML page title.

Discussion

The `BrowserManager` class in Flex 4 enables easy interaction with the DOM of the HTML page that contains your Flex application. Among its features is the ability to change the title of the HTML page that contains your application. The following ActionScript code snippet illustrates how to set the page title:

```
<fx:Script>
    <![CDATA[
        import mx.managers.BrowserManager;
        import mx.managers.IBrowserManager;

        private function changePageTitle( newTitle : String ) : void
        {
            // get an instance of the browser manager
            var bm : IBrowserManager = BrowserManager.getInstance();

            // initialize the browser manager
            bm.init();

            // set the page title
            bm.setTitle( newTitle );
        }
    ]]>
</fx:Script>

<s:Button click="changePageTitle('this is the new title')"/>
```

16.6 Parse the URL via BrowserManager

Problem

You need to read and parse data from the browser's current URL.

Solution

Use the `BrowserManager` and `URLUtil` classes to read and parse the current page URL.

Discussion

The following example shows how to read and parse the current page URL by using the `BrowserManager` and `URLUtil` classes, as well as how to write the parsed results to a `mx:TextArea` instance.

The `URLUtil` class has functions that will help you parse the different pieces of the current URL. When using deep linking within Flex 4, the URL is broken into two parts: the base and the fragment. The URL *base* is everything that is to the left of the # sign, and the *fragment* is everything to the right of the # sign. The fragment is used to pass values into a Flex application, and in history management. A properly constructed fragment can be parsed by the `URLUtil.stringToObject()` method into an ActionScript object that contains the values in the fragment, broken out into string values. Each name/value pair in the URL fragment should be delimited by a semicolon (;). Let's look at an example:

```
<?xml version="1.0" encoding="utf-8"?>
<s:Application xmlns:fx="http://ns.adobe.com/mxml/2009"
               xmlns:s="library://ns.adobe.com/flex/spark"
```

```
                xmlns:mx="library://ns.adobe.com/flex/halo"
                minWidth="1024" minHeight="768"
                xmlns:flex4="oreilly.cookbook.flex4.*"
                creationComplete="parseURL()">

    <fx:Script>
        <![CDATA[
            import mx.managers.BrowserManager;
            import mx.managers.IBrowserManager;
            import mx.utils.ObjectUtil;
            import mx.utils.URLUtil;

            import spark.utils.TextFlowUtil;

        private function parseURL() : void
        {
            // get an instance of the browser manager
            var bm:IBrowserManager = BrowserManager.getInstance();

            // initialize the browser manager
            bm.init();

            // output the URL parameter values
            var outputString:String = "<p>Full URL: <br></br>" + bm.url + "</p>";
            outputString += "<p>Base URL: <br></br>" + bm.base + "</p>";
            outputString += "<p>URL Fragment: <br></br>" + bm.fragment + "</p>";

            // convert URL parameters to an actionscript object using URLUtil
            var o:Object = URLUtil.stringToObject(bm.fragment);
            outputString += "<p>Object: <br></br>" + ObjectUtil.toString( o ) +
                            "</p>";
            outputString += "<p>name: <br></br>" + o.name + "</p>";
            outputString += "<p>index: <br></br>" + o.index + "</p>";
            outputString += "<p>productId: <br></br>" + o.productId + "</p>";

            // parse URL using URLUtil
            outputString += "<p>URL Port: <br></br>" + URLUtil.getPort( bm.url ) +
                            "</p>";
            outputString += "<p>URL Protocol: <br></br>" + URLUtil.getProtocol(
                            bm.url ) + "</p>";
            outputString += "<p>URL Server: <br></br>" + URLUtil.getServerName(
                            bm.url ) + "</p>";
            outputString += "<p>URL Server with Port: <br></br>" +
                            URLUtil.getServerNameWithPort( bm.url )+"</p>";

            output.content = TextFlowUtil.importFromString(outputString);
        }

        ]]>
    </fx:Script>

    <s:TextArea id="output" left="10" top="10" bottom="10" right="10"/>

</s:Application>
```

If the preceding example had the URL *http://localhost:8501/flex4cookbook/main.html #name=Andrew;index=12345;productId=987*, the result would be:

```
Full URL:
http://localhost:8501/flex4cookbook/main.html#name=Andrew;index=12345;productId=987

Base URL:
http://localhost:8501/flex4cookbook/main.html

URL Fragment:
name=Andrew%20Trice;index=12345;productId=987654

Object:
(Object)#0
  index = 12345
  name = "Andrew"
  productId = 987

name:
Andrew

index:
12345

productId:
987

URL Port:
8501

URL Protocol:
http

URL Server:
localhost

URL Server with Port:
localhost:8501
```

16.7 Deep-Link to Data via BrowserManager

Problem

You need to pass data from the browser's URL into Flex controls, and you need to update the value of the browser URL based on data within your Flex application, which should also work the browser's Forward and Back navigational buttons.

Solution

Use the `BrowserManager` class and `BrowserChangeEvent`s to read and write data in the browser's URL.

Discussion

Whenever the browser's URL changes, either by text input on the address bar or through the usage of the navigation controls (Forward and Back buttons), a `Browser ChangeEvent.BROWSER_URL_CHANGE` event is dispatched through the `BrowserManager` instance. Whenever this type of event is encountered, you can simply invoke the `update Values()` method to update the values within the Flex controls. This lets you easily link to and cycle through your input values.

The following example shows how to read data from the browser's URL and put those values into Flex `TextInput` fields. When the sample application loads, it will read the data from the current URL and write the values of the `firstName` and `lastName` parameters into the text boxes. When the value of either the `firstName` or the `lastName` in the `TextInput` field is changed, the application will call the `setFragment()` method on the browser manager, which will update the browser's URL with the new values for the `firstName` and `lastName` parameters. This enables you to copy and paste the URL, so you can easily link directly into the current view. It also adds every change to the browser history. The sample application looks like this:

```
<s:Application xmlns:fx="http://ns.adobe.com/mxml/2009"
               xmlns:s="library://ns.adobe.com/flex/spark"
               xmlns:mx="library://ns.adobe.com/flex/halo"
               minWidth="1024" minHeight="768"
               creationComplete="onCreationComplete()" >

    <fx:Script>
        <![CDATA[
            import mx.events.BrowserChangeEvent;
            import mx.managers.IBrowserManager;
            import mx.managers.BrowserManager;
            import mx.utils.URLUtil;

            private var bm:IBrowserManager

            private function onCreationComplete():void
            {
                // get an instance of the browser manager
                bm = BrowserManager.getInstance();

                // initialize the browser manager
                bm.init();

                // set initial values based on url parameters
                updateValues();

                // add event listeners to handle back/forward browser buttons
                bm.addEventListener( BrowserChangeEvent.BROWSER_URL_CHANGE,
                                     onURLChange );
            }

            private function updateValues():void
            {
```

```
            // update text box values based on url fragment
            var o:Object = URLUtil.stringToObject(bm.fragment);
            firstName.text = o.firstName;
            lastName.text = o.lastName;
        }

        private function updateURL():void
        {
            // update URL fragment
            bm.setFragment( "firstName=" + firstName.text + ";lastName=" +
                            lastName.text );
        }

        private function onURLChange( event : BrowserChangeEvent ):void
        {
            // call update values based on change url
            updateValues();
        }
    ]]>
</fx:Script>

<s:TextInput x="10" y="10" id="firstName" change="updateURL()" />
<s:TextInput x="10" y="40" id="lastName" change="updateURL()" />

</s:Application>
```

16.8 Deep-Link Containers via BrowserManager

Problem

You need to control the visible contents of Flex 4 containers based on URL parameters.

Solution

Use the `BrowserManager` class and `BrowserChangeEvent`s to control the visibility and track the history of Flex components.

Discussion

You can use the URL fragment to control and track which containers and components are visible within a Flex application. When the application loads, you initialize the `BrowserManager` class instance, which helps you parse and handle the browser URL. The `updateContainers()` method (shown in the following code segment) determines which of the tabs within the `TabNavigator` instance is visible. Any time that tab navigator's visible tab changes, you set the `selectedIndex` property in the URL fragment by using the following snippet:

```
    bm.setFragment( "selectedIndex=" + tabNav.selectedIndex );
```

This updates the browser's URL and adds the change to the browser history. If the user were to copy and paste the current browser URL, that URL would link directly to the currently selected tab navigator. The application code follows:

```
<?xml version="1.0" encoding="utf-8"?>
<s:Application xmlns:fx="http://ns.adobe.com/mxml/2009"
               xmlns:s="library://ns.adobe.com/flex/spark"
               xmlns:mx="library://ns.adobe.com/flex/halo"
               minWidth="1024" minHeight="768"
               creationComplete="onCreationComplete()" >

    <fx:Script>
        <![CDATA[
            import mx.events.BrowserChangeEvent;
            import mx.managers.IBrowserManager;
            import mx.managers.BrowserManager;
            import mx.utils.URLUtil;

            private var bm:IBrowserManager;

            private function onCreationComplete() : void
            {
                // get an instance of the browser manager
                bm = BrowserManager.getInstance();

                // initialize the browser manager
                bm.init();

                // set visible containers based on url parameters
                updateContainers();

                // add event listeners to handle back/forward browser buttons
                bm.addEventListener( BrowserChangeEvent.BROWSER_URL_CHANGE,
                onURLChange );

                updateURL();
            }

            private function updateContainers():void
            {
                // convert url parameters to an actionscript object
                var o:Object = URLUtil.stringToObject(bm.fragment);

                // set the selected index
                if ( !isNaN(o.selectedIndex) )
                {
                    var newIndex : Number = o.selectedIndex;
                    if ( newIndex >= 0 && newIndex < tabNav.numChildren )
                    tabNav.selectedIndex = newIndex;
                }
            }
```

```
        private function onURLChange( event:BrowserChangeEvent ):void
        {
            // call updateContainers when url value changes
            updateContainers();
        }

        private function updateURL():void
        {
            bm.setFragment( "selectedIndex=" + tabNav.selectedIndex );
        }

    ]]>
    </fx:Script>

    <mx:TabNavigator bottom="10" top="10" right="10" left="10"
                     id="tabNav" historyManagementEnabled="false">

        <s:NavigatorContent label="Tab 0" show="updateURL()" >
            <mx:Label text="Tab 0 Contents" />
        </s:NavigatorContent>

        <s:NavigatorContent label="Tab 1" show="updateURL()" >
            <mx:Label text="Tab 1 Contents" />
        </s:NavigatorContent>

        <s:NavigatorContent label="Tab 2" show="updateURL()" >
            <mx:Label text="Tab 2 Contents" />
        </s:NavigatorContent>

    </mx:TabNavigator>
</s:Application>
```

You may have noticed that the historyManagementEnabled parameter on the Tab Navigator is set to false. This is because you are using events from the Browser Manager class to determine whether the browser URL has changed and to update the tab contents accordingly. Every change to the visible tab results in a change to the browser history; users can go back and forward through the visible tabs by using the browser's Back and Forward buttons.

CHAPTER 17

Modules and Runtime Shared Libraries

When building Rich Internet Applications, eventually you will have to consider file sizes and download times. The Flex Framework offers several alternatives for separating application code into separate SWF files to enrich the user experience.

Runtime shared libraries (RSLs) are files that can be downloaded and cached on a client. A downloaded RSL persists on the client, and multiple applications can access assets from that cached RSL. Applications can load two types of RSLs: unsigned and signed. *Unsigned RSLs*, such as standard and cross-domain SWF files, are stored in the browser cache. *Signed RSLs*, which are libraries that have been signed by Adobe and have the *.swz* extension, are stored within the Flash Player cache.

As the name suggests, a RSL is loaded at runtime and is considered a dynamically linked library. Statically linked libraries are SWC files that you compile into an application using the `library-path` and `include-libraries` compiler options. Application SWF files compiled against statically linked libraries generally have a larger file size and take longer to download, but they have the benefit of running quickly because all the code is available to the application. Applications employing RSLs load faster and have a smaller initial file size, but they may take more time at startup while loading the RSLs and use more memory as a consequence (the entire library of a RSL is loaded by an application without consideration of which classes the application actually uses). The power of using RSLs becomes apparent when you consider multiple applications that share the same code base. Because RSLs are downloaded once, multiple applications that dynamically link to the same RSL can access assets already available in the client's cache.

Modules are similar to RSLs in that they provide another way of separating application code into SWF files to decrease download times and file sizes. One benefit of using modules is that, unlike with RSLs, the main application shell does not have to load modules when it starts; it can load and unload modules as needed. The development process when using modules also provides an added benefit: you can work on modules separately from the application because they are independent of each other. When changes are needed for a module, you can recompile only that module and not the entire application.

You can create modular applications by using ActionScript and MXML. Flex-based modules use the `<mx:Module>` root tag, while ActionScript-based modules extend either `mx.modules.Module` or `mx.modules.ModuleBase`. Module classes are similar to applications. A module is compiled by using the MXML compiler tool (*mxmlc*), generating a SWF file that can be dynamically loaded and unloaded by an application at runtime. You can manage the loading and unloading of modules in Flex by using `<mx:Module Loader>` and in ActionScript by using the `mx.modules.ModuleLoader` and `mx.modules.ModuleManager` classes.

The capability to create modular applications is a great aspect of the Flex Framework, affording more control over the loading time and file size of an application. By using RSLs and modules, you can separate out code from an application that can be loaded and used by other applications. Both techniques have their benefits, and this chapter addresses how each is used in the development process and in deployment.

17.1 Create a Runtime Shared Library

Problem

You want to create a runtime shared library to be downloaded and cached by an application or multiple applications within the same domain.

Solution

Create a library of custom classes, components, and other assets to be compiled into a SWC file. Then extract the *library.swf* file from the SWC file and include it in the deploy directory for your application, to be used as a RSL.

Discussion

The SWC file format is an archive that contains a *library.swf* file and a *catalog.xml* file. The library is a set of assets compiled into a SWF file, and the catalog describes the hierarchy of dependencies found in the library. To use the library as a RSL, you need to extract the *library.swf* file from the generated SWC and include it within the deploy directory for your application.

Although you must have the library in the same domain as the applications that will access it at runtime, the library SWF file does not have to be present when you compile an application. However, the presence of the SWC file is needed at compile time, because it is used for dynamic linking.

The following example is a MXML component that will be packaged into a SWC archive file. The class will be included in the generated library SWF file, and an instance will be added to the display list of the main application:

```
<s:Group xmlns:fx="http://ns.adobe.com/mxml/2009"
         xmlns:s="library://ns.adobe.com/flex/spark"
         xmlns:mx="library://ns.adobe.com/flex/mx"
         width="300" height="200">

    <fx:Metadata>
        [Event(name="submit", type="flash.events.Event")]
    </fx:Metadata>

    <fx:Script>
        <![CDATA[
            private function handleSubmit():void
            {
                dispatchEvent( new Event( "submit" ) );
            }

            public function get firstName():String
            {
                return firstNameField.text;
            }
            public function get lastName():String
            {
                return lastNameField.text;
            }
        ]]>
    </fx:Script>

    <s:layout>
        <s:VerticalLayout/>
    </s:layout>

    <s:HGroup verticalAlign="bottom">
        <s:Label text="First Name:" />
        <s:TextInput id="firstNameField" />
    </s:HGroup>
    <s:HGroup verticalAlign="bottom">
        <s:Label text="Last Name:" />
        <s:TextInput id="lastNameField" />
    </s:HGroup>
    <s:Button label="submit" click="handleSubmit();" />

</s:Group>
```

This simple component enables a user to enter information and dispatches a submit event. To package this class into a SWC file, you invoke the *compc* utility with the source-path and `include-classes` command-line options. With a path to the */bin* directory of your Flex SDK installation set in your PATH system variable, the following command-line entry will generate a SWC file named *CustomLibrary.swc*:

```
> compc -source-path . -include-classes com.oreilly.f4cb.CustomEntryForm
  -output  CustomLibrary.swc
```

With the MXML component saved as *CustomEntryForm.mxml* in the *com/oreilly/f4cb* subdirectory of the current development directory, the supplied source path input value is the current directory (denoted as a dot). You can supply any number of classes to include by using the fully qualified class name of each, separated by a space.

The *library.swf* file archived in the generated SWC file is used as the RSL. To extract the library file from the generated SWC, you can use any standard unzip utility. When compiling the application, the SWC file is used for dynamic linking. You can rename the extracted library file as you see fit, but you must supply that filename as the runtime shared library value to be linked to your applications. For this example, the extracted library is renamed *CustomLibrary.swf*.

The following example application uses the `CustomEntryForm` component from a loaded RSL:

```
<s:Application xmlns:fx="http://ns.adobe.com/mxml/2009"
               xmlns:s="library://ns.adobe.com/flex/spark"
               xmlns:mx="library://ns.adobe.com/flex/mx"
               xmlns:f4cb="com.oreilly.f4cb.*">

    <fx:Script>
        <![CDATA[
            private function handleFormSubmit():void
            {
                greetingField.text = "Hello " + entryForm.firstName +
                                     " " + entryForm.lastName;
            }
        ]]>
    </fx:Script>

    <s:Panel title="Enter Name" width="400" height="400">
        <s:layout>
            <s:VerticalLayout />
        </s:layout>
        <f4cb:CustomEntryForm id="entryForm" submit="handleFormSubmit();" />
        <s:Label id="greetingField" />
    </s:Panel>

</s:Application>
```

An application using assets from a RSL references classes and declares MXML components just as it would if referencing statically linked libraries and local class files from your development directory. In this example, the `f4cb` namespace is declared in the `<s:Application>` tag and used to add the `CustomEntryForm` component to the display list.

To compile the application to use the RSL you previously generated and renamed to *CustomLibrary.swf*, invoke the *mxmlc* utility and include the `external-library` and `runtime-shared-libraries` command-line options:

```
> mxmlc -external-library-path+=CustomLibrary.swc
  -runtime-shared-libraries=CustomLibrary.swf
  RSLExample.mxml
```

In this command, *CustomLibrary.swc* is used for compile-time link checking, and the URL for the RSL library is declared as being served from the same domain as the generated application SWF. When it is time for deployment, you will place *RSLExample.swf* and *CustomLibrary.swf* in the same directory on a server. At startup, the application will load the `CustomLibrary` RSL and have that code available to present a form on which the user can enter information.

17.2 Use Cross-Domain Runtime Shared Libraries

Problem

You want to store RSLs in a separate location on a server that can be accessed by any application not within the same domain.

Solution

Use the `compute-digest` option of the *compc* utility when creating the RSL, which will be stored in the application during compilation when linking to the RSL. Then create a cross-domain policy file to include along with the locations of any RSLs in the `runtime-shared-library-path` option of the *mxmlc* tool.

Discussion

A *RSL digest* is a hash used to ensure that the RSL being loaded by the Flash Player is from a trusted party. When you create a RSL with the `compute-digest` option set to `true`, the digest is written to the *catalog.xml* file of a SWC archive. When you link a cross-domain RSL to an application during compilation, that digest is stored in the application SWF and is used to verify the authenticity of the requested RSL.

With a path to the */bin* directory of your Flex SDK installation set in your PATH variable, the following command will generate a SWC file named *CustomLibrary.swc*:

```
> compc -source-path . -include-classes com.oreilly.flexcookbook.CustomEntryForm
  -output CustomLibrary.swc -compute-digest=true
```

The default value of the `compute-digest` option is `true`, and you need not include it to create a digest when compiling a library. The digest is required when linking cross-domain RSLs to an application by using the MXML compiler's `runtime-shared-library-path` option.

In Recipe 17.1, you saw an example of a *standard* RSL that resides in the same domain as the application and is linked by using the `runtime-shared-libraries` compiler option. Standard RSLs can use digests as well, but the use of digests is not required for them.

The SWC file generated from this command is an archive folder containing a *library.swf* file and a *catalog.xml* file. To extract the library and catalog from the SWC file, you can use any standard unzip utility. The library is a set of assets compiled into a SWF file and will be used as the RSL. The catalog describes information found in the library along with the digest created by using the `compute-digest` option. The following shows the digest entry for the RSL written to the `<digests>` element of the catalog file:

```
<digests>
    <digest type="SHA-256" signed="false"
        value="2630d7061c913b4cea8ef65240fb295b2797bf73a0db96ceec5c319e2c00f8a5"/>
</digests>
```

The `value` is a hash generated by the compiler using the SHA-256 algorithm. When you compile an application linked to a RSL, this digest value is stored in the application and is used to verify the RSL requested from the server.

Along with a digest to ensure that the RSL is from a trusted resource, a cross-domain policy file is required on the server where the library resides. A cross-domain policy file is a XML file listing remote domains that are granted access to a server. To allow access by multiple applications found in domains other than that in which the RSL resides, list each domain path in a separate `<allow-access-from>` element in the *crossdomain.xml* file. The following is an example of a *crossdomain.xml* file:

```
<?xml version="1.0"?>
<cross-domain-policy>
    <allow-access-from domain="*.mydomain.com" />
    <allow-access-from domain="*.myotherdomain.com" />
    <site-control permitted-cross-domain-policies="all" />
</cross-domain-policy>
```

The preceding cross-domain policy file allows any SWF files from the subdomains of *http://mydomain.com* and *http://myotherdomain.com* to access data on the server, including cross-domain RSLs.

To grant any SWF files held on the listed domains access to data held on the target server, you can place the cross-domain policy file on the root of the server. Although this is a viable option, you may want more control over how applications access RSLs on the target server. By using the `runtime-shared-library-path` option of the MXML compiler, you can specify the location of a cross-domain policy file that lists which domains are permitted to access the libraries.

To compile an application dynamically linked to the cross-domain RSL that was previously generated using the *compc* tool and renamed to *CustomLibrary.swf*, invoke the *mxmlc* utility and include the `runtime-shared-library-path` command-line option and the full URL paths to the RSL and the cross-domain policy file found on the target server:

```
> mxmlc RSLExample.mxml -runtime-shared-library-path=CustomLibrary.swc,
  http://www.mytargetdomain.com/libraries/CustomLibrary.swf,
  http://www.mytargetdomain.com/libraries/crossdomain.xml
```

The comma-delimited argument values of the `runtime-shared-library-path` option are the location of the SWC file to compile against, the full URL path to the RSL residing on a remote server, and the full URL path to the cross-domain policy file that grants permission to an application from another domain to load the RSL. The existence of the runtime shared library SWF file is not checked during compilation, but the URL is stored in the application and is checked at runtime.

The benefit of using cross-domain RSLs, along with decreased file sizes and download times, is that it enables applications not residing in the same domain as a library to have access to trusted data. As more applications are deployed on other servers that use the runtime shared library, you can update the list of domains in the cross-domain policy file.

See Also

Recipe 17.1

17.3 Optimize a Runtime Shared Library

Problem

You want to reduce the file size of a runtime shared library that is loaded by an application.

Solution

Use the *optimizer* command-line tool included in the Flex 4 SDK to remove debugging code and unnecessary metadata included in the library of the SWC file.

Discussion

By default, the *library.swf* file generated when creating a SWC file contains debugging and metadata code. This may add unnecessary performance overhead when an application loads a RSL from a remote server or from the browser cache. To create an optimized RSL, you first create the SWC archive file using the *compc* tool from the Flex 4 SDK, then extract the library file using any standard unzip utility. The *library.swf* file is the RSL that will be loaded by an application that is compiled against the generated SWC. You can then recompile the RSL using the *optimizer* command-line tool.

The generated library within a SWC archive file will vary in size depending on the class libraries included during compilation. However, to get an understanding of the power that the optimizer tool affords, create the following MXML component and save the file as *MyCustomComponent.mxml*:

```
<s:Group xmlns:fx="http://ns.adobe.com/mxml/2009"
         xmlns:s="library://ns.adobe.com/flex/spark">

    <s:TextArea text="Lorem ipsum dolor sit amet" />

</s:Group>
```

This simple file will display an `<s:TextArea>` component with some text.

With a path to the */bin* directory of your Flex SDK installation set in your `PATH`, the following command using the *compc* utility generates a SWC file named *library.swc* within the root of your development directory:

```
> compc -source-path . -include-classes MyCustomComponent -output library.swc
```

Using any standard unzip utility, extract the library file from the generated SWC file. In this example, the extracted library is approximately 830 KB in size.

Using the *optimizer* command-line tool, you can reduce the file size of the target runtime shared library by removing any unnecessary debugging and metadata code within the generated SWF file:

```
> optimizer -keep-as3-metadata=
    "Bindable,Managed,ChangeEvent,NonCommittingChangeEvent,Transient"
    -input library.swf -output optimized.swf
```

The file size of the optimized RSL is now less than half that of the original library (approximately 330 KB).

It is recommended that you include at least the `Bindable`, `Managed`, `ChangeEvent`, `NonCommittingChangeEvent`, and `Transient` metadata names in the argument value for the `keep-as3-metadata` option, because these are common metadata tags associated with components from the Flex Framework. Other metadata, such as `RemoteClass`, can be added to the comma-delimited argument list based on the class dependencies of the RSL library. Metadata tags that are not explicitly specified will be removed by the optimizer.

See Also

Recipes 17.1 and 17.2

17.4 Create a MXML-Based Module

Problem

You want to create a MXML-based module to be loaded by an application at runtime.

Solution

Create a MXML class that extends the `mx.modules.Module` class by using the `<mx:Module>` root tag, and compile the module using the *mxmlc* command-line tool.

Discussion

A *module* is similar to an application and is compiled by using the *mxmlc* utility to generate a SWF file that can be loaded into an application or another module at runtime. To create a MXML-based module, you extend the `mx.modules.Module` class by using `<mx:Module>` as the root tag of the MXML file.

The following example is a module that displays a list of contacts within a data grid:

```
<mx:Module xmlns:fx="http://ns.adobe.com/mxml/2009"
           xmlns:s="library://ns.adobe.com/flex/spark"
           xmlns:mx="library://ns.adobe.com/flex/mx">

    <fx:Declarations>
        <fx:XMLList id="contacts">
            <contact>
                <name>Josh Noble</name>
                <phone>555.111.2222</phone>
                <address>227 Jackee Lane</address>
            </contact>
            <contact>
                <name>Todd Anderson</name>
                <phone>555.333.4444</phone>
                <address>1642 Ocean Blvd</address>
            </contact>
            <contact>
                <name>Garth Braithwaite</name>
                <phone>555.777.8888</phone>
                <address>1984 Winston Road</address>
            </contact>
        </fx:XMLList>
    </fx:Declarations>

    <mx:DataGrid id="contactGrid"
                 width="100%" height="100%"
                 rowCount="4"
                 dataProvider="{contacts}">
        <mx:columns>
            <mx:DataGridColumn dataField="name" headerText="Name" />
            <mx:DataGridColumn dataField="phone" headerText="Phone" />
            <mx:DataGridColumn dataField="address" headerText="Address" />
        </mx:columns>
    </mx:DataGrid>

</mx:Module>
```

The structure of this module is similar to an application or custom component. When an application is required to display a list of contacts, it can load this module and add it to the display list.

To compile this example into a SWF file to be loaded by an application, use the *mxmlc* tool just as you would when compiling a simple application, with the file argument being that of the `Module` class:

```
> mxmlc ContactList.mxml
```

This command generates a SWF file named *ContactList.swf*, though you can use the `output` option to specify a different name as long as the application knows the correct name when it is time to load the module. The size of the generated SWF file is approximately 40 KB. By separating this code into a module, you reduce the download time as well as the file size of any application that may require loading this module.

17.5 Create an ActionScript-Based Module

Problem

You want to create an ActionScript-based module to be loaded by an application at runtime.

Solution

Create an ActionScript class that extends either the `mx.modules.Module` or `mx.mod ules.ModuleBase` class, and compile the module using the *mxmlc* command-line tool.

Discussion

You can create ActionScript-based modules by extending the `Module` and `ModuleBase` classes of the module API. Depending on the role the module plays within the application, the choice to extend either `Module` or `ModuleBase` is based on the necessity of a display list. The `Module` class is a display container that is an extension of `Flex Sprite` and will include some framework code. The `ModuleBase` class extends `EventDispatcher` and can be used to separate logic code from an application that does not depend on visual elements.

MXML-based modules are an extension of `mx.modules.Module` and use the `<mx:Mod ule>` root tag. If you are creating a module that contains visual elements, you can extend the `Module` class and override protected methods, such as the `createChildren()` method inherited from `UIComponent`, as you see fit. The following example shows a module that adds input elements to the display to enable a user to enter information:

```
package {
    import mx.core.IVisualElement;
    import mx.modules.Module;

    import spark.components.HGroup;
    import spark.components.Label;
    import spark.components.TextInput;
    import spark.components.VGroup;
```

```
public class ASContactList extends Module
{
    public function ASContactList()
    {
        super();
        percentWidth = percentHeight = 100;
    }

    override protected function createChildren():void
    {
        super.createChildren();
        var container:VGroup = new VGroup();
        var firstNameItem:IVisualElement = createInputItem( "First Name:" );
        var lastNameItem:IVisualElement = createInputItem( "Last Name:" );
        container.addElement( firstNameItem );
        container.addElement( lastNameItem );
        addChild( container );
    }

    private function createInputItem( label:String ):IVisualElement
    {
        var container:HGroup = new HGroup();
        var field:Label = new Label();
        field.text = label;
        var input:TextInput = new TextInput();
        container.addElement( field );
        container.addElement( input );
        return container;
    }
}
```

You compile an ActionScript-based module as you would a MXML-based module, by using the *mxmlc* utility with the file input value being the name of the ActionScript file:

```
> mxmlc ASContactList.as
```

This command generates a SWF file named *ASContactList.swf*, though you can use the output option to specify a different name as long as the application knows the correct name when it is time to load the SWF. The Module class is an extension of mx.core.Container, and as such internally casts children to be added to the display list as being of type mx.core.IUIComponent. You can add components from the Flex Framework to the display list of an ActionScript-based module by using the addChild() method or the addElement() method. To add components from the ActionScript API, such as flash.text.TextField and flash.media.Video, you need to wrap them in an instance of UIComponent.

The Module class contains framework code that enables interaction with and display of user interface objects. If your module does not rely on framework code, you can create a class that extends ModuleBase. The mx.modules.ModuleBase class extends EventDispatcher and provides a convenient way to separate logic code from your modular application.

The following is an example of a module that extends the `ModuleBase` class:

```
package
{
    import mx.modules.ModuleBase;

    public class EntryStateModule extends ModuleBase
    {
        public function greet( first:String, last:String ):String
        {
            return "Hello, " + first + " " + last + ".";
        }
        public function welcomeBack( first:String, last:String ):String
        {
            return "Nice to see you again, " + first + ".";
        }
    }
}
```

When loaded by an application, this simple module provides a way to structure salutations through the public `greet()` and `welcomeBack()` methods. This module contains no framework code and as a consequence is significantly smaller in file size than a module created using the `Module` class.

Compilation of a module extending the `ModuleBase` class is the same as that of a file extending `Module`:

```
> mxmlc EntryStateModule.as
```

This command generates a SWF file named *EntryStateModule.swf*. To access the public methods available on the module in this example, the parent application or parent module references the `child` property of the `ModuleLoader` instance or the `factory` property of an `IModuleInfo` implementation, which is discussed in Recipe 17.7.

See Also

Recipes 17.4 and 17.7

17.6 Use ModuleLoader to Load Modules

Problem

You want to load modules into your Flex application.

Solution

Use the `<mx:ModuleLoader>` container to load modules into your application.

Discussion

The `mx.modules.ModuleLoader` class is a container that acts similarly to the `mx.con` `trols.SWFLoader` component. It loads SWF files and adds modules to the display list of an application. `ModuleLoader` differs from `SWFLoader` in that it has a contract that dictates that the SWF file that is loaded implements `IFlexModuleFactory`. Compiled modules contain the `IFlexModuleFactory` class factory, which allows an application to dynamically load the modular SWF files at runtime without requiring the class implementations within the main application shell.

Though the `ModuleLoader` object is a display container, it can load modules that extend `Module` and `ModuleBase` and does not rely on the modules to contain framework code or display visual objects. The `url` property of the `ModuleLoader` class is a reference to the location of a module expressed as a URL. Setting the `url` property internally calls the public `loadModule()` method of the `ModuleLoader` class and begins the process of downloading the module.

The following example loads a module from the same domain as the application:

```
<s:Application xmlns:fx="http://ns.adobe.com/mxml/2009"
              xmlns:s="library://ns.adobe.com/flex/spark"
              xmlns:mx="library://ns.adobe.com/flex/mx">

    <s:Panel title="Contacts:" width="350" height="180">
        <mx:ModuleLoader url="Contacts.swf" />
    </s:Panel>

</s:Application>
```

When this application starts up, the `ModuleLoader` is instructed to load a module titled *Contacts.swf* from the same domain. After the module has loaded successfully, it is added to the display list of the application.

The `ModuleLoader` component also allows you to unload and load different modules dynamically. Setting the `url` property of a `ModuleLoader` instance internally calls the public `loadModule()` method of `ModuleLoader` and adds the module as a child. To remove the module from the display, you call the public `unloadModule()` method of the `Module` `Loader` class. Calling `unloadModule()` sets the module reference to `null`, but does not change the `url` property value.

The following example is an application that loads and unloads modules based on user interaction:

```
<s:Application xmlns:fx="http://ns.adobe.com/mxml/2009"
              xmlns:s="library://ns.adobe.com/flex/spark"
              xmlns:mx="library://ns.adobe.com/flex/mx">

    <fx:Script>
        <![CDATA[
            private function displayModule( moduleURL:String ):void
```

```
        {
            if( moduleLoader.url != moduleURL )
                moduleLoader.url = moduleURL;
        }
    ]]>
    </fx:Script>

    <s:Panel title="Contacts:" width="350" height="210">
        <s:layout>
            <s:VerticalLayout />
        </s:layout>
        <mx:ModuleLoader id="moduleLoader" width="100%" height="190" />
        <s:HGroup>
            <s:Button label="show list"
                    click="displayModule('Contacts.swf');" />
            <s:Button label="enter contact"
                    click="displayModule('ContactEntry.swf');" />
        </s:HGroup>
    </s:Panel>

</s:Application>
```

The click event handlers of the Button controls update the module to be loaded into the ModuleLoader. This application alternates between displaying a list of contact information and displaying a form to enter new contacts, by loading the *ContactList.swf* module and the *ContactEntry.swf* module, respectively.

When a module is loaded into an application, it is added to the module list of the mx.modules.ModuleManager object. When it's removed, the reference is turned to null to free memory and resources. Using the ModuleLoader is a convenient way to manage the loading and unloading of modules in a Flex-based application.

See Also

Recipes 17.4, 17.5, and 17.7

17.7 Use ModuleManager to Load Modules

Problem

You want more granular control over the loading and unloading of modules in your Flex- and ActionScript-based applications.

Solution

Access methods of the ModuleManager class directly to listen for status events of loading modules.

Discussion

The `ModuleManager` class manages loaded modules. The `<mx:ModuleLoader>` component internally communicates with this manager when the public `ModuleLoader.loadMod ule()` and `ModuleLoader.unloadModule()` methods are invoked. You can directly access the modules managed by the `ModuleManager` using ActionScript. When a module URL is passed into the public `ModuleManager.getModule()` method, the location is added to the managed list of modules and an instance of `mx.modules.IModuleInfo` is returned.

Modules are essentially instances of the private `ModuleInfo` class of `ModuleManager`. `ModuleInfo` objects load a target SWF file and are wrapped in a proxy class implementing `IModuleInfo`, which is returned from the `ModuleManager.getModule()` method. You can listen for status events on this proxy to have more control over how your application interacts with loaded modules.

The following example shows how an application uses the `ModuleManager` to control how a module is added to the display:

```
<s:Application xmlns:fx="http://ns.adobe.com/mxml/2009"
               xmlns:s="library://ns.adobe.com/flex/spark"
               xmlns:mx="library://ns.adobe.com/flex/mx"
               creationComplete="handleCreationComplete();">

    <fx:Script>
        <![CDATA[
            import mx.core.IVisualElement;
            import mx.events.ModuleEvent;
            import mx.modules.IModuleInfo;
            import mx.modules.ModuleManager;

            private var moduleInfo:IModuleInfo;

            private function handleCreationComplete():void
            {
                moduleInfo = ModuleManager.getModule( "Contacts.swf" );
                moduleInfo.addEventListener( ModuleEvent.READY, handleModuleLoad );
                moduleInfo.load();
            }
            private function handleModuleLoad( evt:ModuleEvent ):void
            {
                contactPanel.addElement( moduleInfo.factory.create() as
                                         IVisualElement );
            }
        ]]>
    </fx:Script>

    <s:Panel id="contactPanel"
             title="Contacts"
             width="350" height="300" />

</s:Application>
```

When this application has completed its initial layout operations, the `ContactList` module is loaded by the `IModuleInfo` object, which is returned from the static `ModuleManager.getModule()` method. The `IModuleInfo` implementation acts as a proxy to the `Loader` instance, which is instructed to download the module.

After the module is successfully downloaded, it is added to the display list using the `IFlexModuleFactory.create()` method. This method returns the instance of the module that is cast as an `IVisualElement` instance to be added to the display of the `Panel` container.

You can listen to events related to the download status of a module by using the `IModuleInfo` object proxy returned from the `getModule()` method. In this example, the application waits until the module is completely loaded before adding it to the display list. The events are dispatched as instances of the `ModuleEvent` class and range from progress to error states related to the download status of a SWF module (see Table 17-1). You can also assign event handlers for these events inline in MXML when declaring an instance of the `ModuleLoader` class.

Table 17-1. The mx.events.ModuleEvent class

Constant variable	String value	Description
PROGRESS	`"progress"`	Dispatched while the module is loading. From this event, you can access the bytesLoaded and bytesTotal properties of the module being loaded.
SETUP	`"setup"`	Dispatched when enough information about the loading module is available.
READY	`"ready"`	Dispatched when the module has finished loading.
UNLOAD	`"unload"`	Dispatched when the module has been unloaded.
ERROR	`"error"`	Dispatched when an error has occurred while downloading the module.

The `unload()` method of the `IModuleInfo` implementation will remove references to the specified module from the `ModuleManager` but will not unload its SWF file from the display. To remove the module from the display, you must explicitly call the `removeElement()` method of the parent display.

In comparison to the `ModuleLoader` class, which internally begins loading a module based on an update to its `url` property, using the `IModuleInfo` implementation returned from the `getModule()` method affords you the capability to defer the loading and subsequent display of a module in your applications. This allows you to preload modules and have them immediately available for display, to reduce the delay in requesting and rendering modules upon user interaction.

See Also

Recipes 17.4, 17.5, and 17.6

17.8 Load Modules from Different Servers

Problem

You want to store modules on a server that is separate from the server you use to deploy applications.

Solution

Use the `flash.system.Security` class to establish trust between the main application SWF file and the loaded module SWF file.

Discussion

Flash Player security is domain based, allowing a SWF file from a specific domain to access data from that same domain without restriction. When a SWF file is loaded into the Flash Player, a security sandbox is set up for its domain and access is granted to any assets within that sandbox. This model is in place to ensure that SWF files do not access external resources and communicate with other SWF files from untrusted sources.

In order to allow a SWF file in a specific domain to access assets, including modules, from another domain, a cross-domain policy file permitting the access must be available on the remote server and you must use the `Security.allowDomain()` method in your main application. To allow a loaded module to interact with the parent SWF file—a communication known as *cross-scripting*—the module needs to call the `allowDomain()` method as well.

Consider the following module that is available from a remote server:

```
<mx:Module xmlns:fx="http://ns.adobe.com/mxml/2009"
           xmlns:s="library://ns.adobe.com/flex/spark"
           xmlns:mx="library://ns.adobe.com/flex/mx"
           initialize="handleInitialization();">

    <fx:Script>
        <![CDATA[
            private function handleInitialization():void
            {
                Security.allowDomain( "appserver" );
            }
        ]]>
    </fx:Script>

    <s:RichText width="100%" text="{loaderInfo.url}" />

</mx:Module>
```

When a parent SWF loads this module and the `initialize` event is fired, the module grants access to the loading SWF file and displays the URL from which the module was loaded.

When this module is compiled and placed on a remote server (in this example, `module server`), a cross-domain policy file is added to the root of that domain, allowing the parent SWF file (residing on `appserver`) to load the module:

```xml
<?xml version="1.0"?>
<cross-domain-policy>
    <allow-access-from domain="appserver" to-ports="*" />
    <site-control permitted-cross-domain-policies="all" />
</cross-domain-policy>
```

To enable the parent SWF to load and establish cross-scripting communication with the module, you must call the `Security.allowDomain()` method (passing in the domain name of the remote server) and load the *crossdomain.xml* file, as shown here:

```
<s:Application xmlns:fx="http://ns.adobe.com/mxml/2009"
               xmlns:s="library://ns.adobe.com/flex/spark"
               xmlns:mx="library://ns.adobe.com/flex/mx"
               preinitialize="handlePreinitialize();">

    <fx:Script>
        <![CDATA[
            private function handlePreinitialize():void
            {
                Security.allowDomain( "moduleserver" );
                Security.loadPolicyFile( "http://moduleserver/crossdomain.xml" );

                var loader:URLLoader = new URLLoader();
                loader.addEventListener( Event.COMPLETE, handleLoadComplete );
                loader.load( new URLRequest(
                        "http://moduleserver.crossdomain.xml" ) );
            }
            private function handleLoadComplete( evt:Event ):void
            {
                moduleLoader.url = "http://moduleserver/modules/MyModule.swf";
            }
        ]]>
    </fx:Script>

    <mx:ModuleLoader id="moduleLoader" />

</s:Application>
```

The `preinitialize` event handler for the main application establishes communication with any resources loaded from the `moduleserver` server by calling the `Security Domain.allowDomain()` method. The application also invokes the `Security.loadPolicy File()` method, passing it the location of the cross-domain policy file found on the remote server. The Flash Player retrieves the policy file and ensures that the application SWF file from `appserver` can be trusted. The `loadPolicyFile()` method must be called prior to loading the cross-domain policy file using an instance of URLLoader; otherwise, security exceptions will be thrown.

After the policy file has finished loading, the application SWF assigns the url property of a ModuleLoader instance to the location of the desired module on the remote server. With the application and module granting access to each other's specified servers, cross-scripting is permitted and the communication lines are open.

See Also

Recipes 17.6 and 17.7

17.9 Communicate with a Module

Problem

You want to access and pass data between the parent SWF and a loaded module.

Solution

Use the child property of mx.modules.ModuleLoader and the factory property of a mx.modules.IModuleInfo instance to listen for events, invoke public methods, and access public properties available from the parent SWF and the loaded module.

Discussion

An application shell can communicate with a loaded module by using properties of ModuleLoader and ModuleManager. Communication is not limited to an Application instance; modules can load other modules as well, making the loading module a parent to the loaded module, with the access points being the same as for an application.

To access data from a loaded module, you can typecast the returned properties of the specified loader instance to the loaded module class. When using a ModuleLoader object, the module instance is available from the child property:

```
<mx:Script>
    <![CDATA[
        private var myModule:MyModule;

        private function handleModuleReady():void
        {
            myModule = moduleLoader.child as MyModule;
            myModule.doSomething();
        }
    ]]>
</mx:Script>

<mx:ModuleLoader id="moduleLoader"
                 url="MyModule.swf"
                 ready="handleModuleReady();" />
```

When access to data of the loaded module is made available to the parent application, the `handleModuleReady()` event handler of the application is invoked. By typecasting the `child` property of the `<mx:ModuleLoader>` to the module's class, you can access data and call public methods available on the module.

When using the `ModuleManager` class in a parent application, the module instance is returned from the public `create()` method of the `IFlexModuleFactory` instance held on the `IModuleInfo` implementation:

```
private var moduleInfo:IModuleInfo;

private function creationHandler():void
{
    moduleInfo = ModuleManager.getModule( 'MyModule.swf' );
    moduleInfo.addEventListener( ModuleEvent.READY, handleModuleLoad );
    moduleInfo.load();
}

private function handleModuleLoad( evt:ModuleEvent ):void
{
    var myModule:MyModule = moduleInfo.factory.create() as MyModule;
    myModule.doSomething();
}
```

When you typecast the values returned from the child property of `ModuleLoader` or the `Object` returned from the `IFlexModuleFactory.create()` method to the loaded module, you introduce a tight coupling between the module and the loading application. To diminish the dependency created by typecasting the module to its class instance, as a general rule you should use interfaces. By typing to an interface, you introduce flexibility into your code and allow the parent application to interface with more than one instance of a particular class.

To exemplify the flexibility that typing to an interface affords you when developing modular applications, consider a situation where you have created a module that is loaded and used as a form for users to input information. As requirements in the application progress and change, you may find that you need to display more than one type of form. Though they may appear different visually, and perhaps perform different operations related to user data, access to the data of modules remains the same in their method signatures. Having different modules implement an interface introduces flexibility in your application, as they can be typed to a common API.

The following example is an interface exposing properties related to user information that separate modules can implement:

```
package com.oreilly.f4cb
{
    import flash.events.IEventDispatcher;

    public interface IUserEntry extends IEventDispatcher
    {
        function getFullName():String;
        function get firstName():String;
```

```
            function set firstName( str:String ):void;
            function get lastName():String;
            function set lastName( str:String ):void;
        }
    }
```

To create a module that implements this interface, declare the implements property value in the markup of the <mx:Module> node to be that of the IUserEntry interface:

```
<mx:Module implements="com.oreilly.f4cb.IUserEntry"
        xmlns:fx="http://ns.adobe.com/mxml/2009"
        xmlns:s="library://ns.adobe.com/flex/spark"
        xmlns:mx="library://ns.adobe.com/flex/mx"
        layout="vertical" width="100%" height="100%">

    <fx:Metadata>
        [Event(name="submit", type="flash.events.Event")]
    </fx:Metadata>

    <fx:Script>
        <![CDATA[
            private var _firstName:String;
            private var _lastName:String;

            private function handleSubmit():void
            {
                firstName = firstNameInput.text;
                lastName = lastNameInput.text;
                dispatchEvent( new Event( "submit" ) );
            }

            public function getFullName():String
            {
                return _lastName + ", " + _firstName;
            }

            [Bindable]
            public function get firstName():String
            {
                return _firstName;
            }
            public function set firstName( value:String ):void
            {
                _firstName = value;
            }

            [Bindable]
            public function get lastName():String
            {
                return _lastName;
            }
            public function set lastName( value:String ):void
            {
                _lastName = value;
            }
        ]]>
```

```
    </fx:Script>

    <s:HGroup verticalAlign="bottom">
        <s:Label text="First Name:" />
        <s:TextInput id="firstNameInput" width="100%" />
    </s:HGroup>
    <s:HGroup verticalAlign="bottom">
        <s:Label text="Last Name:" />
        <s:TextInput id="lastNameInput" width="100%" />
    </s:HGroup>
    <s:Button label="submit" click="handleSubmit();" />

</mx:Module>
```

This module presents display controls for entering and submitting information regarding the user's first and last name. The getter/setter properties and the public `getFull Name()` method are implemented in the `<mx:Script>` tag of the module. Data binding to the `firstName` and `lastName` attributes is established by the `IUserEntry` interface extending the `IEventDispatcher` interface, of which the `mx.modules.Module` and `mx.mod ules.ModuleBase` classes are both implementations.

To access data from this or any module that implements the `IUserEntry` interface, the parent application can typecast the corresponding property value based on the module loader instance.

The following example uses the `child` property of a `ModuleLoader` instance to access data from the `IUserEntry` module implementation:

```
<s:Application xmlns:fx="http://ns.adobe.com/mxml/2009"
               xmlns:s="library://ns.adobe.com/flex/spark"
               xmlns:mx="library://ns.adobe.com/flex/mx">

    <fx:Script>
        <![CDATA[
            import com.oreilly.f4cb.IUserEntry;

            private var myModule:IUserEntry;

            private function handleModuleReady():void
            {
                myModule = moduleLoader.child as IUserEntry;
                myModule.addEventListener( "submit", handleSubmit );
            }
            private function handleSubmit( evt:Event ):void
            {
                welcomeField.text = "Hello " + myModule.getFullName();
            }

            public function getInformation():String
            {
                return "Greetings!";
            }
        ]]>
    </fx:Script>
```

```
    <s:layout>
        <s:VerticalLayout />
    </s:layout>

    <mx:ModuleLoader id="moduleLoader"
        url="ContactForm.swf"
        ready="handleModuleReady();"
        />
    <s:RichText id="welcomeField" />

</s:Application>
```

The **ready** event handler for the `ModuleLoader` instance establishes an event handler for user information submission. When the `handleSubmit()` method is invoked, it prints the return string from the `getFullName()` implementation of the loaded module. By typing the `child` property of the `ModuleLoader` instance to the `IUserEntry` interface, you ensure a loose coupling between the parent application and the module. This allows you to dynamically interface with modules of different class types that have the same implementation.

Communication is not limited to the parent SWF accessing data on the module. Modules can also access data from their parent (loading) applications by using the `parentApplication` property:

```
<mx:Module xmlns:fx="http://ns.adobe.com/mxml/2009"
           xmlns:s="library://ns.adobe.com/flex/spark"
           xmlns:mx="library://ns.adobe.com/flex/mx"
           creationComplete="handleCreationComplete();">

    <fx:Script>
        <![CDATA[
            private function handleCreationComplete():void
            {
                infoField.text = parentApplication.getInformation();
            }
        ]]>
    </fx:Script>

    <s:RichText id="infoField" />

</mx:Module>
```

When the module has finished its initial layout, the `handleCreationComplete()` method is invoked and the returned data from the `getInformation()` method of the parent application is displayed in the child `RichText` component.

The `parentApplication` property of a `Module` instance is inherited from the `UICompo-nent` superclass and is of type `Object`. The dynamic `Object` class is at the root of the ActionScript runtime class hierarchy. As such, you can access data on the `parentApplication` instance by using dot notation, without respect to the parent class implementation, meaning that modules call properties held on the parent application regardless of whether those properties were explicitly declared.

As a general rule, a module should not access the data of a parent application by using the `parentApplication` property, because that creates a tightly coupled relationship between the module and the loading parent. To reduce this coupling, you can type applications that will load a specific module to an interface, as has been done with modules in the previous examples of this recipe. To ensure that different applications have the same communication with a module, however, it is recommended to supply data to the module directly from the parent application as opposed to accessing the data via the dynamic `parentApplication` property. Doing so will enable you to develop modular applications without requiring the module to be knowledgeable about its loading parent.

See Also

Recipes 17.6, 17.7, and 17.8

17.10 Use Query Strings to Pass Data to Modules

Problem

You want to pass data to a module during the loading phase.

Solution

Append a query string to the URL of a module SWF to be loaded. After the module has loaded, parse the URL string by using the `loaderInfo` property of the module.

Discussion

You can append query string parameters to the URL used to load a module. A query string is assembled by following the module location with a question mark (?) and separating each key/value pair with an ampersand (&). When the module is loaded, you can access the URL by using the `loaderInfo` property of the `mx.modules.Module` class. Using ActionScript, you can parse the available parameters of the URL of a module loaded into a parent application.

The following example application appends a query string to the URL of a module:

```
<s:Application xmlns:fx="http://ns.adobe.com/mxml/2009"
               xmlns:s="library://ns.adobe.com/flex/spark"
               xmlns:mx="library://ns.adobe.com/flex/mx"
               creationComplete="handleCreationComplete();">

    <fx:Script>
        <![CDATA[
            private function handleCreationComplete():void
```

```
        {
            var params:String = "firstName=Ted" + "&lastName=Henderson";
            moduleLoader.url = "com/oreilly/f4cb/ContactModule.swf?" + params;
        }
    ]]>
    </fx:Script>

    <mx:ModuleLoader id="moduleLoader" />

</s:Application>
```

After the creation of the `ModuleLoader` instance and the completion of the initial layout of the parent application, the `url` property value is supplied. The `firstName` and `last Name` key/value pairs are passed into the loaded module as constant variables in this example, but they could very well be values received from a service.

A loaded module can parse the appending URL query by using the `loaderInfo` property:

```
<mx:Module xmlns:fx="http://ns.adobe.com/mxml/2009"
           xmlns:s="library://ns.adobe.com/flex/spark"
           xmlns:mx="library://ns.adobe.com/flex/mx"
           layout="vertical" width="100%" height="100%"
           creationComplete="handleCreationComplete();">

    <fx:Script>
        <![CDATA[
            import mx.utils.ObjectProxy;

            [Bindable] public var contact:ObjectProxy;

            private function handleCreationComplete():void
            {
                contact = new ObjectProxy();

                var pattern:RegExp = /.*\?/;
                var query:String = loaderInfo.url.toString();
                query = query.replace( pattern, "" );

                var params:Array = query.split( "&" );
                var i:int = 0;
                var kvPair:Array;
                for( i; i < params.length; i++ )
                {
                    kvPair = params[i].toString().split("=");
                    contact[kvPair[0]] = kvPair[1];
                }
            }

        ]]>
    </fx:Script>

    <s:RichText text="{'Hello, ' + contact.firstName + ' ' + contact.lastName}" />

</mx:Module>
```

The loaded module parses the query string parameters in the appended URL and adds them as properties to the `ObjectProxy` class. Using the inherent data-binding capability of the `ObjectProxy` class, the `firstName` and `lastName` parameter values are displayed in the `RichText` control as those properties are updated.

Passing data by using a query string is a convenient way for a loaded module to receive and operate on data upon initialization. Using query strings does not enforce tight coupling between the parent application and the module, because it is the responsibility of the module to handle the data as it sees fit and ensure that it does not throw runtime errors. However, this technique for supplying data to a module is prone to human development error; a misspelling in the query string can lead to miscommunication between the parent/loading application and the module.

See Also

Recipe 17.9

17.11 Use Linker Reports to Optimize Modules

Problem

You want to reduce the file size and subsequent download time of a module.

Solution

Use the `link-report` command-line option of the *mxmlc* utility when compiling the application to generate a linker report file. Then use that report file as the input value for the `load-externs` command-line option when compiling a module to ensure that only classes that the module requires are compiled.

Discussion

When you compile a module, all custom and framework code that the module depends on is included in the generated SWF file. Some of this code may be common to both the module and its loading parent application. You can remove redundancies and reduce the module's file size by compiling it against a linker report file.

A *linker report file* is an externalized list of classes that the application is dependent on. It can be generated by using the `link-report` command-line option when compiling an application. The following command will generate a linker report named *report.xml* in the current directory:

```
> mxmlc -link-report=report.xml MyApplication.mxml
```

You can then compile your module against this generated linker report file, to remove code redundancy and reduce the module's file size. Use the `load-externs` command-line option, specifying the generated file as the report input value:

```
> mxmlc -load-externs=report.xml MyModule.mxml
```

The result is a generated module SWF file that does not contain any code that both the application and the module depend on. This is a great optimization tool when you take into account the framework code that may be compiled into both the application and a module. Externalizing code and compiling modules against linker reports does create a development dependency between the application and the module, however. If changes are made to the application, you may need to regenerate a linker report and recompile the module to ensure that the code on which it depends is available.

If your application uses more than one module, this optimization technique can also be used to compile code that may not necessarily be used in the parent application, but is common to more than one module. In fact, as a general rule you should compile any manager classes that modules may depend on, such as `mx.managers.DragManager` and `mx.managers.PopUpManager`, into the main application. This is because modules cannot access code resources from other modules, and runtime exceptions will be thrown if, for instance, one module is trying to reference the `DragManager` from another module.

To ensure that modules can access the same manager within an application, you need to import and declare a class local variable in the main application file:

```
import mx.managers.PopUpManager;
var popUpManager:PopUpManager;
```

You can then generate the linker report to compile the modules against, ensure that the modules are using the same manager reference, and reduce code redundancy and module file size.

See Also

Recipes 17.4 and 17.5

CHAPTER 18

AIR Basics

The Adobe Integrated Runtime (AIR) allows you to create applications using HTML, JavaScript, and Flash that users can run on their desktops. The next three chapters of this book cover various aspects of creating AIR applications. In this chapter you'll learn the basics of creating an AIR application in Flash Builder 4.

18.1 Create and Run an AIR Application with Flash Builder 4

Problem

You need to create an AIR application using Flash Builder 4.

Solution

Use the built-in support for AIR application development in Flash Builder 4.

Discussion

Flash Builder 4 has built-in support for creating AIR applications. In many ways, working with an AIR application is similar to working with a Flex application.

Creating a new AIR application

To create a new AIR application project within Flash Builder, you first must create a new project. From the File menu, choose New→Flex Project. If you don't see this option, you may need to choose Other and then select Flex Project from the resulting list.

When the New Flex Project dialog box appears (Figure 18-1), you will notice an option to make this a Flex web application or a Flex-based AIR application. Be sure that the option for an AIR application is selected, and then click the Next button to proceed through the wizard-like interface.

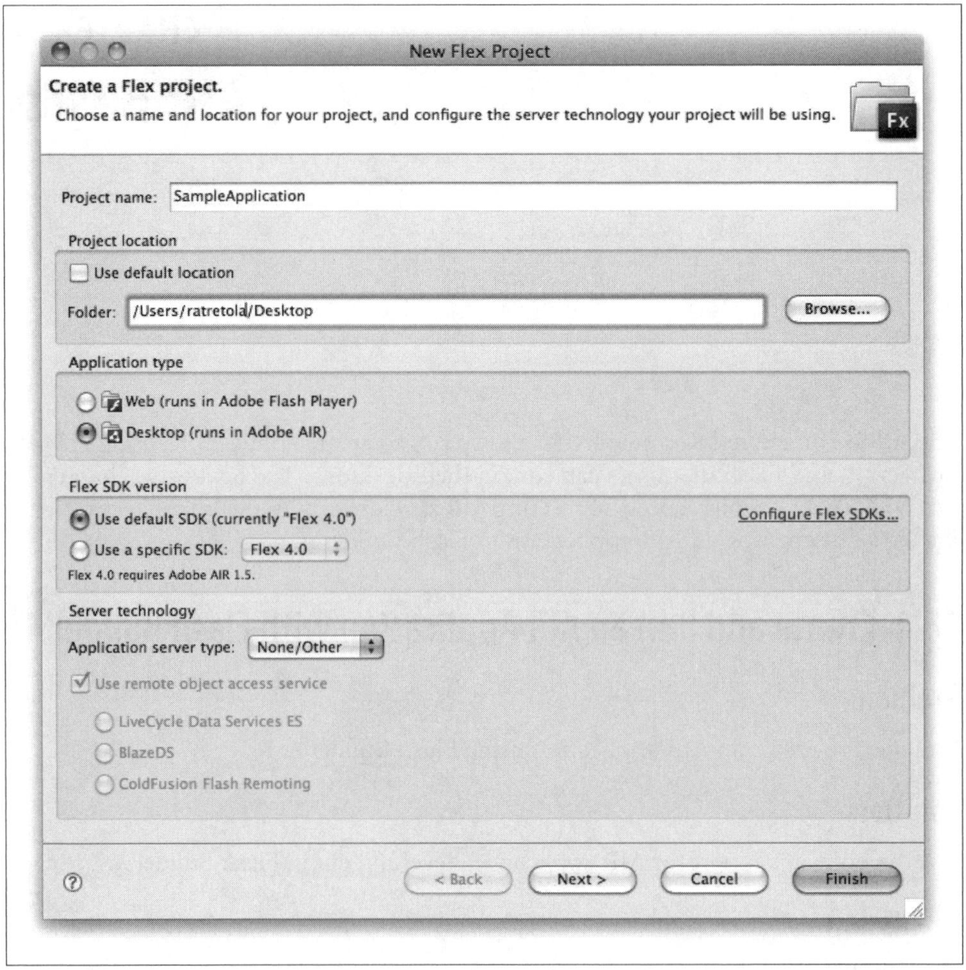

Figure 18-1. New Flex Project dialog box

As you proceed through the dialog box, you can set the application ID and default application MXML filename, as shown in Figure 18-2. (For more information on setting your application ID, see Recipe 18.4.) The application ID will be pre-populated in the application descriptor file for your AIR application once you've created the project. You will also notice that you have the option to target either MX and Spark, for hybrid Flex 3/4 applications, or just MX, for Flex 3-only applications.

When you click Finish, Flash Builder creates a new project that includes the application MXML file as well as the application descriptor XML file.

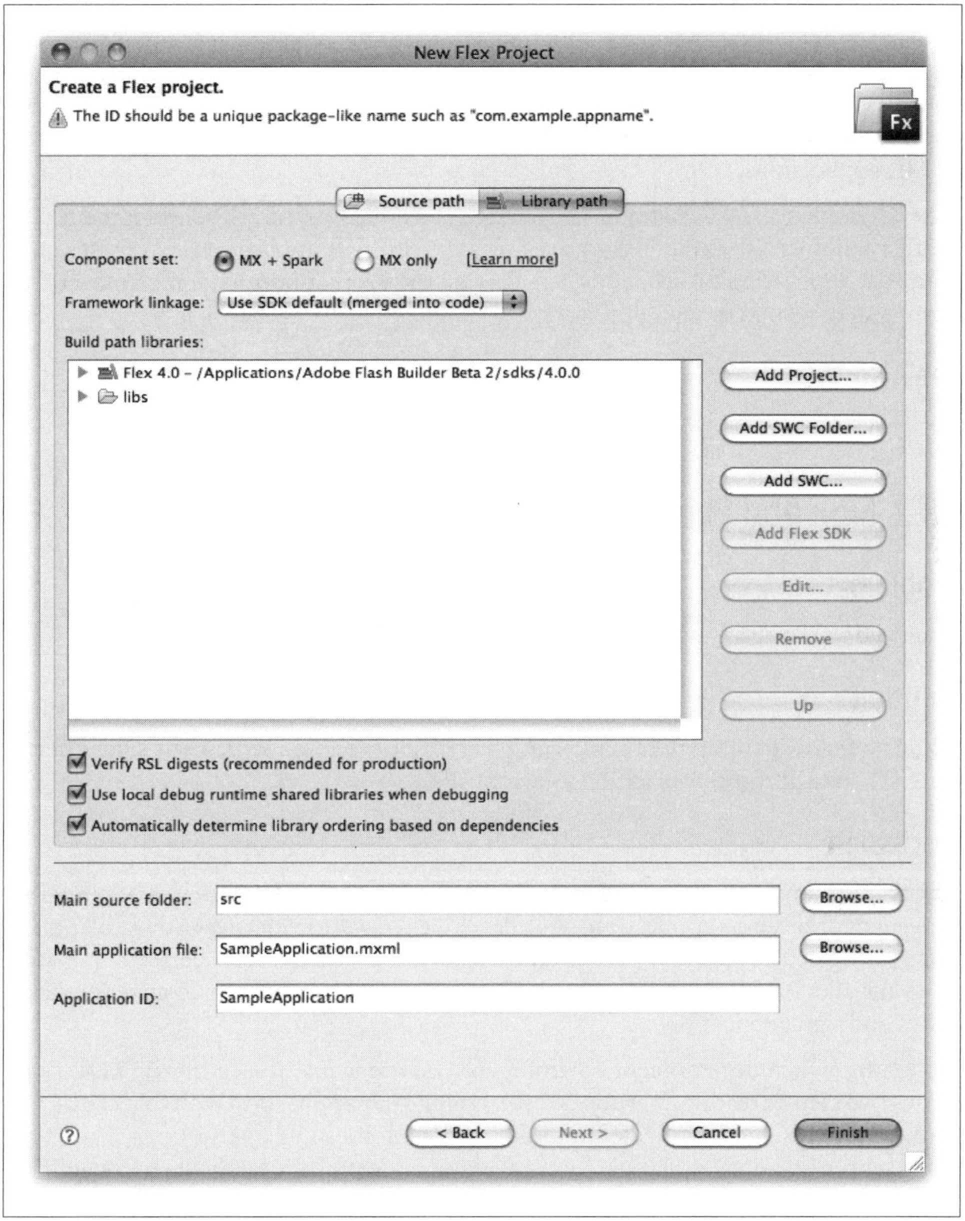

Figure 18-2. Setting application information in Flash Builder

Running and debugging your AIR application

In Flash Builder, you can run an AIR application by selecting the application and clicking the Run button. Flash Builder takes care of calling *adl* (the AIR Debug Launcher) and passing in your application descriptor file. Likewise, you can debug your application by clicking the Debug button. All the regular debugging tools are available to AIR applications.

Flex developers also have another advantage when it comes to AIR development. The profiler within Flash Builder works seamlessly with AIR applications, so by selecting your AIR application project and then clicking the Profiler button, you can determine what system resources your application is using.

See Also

Recipe 18.4

18.2 Sign and Export an AIR Application

Problem

You need to create an installable packaged AIR application.

Solution

Using your AIR development tool, sign your AIR application with a self-signed certificate. Then export the application as an *.air* file.

Discussion

AIR applications must be signed to be installable. This provides a level of security that is needed for desktop applications. For developers used to working with web applications, using certificates may seem scary. However, AIR makes the certificate process easy, and the development environments for AIR provide easy ways to generate certificates and sign applications.

No matter which development environment you are using, the certificate process requires two steps: creating a certificate and signing your application with that certificate. You can use a single certificate multiple times with multiple applications. Each time you package an application into an installable AIR application, you have to sign it.

Figure 18-3 shows the installation dialog box for an application signed with a self-signed certificate. When you sign an application with this kind of certificate, the publisher listed in the installer is not verified. To have the publisher value verified, you will need to use a trusted certificate authority. (You can find a list of supported certificate types in Recipe 18.3.)

Signing and exporting in Flash Builder

When you attempt to package and export your AIR application in Flash Builder, you will be asked which certificate you will be using to sign your application. An alternate option lets you export an AIR application as an unsigned package; this type of packaged file has the extension *.airi* and is not installable. To export an installable application, you need to select the first option: "Export and sign an AIR file with a digital certificate" (Figure 18-4).

The Export Release Build dialog box also gives you the option to create a certificate if you do not already have one. If you click the Create button, you will be presented with a new dialog box that enables you to create a new certificate (Figure 18-5). This dialog box requires you to enter a publisher name, a password, and the location where you want to save your certificate. You can enter a unique identifying piece of information for the publisher name. You need to remember the password you enter when creating your certificate, because you'll have to enter this value each time you sign an application. Be sure to remember where you save your certificate too, because you can use it to sign all your AIR applications. You should also back it up.

When you click the OK button you will be taken back to the Export Release Build dialog box, and the information for your certificate will be populated in the Certificate field. You will need to enter your password in the Password entry field. You can also click the "Remember password for this session" checkbox so you will not have to enter the password each time you export this AIR application during your current session (if you close and reopen Flash Builder, you will have to reenter the password). Once you've entered the password, you can proceed through the dialog box and export your AIR application as an installable AIR file.

See Also

Recipe 18.3

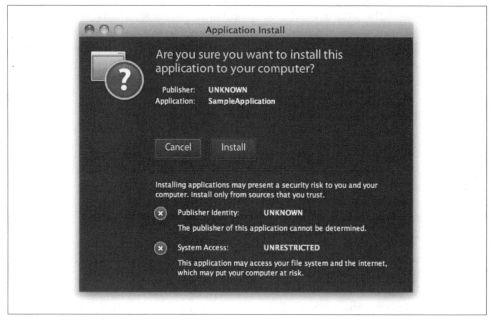

Figure 18-3. Installation dialog box with self-signed certificate

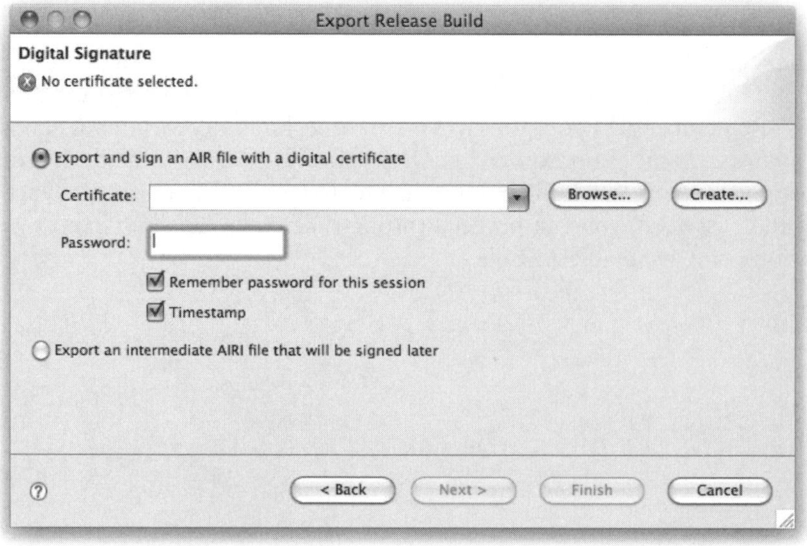

Figure 18-4. Export Release Build dialog box

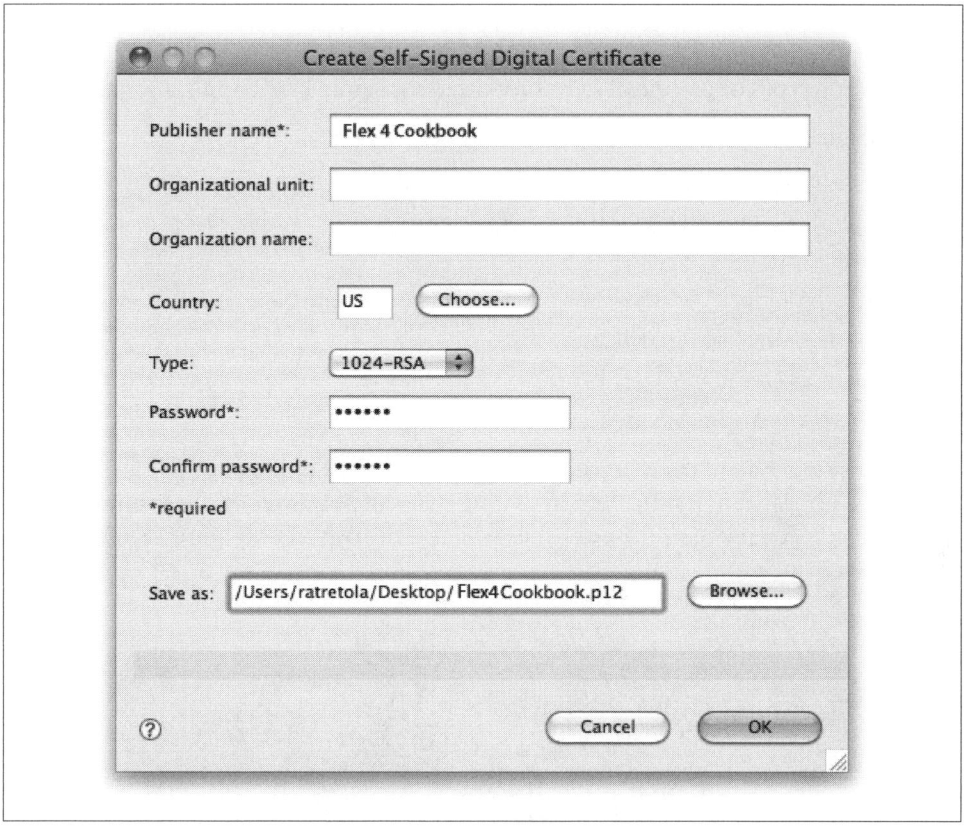

Figure 18-5. Create Self-Signed Digital Certificate dialog box

18.3 Sign an AIR File with a Trusted Certificate

Problem

You need to sign your AIR application with a commercial trusted certificate for deployment.

Solution

Obtain a trusted certificate from one of the vendors selling code-signing certificates for AIR applications.

Discussion

Signing an AIR application with a commercial certificate is done through the same process as signing an AIR application with a self-signed certificate. The only difference is the certificate used. The two companies that currently offer trusted certificates that can be used with AIR are VeriSign and Thawte.

It is important to note that the certificates used with AIR are code-signing certificates. These certificates are different from certificates used with secure web servers. Currently, the following types of certificates are supported for signing AIR applications:

- VeriSign:
  — Microsoft Authenticode Digital ID
  — Sun Java Signing Digital ID
- Thawte:
  — AIR Developer Certificate
  — Apple Developer Certificate
  — JavaSoft Developer Certificate
  — Microsoft Authenticode Certificate

You can use any one of these certificates to sign your AIR application. This causes the installer to appear differently, demonstrating that the publisher of the application has been verified. The name of the publisher will also be displayed (Figure 18-6).

Figure 18-6. Installation dialog box with a commercial certificate

You can read more about code-signing certificates for AIR at these addresses:

- VeriSign: *http://www.verisign.com/products-services/security-services/code-signing/*
- Thawte: *http://www.thawte.com/code-signing/*

Once you have your code-signing certificate, the packaging process for your application is the same as that demonstrated in Recipe 18.2.

18.4 Targeting a Specific Version of AIR

Problem

You need to ensure that your application is targeting AIR 2.0.

Solution

Specify the version of the runtime in the XML namespace within the application descriptor file.

Discussion

The XML namespace that is referenced in the `application` node of the application descriptor file is what tells the compiler which version of AIR you are targeting. If you want to target the latest release, AIR 2.0, you will want to be sure that your opening `application` tag has the XML namespace defined as follows:

```
<?xml version="1.0" encoding="UTF-8"?>
<application xmlns="http://ns.adobe.com/air/application/2.0">
...
</application>
```

If you were targeting the previous version of AIR, you could change the `2.0` in the XML namespace to `1.5`.

18.5 Set the Application ID

Problem

You need to enable the runtime to distinguish your AIR application from other AIR applications.

Solution

Set the application ID in the application descriptor file; this required ID serves as a unique identifier for each AIR application.

Discussion

The most important setting in the application descriptor file, the *application ID*, is a piece of the unique identification signature for each AIR application. Because of the importance of this setting, you should set this value immediately upon creating your application. You should also avoid changing this value once you've set it.

The end user of your application will not see the application ID while installing or using your application. In most cases, developers use *reverse domain notation* for the application ID. For example, if you owned the domain *http://oreilly.com* and you wanted to create an application named Flex 4 Cookbook, you could reverse the order of the domain and then add the name of your application. This would result in an application ID of com.oreilly.flex4cookbook. If you choose a domain you own or control, it will help ensure that your application ID is unique.

The application ID is one piece of the identification puzzle when doing an application update using the Adobe Update Framework (see Recipe 18.17). In order to have a successful update, both the application ID and the secure certificate must match those of the original application, so it is important that you do not change the application ID once you have distributed your application.

In AIR applications, you set the application ID by manually editing the application descriptor file. The application ID is specified in the `id` node:

```xml
<?xml version="1.0" encoding="utf-8" ?>
<application xmlns="http://ns.adobe.com/air/application/2.0">

    <id>com.oreilly.flex4cookbook</id>
    ...

</application>
```

18.6 Set the Application Name and Filename

Problem

You need to give your AIR application a name for the installer as well as a name for the executable file on the end user's computer.

Solution

Set the name and filename of your AIR application in the application descriptor file.

Discussion

Two additional items in the application descriptor file let you customize identification information about your application (its name and filename). Unlike the application ID, the name and filename are visible to the end user and are not part of the way the runtime identifies applications.

The application name appears in multiple locations. The user first encounters it on the application installer's initial screens (Figures 18-7 and 18-8). The application name also appears in the taskbar (Windows) or Dock (Mac) when the application is running.

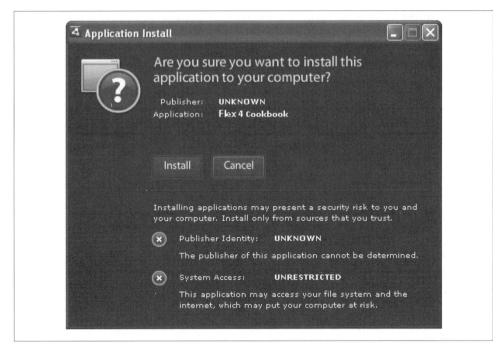

Figure 18-7. Initial application installation screen

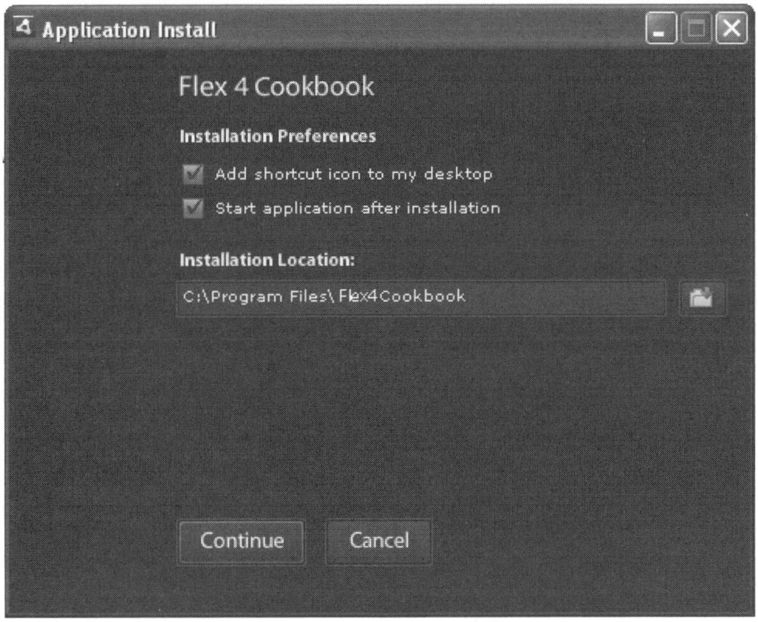

Figure 18-8. Final application installation screen

The filename determines the name of the executable file for your application as well as the name of the installation folder. For example, if the filename of your application is *Flex4Cookbook* and it is installed in the default location on a Windows computer, the path to the executable file will be *C:\Program Files\Flex4Cookbook\Flex4Cookbook.exe*.

In AIR applications, you set the name and filename by manually editing the application descriptor file. In the default template, these values immediately follow the application ID, as shown here:

```xml
<?xml version="1.0" encoding="utf-8" ?>
<application xmlns="http://ns.adobe.com/air/application/2.0">

    <id>com.oreilly.flex4cookbook</id>
    <filename>Flex4Cookbook</filename>
    <name>Flex 4 Cookbook</name>
    ...

</application>
```

18.7 Set the Application Version

Problem

You need to distinguish between different versions of your application.

Solution

Designate a version string for your AIR application as required by the application descriptor file.

Discussion

The version setting in the application descriptor file is not required to be a number. For example, you could set your application version to be 2.0.1, or Alpha 2. In addition, it's not required that your version string be sequential. This is because the version number is parsed as a string and not a number. In many ways, you decide how you will define the versioning of your application.

The version string is crucial, however, when it comes to updating your application. The updating process requires you to know both the current version string and the new version string.

Another important point to understand is that although the runtime can distinguish between two different versions of an application even if they both have the same version number, end users and developers can easily become confused if a consistent versioning string is not in place.

In AIR applications, you set the version string by modifying the application descriptor file directly. For example:

```
<?xml version="1.0" encoding="utf-8" ?>
<application xmlns="http://ns.adobe.com/air/application/2.0">

    <id>com.oreilly.flex4cookbook</id>
    <filename>Flex4Cookbook</filename>
    <name>Flex 4 Cookbook</name>
    <version>1.1</version>
    ...

</application>
```

18.8 Edit the Application Description and Copyright Information

Problem

You want to give the end user more information about your application and your company, both during the installation process and after the application is installed.

Solution

Provide a description and copyright information for your AIR application in the application descriptor file.

Discussion

The description and copyright values in the application descriptor files are both optional but provide useful information to the end user. Any description you specify is displayed in the application installer (Figure 18-9). Your users will see this dialog box after they download your application file, when they start the installation process.

Mac OS X displays any copyright information and the filename you provide in the About dialog box for your application (Figure 18-10). Currently, this information is not displayed for the Windows version of your application. On a Mac, the About dialog box also displays version information.

In AIR applications, you specify the copyright and description settings by modifying the application descriptor file directly, as shown here:

```
<?xml version="1.0" encoding="utf-8" ?>
<application xmlns="http://ns.adobe.com/air/application/2.0">

    <id>com.oreilly.flex4cookbook</id>
    <filename>Flex4Cookbook</filename>
    <name>Flex 4 Cookbook</name>
    <version>1.1</version>
```

```
<description>
    This AIR application provides code samples from the Flex 4 Cookbook
    from O'Reilly.
</description>
<copyright>2010 O'Reilly, Inc.</copyright>

...


</application>
```

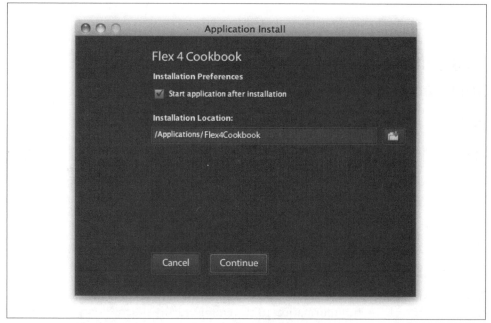

Figure 18-9. Description displayed in application installer

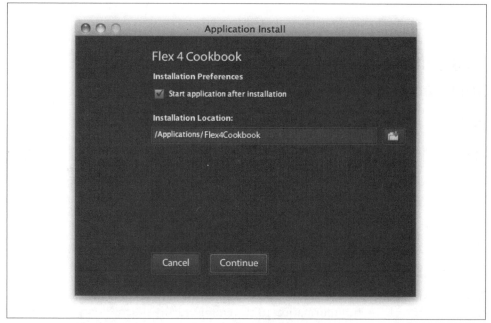

Figure 18-10. Copyright information displayed in the About dialog box

18.9 Edit the Initial Window Settings

Problem

You need to create an initial window that is 640 × 480 pixels with a minimum size of 320 × 240 and a maximum size of 800 × 600. In addition, the window needs to be maximizable, minimizable, resizable, and visible when the application launches. The initial window should be positioned 10 pixels below the top of the desktop and 10 pixels from the left edge of the desktop.

Solution

Use the `initialWindow` node in the application descriptor file to configure the initial window that is launched by your application.

Discussion

The `initialWindow` node enables you to configure virtually every aspect of the window displayed when your application launches. In addition to setting these values in the application descriptor file, you can change many of these values at runtime within your application by editing the window's properties. The many child nodes that set the values of different properties for the initial window are as follows:

content
> The `content` node is required; it specifies the location of the file (*.html* or *.swf*) that will be used as the content of the main application window. In a HTML/JavaScript application, this is the name of the HTML file for the initial window. In Flash Builder and Flash, this value is automatically populated for you with the name of the default application SWF.

title
> The optional `title` node designates the title of the initial window. If this value is not defined, the name of the application is used for the title.

systemChrome
> AIR applications can either use the default operating system look and feel, or a custom look and feel. You can set this node to `standard` for the default look, or `none` if you plan to add a custom look. Unlike many of the other properties, this value cannot be changed at runtime.

transparent
> AIR applications can have transparent windows. This requires extra system resources but can enhance the visual appeal of an application. This node can be set to `true` or `false` to enable or disable transparency.

visible

> In some situations you may want the initial window to be hidden until some task has been completed. In these cases, you can set the `visible` property to `false` and make it visible later from within the application.

minimizable, maximizable, *and* resizable

> In some applications, you may want to control whether the user can maximize, minimize, and resize the initial window. Each of the corresponding nodes can be set to `true` or `false`, and they are all `true` by default.

width *and* height

> Using these nodes, you can set the width and height of the initial window. In the case of Flash and Flex, the initial window's width and height are set by the SWF if these values are undefined.

x *and* y

> The x and y nodes correspond to the *x* and *y* pixel coordinates at which the application will be placed on the desktop.

minSize *and* maxSize

> If the `resizable` value is set to `true`, you can control to what extent the user can resize the application. If you set pixel values for these nodes, the user will be able to resize the application no larger than the `maxSize` and no smaller than the `minSize`.

In AIR applications, you specify the initial window settings by modifying the application descriptor file directly, as in the following example:

```
<?xml version="1.0" encoding="utf-8" ?>
<application xmlns="http://ns.adobe.com/air/application/2.0">

    <id>com.oreilly.flex4cookbook</id>
    <filename>Flex4Cookbook</filename>
    <name>Flex 4 Cookbook</name>
    <version>1.1</version>
    <description>
        This AIR application provides code samples from the Flex 4 Cookbook
        from O'Reilly.
    </description>
    <copyright>2010 O'Reilly, Inc.</copyright>

    <initialWindow>
        <content>Flex4Cookbook.swf</content>
        <systemChrome>standard</systemChrome>
        <transparent>false</transparent>
        <visible>true</visible>
        <width>640</width>
        <height>480</height>
        <x>10</x>
        <y>10</y>
        <minSize>320 240</minSize>
        <maxSize>800 600</maxSize>
        <maximizable>true</maximizable>
        <minimizable>true</minimizable>
```

```
    <resizable>true</resizable>
  </initialWindow>

</application>
```

18.10 Set the Installation Folder for an Application

Problem

You want your AIR application to have a different default value for the installation folder.

Solution

Define a different default folder name in the `installFolder` node of the application descriptor.

Discussion

On each platform that AIR supports, the base path for AIR applications is the default location for programs on that specific operating system. Ordinarily, AIR installs your application in this default directory, but if you specify a folder in the `installFolder` node, AIR installs your application in that folder instead.

This can be especially useful if you want to install a set of specific applications in a single folder. For example, if the Flex 4 Cookbook application provided a set of utilities, you could set the `installFolder` name to `OReilly` and then each application would be installed in that folder. On Windows, this directory will be a subdirectory of the *Program Files* directory. On a Mac, it will be a subdirectory of the *Applications* directory.

To set the `installFolder` value in an AIR application, you must edit the application descriptor file directly, as shown here:

```
<?xml version="1.0" encoding="utf-8" ?>
<application xmlns="http://ns.adobe.com/air/application/2.0">

    <id>com.oreilly.flex4cookbook</id>
    <filename>Flex4Cookbook</filename>
    <name>Flex 4 Cookbook</name>
    <version>1.1</version>
    <description>
        This AIR application provides code samples from the Flex 4 Cookbook
        from O'Reilly.
    </description>
    <copyright>2010 O'Reilly, Inc.</copyright>

    <initialWindow>
        <content>Flex4Cookbook.swf</content>
        <systemChrome>standard</systemChrome>
        <transparent>false</transparent>
        <visible>true</visible>
```

```
        <width>640</width>
        <height>480</height>
        <x>10</x>
        <y>10</y>
        <minSize>320 240</minSize>
        <maxSize>800 600</maxSize>
        <maximizable>true</maximizable>
        <minimizable>true</minimizable>
        <resizable>true</resizable>
    </initialWindow>

    <installFolder>OReilly</installFolder>

</application>
```

18.11 Set the Default Programs Menu Folder

Problem

You want your application to default to a specific folder in the Programs menu on a Windows computer.

Solution

Use the `programMenuFolder` node of the application descriptor file to set the default Programs menu subfolder.

Discussion

On Windows computers, you can group programs into folders in the Programs menu. By default, a shortcut to your AIR application will be installed in the root *Programs* folder, but you can specify a subfolder name in the `programMenuFolder` node.

For example, if you had a group of AIR applications that were all related to Flex 4 Cookbook, you could set the `programMenuFolder` value of each of these applications to `Flex 4 Cookbook`. When the Flex 4 Cookbook application is installed on a Windows machine, a program folder named *Flex 4 Cookbook* would be created with a shortcut to the application in it. All other applications that have the same path set in the `pro gramMenuFolder` property will have their shortcuts added to the same folder upon installation.

 This setting has no effect if the application is installed on a Mac.

To set the `programMenuFolder` for an AIR application, you edit the application descriptor file directly. For example:

```xml
<?xml version="1.0" encoding="utf-8" ?>
<application xmlns="http://ns.adobe.com/air/application/2.0">

    <id>com.oreilly.flex4cookbook</id>
    <filename>Flex4Cookbook</filename>
    <name>Flex 4 Cookbook</name>
    <version>1.1</version>
    <description>
        This AIR application provides code samples from the Flex 4 Cookbook
        from O'Reilly.
    </description>
    <copyright>2010 O'Reilly, Inc.</copyright>

    <initialWindow>
        <content>Flex4Cookbook.swf</content>
        <systemChrome>standard</systemChrome>
        <transparent>false</transparent>
        <visible>true</visible>
        <width>640</width>
        <height>480</height>
        <x>10</x>
        <y>10</y>
        <minSize>320 240</minSize>
        <maxSize>800 600</maxSize>
        <maximizable>true</maximizable>
        <minimizable>true</minimizable>
        <resizable>true</resizable>
    </initialWindow>

    <installFolder>OReilly</installFolder>
    <programMenuFolder>Flex 4 Cookbook</programMenuFolder>

</application>
```

18.12 Set a Custom Application Icon

Problem

You need to brand your application with a specific icon.

Solution

Set the custom icon in the descriptor file for your application.

Discussion

A default set of application icons comes with the AIR SDK. In addition, both Mac OS X and Windows provide a default icon for applications that do not have a predefined icon. In most cases, however, you will want to define an icon that is specific to your application.

In both Windows and Mac OS X, the application icon is used in multiple locations at different sizes. For example, in Windows the application icon appears on the desktop and also next to the title of the application's initial window in the taskbar. In the application descriptor file, AIR lets you define up to four different icons for the different sizes and uses.

When you add icon files to your AIR application, the images must be in PNG format. AIR converts these images to the necessary format for each operating system. In addition, if you provide only the largest size of the icon, AIR will resize that image for the smaller icons, but in most cases resizing the image yourself will result in better quality. If you only provide the smaller icons, the application will still compile: the smaller images will be upsized, which will result in very poor-quality icons.

You can add a custom icon to your AIR application by editing the application descriptor file directly. The relevant settings exist in the `icon` node. The four child nodes of the `icon` node are `image16x16`, `image32x32`, `image48x48`, and `image128x128`, which relate to the sizes of each needed icon.

The following example assumes you have a folder named *icon* at the root of your application with the referenced images in it:

```xml
<?xml version="1.0" encoding="utf-8" ?>
<application xmlns="http://ns.adobe.com/air/application/2.0">

    <id>com.oreilly.flex4cookbook</id>
    <filename>Flex4Cookbook</filename>
    <name>Flex 4 Cookbook</name>
    <version>1.1</version>
    <description>
        This AIR application provides code samples from the Flex 4 Cookbook
        from O'Reilly.
    </description>
    <copyright>2010 O'Reilly, Inc.</copyright>

    <initialWindow>
        <content>Flex4Cookbook.swf</content>
        <systemChrome>standard</systemChrome>
        <transparent>false</transparent>
        <visible>true</visible>
        <width>640</width>
        <height>480</height>
        <x>10</x>
        <y>10</y>
        <minSize>320 240</minSize>
        <maxSize>800 600</maxSize>
        <maximizable>true</maximizable>
        <minimizable>true</minimizable>
        <resizable>true</resizable>
    </initialWindow>

    <installFolder>OReilly</installFolder>
    <programMenuFolder>Flex 4 Cookbook</programMenuFolder>
```

```
<icon>
    <image16x16>icon/icon-16.png</image16x16>
    <image32x32>icon/icon-32.png</image32x32>
    <image48x48>icon/icon-48.png</image48x48>
    <image128x128>icon/icon-128.png</image128x128>
</icon>

</application>
```

18.13 Allow an AIR Application to Interact with the Browser

Problem

You need your application to be able to be launched from the browser.

Solution

Enable the application to interact with the AIR browser API by setting the `allowBrowserInvocation` option in the application descriptor file to `true`.

Discussion

The browser API allows an AIR application to interact with the browser through a SWF file. This enables the application to be launched from the browser. Because this opens up some level of access to the application from other AIR applications or from the browser and adds minimal overhead, the default setting of `allowBrowserInvocation` is `false`, so you will need to enable it to take advantage of this functionality.

To enable your AIR application to be launched from the browser, you modify the application descriptor file directly. For example:

```
<?xml version="1.0" encoding="utf-8" ?>
<application xmlns="http://ns.adobe.com/air/application/2.0">

    <id>com.oreilly.flex4cookbook</id>
    <filename>Flex4Cookbook</filename>
    <name>Flex 4 Cookbook</name>
    <version>1.1</version>
    <description>
        This AIR application provides code samples from the Flex 4 Cookbook
        from O'Reilly.
    </description>
    <copyright>2010 O'Reilly, Inc.</copyright>

    <initialWindow>
        <content>Flex4Cookbook.swf</content>
        <systemChrome>standard</systemChrome>
        <transparent>false</transparent>
        <visible>true</visible>
        <width>640</width>
        <height>480</height>
```

```
        <x>10</x>
        <y>10</y>
        <minSize>320 240</minSize>
        <maxSize>800 600</maxSize>
        <maximizable>true</maximizable>
        <minimizable>true</minimizable>
        <resizable>true</resizable>
    </initialWindow>

    <installFolder>OReilly</installFolder>
    <programMenuFolder>Flex 4 Cookbook</programMenuFolder>

    <icon>
        <image16x16>icon/icon-16.png</image16x16>
        <image32x32>icon/icon-32.png</image32x32>
        <image48x48>icon/icon-48.png</image48x48>
        <image128x128>icon/icon-128.png</image128x128>
    </icon>

    <allowBrowserInvocation>true</allowBrowserInvocation>

</application>
```

18.14 Set the Application to Handle All Updates

Problem

You need to ensure that users of your application always update to the newest version.

Solution

Set the customUpdateUI property of the application descriptor file to true.

Discussion

In many cases, it is advantageous to ensure that users do not accidentally downgrade to an older version of your application. In addition, you might need to take certain steps before the application is updated, such as backing up application data. In these cases, the customUpdateUI setting can be very useful.

When this property is set to true, AIR prevents the normal update process when a user clicks a packaged AIR file for an application that is already installed. Instead, AIR launches the existing application and dispatches an InvokeEvent to which it can respond. If the application is properly configured, it can ensure that the version the user has grabbed is the newest version and, if an update is required, check to see whether any last-minute maintenance is needed before the process begins.

This setting does not change the install process for an application that is not yet installed on the user's computer.

To allow an AIR application to intercept the usual update process, you need to edit the application descriptor file directly. For example:

```xml
<?xml version="1.0" encoding="utf-8" ?>
<application xmlns="http://ns.adobe.com/air/application/2.0">

    <id>com.oreilly.flex4cookbook</id>
    <filename>Flex4Cookbook</filename>
    <name>Flex 4 Cookbook</name>
    <version>1.1</version>
    <description>
        This AIR application provides code samples from the Flex 4 Cookbook
        from O'Reilly.
    </description>
    <copyright>2010 O'Reilly, Inc.</copyright>

    <initialWindow>
        <content>Flex4Cookbook.swf</content>
        <systemChrome>standard</systemChrome>
        <transparent>false</transparent>
        <visible>true</visible>
        <width>640</width>
        <height>480</height>
        <x>10</x>
        <y>10</y>
        <minSize>320 240</minSize>
        <maxSize>800 600</maxSize>
        <maximizable>true</maximizable>
        <minimizable>true</minimizable>
        <resizable>true</resizable>
    </initialWindow>

    <installFolder>OReilly</installFolder>
    <programMenuFolder>Flex 4 Cookbook</programMenuFolder>

    <icon>
        <image16x16>icon/icon-16.png</image16x16>
        <image32x32>icon/icon-32.png</image32x32>
        <image48x48>icon/icon-48.png</image48x48>
        <image128x128>icon/icon-128.png</image128x128>
    </icon>

    <allowBrowserInvocation>true</allowBrowserInvocation>
    <customUpdateUI>true</customUpdateUI>

</application>
```

See Also

Recipe 18.17

18.15 Determine the Application Version at Runtime

Problem

You need to determine the version of an application at runtime.

Solution

Extract the version number from the application's descriptor file at runtime.

Discussion

Often, you may need to know the version number of an application. For AIR applications, the application version is not exposed in a variable; rather, you must extract it from the application's descriptor file.

In ActionScript, the application descriptor file is exposed in the `NativeApplication.nativeApplication.applicationDescriptor` property. To extract the version number from your AIR application, you will need to first define the namespace in which the data is located. In this case, you can just use the first XML namespace and then extract the `version` property, as shown here:

```
private var airApplicationVersion:String = "";

private function getVersion():void
{
    // get the application descriptor file
    var appXML:XML = NativeApplication.nativeApplication.applicationDescriptor;
    // define the default AIR namespace
    var air:Namespace = appXML.namespaceDeclarations()[0];
    // use E4X to extract the application version
    this.airApplicationVersion = appXML.air::version;
}
```

18.16 Create Multilingual AIR Installations

Problem

You need to display language-specific text in the installation dialog box.

Solution

Add language-specific text in the application descriptor file for the appropriate basic `text` property used in the installation dialog box.

Discussion

Within the application descriptor file, you can define multiple translations for the
`name` and `description` nodes. In these cases, you can define child nodes that will include
the locale-specific text.

 AIR supports these languages: Brazilian, Czech, Dutch, English, French,
German, Italian, Japanese, Korean, Polish, Portuguese, Russian, Simplified Chinese, Spanish, Swedish, Traditional Chinese, and Turkish.

In the following example, the name and description are wrapped in a `text` tag and the
language is defined with the `xml:lang="en"` attribute. You can provide the name or
description in an alternate language by including another `text` tag with a different
standard country code and putting the needed text in that tag:

```
<?xml version="1.0" encoding="utf-8" ?>
<application xmlns="http://ns.adobe.com/air/application/2.0">

    <id>com.oreilly.flex4cookbook</id>
    <filename>Flex4Cookbook</filename>
    <name>
        <text xml:lang="en">Flex 4 Cookbook</text>
    </name>
    <version>1.1</version>
    <description>
        <text xml:lang="en">
            This AIR application provides code samples from the
            Flex 4 Cookbook from O'Reilly.
        </text>
    </description>
    <copyright>2010 O'Reilly, Inc.</copyright>

    <initialWindow>
        <content>Flex4Cookbook.swf</content>
        <systemChrome>standard</systemChrome>
        <transparent>false</transparent>
        <visible>true</visible>
        <width>640</width>
        <height>480</height>
        <x>10</x>
        <y>10</y>
        <minSize>320 240</minSize>
        <maxSize>800 600</maxSize>
        <maximizable>true</maximizable>
        <minimizable>true</minimizable>
        <resizable>true</resizable>
    </initialWindow>

    <installFolder>OReilly</installFolder>
    <programMenuFolder>Flex 4 Cookbook</programMenuFolder>
```

```
<icon>
    <image16x16>icon/icon-16.png</image16x16>
    <image32x32>icon/icon-32.png</image32x32>
    <image48x48>icon/icon-48.png</image48x48>
    <image128x128>icon/icon-128.png</image128x128>
</icon>

<allowBrowserInvocation>true</allowBrowserInvocation>
<customUpdateUI>true</customUpdateUI>

</application>
```

To add localization information in an AIR application, you will need to edit your application descriptor file as demonstrated previously.

18.17 Create Applications with Update Capabilities

Problem

You are creating an AIR application that you plan to distribute. You already have plans for the next version and would like to be able to get your users on the new version as soon as possible.

Solution

Use the Adobe AIR Update Framework library, which makes it easier for your applications to handle the various update scenarios that may arise.

Discussion

In the past, when bug fixes or enhancements were needed, developers working on Internet-based applications have enjoyed the ability to quickly update applications running on their servers. This model changes when developing applications for the desktop via Adobe AIR, as updates need to be distributed to the complete user base.

To avoid the possibility of having applications in the wild with no way to "phone home" to get updates, it is imperative that you include update procedures in your application before you ever allow it to be distributed.

The Adobe AIR Update Framework offers you all the functionality you need to be able to create AIR applications that can remotely update themselves. The Update Framework requires a XML file that holds information about application versioning and where the update files are available. This file is accessed whenever a request to check for an update is made. Consider the following example, called *update.xml*:

```
<?xml version="1.0" encoding="utf-8"?>
<update xmlns="http://ns.adobe.com/air/framework/update/description/1.0">
    <version>1.1</version>
    <url>http://mydomain.com/air/myapplication.air</url>
```

```
    <description><![CDATA[Various Bug Fixes ]]></description>
</update>
```

The properties of this file are:

version

The newest version available

url

The download URL for the AIR package

description

Additional text to provide the user with a description of what the update contains

You can also provide language-specific descriptions by adding a text subnode to the description node. For example:

```
<description>
    <text xml:lang="en">English description</text>
    <text xml:lang="it">Italian description</text>
</description>
```

A second, optional XML configuration file can be used to set additional configuration properties. Although you can set these properties manually on the Application UpdaterUI class, the best practice is to include a XML file within your application distribution. The *updaterConfig.xml* shown here is a good example of such a file:

```
<?xml version="1.0" encoding="utf-8"?>
<configuration xmlns="http://ns.adobe.com/air/framework/update/configuration/1.0">
    <url>http://mydomain.com/myairapp/update.xml</url>
    <delay>1</delay>
    <defaultUI>
        <dialog name="checkForUpdate" visible="true" />
        <dialog name="downloadUpdate" visible="true" />
        <dialog name="downloadProgress" visible="true" />
        <dialog name="installUpdate" visible="true" />
    </defaultUI>
</configuration>
```

The properties of this file are:

url

Specifies the path to the *update.xml* file (the example XML file mentioned earlier).

delay

Specifies the interval at which the Update Framework will check to see if updates are available. This is configured in days, so a value of 1 would represent one day and a value of .04 would be about one hour.

defaultUI

The dialog subnodes within the defaultUI node allow you to show or hide specific sections of the Update Framework user interface. By default, all sections are displayed.

Because you will be using the built-in updater interface of the `ApplicationUpdaterUI` class, you need to make sure that you have the *applicationupdater_ui.swc* file linked to your project.

To use this updater class, create an instance of `ApplicationUpdaterUI`, set the path to the *updaterConfig.xml* file, and initialize the updater. The upcoming example shows how to do this.

Upon initialization, you can check several properties of the updater by listening for the `UpdateEvent.INITIALIZED` event. These properties include:

isFirstRun
> This will be `true` only if an update has just occurred.

previousVersion
> This will have a value only if `isFirstRun` was `true`.

currentVersion
> This will always contain the version information of the currently running application.

Because *updaterConfig.xml* sets the delay to `1`, the updater will not automatically check for a new version until the application has been open for a full day. So, the updater also provides a way for you to manually check for updates by calling the `checkNow()` method.

The `ApplicationUpdaterUI` will handle all of the functionality of the update process. For information on how to create your own updater with a custom interface, see Recipe 18.18.

The following example sets the path to the configuration file, adds an event listener to listen for the `UpdateEvent.INITIALIZED` event, and then initializes the updater on the `applicationComplete` event of the application when the `init()` function is called. Finally, when the `updaterInitialized()` method is called, the event's properties are displayed on the screen.

 You must include *applicationupdater_ui.swc* (if you are compiling to Halo) or *applicationupdater_ui4.swc* (if you are compiling to Spark) in your Flex build path. You can find these files in the */frameworks/libs/ air* folder of the AIR SDK.

Here's the complete example code:

```
<?xml version="1.0" encoding="utf-8"?>
<s:WindowedApplication xmlns:fx="http://ns.adobe.com/mxml/2009"
                       xmlns:s="library://ns.adobe.com/flex/spark"
                       xmlns:mx="library://ns.adobe.com/flex/halo"
                       applicationComplete="init()">
    <fx:Declarations>
        <!-- Place nonvisual elements (e.g., services, value objects) here -->
    </fx:Declarations>
```

```
<fx:Script>
<![CDATA[
    import air.update.ApplicationUpdaterUI;
    import air.update.events.UpdateEvent;

    private var updater:ApplicationUpdaterUI = new ApplicationUpdaterUI();

    private function init():void {
        updater.configurationFile = new File("app:/config/updaterConfig.xml");
        updater.addEventListener(UpdateEvent.INITIALIZED, updaterInitialized);
        updater.initialize();
    }

    private function updaterInitialized(event:UpdateEvent):void {
        isFirstRun.text = event.target.isFirstRun;
        previousVersion.text = event.target.previousVersion;
        currentVersion.text = event.target.currentVersion;
    }

]]>
</fx:Script>

<s:Group width="300" height="200" horizontalCenter="0" verticalCenter="0">
    <s:layout>
        <s:BasicLayout/>
    </s:layout>

    <s:Label text="isFirstRun:" x="80" y="45"/>
    <s:Label id="isFirstRun" x="180" y="45"/>
    <s:Label text="previousVersion:" x="78" y="75"/>
    <s:Label id="previousVersion" x="180" y="75"/>
    <s:Label text="currentVersion:" x="78" y="105"/>
    <s:Label id="currentVersion" x="180" y="105"/>
    <s:Button click="updater.checkNow();" label="Check for Update"
              x="88" y="135"/>

</s:Group>

</s:WindowedApplication>
```

In this recipe, the default `ApplicationUpdaterUI` was used. Figures 18-11 through 18-14 show the phases of this user interface.

See Also

Recipes 18.14 and 18.18

Figure 18-11. Default "Check for updates" window

Figure 18-12. "Update available" window with "Release notes" expanded

Figure 18-13. "Download progress" dialog

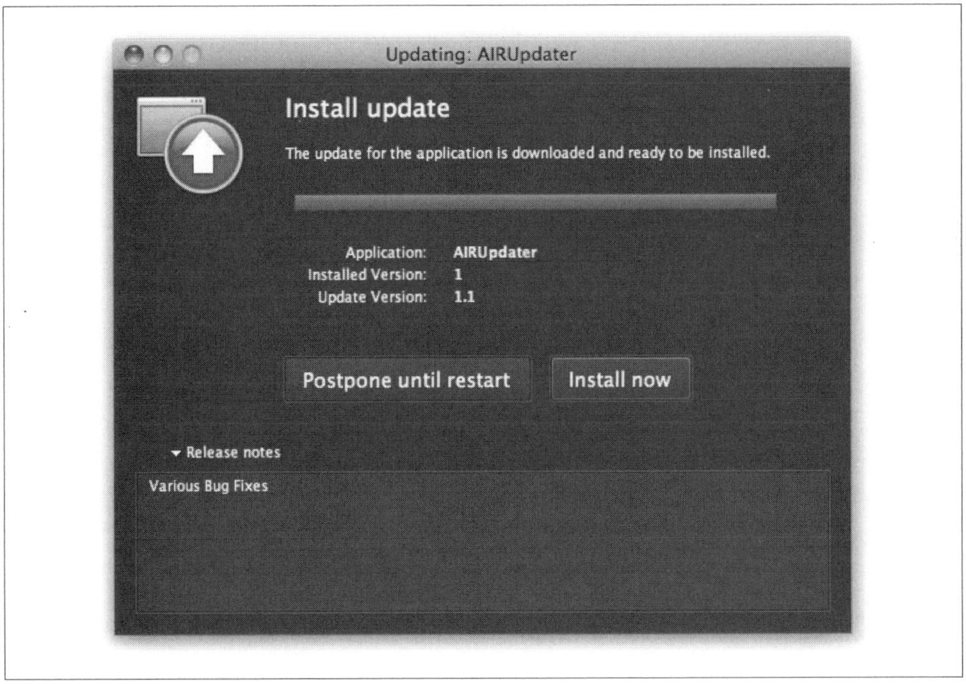

Figure 18-14. Download completed, ready to install

18.18 Create Applications with Update Capabilities with a Custom Interface

Problem

You would like to use the Update Framework for Adobe AIR; however, your client requires specific information to appear in the updater dialog.

Solution

Use the Adobe AIR Update Framework's *applicationupdater.swc* and *applicationupdater.swf* files, which do not include a user interface for the updater dialog.

Discussion

Recipe 18.17 showed an example of using the Adobe AIR Update Framework with the built-in dialog screens. By following the steps and listening for additional events described in this recipe, you can use the `ApplicationUpdater` to build your own update dialogs.

As mentioned in Recipe 18.17, you can configure the Update Framework in two ways. Recipe 18.17 used a XML file (*updaterConfig.xml*) that included information about delay timing, the update URL path, and user interface settings. This recipe will show how to configure the updater through direct property settings.

To build a custom experience, the examples will rely on events being broadcast from the `ApplicationUpdater` class. Here are the relevant events and their properties:

`UpdateEvent.INITIALIZED`
> This event has the following properties:

> `isFirstRun`
>> This will be `true` only if an update has just occurred.

> `previousVersion`
>> This will have a value only if `isFirstRun` was `true`.

> `currentVersion`
>> This will always contain the version information of the currently running application.

`StatusUpdateEvent.UPDATE_STATUS`
> This event has the following properties:

> `available`
>> This will be `true` if the `version` property value in the *update.xml* file does not match the version of the running application.

> `version`
>> This will hold the value of the `version` property in the *update.xml* file.

details

> This will hold the value of the `details` property in the *update.xml* file.

StatusUpdateErrorEvent.UPDATE_ERROR

> This event has no properties and will be dispatched only when an error occurs while trying to read the *update.xml* file.

UpdateEvent.DOWNLOAD_START

> This event has no properties; it will fire when the download starts.

ProgressEvent.PROGRESS

> This event is the standard `ProgressEvent` that contains the standard `bytesLoaded` and `bytesTotal` that you would use to display progress on any upload or download.

UpdateEvent.DOWNLOAD_COMPLETE

> This event is dispatched after the download has completed and has no properties. After the download completes, the default behavior is to automatically start the install process. This event will allow you to stop this automatic install.

DownloadErrorEvent.DOWNLOAD_ERROR

> This event has one property:

> subErrorID

>> This is broadcast when an error occurs during the download of the new AIR file. It also contains the standard errors of its parent, the `ErrorEvent` class.

> This is not a complete list of the events available for the Update Framework, but it does include all the ones that are necessary to create a custom updater interface in the examples that follow.

The example consists of two files: the main `WindowedApplication` file and a `Window` component that acts as the user interface for the update process. This `Window` component will be referred to as the `UpdateWindow` throughout the rest of this recipe. The main application window simply contains a single `Button` component that, when clicked, launches a new window. The code for the main application window follows:

```
<?xml version="1.0" encoding="utf-8"?>
<s:WindowedApplication xmlns:fx="http://ns.adobe.com/mxml/2009"
                       xmlns:s="library://ns.adobe.com/flex/spark"
                       xmlns:mx="library://ns.adobe.com/flex/halo">
    <fx:Declarations>
        <!-- Place nonvisual elements (e.g., services, value objects) here -->
    </fx:Declarations>
    <fx:Script>
        <![CDATA[
            private function openUpdateWindow():void {
                var updateWindow:UpdateWindow = new UpdateWindow();
                updateWindow.open();
            }
        ]]>
    </fx:Script>
```

```
<s:Button click="openUpdateWindow()" label="Open Update Window"
          horizontalCenter="0" verticalCenter="0"/>

   </s:WindowedApplication>
```

The `UpdateWindow` is the guts of this example, as it contains all of the methods and event listeners to handle each step of the update process. This file contains five different states that contain the controls and feedback required to give the user full control over the update.

Upon `CreationComplete` of the window, the `init()` method is called. This method creates a new instance of the `ApplicationUpdater` class, sets the `delay` property of the updater to `0`, sets the updater's `updateURL`, adds six different event listeners, and then calls the `initialize()` method on the new instance of `ApplicationUpdater`.

The `UpdateWindow` defaults to the `Main` state, which shows the user information about the currently installed application, including the updater's `isFirstRun`, `previousVersion`, and `currentVersion` properties. It also contains a `Button` component, which allows the user to check to see if an update is available.

Because the delay was set to `0` in this example, the updater will never automatically check for an update. When the user clicks the "Check for Update" button, the updater's `checkNow()` method is called and the `UpdateWindow` shows updater's first run and current version properties (Figure 18-15).

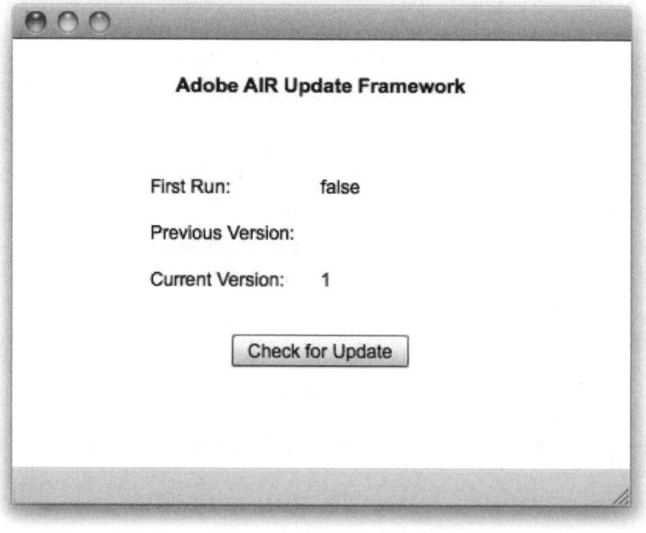

Figure 18-15. Custom "Check for Update" window

The checkNow() method dispatches the StatusUpdateEvent.UPDATE_STATUS event, which then calls the statusUpdate() method. If the available property of this event is true, the state of the UpdateWindow is set to Available. If there is no update available, the state is set to None and the user is shown a message stating this.

If an update is available and the user is now seeing the Available state, information about the update is displayed and the user is given the option to cancel or download the update (Figure 18-16).

Figure 18-16. Custom update available window showing release notes

If the user clicks the Download Now button, the downloadUpdate() method is called on the ApplicationUpdater. The ApplicationUpdater will now attempt to download the new AIR file from the URL that has been supplied in the *update.xml* file. If the ApplicationUpdater is able to begin the download, the UpdateEvent.DOWNLOAD_START event is dispatched and the downloadStarted() method is called, which changes the UpdateWindow to the Downloading state. If the ApplicationUpdater cannot begin the download, the DownloadErrorEvent.DOWNLOAD_ERROR event is dispatched, which calls the downloadError() method. The downloadError() method simply alerts the user that a problem occurred when attempting the download.

Assuming that the download has started correctly, the ProgressEvent.PROGRESS event begins to be dispatched as the file is downloading. This event calls the download Progress() method, which updates a progress bar that is part of the Downloading state (Figure 18-17).

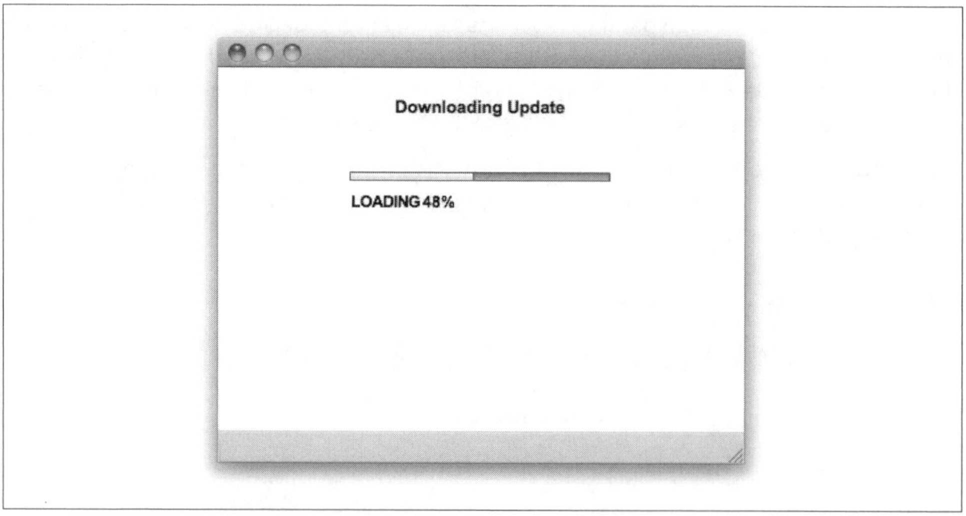

Figure 18-17. Download progress

Upon completion of the download, the `UpdateEvent.DOWNLOAD_COMPLETE` event is dispatched, which calls the `downloadComplete()` method. If this event is ignored, the `ApplicationUpdater` will automatically begin the installation of the new AIR application. In this example, the `preventDefault()` method is called on the `UpdateEvent` and the state of the `UpdateWindow` is set to `InstallNow`. The `preventDefault()` method halts the automatic install by the `ApplicationUpdater`. In Figure 18-18, the `UpdateWindow` asks the user whether to install the update.

Figure 18-18. Download complete, install now?

The `InstallNow` state gives the user the option to cancel or install the update. If the user chooses to install the update, the `installUpdate()` method is called on the `ApplicationUpdater`. At this time the application will close, install the new AIR application, and relaunch. Upon relaunch, if the user launches the `UpdateWindow`, the `isFirstRun` property will show as `true` and the new version information will be displayed (Figure 18-19).

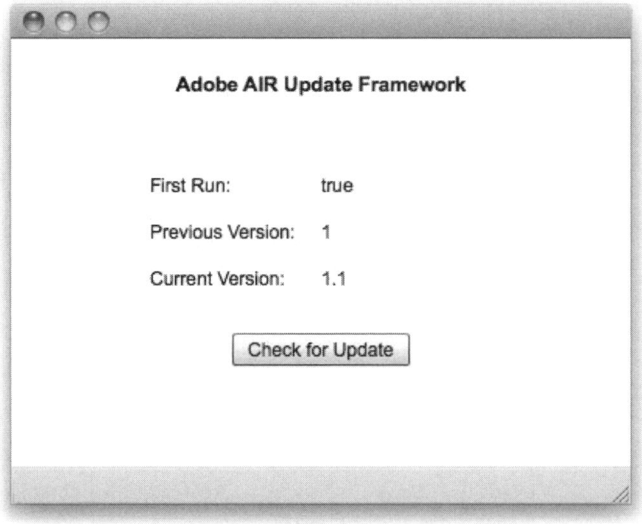

Figure 18-19. First run after update showing application properties

The full source code for the `UpdateWindow` is shown here:

```
<?xml version="1.0" encoding="utf-8"?>
<s:Window xmlns:fx="http://ns.adobe.com/mxml/2009"
        xmlns:s="library://ns.adobe.com/flex/spark"
        xmlns:mx="library://ns.adobe.com/flex/halo"
        width="400" height="300" currentState="main"
        creationComplete="init()">
    <s:states>
        <s:State name="main"/>
        <s:State name="available"/>
        <s:State name="downloading"/>
        <s:State name="none"/>
        <s:State name="installnow"/>
    </s:states>
    <fx:Declarations>
        <!-- Place nonvisual elements (e.g., services, value objects) here -->
    </fx:Declarations>
    <fx:Script>
        <![CDATA[
            import mx.controls.Alert;
```

```
import air.update.events.StatusUpdateErrorEvent;
import air.update.events.StatusUpdateEvent;
import air.update.events.DownloadErrorEvent;
import air.update.events.UpdateEvent;
import air.update.ApplicationUpdater;

public var updater:ApplicationUpdater;

private function init():void {
    updater = new ApplicationUpdater();
    updater.delay = 0;
    updater.updateURL = "http://mydomain.com/myairapp/update.xml";
    updater.addEventListener(UpdateEvent.INITIALIZED,
                            updaterInitialized);
    updater.addEventListener(StatusUpdateEvent.UPDATE_STATUS,
                            statusUpdate);
    updater.addEventListener(StatusUpdateErrorEvent.UPDATE_ERROR,
                            statusUpdateError);
    updater.addEventListener(UpdateEvent.DOWNLOAD_START,
                            downloadStarted);
    updater.addEventListener(ProgressEvent.PROGRESS,
                            downloadProgress);
    updater.addEventListener(UpdateEvent.DOWNLOAD_COMPLETE,
                            downloadComplete);
    updater.addEventListener(DownloadErrorEvent.DOWNLOAD_ERROR,
                            downloadError);
    updater.initialize();
}

private function updaterInitialized(event:UpdateEvent):void {
    isFirstRun.text = event.target.isFirstRun;
    previousVersion.text = event.target.previousVersion;
    currentVersion.text = event.target.currentVersion;
}


private function statusUpdate(event:StatusUpdateEvent):void {
    event.preventDefault();
    if(event.available) {
        currentState="available";
        version.text =  event.version;
        details.text = String(event.details);
    } else {
        currentState="none";
    }
}


private function statusUpdateError(event:StatusUpdateErrorEvent):void {
    currentState="";
    Alert.show("An error has occurred while checking for updates",
                "StatusUpdateEvent.UPDATE_STATUS");
    close();
}
```

```
            private function downloadStarted(event:UpdateEvent):void {
                currentState="downloading";
            }

            private function downloadError(event:DownloadErrorEvent):void {
                currentState="main";
                Alert.show("An error has occurred while downloading the update",
                          "DownloadErrorEvent.DOWNLOAD_ERROR");
                close();
            }

            private function downloadProgress(event:ProgressEvent):void {
                dBar.setProgress(event.bytesLoaded, event.bytesTotal);
            }

            private function downloadComplete(event:UpdateEvent):void {
                event.preventDefault();
                currentState="installnow";
            }

        ]]>
</fx:Script>
<s:Label y="24"
         text.main="Adobe AIR Update Framework"
         text.available="There is an update available"
         text.none="You already have the most current version"
         text.installnow="Would you like to install the update now?"
         text.downloading="Downloading Update"
         horizontalCenter="0" width="100%"
         textAlign="center" fontWeight="bold" fontSize="13"
         id="mainTitle"
         includeIn="main,available,none,installnow,downloading"/>

<s:Label x="90" y="90" text="First Run:" includeIn="main"/>
<s:Label x="90" y="120" text="Previous Version:" includeIn="main"/>
<s:Label x="90" y="150" text="Current Version:" includeIn="main"/>
<s:Label x="200" y="90" id="isFirstRun" includeIn="main"/>
<s:Label x="200" y="120" id="previousVersion" includeIn="main"/>
<s:Label x="200" y="150" id="currentVersion" includeIn="main"/>

<s:Button y="190"
          label.main="Check for Update"
          label.available="Download Now"
          label.installnow="Install Now"
          horizontalCenter="0"
          click.main="updater.checkNow()"
          click.available="updater.downloadUpdate()"
          click.installnow="updater.installUpdate()"
          includeIn="main,available,installnow"
          y.installnow="64"
          horizontalCenter.installnow="0"/>

<mx:ProgressBar horizontalCenter="0" y="78" id="dBar" mode="manual"
                includeIn="downloading"/>
```

```
<s:Button label="Close" click="close();"
          y="223" horizontalCenter="0"
          includeIn="available,installnow,none"
          y.none="56" horizontalCenter.none="0" y.installnow="97"
          horizontalCenter.installnow="0"/>

<s:Label id="version" x="181.5" y="64" includeIn="available"/>
<s:Label x="98.5" y="64" text="New version:" includeIn="available"/>
<s:Label x="98" y="90" text="Details:" includeIn="available"/>
<s:TextArea x="181" y="89" id="details" width="175"
            height="76" editable="false" includeIn="available"/>

</s:Window>
```

18.19 Package an Application in a Native Installer (.exe, .dmg, .rpm)

Problem

You would like to package your AIR application into a native installer so that your audience can install it just as they do other native applications.

Solution

Using AIR 2.0's new functionality, you can compile your application into a native operating system installer file.

Discussion

Using the AIR 2.0 SDK, you can compile your application to a native installer file for Windows (*.exe*), Mac OS X (*.dmg*), or Linux (*.rpm*). Using a native installer allows your application to interact with and run native operating system code (such as C code). Although you certainly get many benefits when you compile to a native executable that you wouldn't get with a standard AIR application, you also have more work to do, as each executable needs to be compiled on the operating system to which it will be deployed.

To package an application within a native installer, first create a new AIR application called AIRSample and add to it a Label component with the text "Hello World," as shown here:

```
<?xml version="1.0" encoding="utf-8"?>
<s:WindowedApplication xmlns:fx="http://ns.adobe.com/mxml/2009"
                       xmlns:s="library://ns.adobe.com/flex/spark"
                       xmlns:mx="library://ns.adobe.com/flex/halo">
    <fx:Declarations>
        <!-- Place nonvisual elements (e.g., services, value objects) here -->
    </fx:Declarations>
```

```
    <s:Label text="Hello World" horizontalCenter="0"
            verticalCenter="0" fontSize="48"/>
</s:WindowedApplication>
```

Next, update the *AIRSample-app.xml* file to include the following node right below the `id` node. This configuration entry will allow your application to make calls to native code that you include within your application (for more information on this functionality, see Recipe 18.20):

```
<supportedProfiles>extendedDesktop desktop</supportedProfiles>
```

Next, export your application to an AIR file.

Now that you have a compiled file called *AIRSample.air*, you can package it up into a native operating system installer file for use on Microsoft Windows, Mac OS X, or Linux. Just be sure you have the AIR SDK within your class path, and remember that you can compile an application only to the native installer of the operating system in which you are currently working. For example, if you are working on Windows, you can only compile to *.exe*. The following example commands assume the *AIRSample.air* file is located within a folder called *AIRSamples* at the root of the filesystem:

Mac OS X

```
adt -package -target native /AIRSamples/AIRSample.dmg
/AIRSamples/AIRSample.air
```

Linux (rpm)

```
adt -package -target native /AIRSamples/AIRSample.rpm
/AIRSamples/AIRSample.air
```

Linux (deb)

```
adt -package -target native /AIRSamples/AIRSample.deb
/AIRSamples/AIRSample.air
```

Windows

```
adt -package -target native C:\AIRSamples\AIRSample.exe
C:\AIRSamples\AIRSample.air
```

See Also

Recipes 18.2 and 18.20

18.20 Include Native Code Within Your AIR Application

Problem

You would like to use some native operating system code within your AIR application.

Solution

Use AIR 2.0's new `flash.desktop.NativeProcess` class to interact directly with native operating system processes.

Discussion

This recipe demonstrates how to create an application that interacts with a `NativeProcess` and then package up the application using *adt* with the AIR 2.0 SDK. (Thanks to John Barlow for his assistance in getting me on the right track to do the C programming in this example.)

Here is the C code to be called from the AIR application:

```
#include <stdio.h>

int main (int argc, const char * argv[]) {
    printf("Hello from ");
    printf(argv[1]);
    printf("\n\n");
    if(argc > 1) {
        printf("You passed in the following arguments:\n");
        int i;
        for(i=1; i<argc; i++) {
            printf("\n");
            printf(argv[i]);
        }
    }
    printf("\n");
    return 0;
}
```

This code will output "`Hello from` " followed by the first argument passed in, which will be the operating system name, and then "`You passed in the following arguments:`". This intro is followed by a list of all the arguments passed in from AIR. The following example commands illustrate how to run the application directly from the command line (assuming you are already in the directory that contains the executable):

```
sample 'Mac OS X' 'argument 1' 'argument 2' 'argument 3';

sample.exe "Windows XP" "argument 1" "argument 2" "argument 3"

sample 'Linux ...' 'argument 1' 'argument 2' 'argument 3';
```

Figure 18-20 shows the results on Windows XP.

The first thing that is necessary for the AIR code is an update to the configuration XML file. You must add the following XML node to allow your AIR application to access native operating system applications:

```
<supportedProfiles>extendedDesktop desktop</supportedProfiles>
```

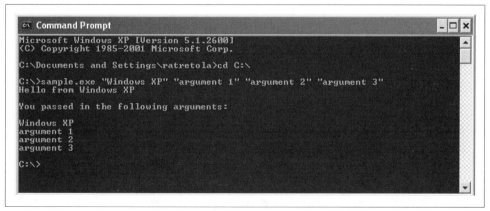

Figure 18-20. The executable running within a Windows XP command prompt

Upon the `applicationComplete` event of the AIR application, the `init()` method is called as defined within the `s:WindowedApplication`. This function uses the `NativeProcess` class to test if native processes are supported. If they are, the `callButton` component is enabled; if not, a message is displayed to the user.

Assuming native processes are supported, the user can then enter up to three arguments to be passed to the native application by filling in the `TextInput` components. To send them to the native application, the user clicks the `callButton`, which calls the `callNativeApp()` method.

Within the `callNativeApp()` method, the path to the `NativeApps` directory is resolved. Then, depending on which operating system is currently being used, the `file` property is set to either `Windows/sample.exe`, `Mac/sample`, or `Linux/sample`. Next, a variable called `nativeProcessStartupInfo` of type `flash.desktop.NativeProcessStartupInfo` is created. The `nativeProcessStartupInfo`'s `executable` property is set to the file variable that was previously resolved. Next, a variable named `args` of type `Vector.<String>` is created and the operating system version is added, using the `Capabilities.os` property. The text values from the `TextInput` components are then pushed onto the `args` vector, which is assigned to the `nativeProcessStartupInfo`'s `arguments` property. Next, the `process` class variable (of type `flash.desktop.NativeProcess`) is initialized, and an event listener listening for `ProgressEvent.STANDARD_OUTPUT_DATA` is added. Finally, the process's `start()` method is called on the `nativeProcessStartupInfo` and the `closeInput()` method is called:

```
<?xml version="1.0" encoding="utf-8"?>
<s:WindowedApplication xmlns:fx="http://ns.adobe.com/mxml/2009"
                       xmlns:s="library://ns.adobe.com/flex/spark"
                       xmlns:mx="library://ns.adobe.com/flex/halo"
                       applicationComplete="init()">
    <fx:Script>
        <![CDATA[
            private var process:NativeProcess;
```

```
                private function init():void {
                    if(NativeProcess.isSupported) {
                        callButton.enabled = true;
                    } else {
                        textReceived.text = "NativeProcess not supported.";
                    }
                }

                private function callNativeApp():void {
                    var file:File = File.applicationDirectory;
                    file = file.resolvePath("NativeApps");
                    if (Capabilities.os.toLowerCase().indexOf("win") > -1) {
                        file = file.resolvePath("Windows/sample.exe");
                    } else if(Capabilities.os.toLowerCase().indexOf("mac") > -1) {
                        file = file.resolvePath("Mac/sample");
                    } else if(Capabilities.os.toLowerCase().indexOf("linux") > -1) {
                        file = file.resolvePath("Linux/sample");
                    }

                    var nativeProcessStartupInfo:NativeProcessStartupInfo =
                            new NativeProcessStartupInfo();
                    nativeProcessStartupInfo.executable = file;
                    var v:Vector.<String> = new Vector.<String>();
                    v.push(Capabilities.os);
                    v.push(arg1.text);
                    v.push(arg2.text);
                    v.push(arg3.text);
                    nativeProcessStartupInfo.arguments = v;
                    process = new NativeProcess();
                    process.addEventListener(ProgressEvent.STANDARD_OUTPUT_DATA,
                                        onStandardOutputData);
                    process.start(nativeProcessStartupInfo);
                    process.closeInput();
                }

                private function onStandardOutputData(event:ProgressEvent):void {
                    textReceived.text = process.standardOutput.readUTFBytes(
                                        process.standardOutput.bytesAvailable );
                }


        ]]>
    </fx:Script>

    <s:Group horizontalCenter="0" verticalCenter="0">
        <s:layout>
            <s:VerticalLayout/>
        </s:layout>
        <s:Label text="Enter a few values and then click the button:"/>
        <s:Label text="Argument 1:"/><s:TextInput id="arg1"/>
        <s:Label text="Argument 2:"/><s:TextInput id="arg2"/>
        <s:Label text="Argument 3:"/><s:TextInput id="arg3"/>
        <s:Button id="callButton" label="Call Native App"
                click="callNativeApp()" enabled="false"/>
        <s:Label id="textReceived"/>
```

```
            </s:Group>
        </s:WindowedApplication>
```

You have two options for packaging the application for distribution as a native installer. The first is to compile the AIR file from within Flash Builder using the Export→Release Build method and then package that AIR file into a native installer, using the appropriate command:

```
adt -package -target native NativeSample.dmg NativeSample.air

adt -package -target native NativeSample.exe NativeSample.air

adt -package -target native NativeSample.rpm NativeSample.air

adt -package -target native NativeSample.deb NativeSample.air
```

The second is to bypass the step of creating the AIR file and to use *adt* to package up the raw SWF. In the following examples, assume the commands are being run from a directory containing the *NativeSample-app.xml* and *NativeSample.exe* files as well as the executables within the directory structures *NativeApps/Mac*, *NativeApps/Windows*, and *NativeApps/Linux*:

```
adt -package -storetype pkcs12 -keystore cert.p12 -target native NativeSample.dmg
NativeSample-app.xml NativeSample.swf NativeApps/Mac/sample

adt -package -storetype pkcs12 -keystore cert.p12 -target native NativeSample.exe
NativeSample-app.xml NativeSample.swf NativeApps/Windows/sample.exe

adt -package -storetype pkcs12 -keystore cert.p12 -target native NativeSample.rpm
NativeSample-app.xml NativeSample.swf NativeApps/Linux/sample

adt -package -storetype pkcs12 -keystore cert.p12 -target native NativeSample.deb
NativeSample-app.xml NativeSample.swf NativeApps/Linux/sample
```

Congratulations! You have now created an AIR application that includes native operating system executables for Windows, Mac OS X, and Linux. With this new capability, the possibilities of what type of application you can build with AIR 2.0 are truly limitless.

CHAPTER 19

Working with Data in AIR

To many Flex developers who are new to AIR, some of its functionality may appear foreign. Because of this, developers will sometimes create applications that don't take full advantage of the powerful capabilities AIR provides. Prime examples are AIR's capabilities for storing and working with local data.

The first area of functionality that deals with storing and working with local data is the *Encrypted Local Store*. This provides secure key/value local storage of binary data. The data can only be accessed by your AIR application.

The second area is the *embedded data support with SQLite* in AIR. This provides full relational database support directly on the user's computer. This allows the developer to store and retrieve almost any type of data using SQL queries.

The final area is the *local filesystem support*. AIR gives you full access to the local filesystem, including the ability to create, delete, copy, and edit files and folders on the user's computer.

By learning to work with these three key features of the AIR API, you can take full advantage of the power AIR provides.

19.1 Safeguard Files with the Encrypted Local Store

Contributed by Ryan Stewart

Problem

You need to protect entire files inside an AIR application.

Solution

Use the Encrypted Local Store and the file APIs to put a file in a safe and secure location.

Discussion

Most people associate the Encrypted Local Store with storing usernames and passwords or other bits of text. In reality, the Encrypted Local Store can store any piece of binary data with the `ByteArray` class, so it's easy to throw any type of data in there. In the following example, the application stores the binary data from a user-selected file into the Encrypted Local Store.

 The Encrypted Local Store supports storage of up to 10 MB of data. It can go higher, but you may see performance problems. In addition, the Encrypted Local Store isn't cleared out automatically when the application is uninstalled; you may have to manually clear it out using the `EncryptedLocalStore.reset()` method.

In the following example, there are two methods that handle the interaction with the `EncryptedLocalStore` class: `saveFile()` and `loadFile()`. Both of these methods are event handlers for the `Event.SELECT` event that is dispatched when the user either selects a file to store in the Encrypted Local Store or selects a location to save the file to the Encrypted Local Store accordingly.

The `saveFile()` function retrieves the instance of the `File` class by getting the `target` property of the `SELECT` event. Next, it creates an instance of the `FileStream` class that will be used to stream the bytes from the file into a `ByteArray`. Next, the filename is stored because it will be used as the key for the Encrypted Local Store. Finally, the value is stored in the Encrypted Local Store and the `resultLabel` is populated to inform the user that the process has completed.

The next function is the `loadFile()` function. It retrieves the instance of the `File` class by getting the `target` property of the event and creates an instance of the `ByteArray` class to store the data that will be loaded from the Encrypted Local Store. Next, the data is loaded from the Encrypted Local Store into the `ByteArray`. Finally, the instance of the `FileStream` class is used to stream the `ByteArray` into the instance of the `File` class and the `resultLabel` is populated to inform the user that the process has completed. This code demonstrates the use of both functions:

```
<s:WindowedApplication xmlns:fx="http://ns.adobe.com/mxml/2009"
                       xmlns:mx="library://ns.adobe.com/flex/mx"
                       xmlns:s="library://ns.adobe.com/flex/spark">

    <fx:Script>
        <![CDATA[
            import flash.events.Event;
            import flash.events.MouseEvent;
            import flash.utils.ByteArray;

            protected var fileName:String = "";
```

```actionscript
protected function loadButton_clickHandler( event:MouseEvent ):void
{
    resultLabel.text = "";

    var file:File = File.desktopDirectory.resolvePath( fileName );
    file.addEventListener( Event.SELECT, loadFile );
    file.browseForSave( "Load File From Encrypted Local Store" );
}

protected function loadFile( event:Event ):void
{
    var file:File = File( event.target );
    var fileData:ByteArray = new ByteArray();
    fileData = EncryptedLocalStore.getItem( fileName );

    var stream:FileStream = new FileStream();
    stream.open( file, FileMode.WRITE );
    stream.writeBytes( fileData );
    stream.close();

    resultLabel.text = "File Loaded from Encrypted Local Store";
}

protected function saveButton_clickHandler( event:MouseEvent ):void
{
    resultLabel.text = "";

    EncryptedLocalStore.reset();

    var file:File = File.documentsDirectory;
    file.browseForOpen( "Save File Into Encrypted Local Store" );
    file.addEventListener( Event.SELECT, saveFile );
}

protected function saveFile( event:Event ):void
{
    var file:File = File( event.target );
    var stream:FileStream = new FileStream();

    var fileData:ByteArray = new ByteArray();
    stream.open( file, FileMode.READ );
    stream.readBytes( fileData, 0, file.size );
    stream.close();
    fileName = file.name;

    EncryptedLocalStore.setItem( fileName, fileData );

    resultLabel.text = "File Saved To Encrypted Local Store";
}
        ]]>
    </fx:Script>
```

```
<s:layout>
    <s:VerticalLayout horizontalAlign="center"
                      paddingBottom="10"
                      paddingLeft="10"
                      paddingRight="10"
                      paddingTop="10" />
</s:layout>

<s:Button id="saveButton"
          label="Save File Into Encrypted Local Store"
          click="saveButton_clickHandler( event );" />

<s:Button id="loadButton"
          label="Load File From Encrypted Local Store"
          click="loadButton_clickHandler( event );" />

<s:Label id="resultLabel" />

</s:WindowedApplication>
```

19.2 Migrate Serialization Changes

Contributed by Greg Jastrab

Problem

Your AIR application stores a custom `IExternalizable` class to disk, and a later update to the application adds new variables to the class that would cause a runtime error in your `readExternal()` method call if you tried to read them in.

Solution

Include a version marker in your serialization class so that you may parse the data according to the appropriate version that is stored.

Discussion

Assume you're writing an AIR application that stores historical weather data about a town. You've written the data object as a class implementing `IExternalizable` so that reading and writing the data is as simple as calling `readObject()` or `writeObject()`. Assume as well that the first version of the serialization class simply stores the date and the highest temperature recorded for that date:

```
public class WeatherData {
    public var date:Date;
    public var high:Number;
}
```

Poor serialization choice

Typically, the `readExternal()` and `writeExternal()` functions would be implemented in a straightforward manner:

```
function readExternal(input:IDataInput):void {
    date = input.readObject() as Date;
    high = input.readFloat();
}
function writeExternal(output:IDataOutput):void {
    output.writeObject(date);
    output.writeFloat(high);
}
```

This may seem fine, but what if you want to add the lowest recorded temperature for the day in a later version? You could add `low = input.readFloat()` to the `readExternal()` function, but because the data was written to disk without the `low` value, a runtime error would be raised when a user who had upgraded the application ran this function again.

Migratable serialization

To avoid this error, you should add a version marker to the beginning of the serialization, so the application knows which data scheme to use before reading data back:

```
public class WeatherData {
    namespace wd1_0 = "WD1.0";
    namespace wd1_1 = "WD1.1";

    protected var version:String;
    public var date:Date;
    public var low:Number;
    public var high:Number;

    public function WeatherData() {
        version = "WD1.1";
        date = new Date();
        low = high = 0;
    }
    public function readExternal(input:IDataInput):void {
        version = input.readUTF();
        var ns:Namespace = new Namespace(version);
        ns::parse(input);
    }
    public function writeExternal(output:IDataOutput):void {
        output.writeUTF(version);
        output.writeObject(date);
        output.writeFloat(low);
        output.writeFloat(high);
    }
    wd1_0 function parse(input:IDataInput):void {
        date = input.readObject() as Date;
        high = input.readFloat();
```

```
        }
        wd1_1 function parse(input:IDataInput):void {
            date = input.readObject() as Date;
            low = input.readFloat();
            high = input.readFloat();
        }
    }
```

This allows the class to be properly read if the user has run the initial version of the application that writes the WD1.0 version of the WeatherData and then runs an updated version for the first time with this as the WeatherData code.

Adding members in future versions

Whenever you need to add an additional field to the class, you need to follow these steps:

1. Add the variable to the class.
2. Modify writeExternal() to include that variable in the serialization.
3. Increment the version string in the constructor.
4. Add a namespace for this new version.
5. Add a parse function scoped to the namespace you just added and implement readExternal() to correspond with your updated writeExternal() method.

19.3 Create an In-Memory Database

Problem

You need to create an in-memory database without creating a local file.

Solution

Set the reference parameter of the open() and openAsync() methods to null to create an in-memory database.

Discussion

For a desktop application, it is often useful to be able to manage the data structurally by using a powerful language such as SQL, without having to save the data locally.

You can create an in-memory database by passing a null value to the reference parameter of either the synchronous open() method or the asynchronous openAsync() method. The temporary database will exist while your application is open, but it is not saved to disk; instead, it's deleted when your application closes.

The reference parameter is an Object that specifies the location of the database file that is being opened. Set it to null to create an in-memory database:

```
var _dbConn:SQLConnection = new SQLConnection();
_dbConn.openAsync(null);
```

19.4 Encrypt a Database with a Password

Problem

You need to encrypt a database based on a user's password. In addition, you need to allow the user to change his password and update the encryption accordingly.

Solution

Use the user's password as the basis for the encryption key, and use the `reencrypt()` method of the `SQLConnection` class to change the encryption key for a database.

Discussion

Although creating a random key may work for many situations, in some cases it is preferable to base the key on user input. This is ideal in situations where you are downloading password-protected data from an online service, for example, as it allows the same password that secures the data online to secure the data in the AIR application.

Because the `open()` and `openAsync()` methods of the `SQLConnection` class expect a 16-byte binary key, you will need to create a MD5 hash of the user's password by utilizing the AS3Crypto library. This creates the needed 16-byte `ByteArray` that can then be passed into the `open()` or `openAsync()` method.

When the user changes his password, the `reencrypt()` method of the `SQLConnection` class allows the application to change the encryption key for a specific database, as long as the database connection has already been opened with the old encryption key. Once this method has been called, a transaction-like process is executed. If the process is interrupted before completion, the database retains the old encryption key. If the process is completed successfully, a `SQLEvent.REENCRYPT` event is dispatched. If it fails, a `SQLError.ERROR` event is dispatched.

> Remember that a database that is not encrypted cannot be encrypted; its data must be imported into a new encrypted database.

In this example, the user must specify a password to connect to the database. If the database does not exist, a new database is created using the password hash as the encryption key. While the database is connected, the user can enter a new password and click the Change Password button. This triggers the `reencrypt()` method, which changes the encryption key for the database.

You will need to include the AS3Crypto library for this project, because it will be used to generate the random encryption key. Download the *as3crypto.swc* file from *http://code.google.com/p/as3crypto/* and add it to your project's build path.

To create the encryption key, the MD5 class from the AS3Crypto library is used along with the password entered by the user. The password, which is passed into the function as a string, is converted into a ByteArray by using the writeUTFBytes() method. Next, the MD5 class is instantiated, and the hash() method is called on the ByteArray. The returned value is used as the encryption key for the database:

```
private function createEncryptionKey(password:String):ByteArray {
    var ba:ByteArray = new ByteArray();
    ba.writeUTFBytes(password);
    var md5:MD5 = new MD5();
    var output:ByteArray = md5.hash(ba);
    return output;
}
```

To allow the changing of the password, the reencrypt() method of the SQLConnection class is used. This method must be called while the SQLConnection is open:

```
connection.addEventListener(SQLEvent.REENCRYPT, handleDatabaseReencrypt);
connection.reencrypt( createEncryptionKey(newPassword.text) );
```

The completed example, shown here, integrates all this functionality into a single AIR application:

```
<?xml version="1.0" encoding="utf-8"?>
<s:WindowedApplication xmlns:mx="http://www.adobe.com/2006/mxml"
                       xmlns:s= "library://ns.adobe.com/flex/spark"
                       xmlns:mx="library://ns.adobe.com/flex/halo"
                       horizontalAlign="left">
    <s:layout><s:HorizontalLayout/></s:layout>
    <fx:Script>
        <![CDATA[
            import flash.utils.ByteArray;
            import mx.collections.ArrayCollection;
            import com.hurlant.crypto.hash.MD5;

            public static const ENCRYPTED_DB_FILE:String = "encrypted.db";

            [Bindable]
            private var results:ArrayCollection = new ArrayCollection();

            private var connection:SQLConnection;
            private var dbFile:File;

            private function createEncryptionKey(password:String):ByteArray {
                var ba:ByteArray = new ByteArray();
                ba.writeUTFBytes(password);
                var md5:MD5 = new MD5();
                var output:ByteArray = md5.hash(ba);
                results.addItem("[ACTION]: Hash Key Created " +
                            output.toString());
                return output;
```

```
            }

            private function handleConnectClick(event:MouseEvent):void {
                results.addItem("[ACTION]: Attempting Database Connection");
                dbFile = File.applicationStorageDirectory.resolvePath(
                        ENCRYPTED_DB_FILE );
                connection = new SQLConnection();
                connection.addEventListener(SQLEvent.OPEN,
                                            handleDatabaseOpen);
                connection.addEventListener(SQLErrorEvent.ERROR,
                                            handleDatabaseError);
                connection.openAsync(dbFile,SQLMode.CREATE,null,false,1024,
                                    createEncryptionKey(password.text));
            }

            private function handleDisconnectClick(event:MouseEvent):void {
                connection.close();
                disconnectButton.enabled = false;
                password.enabled = true;
                connectButton.enabled = true;
                newPassword.enabled = false;
                reencryptButton.enabled = false;
            }

            private function handleReencryptClick(event:MouseEvent):void {
                connection.addEventListener(SQLEvent.REENCRYPT,
                                            handleDatabaseReencrypt);
                connection.reencrypt(createEncryptionKey(newPassword.text));
            }

            private function handleDatabaseOpen(event:SQLEvent):void {
                results.addItem("[ACTION]: Database Connection Successful");
                disconnectButton.enabled = true;
                newPassword.enabled = true;
                reencryptButton.enabled = true;
                password.enabled = false;
                connectButton.enabled = false;
            }

            private function handleDatabaseReencrypt(event:SQLEvent):void {
                connection.removeEventListener(SQLEvent.REENCRYPT,
                                                handleDatabaseReencrypt);
                results.addItem("[ACTION]: Database Reencrypted");
            }

            private function handleDatabaseError(event:SQLErrorEvent):void {
                results.addItem("[ERROR]: Database Error " +
                                event.error.detailArguments.toString() );
            }

        ]]>
    </fx:Script>

    <mx:Label text="Encryption By Password" fontWeight="bold" fontSize="18" />
```

```
<mx:Label text="Connect To Database" fontWeight="bold"/>
<s:HGroup>
    <s:Label text="Password" />
    <s:TextInput id="password" />
    <s:Button id="connectButton" label="Connect"
            click="handleConnectClick(event)" />
    <s:Button id="disconnectButton" label="Disconnect"
            click="handleDisconnectClick(event)" enabled="false" />
</s:HGroup>

<s:Label text="Change Password / ReEncrypt" fontWeight="bold"/>
<s:HGroup>
    <s:Label text="New Password" />
    <s:TextInput id="newPassword" enabled="false" />
    <s:Button id="reencryptButton" label="Change Password"
            click="handleReencryptClick(event)" enabled="false" />
</s:HGroup>
</s:WindowedApplication>
```

19.5 Use Parameters in Queries

Problem

You want to use parameters in queries to create reusable SQL statements and prevent the risk of SQL injection attacks.

Solution

Use the `parameters` property to specify named or unnamed parameters in SQL queries and to create reusable SQL statements.

Discussion

Parameters enable you to create reusable SQL statements to work with the same `SQLStatement` instance and carry out multiple SQL operations. For example, you can use an `INSERT` statement several times during the lifecycle of the application to allow the user to insert multiple values into the database, populating it with data. Both named and unnamed parameters can be declared.

Named parameters are declared with a specific name, which the database uses as a placeholder in the SQL statement. They can be specified by using the `:` or `@` character. In the following example, the `:name` and `:surname` parameters are inserted in the SQL text statement:

```
var statementInstance:SQLStatement = new SQLStatement();
var sqlText:String = "INSERT INTO Students (firstName, lastName) VALUES (:name,
                    :surname)";
statementInstance.parameters[":name"] = "Marco";
statementInstance.parameters[":surname "] = "Casario";
```

Unnamed parameters, on the other hand, are specified with the ? character in the SQL statement, and they are set by using a numerical index in the same order they are written in the SQL statement:

```
var statementInstance:SQLStatement = new SQLStatement();
var sqlText:String = "INSERT INTO Students (firstName, lastName) VALUES (?, ?)";
statementInstance.parameters[0] = "Marco";
statementInstance.parameters[1] = "Casario";
```

The `parameters` property is an associative array, and the indexes are zero-based.

Using parameters makes an application both more robust and more secure. It's more robust because the parameters are typed substitutions of values and they guarantee the storage class for values passed into the database. It's more secure because the parameters aren't written in the SQL text and they don't link the user input to the SQL text. This prevents possible SQL injection attacks. In fact, when you use parameters, the values are treated as substituted values instead of being part of the SQL text.

It's necessary to use parameters in SQL statements in most AIR applications. To use parameters, you need to have an instance of the `SQLStatement` class where you can define the `parameters` property as an associative array. The SQL text will also have to be changed by defining the placeholder values that will be associated to the parameters of the `SQLStatement` instance.

In this solution, you will add a public method to the ActionScript class shown here (named *InsertParam.as*) to create a parameterized `INSERT` SQL operation:

```
package com.oreilly.flex4cookbook.ch19
{
    import flash.data.SQLConnection;
    import flash.data.SQLStatement;
    import flash.errors.SQLError;
    import flash.events.SQLErrorEvent;
    import flash.events.SQLEvent;
    import flash.filesystem.File;

    import mx.controls.Alert;

    public class InsertParam
    {
        private var _myDB:File;
        private var _isOpen:Boolean = false;

        private var _dbConn:SQLConnection;

        private var sqlString:String;

        public function get myDB():File
        {
            return _myDB;
        }

        public function get isOpen():Boolean
```

```
    {
        return _isOpen;
    }


    public function InsertParam()
    {
        createLocalDB();
        sqlString = "CREATE TABLE IF NOT EXISTS Students(" +
                    "stuId INTEGER PRIMARY KEY AUTOINCREMENT, " +
                    "firstName TEXT, " +
                    "lastName TEXT" + ")";
    }

    private function createLocalDB():void
    {
        var folder:File= File.applicationStorageDirectory.resolvePath( "db"
);

        folder.createDirectory();

        _myDB = folder.resolvePath( "myDBFile.db" );
    }

    public function createTableDB(dbFile:File,isAsync:Boolean=true):void
    {
        _dbConn = new SQLConnection();

        if(isAsync)
        {
            _dbConn.openAsync(dbFile);

            _dbConn.addEventListener(SQLEvent.OPEN, openHandler);
            _dbConn.addEventListener(SQLErrorEvent.ERROR, errorHandler);

        } else {

            try
            {
                _dbConn.open(dbFile);

                var createStm:SQLStatement = new SQLStatement();
                createStm.sqlConnection = _dbConn;
                createStm.text = sqlString;

                createStm.addEventListener(SQLEvent.RESULT,
                                            onStatementResult);
                createStm.addEventListener(SQLErrorEvent.ERROR,
                                            onStatementError);

                createStm.execute();
            }
            catch (error:SQLError)
            {
                trace("Error message:", error.message);
```

```
                trace("Details:", error.details);
            }
        }
    }

    private function openHandler(event:SQLEvent):void
    {

        _isOpen = _dbConn.connected;

        var createStm:SQLStatement = new SQLStatement();
        createStm.sqlConnection = _dbConn;
        createStm.text = sqlString;

        createStm.addEventListener(SQLEvent.RESULT, onStatementResult);
        createStm.addEventListener(SQLErrorEvent.ERROR, onStatementError);

        createStm.execute();

    }

    private function errorHandler(event:SQLErrorEvent):void
    {
        Alert.show("Error message:", event.error.message);
        Alert.show("Details:", event.error.details);
        _isOpen = _dbConn.connected;
    }

    private function onStatementResult(event:SQLEvent):void
    {
        Alert.show("Table created");
    }

    private function onStatementError(event:SQLErrorEvent):void
    {
        Alert.show("Error message:", event.error.message);
        Alert.show("Details:", event.error.details);
    }

    }
}
```

Use the preceding ActionScript class and add a private **String** property called **sqlAdd**. Next, change the constructor by adding a SQL statement that will use the parameters shown here:

```
private var sqlAdd:String;
public function insertParam():void
{
    this.createLocalDB();

    sqlString = "CREATE TABLE IF NOT EXISTS Students(" +
            "stuId INTEGER PRIMARY KEY AUTOINCREMENT, " +
            "firstName TEXT, " +
            "lastName TEXT" + ")";
```

```
        sqlInsert = "INSERT INTO Students (firstName, lastName) " +
                    "VALUES ('Marco', 'Casario')";

        sqlSelect = "SELECT * FROM Students";

        sqlAdd = "INSERT INTO Students (firstName, lastName)" +
                 "VALUES (:name, :surname)";
    }
```

Now write a new public method that will be invoked by the application and that will be responsible for executing the SQL statement and associating the parameters to the SQL text:

```
    public function insertParameters(paramName:String, paramLast:String):void
    {
        var paramStmt:SQLStatement = new SQLStatement();
        paramStmt.sqlConnection = _dbConn;
        paramStmt.text = sqlAdd;

        paramStmt.parameters[":name"] = paramName;
        paramStmt.parameters[":surname"] = paramLast;

        paramStmt.execute();

        paramStmt.addEventListener(SQLEvent.RESULT, paramAddHandler);

        paramStmt.addEventListener(SQLErrorEvent.ERROR, errorHandler);
    }

    private function paramAddHandler(event:SQLEvent):void
    {
        trace("Data added using parameters");
    }
```

The `insertParam()` method accepts two parameters: `paramName:String` and `paramLast:String`. These are used by the `parameters` property of the `SQLStatement` instance:

```
    paramStmt.parameters[":name"] = paramName;
    paramStmt.parameters[":surname"] = paramLast;
```

The MXML page that imports the new ActionScript class has a container with two TextInput controls. The text you will insert into these two controls will be passed on to the `insertParam()` method, which will use those values as parameters in the SQL statement:

```
    <?xml version="1.0" encoding="utf-8"?>

    <s:WindowedApplication xmlns:mx="http://www.adobe.com/2006/mxml"
                           xmlns:s="library://ns.adobe.com/flex/spark"
                           xmlns:mx="library://ns.adobe.com/flex/halo"
                           initialize="init()">
        <s:layout><s:HorizontalLayout/></s:layout>
```

```
<fx:Script>
<![CDATA[
    import com.oreilly.flex4cookbook.ch19.InsertParam;

    private var myDB:File;
    [Bindable]
    private var myDBclass:InsertParam;

    private function init():void
    {
        createBtn.addEventListener(MouseEvent.CLICK, onClick);
        openBtn.addEventListener(MouseEvent.CLICK, onClickOpen);
        insertBtn.addEventListener(MouseEvent.CLICK, onClickInsert);
        selectBtn.addEventListener(MouseEvent.CLICK, onClickSelect);
        addBtn.addEventListener(MouseEvent.CLICK, onClickAdd);
    }

    private function onClick(evt:MouseEvent):void
    {
        myDBclass = new InsertParam();
        myDB = myDBclass.myDB;

        openBtn.enabled = true;

        mx.controls.Alert.show("Database File Was Created :\n" +
                            myDB.nativePath );
    }

    private function onClickOpen(evt:MouseEvent):void
    {
        insertBtn.enabled = true;
        selectBtn.enabled = true;
    }

    private function onClickInsert(evt:MouseEvent):void
    {
        myDBclass.insertData(myDB);
        mx.controls.Alert.show("Data was inserted into the database : \n" +
                            myDB.nativePath );
    }

    private function onClickSelect(evt:MouseEvent):void
    {
        myDBclass.selectData(myDB);

        myDG.dataProvider = myDBclass.myResultAC;
    }

    private function onClickAdd(evt:MouseEvent):void
    {
        myDBclass.insertParameters(nameTxt.text, lastTxt.text);
    }

]]>
```

```
        </fx:Script>

        <s:VGroup>
            <s:HGroup>
                <s:Button id="createBtn" label="Create DB" />

                <s:Button label="Open DataBase" id="openBtn" enabled="false" />

                <s:Button label="Insert Data Asynchronously" enabled="false"
                          id="insertBtn" />

                <s:Button label="Show Data" id="selectBtn" enabled="false" />
            </s:HGroup>

            <mx:DataGrid id="myDG" width="100%" height="60%"/>

            <s:VGroup width="100%">
                <s:Label text="Insert Values into the Database" />
                <s:TextInput id="nameTxt"/>
                <s:TextInput id="lastTxt"/>
                <s:Button label="Insert Values" id="addBtn"/>
            </s:VGroup>
        </s:VGroup>
    </s:WindowedApplication>
```

In the event handler that is triggered with the click of the button, the `insertParam()` method of the ActionScript class is invoked, and the values inserted in the two `TextInput` controls are passed into it.

You can test this by launching the AIR application, inserting values in the text fields, and clicking the button to send the data. This data will be inserted in the database and shown in the `DataGrid` control that is associated with the `ArrayCollection` that contains the `SELECT` SQL statement.

19.6 Include a Database in an Application

Problem

You want to include an existing SQLite database with an Adobe AIR application.

Solution

Embed an existing SQLite database in the AIR application and copy it to another folder to interact with it.

Discussion

Many desktop applications use databases to store data locally on the user's computer. In some AIR applications, you need to embed an existing SQLite database within the packaged *.air* file.

The *.air* file is a package with some files inside. When you install an AIR application on your computer, you copy those files into the application folder or a subfolder. Any files you want to include in an AIR application must be packaged with it when you create it. This applies to images, text files, and database files, including an existing SQLite database created for another application or with another program. Note that the application folder, `File.applicationDirectory`, is read-only. If you try to work with a database file in this directory, it will fail with a silent error. To make this work, you must copy the database file into another folder, such as the *Documents* folder or the desktop folder, using the `copyTo()` method of the `File` class. You can then work with your database and create new records, update records, or delete them.

In this ActionScript example, the file *software.db* is copied from the application directory of the AIR application to the *Documents* directory of the user's computer. After the file is copied, you can then interact with it as needed:

```
var dbFile:File = File.applicationDirectory.resolvePath("db/software.db");
var dbWorkFile:File = File.documentsDirectory.resolvePath("software.db");

if(!dbWorkFile.exists){
    dbFile.copyTo(dbWorkedFile);
}
```

19.7 Store Simple Relationships with an Object Relational Mapping

Problem

You need the ability to easily store and retrieve class instances from an embedded database.

Solution

Use the FlexORM open source project, which provides a powerful Object Relational Mapping (ORM) solution for AIR developers.

Discussion

Object Relational Mapping libraries are common across many languages. In short, an ORM gives you the ability to think of your data in terms of classes and not database tables. The ORM does the heavy lifting of converting your classes to data that can be stored in database tables based on a mapping that you define. It also provides a simple API for performing normal CRUD operations on your data. Because of the ORM, all of this is possible without having to write any SQL code to interact with the local database.

When AIR was first released, many developers wanted the ability to work with local databases in AIR in the same way they could work with it using other ORM tools such as Hibernate. After a year had passed, there were several different libraries in development that provided similar functionality. One of those was FlexORM, developed by Mark Moloney.

 FlexORM is hosted at *http://flexorm.riaforge.org*. The FlexORM library will be required for this example.

Defining the object mapping

The FlexORM library allows you to use metadata on your model classes to define the mapping between your classes and the database tables. One of the advantages of this approach over other solutions is that it does not require you to extend framework classes. Your model can remain entirely unchanged except for the metadata (which is ignored by the compiler if not used).

In the following example, there is a single class that defines a browser bookmark. It includes id, name, url, and notes properties:

```
package vo
{

    [Bindable]
    [Table(name="BOOKMARKS")]
    public class Bookmark
    {

        [Id]
        public var id:int;
        [Column( name="bookmark_name" )]
        public var name:String;
        [Column( name="bookmark_url" )]
        public var url:String;
        [Column( name="bookmark_notes" )]
        public var notes:String;

    }
}
```

The [Bindable] metadata tag should already look familiar to you, as it is core to the Flex framework. However, the [Table], [Column], and [Id] metadata tags are specific to FlexORM. The [Table] metadata tag marks a specific class as being managed by FlexORM. You can also optionally define the name of the table as an argument in the metadata tag. The [Id] metadata tag specifies the field that will be used as the primary key of the object. FlexORM includes primary key generation, so you don't have to worry about defining this value. Finally, the [Column] metadata tag allows you to specify a column name for the specific property on which it's set. In most cases, this is optional; if not defined, the column name will default to the name of the property.

Using the EntityManager

FlexORM provides a singleton class, EntityManager, that handles all the CRUD tasks for all the classes that are managed by FlexORM. This class makes it extremely easy to create, retrieve, update, and delete any instances of classes that have the [Table] metadata tag defined on them.

The first task is to properly set up the EntityManager. Before it can perform any operations, you must provide it with an instance of the SQLConnection class:

```
protected var entityManager:EntityManager=EntityManager.getInstance();

protected function application_creationCompleteHandler(event:FlexEvent):void
{
    var databaseFile:File=File.applicationStorageDirectory.resolvePath(
        "bookmarks.db");
    var connection:SQLConnection=new SQLConnection();
    connection.open(databaseFile);

    entityManager.sqlConnection=connection;
}
```

In the preceding example, the EntityManager is configured to use the database file *bookmarks.db* in the application storage directory. After the sqlConnection property has been set, you can perform CRUD operations on your data.

Retrieving all the items of a specific type is easy with the EntityManager. You just need to pass the class you want to retrieve into the EntityManager's findAll() method:

```
[ArrayElementType( "vo.Bookmark" )]
[Bindable]
public var bookmarks:ArrayCollection;

public function getAllBookmarks():void
{
    bookmarks = entityManager.findAll( Bookmark );
}
```

Saving an instance of a class is equally simple with the EntityManager:

```
public function saveBookmark():void
{
    var bookmark:Bookmark = new Bookmark();
    bookmark.name = "Google";
    bookmark.url = "http://www.google.com/"
    bookmark.notes = "Search Engine";

    entityManager.save( bookmark );
}
```

The process of deleting an instance follows the same pattern, but it requires you to pass in the class you want to delete and the instance's `id`:

```
public function deleteFirstBookmark():void
{
    var bookmarks:ArrayCollection = entityManager.findAll( Bookmark );
    var firstBookmark:Bookmark = bookmarks.getItemAt( 0 );
    entityManager.removeItem( Bookmark, firstBookmark.id );
}
```

Creating a complete application

By implementing the preceding examples for working with data, you can create a sample application that handles CRUD actions solely through the `EntityManager`. In this example, a simple browser stores the bookmarks (as described earlier). In addition to the MXML file shown here, you will also need the FlexORM SWC file defined on the build path as well as the `Bookmark` class defined previously (place it in the **vo** package):

```
<?xml version="1.0" encoding="utf-8"?>
<s:WindowedApplication xmlns:fx="http://ns.adobe.com/mxml/2009"
                       xmlns:mx="library://ns.adobe.com/flex/mx"
                       xmlns:s="library://ns.adobe.com/flex/spark"
                       currentState="default"
                       height="600"
                       width="800"
                       creationComplete="application_creationCompleteHandler(
                                event )"
                       title="{ browserPageTitle }">

    <s:states>
        <s:State name="default" />
        <s:State name="viewBookmarks" />
        <s:State name="bookmark" />
    </s:states>

    <s:layout>
        <s:VerticalLayout horizontalAlign="center"
                          paddingBottom="10"
                          paddingLeft="10"
                          paddingRight="10"
                          paddingTop="10" />
    </s:layout>

    <fx:Script>
        <![CDATA[
            import mx.collections.ArrayCollection;
            import mx.events.FlexEvent;
            import nz.co.codec.flexorm.EntityManager;
            import vo.Bookmark;

            [Bindable]
            public var bookmarks:ArrayCollection;
```

```
        [Bindable]
        protected var browserPageTitle:String = "";

        protected var entityManager:EntityManager =
                EntityManager.getInstance();

        protected function application_creationCompleteHandler(
                event:FlexEvent ):void
        {
            var databaseFile:File =
                    File.applicationStorageDirectory.resolvePath(
                    "bookmarks.db" );
            var connection:SQLConnection = new SQLConnection();
            connection.open( databaseFile );

            entityManager.sqlConnection = connection;
            loadBookmarks();
        }

        protected function deleteBookmark( bookmark:Bookmark ):void
        {
            entityManager.remove( bookmark );
            loadBookmarks();
        }

        protected function loadBookmarks():void
        {
            bookmarks = entityManager.findAll( Bookmark );
            currentState = "default";
        }

        protected function saveBookmark():void
        {
            var bookmark:Bookmark = new Bookmark();
            bookmark.name = nameInput.text;
            bookmark.url = bookmarkUrlInput.text;
            bookmark.notes = notesInput.text;

            entityManager.save( bookmark );
            loadBookmarks();
            currentState = "default";
        }
    ]]>
</fx:Script>

<s:HGroup width="100%">

    <s:TextInput id="urlInput"
                width="75%"
                enter="browser.location = urlInput.text;" />

    <s:Button label="Bookmark This"
            width="25%"
            click="currentState = 'bookmark';" />
```

```
    <s:Button label="View Bookmarks"
            width="25%"
            click="currentState = 'viewBookmarks';" />

</s:HGroup>

<mx:HTML height="100%"
        id="browser"
        width="100%"
        complete="browserPageTitle =
                browser.htmlLoader.window.document.title;"
        location="http://www.oreilly.com/"
        locationChange="urlInput.text = browser.location;" />

<s:VGroup id="bookmarkForm"
        width="100%"
        includeIn="bookmark">

    <s:Label text="Add Bookmark"
            fontSize="16"
            fontWeight="bold" />
    <s:TextInput id="nameInput"
                text="{ browserPageTitle }"
                width="100%" />
    <s:TextInput enabled="false"
                id="bookmarkUrlInput"
                text="{ browser.location }"
                width="100%" />
    <s:TextArea height="100"
                id="notesInput"
                width="100%" />

    <s:HGroup>

        <s:Button id="saveButton"
                label="Save Bookmark"
                click="saveBookmark();" />

        <s:Button id="cancelButton"
                label="Cancel"
                click="currentState = 'default';" />
    </s:HGroup>

</s:VGroup>

<s:VGroup id="bookmarkList"
        width="100%"
        includeIn="viewBookmarks">

    <mx:DataGrid dataProvider="{ bookmarks }"
                id="bookmarkGrid"
                width="100%" />
```

```
        <s:HGroup>

            <s:Button enabled="{ bookmarkGrid.selectedIndex > -1 }"
                    label="Load Bookmark"
                    click="browser.location = Bookmark(
                            bookmarkGrid.selectedItem ).url;" />

            <s:Button enabled="{ bookmarkGrid.selectedIndex > -1 }"
                    label="Delete Bookmark"
                    click="deleteBookmark( Bookmark(
                            bookmarkGrid.selectedItem ) );" />

            <s:Button label="Close Bookmarks"
                    click="currentState = 'default';" />

        </s:HGroup>
    </s:VGroup>
</s:WindowedApplication>
```

CHAPTER 20

Operating System Integration with AIR

Adobe AIR enables applications to move beyond the browser and interact with many aspects of the end user's native operating system. One of the main benefits of developing applications for the Adobe AIR runtime is the absence of some of the security sandbox restrictions that are normally found in the browser-based Flash Player.

AIR applications are installed on the local computer with permissions to access and interact with the operating system: they can interact with the filesystem, open files with default applications, and establish connections with XML Sockets.

As Rob Christensen, senior product manager of Adobe AIR, wrote, "as the definition of AIR 2 evolved, it became clear that Adobe would focus our efforts on the following themes: providing deeper integration with the operating system, making developers more productive, and improving performance." (His "Introducing Adobe AIR 2" article is available at *http://www.adobe.com/devnet/logged_in/rchristensen_air_2.html*.)

This chapter focuses on the key areas that have been improved in and added to the new version of AIR and how you can leverage them to make your AIR applications work in close contact with the operating system. Specifically, the solutions presented within this chapter will show you how to do all of the following:

- Read, write, move, and delete files. AIR 1 and 1.5 already provided a very rich set of API files for working with the filesystem, but AIR 2 increases the API file set even further by adding the ability to open files with their default registered applications, flag files as "downloaded" so that (some) operating systems will warn users before opening them for the first time, and receive notifications about mounted and unmounted storage volumes.

- Package and release AIR 2 applications via a native installer application. This means you can deliver an EXE installer file on Windows, a DMG file on Mac OS X, and a RPM or DEB file on Linux, and you can launch and communicate with the native operation systems process using the `NativeProcess` class.

- Listen on a socket using the new AIR 2 server socket support (with the Socket
  Server class within the flash.net package). This means that you can send and
  receive data over a TCP socket without having to initiate a socket connection.

Moreover, in this chapter you'll learn how to interact with and manage the windows
of your main application, and learn some basics of working efficiently and seamlessly
on remote systems.

20.1 Close All Open Windows at Once

Problem

You want to close all the open windows when the main application window is closed.

Solution

Listen for the closing event (Event.CLOSING), cancel the close operation, and loop
through all the open windows to close them manually.

Discussion

When building a multiwindow application, you may need to provide the ability to close
all open windows when the main application window is closed.

By calling the preventDefault() method of the Event class, you can cancel the default
behavior of the closing event so that it does not automatically close the main window.
Then, you can close any opened windows first in the opposite order from which they
were opened (i.e., closing the more recent windows first). In this way, you can be sure
your application is fully exited when the user clicks the close button. Here is the complete code you need:

```
<s:WindowedApplication xmlns:fx="http://ns.adobe.com/mxml/2009"
                       xmlns:s="library://ns.adobe.com/flex/spark"
                       xmlns:mx="library://ns.adobe.com/flex/halo"
                       applicationComplete="init()"
                       title="Main window">
    <s:layout>
        <s:BasicLayout/>
    </s:layout>
    <fx:Declarations>
        <!-- Place nonvisual elements (e.g., services, value objects) here -->
    </fx:Declarations>

    <fx:Script>
        <![CDATA[
            import mx.core.Window;
```

```
private function init() : void
{
    var firstWindow : Window = new Window();
    firstWindow.title = "First Window";
    firstWindow.width = 400;
    firstWindow.height = 200;
    firstWindow.open( true );

    var secondWindow : Window = new Window();
    secondWindow.title = "Second Window";
    secondWindow.width = 400;
    secondWindow.height = 200;
    secondWindow.open( true );
    this.addEventListener(Event.CLOSE,closeAllWindows);

}

private function closeAllWindows( event : Event ) : void
{
    event.preventDefault();
    // loop through all windows and close them
    for ( var i : int =
        NativeApplication.nativeApplication.openedWindows.length -1;
        i >= 0; --i )
    {

        var closeWin : NativeWindow =
            NativeApplication.nativeApplication.openedWindows[ i ]
            as NativeWindow;
        closeWin.close();
    }
}
]]>
</fx:Script>
</s:WindowedApplication>
```

20.2 Add a Drop Shadow for a Custom Chrome Window

Problem

You want to add a drop shadow to the border of a window that has custom chrome
applied.

Solution

Pass a DropShadowFilter instance to the filters Array of the NativeWindow instance, or
set the dropShadowEnabled and dropShadowColor styles.

Discussion

A window that has custom chrome applied can have a drop shadow around its borders. This window can be your main application window or any other window in the application. When you want to add a shadow around your main application window, make sure to set the transparency of this window using the `systemChrome` and `transparent` attributes in the application descriptor file:

```
<systemChrome>none</systemChrome>
<transparent>true</transparent>
```

You can then add a drop shadow to your window in two ways. The first way is to instantiate a `DropShadowFilter` (a subclass of the `BitmapFilter` class) object and set the properties you want for the drop shadow. Every `DisplayObject` has a `filters Array` property where you can store `BitmapFilter` instances you want to use on that `DisplayObject`. For the `DropShadowFilter`, you can define many properties, such as `color`, `alpha`, `blurX`, `blurY`, `distance`, and `angle`, to customize the look and feel of your drop shadow.

The following example is a basic AIR application with custom chrome applied (Figure 20-1). Actually, the chrome consists of just three `Canvas` components from the Flex Framework.

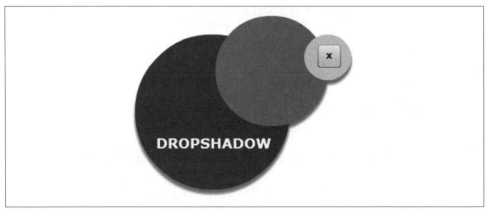

Figure 20-1. A custom chrome window

The drop shadow is configured as follows:

```
shadowFilter = new DropShadowFilter();
shadowFilter.color = 0xFF0000;
shadowFilter.alpha = 0.75;
shadowFilter.blurX = 5;
shadowFilter.blurY = 5;
shadowFilter.distance = 5;
shadowFilter.angle = 90;
```

To cast the drop shadow on the window's transparent background, assign the shadow Filter instance to the `filters` Array of the WindowedApplication instance. In this example, the keyword refers to the WindowedApplication instance:

```
this.filters = [shadowFilter];
```

Here is the complete MXML code for the example:

```
<s:WindowedApplication xmlns:fx="http://ns.adobe.com/mxml/2009"
                       xmlns:s="library://ns.adobe.com/flex/spark"
                       xmlns:mx="library://ns.adobe.com/flex/halo"
                       applicationComplete="init()"
                       backgroundAlpha="0"
                       showStatusBar="false"
                       title="Main window">
    <s:layout>
        <s:BasicLayout/>
    </s:layout>
    <fx:Declarations>
        <!-- Place nonvisual elements (e.g., services, value objects) here -->
    </fx:Declarations>

    <fx:Style>
        Canvas{
            border-style:solid;
            border-thickness:0;
            corner-radius:150;
        }
        WindowedApplication{
            drop-shadow-enabled:"true";
            drop-shadow-color:"0xFF0000";
        }
    </fx:Style>

    <fx:Script>
        <![CDATA[
            import mx.core.Window;
            import spark.filters.DropShadowFilter;

            private var shadowFilter:DropShadowFilter;
            private var newWindow:Window;

            private function init():void {
                shadowFilter = new DropShadowFilter();
                shadowFilter.color = 0xFF0000;
                shadowFilter.alpha = 0.75;
                shadowFilter.blurX = 5;
                shadowFilter.blurY = 5;
                shadowFilter.distance = 5;
                shadowFilter.angle = 90;
                // attach the drop shadow to the NativeWindow

                this.filters = [shadowFilter];
                this.stage.addEventListener(MouseEvent.MOUSE_DOWN,onMouseDown);
```

```
            }
            private function closeWindow(event:MouseEvent):void {
                this.nativeWindow.close();
            }
            private function onMouseDown(event:MouseEvent):void {
                this.nativeWindow.startMove();
            }
        ]]>
    </fx:Script>

    <mx:Canvas x="29" y="34" width="200" height="200" backgroundColor="#343434">
        <mx:Label x="25" y="127" text="DROPSHADOW"
                    fontSize="18" color="#FFFFFF" fontWeight="bold"/>
        <mx:Canvas x="9.7" y="10" width="180" height="180"
                    backgroundColor="#7A7C7E" >
            <mx:Canvas x="110.3" y="9" width="60" height="59"
                        backgroundColor="#D7D7D7" >
                <mx:Button label="X" width="30" paddingLeft="0" paddingRight="0"
                            paddingTop="0" paddingBottom="0" height="30"
                            color="#000000" right="12" top="13"
                            themeColor="#949698" click="closeWindow(event)"/>
            </mx:Canvas>
        </mx:Canvas>
    </mx:Canvas>

</s:WindowedApplication>
```

The second way to show a drop shadow is by setting the drop-shadow-color and drop-shadow-enabled style properties of the displayObject you are using as the background of your application. In a basic AIR application with a Canvas component as a background container, set the style properties for the Canvas component as follows:

```
Canvas.BgCanvas {
    background-color:"0xE6E6E6";
    border-style:solid;
    border-color:"0xFFFFFF";
    border-thickness:10;
    corner-radius:20;

    drop-shadow-color:"0x000000";
    drop-shadow-enabled:true;

    shadow-direction:top;
    shadow-distance:5;

}
```

You can also set the shadow-distance as you like, and you can set shadow-direction to be centered, left, or right.

Make sure the systemChrome attribute is set to none and the transparent attribute is set to true; otherwise, you will not see the shadow. Figure 20-2 shows the resulting application.

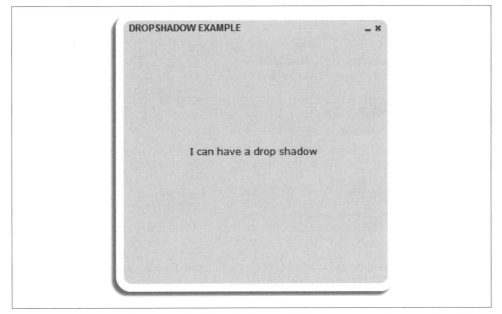

Figure 20-2. An AIR application with a drop shadow applied by setting drop shadow style attributes

Here is the full MXML code for the example:

```
<s:WindowedApplication xmlns:fx="http://ns.adobe.com/mxml/2009"
                       xmlns:s="library://ns.adobe.com/flex/spark"
                       xmlns:mx="library://ns.adobe.com/flex/halo"
                       applicationComplete="init()"
                       backgroundAlpha="0"
                       showStatusBar="false"
                       title="Main window">
    <s:layout>
        <s:BasicLayout/>
    </s:layout>
    <fx:Declarations>
        <!-- Place nonvisual elements (e.g., services, value objects) here -->
    </fx:Declarations>

    <fx:Style>

        @namespace "library://ns.adobe.com/flex/spark";

        WindowedApplication {
            padding-right:"5";
            padding-left:"5";
            padding-top:"5";
            padding-bottom:"5";
            show-flex-chrome:false;
        }
        Border.BgCanvas {
            background-color:"0xE6E6E6";
            border-style:solid;
```

```
                border-color:"0xFFFFFF";
                border-thickness:10;
                corner-radius:20;

                drop-shadow-color:"0x000000";
                drop-shadow-enabled:true;

                shadow-direction:left;
                shadow-distance:15;
            }
        </fx:Style>

        <fx:Script>
            <![CDATA[
                import flash.display.NativeWindowSystemChrome;

                private function init() : void {
                    stage.addEventListener( MouseEvent.MOUSE_DOWN, onMouseDown )
                }

                private function closeWindow( event : MouseEvent ) : void {
                    this.nativeWindow.close();
                }

                private function onMouseDown( event : MouseEvent ) : void {
                    this.nativeWindow.startMove();
                }
            ]]>
        </fx:Script>

        <s:Border styleName="BgCanvas"
                right="20"
                bottom="20"
                top="20"
                left="20">
            <s:HGroup y="0"
                    right="15"
                    left="5"
                    verticalAlign="middle"
                    direction="ltr"
                    width="100%">
                <mx:Spacer width="100%"/>
                <mx:LinkButton label="close"
                            click="closeWindow(event)"/>
            </s:HGroup>
            <s:Label text="I can have a drop shadow "
                    horizontalCenter="0"
                    verticalCenter="0"
                    fontSize="12"/>
        </s:Border>

    </s:WindowedApplication>
```

20.3 Use Deferred Rendering with Clipboard Data

Problem

You have large or computationally expensive data on the clipboard that you want to be processed or rendered when the user pastes data instead of when the user copies it.

Solution

Use the `setDataHandler()` method, which doesn't store the actual data in the clipboard but rather references a method for rendering the data.

Discussion

In cases where rendering the clipboard data requires a large amount of system resources or where the data changes on a regular basis, you may want the data to be rendered when it is pasted instead of when it is copied to the clipboard. To accomplish this in AIR, you can use the `setDataHandler()` method.

The `setDataHandler()` method works in a similar manner to the `setData()` method. Instead of passing in the actual data, however, you pass in a function that will render the data and that is called only when the data is needed. The first time the data is requested, the function is called, and the return value of the function populates the clipboard with the correct data. Subsequent calls to that data return that value. The function is not called again until the data is copied and requested again. It is important to remember this to avoid undesired effects when working with stale data. Also noteworthy is that when data of a particular format is set using both the `setData()` method and the `setDataHandler()` method, `setData()` takes priority. In this case, the handler function is never called when retrieving the data.

To demonstrate, consider a Flex example with three user interface elements, a Copy button, a Paste button, and a text element to contain the result text:

```
<mx:Button label="Copy" click="handleCopyClick(event)" />
<mx:Button label="Paste" click="handlePasteClick(event)" />
<mx:Text id="resultText" />
```

When the user clicks the Copy button, the current application time is stored, and the data is added to the clipboard with deferred rendering:

```
import flash.desktop.Clipboard;
import flash.desktop.ClipboardFormats;
import flash.utils.getTimer;

private var timeCopied:int;

private function handleCopyClick( event:MouseEvent ):void {
    timeCopied = getTimer();
    Clipboard.generalClipboard.setDataHandler( ClipboardFormats.TEXT_FORMAT,
                                               dataHandler );
```

```
    }

    private function dataHandler():String {
        return "[Time Copied]: " + timeCopied + " [Time First Pasted]: " + getTimer();
    }
```

When the user clicks the Paste button, the data is retrieved from the clipboard using deferred rendering. It lists both the time when the data was pasted and the time the data was copied:

```
    private function handlePasteClick( event:MouseEvent ):void {
        var data:String = Clipboard.generalClipboard.getData( Clipboard
              Formats.TEXT_FORMAT ) as String;
        resultText.text = data;
    }
```

If the user clicks the Paste button twice, the result stays the same. This is because the `dataHandler()` method is called only the first time the data is requested. If you want the method to be called each time the Paste button is clicked, you must call the `setData Handler()` method again at the end of the `handlePasteClick()` method.

20.4 Create Custom Clipboard Data Formats

Problem

You want to use a data format for the clipboard that is not one of the five default formats defined in `ClipboardFormats`.

Solution

Create a custom `Clipboard` data format using the built-in support for custom formats within AIR.

Discussion

In some situations, the standard clipboard data formats do not meet the needs of your application. For these situations, you can take advantage of the custom data formats of the `Clipboard` class.

To create a custom data format in AIR, you need a string that identifies your format. You will pass this to the `Clipboard` methods instead of a constant from the `Clipboard DataFormats` class. The only limitation on this string is that it cannot begin with `air:`. The AIR documentation suggests you use your application ID as the prefix for the format. For example:

```
    com.comtaste.oreilly.f4cookbook.MyApplication:customdata
```

This helps to ensure your custom data format identifier will not match any other custom data formats from other AIR applications.

Transfer modes

When you are dealing with custom data formats, you use the third parameter of the `setData()` and `setDataHandler()` methods to control how your data is placed on the clipboard. Essentially, there are two ways to place your data: as a copy and as a reference to the original object. Almost any object can be added to the clipboard as a reference, but classes that are copied onto the clipboard must be serializable. If your class is serializable, you can pass `true` as the third parameter of these methods, and your data will be placed on the clipboard as a copy. If you pass `false`, it will be passed as a reference.

The transfer mode is not just important when pasting data; it also plays a key role in retrieving data. The `getData()` method has a third parameter that lets you indicate whether you want to retrieve a copy of the data or a reference to the original data. The values for this parameter are defined as constants in the `ClipboardTransferMode` class:

`ClipboardTransferMode.ORIGINAL_ONLY`
> This mode takes only a reference to the data. If this is passed as the third parameter of the `getData()` method, the method will take the original data only. If only a copy of the data is available, no data will be returned.

`ClipboardTransferMode.CLONE_ONLY`
> This mode takes only a copy of the clipboard data. If only a reference to the original object is available, no data will be returned.

`ClipboardTransferMode.ORIGINAL_PREFERRED`
> In this mode, the `getData()` method is requesting a reference to the original object, but if a copy is all that is available, the method will take that value.

`ClipboardTransferMode.CLONE_PREFERRED`
> In this mode, the `getData()` method is requesting a copy of the original data, but if a reference to the original is all that is available, the method will take that value.

In some cases, it might not be apparent which transfer mode is appropriate. However, this value can become extremely important when working with clipboard data in the file list format. It could mean the difference between deleting a file and deleting a copy of a file. Unless you are performing actual filesystem operations, you will probably want to use `ClipboardTransferMode.CLONE_ONLY` when working with file list format data.

Sharing data between AIR applications

If you want your custom data format to be available to other AIR applications, the data must be passed as a copy. When using a reference to the original data, you can paste the data only within the same AIR application.

The first step in creating a custom data format in ActionScript is to define your data. For your data class to be serializable, it must implement the `IExternalizable` interface. This requires that you define two methods, `readExternal()` and `writeExternal()`, which allow your data class to be broken down into binary data and copied onto the clipboard.

In the writeExternal() method, you use the methods of the IDataOutput interface to write your data into binary form. Each standard ActionScript data type has a corresponding method that enables you to write the data. Be sure to pay attention to the order the data is written in this method. This order must be repeated in the readExternal() method.

For the readExternal() method, you use the read methods of the IDataInput interface to read your data back into your class. They do not need to appear in the same order as they were written in the writeExternal() method. For example:

```
package
{
    import flash.utils.IExternalizable;
    import flash.utils.IDataInput;
    import flash.utils.IDataOutput;
    import flash.net.registerClassAlias;

    [Bindable]
    public class Person implements IExternalizable {

        public var firstName:String;
        public var lastName:String;
        public var age:int;

        public function Person() {
            registerClassAlias( "Person", Person );
        }

        public function readExternal(input:IDataInput):void {
            firstName = input.readUTF();
            lastName = input.readUTF();
            age = input.readInt();
        }

        public function writeExternal(output:IDataOutput):void {
            output.writeUTF(firstName);
            output.writeUTF(lastName);
            output.writeInt(age);
        }
    }
}
```

In this example, the custom data defines a person. It has the properties firstName, lastName, and age. Because the data has been defined, you can now add it to the clipboard as a custom data format. For this example, you will be using the following Flex user interface:

```
<s:WindowedApplication xmlns:fx="http://ns.adobe.com/mxml/2009"
                       xmlns:s="library://ns.adobe.com/flex/spark"
                       xmlns:mx="library://ns.adobe.com/flex/halo">
    <s:layout>
        <s:VerticalLayout />
    </s:layout>
```

```
<fx:Declarations>
    <!-- Place nonvisual elements (e.g., services, value objects) here -->
</fx:Declarations>

<s:Label text="Input Data" fontSize="20" fontWeight="bold" />

<s:Label text="First Name" />
<s:TextInput id="firstName" />
<s:Label text="Last Name" />
<s:TextInput id="lastName" />
<s:Label text="Age" />
<s:TextInput id="age" />

<s:HGroup>
    <s:Button label="Copy" click="handleCopyClick(event)" />
    <s:Button label="Paste" click="handlePasteClick(event)" />
    <s:Button label="Clear All Data" click="handleClearClick(event)" />
</s:HGroup>

<s:Label text="Result" fontSize="20" fontWeight="bold" />

<s:Label text="First Name" />
<s:TextInput id="resultFirstName" enabled="false" />
<s:Label text="Last Name" />
<s:TextInput id="resultLastName" enabled="false" />
<s:Label text="Age" />
<s:TextInput id="resultAge" restrict="0-9" enabled="false" />

</s:WindowedApplication>
```

The application should allow the user to fill in the fields at the top with the first name, last name, and age of the person. Then, if the user clicks the Copy button, the data will be added to the clipboard through a custom data type identified by the string person. Next, if the user clicks the Paste button, that data will be retrieved from the clipboard and used to populate the values in the lower form. The handleCopyClick() method handles adding the data to the clipboard:

```
public function handleCopyClick( event:MouseEvent ):void {
    var data:Person = new Person();
    data.firstName = firstName.text;
    data.lastName = lastName.text;
    data.age = parseInt( age.text );
    var setResult:Boolean = Clipboard.generalClipboard.setData( "person", data,
                                                                true );
}
```

First, an instance of the data class Person is created. Then its properties are assigned the values of their respective text inputs. Finally, the data is added to the operating system clipboard with the setData() method. The data is passing a copy of itself because the value true was passed as the third parameter, indicating that the data is to be serialized:

```
public function handlePasteClick(event:MouseEvent):void {
    var result:Person = Clipboard.generalClipboard.getData(
            "person", ClipboardTransferMode.CLONE_PREFERRED ) as Person;
    if (result) {
        resultFirstName.text = result.firstName;
        resultLastName.text = result.lastName;
        resultAge.text = result.age.toString();
    }
}
```

The `handlePasteClick()` method gets the data from the clipboard using the same identifier that was used to set it on the clipboard. It also indicates that it wants a copy of the data if available, as opposed to the original object. Finally, the values of the lower form are set. After using the Paste button, the user can click the Clear All Data button to clear all the data from the form fields as well as the clipboard. Note that after clearing the clipboard, attempting to paste will cause the Flash Player to throw an "end of file" error, because there is no relevant data to be read:

```
public function handleClearClick( event:MouseEvent ):void {
    firstName.text = "";
    lastName.text = "";
    age.text = "";
    resultFirstName.text = "";
    resultLastName.text = "";
    resultAge.text = "";
    Clipboard.generalClipboard.clearData( "person" );
}
```

20.5 Assign Keyboard Shortcuts to Menu Items

Problem

You want to give the user the option to use keyboard shortcuts to control your native menu.

Solution

Set a key equivalent to every menu item that needs a keyboard shortcut by setting the `keyEquivalent` property of the `NativeMenuItem` instance.

Discussion

A good way to make your menu more accessible and usable is by utilizing keyboard shortcuts. To assign a key equivalent to a native menu item in ActionScript, use these lines:

```
var menuItemC:NativeMenuItem = new NativeMenuItem("Menu Item C");
menuItemC.keyEquivalent = "c";
```

A key equivalent consists of two parts: a primary key `String` and an `Array` of modifier keys that must be pressed at the same time. For Windows, the default modifier key is the Control (Ctrl) key. For the Mac, it is the Command (Cmd) key.

Because the previous code does not specify any special key modifier, the actual shortcuts will be Ctrl-C on Windows and Cmd-C on the Mac.

If you want to add the Shift key to the modifier array, simply specify the primary key in uppercase. AIR automatically will add the Shift key to the modifier array. For example, this ActionScript code:

```
var menuItemC:NativeMenuItem = new NativeMenuItem("Menu Item C");
menuItemC.keyEquivalent = "C";
```

specified the shortcut Ctrl-Shift-C for Windows and the shortcut Cmd-Shift-C for the Mac.

The Shift key is always added to a modifier array, even if you define the modifier array yourself. You can define the modifier array in ActionScript as follows:

```
var menuItemC:NativeMenuItem = new NativeMenuItem("Menu Item C");
menuItemC.keyEquivalent = "C";
menuItemC.keyEquivalentModifiers = [Keyboard.CONTROL];
```

This code does the same thing as the previous snippet. The only difference is that you now define the Ctrl modifier yourself instead of using the default value.

20.6 Notify the User Through the Dock (Mac) and the Taskbar (Windows)

Problem

You want to attract the user's attention through the Dock or the taskbar.

Solution

If the operating system supports window-level notification, you can make the application's Dock icon "bounce" by calling the `DockItem.bounce()` method or its taskbar button (and the application window) flash by calling the `notifyUser()` method.

Discussion

When using the Dock's bounce feature, you can pass a `NotificationType` to the `bounce()` method to inform the user that something critical has happened (the application continuously bounces until the application is brought to the foreground) or just to give the user some information (a single bounce).

Similarly, in Windows you can pass a `NotificationType` to the `notifyUser()` method to draw the user's attention by making the application window and its taskbar button flash either continuously (for a critical notification) or once (for an informational notification).

The two appropriate `NotificationType` constants are `NotificationType.CRITICAL` and `NotificationType.INFORMATIONAL`. To determine whether the operating system has this notification capability, access `NativeWindow.supportsNotification`.

Notifying using the Dock (Mac)

The following example shows a small application that has two buttons defined. When clicked, the buttons notify the user in either a critical or informational way. After checking that the operating system supports Dock icons, you can cast the `NativeAppli` `cation.icon` property to an instance of the `DockIcon` class:

```
<?xml version="1.0" encoding="utf-8"?>
<s:WindowedApplication xmlns:fx="http://ns.adobe.com/mxml/2009"
                       xmlns:s="library://ns.adobe.com/flex/spark"
                       xmlns:mx="library://ns.adobe.com/flex/halo"
                       title="Recipe 20.6: Notifying using the Dock (Mac)"
                       deactivate="bounce()">
    <s:layout>
        <s:BasicLayout />
    </s:layout>
    <fx:Declarations>
        <!-- Place nonvisual elements (e.g., services, value objects) here -->
        <s:RadioButtonGroup id="notificationType" />
    </fx:Declarations>

    <fx:Script>
        <![CDATA[

            private function bounce():void
            {
                if (NativeApplication.supportsDockIcon)
                {
                    var myIcon:DockIcon =
NativeApplication.nativeApplication.icon as DockIcon;
                    var type:String = critical.selected ?
                        NotificationType.CRITICAL :
                        NotificationType.INFORMATIONAL;
                    myIcon.bounce(type);
                }
            }

        ]]>
    </fx:Script>
    <s:RadioButton id="critical" group="{notificationType}"
                   label="NOTIFY THE USER CRITICAL"
                   selected="true" x="32" y="64"/>
```

```
<s:RadioButton id="informational" group="{notificationType}"
               label="NOTIFY THE USER INFORMATIONAL"
               x="32" y="90"/>

</s:WindowedApplication>
```

Notifying using the taskbar (Windows)

If the operating system supports window-level notification, you can make the application's taskbar button and window flash by calling the `NativeWindow.notifyUser()` method.

You can pass a `NotificationType` to the `notifyUser()` method to inform the user that something critical has happened (the taskbar button and application window flash until the application is brought to the foreground) or just to give the user some information (the taskbar button and window flash only once). The two appropriate `Notification Type` constants are `NotificationType.CRITICAL` and `NotificationType.INFORMATIONAL`. To determine whether the operating system has this notification capability, access `NativeWindow.supportsNotification`.

The following example shows how to implement this notification with the `Native Window` class. When the application window is deactivated (i.e., is not in the foreground), the taskbar button and window flash to get the attention of the user:

```
<?xml version="1.0" encoding="utf-8"?>
<s:WindowedApplication xmlns:fx="http://ns.adobe.com/mxml/2009"
                       xmlns:s="library://ns.adobe.com/flex/spark"
                       xmlns:mx="library://ns.adobe.com/flex/halo"
                       title="Recipe 20.6: Notifying using the taskbar (Windows)"
                       deactivate="bounce()">
    <s:layout>
        <s:BasicLayout />
    </s:layout>
    <fx:Declarations>
        <!-- Place nonvisual elements (e.g., services, value objects) here -->
        <s:RadioButtonGroup id="notificationType" />
    </fx:Declarations>

    <fx:Script>
        <![CDATA[

            private function bounce():void
            {
                if( NativeWindow.supportsNotification &&
                        NativeApplication.supportsSystemTrayIcon)
                {
                    var type:String = critical.selected ?
                            NotificationType.CRITICAL :
                            NotificationType.INFORMATIONAL;
                    this.nativeWindow.notifyUser(type);
                }
            }
```

```
            ]]>
          </fx:Script>
          <s:RadioButton id="critical" group="{notificationType}"
                         label="NOTIFY THE USER CRITICAL"
                         selected="true" x="32" y="64"/>
          <s:RadioButton id="informational" group="{notificationType}"
                         label="NOTIFY THE USER INFORMATIONAL"
                         x="32" y="90"/>

      </s:WindowedApplication>
```

20.7 Register Custom File Types

Problem

You want to register a custom file type so that the operating system will associate it with your AIR application.

Solution

Use the `fileTypes` element in the application descriptor file to declare the file types associated with your AIR application.

Discussion

When a file type is associated with your AIR application, every associated file of that type will open itself in your AIR application. This gives you great opportunities to work with external files in your AIR application.

Before you begin, you should note that you make associations for an AIR application when installing the application, not at compile or debug time. This means you can't test file associations until you package and install your application. When your application is packaged, the application descriptor XML file is read, and the file associations are set. This is not automatically done if another application on the system is already the default application; in other words, the AIR application install process does not override an existing file type association.

Associations between your application and a file type must be declared in the application descriptor file. Depending on your environment and compiler settings, this descriptor file is typically the *-app.xml* file in your Adobe AIR project, characterized by the application root nodes. In that XML file you can manipulate, for example, the initial, minimum, and maximum width and height; the initial position of your main AIR application window; and the file type associations.

An empty `fileTypes` node in the application descriptor file typically looks like this:

```
<fileTypes>
    <fileType>

        <name></name>
        <extension></extension>
        <description></description>
        <contentType></contentType>
        <icon>
            <image16x16></image16x16>
            <image32x32></image32x32>
            <image48x48></image48x48>
            <image128x128></image128x128>
        </icon>
    </fileType>
</fileTypes>
```

For each file type you want to register, you need to define a `fileType` node in the `fileTypes` element in your application descriptor XML file. The `name` and `extension` values are required, but the `description` and `contentType` values are optional. The `name` value is the name the system displays for the registered file. The `extension` is the extension for the file (not including the leading dot). You can use the same name for multiple extensions.

The description is shown to the user by the operating system user interface when the user looks at the file properties, for example.

The `contentType` property helps the operating system locate the best application to open a file in special circumstances, such as when the extension is not recognized. The `contentType` property is required for any `fileType` defined in the application descriptor file. The value of the `contentType` node is the name of the MIME type for the files.

 MIME stands for Multipurpose Internet Mail Extensions, and MIME types form standard ways of classifying file types. You can find an overview of common MIME types and their corresponding file extensions at *http://en.wikipedia.org/wiki/MIME*.

Last but not least, you can also specify icons for your file types. The icon files must be included in the AIR installation file because they are not packaged automatically.

Setting an icon is also optional. The path specified is relative to the installed AIR application root directory at runtime. Icon files must be in the PNG format, but you can specify different icon sizes. When all sizes are not provided, the closest size is scaled to fit for a given use of the icon by the operating system.

The following example shows a full `fileTypes` node from an application descriptor XML file:

```
<fileTypes>
    <fileType>
        <name>Example.myOwnfileType</name>
        <extension>koen</extension>
        <description>
            This is a custom fileType that has my name
        </description>
        <contentType>text/plain</contentType>
        <icon>
            <image16x16>KOEN16.PNG</image16x16>
            <image32x32>KOEN32.PNG</image32x32>
            <image48x48>KOEN48.PNG</image48x48>
            <image128x128>KOEN128.PNG</image128x128>
        </icon>
    </fileType>
</fileTypes>
```

According to this `fileTypes` node, if the user double-clicks a file called *file.koen*, the associated AIR application will launch.

To retrieve the path to the specific file, you need to write a handler function for the `InvokeEvent` object dispatched by the `NativeApplication` object. The `Native Application` object represents the AIR application, and it can dispatch application-level events. If you want to open the file, you can use that specific path.

When the AIR application is invoked a second time, another instance of the application is not started. Instead, the first instance receives an additional `invoke` event.

If your AIR application is already running when the user double-clicks the associated file, AIR will immediately dispatch the `InvokeEvent` object to the running AIR application.

The following code illustrates how your AIR application can handle an `invoke` event dispatched by the runtime when an associated file is opened:

```
<?xml version="1.0" encoding="utf-8"?>
<s:WindowedApplication xmlns:fx="http://ns.adobe.com/mxml/2009"
                       xmlns:s="library://ns.adobe.com/flex/spark"
                       xmlns:mx="library://ns.adobe.com/flex/halo"
                       applicationComplete="init()">
    <s:layout>
        <s:BasicLayout/>
    </s:layout>
    <fx:Declarations>
        <!-- Place nonvisual elements (e.g., services, value objects) here -->
    </fx:Declarations>

    <fx:Script>
        <![CDATA[
            private function init() : void
```

```
            {
                this.nativeApplication.addEventListener( InvokeEvent.INVOKE,
                                                          invokeHandler );
            }

            private function invokeHandler( event : InvokeEvent ) : void
            {
                pathLabel.text = event.arguments[ 0 ];
            }
        ]]>
    </fx:Script>
    <s:Label id="pathLabel" x="86" y="97" text="" fontSize="15"/>
</s:WindowedApplication>
```

20.8 Open a File with Its Default Application

Problem

You need to open a file directly in its default application.

Solution

Use the `openWithDefaultApplication()` method on a file to open whichever application the operating system associates with that file, and then to activate that application.

Discussion

Adobe AIR 1.5 allowed you to copy, move, create, and make changes to files and folders on the filesystem. AIR 2 builds on this: you now have the additional ability to open files with their default applications.

The `File` class in AIR 2 allows you to:

- Request that a file or folder be opened using the default application registered for that file type on the operating system.

- Receive a notification every time an external volume is added or removed.

- Flag a file as "downloaded," which will notify the operating system that the file was downloaded from the Web.

AIR 2 adds the `openWithDefaultApplication()` method to the `File` class. When you invoke the `openWithDefaultApplication()` method on a `File` object, you ask the operating system to open that file with the default application registered for files of its type. The default application that is associated with a given file extension is defined by user and operating system preferences. There is no way of changing these preferences from AIR.

Suppose you have a file object pointing to a PDF. If you invoke the `openWithDefault` `Application()` method, AIR will try to open it with the registered default application. Depending on the operating system and user preferences, it could be opened with Acrobat Reader, Preview, or another application.

The following code shows how to open a *Readme.pdf* file that is on the computer desktop with the default application:

```
// point to a .pdf file
var pdf:File = File.desktopDirectory.resolvePath("Readme.pdf");
// request to open with default application
pdf.openWithDefaultApplication();
```

If the user doesn't have a registered default application for PDF documents, Adobe AIR generates an error. It is important to intercept this error by using a `try...catch` construct, to avoid the user receiving unwanted or uncontrolled error messages.

If you want to use the `openWithDefaultApplication()` method of the `File` class, remember:

- If the file contains errors, the default application may not be able to open it.
- If the file has the wrong extension, the default application may not be able to open it.
- If you invoke `openWithDefaultApplication()` on a folder it will open in the default explorer application, such as the Finder in Mac OS X.
- You can't launch an application without having a valid file reference name.
- You can't communicate with the default application associated to a file; to do so you have to use the *NativeProcess API* (introduced later, in Recipe 20.12).
- You cannot invoke `openWithDefaultApplication()` for executable files, unless the AIR application has been installed using a *native installer* (also introduced in Recipe 20.12).

Now you will see how to create an application that allows you to select files and folders on the computer and open them with their default applications.

The first step is to define a project that runs in Adobe AIR by creating a new project in Flash Builder and specifying Desktop as its application type. Next, insert two labels and two buttons (`browseFileBtn` and `browseFolderBtn`) contained in two `HGroup` containers in the file:

```
<mx:Spacer height="100" />
<s:HGroup width="100%">
    <s:Label text="Choose File to open: " width="100%" />
    <mx:Spacer width="10" />
    <s:Button id="browseFileBtn" label="Browse File" />
</s:HGroup>
<s:HGroup width="100%">
    <s:Label text="Choose Folder to browse: " width="100%" />
    <mx:Spacer width="10" />
```

```
        <s:Button id="browseFolderBtn" label="Browse Folder" />
    </s:HGroup>
```

When clicked, the `browseFileBtn` and `browseFolderBtn` buttons open a dialog box that allows the user to select a file or folder, respectively, from the local filesystem. You can retrieve the complete file from the *ch20* folder in the book's source code files (available from the downloads section on the book's website, *http://oreilly.com/catalog/9780596805616*).

To create the ActionScript code that will operate with the file and folder, first create a `Script` block and import the necessary classes:

```
<fx:Script>
    <![CDATA[
        import flash.events.Event;
        import flash.events.MouseEvent;
        import mx.controls.Alert;

        private var file : File;
    ]]>
</ fx:Script>
```

The private `file` variable will contain a reference to the file or folder that the user selects through the dialog box:

```
private var file : File;
```

On the `applicationComplete` event of the `WindowedApplication`, the application will invoke the `init()` method:

```
<s:WindowedApplication xmlns:fx="http://ns.adobe.com/mxml/2009"
                       xmlns:s="library://ns.adobe.com/flex/spark"
                       xmlns:mx="library://ns.adobe.com/flex/halo"
                       title="Recipe 20.8: Open a File with Its Default Application"
                       applicationComplete="init()">
```

The `init()` method instantiates a `File` object that will be used to select files and folders. You register the event handlers that you need for the application to work as shown here:

```
private function init() : void
{
    file = File.desktopDirectory;
    file.addEventListener( Event.SELECT, openSelection );

    browseFileBtn.addEventListener( MouseEvent.CLICK, onBrowseFile );
    browseFolderBtn.addEventListener( MouseEvent.CLICK, onBrowseFolder );
}
```

The `onBrowseFile()` and `onBrowseFolder()` event listeners are associated with the two buttons. They allow the user to select the file or the folder to open with its default application. Here's the code to accomplish these tasks:

```
private function onBrowseFile( event : MouseEvent ) : void
{
    file.browseForOpen( "Choose a file to open" );
}
```

```
private function onBrowseFolder( event : MouseEvent ) : void
{
    file.browseForDirectory( "Choose a folder to browse" );
}
```

When a file or a folder is selected, the openSelection() function invokes the opening of the selection in its default application, as shown here:

```
private function openSelection( event : Event ) : void
{
    try
    {
        file.openWithDefaultApplication();
    }
    catch( error : Error )
    {
        Alert.show( "Error: " + error.message, "Error" );
    }
}
```

Here is the complete code for the application:

```
<s:WindowedApplication xmlns:fx="http://ns.adobe.com/mxml/2009"
                       xmlns:s="library://ns.adobe.com/flex/spark"
                       xmlns:mx="library://ns.adobe.com/flex/halo"
                       title="Recipe 20.8: Open a File with Its Default Application"
                       applicationComplete="init()">

    <s:layout>
        <s:VerticalLayout />
    </s:layout>

    <fx:Script>
        <![CDATA[
            import flash.events.Event;
            import flash.events.MouseEvent;

            import mx.controls.Alert;

            private var file : File;

            private function init() : void
            {
                file = File.desktopDirectory;
                file.addEventListener( Event.SELECT, openSelection );

                browseFileBtn.addEventListener( MouseEvent.CLICK, onBrowseFile );
                browseFolderBtn.addEventListener( MouseEvent.CLICK,
                                                  onBrowseFolder );
            }

            private function onBrowseFile( event : MouseEvent ) : void
            {
                file.browseForOpen( "Choose a file to open" );
            }
```

```
            private function onBrowseFolder( event : MouseEvent ) : void
            {
                file.browseForDirectory( "Choose a folder to browse" );
            }

            private function openSelection( event : Event ) : void
            {
                try
                {
                    file.openWithDefaultApplication();
                }
                catch( error : Error )
                {
                    Alert.show( "Error: " + error.message, "Error" );
                }
            }
        ]]>
    </fx:Script>
    <mx:Spacer height="100" />
    <s:HGroup width="100%">
        <s:Label text="Choose File to open: " width="100%" />
        <mx:Spacer width="10" />
        <s:Button id="browseFileBtn" label="Browse File" />
    </s:HGroup>
    <s:HGroup width="100%">
        <s:Label text="Choose Folder to browse: " width="100%" />
        <mx:Spacer width="10" />
        <s:Button id="browseFolderBtn" label="Browse Folder" />
    </s:HGroup>

</s:WindowedApplication>
```

Run the application and try to select files and folders from your computer. You will see that they will be opened by their default applications.

20.9 Check for Mounted and Unmounted Drives

Problem

You need to determine if an external drive has been added to or removed from the system.

Solution

Use AIR 2's new StorageVolumeInfo.storageVolumeInfo object.

Discussion

AIR 2 offers the ability to control the addition and removal of external drives, as well as to obtain specific information on them. For example, you can recognize and access USB keys and video cameras connected to the computer.

To know when a drive has been connected or is mounted or unmounted, you need to register an event listener method to the Singleton `StorageVolumeInfo.storageVolume Info` object. The following code shows how to recognize the mounting, connection, and disconnection of a drive:

```
StorageVolumeInfo.storageVolumeInfo.addEventListener(
        StorageVolumeChangeEvent.STORAGE_VOLUME_MOUNT, onVolumeMount );
StorageVolumeInfo.storageVolumeInfo.addEventListener(
        StorageVolumeChangeEvent.STORAGE_VOLUME_UNMOUNT, onVolumeUnmount );
```

Every time a drive is mounted or unmounted, a `StorageVolumeChangeEvent` object containing information regarding the drive is passed to the event handler functions. Every `StorageVolumeChangeEvent` object transports two relevant properties: `rootDirectory` is a `File` object that indicates the absolute pathway of the drive, while `storageVolume` is a `StorageVolume` object that contains the details that are available for the drive. This property is `null` if the event indicates that the drive is unmounted.

The `StorageVolume` class provides the specific information for the drive that is connected to the computer. The properties are:

`fileSystemType`
Indicates the type of filesystem on the storage volume (such as "FAT" or "NTFS").

`isRemovable`
Shows whether or not the drive is removable.

`isWritable`
Shows if the drive is writable.

`drive`
Indicates the volume letter. Only valid for Windows; this is null on Mac and Linux.

`name`
Specifies the drive name.

`rootDirectory`
Specifies a `File` object with the absolute pathway of the drive.

All properties of the `StorageVolume` class are read-only.

20.10 Obtain a List of Available External Drives

Problem

You want to obtain a list of external drives that are available to the system.

Solution

Query the `StorageVolumeInfo` class using the `getStorageVolumes()` function to obtain a list of external drives connected to the computer.

Discussion

To obtain information on the external drives that are available, it is not necessary to listen to the events of the `StorageVolumeInfo` class. Instead, use the following code to obtain a list of external drives that are connected to the computer:

```
var volumes:Vector.<StorageVolume> =
        StorageVolumeInfo.storageVolumeInfo.getStorageVolumes();
```

As you can see, the `getStorageVolumes()` function returns a `Vector`-type list, to guarantee the validity of the objects it contains.

This recipe will show you how to create an application that checks if any external drives are mounted on the computer. When a drive is mounted on the system, a new window is created that shows the content of the drive. Every time a drive is unmounted, the relevant window will close.

First, create a new MXML file from the AIR project that you created in Recipe 20.9. Then insert one `Label` control in the file with the following properties:

```
<s:Label width="100%" textAlign="center" text="Plug a removable volume."
        x="0" y="34"/>
```

Next, add a `Script` block and import the classes you need to manage the external drives:

```
<fx:Script>
    <![CDATA[
        import com.comtaste.oreilly.f4cookbook.VolumeWindow;

        import flash.events.StorageVolumeChangeEvent;

        private var stageRef : Stage;

        private var volumes : Array;
    ]]>
</fx:Script>
```

The first import regards a custom ActionScript class named `VolumeWindow` that is in the `com.comtaste.oreilly.f4cookbook` package and that extends the `flash.display.Native Window` class. This class will create a window that will be used to view the content of the external drives that are connected to the computer. The class will receive a `StorageVolume`-type object as an argument of the constructor function.

You next need to create a method called `init()`, which will be executed upon the `applicationComplete` event of the application. Three event listener functions will be registered in this method: two to track the mounting and unmounting of external drives and a third for the closing event of the application. Finally, you instantiate the array that will contain a reference to the open windows:

```
private function init() : void
{
    // listen for VolumeChangeEvents, to monitor when new volumes are
    // mounted or unmounted
    StorageVolumeInfo.storageVolumeInfo.addEventListener(
            StorageVolumeChangeEvent.STORAGE_VOLUME_MOUNT, addVolume );
    StorageVolumeInfo.storageVolumeInfo.addEventListener(
            StorageVolumeChangeEvent.STORAGE_VOLUME_UNMOUNT, removeVolume );

    // event handler for application closing event
    this.stage.nativeWindow.addEventListener( Event.CLOSING, onClosingWindow );

    // open pop ups
    volumes = new Array();
}
```

When you connect a new external drive, the application executes the addVolume() function. This function creates a new VolumeWindow-type window and saves a reference in the volumes array:

```
private function addVolume(e:StorageVolumeChangeEvent):void
{
    if (e.storageVolume.isRemovable)
    {
        var popup : VolumeWindow = new VolumeWindow( e.storageVolume );
        popup.width = 600;
        popup.height = 450;
        popup.activate();

        // store popup reference
        var id : String = e.rootDirectory.name;
        volumes.push( { url: id, popup: popup } );
    }
}
```

Now every time a new external drive is added, the application creates a new window showing the content of the drive. However, you also have to manage the unmounting of the external drives. You want the relevant window to close every time an external drive is removed. That is why the volumes array maintains its references to the open windows.

Every time an external drive is removed, the removeVolume() function is executed. The removeVolume() function searches the volumes array for the window that corresponds to the external drive that has just been removed. If it finds it, it removes the reference from the volumes array and invokes the close() function of the window:

```
private function removeVolume(e:StorageVolumeChangeEvent):void
{
// get ID REF
var id : String = e.rootDirectory.name;
```

```
// search reference
var popup : VolumeWindow;
for( var i : int = 0; i < volumes.length; i++ )
{
var obj : Object = volumes[ i ];
if( obj != null )
{
var url : String = obj[ "url" ];
if( url == id )
{
// get popup pointer
popup = obj[ "popup" ] as VolumeWindow;

// delete popup reference
volumes.splice( i, 1 );

// break loop
break;
}
}
}

// close popup
if( popup != null )
popup.close();
}
```

When you ask the main window of the application to close, it is also necessary to close all the open windows for any external drives that are connected. This is why you execute the onClosingWindow() function. This function looks for any references to windows in the volumes array and, if it finds any, forces them to close with the close() method. The code for onClosingWindow() is:

```
private function onClosingWindow(e:Event):void
{
for (var i:int = volumes.length - 1; i >= 0; --i)
{
var popup : VolumeWindow = volumes[ i ][ "popup" ];
popup.close();
}
volumes = null;
}
```

Now it's time to create the new VolumeWindow class in the com.comtaste.oreilly.f4cook book package. The VolumeWindow class extends NativeWindow and will be used to view the content of the external drives that are connected. The class receives a StorageVolume-type object as an argument of the constructor function. This object allows the class to access the list of files and folders on the external drive. To access the list of drives that are available, you invoke the getDirectoryListingAsync() function of the File class. The icons of the files and folders that are available are then presented in a fl.controls.TileList component.

Here is the complete code of the VolumeWindow class:

```
package com.comtaste.oreilly.f4cookbook
{
    import fl.controls.ScrollBarDirection;
    import fl.controls.TileList;

    import flash.display.Bitmap;
    import flash.display.BitmapData;
    import flash.display.Loader;
    import flash.display.NativeWindow;
    import flash.display.NativeWindowInitOptions;
    import flash.display.NativeWindowSystemChrome;
    import flash.display.NativeWindowType;
    import flash.display.StageAlign;
    import flash.display.StageScaleMode;
    import flash.events.Event;
    import flash.events.FileListEvent;
    import flash.events.NativeWindowBoundsEvent;
    import flash.filesystem.File;
    import flash.filesystem.FileMode;
    import flash.filesystem.FileStream;
    import flash.filesystem.StorageVolume;
    import flash.geom.Matrix;
    import flash.utils.ByteArray;

    public class VolumeWindow extends NativeWindow
    {
        private var volume : StorageVolume;

        private var tileSide : uint = 128;

        private var tileList : TileList;

        public function VolumeWindow( volume : StorageVolume )
        {
            this.volume = volume;

            var initOptions:NativeWindowInitOptions = new
                    NativeWindowInitOptions();
            initOptions.type = NativeWindowType.UTILITY;
            initOptions.systemChrome = NativeWindowSystemChrome.STANDARD;
            initOptions.transparent = false;
            super(initOptions);

            this.title = "Volume: " + volume.name;

            this.stage.align = StageAlign.TOP_LEFT;
            this.stage.scaleMode = StageScaleMode.NO_SCALE;

            this.addEventListener( NativeWindowBoundsEvent.RESIZE, onResize );

            createIcons();
        }
```

```
private function createIcons():void
{
    // init TileList
    tileList = new TileList();

    // Set scroll bar direction
    tileList.direction = ScrollBarDirection.HORIZONTAL;

    // position TileList and set column and row values
    tileList.move(0,0);
    tileList.columnWidth = tileSide;
    tileList.rowHeight = tileSide;

    tileList.columnCount = Math.floor( this.width / tileList.columnWidth );
    tileList.rowCount = Math.floor( ( this.height - 15) /
                                    tileList.rowHeight );

    tileList.width = tileList.columnCount * tileList.columnWidth;
    tileList.height = tileList.rowCount * tileList.columnWidth;

    // add to the display
    this.stage.addChild(tileList);

    volume.rootDirectory.addEventListener( FileListEvent.DIRECTORY_LISTING,
                                           onFileListReady );
    volume.rootDirectory.getDirectoryListingAsync();
}

private function onFileListReady( event : FileListEvent ):void
{
    volume.rootDirectory.removeEventListener(
            FileListEvent.DIRECTORY_LISTING, onFileListReady );
    var files : Array = event.files;

    var file : File;
    var ext : String;
    var bitmap : Bitmap;
    var imageBytes:ByteArray;
    var stream:FileStream;
    var loader:Loader;
    for each( file in files )
    {
        ext = file.extension;
        if (ext != null && (ext.toLocaleLowerCase() == "jpg" ||
            ext.toLocaleLowerCase() == "png" || ext.toLocaleLowerCase() ==
            "gif") )
        {
            imageBytes = new ByteArray();

            // read image bytes
            stream = new FileStream();
            stream.open(file, FileMode.READ);
            stream.readBytes(imageBytes);
            stream.close();
```

```
        // handler for image loaded
        var imageDataLoaded : Function = function(event:Event):void
        {
            // set correct scaling
            var scaleFactor:Number = 1;
            if ( loader.width > loader.height && loader.width >
                 tileSide )
            {
                scaleFactor = tileSide / loader.width;
            }
            if ( loader.height > loader.width && loader.height >
                 tileSide)
            {
                scaleFactor = tileSide / loader.height;
            }

            // access image and scale it
            var bmd:BitmapData = Bitmap(loader.content).bitmapData;
            var scaledBMD:BitmapData = new BitmapData(loader.width *
                    scaleFactor, loader.height * scaleFactor);
            var matrix:Matrix = new Matrix();
            matrix.scale(scaleFactor, scaleFactor);
            scaledBMD.draw(bmd, matrix, null, null, null, true);

            // create new bitmap
            bitmap = new Bitmap(scaledBMD);


            // clear memory
            loader.unload();
            bmd = null;
        };

        // load image
        loader = new Loader();
        loader.contentLoaderInfo.addEventListener( Event.COMPLETE,
                                                imageDataLoaded );
        loader.loadBytes(imageBytes);
    }
    else
    {
        var bitmaps:Array = file.icon.bitmaps;
        var iconData:BitmapData = this.getBiggestIcon(bitmaps);
        bitmap = new Bitmap(iconData, "auto", true);
        bitmap.opaqueBackground = null;
        bitmap.width = tileSide;
        bitmap.height = tileSide;
    }

    // store new bitmap
    tileList.addItem({label: file.name, source: bitmap});
    }
}
```

```
private function getBiggestIcon(icons:Array):BitmapData
{
    var biggest:BitmapData = icons[0] as BitmapData;
    for each (var icon:BitmapData in icons)
    {
        if (icon.width > biggest.width || icon.width == tileSide)
        {
            biggest = icon;
        }
    }
    return biggest;
}

private function onResize( event : NativeWindowBoundsEvent ) : void
{
    var w : Number = event.afterBounds.width;
    var h : Number = event.afterBounds.height;

    tileList.move(0,0);
    tileList.columnWidth = tileSide;
    tileList.rowHeight = tileSide;

    tileList.columnCount = Math.floor( w / tileList.columnWidth );
    tileList.rowCount = Math.floor( ( h - 15) / tileList.rowHeight );

    tileList.width = tileList.columnCount * tileList.columnWidth;
    tileList.height = tileList.rowCount * tileList.columnWidth;
}

    }
}
```

When you run the project, try adding external drives to or removing them from the computer. The application should open new windows and close them accordingly, as shown in Figure 20-3.

20.11 Tell the Operating System That a File Has Been Downloaded from the Web

Problem

You need to know when a file has been downloaded from the Internet.

Solution

In AIR 2, create a File object that refers to the relevant document, then set the down loaded property to true to flag the file.

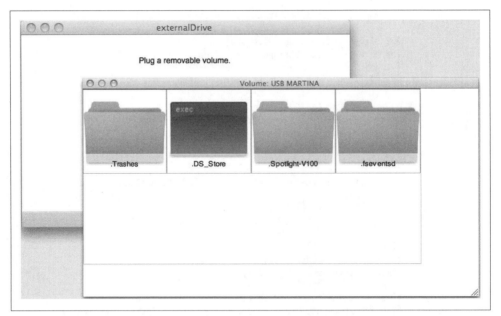

Figure 20-3. The pop-up window shows the external drives that are connected to the computer

Discussion

Some operating systems allow you to flag files as having been downloaded from the Web. This way, when you try to execute or open a downloaded file, the system will ask you for confirmation before it proceeds. This technique allows you to know which files you have created locally and which ones you have downloaded from external sources. To flag downloaded files using AIR 2, use the following code:

```
// get File object pointing to desired file
var remoteSong : File = File.desktopDirectory.resolvePath("remoteSong.mp3");
// mark the file as downloaded
remoteSong.downloaded = true;
```

 Files downloaded using the `FileReference.download()` method are marked as downloaded by the Flash Player.

20.12 Deploy an AIR Application as a Native Installer

Problem

You need to interact directly with the native processes of the operating system.

Solution

In AIR 2, use the new `NativeProcess` class and an application distributed via a native installer.

Discussion

Adobe AIR 2 introduces the concept of native installers and the possibility of interacting directly with the native processes of the operating system. This new addition means that now it is possible to package and distribute an AIR application via a native installer (e.g., a DMG file on Mac OS X, EXE file on Windows, or RPM or DEB file on Linux). Applications that are distributed via a native installer allow you to interact with the operating system's native processes, using the new `NativeProcess` class. This new class allows you to create much more complex and refined applications compared to the possibilities of AIR 1.5.

It is only possible to create a native installer for the operating system on which you are working. That is, to create a native installer for Windows, the executable file must be compiled on Windows, and to create a native installer for Mac OS X, you need to compile the executable file on a Mac OS platform.

You can create a native installer by starting from either the original Flash CS4 project or an *.air* file you have already compiled.

The `NativeProcess` class has the `isSupported` property to check whether the application in execution can interact with the operating system's native processes. To use the native processes, you need to add the following node to the XML file of the application descriptor file, as well as creating the native installer:

```
<supportedProfiles>extendedDesktop</supportedProfiles>
```

If this node is not defined, the `NativeProcess.isSupported` property will always be `false` and it will not be possible to interact with the native processes.

Invoking and interacting with native processes

You can easily create an application that invokes a native process, receives information in response, and interrupts communication. This recipe's example application uses the *ping* executable, as it is available for most operating systems supported by Adobe AIR 2.

The first step is to create a new MXML file and insert the following controls:

startProcessBtn
> A `Button` control on the stage; clicking it launches the ping process

stopProcessBtn
> A `Button` control on the stage; clicking it stops the ping process

siteURL

A **TextInput** on the stage; used to define the remote address to ping

outputConsole

A **TextArea** on the stage; prints the ping process output

The code you need to insert is:

```
<s:HGroup width="100%">

    <s:Button id="startProcessBtn"
            label="Start Process"/>
    <s:Button id="stopProcessBtn"
            label="Stop Process"/>
    <s:TextInput id="siteURL"
            width="100%"
            text="www.google.com"/>

</s:HGroup>

<mx:Text width="100%"
        text="Try to ping given website using native ping command offered by
            your system"/>
<s:TextArea id="outputConsole"
        width="100%"
        height="100%"/>
```

This file will deal with starting and stopping the native process.

Next, create a script block within the MXML file with the following code to check if the application can interact with the native processes of the operating system:

```
<fx:Script>
    <![CDATA[
        import flash.events.MouseEvent;

        import mx.controls.Alert;

        private var nativeProc:NativeProcess;

        private var executablePaths : Object;

    ]]>
</fx:Script>

// Add an init() method right away invoked on the applicationComplete:
public function init():void
{
    if (!NativeProcess.isSupported)
    {
        // You could also get this error if you forgot to add the extendedDesktop
        // flag to your app.xml descriptor.
        // This line must be within the <application> tags:
        // <supportedProfiles>extendedDesktop</supportedProfiles>
```

```
            Alert.show("NativeProcess is not supported");
        }
        else
        {
            // register mouse events for buttons
            startProcessBtn.addEventListener( MouseEvent.CLICK, runProcess );
            stopProcessBtn.addEventListener( MouseEvent.CLICK, stopProcess );

            // init ping executable paths
            executablePaths = new Object();
            executablePaths[ "unix1" ] = "/sbin/ping";
            executablePaths[ "unix2" ] = "/bin/ping";
            executablePaths[ "unix3" ] = "/usr/bin/ping";
            executablePaths[ "win" ] = "c:\windows\system32\ping.exe";
        }
    }
}
```

If the method determines the application cannot interact with the native processes, it
displays an alert window that states "NativeProcess is not supported." If it is possible
to use the native processes, two event listeners are registered for click events on two
buttons: startProcessBtn and stopProcessBtn. Finally, as shown here, you need to define the possible pathways of the *ping* executable:

```
executablePaths = new Object();
executablePaths[ "unix1" ] = "/sbin/ping";
executablePaths[ "unix2" ] = "/bin/ping";
executablePaths[ "unix3" ] = "/usr/bin/ping";
executablePaths[ "win" ] = "c:\windows\system32\ping.exe";
```

When the user clicks on the startProcessBtn button, the runProcess() function is executed. This function checks for the existence of the *ping* executable in a try...catch
construct. Here is the code:

```
public function runProcess( event : MouseEvent ):void
{
    var file:File = new File();
    try
    {
        // use default paths for ping
        // (modify if your system does not use the default path)
        if ( Capabilities.os.toLowerCase().indexOf( "win" ) > -1 )
        {
            file = new File( executablePaths[ "win" ] );
        }
        else if ( Capabilities.os.toLowerCase().indexOf( "mac" ) > -1 ||
                  Capabilities.os.toLowerCase().indexOf( "linux" ) > -1 )
        {
            file = new File( executablePaths[ "unix1" ] );
            if ( file == null )
            file = new File( executablePaths[ "unix2" ] );
            else
            if ( file == null )
            file = new File( executablePaths[ "unix3" ] );
        }
```

```
            // create object to specify arguments to send to ping process
            var nativeProcessStartupInfo : NativeProcessStartupInfo =
                new NativeProcessStartupInfo();

            // point to executable
            nativeProcessStartupInfo.executable = file;

            // define a vector with argument
            var args : Vector.<String> = new Vector.<String>;

            // URL to ping
            args.push( siteURL.text );
            nativeProcessStartupInfo.arguments = args;

            // create native process object
            nativeProc = new NativeProcess();

            // register process data output handler
            nativeProc.addEventListener( ProgressEvent.STANDARD_OUTPUT_DATA,
                                    onDataOutput );

            // register process error handler
            nativeProc.addEventListener( ProgressEvent.STANDARD_ERROR_DATA,
                                    onDataError );

            // start defined process
            nativeProc.start( nativeProcessStartupInfo );
        }
        catch (e:Error)
        {
            Alert.show(e.message, "Error");
        }
    }
}
```

After the function finds the executable, you create a `NativeProcessStartupInfo` object. This class allows you to define the executable to invoke and the arguments to pass to it. The arguments are defined in a `Vector.<String>` object. The only argument passed to the executable in this case is the ping address, as shown here:

```
            // create object to specify arguments to send to ping process
            var nativeProcessStartupInfo : NativeProcessStartupInfo = new
                NativeProcessStartupInfo();

            // point to executable
            nativeProcessStartupInfo.executable = file;

            // define a vector with argument
            var args : Vector.<String> = new Vector.<String>;

            // URL to ping
            args.push( siteURL.text );
            nativeProcessStartupInfo.arguments = args;
```

After defining the properties of the call to the ping process, you create a `Native Process` object that has the task of actually executing the invocation of the native process. You register two event listeners on the `nativeProcess` object: the `onDataOutput()` function will receive the output during the execution of the process, and `onData Error()` will receive any errors in the execution of the process. Finally, execute the `start()` function of the `nativeProcess` object:

```
// create native process object
nativeProc = new NativeProcess();

// register process data output handler
nativeProc.addEventListener( ProgressEvent.STANDARD_OUTPUT_DATA,
                             onDataOutput );

// register process error handler
nativeProc.addEventListener( ProgressEvent.STANDARD_ERROR_DATA,
                             onDataError );

// start defined process
nativeProc.start( nativeProcessStartupInfo );

} catch ( e : Error ) {

    Alert.show(e.message, "Error");
}
}
```

The `stopProcess()` function is executed when the user clicks on the `stopProcessBtn` button. This function requests that the execution of the process be interrupted:

```
/**
 * Stop and exit from native process execution.
 * Print in a textfield if any errors occur.
 */
private function stopProcess( event : MouseEvent ) : void
{
    try
    {
        // close process execution
        nativeProc.exit();
        outputConsole.text += "Exit Process Done";
    }
    catch( error : Error )
    {
        outputConsole.text += "Exit Process Error:\n " + error.message;
    }
}
```

During the execution of the native process, the `onDataOutput()` and `onDataError()` functions write the information they have received from the process in the `out putConsole` text field. These are the two methods:

```
/**
 * Receive data sent back from process execution.
 * Print the data in a textfield.
 */
public function onDataOutput( event : ProgressEvent ) : void
{
    // data received
    var data : String = nativeProc.standardOutput.readUTFBytes(
            nativeProc.standardOutput.bytesAvailable );
    outputConsole.text += data;
}

/**
 * Receive error sent back from process execution.
 * Print the error in a textfield.
 */
public function onDataError( event : ProgressEvent ) : void
{
    // error received
    var data : String = nativeProc.standardError.readUTFBytes(
            nativeProc.standardError.bytesAvailable );
    outputConsole.text += data;
}
```

Now the project is complete and you can run it. Try running the ping process on various remote addresses. The output of the ping process will be shown in the `outputConsole` text field.

You can create a native installer by invoking the *adt* executable from the command line:

1. Create an AIR installer for the Flex project.
2. Open Terminal on Mac OS X or a command-line session on Windows and navigate to the folder containing *nativeProcess.air*.
3. Invoke the *adl* executable to create the native installer. The syntax to create a native installer from an AIR application is:

   ```
   adt -package -target native installer_file air_file
   ```

   If you are operating on Mac OS X, the following code generates a native installer:

   ```
   adt -package -target native nativeProcess.dmg nativeProcess.air
   ```

   If you are operating on Windows, the following code generates a native installer:

   ```
   adt -package -target native nativeProcess.exe nativeProcess.air
   ```

If everything has gone well, you should now have a native installer. Figure 20-4 shows the creation of a native installer on Mac OS X.

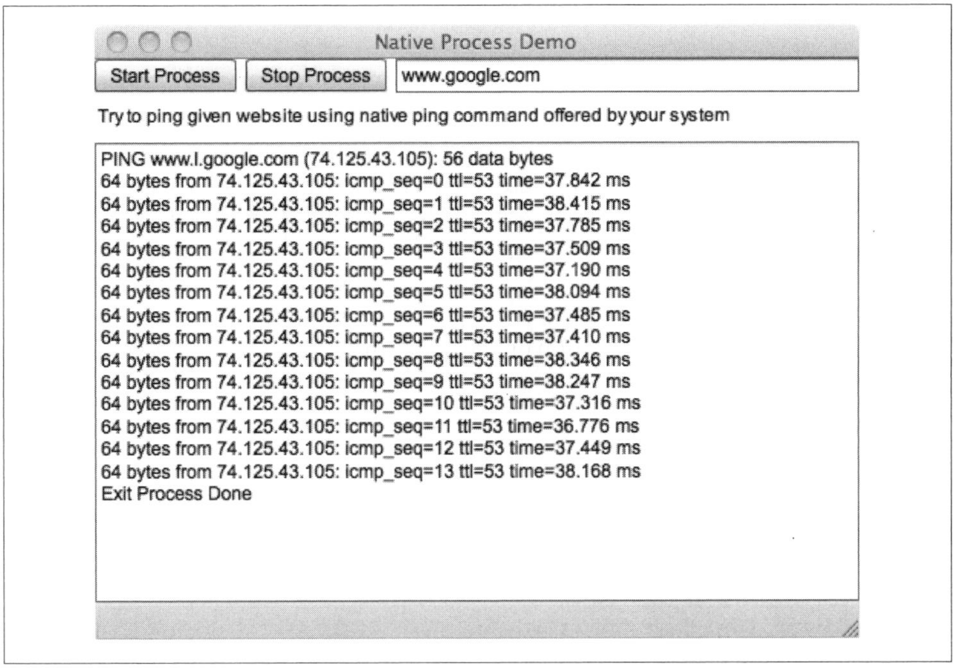

Figure 20-4. The native installer created

20.13 Create a HTTP Proxy Using the ServerSocket Class

Problem

You need to create a simple HTTP proxy that listens to all incoming calls to a given port.

Solution

Use AIR 2's new `ServerSocket` class.

Discussion

With AIR 2, you can not only connect to XML and binary sockets, but also receive messages through sockets. Now AIR applications can behave like servers. This opens the door to new and interesting scenarios, such as:

- Peer-to-peer communication in which applications exchange data on an intranet without needing a server as an intermediary in the communication process.

- Communication between different applications on the same machine, making it possible to create an ecosystem of applications that is much more integrated and functional than was possible in the past.

- Testing your own applications via local mini-web servers.

Your operating system may not allow you to use the `ServerSocket` class with ports under 1024, so unless it is specifically required, you are advised to use ports over 1024.

In this recipe you will see how to create a `ServerSocket` that listens on a given port, allowing you to simulate a local web server with very limited functionality. The server will allow you to view simple HTML pages without any advanced functions or external files. For a preview of what you'll create, you can view the completed *socketServer.fxp* project file found in the */ch20* folder in the book's source code files (available from the downloads section on the book's website, *http://oreilly.com/catalog/ 9780596805616*).

To begin, create a new MXML file in the AIR project you created earlier in this recipe, and insert the following containers and controls:

```
<s:HGroup width="100%" verticalAlign="middle">
    <s:Label text="Port to listen:"/>
    <s:TextInput id="port"
                 text="8888"
                 width="50"/>
    <s:Button label="open connection"
              click="listen()"/>

    <mx:Spacer width="10" />

    <s:Label text="WebRoot:"/>
    <s:TextInput id="path"
                 editable="false"
                 text=""
                 width="100%"/>
    <s:Button label="Choose webroot folder"
              click="changeWebRoot()" />
</s:HGroup>

<s:TextArea id="outputConsole"
            width="100%"
            height="100%"/>
```

Next, add a `Script` block and start importing the classes and properties you need for the project. In particular:

```
<fx:Script>
    <![CDATA[

        import flash.events.Event;
        import flash.events.ProgressEvent;
        import flash.events.ServerSocketConnectEvent;
        import flash.net.ServerSocket;
        import flash.net.Socket;
        import flash.utils.ByteArray;

        import mx.controls.Alert;
```

```
                private var server : ServerSocket;

                private var validMimeTypes : Object = new Object();

                private var webRootFolder : File;
        ]]>
    </fx:Script>
```

The class defines the **server** property, typed as **ServerSocket**, the **validMimeTypes** property, typed as **Object**, and the **webRootFolder** property, typed as **File**. The **server** property will be the server that receives the calls on the relevant port. The **validMime Types** property defines the MIME types that the server accepts, and **webRootFolder** specifies the folder where the server will look for the requested files.

Next, add an **init()** method, which launches upon receipt of the **application Complete** event, defines the valid MIME types, and registers two event listeners on two buttons that start and stop the **ServerSocket**:

```
private function init() : void
{
    // define the MIME types the socket server will support
    validMimeTypes[ ".swf" ] = "application/x-shockwave-flash ";
    validMimeTypes[ ".js" ] = "application/x-javascript";
    validMimeTypes[ ".htm" ] = "text/html";
    validMimeTypes[ ".html" ] = "text/html";
    validMimeTypes[ ".css" ] = "text/css";
    validMimeTypes[ ".ico" ] = "image/x-icon";
    validMimeTypes[ ".jpg" ] = "image/jpeg";
    validMimeTypes[ ".png" ] = "image/png";
    validMimeTypes[ ".gif" ] = "image/gif";

    this.addEventListener( Event.CLOSING, onClosingApp );
}
// you also create an event listener on the CLOSING event, which
// executes the onClosingApp() method:
private function onClosingApp( event : Event ) : void
{
    try
    {
        server.close();
    }
    catch( error : Error )
    {}
}
```

When the **chooseServerRootBtn** button is clicked, it executes the **changeWebRoot()** function. This function deals with letting the user choose the folder for the web server:

```
private function changeWebRoot() : void
{
    webRootFolder = File.desktopDirectory;
    webRootFolder.addEventListener( Event.SELECT, onWebRootFolderSelected )
    webRootFolder.browseForDirectory( "Choose root folder for AIR Socket Server" );
}
```

Next, create an event listener for the SELECT event, which is triggered only when the user has selected the folder from the dialog window that opens with the browseForDirectory() method:

```
webRootFolder.addEventListener( Event.SELECT, onWebRootFolderSelected )
webRootFolder.browseForDirectory( "Choose root folder for AIR Socket Server" );
```

Once the folder has been selected the onWebRootFolderSelected() method is invoked:

```
private function onWebRootFolderSelected( event : Event ) : void
{
    webRootFolder.removeEventListener( Event.SELECT, onWebRootFolderSelected )

    // update text on screen
    path.text = webRootFolder.nativePath;
}
```

When the user clicks the openServerConnectionBtn button, it executes the listen() function. This function opens the connection of the ServerSocket on the specified port, which will start the HTTP proxy. Here is the code:

```
private function listen() : void
{
    if( webRootFolder == null )
    setDefaultWebRoot();

    try
    {
        server = new ServerSocket();
        server.addEventListener( Event.CONNECT, onSocketConnected );
        server.bind( Number( port.text ) );
        server.listen();
        outputConsole.text += "Server now listening on port [ " + port.text
                                                        + "]\n";
    }
    catch ( error : Error )
    {
        outputConsole.text += "ERROR -- Port [ " + port.text + " ] NOT AVAILABLE,
                try another one.\n";
        Alert.show( "Port " + port.text + " not available. Try again with another
                port number.", "Error" );
    }
}
// If the webRootFolder property is null, it will execute the setDefaultWebRoot()
// method to set the default web root:
private function setDefaultWebRoot() : void
{
    // copy sample HTML to a folder on the desktop
    webRootFolder = File.desktopDirectory.resolvePath( "AIRsocketServerRoot" );
```

```
            // if folder doesn't exist, populate it with a sample file
            if ( !webRootFolder.exists )
            File.applicationDirectory.resolvePath( "AIRsocketServerRoot" ).copyTo(
                    webRootFolder );

            // update text on screen
            path.text = webRootFolder.nativePath;
        }
```

When the ServerSocket begins running, it invokes the onSocketConnected() function every time the server receives a call on the specified port, which registers an event listener on the SOCKET_DATA event:

```
    private function onSocketConnected( event : ServerSocketConnectEvent ) : void
    {
        var socket : Socket = event.socket;
        socket.addEventListener( ProgressEvent.SOCKET_DATA, onSocketDataReceived );
    }
```

The onSocketDataReceived() event listener receives a ByteArray object containing the message it has received from the ServerSocket. The pathway of the requested file is extracted from this message. The existence of the requested file is checked in the webRootFolder folder. If the file exists, its content is sent back via the ServerSocket. If the file does not exist or it is not a valid MIME type, the ByteArray object returns the text equivalent of a HTML page with the getMimeType() method, which shows that the requested file does not exist. The onSocketDataReceived() event handler is shown here:

```
    private function onSocketDataReceived( event : ProgressEvent ) : void
    {
        try
        {
            var socket : Socket = event.target as Socket;
            var bytes : ByteArray = new ByteArray();
            socket.readBytes( bytes );

            var request : String = "" + bytes;
            outputConsole.text += request;

            var filePath : String = request.substring( 5, request.indexOf( "HTTP/" )
                    - 1 );
            var file : File = webRootFolder.resolvePath( filePath );
            if ( file.exists && !file.isDirectory )
            {
                var content : ByteArray = new ByteArray();
                var stream : FileStream = new FileStream();
                stream.open( file, FileMode.READ );
                stream.readBytes( content );
                stream.close();
```

```
        socket.writeUTFBytes( "HTTP/1.1 200 OK\n" );
        socket.writeUTFBytes( "Content-Type: " + getMimeType( filePath )
                + "\n\n" );
        socket.writeBytes( content );
    }
    else
    {
        socket.writeUTFBytes( "HTTP/1.1 404 Not Found\n" );
        socket.writeUTFBytes( "Content-Type: text/html\n\n" );
        socket.writeUTFBytes( "<html><body><h1>Impossible load the requested
                page.</h1></body></html>" );
    }
    socket.flush();
    socket.close();
    }
    catch ( error : Error )
    {
        outputConsole.text += error.message + "\n\n";
        Alert.show( error.message, "Error" );
    }
}
```

Finally, here is the getMimeType() method that is executed if the file does not exist or is
not a valid MIME type (in which case, it returns the text equivalent of a HTML page
showing that the requested file does not exist):

```
private function getMimeType( path : String ) : String
{
    var mimeType : String;
    var index : int = path.lastIndexOf( "." );
    if ( index > -1 )
    mimeType = validMimeTypes[ path.substring( index ) ];

    // if mimetype is unknown, always set it to html
    if( mimeType == null )
    mimeType = "text/html";

    return mimeType;
}
```

Now the project is complete, and you can run the file. Start the server and specify a
folder on the computer that contains HTML documents. Set the port to 8888. Open
an Internet browser and, supposing that there is a file called *test1.html* in your webroot,
type *http://localhost:8888/test1.html*.

The output of the HTTP call will be shown in the `outputConsole` text field and the browser will show the HTML page you requested, as in Figure 20-5.

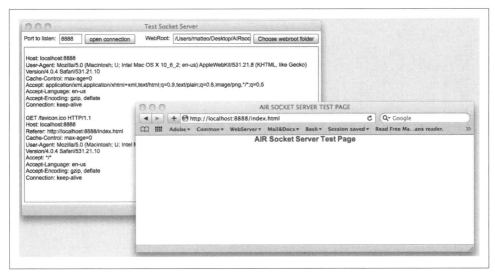

Figure 20-5. The output of the HTTP call

CHAPTER 21

Charting

The Flex Charting Framework is a powerful series of data-rich controls that lets you create deep and interactive displays of many types of data. Flex defines a few of the most commonly used charts—bar charts, pie charts, and column charts—and gives you a great deal of control over their appearance. A Chart contains a ChartSeries that creates the item renderers based on the dataProvider passed to the Chart. The ChartSeries object can use an itemRenderer, have distinct dataFields from the dataProvider used to display data in that ChartSeries, use display effects, and have distinct properties set to handle user interaction. The Flex Charting Framework is an immense topic, and as such the recipes in this chapter can cover only a small set of the possibilities. It should also be noted that the Flex Charting components are part of the Flex data visualization package, which is included in the Flex Builder Professional Edition and not in the Standard Edition or with the free Flex 4 SDK.

21.1 Create a Chart

Problem

You want to add a chart to your application.

Solution

Create a chart of the desired type and add the appropriate ChartSeries object for that ChartType, and then add a dataProvider to the ChartSeries.

Discussion

Charts come in a variety of types, and it's important to know what you have in your toolbox before you start working.

For every chart type, there is a corresponding `ChartSeries`. To add a series of data visualized as a particular type, you add the corresponding series type and bind it to a `dataProvider`. The `ChartSeries` defines the data that is shown on the *x* and *y* axes and the name of the series. A series can also have filters applied to give drop shadows and blur or glow effects.

Depending on the form of your data, you may need to define a horizontal or vertical axis. If your data is grouped into categories, such as dates, countries, or people, you'll need a `CategoryAxis`. If you are using numeric data, use a `LinearAxis`.

The `dataProvider` of a chart can be an array or collection of objects; it can also be an `XMLList` object. If you set a `dataProvider` in your chart tag, your series objects will inherit that `dataProvider`, or you can specify a `dataProvider` for each series object. Different series objects can use different `dataProviders`. A chart does not have to use all the data in the `dataProvider`; it can use only a specified range.

To create bar and pie charts, you would use code similar to this:

```
<s:Application xmlns:fx="http://ns.adobe.com/mxml/2009"
               xmlns:s="library://ns.adobe.com/flex/spark"
               xmlns:mx="library://ns.adobe.com/flex/mx"
               backgroundColor="0xFFFFFF">
    <s:layout><s:HorizontalLayout/></s:layout>
    <fx:Script>
        <![CDATA[

            // a basic data set

            [Bindable] public var chartDP:Array = [
                {day:'Monday',rainfall:10,elevation:100,temperature:78},
                {day:'Tuesday',rainfall:7,elevation:220,temperature:66},
                {day:'Wednesday',rainfall:5,elevation:540,temperature:55},
                {day:'Thursday',rainfall:8,elevation:60,temperature:84},
                {day:'Friday',rainfall:11,elevation:390,temperature:52},
                {day:'Saturday',rainfall:12,elevation:790,temperature:45},
                {day:'Sunday',rainfall:14,elevation:1220,temperature:24}
            ];

        ]]>
    </fx:Script>
    <mx:ToggleButtonBar dataProvider="{simpleCharts}" direction="vertical" />
    <mx:ViewStack id="simpleCharts" >

        <s:Group label="Bar">
            <mx:BarChart dataProvider="{chartDP}" >
                <mx:verticalAxis>
                    <mx:CategoryAxis dataProvider="{chartDP}"
                                     categoryField="day" />
                </mx:verticalAxis>
                <mx:series>

                    <!-- bar chart uses a BarSeries -->
```

```
                    <mx:BarSeries yField="day" xField="rainfall"
                                  displayName="day" />
                </mx:series>
            </mx:BarChart>
        </s:Group>

        <s:Group label="Pie">
            <mx:PieChart dataProvider="{chartDP}" >
                <!-- no axes need to be defined in a pie chart -->

                <mx:series>

                    <!-- pie chart uses a pie series -->

                    <mx:PieSeries field="rainfall"
                                  nameField="day"
                                  labelPosition="callout"
                                  displayName="rainfall" />
                </mx:series>
            </mx:PieChart>
        </s:Group>
    </mx:ViewStack id="simpleCharts" >
</s:Application>
```

The `CandlestickChart` and `HLOCChart` (High, Low, Open, Close) chart types need a
slightly different kind of data set, taking a date and four different values for each point
in the data set:

```
<s:Application xmlns:fx="http://ns.adobe.com/mxml/2009"
               xmlns:s="library://ns.adobe.com/flex/spark"
               xmlns:mx="library://ns.adobe.com/flex/mx"
               backgroundColor="0xFFFFFF">
    <s:layout><s:HorizontalLayout/></s:layout>
    <fx:Script>
        <![CDATA[
            // the field names don't need to be 'high','open','low', and 'close',
            // but you need four different fields to get this kind of chart to work
            [Bindable] public var highLowChartDP:Array = [
                {date:"1-Aug-05",open:42.57,high:43.08,low:42.08,close:42.75},
                {date:"2-Aug-05",open:42.89,high:43.5,low:42.61,close:43.19},
                {date:"3-Aug-05",open:43.19,high:43.31,low:42.77,close:43.22},
                {date:"4-Aug-05",open:42.89,high:43,low:42.29,close:42.71},
                {date:"5-Aug-05",open:42.49,high:43.36,low:42.02,close:42.99},
                {date:"8-Aug-05",open:43,high:43.25,low:42.61,close:42.65},
                {date:"9-Aug-05",open:42.93,high:43.89,low:42.91,close:43.82},
                {date:"10-Aug-05",open:44,high:44.39,low:43.31,close:43.38},
                {date:"11-Aug-05",open:43.39,high:44.12,low:43.25,close:44},
                {date:"12-Aug-05",open:43.46,high:46.22,low:43.36,close:46.1}
            ];
        ]]>
    </fx:Script>
    <mx:CandlestickChart dataProvider="{highLowChartDP}"
                         showDataTips="true">
```

```
<mx:verticalAxis>
    <mx:LinearAxis minimum="40" maximum="50" />
</mx:verticalAxis>

<mx:horizontalAxis>
    <mx:CategoryAxis categoryField="date" />
</mx:horizontalAxis>

    <mx:series>
        <mx:CandlestickSeries dataProvider="{highLowChartDP}"
                              openField="open"
                              highField="high"
                              lowField="low"
                              closeField="close"
                              displayName="Rainfall"/>
    </mx:series>

    </mx:CandlestickChart>
</s:Application>
```

21.2 Add Effects to Charts

Problem

You want to use effects for a chart.

Solution

Add an effect of the desired type to the chart's axis or data series objects by using
`<mx:rollOverEffect>` or `<mx:rollOutEffect>` within the definition of the `Axis`.

Discussion

You can add any `Effect` from the `mx.effects` package to the `Series` or `Axis` of a `Chart`.
A simple rollover effect can enhance the look and feel of your chart. Here's a basic
example of how to add a fade-in and fade-out effect on rollover and rollout of chart
elements:

```
<?xml version="1.0" encoding="utf-8"?>
<s:Application xmlns:fx="http://ns.adobe.com/mxml/2009"
               xmlns:s="library://ns.adobe.com/flex/spark"
               xmlns:mx="library://ns.adobe.com/flex/mx"
               backgroundColor="0xFFFFFF">

    <s:layout><s:HorizontalLayout/></s:layout>
    <fx:Script>
        <![CDATA[

            [Bindable] public var chartDP:Array = [
                {day:'Monday',rainfall:10,elevation:100,temperature:78},
                {day:'Tuesday',rainfall:7,elevation:220,temperature:66},
```

```
                    {day:'Wednesday',rainfall:5,elevation:540,temperature:55},
                    {day:'Thursday',rainfall:8,elevation:60,temperature:84},
                    {day:'Friday',rainfall:11,elevation:390,temperature:52},
                    {day:'Saturday',rainfall:12,elevation:790,temperature:45},
                    {day:'Sunday',rainfall:14,elevation:1220,temperature:24}
            ];

        ]]>
    </fx:Script>
    <mx:AreaChart dataProvider="{chartDP}" >
        <mx:horizontalAxis>
            <mx:CategoryAxis dataProvider="{chartDP}"
                             categoryField="day" />
        </mx:horizontalAxis>
        <mx:series>
            <mx:AreaSeries alpha=".5"
                           yField="rainfall"
                           displayName="rainfall">
```

Here, a `Fade` effect is set for the `rollover` and `rollout` of the `AreaSeries`; these effects will affect only this particular series, not the chart as a whole:

```
                <mx:rollOverEffect>
                    <s:Fade alphaFrom=".5" alphaTo="1" duration="500" />
                </mx:rollOverEffect>
                <mx:rollOutEffect>
                    <s:Fade alphaFrom="1" alphaTo=".5" duration="500" />
                </mx:rollOutEffect>
            </mx:AreaSeries>
        </mx:series>
    </mx:AreaChart>
</s:Application>
```

To add a little more action to your chart, you can use `SeriesInterpolate`, `SeriesZoom`, and `SeriesSlide` to animate changing data. `SeriesInterpolate` animates the data points moving from their old positions to their new positions. `SeriesZoom` shrinks the old data to nothing and grows the new data from nothing. `SeriesSlide` slides out the old data and slides in the new data. These effects are typically assigned to the `showDataEffect` and `hideDataEffect` event attributes of a series object. `SeriesInterpolate` can be assigned to only the `showDataEffect` event attribute and has no effect when assigned to the `hideDataEffect` event attribute.

This example shows a slide effect that can be used when switching a chart between two data sets. To see `SeriesZoom` in action, add comment tags around the other effects and remove the comment tags from around the `SeriesZoom` effect. To see how `SeriesInter polate` works, comment out the other effects, comment in the `SeriesInterpolate` effect, and remove the `hideDataEffect` property from the `ColumnSeries` tag:

```
<?xml version="1.0" encoding="utf-8"?>
<s:Application xmlns:fx="http://ns.adobe.com/mxml/2009"
               xmlns:s="library://ns.adobe.com/flex/spark"
               xmlns:mx="library://ns.adobe.com/flex/halo"
               minWidth="1024" minHeight="768">
```

```
    <fx:Declarations>
        <mx:SeriesSlide id="dataIn" duration="500" direction="up"/>
        <mx:SeriesSlide id="dataOut" duration="500" direction="up"/>
<!--    <mx:SeriesZoom id="dataOut" duration="500"/>
        <mx:SeriesInterpolate id="dataIn" duration="1000"/> -->
    </fx:Declarations>

    <s:layout><s:HorizontalLayout/></s:layout>
    <fx:Script>
        <![CDATA[
            [Bindable] public var chartDP1:Array = [
                {day:'Monday',rainfall:10,elevation:100,temperature:78},
                {day:'Tuesday',rainfall:7,elevation:220,temperature:66},
                {day:'Wednesday',rainfall:5,elevation:540,temperature:55},
                {day:'Thursday',rainfall:8,elevation:60,temperature:84},
                {day:'Friday',rainfall:11,elevation:390,temperature:52},
                {day:'Saturday',rainfall:12,elevation:790,temperature:45},
                {day:'Sunday',rainfall:14,elevation:1220,temperature:24}
            ];

            [Bindable] public var chartDP2:Array = [
                {day:'Sunday',rainfall:10,elevation:100,temperature:78},
                {day:'Saturday',rainfall:7,elevation:220,temperature:66},
                {day:'Friday',rainfall:5,elevation:540,temperature:55},
                {day:'Thursday',rainfall:8,elevation:60,temperature:84},
                {day:'Wednesday',rainfall:11,elevation:390,temperature:52},
                {day:'Tuesday',rainfall:12,elevation:790,temperature:45},
                {day:'Monday',rainfall:14,elevation:1220,temperature:24}
            ];
        ]]>
    </fx:Script>
    <mx:BarChart id="rainfallChart" dataProvider="{chartDP1}" >
        <mx:horizontalAxis>
            <mx:CategoryAxis dataProvider="{chartDP1}"
                            categoryField="day" />
        </mx:horizontalAxis>
        <mx:series>
            <mx:ColumnSeries yField="rainfall" xField="day"
                            displayName="rainfall"
                            showDataEffect="{dataIn}"
                            hideDataEffect="{dataOut}" />
        </mx:series>
    </mx:BarChart>

    <s:HGroup>
        <mx:RadioButton groupName="dataProvider" label="Data Provider 1"
                        selected="true"
                        click="rainfallChart.dataProvider=chartDP1;"/>
        <mx:RadioButton groupName="dataProvider" label="Data Provider 2"
                        click="rainfallChart.dataProvider=chartDP2;"/>
    </s:HGroup>

</s:Application>
```

21.3 Select Regions of a Chart

Problem

You need to select regions of or specific items on your chart.

Solution

Use the `selectionMode` attribute of your chart to set the selection type you want; then use mouse, keyboard, or programmatic means to select items on your chart.

Discussion

Just as with the different list components, chart elements are selectable, which is useful when you need to show more detail on a data point with data grids or a secondary chart. To make a chart selectable, you set the `selectionMode` attribute to `single` or `multiple` (the default value of this attribute is `none`). A `none` value does not allow any selection, a `single` value allows only one item to be selected at a time, and a `multiple` value allows multiple items to be selected.

Chart selection can be done via the mouse, via the keyboard, by dragging a rectangular region to select multiple points, or programmatically in ActionScript. When you select multiple items, the first item selected is known as the *anchor* and the last as the *caret*. Mouse selection is very straightforward. Simply clicking a chart item puts it in a selected state. For multiple selections, hold down the Shift key to select all the items between your first and last selection, or hold down the Control key (or on a Mac, the Command key) to make noncontiguous multiple selections. Using the left and right arrow keys lets you cycle through the items in a chart. Chart items cycle per series. When the `selectionMode` attribute is set to `multiple`, drawing a rectangle in a chart selects all chart items that overlap with that rectangle.

Programmatic selection is a little more complex. A charting selection API lets you access which items are selected and manipulate the selection. You can use these attributes of a `ChartSeries` object to get and set the selection state:

- `selectedItem`
- `selectedItems`
- `selectedIndex`
- `selectedIndices`

Alternatively, you can use methods defined in the `ChartBase` class:

- `getNextItem()`
- `getPreviousItem()`
- `getFirstItem()`
- `getLastItem()`

Using the Change event of the chart enables you to be notified when the selection changes based on mouse or keyboard interaction (but not programmatic changes).

The following example shows the data for all of the chart's selected items in a Data Grid. There are also Next and Previous buttons for navigating through the selection programmatically:

```
<s:Application xmlns:fx="http://ns.adobe.com/mxml/2009"
               xmlns:s="library://ns.adobe.com/flex/spark"
               xmlns:mx="library://ns.adobe.com/flex/mx"
               backgroundColor="0xFFFFFF">
    <s:layout><s:HorizontalLayout/></s:layout>
    <fx:Script>
        <![CDATA[
            [Bindable] public var chartDP:Array = [
                {day:'Monday',rainfall:10,elevation:100,temperature:78},
                {day:'Tuesday',rainfall:7,elevation:220,temperature:66},
                {day:'Wednesday',rainfall:5,elevation:540,temperature:55},
                {day:'Thursday',rainfall:8,elevation:60,temperature:84},
                {day:'Friday',rainfall:11,elevation:390,temperature:52},
                {day:'Saturday',rainfall:12,elevation:790,temperature:45},
                {day:'Sunday',rainfall:14,elevation:1220,temperature:24}
            ];

            private function changeSelectedIndex(offset:int):void
            {
                barSeries.selectedIndex+=offset;
                onSelectionChange();
            }

            private function onSelectionChange():void
            {
                // programmatic changes to chart selection don't fire a Change
                // event, so we need to manually reset the dataProvider of
                // our detail grid when we programatically change the selection
                detailGrid.dataProvider = barChart.selectedChartItems;
            }
        ]]>
    </fx:Script>
    <!-- use the change event to set the dataProvider of our detail grid to our
    chart's selected items -->
    <mx:BarChart id="barChart" dataProvider="{chartDP}" selectionMode="multiple"
                 change="onSelectionChange()">
        <mx:verticalAxis>
            <mx:CategoryAxis dataProvider="{chartDP}"
                             categoryField="day" />
        </mx:verticalAxis>
        <mx:series>
            <mx:BarSeries id="barSeries" selectedIndex="0"
                          yField="day" xField="rainfall"
                          displayName="day" />
        </mx:series>
    </mx:BarChart>
```

```
    <s:HGroup>
        <mx:Button click="changeSelectedIndex(1)" label="Previous" />
        <mx:Button click="changeSelectedIndex(-1)" label="Next" />
    </s:HGroup>
    <mx:DataGrid id="detailGrid" >
        <mx:columns>
            <mx:DataGridColumn dataField="xValue" headerText="rainfall" />
            <mx:DataGridColumn dataField="yValue" headerText="day" />
        </mx:columns>
    </mx:DataGrid>
</s:Application>
```

21.4 Format Tick Marks for a Chart

Problem

You want to use a custom look for the chart tick marks.

Solution

Use styles on an `AxisRenderer` to set the desired look for your chart.

Discussion

Using styles, Flex gives you quite a bit of control over where and how tick marks are displayed. There are two types of tick marks in Flex charts: major and minor. *Major tick marks* correspond to axis labels, and *minor tick marks* appear in between the major tick marks.

Styles that control tick mark appearance are defined in the `AxisRenderer` for a chart axis. To customize major tick marks, use `tickPlacement`, `tickAlignment`, and `tick Length`. For customizing minor tick marks, use `minorTickPlacement`, `minorTickAlign ment`, and `minorTickLength`.

The `tickMarkPlacement` and `minorTickPlacement` styles define where the tick mark is in relation to the axis line. Possible values are listed in Table 21-1.

Table 21-1. Tick mark values and their placement

Value	Placement
cross	Across the axis
inside	Inside the axis
outside	Outside the axis
none	No tick mark

This example places the major tick marks inside the chart axis and the minor ones outside. The length of the minor tick marks is 10 pixels (`minorTickLength` property), and the length of the major tick marks is 5 pixels (`tickLength` property):

```
<s:Application xmlns:fx="http://ns.adobe.com/mxml/2009"
               xmlns:s="library://ns.adobe.com/flex/spark"
               xmlns:mx="library://ns.adobe.com/flex/mx"
               backgroundColor="0xFFFFFF">
    <s:layout><s:HorizontalLayout/></s:layout>

    <fx:Script>
        <![CDATA[
            [Bindable] public var chartDP:Array = [
                {day:'Monday',rainfall:10,elevation:100,temperature:78},
                {day:'Tuesday',rainfall:7,elevation:220,temperature:66},
                {day:'Wednesday',rainfall:5,elevation:540,temperature:55},
                {day:'Thursday',rainfall:8,elevation:60,temperature:84},
                {day:'Friday',rainfall:11,elevation:390,temperature:52},
                {day:'Saturday',rainfall:12,elevation:790,temperature:45},
                {day:'Sunday',rainfall:14,elevation:1220,temperature:24}
            ];

        ]]>
    </fx:Script>

    <fx:Style>
        .customTicks {
            tickPlacement:inside;
            minorTickPlacement:outside;
            tickLength:5;
            minorTickLength:10;
        }
    </fx:Style>

    <s:Group label="Area">
        <mx:AreaChart dataProvider="{chartDP}" >
            <mx:horizontalAxis>
                <mx:CategoryAxis
                    dataProvider="{chartDP}"
                    categoryField="day" />
            </mx:horizontalAxis>
            <mx:verticalAxis>
                <mx:LinearAxis id="vertAxis" />
            </mx:verticalAxis>
            <mx:verticalAxisRenderers>
                <mx:AxisRenderer axis="{vertAxis}" styleName="customTicks" />
            </mx:verticalAxisRenderers>
            <mx:series>
                <mx:AreaSeries
                    yField="rainfall"
                    displayName="rainfall" />
            </mx:series>
        </mx:AreaChart>
    </s:Group>
</s:Application>
```

21.5 Create a Custom Label for a Chart

Problem

You want to customize the chart labels.

Solution

Use styles and label functions.

Discussion

Charts use two kinds of labels: axis labels and data labels. *Axis labels* are used to show the values at points along an axis. *Data labels* show the data values at the locations of data points and chart elements.

Using label functions, you can gain greater control over how your axis labels are formatted. If you need specific date formatting or currency formatting, for example, you can use a label function. Label functions also work for data labels.

The numeric axis label function has the following signature:

```
function_name(labelValue:Object, previousLabelValue:Object, axis:IAxis):String
```

The parameters are:

labelValue
> The value of the current label

previousLabelValue
> The value of the label preceding this label; if this is the first label, the value of previousLabelValue is null

axis
> The axis object, such as CategoryAxis or NumericAxis

The category axis label function has this signature:

```
function_name(labelValue:Object, previousLabelValue:Object, axis:axis_type,
              labelItem:Object):String
```

The parameters are:

categoryValue
> The value of the category to be represented

previousCategoryValue
> The value of the previous category on the axis

axis
> The CategoryAxis being rendered

categoryItem
> The item from the data provider that is being represented

This example uses a `CurrencyFormatter` for formatting the vertical axis labels and the data labels:

```
<s:Application xmlns:fx="http://ns.adobe.com/mxml/2009"
               xmlns:s="library://ns.adobe.com/flex/spark"
               xmlns:mx="library://ns.adobe.com/flex/halo"
               backgroundColor="0xFFFFFF" initialize="onInit()">
    <s:layout><s:HorizontalLayout/></s:layout>
    <fx:Script>
        <![CDATA[
            import mx.charts.chartClasses.Series;
            import mx.charts.ChartItem;
            import mx.charts.chartClasses.IAxis;
            import mx.formatters.CurrencyFormatter;

            [Bindable] public var chartDP:Array = [
                {month:'Jan',costs:10000,sales:100000},
                {month:'Feb',costs:7000,sales:220000},
                {month:'Mar',costs:5000,sales:540000},
                {month:'April',costs:8000,sales:60000},
                {month:'May',costs:11000,sales:390000},
                {month:'June',costs:12000,sales:790000},
                {month:'July',costs:14000,sales:1220000}
            ];

            private var formatter:CurrencyFormatter;

            private function onInit():void
            {
                formatter = new CurrencyFormatter();
                formatter.currencySymbol = '$';
                formatter.precision = 0;
                formatter.useThousandsSeparator = true;
            }

            private function currencyAxisLabel(value:Object, previousValue:Object,
                                               axis:IAxis):String
            {
                return formatter.format(value);
            }

        ]]>
    </fx:Script>
    <mx:LineChart dataProvider="{chartDP}">
        <mx:horizontalAxis>
            <mx:CategoryAxis dataProvider="{chartDP}"
                             categoryField="month" />
        </mx:horizontalAxis>
        <mx:verticalAxis>
            <mx:LinearAxis labelFunction="{currencyAxisLabel}" />
        </mx:verticalAxis>
```

```
            <mx:series>
                <mx:LineSeries yField="costs" xField="month"
                                displayName="Costs" />
            </mx:series>
        </mx:LineChart>
    </s:Application>
```

21.6 Create a Drill-Down Effect for a Column Chart

Problem

You want to display an effect when drilling down into chart data.

Solution

Create a new array to populate with data from the chosen item and set the
dataProvider of the ColumnChart to that array. Use a SeriesZoom to transition from the
overview data set to the specific data set.

Discussion

The idea of *drilling down* into a chart is a user interface concept that refers to allowing
a user to select a particular data item from a larger set for closer inspection. A chart's
drill-down effect enables you to select items in the chart and then display more specific
data about those items. This is achieved simply by setting the dataProvider of the
ChartSeries. You can play an effect when the dataProvider is changed by setting the
showDataEffect and hideDataEffect properties. There are three effects defined in the
mx.charts.effects package: SeriesInterpolate, SeriesSlide, and SeriesZoom. Used in
the example that follows, the SeriesZoom effect zooms in and out of the data displayed
in the chart by using a focal point set via the horizontalFocus and verticalFocus
attributes:

```
    <s:Application xmlns:fx="http://ns.adobe.com/mxml/2009"
                xmlns:s="library://ns.adobe.com/flex/spark"
                xmlns:mx="library://ns.adobe.com/flex/mx">
        <fx:Declarations>
            <mx:SeriesZoom id="slideZoomIn" duration="1000" verticalFocus="bottom"/>
            <mx:SeriesZoom id="slideZoomOut" duration="1000" verticalFocus="bottom"/>
        </fx:Declarations>
        <fx:Script>
            <![CDATA[
                import mx.charts.series.items.ColumnSeriesItem;
                import mx.graphics.SolidColor;
                import mx.charts.ChartItem;
                import mx.graphics.IFill;
                import mx.collections.ArrayCollection;
                import mx.charts.HitData;
                import mx.charts.events.ChartItemEvent;
```

This deep data set allows the display of all the items together, as well as allowing each item to be shown individually:

```
[Bindable]
public var overview:ArrayCollection = new ArrayCollection ([
        { date:"01/02/2006", total:3000, food:1300, drinks:1700,
        other:0, expenses:2700, profit:300},
        { date:"01/08/2006", total:3500, food:1800, drinks:1500,
        other:200, expenses:2900, profit:600},
        { date:"01/15/2006", total:2600, food:1000, drinks:1600,
        other:0, expenses:2700, profit:-100},
        { date:"01/22/2006", total:3200, food:1300, drinks:1900,
        other:0, expenses:2900, profit:200 },
        { date:"02/1/2006", total:2200, food:1200, drinks:1000,
        other:0, expenses:2100, profit:100 },
        { date:"02/8/2006", total:2600, food:1300, drinks:1600,
        other:100, expenses:2700, profit:400 },
        { date:"02/16/2006", total:4100, food:2300, drinks:1700,
        other:100, expenses:2700, profit:200 },
        { date:"02/22/2006", total:4300, food:2300, drinks:1700,
        other:300, expenses:3300, profit:1000 }]);

[Bindable]
public var drillDownDataSet:ArrayCollection;

[Bindable]
public var mainDataProvider:ArrayCollection = overview;

private function zoomIntoSeries(e:ChartItemEvent):void {
    if (mainDataProvider == overview) {

        drillDownDataSet = new ArrayCollection(createDataForDate(e));
        columnSeries.displayName = "Daily Breakdown";
        columnSeries.yField = "amount";
        columnSeries.xField = "type";

        ca1.categoryField = "type";

        mainPanel.title = "Profits for " + e.hitData.item.date;
        mainDataProvider = drillDownDataSet;

    } else {

        mainDataProvider = overview;

        columnSeries.displayName = "Profit by date";
        columnSeries.yField = "profit";
        columnSeries.xField = "date";

        ca1.categoryField = "date";

        mainPanel.title = "Profit Overview";
    }
}
```

```
            private function profitFunction(element:ChartItem, index:Number):IFill
            {
                // black for profit
                var dateColor:SolidColor = new SolidColor(0x000000);

                var item:ColumnSeriesItem = ColumnSeriesItem(element);
                var profit:Number = Number(item.yValue);

                if (profit < 0) {
                    // red for not profitable
                    dateColor.color = 0xFF0000;
                }
                return dateColor;
            }
```

Here, the `hitData` property of the `ChartItemEvent` is used to generate the data for the specific column in the `ColumnChart` that has been clicked. This will be the data set for the drilled-down view:

```
            private function createDataForDate(e:ChartItemEvent):Array {
                var result:Array = [];

                var food:Object = { type:"food", amount:e.hitData.item.food };
                var drinks:Object = { type:"drinks",
                                      amount:e.hitData.item.drinks };
                var other:Object = { type:"other", amount:e.hitData.item.other };
                var expenses:Object = { type:"expenses",
                                        amount:e.hitData.item.expenses };

                result.push(food);
                result.push(drinks);
                result.push(other);
                result.push(expenses);
                return result;
            }

        ]]>
    </fx:Script>

    <s:Panel id="mainPanel" title="Profitability">
        <mx:ColumnChart id="chart" showDataTips="true"
                    itemClick="zoomIntoSeries(event)"
                    dataProvider="{mainDataProvider}">
            <mx:series>
```

The `showDataEffect` and `hideDataEffect` properties indicate which effects will be played when the `dataProvider` for a `ChartSeries` is changed:

```
            <mx:ColumnSeries id="columnSeries" displayName="Total profit"
                        fillFunction="profitFunction"
                        yField="profit" xField="date"
                        hideDataEffect="slideZoomOut"
                        showDataEffect="slideZoomIn"/>
            </mx:series>
```

```
            <mx:horizontalAxis>
                <mx:CategoryAxis id="ca1" categoryField="date"/>
            </mx:horizontalAxis>
        </mx:ColumnChart>
    </s:Panel>
</s:Application>
```

21.7 Skin Chart Items

Problem

You need to skin (change the appearance of) the items displayed in a chart.

Solution

Create a class that extends the `ProgrammaticSkin` class and implements the `IDataRenderer` interface. Set that skin class to be the `itemRenderer` for the `ChartSeries` of the chart.

Discussion

The `mx.charts.ChartItem` is the representation of a data point in the series, so there is one `ChartItem` for each item in the series's `dataProvider`. The `ChartItem` defines the following properties:

currentState : String
> The appearance of the `ChartItem`

element : IChartElement
> The series or element that owns the `ChartItem`

index : int
> The index of the data from the series's `dataProvider` that the `ChartItem` represents

item : Object
> The item from the series's `dataProvider` that the `ChartItem` represents

itemRenderer : IFlexDisplayObject
> The instance of the chart's item renderer that represents this `ChartItem`

The `ChartItems` are owned by a `ChartSeries`, which uses the items to display the data points. A `ChartSeries` is in turn owned by a `Chart`, which may have one or more `ChartSeries` items with distinct data properties. Each series has a default renderer that Flex uses to draw that series's `ChartItem` objects, as listed in Table 21-2. You can specify a new renderer to use with the series's `itemRenderer style` property. This property points to a class that defines the appearance of the `ChartItem` object.

Table 21-2. Available itemRenderers for charts

Chart type	Renderer classes
AreaChart	AreaRenderer
BarChart	BoxItemRenderer
BubbleChart	CircleItemRenderer
ColumnChart	CrossItemRenderer
PlotChart	DiamondItemRenderer
	ShadowBoxRenderer
	TriangleItemRenderer
CandlestickChart	CandlestickItemRenderer
HLOCChart	HLOCItemRenderer
LineChart	LineRenderer
	ShadowLineRenderer
PieChart	WedgeItemRenderer

To set an image as the `itemRenderer` for a series in a chart, simply set an embedded image as the `itemRenderer` property value:

```
<mx:PlotSeries xField="goals" yField="games" displayName="Goals per game"
                itemRenderer="@Embed(source='../assets/soccerball.png')"
    radius="20"
                legendMarkerRenderer="@Embed(source='../assets/soccerball.png')"/>
```

To create a skin for a chart item, create a `ProgrammaticSkin` and override the `updateDisplayList()` method:

```
package oreilly.cookbook
{
    import flash.display.BitmapData;
    import flash.display.DisplayObject;
    import flash.display.IBitmapDrawable;

    import mx.charts.series.items.ColumnSeriesItem;
    import mx.core.IDataRenderer;
    import mx.skins.ProgrammaticSkin;

    public class CustomRenderer extends ProgrammaticSkin implements IDataRenderer {

        private var _chartItem:ColumnSeriesItem;

        [Embed(source="assets/Shakey.png")]
        private var img:Class;

        public function get data():Object {
            return _chartItem;
        }
```

```
        public function set data(value:Object):void {
            _chartItem = value as ColumnSeriesItem;
            invalidateDisplayList();
        }

        override protected function updateDisplayList(
                unscaledWidth:Number,unscaledHeight:Number):void {
            super.updateDisplayList(unscaledWidth, unscaledHeight);
            var img_inst = new img();
            var bmd:BitmapData = new BitmapData((img_inst as DisplayObject).height,
                    (foo_inst as DisplayObject).width, true);
            bmd.draw(img_inst as IBitmapDrawable);
            graphics.clear();
            graphics.beginBitmapFill(bmd);
            graphics.drawRect(0, 0, unscaledWidth, unscaledHeight);
            graphics.endFill();
        }
    }
}
```

Now the `CustomRenderer` that extends the `ProgrammaticSkin` class can be set as the `itemRenderer` of a `ColumnSeries`:

```
<mx:ColumnChart id="column" dataProvider="{expenses}">
    <mx:horizontalAxis>
        <mx:CategoryAxis dataProvider="{expenses}"
                        categoryField="Month" />
    </mx:horizontalAxis>
    <mx:series>
        <mx:Array>
            <mx:ColumnSeries xField="Month"
                            yField="Expenses"
                            displayName="Expenses"
                            itemRenderer="oreilly.cookbook.CustomRenderer" />
        </mx:Array>
    </mx:series>
</mx:ColumnChart>
```

21.8 Use ActionScript to Dynamically Add Columns to and Remove Columns from a Chart

Problem

You need to add or remove columns of data in a chart at runtime.

Solution

Create a `ColumnSet` in ActionScript and add or remove `ColumnSeries` objects.

Discussion

A `ColumnSet` allows you to add or remove multiple `ColumnSeries` objects in a chart. There are different `Set` types for each chart type; for example, a `ColumnChart` uses a `ColumnSet` to group multiple `ColumnSeries` instances. `Series` instances use a `type` attribute to determine how the series items are grouped (Table 21-3).

Table 21-3. Types of groupings for ColumnSet

Attribute	Description
clustered	Series items are grouped side by side in each category. This is the default for BarCharts and ColumnCharts.
stacked	Series items are stacked on top of each other. Each item represents the cumulative value of the items beneath it.
overlaid	Series items are overlaid on top of each other, with the last item on top.
100%	Series items are stacked on top of each other, with each item representing its percentage value within the whole set. The total adds up to 100 percent.

Chart sets have a `series` attribute that accepts an array of series objects. Using sets enables you to group your data in many ways. For example, your chart can have two sets of stacked sets, each of which can contain a set of clustered series.

The following example uses a data set that tracks millimeters of rainwater throughout the day over the course of a week. Each time of day is a series and is initialized in ActionScript. For each series, there is a checkbox; when the checkbox values are changed, the `ColumnSet` is reinitialized and adds a series for each selected checkbox. Finally, the `ColumnSet` is added to a new array and set to the `series` attribute of the `ColumnChart`:

```
<s:Application xmlns:fx="http://ns.adobe.com/mxml/2009"
               xmlns:s="library://ns.adobe.com/flex/spark"
               xmlns:mx="library://ns.adobe.com/flex/mx"
               backgroundColor="0xFFFFFF" creationComplete="onComplete()">

    <s:layout><s:HorizontalLayout/></s:layout>

    <fx:Script>
        <![CDATA[
            import mx.charts.series.ColumnSet;
            import mx.charts.series.ColumnSeries;

            [Bindable] private var chartDP:Array = [{day:'Monday',dawnRainfall:10,
                morningRainfall:12,midDayRainfall:6,afternoonRainfall:4,
                duskRainfall:5},{day:'Tuesday',dawnRainfall:7,morningRainfall:10,
                midDayRainfall:5,afternoonRainfall:5,duskRainfall:6},
                {day:'Wednesday',dawnRainfall:5,morningRainfall:9,
                midDayRainfall:3,afternoonRainfall:2,duskRainfall:3},
                {day:'Thursday',dawnRainfall:8,morningRainfall:9,
                midDayRainfall:6,afternoonRainfall:6,duskRainfall:6},
                {day:'Friday',dawnRainfall:11,morningRainfall:13,
                midDayRainfall:4,afternoonRainfall:5,duskRainfall:7},
```

```
        {day:'Saturday',dawnRainfall:12,morningRainfall:13,
        midDayRainfall:9,afternoonRainfall:3,duskRainfall:4},
        {day:'Sunday',dawnRainfall:14,morningRainfall:12,
        midDayRainfall:5,afternoonRainfall:1,duskRainfall:3}
];

private var dawnSeries:ColumnSeries;
private var morningSeries:ColumnSeries;
private var midDaySeries:ColumnSeries;
private var afternoonSeries:ColumnSeries;
private var duskSeries:ColumnSeries;

private var columnSet:ColumnSet;

private function onComplete():void
{
    // initialize our clustered ColumnSet
    columnSet = new ColumnSet();
    columnSet.type = "clustered";

    // initialize all of our series
    dawnSeries = new ColumnSeries();
    dawnSeries.yField = "dawnRainfall";
    dawnSeries.xField = "day";
    dawnSeries.displayName = "Dawn Rainfall";

    morningSeries = new ColumnSeries();
    morningSeries.yField = "morningRainfall";
    morningSeries.xField = "day";
    morningSeries.displayName = "Morning Rainfall";

    midDaySeries = new ColumnSeries();
    midDaySeries.yField = "midDayRainfall";
    midDaySeries.xField = "day";
    midDaySeries.displayName = "Mid-day Rainfall";

    afternoonSeries = new ColumnSeries();
    afternoonSeries.yField = "afternoonRainfall";
    afternoonSeries.xField = "day";
    afternoonSeries.displayName = "Afternoon Rainfall";

    duskSeries = new ColumnSeries();
    duskSeries.yField = "duskRainfall";
    duskSeries.xField = "day";
    duskSeries.displayName = "Dusk Rainfall";

    updateSeries();

}
```

Here the series is pushed into the column set, updating the chart:

```
private function updateSeries():void
{
    // reinit columnSet
    columnSet.series = new Array();
    // for each checkbox, add the corresponding series
    // if it's checked
    if(showDawnCheckBox.selected) {
        columnSet.series.push(dawnSeries);
    }
    if(showMorningCheckBox.selected) {
        columnSet.series.push(morningSeries);
    }
    if(showMidDayCheckBox.selected) {
        columnSet.series.push(midDaySeries);
    }
    if(showAfternoonCheckBox.selected) {
        columnSet.series.push(afternoonSeries);
    }
    if(showDuskCheckBox.selected) {
        columnSet.series.push(duskSeries);
    }
    // put columnSet in an array and set it to
    // the chart's "series" attribute
    rainfallChart.series = [columnSet];
}

        ]]>
    </fx:Script>
    <mx:ColumnChart id="rainfallChart" dataProvider="{chartDP}" >
        <mx:horizontalAxis>
            <mx:CategoryAxis categoryField="day" />
        </mx:horizontalAxis>
        <mx:verticalAxis>
            <mx:LinearAxis minimum="0" maximum="14" />
        </mx:verticalAxis>
        <!-- notice there is no series attribute defined; we did that in AS -->
    </mx:ColumnChart>
    <s:HGroup>
        <s:CheckBox id="showDawnCheckBox"
                    label="Dawn Rainfall" selected="true"
                    change="updateSeries()" />
        <s:CheckBox id="showMorningCheckBox"
                    label="Morning Rainfall" change="updateSeries()" />
        <s:CheckBox id="showMidDayCheckBox"
                    label="Mid-day Rainfall" change="updateSeries()" />
        <s:CheckBox id="showAfternoonCheckBox"
                    label="Afternoon Rainfall" change="updateSeries()" />
        <s:CheckBox id="showDuskCheckBox"
                    label="Dusk Rainfall" change="updateSeries()" />
    </s:HGroup>
</s:Application>
```

21.9 Overlap Multiple ChartSeries

Problem

You want to be able to use different chart types to represent overlapping data sets.

Solution

Use a `ColumnChart` to hold the multiple charts, and then use an `<mx:Series>` tag to define the multiple charts and their properties.

Discussion

Any chart can contain multiple `ChartSeries` within its series array, each of which can represent different fields within the same data provider or different data providers. In the following example, multiple `ChartSeries` items are passed to the `ColumnChart`:

```
<s:Application xmlns:fx="http://ns.adobe.com/mxml/2009"
               xmlns:s="library://ns.adobe.com/flex/spark"
               xmlns:mx="library://ns.adobe.com/flex/mx"
               creationComplete="genData()">
    <fx:Declarations>
        <mx:SeriesInterpolate id="eff" elementOffset="1"
                              minimumElementDuration="40"
                              duration="2000"/>
    </fx:Declarations>
    <fx:Script>
        <![CDATA[

            private var DJIA:Number = Math.random()*50 - 20;
            private var NASDAQNumber = DJIA - Math.random() * 20;
            private var SP500:Number = Math.random()*40;

            public function genData():void
            {
                // assigning the data that the chart is bound to
                // is best done via a local variable that is then
                // set to the chart data, rather than by adding values
                // to the dataProvider of the chart
                var newArr:Array = [];
                for(var i:int = 0; i<10; i++)
                {
                    DJIA = DJIA + Math.random()*10 - 5;
                    NASDAC = NASDAC - Math.random() * 5;
                    SP500 = Math.random()*40;
                    newArr.push({"DJIA": DJIA, "NASDAC": NASDAC, "SP500": SP500 });
                }
                chartData = newArr;
            }
            [Bindable] public var chartData:Array = [];


        ]]>
```

```
        </fx:Script>
        <mx:Button click="genData()" label="Generate data"/>
        <mx:ColumnChart y="100" width="100%" height="100%"
                            dataProvider="{chartData}">
            <mx:series>
                <mx:ColumnSeries showDataEffect="{eff}" yField="DJIA"/>
                <mx:ColumnSeries showDataEffect="{eff}" yField="NASDAC"/>
                <mx:ColumnSeries showDataEffect="{eff}" yField="SP500"/>
            </mx:series>
        </mx:ColumnChart>
    </s:Application>
```

The multiple `ColumnSeries` objects will be rendered one atop the other in the `ColumnChart`.

21.10 Drag and Drop Items in a Chart

Problem

You need to drag items from a data source into a chart.

Solution

Override the `dragEnterHandler()` and `dragDropHandler()` methods of a chart component to create a chart with dragging and dropping enabled.

Discussion

The drag-and-drop feature of a chart works much the same as the drag-and-drop feature of any other component in the Flex Framework: the parent component defines a handler for the `mouseMove` event of the chart from which the data will be dragged and a handler for the `dragDrop` event of the chart that will receive the dropped data. In the following example, the two pie charts have their `dragEnabled` and `dropEnabled` properties set to `true` and have two separate `ArrayCollection`s used as their `dataProvider`s. When data is dragged from one component to the other, it is removed from the first component's `dataProvider` and added to the other's:

```
    <s:Application xmlns:fx="http://ns.adobe.com/mxml/2009"
                   xmlns:s="library://ns.adobe.com/flex/spark"
                   xmlns:mx="library://ns.adobe.com/flex/mx"
                   xmlns:cookbook="oreilly.cookbook.*">
        <fx:Script>
            <![CDATA[
                import mx.events.DragEvent;
                import mx.charts.PieChart;
                import mx.core.IUIComponent;
                import mx.core.DragSource;
                import mx.containers.Panel;
                import mx.managers.DragManager;
                import mx.collections.ArrayCollection;
```

```
[Bindable]
private var masterArrColl:ArrayCollection = new ArrayCollection([{
    "name":"C Ronaldo", "sog":128, "goals":20, "games":33 },
    { "name":"A Adebayor", "sog":128, "goals":20, "games":35 },
    { "name":"F Torres", "sog":98, "goals":18, "games":32 },
    { "name":"W Rooney", "sog":89, "goals":17, "games":34 },
    { "name":"D Drogba", "sog":114, "goals":16, "games":31 }]);

[Bindable]
private var subColl:ArrayCollection = new ArrayCollection([{ "name":
    "C Ronaldo", "sog":128, "goals":20, "games":33 },
    { "name":"A Adebayor", "sog":128, "goals":20, "games":35 }]);

// initializes the drag-and-drop operation
private function mouseMoveHandler(event:MouseEvent):void {

    event.preventDefault();

    // get the drag initiator component from the event object
    var dragInitiator:PieChart = PieChart(event.currentTarget);

    // create a DragSource object
    var ds:DragSource = new DragSource();
    // make sure that the chart has a selected item
    if(dragInitiator.selectedChartItem == null) return;
    // call the DragManager doDrag() method to start the drag
    DragManager.doDrag(dragInitiator, ds, event);
}
```

The `mouseMoveHandler()` method passes the `dragInitiator` (the component that has dispatched the dragging event) to the `DragManager` along with the `DataSource` object and the mouse event that initiated the action:

```
// called if the target accepts the dragged object and the user
// releases the mouse button while over the Canvas container
private function dragDropHandler(event:DragEvent):void {

    // get the selected data from the chart
    var index:Number = (event.dragInitiator as
            PieChart).selectedChartItem.index;
    (event.currentTarget as PieChart).dataProvider.addItem((event.
            dragInitiator as PieChart).dataProvider.getItemAt(index));
    (event.dragInitiator as PieChart).dataProvider.removeItemAt(index);
}
```

The object is first added to the `dataProvider` of the `currentTarget` of the `dragEvent`—that is, the `PieChart` where the component is being dropped. The data (and corresponding object) is then removed from the `DragEvent.dragInitiator` and the Pie Chart that has had the data dragged from it:

```
        ]]>
    </fx:Script>
    <mx:PieChart dataProvider="{subColl}" selectionMode="single" dragEnabled="true"
            dropEnabled="true" mouseMove="mouseMoveHandler(event)"
```

```
                dragDrop="dragDropHandler(event)">
        <mx:series>
            <mx:PieSeries field="goals" nameField="name" labelField="name"
                        labelPosition="callout" selectable="true"/>
        </mx:series>
    </mx:PieChart>
    <mx:PieChart dataProvider="{masterArrColl}" dragEnabled="true"
                dropEnabled="true" selectionMode="single"
                mouseMove="mouseMoveHandler(event)"
                dragDrop="dragDropHandler(event)">
        <mx:series>
            <mx:PieSeries field="goals" nameField="name" labelField="name"
                        labelPosition="callout" selectable="true"/>
        </mx:series>
    </mx:PieChart>
</s:Application>
```

The `selectable` property of both `PieSeries` components must be set to `true`, as must
the `dragEnabled` and `dropEnabled` properties of both `PieCharts`. When a `ChartItem` is
dragged from the `Chart`, the `dragProxy` is rendered as a bitmap copy of the `ChartItem`
being dragged.

21.11 Create an Editable Line Chart

Problem

You need to update the values of one property in the data provider of a chart based on
changes to the other properties.

Solution

Create a `Chart` with multiple `ChartSeries` objects and set the `selectable` property of
each changeable `ChartSeries` to `true`. Then create drag-and-drop event handlers that
will perform any calculations that need to be made when a value is changed.

Discussion

In the following example, a series of charts are set up to represent the profit relationship
between expenses and sales for a given date. The `LineSeries` objects that represent the
expenses and sales both have their `selectable` property set to `true`:

```
<s:Application xmlns:fx="http://ns.adobe.com/mxml/2009"
            xmlns:s="library://ns.adobe.com/flex/spark"
            xmlns:mx="library://ns.adobe.com/flex/mx">
    <fx:Script>
        <![CDATA[
            import mx.charts.chartClasses.AxisLabelSet;
            import mx.core.DragSource;
            import mx.charts.series.LineSeries;
            import mx.events.DragEvent;
```

```
import mx.managers.DragManager;
import mx.collections.ArrayCollection;

[Bindable]
private var expensesAC:ArrayCollection = new ArrayCollection( [
        { Month: "Jan", Profit: 2000, Expenses: 1500, Sales: 3550},
        { Month: "Feb", Profit: 1000, Expenses: 200, Sales: 1200},
        { Month: "Mar", Profit: 1500, Expenses: 500, Sales: 2000},
        { Month: "Apr", Profit: 1800, Expenses: 1200, Sales: 3000},
        { Month: "May", Profit: 2400, Expenses: 575, Sales: 2975}]);

// initializes the drag-and-drop operation
private function mouseMoveHandler(event:MouseEvent):void {

    event.preventDefault();

    // get the drag initiator component from the event object
    var dragInitiator:LineSeries = LineSeries(event.currentTarget);
    // if a selectedItem isn't set, ignore the mouse event
    if(dragInitiator.selectedItem == null) return;

    // create a DragSource object
    var ds:DragSource = new DragSource();

    // call the DragManager doDrag() method to start the drag
    DragManager.doDrag(dragInitiator, ds, event);
}
```

The `mouseMoveHandler` processes mouse movements for each of the selection-enabled
`LineSeries` objects. Dragging calls the `DragManager.doDrag()` method, which has the
`dragInitiator` (in this case, a `LineSeries` object):

```
private function setDragDropData(event:DragEvent):void {

    var index:Number = (event.dragInitiator as
            LineChart).selectedChartItem.index;
    var newYVal:Number = (event.dragInitiator as LineChart).mouseY;
    var selectedSeries:LineSeries = (event.dragInitiator as
            LineChart).selectedChartItem.element as LineSeries;
    var editedObj:Object = (event.dragInitiator as
            LineChart).dataProvider.getItemAt(index);
    var als:AxisLabelSet =
            linechart.verticalAxis.getLabelEstimate();
    var maxValue:Number = als.labels[als.labels.length - 1].value;
```

The `getLabelEstimate()` method of the `IAxis` interface, which both the horizontal and
vertical axes of a chart implement, returns an `AxisLabelSet` object. The `AxisLabelSet`
object defines a `label` property of type **array** that contains all the labels that are used
in that particular axis. In this case, the last value is used to determine the maximum
value of the chart. Because this can change each time the user alters the values, it is
important to read this value each time a value is dropped to ensure that the correct
maximum for the chart is used to calculate the value that the user intended:

```
            if(selectedSeries.yField == "Expenses") {
                var yPos:Number = ((linechart.height - newYVal) /
                                    linechart.height);
                var newVal:Number = maxValue * yPos;
                editedObj.Expenses = newVal;
            } else {
                var yPos:Number = ((linechart.height - newYVal) /
                                    linechart.height);
                var newVal:Number = maxValue * yPos;
                editedObj.Sales = newVal;
            }
```

It is also important to call the `clearSelection()` method for the parent chart to ensure that the chart selection does not interfere with the processing of mouse events in the chart. The `dataProvider` for the `LineChart` is refreshed, forcing the component to redraw:

```
            editedObj.Profit = editedObj.Sales - editedObj.Expenses;
            (event.dragInitiator as LineChart).clearSelection();
            // force the chart to redraw - note that if we weren't using a
            // simple array collection the data object in the array could
            // dispatch an event, forcing the binding to update
            (event.dragInitiator as LineChart).dataProvider = expensesAC;

        }

    ]]>
</fx:Script>

<s:Panel title="LineChart and AreaChart Controls Example"
         height="100%" width="100%" layout="horizontal">

    <mx:LineChart id="linechart" height="100%" width="100%"
                  paddingLeft="5" paddingRight="5"
                  dragDrop="setDragDropData(event)"
                  showDataTips="true" dataProvider="{expensesAC}"
                  selectionMode="single"
                  dragEnabled="true" dropEnabled="true">

        <mx:horizontalAxis>
            <mx:CategoryAxis categoryField="Month"/>
        </mx:horizontalAxis>
```

The `CircleItemRenderer` used for each `LineSeries` is draggable if its `selectable` property is set to `true`. Because the `LineSeries` representing the `Profit` property should be calculated by the component when the expenses or sales are altered, its `selectable` property is set to `false`:

```
        <mx:series>
            <mx:LineSeries selectable="false" id="profitSeries" yField="Profit"
                           form="curve" displayName="Profit"
                           itemRenderer = "mx.charts.renderers.
                                                CircleItemRenderer"/>
```

```
                <mx:LineSeries mouseMove="mouseMoveHandler(event)"
                               yField="Expenses" form="curve"
                               displayName="Expenses" selectable="true"
                               itemRenderer = "mx.charts.renderers.
                                                       CircleItemRenderer"/>
                <mx:LineSeries mouseMove="mouseMoveHandler(event)" yField="Sales"
                               form="curve" displayName="Sales"
                               selectable="true"
                               itemRenderer = "mx.charts.renderers.
                                                       CircleItemRenderer"/>
            </mx:series>
        </mx:LineChart>

        <mx:Legend dataProvider="{linechart}"/>

    </s:Panel>
</s:Application>
```

CHAPTER 22

Unit Testing with FlexUnit

Unit testing is a practice and concept that has been gaining in popularity and acceptance in the Flex community as Flex applications have grown larger and more complex. *Unit testing*, the process of ensuring that new additions or changes to a project do not introduce bugs or modify expected behavior, enables large teams to work in tandem without introducing bugs and confirm that individual parts of a program, down to specific methods, all return the expected results. This pinpoints bugs and errors much more quickly, because a properly written unit test will test the behavior of a very small piece of functionality.

The core of unit testing is the *test case*, an evaluation that passes a value into a method of an application and reports the test as passing if the correct value is returned. These can be as simple as checking whether a method returns the correct integer value for an operation or as complex as ensuring that some display logic is appropriately performed or that a service has returned the correct object type. A group of test cases that can be used to test an entire application or a specific aspect of a very large application are referred to as a *test suite*. The test suite will show all test cases that have passed or failed. As a developer adds new code to the application, new test cases are written to provide coverage for that new code and are added to the test suite, and then the entire test suite is run. This ensures that any added code does not interfere with previously functional code and that the new code integrates as expected with the application. In the previous version of FlexUnit, the test cases extended a class called `TestCase` and the test suites were `TestSuite` instances. All test method names needed to begin with `test` to be picked up by the unit test runner. In FlexUnit 4, test cases and suites can be of any type and have any names you like. Metadata tags are used to mark tests within a test case and suites of tests: you include the tag `[Test]` above a test to be run and `[Suite]` to mark a suite of tests.

The FlexUnit Framework allows you to create tests and evaluate them in a test harness application that provides a visual display of all the tests in a test suite. The recipes in this chapter show how to develop meaningful test cases and integrate them into coherent test suites.

22.1 Create an Application That Uses the FlexUnit Framework

Problem

You want to create an application that uses the FlexUnit Framework classes to create and run tests.

Solution

If you're not using Flash Builder, download and unpack the FlexUnit Framework and include the *flexunit.swc* file in your application's compilation path. If you are using Flash Builder, the libraries are included and can be added by creating a test suite.

Discussion

The FlexUnit Framework includes a graphical test runner and base classes that can be used to create custom tests. If you prefer the command line, you can download it from Google Code at *http://code.google.com/p/as3flexunitlib/*. Be sure you download the most recent version. After you unpack the ZIP file into a location of your choice, you simply include *flexunit.swc* in your application's compilation path to use the FlexUnit Framework. Then modify the *mxmlc* arguments to include `-library-path+=flexunit/bin/flexunit.swc`, adjusting the path as needed.

If you're using Flash Builder, these libraries are included by default in your application and you can simply create a test suite as shown in the next recipe to have the relevant SWC libraries included in your project.

22.2 Create an Application to Run FlexUnit Tests

Problem

You need to create an application to run FlexUnit tests and graphically view the results.

Solution

Create a class containing one or more tests, mark that class with the `[Suite]` metadata tag and pass it to a `TestRunnerBase` component to run the tests.

Discussion

If you're using Flash Builder, create your application, then right-click on the project in the Project Explorer window and select New→Test Suite Class. This will import the necessary FlexUnit 4 SWCs so that you don't receive any compilation errors while building out the tests and suites in the next steps.

TestRunnerBase is the new default graphical test runner included with FlexUnit 4. An application that will run tests using TestRunnerBase is shown here:

```
<s:Application xmlns:fx="http://ns.adobe.com/mxml/2009"
               xmlns:s="library://ns.adobe.com/flex/spark"
               xmlns:mx="library://ns.adobe.com/flex/mx"
               xmlns:flexui="flexunit.flexui.*">
    <flexui:FlexUnitTestRunnerUI id="testRunner" width="100%" height="100%"/>
</s:Application>
```

You can also use the TraceListener class to output the results of the tests to a console or the TextListener class to log the results of your tests to a log file. After you compile and run the application, the output will look like Figure 22-1.

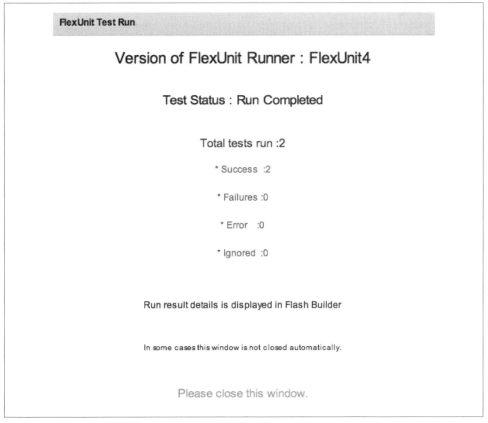

Figure 22-1. The initial appearance of a FlexUnit test application

Next, create a test suite to hold the collection of tests to be run. Create an object in a separate file as shown here and simply use the [Suite] metadata tag to mark it as a test suite:

```
package flexUnitTests
{
    [Suite]
    [RunWith("org.flexunit.runners.Suite")]
    public class FirstTestSuite {
    }
}
```

This tells FlexUnit to treat this object as a test suite and inspect it for test case instances, which will be discussed in the next recipe. If you're using Flash Builder, you can use the IDE to help you create the test suite: right-click or Ctrl-click (Mac) on the project name and select Add TestSuite from the context menu to display the New Test Suite Class dialog (Figure 22-2).

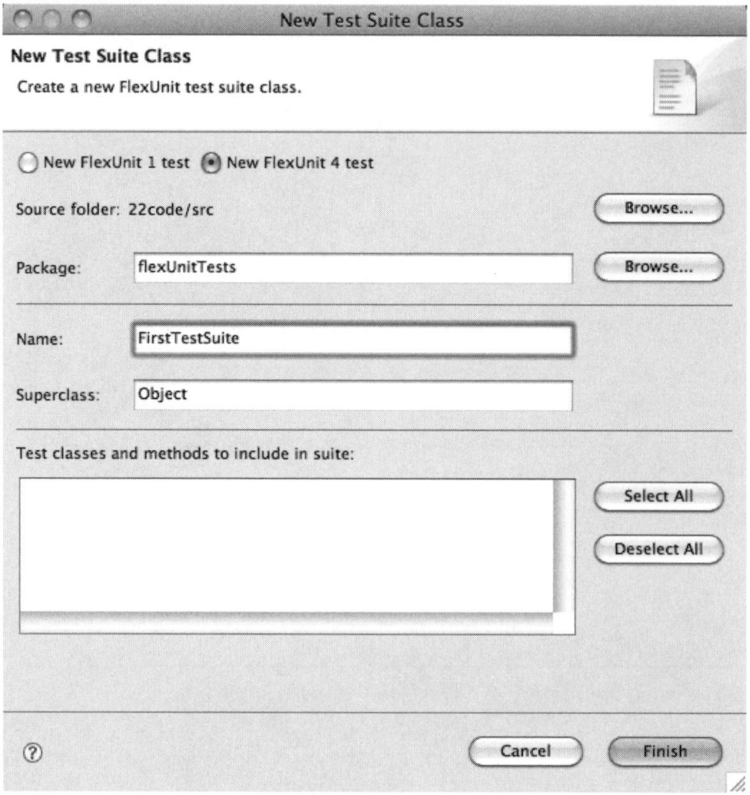

Figure 22-2. The New Test Suite Class dialog in Flash Builder

The real work of looking through all the suites for tests to run, running those tests, and returning the results is encapsulated in the `FlexUnitCore` class. It has two primary responsibilities: first, to get whatever will be listening for the results of your tests, and second, to begin running all of the tests in one or more test suites. To run a test suite, pass it to an instance of the `FlexUnitCore` class, as shown here:

```
<s:Application xmlns:fx="http://ns.adobe.com/mxml/2009"
               xmlns:s="library://ns.adobe.com/flex/spark"
               xmlns:mx="library://ns.adobe.com/flex/halo"
               minWidth="1024" minHeight="768"
               creationComplete="runTests()">

    <fx:Script>
        <![CDATA[
            import flexUnitTests. FirstTestSuite;

            import org.flexunit.internals.TraceListener;
            import org.flexunit.listeners.UIListener;
            import org.flexunit.runner.FlexUnitCore;


            public function runTests():void
            {
```

First, instantiate an instance of the `FlexUnitCore` class:

```
            var core:FlexUnitCore = new FlexUnitCore();
```

Next, add a listener to display the results of your tests. In this case it's the `TraceListener`, which writes the output from a test to the console:

```
            core.addListener( new TraceListener());
```

Finally, pass the `FirstTestSuite` class to the `run()` method of the `FlexUnitCore`. This starts the application running the test suites:

```
            core.run(FirstTestSuite);
        }

        ]]>
    </fx:Script>
</s:Application>
```

Now you're ready to begin adding specific tests to your test suite.

22.3 Create a FlexUnit Test Case

Problem

You need to create a FlexUnit test case class for testing code.

Solution

Create a class that has one or more methods marked with the [Test] metadata tag.

Discussion

When creating a test case, the standard convention is to name it after the class being tested and to add Test as a suffix. For example, if the class to be tested is called RegExp, the test case class would be called RegExpTest. Create a new ActionScript class called RegExpTest with a method in it marked with the [Test] metadata tag. This tells FlexUnit that the method should be run as a test and any results should be reported by the listener:

```
package test
{
    public class RegExpTest
    {
        [Test]
        public function testRegExp():void
        {
        }
    }
}
```

The next step is to make one or more assertions. An *assertion* is a programmatic way of verifying a statement of fact. The most common form of assertion is comparing an expected value to the actual value returned by some operation. FlexUnit includes a number of assertion types that can be used to test different situations. The most common assertions and their functions are as follows:

assertEquals
: Compare with ==

assertTrue
: Check that the condition is true

assertNull
: Check that the condition is null

assertStrictlyEquals
: Compare with ===

FlexUnit also provides various convenience assertions that test for the opposite condition, such as assertFalse and assertNotNull. (See the Assert API documentation included with FlexUnit for a complete list of assertions.)

Each assertion function can take an optional string as the first argument. If the assertion fails, the string will be prefixed before the default "expected X but was Y" failure message that the assertion outputs. When writing assertions, keep in mind that if an assertion fails, the rest of the test method will not be executed. The following code demonstrates the various assertion methods and should be added to the `testRegExp()` function:

```
var regExp:RegExp = new RegExp("a", "i");
assertFalse(regExp.test("b"));
assertFalse("regExp doesn't match", regExp.test("b"));

assertNull(regExp.exec("b"));
assertNull("regExp doesn't match", regExp.exec("b"));

assertNotNull(regExp.exec("Apple"));
assertNotNull("regExp matches", regExp.exec("Apple"));

assertTrue(regExp.exec("Apple") is Array);
assertTrue("regExp exec returned an Array",
regExp.exec("Apple") is Array);

assertEquals("A", regExp.exec("Apple")[0]);
assertEquals("regExp matched A in Apple", "A", regExp.exec("Apple")[0]);

assertStrictlyEquals(regExp, regExp);
assertStrictlyEquals("regExp object identity", regExp, regExp);
```

You can add new test methods to the test case to test other logical groups of operations. It is convention for each test method to focus on testing a specific operation or task. For example, when testing create, retrieve, update, and delete operations, each one should be put into its own test method (`testCreate()`, `testRetrieve()`, and so forth). This way, should assertions start to fail, multiple failures will be reported, which will help you diagnose the issue.

Keep in mind, however, that the order in which the test methods in a test case are run is random. Each test should create its own data and make no assumptions about another test having already run. If you need some control over the test order, you can use the [Before] and [After] tags or use asynchronous tests. Those mechanisms will be covered in later recipes in this chapter.

The sample `testRegExp()` function looks like this:

```
package test
{
    public class RegExpTest
    {
        [Test]
        public function testRegExp():void
        {
            var regExp:RegExp = new RegExp("a", "i");
            assertFalse(regExp.test("b"));
            assertFalse("regExp doesn't match", regExp.test("b"));

            assertNull(regExp.exec("b"));
            assertNull("regExp doesn't match", regExp.exec("b"));

            assertNotNull(regExp.exec("Apple"));
            assertNotNull("regExp matches", regExp.exec("Apple"));
```

```
        assertTrue(regExp.exec("Apple") is Array);
        assertTrue("regExp exec returned an Array", regExp.exec("Apple")
                is Array);

        assertEquals("A", regExp.exec("Apple")[0]);
        assertEquals("regExp matched A in Apple", "A",
                regExp.exec("Apple")[0]);

        assertStrictlyEquals(regExp, regExp);
        assertStrictlyEquals("regExp object identity", regExp, regExp);
    }
  }
}
```

Now you're ready to add your test case to the test suite, which you can do by adding an instance of the test case class to the Test suite, as shown here. Note the [Suite] and [RunWith] tags added to the Test suite declaration:

```
package tests
{
    [Suite]
    [RunWith("org.flexunit.runners.Suite")]
    public class FirstTestSuite
    {
        public var regexpTest:RegExpTest;
    }
}
```

Behind the scenes, FlexUnit will create new instances of your test suite and execute all the test cases included within it.

See Also

Recipes 22.2 and 22.4

22.4 Run Code Before and After Every Test

Problem

You need to run specific code before and after every test in a test case.

Solution

Add the [Before] metadata tag to a method that should be run before the rest of the tests are run and the [After] tag to a method that should be run after all the other tests have been run.

Discussion

By default, every test method defined in a test case runs in its own instance of the test case class. When multiple test methods require the same system state or data, you can use an initialization method to centralize setting up the tests without having to explicitly call a method at the start of every test. In FlexUnit 1, this was called the `setup()` method. In FlexUnit 4, you can instead set the `[Before]` metadata tag on any method to specify that it be run before the tests are begun. Throughout this recipe the method marked `[Before]` will be referred to as the *setup method* to follow convention, even though the method need not be named `setup()`. Likewise, if after every test you need to clean up certain objects or test assertions, you can set the `[After]` metadata tag on the cleanup method you want to run. This method (referred to as the *teardown method*) is guaranteed to run, regardless of any assertion failures or errors. Remember that a test method stops executing as soon as the first assertion fails or an error is generated. The teardown method is thus particularly useful if tests use external resources or objects that should always be freed up when they stop executing.

 If the setup method stops executing because an assertion fails or it throws an error, neither the intended test method nor the teardown method marked with `[After]` will be called.

To create code that runs before every test in a test case, create a method like so:

```
[Before]
public function setUp():void // this can be any method name
{
}
```

Complex tests may require hooking up multiple objects or connecting to external resources. You can place any code, including assertions, in the `[Before]` method. The ability to use assertions in a setup method allows for quick canceling of a test if a resource or object isn't available.

Analogous to the setup method is the teardown method, which is run after every test in the test case, regardless of failed assertions or errors. Think of it as the `finally` part of a `try...catch...finally` block that is wrapped around the test method call. With that said, a teardown method is not usually needed. Remember that by default every test method runs in its own instance of the test case. This means that class-level variables will be set to instantiation values, negating any changes a previous test method may have made. Common situations in which a teardown method is handy include for executing shared assertions that should be made after every test method is run, or releasing resources that are external to the system, such as disconnecting a `Socket`.

To create code that runs after every test method in a test case, create a teardown method as follows. In FlexUnit 4, the teardown method is marked with an [After] tag:

```
[After]
public function tearDown():void
{
}
```

The following code demonstrates how each test method, when run, calls the setup method, the test code, and the teardown method:

```
package flexUnitTests
{

    public class SetUpTearDownTestEx
    {
        private var _phase:String = "instance";

        [Before]
        public function setUp():void
        {
            updatePhase("setUp()");
        }

        [After]
        public function tearDown():void
        {
            updatePhase("tearDown()");
        }

        [Test( description = "This test calls the updatePhase" )]
        public function testOne():void
        {
            updatePhase("testOne()");
        }

        [Test( description = "This test will fail" )]
        public function testFail():void
        {
            updatePhase("testFail()");
            fail("testFail() always fails");
        }

        [Test( description = "This test will error" )]
        public function testError():void
        {
            updatePhase("testError()");
            this["badPropertyName"] = "newValue";
        }

        private function updatePhase(phase:String):void
        {
            trace("Running test", methodName, "old phase", _phase,
                "new phase", phase);
```

```
            _phase = phase;
        }
    }
}
```

Sample output from running SetUpTearDownTest looks like this:

```
Running test testFail old phase instance new phase setUp()
Running test testFail old phase setUp() new phase testFail()
Running test testFail old phase testFail() new phase tearDown()
Running test testError old phase instance new phase setUp()
Running test testError old phase setUp() new phase testError()
Running test testError old phase testError() new phase tearDown()
Running test testOne old phase instance new phase setUp()
Running test testOne old phase setUp() new phase testOne()
Running test testOne old phase testOne() new phase tearDown()
```

Notice that each test starts with a _phase value of instance and that regardless of any assertion failures or errors in the tests, both the setup and teardown methods are executed.

22.5 Share Test Data Between Test Cases

Problem

You want to share simple and complex test data instances between multiple test cases.

Solution

Create a factory class that can generate required test data instances.

Discussion

A common unit-testing need is to have multiple test cases share the same or similar test data. This data may be simple, such as an object that represents an address, or it may be complex, such as an order that has many interrelated entities that must be set up in a particular manner. Instead of cutting and pasting code or trying to load data from an external resource to create and initialize such objects in each test case, the creation can be centralized into a factory. This type of test data centralization is referred to as the ObjectMother pattern.

In its simplest form, the ObjectMother is a single utility class with a static method for creating each type of object that is needed. Typically, the creation methods will come in two forms. The first form requires passing in values for each property that needs to be set, and the method just assembles the object. The second form requires few or no arguments, and the method provides realistic, intelligent defaults for each field. As additional object types are needed, lower-level creation methods can be used to build more and more complex objects.

The ObjectMother class is also useful for providing testing constants or other magic values that many tests will reference. The following is an example of what a simple ObjectMother implementation could look like:

```
package
{
    public class ObjectMother
    {
        public static const SHIPPING_ZIP_CODE:String = "01234";

        public static function createAddress(line:String, city:String,
                                    state:String, zip:String):Address
        {
            var address:Address = new Address();
            address.line = line;
            address.city = city;
            address.state = state;
            address.zip = zip;
            return address;
        }

        public static function createAddressShipping():Address
        {
            return createAddress("123 A Street", "Boston", "MA",
                            SHIPPING_ZIP_CODE);
        }

        public static function createAddressBilling():Address
        {
            return createAddress("321 B Street", "Cambridge", "MA", "02138");
        }

        public static function createOrder(lineItems:Array = null):Order
        {
            var order:Order = new Order();
            order.shippingAddress = createAddressShipping();
            order.billingAddress = createAddressBilling();
            for each (var lineItem:LineItem in lineItems)
            {
                addLineItemToOrder(order, lineItem);
            }
            return order;
        }

        public static function addLineItemToOrder(order:Order,
                                        lineItem:LineItem):void
        {
            order.addLineItem(lineItem);
        }
    }
}
```

Starting with a simple `Address` object, the standardized parameter-creation method `createAddress()` is defined. Two helper functions, `createAddressShipping()` and `createAddressBilling()`, are added to provide a quick way for test case methods to get access to fully fleshed-out `Address` instances. The helper functions build on the generic `createAddress()` function by using any creation logic already written in that method. This tiered creation policy becomes handy when the types of objects being created become more complex, as shown in the `createOrder()` example, or when there are many steps involved in creating a single object.

Because new instances of objects are created each time a method is called, changes made by one test case won't have unintended side effects on other test case instances. Conversely, because the test data objects are centralized, changing the data in the `ObjectMother` to support a new test may break existing brittle tests. This is usually a minor concern, though, compared to the benefit of having readily accessible test data.

22.6 Handle Events in a Test Case

Problem

You need to wait for an event in a test case.

Solution

Use the `[Async]` metadata tag to mark a method as containing an asynchronous test. Then, within that method, use the `Async.asyncHandler()` method to add event listeners for the completion of the asynchronous event or its failure.

Discussion

Testing behavior in a test case often involves waiting for asynchronous events. If the test case methods concern only synchronous events, such as property change events fired immediately when a property is set, no special handling is required. When asynchronous events are involved, however, you need to take extra care in testing. A common example requiring listening for asynchronous events in a test is waiting for a `URLLoader` to finish or a `UIComponent` to finish creating children. This recipe discusses the syntax and common pitfalls of handling events in a sample test case using the `URLLoader` class and a fictitious `Configuration` object.

Events need to be treated specially in test cases because unless FlexUnit is informed that it should be waiting for an event, as soon as the test method ends, FlexUnit will think that the method has passed and start running the next one. This can lead to false-positive tests, where FlexUnit reports that a test has passed when behind the scenes it has silently failed or, worse, thrown an uncaught error.

To inform FlexUnit that it should wait for an event to fire before marking a test as passed or failed, the listener passed to `addEventListener()` must be replaced by a call to `Async.asyncHandler()`. This method has the following signature:

```
asyncHandler(testCase:Object, eventHandler:Function, timeout:int,
            passThroughData:Object = null,
            timeoutHandler:Function = null):Function
```

The first argument is the object that acts as the test case. In most cases the test case will be the class within which the test is contained. The second argument is the listener that should be called when the event is fired. This is the method that would have been used as the listener before introducing `asyncHandler()`. It needs to accept two parameters, an `Event` and an `Object`:

```
function eventHandler(event:Event, passThroughData:Object):void
```

The third argument is the timeout in milliseconds for waiting for the event to fire. Should the event not fire within the timeout period, FlexUnit will mark the test as failed and continue running the other test methods. `passThroughData` is an `Object` that can be given information about the current test so that this information will be available for both the `eventHandler()` and `timeoutHandler()` functions. The `timeoutHandler()` function will be triggered if the asynchronous event doesn't complete in enough time:

```
function timeoutHandler(event:Event, passThroughData:Object):void
```

Here is a typical usage of an asynchronous test:

```
package flexUnitTests.first
{

    import flash.events.Event;
    import flash.net.URLLoader;
    import flash.net.URLRequest;

    import org.flexunit.asserts.*;
    import org.flexunit.async.Async;

    public class AsyncClassTest {


        [Test(async, description="Async Example")]
        public function testLoad():void
        {
            var urlLoader:URLLoader = new URLLoader();
            urlLoader.addEventListener(Event.COMPLETE, Async.asyncHandler(this,
                                    verifyParse, 1000, null, handleTimeout));
            urlLoader.load(new URLRequest("note.xml"));
        }


        private function verifyParse(event:Event, passThroughData:Object):void
        {
            assertTrue( (event.target as URLLoader).data != "");
        }
```

```
            private function handleTimeout(event:Event):void
            {
                fail(" testLoad didn't didn't execute ");
            }
        }
    }
```

At this point, you should keep in mind two important caveats about `asyncHandler()`. First, never have more than one `asyncHandler()` waiting at a time. The FlexUnit Framework doesn't correctly handle detecting and failing a test if more than one `asyncHandler()` is defined. It is possible to chain asynchronous calls though, so that in the listener called by one `asyncHandler()`, a new asynchronous handler can be created. Second, don't register an `asyncHandler()` for an event that will be fired multiple times during a test. Because the `asyncHandler()` mechanism is used by the FlexUnit Framework to determine whether a test has finished or failed, having the same `asyncHandler()` called multiple times can produce false positives and odd behavior.

See Also

Recipe 22.7

22.7 Test Visual Components with FlexUnit

Problem

You need to test a visual component.

Solution

Temporarily place the component on the display hierarchy and then test it.

Discussion

Some may argue that testing the behavior of visual components strays from the goal of unit testing because it is hard to isolate the class being tested to allow for controlled test conditions. The testing of components is complicated by the richness of the Flex Framework in terms of how it determines when certain methods, such as `measure()`, get called. The influence of styles and parent containers can also impact how a component behaves. As such, you're better off thinking of the testing of visual components as automated functional testing.

Before you can test the behavior of a visual component, the component must go through the various lifecycle steps. The Flex Framework automatically handles this when a component is added to the display hierarchy. Test cases are not visual components, however, which means that the component must be associated with an object external to the test case. This external association means that you must take extra care to clean up after both failed and successful tests; otherwise, stray components could inadvertently impact other tests.

Component testing pattern

The simplest way to get a reference to a display object to which you can add the component being tested is to use `parentApplication`. Because the test case is running within a Flex application, this singleton instance is available. The creation and activation of a visual component is not a synchronous activity; before it can be tested, the test case needs to wait for the component to get into a known state. Waiting for the `FlexEvent.CREATION_COMPLETE` event by using `asyncHandler()` is the easiest way to reach that known state for a newly created component. To ensure that one method within your test case doesn't impact the running of another method, the component created needs to be cleaned up and any external references to it removed. Using the teardown method and a class instance variable is the best way to accomplish these two tasks. The following sample code shows the creation, attachment, activation, and cleanup pattern for an instance of `Tile`:

```
package test.mx.containers
{

    import mx.core.Application;
    import mx.events.FlexEvent;

    public class TileTest
    {
        // class variable allows tearDown() to access the instance
        private var _tile:Tile;

        [After]
        public function tearDown():void
        {
            try
            {
                parentApplication.removeChild(_tile);
            }
            catch (argumentError:ArgumentError)
            {
                // safe to ignore, just means component was never added
            }
            _tile = null;
        }

        [Test]
        public function testTile():void
        {
            _tile = new Tile();
            _tile.addEventListener(FlexEvent.CREATION_COMPLETE, Async.asyncHandler
                                (verifyTile, 1000));
            parentApplication.addChild(_tile);
        }
```

```
        private function verifyTile(flexEvent:FlexEvent,
                                        passThroughData:Object):void
        {
            // component now ready for testing
            assertTrue(_tile.initialized);
        }
    }
}
```

The key points to note are that a class variable is defined to allow the teardown method to reference the instance that was created and added to parentApplication. The addition of the component to parentApplication may not have succeeded, which is why the teardown method wraps the removeChild() call in a try...catch block to prevent any erroneous errors from being reported. The test method uses Async.asyncHandler() to wait for the component to be in a stable state before running tests against it.

Component creation testing

Although you can manually call measure() and the various other Flex Framework methods on a component instance by making it part of the display hierarchy, the test() method better simulates the environment in which the object will run. Unlike a unit test, the environment external to the component isn't tightly controlled, which means extra care must be taken to focus the testing on the component and not the surrounding environment. As an example, you can test the layout logic of the Tile container created earlier by adding children to it:

```
[Test]
public function testTileLayout():void
{
    _tile = new Tile();
    var canvas:Canvas = new Canvas();
    canvas.width = 100;
    canvas.height = 100;
    _tile.addChild(canvas);
    canvas = new Canvas();
    canvas.width = 50;
    canvas.height = 50;
    _tile.addChild(canvas);
    canvas = new Canvas();
    canvas.width = 150;
    canvas.height = 50;
    _tile.addChild(canvas);
    _tile.addEventListener(FlexEvent.CREATION_COMPLETE, Async.asyncHandler
                            (verifyTileLayout, 1000));
    parentApplication.addChild(_tile);
}

private function verifyTileLayout(flexEvent:FlexEvent):void
{
    var horizontalGap:int = int(_tile.getStyle("horizontalGap"));
    var verticalGap:int = int(_tile.getStyle("verticalGap"));
    assertEquals(300 + horizontalGap, _tile.width);
    assertEquals(200 + verticalGap, _tile.height);
```

```
        assertEquals(3, _tile.numChildren);
        assertEquals(0, _tile.getChildAt(0).x);
        assertEquals(0, _tile.getChildAt(0).y);
        assertEquals(150 + horizontalGap, _tile.getChildAt(1).x);
        assertEquals(0, _tile.getChildAt(1).y);
        assertEquals(0, _tile.getChildAt(2).x);
        assertEquals(100 + verticalGap, _tile.getChildAt(2).y);
    }
```

In this example, three children of various sizes are added to the `Tile`. Based on the
`Tile` layout logic, this example should create a 2 × 2 grid and make each tile within the
grid the maximum width and height found among the children. The `verify()` method
asserts that the default logic does in fact produce this result. It is important to note that
the test is focusing only on the logic used by the component. It doesn't test whether
the layout looks good, just that its behavior matches the documentation. Another important point to note about testing components at this level is the effect that styles can
have on a component. The dynamic lookup of the `horizontalGap` and `verticalGap` in
the asynchronous event handler is one way to make the test less brittle in case the default
values change. This test method could have instead set the style values when it created
the instance to control the values being used.

Postcreation testing

After a component is created, additional changes made to it can be tricky to test. The
generic `FlexEvent.UPDATE_COMPLETE` event is tempting to use, but it can fire multiple
times as a result of a single change made to a component. Although it's possible to set
up logic that correctly handles these multiple events, the test case ends up inadvertently
testing the Flex Framework's event and UI update logic instead of the logic just within
the component. As such, designing the test to focus just on the component's logic
becomes something of an art. This is another reason why most consider component
testing at this level to be functional testing instead of unit testing.

The following is an example of adding another child to the `Tile` created previously and
detecting that the change has been made:

```
// class variable to track the last asyncHandler() function instance
private var _async:Function;

public function testTileLayoutChangeAfterCreate():void
{
    _tile = new Tile();
    var canvas:Canvas = new Canvas();
    canvas.width = 100;
    canvas.height = 100;
    _tile.addChild(canvas);
    canvas = new Canvas();
    canvas.width = 50;
    canvas.height = 50;
    _tile.addChild(canvas);
    canvas = new Canvas();
    canvas.width = 150;
```

```
        canvas.height = 50;
        _tile.addChild(canvas);
        _tile.addEventListener(FlexEvent.CREATION_COMPLETE,
                Async.asyncHandler (verifyTileLayoutAfterCreate, 1000));
        parentApplication.addChild(_tile);
}

private function verifyTileLayoutAfterCreate(flexEvent:FlexEvent):void
{
        var horizontalGap:int = int(_tile.getStyle("horizontalGap"));
        var verticalGap:int = int(_tile.getStyle("verticalGap"));
        assertEquals(300 + horizontalGap, _tile.width);
        assertEquals(200 + verticalGap, _tile.height);
        assertEquals(3, _tile.numChildren);
        assertEquals(0, _tile.getChildAt(0).x);
        assertEquals(0, _tile.getChildAt(0).y);
        assertEquals(150 + horizontalGap, _tile.getChildAt(1).x);
        assertEquals(0, _tile.getChildAt(1).y);
        assertEquals(0, _tile.getChildAt(2).x);
        assertEquals(100 + verticalGap, _tile.getChildAt(2).y);

        var canvas:Canvas = new Canvas();
        canvas.width = 200;
        canvas.height = 100;
        _tile.addChild(canvas);
        _async = Async.asyncHandler(verifyTileLayoutChanging, 1000);
        _tile.addEventListener(FlexEvent.UPDATE_COMPLETE, _async);
}

private function verifyTileLayoutChanging(flexEvent:FlexEvent,
        passThroughData:Object):void
{
        _tile.removeEventListener(FlexEvent.UPDATE_COMPLETE, _async);
        _tile.addEventListener(FlexEvent.UPDATE_COMPLETE, Async.asyncHandler
                (verifyTileLayoutChangeAfterCreate, 1000));
}

private function verifyTileLayoutChangeAfterCreate(flexEvent:FlexEvent,
        passThroughData:Object):void
{
        var horizontalGap:int = int(_tile.getStyle("horizontalGap"));
        var verticalGap:int = int(_tile.getStyle("verticalGap"));
        assertEquals(400 + horizontalGap, _tile.width);
        assertEquals(200 + verticalGap, _tile.height);
        assertEquals(4, _tile.numChildren);
        assertEquals(0, _tile.getChildAt(0).x);
        assertEquals(0, _tile.getChildAt(0).y);

        assertEquals(200 + horizontalGap, _tile.getChildAt(1).x);
        assertEquals(0, _tile.getChildAt(1).y);

        assertEquals(0, _tile.getChildAt(2).x);
        assertEquals(100 + verticalGap, _tile.getChildAt(2).y);
```

```
        assertEquals(200 + horizontalGap, _tile.getChildAt(3).x);
        assertEquals(100 + verticalGap, _tile.getChildAt(3).y);
    }
```

The event-handling logic now uses a `class` variable to track the last asynchronous function created by `asyncHandler()`, in order to allow it to be removed and a different listener added to handle the second time the same event type is fired. If an additional change was going to be made that would fire another `FlexEvent.UPDATE_COMPLETE` event, the `verifyTileLayoutChanging()` method would also have to store its `asyncHandler()` function to allow it to be removed. This chained event handling is brittle in that if the Flex Framework logic changes how such events are fired, the code might fail. The test doesn't care that two `FlexEvent.UPDATE_COMPLETE` events fire as the component completes laying out its children; this is an unintended effect of trying to capture component logic at this level. If the intermediate state captured in `verifyTileLayoutChanging()` is vital to the logic of the component, the assertions made in that method will have merit and a change in the number of events should warrant this test failing if the events are not fired correctly.

Although a component may dispatch additional events, such as `Event.RESIZE`, the component state at the point at which the event is dispatched is usually unstable. In the case of a `Tile`, when `Event.RESIZE` is dispatched the component's width has changed but the positioning of its children has not. Additionally, there may be actions queued via `callLater()`, and removing the component from the display hierarchy may cause errors when those queued actions attempt to execute. You can avoid some of these issues when testing a component whose update logic is synchronous, removing the need for any event handling. Alternatively, the component being tested may dispatch an event that clearly defines when a change has been fully realized. Whichever method you choose to handle such cases, keep in mind how brittle these approaches are and how much they inadvertently test behavior outside the component.

Testing with timers

If many complex changes are being made to a component at once, the number and order of events dispatched may be too cumbersome to manage. Instead of waiting for a specific event, another approach is to wait for a period of time. This approach makes it easy to handle multiple objects that are being updated or a component that uses `Effect` instances that take a known amount of time to play. The primary drawback is that testing based on time can produce false positives if the speed or resources of the testing environment change. Waiting for a fixed amount of time also tends to lengthen the runtime of the entire test suite more than just adding another synchronous or event-driven test would.

The preceding `Tile` example can be rewritten using timer-based triggers as shown here:

```
        private function waitToTest(listener:Function, waitTime:int):void
        {
            var timer:Timer = new Timer(waitTime, 1);
```

```
            timer.addEventListener(TimerEvent.TIMER_COMPLETE,
                            Async.asyncHandler(listener, waitTime + 250));
        timer.start();
    }

    [Test(async)]
    public function testTileLayoutWithTimer():void
    {
        _tile = new Tile();
        var canvas:Canvas = new Canvas();
        canvas.width = 100;
        canvas.height = 100;
        _tile.addChild(canvas);
        canvas = new Canvas();
        canvas.width = 50;
        canvas.height = 50;
        _tile.addChild(canvas);
        canvas = new Canvas();
        canvas.width = 150;
        canvas.height = 50;
        _tile.addChild(canvas);
        parentApplication.addChild(_tile);
        waitToTest(verifyTileLayoutCreateWithTimer, 500);
    }

    private function verifyTileLayoutCreateWithTimer(timerEvent:TimerEvent,
            passThroughData:object):void
    {
        var horizontalGap:int = int(_tile.getStyle("horizontalGap"));
        var verticalGap:int = int(_tile.getStyle("verticalGap"));
        assertEquals(300 + horizontalGap, _tile.width);
        assertEquals(200 + verticalGap, _tile.height);
        assertEquals(3, _tile.numChildren);
        assertEquals(0, _tile.getChildAt(0).x);
        assertEquals(0, _tile.getChildAt(0).y);
        assertEquals(150 + horizontalGap, _tile.getChildAt(1).x);
        assertEquals(0, _tile.getChildAt(1).y);
        assertEquals(0, _tile.getChildAt(2).x);
        assertEquals(100 + verticalGap, _tile.getChildAt(2).y);

        var canvas:Canvas = new Canvas();
        canvas.width = 200;
        canvas.height = 100;
        _tile.addChild(canvas);
        waitToTest(verifyTileLayoutChangeWithTimer, 500);
    }

    private function verifyTileLayoutChangeWithTimer(timerEvent:TimerEvent,
            passThroughData:object):void
    {
        var horizontalGap:int = int(_tile.getStyle("horizontalGap"));
        var verticalGap:int = int(_tile.getStyle("verticalGap"));
        assertEquals(400 + horizontalGap, _tile.width);
        assertEquals(200 + verticalGap, _tile.height);
        assertEquals(4, _tile.numChildren);
```

```
            assertEquals(0, _tile.getChildAt(0).x);
            assertEquals(0, _tile.getChildAt(0).y);
            assertEquals(200 + horizontalGap, _tile.getChildAt(1).x);
            assertEquals(0, _tile.getChildAt(1).y);
            assertEquals(0, _tile.getChildAt(2).x);
            assertEquals(100 + verticalGap, _tile.getChildAt(2).y);
            assertEquals(200 + horizontalGap, _tile.getChildAt(3).x);
            assertEquals(100 + verticalGap, _tile.getChildAt(3).y);
        }
```

Unlike the previous test examples that could complete as fast as the events fired, this
version of the test has a minimum runtime of 1 second. The additional time added to
the timer delay when calling `Async.asyncHandler()` is to handle small variances in when
the timer fires. The intermediate method to swap `FlexEvent.UPDATE_COMPLETE` listeners
from the preceding example is removed, but otherwise the test code remains the same.

Using programmatic visual assertions

The ability to capture the raw bitmap data of a rendered component can make it easy
to programmatically verify certain visual aspects of the component. An example would
be to test that changing the background and border styles of a component change how
it is drawn. After creating an instance of the component, the bitmap data can be captured and examined. The following is a sample test to verify that adding a border to a
`Canvas` produces the intended results:

```
package mx.containers
{
    import flash.display.BitmapData;

    import mx.core.Application;
    import mx.events.FlexEvent;

    public class CanvasTest
    {
        // class variable allows tearDown() to access the instance
        private var _canvas:Canvas;

        [After]
        override public function tearDown():void
        {
            try
            {
                parentApplication.removeChild(_canvas);
            }
            catch (argumentError:ArgumentError)
            {
                // safe to ignore, just means component was never added
            }
            _canvas = null;
        }

        private function captureBitmapData():BitmapData
        {
```

```
            var bitmapData:BitmapData = new BitmapData(_canvas.width,
                                            _canvas.height);
            bitmapData.draw(_canvas);
            return bitmapData;
        }

        [Test(async)]
        public function testBackgroundColor():void
        {
            _canvas = new Canvas();
            _canvas.width = 10;
            _canvas.height = 10;
            _canvas.setStyle("backgroundColor", 0xFF0000);
            _canvas.addEventListener(FlexEvent.CREATION_COMPLETE,
                    Async.asyncHandler(verifyBackgroundColor, 1000));
            parentApplication.addChild(_canvas);
        }

        private function verifyBackgroundColor(flexEvent:FlexEvent):void
        {
            var bitmapData:BitmapData = captureBitmapData();
            for (var x:int = 0; x < bitmapData.width; x++)
            {
                for (var y:int = 0; y < bitmapData.height; y++)
                {
                    assertEquals("Pixel (" + x + ", " + y + ")", 0xFF0000,
                            bitmapData.getPixel(x, y));
                }
            }
        }

        [Test(async)]
        public function testBorder():void
        {
            _canvas = new Canvas();
            _canvas.width = 10;
            _canvas.height = 10;
            _canvas.setStyle("backgroundColor", 0xFF0000);
            _canvas.setStyle("borderColor", 0x00FF00);
            _canvas.setStyle("borderStyle", "solid");
            _canvas.setStyle("borderThickness", 1);
            _canvas.addEventListener(FlexEvent.CREATION_COMPLETE,
                    Async.asyncHandler(verifyBorder, 1000));
            parentApplication.addChild(_canvas);
        }

        private function verifyBorder(flexEvent:FlexEvent):void
        {
            var bitmapData:BitmapData = captureBitmapData();
            for (var x:int = 0; x < bitmapData.width; x++)
            {
                for (var y:int = 0; y < bitmapData.height; y++)
                {
                    if ((x == 0) || (y == 0) || (x == bitmapData.width - 1) ||
                            (y == bitmapData.height - 1))
```

```
            {
                assertEquals("Pixel (" + x + ", " + y + ")", 0x00FF00,
                        bitmapData.getPixel(x, y));
            }
            else
            {
                assertEquals("Pixel (" + x + ", " + y + ")", 0xFF0000,
                        bitmapData.getPixel(x, y));
            }
        }
    }
}
```

The `testBackgroundColor()` method verifies that all pixels in the `Canvas` are assigned
the background color correctly. The `testBorder()` method verifies that when a border
is added to the `Canvas`, the outside pixels switch to the specified border color while all
other pixels remain the background color. The capturing of the bitmap data is handled
in the `captureBitmapData()` method and makes use of the ability to draw any Flex component into a `BitmapData` instance. This is a powerful technique that can be used to
verify programmatic skins and other visual components that may otherwise be hard to
unit-test.

 For an alternative approach to testing the visual appearance of a component, look at the Visual FlexUnit package, available at *http://code*
.google.com/p/visualflexunit/, or the FlexMonkey project, available at
http://code.google.com/p/flexmonkey/.

Hiding the component being tested

One side effect of adding the component to be tested to a `parentApplication` is that it
will be rendered. This can cause the FlexUnit testing harness to resize and reposition
it as the tests are running and components are being added to and removed from the
display hierarchy. To suppress this behavior, you can hide the component being tested
by setting its `visible` and `includeInLayout` properties to `false` prior to adding it to the
display hierarchy. For example, if the `Canvas` should be hidden while being tested in
the preceding code, the addition of that component to the display hierarchy would be
rewritten as follows:

```
_canvas.visible = false;
_canvas.includeInLayout = false;
parentApplication.addChild(_canvas);
```

See Also

Recipes 22.3 and 22.7

22.8 Create Mock Objects for Testing

Problem

You want to test functionality that relies on classes, systems, or services that cannot be created or are overly complex to create.

Solution

Create a mock object that mimics the behavior of the required class or system and allows you test any classes that interact with that class or system.

Discussion

Mock objects are very useful when working with services that are not yet built out or with external systems that are not easily accessible for testing—for instance, to test browser interaction or interaction with other applications. There are several libraries for working with mock objects in ActionScript, with confusingly similar names: *mock-as3* (*http://code.google.com/p/mock-as3*), *asmock* (*http://asmock.sourceforge.net*), and *mock4as* (*http://code.google.com/p/mock4as*). Each of them operates in more or less the same way. The following recipe will show you how to create a mock class with the *mock-as* library, but you can use similar approaches with the other libraries as well.

Imagine that you have an interface to a service that you want to use in tests like the one shown here:

```
package mockas3.examples {

    import flash.events.IEventDispatcher;

    public interface ServiceInterface extends IEventDispatcher {
        function serviceCallWithoutParams():void;
        function dispatchMyEvent():void;
        function serviceCallWithRest(...rest):void;
    }
}
```

You might want to test how other classes interact with these methods but find that the services are inaccessible, so a simple class like the following might be untestable:

```
import oreilly.cookbook.flex4.ServiceInterface;

public class ServiceIntereactionClass
{

    private var serviceInstance:ServiceInterface;

    public function ServiceIntereactionClass() {

    }
```

```
public function set serviceClass(service:ServiceInterface):void {
    serviceInstance = service;
}

public function saveSimple():Object {
    var someObj:Object = serviceInstance.serviceCallWithoutParams();
}

public function saveComplex(id:int, name:String, other:Array):Object {
    return serviceInstance.serviceCallWithRest(id, name, other);
}
}
```

This is where you can delegate the calls to an instance of the mock library. First, create a class that extends the service interface and contains an instance of the Mock class, as shown here:

```
package com.anywebcam.mock.examples {

    import com.anywebcam.mock.Mock;
    import flash.events.Event;
    import flash.events.EventDispatcher;

    public class MockExample implements ServiceInterface {

        public var mock:Mock;

        public function MockExample( ignoreMissing:Boolean = false ) {
            mock = new Mock( this, ignoreMissing );
        }
```

Note that all the methods of the ServiceInterface call the same method on the Mock object. This allows you to easily determine whether all the methods have been called with the correct parameters:

```
public function serviceCallWithoutParams( ):void {
    mock.serviceCallWithoutParams( );
}

public function serviceCallWithRest(...rest):void {
    mock. serviceCallWithRest(rest);
}

public function addEventListener(type:String, listener:Function,
        useCapture:Boolean=false, priority:int=0,
        useWeakReference:Boolean=false):void {
    mock.addEventListener(type, listener, useCapture, priority,
            useWeakReference);
}

public function removeEventListener(type:String, listener:Function,
        useCapture:Boolean=false):void {
    mock.removeEventListener(type, listener, useCapture);
}
```

```
        public function dispatchEvent(event:Event):Boolean {
            return mock.dispatchEvent(event);
        }

        public function hasEventListener(type:String):Boolean {
            return mock.hasEventListener(type);
        }

        public function willTrigger(type:String):Boolean {
            return mock.willTrigger(type);
        }
    }
}
```

Now you're ready to use the methods in a test. In this test, what's being confirmed is that the `ServiceInteractionClass` does the right thing when its methods are called. You use the `Mock` instances to create an interface with which the `ServiceInteractionClass` can interact. This approach works best when testing controllers, commands, or other classes that interact with services. The example here is greatly simplified, but it should help you understand how to use the *as3-mock* library:

```
import oreilly.cookbook.flex4.MockService;
import org.flexunit.asserts.assertEquals;

public class TestWithMock
{
    [Test]
    public function testUsingMock():void {
```

First, create an instance of the `MockService`:

```
        var mockService:MockService = new MockService();
        var serviceResult:String = "Some valid service result";
```

Then tell the `Mock` object of the `MockService` what arguments to expect to be passed to a method and what to return. These are referred to as the *expectations* of the `Mock` object:

```
        mockService.mock.method("serviceCallWithRest").withArgs(6, "Todd Anderson",
            [100, 100]).andReturn(serviceResult);
        var sic:ServiceInteractionClass = new ServiceInteractionClass();
```

Calling the `ServiceInteractionClass` should call the `MockService` in the same way that it would call any other class that implements the `ServiceInterface`:

```
        var newRes:String = sic.saveComplex(6, "Todd Anderson", [100, 100]);
```

Now ensure that the value returned from the service is correct and call the `verify()` method of the `Mock` object to ensure that the expectations were met:

```
        assertEquals(serviceResult, newRes);
        mockService.mock.verify();

    }
}
```

22.9 Use Complex Assertions in a Test Case

Problem

You need to do complex pattern matching in your test case.

Solution

Use the matching functions defined by the *Hamcrest* library to create complex assertions.

Discussion

Hamcrest is a matching library that helps you create complex assertions and test them. A complex assertion, when written out in English, might look like this: "make sure that for every item in an array the item is of type `Sprite` and has no children." To implement this in simple standard ActionScript, you would need to write a `for` loop and two conditions within that loop and store the results in a Boolean, which could then be evaluated for the test. Using the Hamcrest library, you can condense this to the following:

```
assertThat(arr, everyItem(both(isA(
        flash.display.Sprite )).and(hasProperty("numChildren", 0))));
```

This statement contains four methods:

- `everyItem()` takes any operation that returns a Boolean value and applies it to every item in a list. If the operation doesn't return `true` for every item in the list, the `everyItem()` method returns `false`.

- `both()` takes two operations that return Boolean values and returns `true` if both those values are `true`.

- `isA()` returns `true` if an object is of the type passed into it. For instance, calling the `isA()` method on a `String` when `int` has been passed to `isA()` will return `false`.

- `hasProperty()` returns `true` if the object has a property that matches the second parameter passed into this method. In our example, the object is tested whether to see it has a property called `numChildren` and whether that property is equal to `0`.

A different example of using the Hamcrest library to simplify your program logic might look like the following (assuming that there is a class called `ValidDate` that performs some logic and returns a date that is valid for a certain purpose):

```
package flexUnitTests
{
    import org.hamcrest.date.dateBetween;
    import oreilly.cookbook.flex4.ValidDate;

    public class ValidDateTest
    {
        // reference declaration for class to test
        private var classToTestRef : oreilly.cookbook.flex4.ValidDate;
```

```
public function ValidDateTest(methodName:String=null) {
    super(methodName);
}

[After]
override public function tearDown():void {
    classToTestRef = new ValidDate();
    super.tearDown();
}
```

Another example of using the Hamcrest library is the dateBetween() method, which compares two dates with a single very readable line of code:

```
[Test]
public function testReturnDate():void {
    assertThat(classToTestRef.returnDate(), dateBetween(new Date(2000, 1,
            1), new Date(2020, 1, 1)));
}

    }
}
```

Another friendly feature of the Hamcrest library is how easy it makes performing complex assertions on strings or arrays. For instance, to ensure that an array has at least one item with a date before 1999 and at least one item with a date after 2008, you could simply write:

```
assertTrue(array, hasItems( dateBefore(new Date(1999, 1, 1)),
        dateAfter(new Date(2008, 1, 1))));
```

To ensure that a String begins, contains, and ends with certain substrings, you can simply do the following:

```
assertTrue(str, allOf(startsWith("Dependency injection"), endsWith("business"),
        containsString("Flex")));
```

This would return true for the following string:

```
var str:String = "Dependency injection with Flex UI components can be tricky
        business.";
```

You can use the Hamcrest library in Flex Validators and Formatters to help simplify your validation and formatting logic.

CHAPTER 23

Compiling, Debugging, and Deploying

Compiling Flex applications is most often done through Flash Builder or through invoking the MXML compiler (*mxmlc*) on the command line, but there are many other tools that let you compile applications, move files, or invoke applications. Tools such as *make*, Ant, and Rake, for example, enable you to simplify an entire compilation and deployment routine so that you can invoke it using a single command.

Debugging in Flex is done through the debug version of the Flash Player, which enables you to see the results of `trace` statements. With Flash Builder, you can step through code line by line and inspect the properties of variables. Flash Builder also introduces a new profiling view that lets you examine memory usage and the creation and deletion of objects. Outside of Flash Builder, numerous open source tools expand your options. With De MonsterDebugger, for example, you can inspect the values of objects, or you can view the output of `trace` statements with a free open source utility such as Flash-Tracer instead of using the Flash Builder IDE. The recipes in this chapter cover both debugging with the tools provided in Flash Builder, and tracing values and inspecting objects by using De MonsterDebugger and FlashTracer.

23.1 Use trace Statements Without Flash Builder

Problem

You want to create `trace` statements that will assist you in debugging your application, but you do not have Flash Builder.

Solution

Download and use one of the many open source tracing tools available.

Discussion

Since Adobe made the Flex 3 library and compiler freely available, developers have gained more options for viewing `trace` statements output by the Flash Player. No longer are you limited to using the Flash IDE or Flash Builder IDE; now you can choose from several tools. For example, De MonsterDebugger (developed by De Monsters) creates `trace` statement viewers within Flash. De MonsterDebugger allows for not only the viewing of `trace` statements during application execution, but also the basic inspection of objects during execution (Figure 23-1).

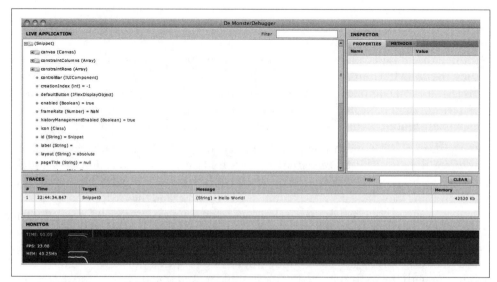

Figure 23-1. Viewing output with De MonsterDebugger

Another option is the FlashTracer utility (developed by Alessandro Crugnola). Installing this plug-in in the Firefox browser enables you to receive any `trace` statements that are executed within the application. You need to have a *flashlog.txt* file created in order for Flash Tracer to work properly.

 You can download De MonsterDebugger from *http://www.demonster debugger.com* and FlashTracer from *http://www.sephiroth.it/firefox*.

Yet another option is to install the Flash debug player and configure it to write to a log file. After installing the debug player, open the *mm.cfg* file. Depending on your operating system, it will be in one of the following locations:

- Mac OS X: *MacHD:Library:Application Support:macromedia:*
- Microsoft Windows Vista or Windows 7: *C:\Users\user_name*
- Microsoft Windows 2000/XP: *C:\Documents and Settings\user_name*
- Linux: */home/user_name*

Open the *mm.cfg* file and enter the following lines:

```
ErrorReportingEnable=1
TraceOutputFileEnable=1
```

The *flashlog.txt* file will be written to one of the following locations, depending on your operating system:

- Mac OS X: *MacHD:Users:user_name:Library:Preferences:Macromedia:Flash Player: Logs:flashlog.txt*
- Windows Vista or Windows 7: *C:\Users\user_name\AppData\Roaming\Macromedia\ Flash Player:Logs:flashlog.txt*
- Windows 2000/XP: *C:\Documents and Settings\user_name\Application Data\ Macromedia\Flash Player:Logs:flashlog.txt*
- Linux: */home/user_name/.macromedia/Flash_Player/Logs/flashlog.txt*

If the *Logs* directory and *flashlog.txt* file do not already exist, you'll need to run a SWF that contains a `trace` statement—after changing *mm.cfg*—to force the Flash Player to create them.

23.2 Use the Component Compiler

Problem

You want to compile a Flex component into a SWC file that can be used as a runtime shared library (RSL).

Solution

Use the component compiler (*compc*), and either pass it command-line arguments or pass a configuration XML file as the `load-config` argument.

Discussion

To invoke the component compiler, use this syntax:

```
compc -source-path . -include-classes oreilly.cookbook.foo -output example.swc
```

To see all of the options available in *compc*, you can simply type the following command line:

```
compc -help list details
```

Compiling many classes into a runtime shared library can result in a very long command. To simplify this, you can use either configuration files or manifest files.

As with the MXML compiler (*mxmlc*), you can use configuration files with *compc* by specifying a `load-config` option. Also like *mxmlc*, *compc* automatically loads a default configuration file called *flex-config.xml*. Unless you want to duplicate the entire contents of *flex-config.xml* (much of which is required) in your configuration file, you can specify a configuration file to use in addition to the default by using the += operator:

```
compc -load-config+=configuration.xml
```

Any flags passed to the compiler can be described in XML and passed to *compc* in the `load-config` option:

```
<include-sources>src/.</include-sources>
```

A configuration file for the *compc* task might look like the following:

```
<flex-config>
    <compiler>
        <source-path>
            <path-element>src.</path-element>
        </source-path>
    </compiler>
    <output>demo.swc</output>
    <include-classes>
        <class>oreilly.cookbook.flex4.First</class>
        <class>oreilly.cookbook.flex4.Second</class>
        <class>oreilly.cookbook.flex4.Third</class>
        <class>oreilly.cookbook.flex4.Fourth</class>
    </include-classes>
</flex-config>
```

23.3 Install the Flex Ant Tasks

Problem

You want to use the Flex Ant tasks included with the Flex 4 SDK.

Solution

Copy the *ant/lib/flexTasks.jar* file to Ant's *lib* directory (*{ANT_root}/lib*).

Discussion

Ant is a Java-based build tool that helps you compile applications, copy and delete files, perform system tasks, and do a wide range of other tasks as part of a build process. Ant can make compiling and deploying your Flex application much easier and allow you to integrate it with other tasks and build processes easily. Flex Ant tasks is a library of Flex-specific tasks for Ant that can invoke the *compc* or *mxmlc* compilers or generate HTML wrappers and other files for your application. To use it, you'll need to have Ant installed on your system (Ant is available from *http://ant.apache.org*). To ensure that Ant always has access to all tasks included in the Flex Ant tasks library provided with the Flex 4 SDK, you must copy the *flexTasks.jar* file into the *lib* directory of the Ant installation. If you do not copy this file to the *lib* directory, you must specify it by using Ant's `lib` option on the command line when you make a project XML file.

 There are many more Ant commands that you can learn about by visiting *http://ant.apache.org*.

Creating an Ant build file is easy, and this is the first step toward using Ant to automate common tasks. Simply create a new XML document named *build.xml* and save it in a directory named *build* in the root of your project directory. Saving the file in this directory is not mandatory, but it's a common convention.

The root node in your build file should look something like this:

```
<project name="MyAntTasks" basedir="..">
</project>
```

You will want to set the `name` attribute to something unique for your project. This is the name that will show up inside the Ant view in Eclipse. Also, make sure the `basedir` attribute is set to the root of your project directory. You will use the `basedir` property frequently when defining other properties that point toward files and directories inside your project folder.

Next, you will likely want to create some additional properties for use throughout the various tasks that you may add later. For instance, to create a property that points toward your project's source folder, you could do something like this:

```
<project name="MyAntTasks" basedir="..">
    <property name="src" value="${basedir}/src" />
</project>
```

The preceding example also demonstrates how to use a property after it has been defined, with the syntax ${*property*}.

If you find that you are defining a lot of properties and you would like to keep your build file as clean as possible, you can declare the properties in a separate file instead. To do this, create a new text file named *build.properties* and save it in the same directory as your *build.xml* file. Inside this file, declaring properties is as simple as this:

```
src="${basedir}/src"
```

That's all there is to it. Some examples of useful properties to define are paths to your source folder(s), your *bin* folder, and the Flex 4 SDK directory. You'll catch on pretty quickly as to what you need.

You are now ready to start adding tasks to your build file. A simple build file might look like this:

```
<?xml version="1.0" encoding="utf-8"?>
<!-- mySimpleBuild.xml -->
<project name="Cookbook Ant Demo!" basedir="src.">
    <taskdef resource="flexTasks.tasks"
                classpath="${basedir}/flexTasks/lib/flexTasks.jar"/>
    <property name="FLEX_HOME" value="C:/FlexHome/flex/sdk"/>
    <property name="APP_ROOT" value="Cookbook4"/>
    <target name="main">
        <mxmlc file="${APP_ROOT}/Cookbook4.mxml"
                keep-generated-actionscript="true">
            <load-config filename="${FLEX_HOME}/frameworks/flex-config.xml"/>
            <source-path path-element="${FLEX_HOME}/frameworks"/>
        </mxmlc>
    </target>
</project>
```

Save the file as *build.xml* and run it by entering the following on the command line:

```
ant -buildfile mySimpleBuild.xml main
```

23.4 Use mxmlc and Ant to Compile Flex Applications

Contributed by Ryan Taylor

Problem

You want to add tasks to your Ant build file for compiling your application.

Solution

Add executable tasks to your Ant build file that use the MXML compiler to compile your files.

Discussion

Compiling targets are by far the most common and useful type of targets you will add to your Ant build files. Flex applications are compiled using *mxmlc*, which is the free command-line compiler included with the Flex 4 SDK. By adding targets for compiling to your build file, you can automate the build process: Ant will compile all your files without you ever having to open up the command prompt or Terminal.

The MXML compiler is included in multiple formats. You can use the executable version of it by creating a target similar to this:

```
<!-- COMPILE MAIN -->
<target name="compileMain" description="Compiles the main application files.">
    <echo>Compiling '${bin.dir}/main.swf'...</echo>
    <exec executable="${FLEX_HOME}/bin/mxmlc.exe" spawn="false">
        <arg line="-source-path '${src.dir}'" />
```

```
            <arg line="-library-path '${FLEX_HOME}/frameworks'" />
            <arg line="'${src.dir}/main.mxml'" />
            <arg line="-output '${bin.dir}/main.swf'" />
        </exec>
    </target>
```

Alternatively, you can use the Java version by writing a task such as this one:

```
<!-- COMPILE MAIN -->
<target name="compileMain" description="Compiles the main application files.">
    <echo>Compiling '${bin.dir}/main.swf'...</echo>
    <java jar="${FLEX_HOME}/lib/mxmlc.jar" fork="true" failonerror="true">
        <arg value="+flexlib=${FLEX_HOME}/frameworks" />
        <arg value="-file-specs='${src.dir}/main.mxml'" />
        <arg value="-output='${bin.dir}/main.swf'" />
    </java>
</target>
```

The final (and perhaps best) approach is to use the optional *mxmlc* tasks that are included with the Flex 4 SDK. Installing these is described in Recipe 23.3. To access them in your build file, first you will need to add a task definition:

```
<!-- TASK DEFINITIONS -->
<taskdef resource="flexTasks.tasks"
         classpath="${FLEX_HOME}/ant/lib/flexTasks.jar" />
```

By importing the optional Flex tasks, you can now compile by using an even more intuitive syntax, as well as leveraging error detection in a tool such as Eclipse as you write out the task. For example:

```
<!-- COMPILE MAIN -->
<target name="compileMain" description="Compiles the main application files.">
    <echo>Compiling '${bin.dir}/main.swf'...</echo>
    <mxmlc file="${src.dir}/main.mxml" output="${bin.dir}/main.swf">
        <source-path path-element="${src.dir}" />
    </mxmlc>
</target>
```

In all of these examples, the same basic rules apply. You need to define properties that point toward your project's *src* and *bin* directories, as well as the Flex 4 SDK. All of the properties in the examples use suggested names, except for FLEX_HOME, which is a mandatory name. The FLEX_HOME property *must* be set to the root of the Flex 4 SDK before you use the *mxmlc* task.

> If you're using the EXE or JAR version of *mxmlc*, you can use a property
> name other than FLEX_HOME.

The true power of compiling your project via Ant lies in the ability to chain targets together. For instance, you could create a `compileAll` target that calls each individual compile target one by one:

```
<!-- COMPILE ALL -->
<target name="compileAll" description="Compiles all application files."
        depends="compileMain, compileNavigation, compileGallery, compileLibrary">
    <echo>Finishing compile process...</echo>
</target>
```

All of this may seem a little intimidating at first; however, when you've spent a little time using Ant and configuration files, you will find that they can greatly improve your workflow. Letting a third-party tool such as Ant automate your compile process means that you are no longer tied to using one particular development tool; you will easily be able to call on Ant to build your project from the development tool of your choice (e.g., Flash Builder, FDT, TextMate, or FlashDevelop).

See Also

Recipe 23.3

23.5 Use Ant to Compile and Deploy Flex Applications That Use RSLs

Problem

You need to deploy a Flex application that uses one or more runtime shared libraries.

Solution

Use the `external-library-path` compiler option to indicate the location of the RSL or RSLs after the application is compiled.

Discussion

When it initializes, a Flex application needs to know the locations of any necessary runtime shared libraries. The `external-library-path` compiler option contains this information; passing it to the compiler enables the Flash Player to begin loading the bytes for the RSL right away, without needing to load a separate SWF file before instantiating components or classes.

In order to use an RSL file, you need to first create an RSL. RSLs are stored within SWC files that are then accessed by the application at runtime. The SWC RSL file is compiled using *compc*, and the application SWF file is compiled using the *mxmlc* compiler. In order for the application to use an RSL, a reference to the RSL's location must be passed to *mxmlc* via the `runtime-shared-libraries` option. In this example, Ant is used to compile both the SWC file and the application that will access it, meaning that you need to use both *compc* and *mxmlc*. In the *build.xml* file that Ant will use, both of the compilers need to be declared as variables:

```
<property name="mxmlc" value="C:\FlexSDK\bin\mxmlc.exe"/>
<property name="compc" value="C:\FlexSDK\bin\compc.exe"/>
```

Next, use *compc* to compile the RSL that the application will access, and use the move task to place it in the *application/rsl* directory:

```
<target name="compileRSL">
    <exec executable="${compc}">
        <arg line="-load-config+=rsl/configuration.xml" />
    </exec>
    <mkdir dir="application/rsl" />
    <move file="example.swc" todir="application/rsl" />
    <unzip src="application/rsl/example.swc" dest="application/rsl/" />
</target>
```

Then compile the application SWF using *mxmlc*. Note that we're passing an XML file called *configuration.xml* to the compiler by using the load-config option. This file will contain all the information about how you want your application compiled, including, in this case, the location of the RSL:

```
<target name="compileApplication">
    <exec executable="${mxmlc}">
        <arg line="-load-config+=application/configuration.xml" />
    </exec>
</target>

<target name="compileAll" depends="compileRSL,compileApplication">
</target>
```

Note that both actual command-line calls to the compilers use a *configuration.xml* file containing information about the locations of the runtime shared libraries that will be passed to *mxmlc*:

```
<flex-config>
    <compiler>
        <external-library-path>
            <path-element>example.swc</path-element>
        </external-library-path>
    </compiler>
    <file-specs>
        <path-element>RSLClientTest.mxml</path-element>
    </file-specs>
    <runtime-shared-libraries>
        <url>example.swf</url>
    </runtime-shared-libraries>
</flex-config>
```

In place of adding the external-library-path flag to the command-line invocation of *mxmlc*, as shown here:

```
mxmlc -external-library-path=example.swc
```

the *configuration.xml* file is passed as the load-config flag in the call to the compiler, and each option is read from the XML file.

A similar file can be passed to *compc*:

```
<flex-config>
    <compiler>
        <source-path>
            <path-element>.</path-element>
        </source-path>
    </compiler>
    <output>example.swc</output>
    <include-classes>
        <class>oreilly.cookbook.shared.*</class>
    </include-classes>
</flex-config>
```

The complete Ant file for this recipe is shown here:

```
<?xml version="1.0"?>
<project name="useRSL" basedir="./">

    <property name="mxmlc" value="C:\FlexSDK\bin\mxmlc.exe"/>
    <property name="compc" value="C:\FlexSDK\bin\compc.exe"/>

    <target name="compileRSL">
        <exec executable="${compc}">
            <arg line="-load-config+=rsl/configuration.xml" />
        </exec>
        <mkdir dir="application/rsl" />
        <move file="example.swc" todir="application/rsl" />
        <unzip src="application/rsl/example.swc" dest="application/rsl/" />
    </target>

    <target name="compileApplication">
        <exec executable="${mxmlc}">
            <arg line="-load-config+=application/configuration.xml" />
        </exec>
    </target>

    <target name="compileAll" depends="compileRSL,compileApplication">
    </target>

</project>
```

23.6 Use Rake to Compile Flex Applications

Problem

You want to compile Flex applications by using Rake, the Ruby *make* tool.

Solution

Download and install Ruby 1.9 from *http://www.ruby-lang.org/en/downloads/* if you have not already, and then download and install Rake (*http://rake.rubyforge.org*).

Discussion

Although written completely in Ruby, Rake functions very similarly both to the classic *make* utility used by C++ and C programmers and to Ant. After you've downloaded and installed both Ruby and Rake, you can write a simple Rake file like so:

```
task :default do
    DEV_ROOT = "/Users/base/flex_development"
    PUBLIC = "#{DEV_ROOT}/bin"
    FLEX_ROOT = "#{DEV_ROOT}/src"
    system "/Developer/SDKs/Flex/bin/mxmlc --show-actionscript-warnings=true
            --strict=true -file-specs #{FLEX_ROOT}/App.mxml"
    system "cp #{FLEX_ROOT}/App.swf #{PUBLIC}/App.swf"
end
```

All tasks in Rake are similar to targets in Ant; that is, they define actions to be done. The default action is always performed, and any extra actions can optionally be called within a different task. Within the task itself, variables can be declared and system arguments can be called, as shown here:

```
system "/Developer/SDKs/Flex/bin/mxmlc --show-actionscript-warnings=true
        --strict=true -file-specs #{FLEX_ROOT}/App.mxml"
```

This is the actual call to the MXML compiler that will generate the SWF file. Because an item in the Rake task won't be run until the previous task returns, the next line can assume that the SWF has been generated and can be copied to a new location:

```
system "cp #{FLEX_ROOT}/App.swf #{PUBLIC}/App.swf"
```

The rest of the Rake file declares variables that will be used to place files in the appropriate folders. The file can now be saved with any name and run from the command line using the **rake** command. For instance, if you save the file as *Rakefile*, you can now run it by entering the following:

```
rake Rakefile
```

23.7 Create and Monitor Expressions in the Flash Builder Debugger

Problem

You want to track the changes to a value in your Flex application as the application executes.

Solution

Use the Flash Builder Debugger to run your application and set a breakpoint where the variable that you would like to inspect is within scope. In the Expressions window of the Flash Builder Debugger, create a new expression.

Discussion

Expressions are powerful debugging tools that let you see the value of any variable within scope. Any object within the scope where the breakpoint is set can be evaluated by creating an expression, as shown in Figure 23-2.

Once you have an expression created, you can inspect the variable, as in Figure 23-3.

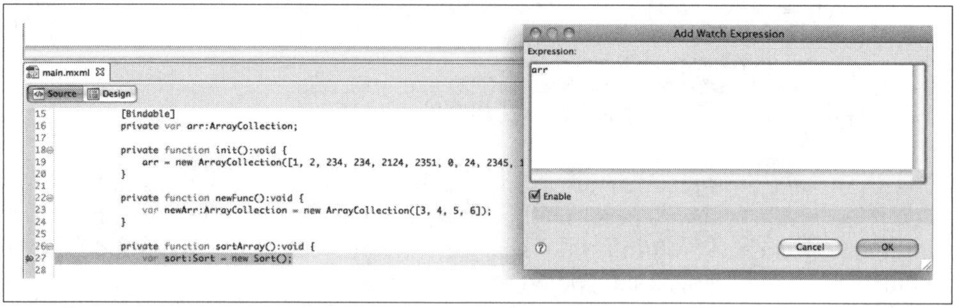

Figure 23-2. Creating an expression

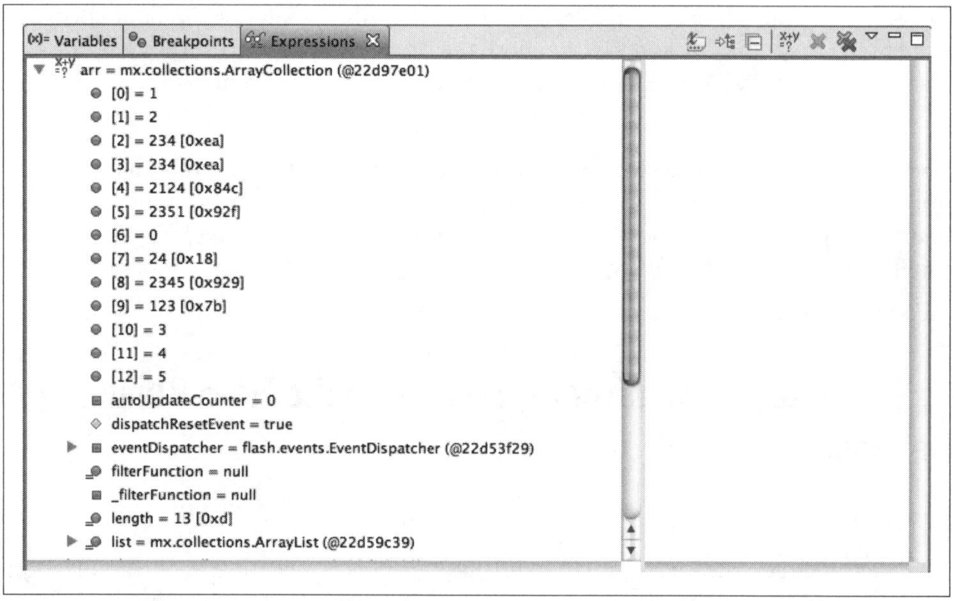

Figure 23-3. The expression evaluated

For example, if you place a breakpoint at the line where an array is instantiated, marked here with *breakpoint here*:

```
<s:Groups:VGroup xmlns:fx="http://ns.adobe.com/mxml/2009"
                 xmlns:s="library://ns.adobe.com/flex/spark"
                 xmlns:mx="library://ns.adobe.com/flex/halo"
```

```
                        creationComplete="init()">
    <fx:Script>
        <![CDATA[
            import mx.collections.ArrayCollection;

            private var arr:ArrayCollection;

            private function init():void {
                arr = new ArrayCollection([1, 2, 3, 4, 5]); // breakpoint here
            }

            private function newFunc():void {
                var newArr:ArrayCollection = new ArrayCollection([3, 4, 5, 6]);
            }

        ]]>
    </fx:Script>
</s:VGroup>
```

the expression **arr** will evaluate to **null**. When you advance the application by pressing the F6 key, the expression will evaluate to an **ArrayCollection** wrapping an **Array** of five integers (Figure 23-4).

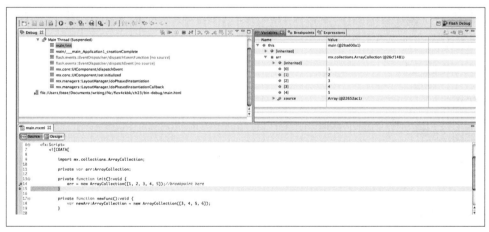

Figure 23-4. The expression showing the variable evaluated

The expression **newArr** evaluates to **null**, however, because the variable **newArr** will not be in scope (Figure 23-5).

If you instead place a breakpoint at line 15, the expressions **newArr** and **arr** both evaluate to **ArrayCollection**s, because both variables are in the current scope.

You can also use a tool like De MonsterDebugger, introduced in Recipe 23.1, to inspect objects at runtime.

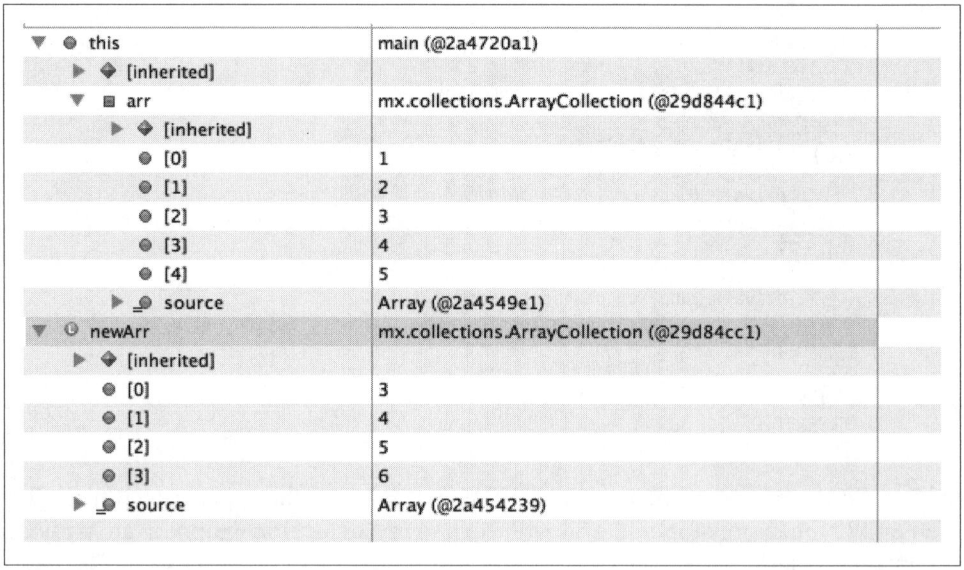

▼ ● this	main (@2a4720a1)	
▶ ◆ [inherited]		
▼ ■ arr	mx.collections.ArrayCollection (@29d844c1)	
▶ ◆ [inherited]		
● [0]	1	
● [1]	2	
● [2]	3	
● [3]	4	
● [4]	5	
▶ ● source	Array (@2a4549e1)	
▼ ● newArr	mx.collections.ArrayCollection (@29d84cc1)	
▶ ◆ [inherited]		
● [0]	3	
● [1]	4	
● [2]	5	
● [3]	6	
▶ ● source	Array (@2a454239)	

Figure 23-5. Only variables in scope can be evaluated

23.8 Install the Ant View in the Standalone Version of Flash Builder

Contributed by Ryan Taylor

Problem

You can't find the Ant view in the standalone version of Flash Builder.

Solution

Install the Eclipse Java Development Tools.

Discussion

To access Ant in Flash Builder's standalone version, you must install the Eclipse Java Development Tools. To do so:

1. In the Flash Builder menu bar, choose Help→Software Updates→Find and Install.
2. Select the "Search for New Features to Install" option and click Next.
3. Choose The Eclipse Project Updates in the dialog box and click Finish.
4. A menu appears, asking you to select a location from which to download the files. Select any location—preferably one that is geographically near you for faster download times—and then click OK.

5. Browse the various SDK versions in the Eclipse Project Updates tree until you find Eclipse Java Development Tools. Select the checkbox next to it and click Next.

6. After the Update Manager finishes downloading the necessary files, you will be prompted with a feature verification dialog box. Click Install All.

7. After installation is completed, restart Flash Builder.

You can now find the Ant view in Flash Builder by browsing to Window→Other Views→Ant.

23.9 Use ASDoc and Ant to Generate Documentation

Contributed by Ryan Taylor

Problem

You want to easily generate documentation for your application.

Solution

Add an executable task to your Ant build file that uses ASDoc (included with the Flex 4 SDK) to generate the documentation for you.

Discussion

ASDoc is a free command-line utility that is included with the Flex 4 SDK. If you have ever used Adobe's LiveDocs, you are already familiar with the style of documentation that ASDoc produces. Although using the command prompt or a Terminal window isn't terribly difficult, a better solution is to add a target to your Ant build file to automate the process even further.

Before creating a target for generating your documentation, it is a good idea to create an additional target that cleans out your *docs* directory. When you define the `docs.dir` property, simply point it toward your project's *docs* directory:

```
<!-- CLEAN DOCS -->
<target name="cleanDocs" description="Cleans out the documentation directory.">
    <echo>Cleaning '${docs.dir}'...</echo>
    <delete includeemptydirs="true">
        <fileset dir="${docs.dir}" includes="**/*" />
    </delete>
</target>
```

With the target for cleaning out the *docs* directory in place, you are ready to create the target that actually generates the documentation. Notice in the sample code that the `depends` attribute mandates that the `cleanDocs` target is executed before the instructions for generating the documentation:

```
<!-- GENERATE DOCUMENTATION -->
<target name="generateDocs"
```

```
            description="Generates application documentation using ASDoc."
            depends="cleanDocs">
        <echo>Generating documentation...</echo>
        <exec executable="${FLEX_HOME}/bin/asdoc.exe" failOnError="true">
            <arg line="-source-path ${src.dir}" />
            <arg line="-doc-sources ${src.dir}" />
            <arg line="-main-title ${docs.title}" />
            <arg line="-window-title ${docs.title}" />
            <arg line="-footer ${docs.footer}" />
            <arg line="-output ${docs.dir}" />
        </exec>
    </target>
```

The FLEX_HOME property needs to point toward the root directory of the Flex 4 SDK on your machine. The src.dir and docs.dir properties represent your project's *src* and *docs* directories, respectively. Last but not least are the docs.title and docs.footer properties, which set the title and footer text that appears in the documentation. A common convention for the documentation title is "*<Your Project>* Reference," where *<Your Project>* is the name of the project you are working on. The footer is a good place to put copyright information and a URL.

ASDoc will successfully generate documentation from your code even if you haven't written a single comment. It is, however, highly recommended that you thoroughly document your code by using Javadoc commenting. Not only will this produce much more in-depth documentation, but it will enable programmers unfamiliar with your code to follow along inside the code itself.

23.10 Use Express Install for Your Application

Problem

You want to ensure that if a user does not have the correct version of Flash Player installed to view a Flex application, the correct version can be installed.

Solution

Use the Express Install option when compiling to let the SWF file redirect the user to the Adobe website, where the most current version of Flash Player can be downloaded.

Discussion

To use Express Install, you can set the Use Express Install option in Flash Builder, in the compiler options (Figure 23-6).

If you are not using Flash Builder for development, you can download the SWFObject library from *http://code.google.com/p/swfobject*. There are two important files in this download: *swfobject.js* and *expressInstall.swf*. The first file generates the embedding code for your application, and the second handles determining whether you have the

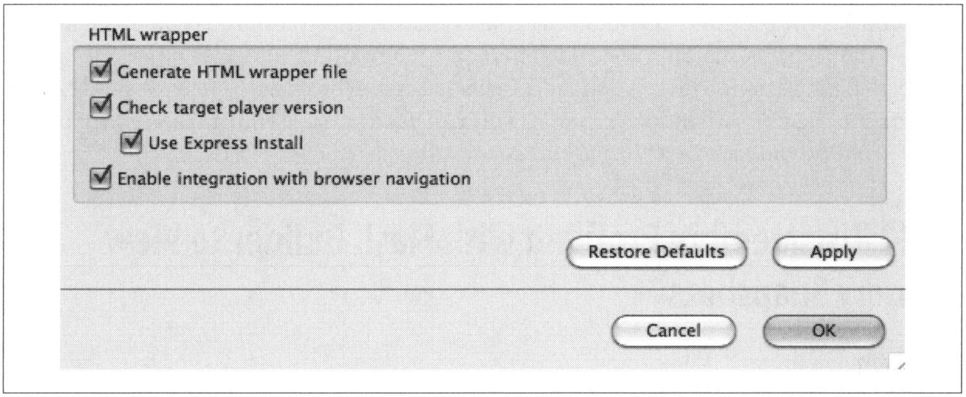

Figure 23-6. Enabling the Express Install option

correct version of the Flash Player installed, and installing it if you do not. Take a look at the following HTML document:

```html
<html xmlns="http://www.w3.org/1999/xhtml" lang="en" xml:lang="en">
    <head>
        <title></title>
        <meta http-equiv="Content-Type" content="text/html; charset=iso-8859-1" />
        <script type="text/javascript" src="swfobject.js"></script>
        <script type="text/javascript">
                swfobject.registerObject("contentObj", "10.0.0",
                                         "expressInstall.swf");
        </script>
    </head>
    <body>
        <div>
            <object classid="clsid:D27CDB6E-AE6D-11cf-96B8-444553540000"
                    width="800" height="600" id="contentObj">
                <param name="movie" value="main.swf" />
                <!-- [if !IE]> -->
                <object type="application/x-shockwave-flash" data="main.swf"
                        width="800" height="600">
                    <!-- <![endif] -->
                    <a href="http://www.adobe.com/go/getflashplayer">
                        <img src="http://www.adobe.com/images/shared/
                                  download_buttons/get_flash_player.gif"
                             alt="Get Adobe Flash player" />
                    </a>
                    <!-- [if !IE]> -->
                </object>
                <!-- <![endif] -->
            </object>
        </div>
    </body>
</html>
```

Notice in the bold section the parameters that are being passed to the **swfobject** constructor. The first is the ID of the **object** where the SWF information will be written, the second is the required version of the Flash Player, and the third is the name of and path to the Express Install SWF file. There are many other optional parameters that you can pass to `swfobject`, such as `flashvars`, `wmode` for the window mode, and `bgcolor` for the color behind the SWF. You can read more about these at *http://code .google.com/p/swfobject* or at *http://kb2.adobe.com/cps/127/tn_12701.html*.

23.11 Use Memory Profiling with Flash Builder to View Memory Snapshots

Problem

You want to view all the objects allocated in the Flash Player's memory at runtime.

Solution

Use the Memory Profiler view in Flash Builder to run your application and observe the objects being created and destroyed.

Discussion

The Flex Profiler is a powerful tool that enables you to watch an application as it allocates and clears memory and objects. It connects to your application with a local socket connection. You might have to disable your antivirus software to use it, however, if it prevents socket communication.

As the Profiler runs, it takes a snapshot of your application every few milliseconds and records the state of the Flash Player at that snapshot, a process referred to as *sampling*. By parsing this data, the Profiler can show every operation in your application. It records the execution time of each operation it captures, as well as the total memory usage of the objects in the Flash Player at the time of the snapshot.

When an application is run in the Profiler, you'll see the Connection Established dialog box (Figure 23-7). Here you can enable memory profiling to help identify areas of an application where memory allocation problems are occurring, as well as enabling performance profiling to help improve the performance of an application.

If you select the Watch Live Memory Data checkbox, the Profiling view displays live graphs of the objects allocated in the Flash Player (Figure 23-8).

The Profiler enables you to take memory snapshots that provide in-depth data about the number of instances of any object and the amount of memory they require at any given point in your application's execution. You can also compare any two memory snapshots from different times to find *loitering objects* (that is, objects that were created after the first memory snapshot and exist only in the second). Information about the class name, memory size, and number of instances are all included in the Loitering Objects view. This can be very helpful in identifying memory leaks.

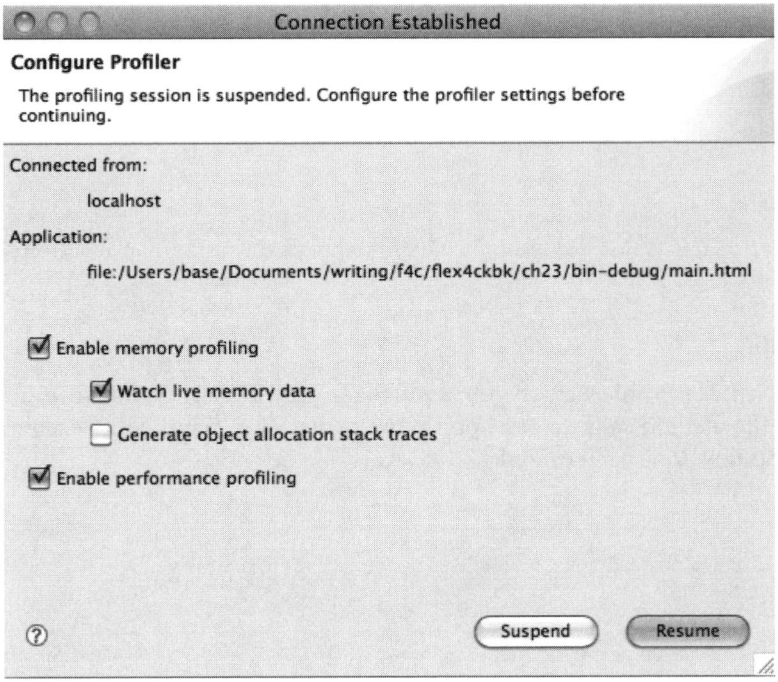

Figure 23-7. Selecting a profiling type

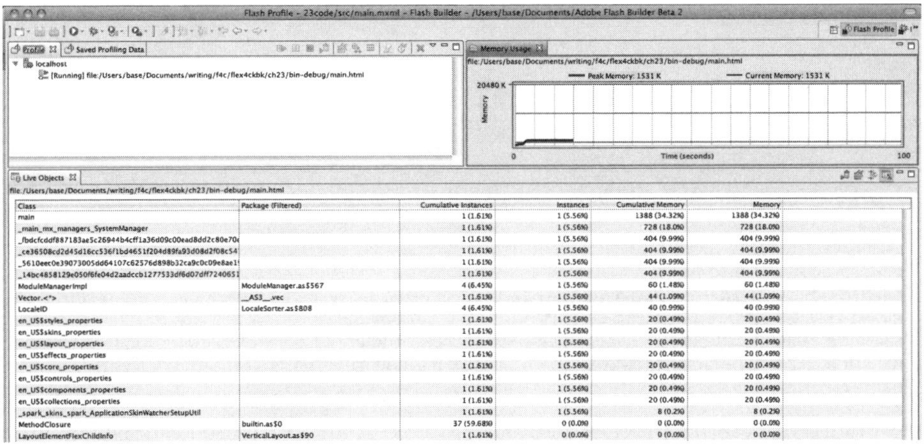

Figure 23-8. Live object and memory allocation data in the Flex Profiling view

23.12 Check the Performance of Specific Methods

Problem

You want to quickly check the performance of a particular method.

Solution

Use the Performance Profile view in Flash Builder to examine your application's method calls.

Discussion

The Performance Profile view (Figure 23-9) is a feature in Flash Builder that allows you to see all the method calls that an application makes, how many times each method is called, and how long each call takes to execute.

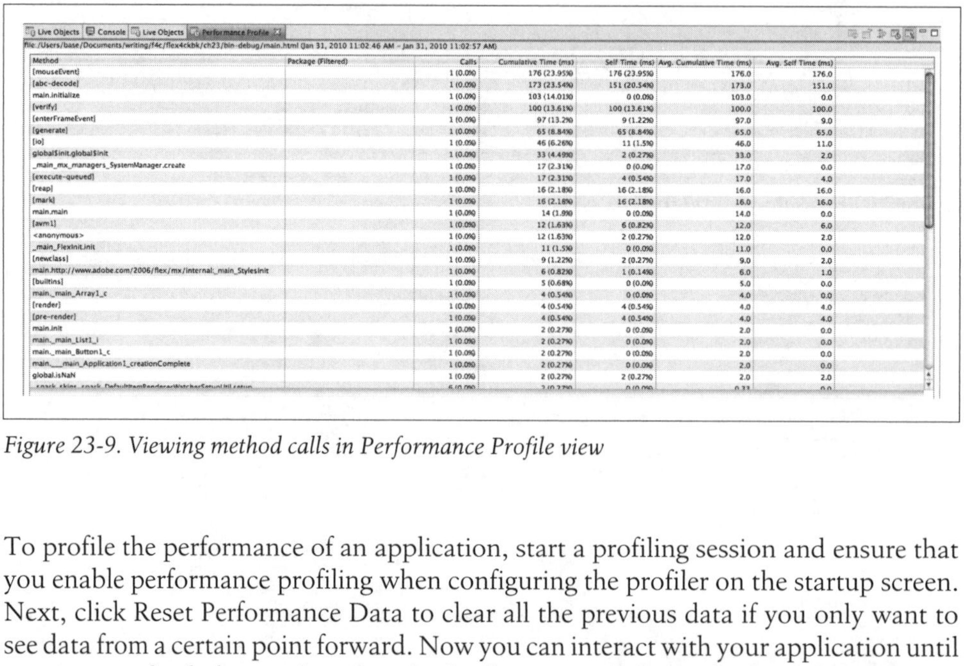

Figure 23-9. Viewing method calls in Performance Profile view

To profile the performance of an application, start a profiling session and ensure that you enable performance profiling when configuring the profiler on the startup screen. Next, click Reset Performance Data to clear all the previous data if you only want to see data from a certain point forward. Now you can interact with your application until you want to check the number of method calls. To see all the method call data gathered since the data was cleared, click the Capture Performance Profile button. Now you can see the Performance Profile view, which shows the number of times that each method was called during the sampling. You can also select a particular method and see what called it, as well as all the other method calls within that method, in a subview of the Performance Profile view called the Method Statistics view (Figure 23-10).

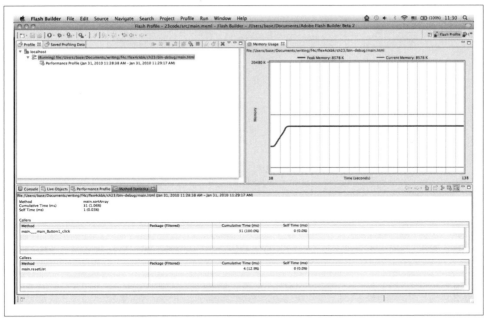

Figure 23-10. Viewing method calls in the Method Statistics view

Both the Callers and Callees tables of the Method Statistics view show the following information:

Package

> The package in which each class resides. If the class is not in a package, the value of this field is the name of the file in which the class is defined. The number following the dollar sign is a unique ID for that class. If the Package field is empty, the class is in the global package or the unnamed package.

Cumulative Time

> The amount of time, in milliseconds, that each called method, and all subsequent methods, spent executing.

Self Time

> The amount of time, in milliseconds, that each called method spent executing. This does not include methods called by subsequent methods.

CHAPTER 24

Internationalization, Accessibility, and Printing

To ensure that your applications are usable by the widest range of users, Flex 4 provides many accessibility, internationalization, and printing options. For example, if your project must comply with accessibility standards, you'll find screen-reader detection and keyboard tab orders to help visually impaired users, or users for whom the use of a pointing device is difficult or impossible. Flex's toolset for internationalization and localization was much improved in Version 4. The localization features include a built-in internationalization resource manager, runtime locale determination, runtime locale switching, and resource modules that can be requested at runtime. If your challenge is closer to home—say, if you need printed deliverables—the latest version of Flex has that covered too. Flex 4 enables you to print Flex components and includes a `Data Grid` component specifically for printing repetitive, multipage output.

This chapter contains recipes that will walk you through formatting many kinds of output for printing, including a solution for formatting collections of components for printing across multiple pages by using `PrintDataGrid` with a custom item renderer. Recipes for displaying non-Western characters, detecting screen readers, and defining tab orders help make your applications more accessible to visually impaired users. Finally, several techniques for localizing applications are presented.

24.1 Add an International Character Set to an Application

Problem

You need to display text from an ideogram-based language, such as Chinese or Korean, in your application.

Solution

Use embedded fonts to ensure that the appropriate font is available to the Flash Player.

Discussion

Flex applications are capable of rendering text using non-Western characters, including Unicode-encoded text such as Chinese or Korean characters, provided that a font including those characters is available to the Flash Player. Developers can ensure that the appropriate font is available by embedding it into the application the same way as you would any Western font. Be aware, however, that the ease of this method comes at a price: the large number of characters in most ideogram-based languages means a bulkier SWF file. When considering this approach, you must weigh the trade-off between the increased size of your SWF file and the proper rendering of your text. The following example, *ChineseFonts.mxml*, illustrates both embedding the font and loading the system font.ch23_FlashBuildDebugger.

> When you open *ChineseFonts.mxml*, you will see the Chinese text next to `System Font` only if your system's font contains the required characters. The `Embedded Font` line will be displayed on all systems.

You can embed a font as shown here:

```
<s:Application xmlns:fx="http://ns.adobe.com/mxml/2009"
               xmlns:s="library://ns.adobe.com/flex/spark"
               xmlns:mx="library://ns.adobe.com/flex/halo" >


    <s:layout><s:BasicLayout/></s:layout>
    <fx:Style>
        @font-face
        {
            src:url("../assets/LiSongPro.ttf");
            fontFamily:"LiSong Pro";
            fontStyle:Light;
        }
    </fx:Style>
    <s:Panel title="Fonts" width="75%" height="75%"
             horizontalCenter="0"  verticalCenter="0">
        <s:layout><s:VerticalLayout/></s:layout>
        <s:Label text="System Font"/>
        <s:Label text="快的棕色狐狸慢慢地跳過了懶惰灰色灰鼠" />

        <s:Label text="Embedded Font"/>
        <s:Label fontFamily="LiSong Pro"
        text="快的棕色狐狸慢慢地跳過了懶惰灰色灰鼠" />
    </s:Panel>

</s:Application>
```

Although the MXML source for the Unicode-encoded method is unremarkable, the XML data it loads contains text in simplified Chinese:

```
<s:Application xmlns:fx="http://ns.adobe.com/mxml/2009"
               xmlns:s="library://ns.adobe.com/flex/spark"
               xmlns:mx="library://ns.adobe.com/flex/halo"
               creationComplete="createComplete()">
    <s:layout><s:BasicLayout/></s:layout>

    <fx:Declarations>
        <fx:XML source="books.xml" id="booksData"/>
    </fx:Declarations>

    <fx:Style>
        @font-face
        {
            src:url("../assets/LiSongPro.ttf");
            fontFamily:"LiSong Pro";
            fontStyle:Light;
        }

    </fx:Style>

    <fx:Script>
        <![CDATA[
            import spark.components.Label;

            private function createComplete():void {

                var booklist:XMLList = booksData.book;
                for(var i:int = 0; i<booklist.length(); i++) {
                    var label:Label = new Label();
                    label.text = booklist[i];
                    vgroup.addElement(label);
                }

            }

        ]]>
    </fx:Script>

    <s:VGroup id="vgroup"/>
</s:Application>
```

The following is the document loaded by the application:

```
<books>
    <book title="阿波罗为 Adobe 导电线开发商口袋指南">
        现在您能建立和部署基于闪光的富有的互联网应用(RIAs) 对桌面使用 Adobe 的导电线框架。
        由阿波罗产品队的成员写, 这是正式指南对于 Adobe 阿波罗, 新发怒平台桌面运行时间阿
        尔法发行从 Adobe 实验室。众多的例子说明怎么阿波罗工作因此您可能立即开始大厦 RIAs
        为桌面。
    </book>
    <book title="编程的导电线 2">
        编程的导电线 2 谈论导电线框架在上下文。作者介绍特点以告诉读者不仅怎样, 而且原因
        为什么使用一个特殊特点, 何时使用它, 和何时不是的实用和有用的例子。这本书被写为
        发展专家。当书不假设观众早先工作了以一刹那技术, 读者最将受益于书如果他们早先建
        立了基于互联网,n tiered 应用。
    </book>
```

```
<book title="ActionScript 3.0 设计样式">
    如果您是老练的闪光或屈曲开发商准备好应付老练编程技术与 ActionScript 3.0,
    这实践介绍逐步设计样式作为您通过过程。您得知各种各样的类型设计样式和修建小
    抽象例子在尝试您的手之前在大厦完全的运作的应用被概述在书。
</book>
</books>
```

24.2 Use a Resource Bundle to Localize an Application

Problem

You need to support a small number of alternate languages in your application.

Solution

Use compiled-in resource bundles to provide localized assets.

Discussion

For basic localization of Flex applications, you can use resource bundles. *Resource bundles* are ActionScript objects that provide an interface for accessing localized content defined in a properties file through data binding or ActionScript code. Each bundle your application uses represents a single localization properties file. The *properties file* is a text file containing a list of localization property keys and their associated values. The key/value pairs are listed in the file in the format key=value, and properties files are saved with a *.properties* extension.

Localized values for text strings, embedded assets such as images, and references to ActionScript class definitions can all be defined in a properties file. When localizing an application, you define an entry in a properties file for each item in that application that would need to be updated in order for the application to fully support an alternate language. The following example properties file defines the values of several properties in American English:

```
#Localization resources in American English
pageTitle=Internationalization Demo
language=American English
flag=Embed("assets/usa.png")
borderSkin=ClassReference("skins.en_US.LocalizedSkin")
```

For each language you want to support, you must create a copy of the properties file that contains values appropriate to that language. If your application must support American English and French, for example, you must create a second properties file containing translated text, a reference to an image of the French flag instead of the American flag, and a reference to the appropriate border skin for the French-language version of the application:

```
#Localization resources, En Francais
pageTitle=Demo d'internationalisation
```

```
language=Francais
flag=Embed("assets/france.png")
borderSkin=ClassReference("skins.fr_FR.LocalizedSkin")
```

When setting up your properties files, there are several factors to consider—most importantly, the size and complexity of your application. You may wish to create a properties file for each custom component in your application, for example, or for packages of related components that share resources. You may also want to define properties files that are useful on a global scale, such as one containing custom application error messages or commonly used labels (like the ones used on buttons).

No matter how you decide to break up your localization properties, you will need to create a directory structure to organize the files. As illustrated in Figure 24-1, a best practice is to create a directory named *locale* or *localization* that contains subdirectories named after the locale identifiers. These subdirectories will house all the properties files for a given locale. Adhering to this practice will make it easy to instruct the compiler how to find the properties files.

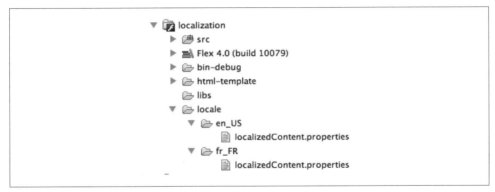

Figure 24-1. Directory structure for localization properties files

When you build your application, the compiler creates subclasses of the ResourceBundle class for each properties file you define. The easiest way to access items defined in your properties files is through the @Resource directive. Using this method, the compiler substitutes the appropriate property values for the @Resource directive. With @Resource directives, you never actually write code that uses a ResourceBundle instance; the compiler does all the work for you. @Resource directives take two arguments, a bundle identifier and a key, which it uses to look up the appropriate property value in the appropriate properties file. For example, to reference the property name applicationTitle in a localization properties file named *localizationProperties.properties*, use the following:

```
@Resource(key='applicationTitle', bundle='localizationProperties')
```

A more complete example, *LocalizationResource.mxml*, defines a small application that consumes the localization properties files defined in the two previous code snippets:

```
<s:Application xmlns:fx="http://ns.adobe.com/mxml/2009"
               xmlns:s="library://ns.adobe.com/flex/spark"
               xmlns:mx="library://ns.adobe.com/flex/halo">
    <fx:Metadata>
        [ResourceBundle("localizedContent")]
    </fx:Metadata>
    <s:VGroup horizontalCenter="0"
              verticalCenter="0"
              horizontalAlign="center"
              borderSkin="@Resource(key='borderSkin', bundle='localizedContent')">
        <s:Label fontSize="24" text="@Resource(key='pageTitle',
                                        bundle='localizedContent')" />
        <s:Label fontSize="24" text="@Resource(key='language',
                                        bundle='localizedContent')" />
        <s:Image source="@Resource(key='flag', bundle='localizedContent')" />
    </s:VGroup>
</s:Application>
```

Note that the [ResourceBundle] metadata tells the compiler which bundles are required for a given component. This is important because resource bundles are built at compile time, and all required resources for the supported languages must be compiled into the application SWF.

The compiler must also be configured to build in localization support for the required locales. In Flash Builder, you set these options in the Project Properties dialog box for the Flex project. In the Flex Build Path panel, you define a source path that points to your localization files. If you followed the best practice of using a locale directory, your source path entry will be locale/{locale}, as shown in Figure 24-2. In addition, you need to identify the locales you wish to support in the Flex Compiler panel's Additional Compiler Arguments field. For example, to support American English and French, enter -locale en_US,fr_FR (Figure 24-3). When the compiler builds your application and looks for properties files, it substitutes each of the locale identifiers into your source path expression: specifically, locale/en_US for American English properties files and locale/fr_FR for French properties files.

The last step you need to perform before building a localized application is to localize relevant Flex Framework content, such as error messages. You can use the Adobe-provided command-line utility called *copylocale* to copy each of the relevant files to a new locale. You will have to perform this step once for every locale, but that copy will then be available for use in any project built against that installation of the Flex Framework. You will not have to repeat this step in each project. Note that *copylocale* will not actually make localized copies of the files for you, but it will let you compile your application. You can find *copylocale* in the *bin* subdirectory of the Flex 4 SDK installation. To run it, simply pass in the default locale identifier and the identifier of the locale for which you want to make a copy. For example:

```
copylocale.exe en_US fr_FR
```

Prior to Flex 3, you could not change locales at runtime. This meant the only possible approach for building localized applications by using resource bundles was to compile a separate copy of the application for each supported locale. This approach may still be valid in certain cases—for example, when minimal localization is required and the smallest possible SWF file size is desired. To use this technique, set the `locale` compiler argument to the desired target locale and build your application. The two main advantages to this option are simplicity and small SWF file size, due to the compiler including only one set of localization properties files. To see this technique in action, you can try compiling the *LocalizationResource.mxml* example application for American English (`en_US`) or for French (`fr_FR`) by setting the locale compiler argument appropriately.

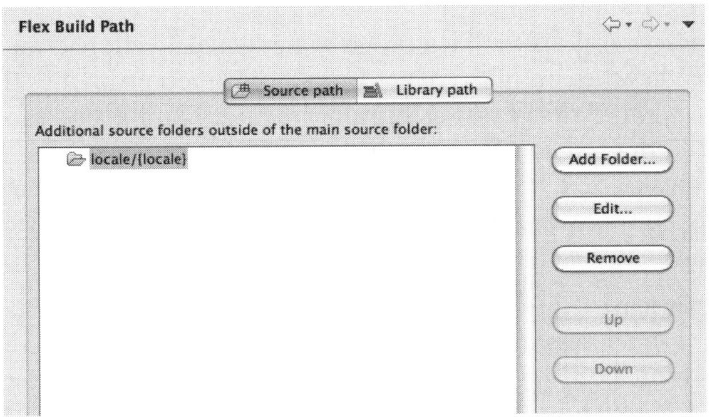

Figure 24-2. Localization build path entry

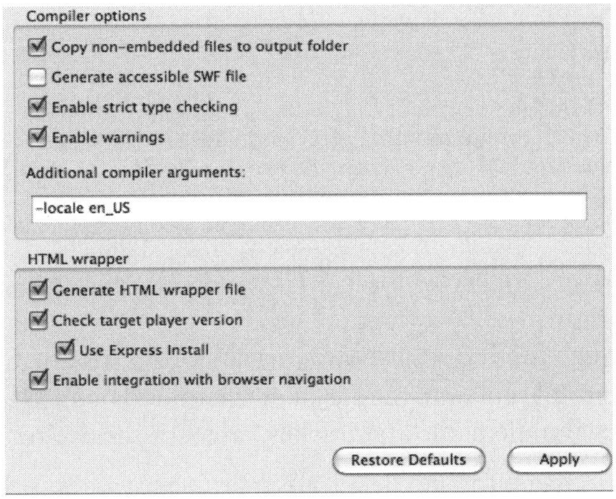

Figure 24-3. Localization compiler arguments

24.3 Use the ResourceManager for Localization

Problem

You want to support a small number of locales and either determine the locale programmatically at runtime or allow the user to choose the locale.

Solution

Use the ResourceManager class to support multiple locales and allow the application to change locales at runtime.

Discussion

The ResourceManager class is the Flex programmer's main ActionScript interface into the resource bundles the compiler creates from localization properties files. It enables you to retrieve various types of resources from resource bundles and provides a mechanism to set the desired locale at runtime. The resource manager is a singleton that manages localization for an entire application. Every class that derives from UIComponent has a protected property named resourceManager that provides a reference to the resource manager singleton.

Although the @Resource directive is convenient for binding localized content into MXML tags, it is much less useful for pure ActionScript components or ActionScript methods that rely on localized resources. In these situations, you're better off using the resource manager, which provides methods that can be used to access localized data or used as the targets of data-binding expressions in ActionScript or MXML. The following example, excerpted from *LocalizationManager.mxml*, substitutes ResourceManager methods for the @Resource directives used in Recipe 24.2's *LocalizationResource.mxml*:

```
<mx:VBox horizontalCenter="0"
        verticalCenter="0"
        horizontalAlign="center"
        borderSkin="{resourceManager.getClass('localizedContent', 'borderSkin')}">
    <mx:Label fontSize="24" text="{resourceManager.getString('localizedContent',
                                    'pageTitle')}" />
    <mx:Label fontSize="24" text="{resourceManager.getString('localizedContent',
                                    'language')}" />
    <mx:Image source="{resourceManager.getClass('localizedContent', 'flag')}" />
</mx:VBox>
```

Although the method names vary according to the type of resource you're retrieving, the arguments here are all similar to the arguments required by an @Resource directive—namely, the resource bundle name and the key value for the desired property.

Using the resource manager to bind localization property values to their targets has an additional benefit. Flex 4 gives you the ability to change the desired locale at runtime; no longer are you forced to build separate localized SWF files for each supported locale.

Binding properties to resource methods enables the application to update itself for the desired locale. In the *LocalizationManager.mxml* example, buttons are provided to let the user switch between English and French:

```
<mx:HBox>
    <mx:Button label="In English"
                click="resourceManager.localeChain = ['en_US']" />
    <mx:Button label="En Francais"
                click="resourceManager.localeChain = ['fr_FR']" />
</mx:HBox>
```

In this example, the `localeChain` property is reset depending on which button the user selects. The `localeChain` property is an array of strings representing an ordered list of desired locales. This is useful if, for example, the application is going to receive information about the user's language preferences from the browser, through either the `Accept-Language` HTTP header or the host operating system's language preferences. For a user from the United Kingdom, the preferred locale is `en_GB`, but the user can also accept `en_US`. When a method call is invoked on the resource manager, it will search for a resource bundle with the specified name in one of the locales defined in the locale chain, in the order they appear. Therefore, an application localized for `en_US` would be delivered to the user from the United Kingdom if you set `localeChain` as follows:

```
resourceManager.localeChain = ["en_GB", "en_US"];
```

It is a good practice to ensure that the American English locale appears in the property chain somewhere. Many of the Flex Framework components assume that framework localization resources exist, and they will throw an error if they are unable to locate their localized content. Appending `en_US` to the end of your property chain will help to ensure that the framework classes themselves do not fail because they could not locate localized resources.

When building an application that utilizes the resource manager simply for binding, you do not need to do anything differently compared to using `@Resource`. However, if your application is going to support multiple locales from which one is selected at runtime, resources for every supported locale must be compiled into the application. You can supply a comma-delimited list of supported locales to the compiler in place of the single locale used in Recipe 24.2.

24.4 Use Resource Modules for Localization

Problem

You need to support a large number of locales in your application.

Solution

Use resource modules to load only the localization support required by your application at runtime.

Discussion

Localization using resource bundles that are compiled into your application will cause the size of your SWF file to grow with each additional locale you need to support. The overwhelming majority of users will require resources for just one locale, adding up to a lot of dead weight in the download size of your application. Flex 4 adds the ability to compile the resource bundles for a given locale into SWF files called *resource modules*, which your application can load dynamically at runtime. You then can prompt for or determine programmatically which locale the user prefers, and load only the resource module required to support that user's locale.

To build resource modules from your localization properties files, you must first determine which resources your application requires. This includes not only resources you define, but also resources required by the Flex Framework. You can use the *mxmlc* compiler to analyze your application and output a list of required resources. You can do this from Flash Builder by modifying the Additional Compiler Arguments field in the Project Properties dialog box, but it's easy enough to do from the command line. This will also save you from having to navigate back to the applicable panel in the Project Properties dialog box each time you need to update the list. When you invoke the compiler, you specify the locale and a file where the compiler will write the results of the analysis in addition to the name of the application MXML file:

```
> mxmlc -locale= -resource-bundle-list=resources.txt ResourceModules.mxml
```

When the command completes, the contents of the *resources.txt* output file look like this:

```
bundles = containers controls core effects localizedContent skins styles
```

You will use this output to tell the compiler which resource bundles to build into your resource module.

To compile an application that uses resource modules, you must use the command-line compiler. You specify the source path for your localization properties files, the resource bundle list from the previous step, and the name of the resulting SWF file. The compiler then builds resource bundles from your localization properties files and packages them into a SWF file with the specified name. For example, to build resource bundles for Recipe 24.4's *ResourceModules.mxml* example, you would use this command:

```
> mxmlc -locale=en_US -source-path=.,locale/{locale}
  -include-resource-bundles=containers,controls,core,effects,localizedContent,
  skins,styles -output en_US_resources.swf
```

To compile French resource modules, you would use this command:

```
> mxmlc -locale=fr_FR -source-path=.,locale/{locale}
  -include-resource-bundles=containers,controls,core,effects,localizedContent,
  skins,styles -output fr_FR_resources.swf
```

There are several items of interest in these commands. First, you define the target locale by using the `locale` argument, just as you do when compiling resource bundles into your application. Second, although the `source-path` argument may look familiar, including the current directory (.) in your source path is important in this case. The example includes an embedded class reference in the `localizedContent` properties file, and the compiler may not be able to resolve the reference to this class without the root of the application in the source path. Note that this assumes you invoke *mxmlc* from your project's source root. Next, the `include-resource-bundles` argument is filled in based on the list generated earlier. This list is comma-delimited and cannot contain spaces between the delimiter and the bundle names. Finally, you specify a name for the output (e.g., *en_US_resources.swf*). You can name the output SWF anything you like, but it's good practice to come up with a naming convention that includes the locale identifier in the filename. This way, you can programmatically determine the name of the resource module your application should load based on a locale identifier.

When you compile resource modules using *mxmlc*, references to embedded assets such as images will be resolved relative to the location of the localization properties file into which that reference is embedded. Therefore, if your application uses compiled-in resource bundles that have embedded assets defined relative to the project's source root, these will have to be updated to work as resource modules.

In your application code, you use the resource manager's `loadResourceModule()` method: you pass a URL to this method identifying the resource module SWF file you want to use. This method works in a similar fashion to other mechanisms for loading ActionScript objects at runtime, such as `SWFLoader` or conventional modules. A request is made to the server for the required SWF, which is then downloaded by the browser. Requests for resources from other domains require a cross-domain policy file. You must wait until the resource module has been loaded into your application before you can make use of it. When the resource module is ready for use, a `ResourceEvent` will be dispatched. You can listen for these events by defining a listener for `ResourceEvent.COMPLETE` events. The `loadResourceModule()` method returns a reference to an object that implements the `IEventDispatcher` interface that you use to register listeners for the `complete` event. The following code is excerpted from the *ResourceModules.mxml* example and demonstrates how a resource module is loaded and utilized:

```
import mx.events.ResourceEvent;
import mx.resources.ResourceManager;

private var selectedLocale:String;

private function setAppLocale(locale:String):void
{
    this.selectedLocale = locale;
    if (resourceManager.getLocales().indexOf(locale) == -1)
    {
        var dispatcher:IEventDispatcher =
                resourceManager.loadResourceModule(locale + "_resources.swf");
        dispatcher.addEventListener(ResourceEvent.COMPLETE, onResourceLoaded);
```

```
        }
        else
        {
            onResourceLoaded(null);
        }
    }

    private function onResourceLoaded(e:ResourceEvent):void
    {
        resourceManager.localeChain = [this.selectedLocale];
        views.selectedIndex = 1;

        contentBackground.setStyle("borderSkin",
                resourceManager.getClass('localizedContent', 'borderSkin'));
        contentBackground.invalidateDisplayList();
        contentBackground.validateNow();
    }
```

In this example, the user is prompted to choose between American English and French. When the user selects a language, the setAppLocale() function is called to load the required resource module. This method first checks whether resources for the requested locale have already been loaded by searching the result of the resource manager's getLocales() method. It is a good practice to test whether you currently have the resources required in order to save the overhead of requesting and loading resources that are already present. If the requested locale isn't already loaded, a call is made to the loadResourceModule() method to retrieve it, and a listener for the complete event is registered so you know when the resource module has been loaded and is ready for use.

In response to the complete event, the application sets the localeChain property to make use of the newly loaded resource module. Of note in this method are the three method calls on the contentBackground object. Style settings are not bound in Flex, so objects referencing style properties from resource modules must be updated programmatically in order to pick up changes to their styling properties.

The loadResourceModule() method can take several optional parameters in addition to the resource module URL. If your application loads multiple resource modules, you will want to load all but the last with the update parameter set to false. This will save overhead by not running the resource manager's update routines repeatedly.

24.5 Support Input Method Editor (IME) Devices

Problem

You need to distribute your application in a language that uses multibyte characters, such as Japanese, Chinese, or Korean.

Solution

Use the `Capabilities` class to detect an input method editor and the `IME` class to control how it interacts with your Flex application.

Discussion

Far Eastern languages such as Chinese represent words with single ideograms, rather than with combinations of letters as in Latin languages. In Latin languages, the number of individual characters is limited and they can easily be mapped onto a keyboard with a limited number of keys. It would be impossible to do the same for Far Eastern languages, as this would require thousands of keys. Input method editors (IMEs) are software tools that allow characters to be composed with multiple keystrokes. An IME runs at the operating system level, external to the Flash Player.

The `Capabilities` class has a property called `hasIME` that you can use to determine whether the user has an IME installed. You can use the `flash.system.IME` object to test whether the IME is enabled and what conversion mode it is set to. The following example tests for an IME and, if it finds one, starts the IME and sets the required conversion mode:

```
private function detectIME():void
{
    if (Capabilities.hasIME == true)
    {
        output.text = "Your system has an IME installed.\n";
        if (flash.system.IME.enabled == true)
        {
            output.text += "Your IME is enabled. and set to " +
                    flash.system.IME.conversionMode;
        }
        else
        {
            output.text += "Your IME is disabled\n";
            try
            {
                flash.system.IME.enabled = true;
                flash.system.IME.conversionMode =
                        IMEConversionMode.JAPANESE_HIRAGANA;
                output.text += "Your IME has been enabled successfully";
            }
            catch (e:Error)
            {
                output.text +="Your IME could not be enabled.\n"
            }
        }
    }
    else
        output.text = "You do not have an IME installed.\n";
}
```

When trying to manipulate the IME settings, you should always use a **try...catch** block. If the current IME does not support the specified settings, the call will fail.

You may wish to disable the IME in some cases, such as for a text field that expects numeric input. If the IME is inappropriate for a given data entry component, you can trigger a function to disable it when that component gets focus and re-enable it after the component loses focus:

```
<fx:Script>
    <[[
        private function enableIME(enable:Boolean):void
        {
            if (Capabilities.hasIME)
            {
                try
                {
                    flash.system.IME.enabled = enable;
                    trace("IME " + (enable ? "enable" : "disable"));
                }
                catch (e:Error)
                {
                    Alert.show("Could not " (enable ? "enable" : "disable") +
                                " IME");
                }
            }
        }
    ]]>
</fx:Script>
<s:VGroup horizontalCenter="0" verticalCenter="0">
    <s:TextInput id="numericInput" focusIn="enableIME(false)"
                 focusOut="enableIME(true)" />
    <s:TextInput id="textInput" />
</s:VGroup>
```

If you want to know when a user has composed a character, you can listen for events on the **System.ime** object:

```
System.ime.addEventListener(IMEEvent.IME_COMPOSITION, onComposition);
```

24.6 Detect a Screen Reader

Problem

You must provide support for visually impaired users and would like to customize your application for screen-reader users.

Solution

Use the **active** static property of the **Accessibility** class to detect a screen reader.

Discussion

Rich media capabilities and a cinematic user experience are hallmarks of a Rich Internet Application. Unfortunately, these capabilities can make using a Flex application difficult for visually impaired users. Screen-reader support is important for visually impaired users, and may in fact be their only method of interacting with your application. If accommodating visually impaired users is a requirement, you may wish to alter the user experience specifically for screen-reader users. The `active` property of the `Accessibility` class can be used to test whether a user is using a screen reader. The following code block, excerpted from *ScreenReader.mxml*, uses `Accessibility.active` to determine whether an animation should play:

```
private function showNextPage():void
{
    if (Accessibility.active == false)
    {
        page2.visible = true;
        pageChangeAnimation.play();
    }
    else
    {
        page1.visible = false;
        page2.alpha = 1;
    }
}
```

24.7 Create a Tabbing Reading Order for Accessibility

Problem

You must support users who may have difficulty using a pointing device.

Solution

Define a tab order for components in your application so that the user may navigate through the application without using a pointing device.

Discussion

Tab order is an important usability concern in an application. It enables users to effectively navigate through the application without having to switch between the keyboard and a pointing device unnecessarily. For users with impairments that make using a pointing device difficult or impossible, tab order is a necessity. You can specify the tab order in your components by setting the `tabIndex` property of each object in the component. The following example, saved as *TabOrder.mxml*, sets a tab order so a user can easily navigate through an address form without using a mouse:

```
<s:Application xmlns:fx="http://ns.adobe.com/mxml/2009"
               xmlns:s="library://ns.adobe.com/flex/spark"
```

```
                    xmlns:mx="library://ns.adobe.com/flex/halo"
                    creationComplete="firstName.setFocus()">
    <s: VGroup width="228" height="215" x="50" y="50" backgroundColor="#FFFFFF">
        <s:Label x="10" y="10" text="First Name" tabIndex="1" />
        <s:TextInput x="10" y="36" width="100" id="firstName" tabIndex="2"/>
        <s:Label x="118" y="10" text="Last Name" tabIndex="3" />
        <s:TextInput x="118" y="36" width="100" id="lastName" tabIndex="4"/>
        <s:Label x="10" y="69" text="Address" tabIndex="5" />
        <s:TextInput x="10" y="95" width="208" id="address" tabIndex="6"/>
        <s:Label x="10" y="125" text="City" tabIndex="7"/>
        <s:TextInput x="10" y="151" width="100" id="city" tabIndex="8"/>
        <s:Label x="118" y="125" text="State" tabIndex="9"/>
        <s:TextInput x="118" y="151" width="34" id="state" tabIndex="10"/>
        <s:Label x="160" y="125" text="Zip" tabIndex="11"/>
        <s:TextInput x="160" y="151" width="58" id="zip" tabIndex="12"/>
        <s:Button x="153" y="181" label="Submit" id="submit" tabIndex="13"/>
    </s:VGroup>
</mx:Application>
```

Note that in this example, the tabIndex property is set for all labels as well as the text inputs and buttons, even though the labels cannot receive focus. For users who require a screen reader, the tab order also dictates the order in which the screen reader will describe items on the page. When considering screen-reader users, it is important that you set the tabIndex property for all accessible components, not just those that can receive focus. Any items that do not have their tabIndex set will be placed at the end of the tab order, which could confuse screen-reader users when those items are read out of order compared to the visual layout.

24.8 Print Selected Items in an Application

Problem

You need to create printed output from an application.

Solution

Use the classes in the mx.printing package to define, format, and produce printed output.

Discussion

The mx.printing package implements several classes used to produce printed output. For example, the FlexPrintJob class defines a print job, adds items to the job, and sends the job to the printer. The following example, saved in *BasicPrintJob.mxml*, creates a print job, adds two pages of output, and sends the job to the printer:

```
<s:SkinnableContainer xmlns:mx="http://www.adobe.com/2006/mxml"
                      width="400" height="300">
    <fx:Script>
        <![CDATA[
```

```
            import mx.printing.FlexPrintJob;

            public function print():void
            {
                var printJob:FlexPrintJob = new FlexPrintJob();
                if (printJob.start())
                {
                    printJob.addObject(pageContainer1);
                    printJob.addObject(pageContainer2);
                    printJob.send();
                }
            }
        ]]>
    </fx:Script>
    <s:VGroup width="380" height="260" verticalCenter="-20" horizontalCenter="0">
        <s:VGroup id="pageContainer1">
            <s:Label text="Page 1" />
            <s:TextArea id="page1" width="100%" height="100%" />
        </s:VGroup>
        <s:VGroup id="pageContainer2">
            <mx:Label text="page 2" />
            <mx:TextArea id="page2" width="100%" height="100%" />
        </s:VGroup>
    </s:VGroup>
    <s:Button bottom="5" right="10" label="Print" click="print();" />
```

When the start() method is called, the operating system displays the Print dialog box. Execution is suspended until the user has finished configuring the print job. If the user decides to cancel the print job, the start() method returns false. Otherwise, the function calls the addObject() method to add the text area to the print job and then calls the send() method to send the job to the printer.

Each time you call addObject(), the item and all of its children are placed on a new page. In the printed output generated by this example, the page labels and text inputs contained in pageContainer1 and pageContainer2 are sent to the printer on separate pages.

The addObject() method also accepts an optional parameter that tells the print job how to scale the added item. If an item is too big to fit, the print job will render it on multiple pages. By default, the item will be scaled to the width of the page, but several other options are available. These options are defined as static constants on the FlexPrint JobScaleType class. You may, for example, want to scale a column chart so that it fits vertically within a single page, ensuring that the value of each column can be read on a single page:

```
public function print():void
{
    if (printJob.start())
    {
        printJob.addObject(columnChart, FlexPrintJobScaleType.MATCH_HEIGHT);
        printJob.send();
    }
}
```

If the chart is too wide to fit within a single page, the excess will be printed on a new page. An example, called *ScaleExample.mxml*, has been provided to demonstrate the effects of the various scale types. This file is available on the book's website, along with all the others.

24.9 Format Application Content for Printing

Problem

You want your application to produce output specifically formatted for printing.

Solution

Build custom print renderer components to format output specifically for printing.

Discussion

Often, the output you want to generate for printing is different from what is displayed to the user in the application. You may wish to create printable versions of application objects or generate reports of data not shown to the user through the application. This is accomplished by using a print renderer, a component you create specifically for generating printed output.

In the *BasicPrintJob.mxml* example from Recipe 24.8, for instance, you may not want to print the page label or the text input control's border. Also, you probably want the entered text printed as if it had been created in a word processor, filling the width of the page without scaling the text and continuing on to the next page when the end of the page is reached. To format a text block for printing, use a component like the one shown here:

```
<s:SkinnableContainer xmlns:mx="http://www.adobe.com/2006/mxml"
                      backgroundColor="0xffffff">
    <fx:String id="textToPrint" />
    <s:TextArea width="100%" text="{textToPrint}" />
</s:SkinnableContainer>
```

When you use a print renderer to format output, you must first add the renderer to a display list in order for Flex to lay out the visual aspects of the component. Take care when considering where to add the component. Unintended consequences, such as shifts in layout or unintended scroll bars, can occur in some cases. In the following code the renderer is added to the parent application's display list in order to avoid the appearance of scroll bars:

```
public function print():void
{
    var printJob:FlexPrintJob = new FlexPrintJob();
    if (printJob.start())
    {
        var printRenderer:BasicTextRenderer = new BasicTextRenderer();
```

```
        printRenderer.width = printJob.pageWidth;
        printRenderer.textToPrint = page1.text;
        printRenderer.visible = false;
        FlexGlobals.topLevelApplication.addChild(printRenderer);
        printJob.addObject(printRenderer);
        printJob.send();
        FlexGlobals.topLevelApplication.removeChild(printRenderer);
    }
}
```

Also of note in this example is the use of the `pageWidth` property of the `printJob` object. Both the `pageWidth` and `pageHeight` properties are set when the `start()` method has returned. When writing a print renderer component, it is important to pay attention to these properties when sizing components. By using these properties, you can ensure that your renderer will work in both portrait and landscape mode, and with varying paper sizes and types of printers.

See Also

Recipe 24.8

24.10 Control Printing of Unknown-Length Content over Multiple Pages

Problem

You need to control the layout of printed output over multiple pages, but you don't know how much data you will be printing or the sizes of the components you need to lay out.

Solution

Use the `PrintDataGrid` component to control how data is printed over multiple pages when printing tabular data.

Discussion

If you have tabular data, such as a spreadsheet-style report, you can use the `PrintData Grid` component to format that data for multipage output. The `PrintDataGrid` component is a specialized data grid that is designed to format printed data across multiple pages and can be used to control a variety of types of repetitive multipage output. The following example, from *MultipageDataGrid.mxml*, utilizes a `PrintDataGrid` to format a report for printing:

```
public function print():void
{
    var printJob:FlexPrintJob = new FlexPrintJob();
    if (printJob.start())
```

```
    {
        var printGrid:PrintDataGrid = new PrintDataGrid();
        printGrid.width = printJob.pageWidth;
        printGrid.height = printJob.pageHeight;
        printGrid.columns = populationGrid.columns;
        printGrid.dataProvider = populationData.state;
        printGrid.visible = false;
        FlexGlobals.topLevelApplication.addChild(printGrid);
        printJob.addObject(printGrid);
        while (printGrid.validNextPage)
        {
            printGrid.nextPage();
            printJob.addObject(printGrid);
        }
        printJob.send();
        parentApplication.removeChild(printGrid);
    }
}
```

When using a PrintDataGrid, you set its size to match your page size. Adding the grid to the print job will add the first page. You can test whether additional pages of data exist by using the validNextPage property, and you can advance to the next page of output by using the nextPage() method.

Used creatively, the PrintDataGrid component can help format many kinds of output. PrintDataGrid isn't restricted to printing only tabular text; it can be used in combination with an item renderer to produce repetitive layouts of things like charts, images, or complex components. In the following example, *GridSquares.mxml*, the PrintData Grid is used in combination with an item renderer to produce a collection of red squares identical to the *ManualMultiPage.mxml* example:

```
public function print(itemSize:int, itemCount:int):void
{
    var printData:Array = new Array();
    for (var i:int = 0;  i < itemCount;  i++)
    {
        printData.push(itemSize);
    }

    var column:DataGridColumn = new DataGridColumn();
    column.headerText = "";
    column.itemRenderer = new ClassFactory(SquareRenderer);

    var printGrid:PrintDataGrid = new PrintDataGrid();
    printGrid.showHeaders = false;
    printGrid.visible = false;
    printGrid.setStyle("horizontalGridLines", false);
    printGrid.setStyle("verticalGridLines", false);
    printGrid.setStyle("borderStyle", "none");
    printGrid.columns = [column];
    printGrid.dataProvider = printData;
    FlexGlobals.topLevelApplication.addChild(printGrid);
```

```
        var printJob:FlexPrintJob = new FlexPrintJob();
        if (printJob.start())
        {
            printGrid.width = printJob.pageWidth;
            printGrid.height = printJob.pageHeight;
            printJob.addObject(printGrid);
            while (printGrid.validNextPage)
            {
                printGrid.nextPage();
                printJob.addObject(printGrid);
            }
            printJob.send();
        }

        parentApplication.removeChild(printGrid);
    }
```

24.11 Add a Header and a Footer When Printing

Problem

You need to produce printed output with headers and footers.

Solution

Create a print renderer component to control the page layout.

Discussion

Combining a print renderer with a `PrintDataGrid` enables much finer control over your printed layouts than the `PrintDataGrid` can provide itself. A common task is to add headers and footers to printed pages. This technique involves manipulating whether the header and footer are included in the layout and testing the results by using the `validNextPage()` property of the `PrintDataGrid`. The following code, *HeaderFooter PrintRenderer.mxml*, defines a print renderer that produces multipage output with header and footer areas included where appropriate:

```
<?xml version="1.0" encoding="utf-8"?>
<s:VGroup xmlns:fx="http://ns.adobe.com/mxml/2009"
        xmlns:s="library://ns.adobe.com/flex/spark"
        xmlns:mx="library://ns.adobe.com/flex/halo"
        horizontalAlign="center">

    <fx:Declarations>
        <mx:DateFormatter id="formatter" formatString="M/D/YYYY" />
        <mx:DateFormatter id="format" formatString="m/d/yyyy" />
    </fx:Declarations>

    <fx:Script>
        <![CDATA[
```

```
            public function startJob():void
            {
                // try to print this on a single page
                header.visible = true;
                header.includeInLayout = true;
                footer.visible = true;
                footer.includeInLayout = true;

                this.validateNow();

                if (printGrid.validNextPage)
                {
                    // the grid is too big to fit on a single page
                    footer.visible = false;
                    footer.visible = false;

                    this.validateNow();
                }
            }

            public function nextPage():Boolean
            {
                header.visible = false;
                header.includeInLayout = false;

                printGrid.nextPage();

                footer.visible = !printGrid.validNextPage;
                footer.includeInLayout = !printGrid.validNextPage;

                this.validateNow();

                return printGrid.validNextPage;
            }
        ]]>
    </fx:Script>
    <s:Panel id="header" height="80" width="100%">
        <s:Label text="Population by State"
                 fontSize="24"
                 color="0x666666"
                 horizontalCenter="0"
                 verticalCenter="0"
                 width="100%"
                 textAlign="center" />
    </s:Panel>
    <s:Panel height="100%" width="80%">
        <mx:PrintDataGrid id="printGrid" width="100%" height="100%">
            <mx:columns>
                <mx:DataGridColumn dataField="@name"
                                    headerText="State" />
                <mx:DataGridColumn dataField="@population"
                                    headerText="Population"/>
            </mx:columns>
        </mx:PrintDataGrid>
```

```
        </s:Panel>
        <s:Group id="footer" height="80" width="100%">
            <s:Label text="{formatter.format(new Date())}"
                    left="20" bottom="5" />
        </s:Group>
    </s:VGroup>
```

This component defines a header containing the report title and a footer that displays the date the report was printed. The startJob() method initializes the print layout to the appropriate first-page layout. It first tries to lay out the page as if all data will fit on a single page. After a call to the validateNow() method forces the layout of the component to occur, you can test whether the report will fit within one page by testing the PrintDataGrid's validNextPage property. If the value is false, the report will fit. If not, the layout is adjusted to hide the footer and the layout is updated again. At this point, whether the report is a single page or multiple pages, the first page is ready to be added to the print job. If the report does require multiple pages, the nextPage() method will prepare the layout appropriately. It hides the header (it will never be used except on the first page) and enables the footer when appropriate.

Building the page-layout intelligence into the renderer greatly simplifies the actual print routine. The following code block, taken from *HeaderFooter.mxml*, demonstrates the use of the example print renderer in an application:

```
public function print():void
{
    var printJob:FlexPrintJob = new FlexPrintJob();
    if (printJob.start())
    {
        var printRenderer:HeaderFooterPrintRenderer =
                new HeaderFooterPrintRenderer();

        printRenderer.visible = false;
        this.addChild(printRenderer);
        printRenderer.width = printJob.pageWidth;
        printRenderer.height = printJob.pageHeight;
        printRenderer.dataProvider = populationData.state;
        printRenderer.startJob()

        do
        {
            printJob.addObject(printRenderer);
        }
        while (printRenderer.nextPage());

        // send the last page
        printJob.addObject(printRenderer);
        printJob.send();

        this.removeChild(printRenderer);
    }
}
```

The print() method begins a print job and sets up a print renderer in a similar fashion to previous examples. This portion of the code finishes by calling the startJob() method on the print renderer, which lays out the renderer for the first page. In the next section of the method, the do...while block continues to add pages to the print job until the nextPage() method returns false, indicating there are no more pages to lay out. However, because the do...while block invokes the nextPage() method at the end of the block, the last page will not yet be added to the print job when the loop completes. The print() function therefore queues the last page manually, sends the print job, and removes the renderer from the display list.

Index

Symbols

! (exclamation mark)
    != (inequality) operator, 439
$ (dollar sign), end of line matching in regular
        expressions, 392, 398
- (hyphen), designating ranges in regular
        expression character classes, 392
. (dot notation)
    defining bindable property chain in MXML,
        360
    using in E4X, 437
    working with dynamic property references,
        374
... (rest) operator, 21
3D effects, 294
: (colon), :: operator following XML namespace
        declarations, 442
= (equals sign)
    == (equality) operator, 439
    == and === operators, equality
        comparisons, 347
? (question mark)
    ?! (negative look-ahead), 400
    ?<! (negative look-behind), 400
    ?<= (positive look-behind), 400
    ?= (positive look-ahead), 400
@ (at sign)
    E4X operator, 437
    shorthand two-way binding syntax, 154,
        355
@font-face declaration (CSS), 181
@Resource directive, 691
[ ] (square brackets)

enclosing character classes in regular
        expressions, 392
    indexed array operator, 437
\ (backslash), escaping characters in regular
        expressions, 393
^ (caret), beginning of line matching in regular
        expressions, 392, 398
{ } (curly braces)
    enclosing event handlers in MXML, 15
    using for data binding in MXML, 351, 361
    wrapping E4X expression in attribute, 363
| (pipe character), alternation in regular
        expression matching, 393

A

<a> tag with href attribute in TextFlow XML
        document, 187
accessibility
    creating tabbing reading order, 701
    detecting a screen reader, 700
Accessibility class, active property, 700
Action Message Format (see AMF)
ActionScript, xv
    assigning event listeners, 140
    creating module based in, 470–472
    defining bindable property chain, 361
    encoding data object as XML, 442
    invoking ActionScript functions from
        JavaScript, 451–453
    invoking JavaScript functions from, 450
    relation to MXML, 1
    using to bind properties, 356–360
ad3httpclient library, 408
AddAction class, Spark, 303
    startDelay property, 304

We'd like to hear your suggestions for improving our indexes. Send email to *index@oreilly.com*.

711

addElement( ) method,
IVisualElementContainer interface,
28
addElementAt( ) method,
IVisualElementContainer interface,
29
adl (AIR Debug Launcher), 492
Adobe Integrated Runtime (see AIR)
AdvancedDataGrid controls, 268
async refresh for grouping collection, 271–
274
displaying hierarchical data, 333
generating summary for flat data, 268–271
grouped collection within, 328
groupItemRenderer property, 268
After metadata tag, 642
AIR (Adobe Integrated Runtime), 3, 489–533
allowing AIR application to interact with
browser, 509
creating AIR application using Flash Builder
4, 489–492
creating application updater with custom
interface, 520–528
creating applications with update
capabilities, 514–520
creating in-memory database, 540
creating multilingual AIR installations, 512
determining application version at runtime,
512
editing application description and
copyright information, 501
editing initial window settings, 503–505
embedding existing SQLite database in
application, 550
encrypting database with password, 541–
544
including native code in application, 529–
533
integration with operating system, 559–
605
checking for mounted or unmounted
drives, 583
closing all open windows at once, 560–
561
creating HTTP proxy using
ServerSocket, 599–605
custom clipboard data formats, 568–
572

deferred rendering of clipboard data,
567
deploying AIR application as native
installer, 592–599
drop shadow for custom chrome
window, 561–567
flagging downloaded files, 591
listing of available external drives, 584–
591
menu item keyboard shortcuts, 572
notifying users, 573–576
opening file with default application,
579–583
registering custom file types, 576–579
local data, storing and working with, 535
migrating serialization changes, 538–540
packaging application in native installer,
528
protecting files with Encrypted Local Store,
535–538
setting application ID, 497
setting application name and filename, 498
setting application to handle all updates,
510
setting application version, 500
setting custom application icon, 507
setting default Programs menu folder, 506
setting installation folder for application,
505
signing AIR file with trusted certificate,
495
signing and exporting AIR application, 492
storing relationships with Object Relational
Mapping, 551–557
targeting specific version of AIR, 497
using parameters in SQL queries, 544–550
.air files, 550
Alert control, 149–151
show( ) method of Alert class, arguments to
configure alert, 151
alignment of child elements in a container, 83
aligning children along x-axis, 84
dynamically changing alignment along y-
axis, 84
using alignment properties to size child
elements, 85
alpha property, 307
AMF (Action Message Format), 346, 418
efficient serialization with AMF3, 424

secure communication with, using
SecureAMFChannel, 433
AMFChannel objects, 419, 420
Animate class, 293, 308
Animate objects
Effect objects versus, 306
passing MotionPath to, 299
AnimateInstance class, 293, 306, 308
creation of ConvolutionFilters, 313
AnimateTransform class
applyChangesPostLayout property, 104
effects based on, 103
AnimateTransitionShader object, applying
Pixel Bender filter to bitmaps, 317–
320
Animation class, 293
target property, 296
animations and effects, 293–320
adding drill-down effect to columnar chart,
619–622
adding effects to charts, 610–613
calling Animate instance in MXML and
ActionScript, 295
creating custom animation effects, 306–
308
creating multiple effects that play in parallel
or sequence, 300
creating show and hide effects for
component, 297–299
defining keyframes for animation, 299–300
dynamically setting filter for component,
294–295
pause, reverse, and restart effect, 302–303
setting effects for adding or removing
component from parent, 303–
306
using convolution filter to create animation,
312–317
using DisplacementMapFilter in effect,
308–312
using Pixel Bender filter to create transition,
317–320
Ant build tool, 668
adding executable task to build file that uses
ASDoc, 679
adding tasks to build file for compiling Flex
applications, 670
compiling and deploying Flex applications
that use RSLs, 672–674

installing Ant view in standalone Flash
Builder, 678
Application class, Spark
applying repeating background image skin,
166
Application containers, Spark
control bars, 55
application descriptor file (AIR), creating in
Flash Builder, 490
application ID, setting for AIR applications,
497
application name (AIR), 498
ApplicationUpdater class, 520–528
ApplicationUpdaterUI class, 516–520
ArrayCollection objects
acting as dataProvider for DataGrid,
creating cursor for, 266
creating deep copy, 345–347
determining when item is modified, 326
filterFunction property, 253
filtering, 325–326
getItemIndex( ) method, 266
retrieving and sorting data from, 323–325
using in button bar, 143–144
ArrayList objects, 321
arrays
multiple values interpolated into, 317
of typed objects, storing, 15
AS3Crypto library, 542
ASDoc utility, 679
assertions in FlexUnit, 640–642
complex assertions in a test case, 662–663
testing visual components, 656–658
Async metadata tag, 647
Async.asyncHandler( ) method, 647–649, 650
asynchronous refresh for grouping collection,
271–274
AsyncListView objects, 242–244
AsyncMessage objects, 418
ASyncToken class, 418, 425
axis and data labels for charts, 617–619
AxisLabelSet objects, 632
AxisRenderer objects, styles for tick marks,
615

B

back-references in regular expressions, 399
backgroundFill property, BorderContainer, 55
backgroundImage property, 55

backgroundImageFillMode property, 55
bar charts, creating, 608
base and fragment (URLs), 454
BaseListData type, 260
BasicLayout class, 82
BasicLayout containers, Spark, 26
Before metadata tag, 642
bidirectional binding, 355
binary data
    sending and receiving via binary socket,
        435
    storing in Encrypted Local Store, 536–538
Bindable metadata tag
    defining, 349
    event attribute, 365
    event attribute, defining function as
        bindable to event, 354
BindingUtils class, 356–360, 374
    bindProperty( ) method, 356, 376
    bindSetter( ) method, 357, 358
    specifying bindable property chain, 361
BitmapData objects, 308
    drawing Flex components into, 658
BitmapDataChannel class, 309
BitmapFill element, 124
    using within MXML fragment, 124
BitmapFillMode class, 55, 124
BitmapFilter objects, 295
BitmapImage element, 124–127
    setting to Bitmap instance at runtime, 126
    source property of element within MXML
        document, 125
    supplying URL to source property within
        FXG document, 125
    using within MXML fragment, 124
bitmaps
    applying Pixel Bender filter to, 320
    copying pixels of a character within
        TextFlow as a bitmap, 202–204
BlazeDS
    configuring HTTPService object to use
        server, 407
    configuring services for application using,
        411–415
    simple chat service (example), 422
blockProgression property, 199
Blur effect, 296
BorderContainer, Spark, 48
    borderStroke property, 49

setting background image, 53–55
setting border styles for IVisualElement
        children, 48
skin part serving as content layer, 43
borderStroke property, setting for
        BorderContainer, 49
breakpoints, setting for expression evaluation,
        675
browser communication, 447–460
    changing HTML page title via
        BrowserManager, 453
    invoking ActionScript functions from
        JavaScript, 451–453
    invoking JavaScript functions from Flex,
        450
    linking to external URL, 447
    using FlashVars, 448–450
BrowserChangeEvent objects, 456, 458
BrowserManager class
    deep-linking containers via, 458–460
    deep-linking data via, 456
    parsing URLs via, 454–456
    setTitle( ) method, 453
browsers
    allowing AIR application to interact with,
        509
bubbling up (events), 17
Button, Spark
    handling button's click event, 139–142
ButtonBar, Spark
    creating custom skin for, 167–169
    using with ArrayCollection to create series
        of buttons, 142–144
buttons
    creating button component with icon, 177
    creating skin for s:Button, 163–165
    handling click event
        assigning handler to click event attribute
            of <s:Button> tag in MXML,
            140
ByteArray objects, 436
    created by ObjectUtil.copy( ) method, 345
bytesLoaded property, LoadEvent objects, 282

C

C/c drawing command, 119
callback( ) function, 452
callbacks

registering for ActionScript functions for exposure to JavaScript, 452
CandlestickChart objects, 609
Capabilities class, hasIME property, 699
captioning plug-in (OSMF), 288
catalog.xml files, 462
category axis label function, 617
CategoryAxis objects, 608
certificates
    creating and signing, 493
    signing AIR file with trusted certificate, 495
ChangeWatcher objects, 356–360
    freeing for garbage collection, 359
channels, 419
ChannelSet objects, 420
character classes in regular expressions, 392
character sets
    adding international character set to application, 687–690
character types, matching using regular expressions, 393
ChartBase class, methods for selection, 613
charting, 607–634
    adding and removing columns at runtime, 624–628
    adding effects to charts, 610–613
    creating charts, 607–610
    creating custom chart labels, 617–619
    creating drill-down effect for columnar chart, 619–622
    creating editable line chart, 631–634
    dragging and dropping items in charts, 629–631
    formatting chart tick marks, 615–617
    overlapping multiple ChartSeries, 628–629
    selecting regions or specific items of charts, 613–615
    skinning chart items, 622–624
ChartItem objects, 622
ChartItemEvent objects, hitData property, 621
ChartSeries objects, 607
    itemRenderer style property, 622
    overlapping multiple in a chart, 628–629
    selectable property, 631
    selection attributes, 613
chat applications

using publish/subscribe messaging, 418–423
CheckBox controls
    adding CheckBox to custom DataGrid header, 255–257
class selector (CSS), 175
classes
    defining to implement an interface, 22
    dynamic, binding to properties on, 370–376
clipAndEnableScrolling property, 42
clipboard data
    custom formats for, 568–572
    deferred rendering with, 567
ClipboardTransferMode class, 569
code-signing certificates for AIR, 496
collectionChange event, 326
CollectionEvent class, 326
collections, 321–348
    ArrayCollection
        creating deep copy, 345–347
        determining if item is modified, 326
        filtering, 325–326
        retrieving and sorting data, 323–325
    ArrayList, 321
    creating HierarchicalViewCollection object, 337–339
    filtering and sorting XMLListCollection, 340–342
    GroupingCollection, creating, 327–330
    hierarchical data provider for control, 330–334
    navigating and saving your position, 334–337
    sorting dates in, 343
    sorting on multiple fields, 342
    using data objects with unique IDs, 347
ColumnChart objects
    creating drill-down effect for, 619–622
    series property, 625
columnCount property, 123
    TextLayoutFormat objects, 211
columnGap property, 123
columnHeight property, HorizontalLayout, 89
columns property, DataGrid, 248
ColumnSeries objects
    adding or removing from ColumnSet, 624–628
ColumnSet objects

adding or removing ColumnSeries objects, 625–628

types of groupings, 625

columnWidth property, 123

columnWidth property, HorizontalLayout, 89

ComboBox components, validating, 385–387

command line

invoking mxmlc directly from without full SDK path provided, 12

compc (component compiler)

compiling component into SWC to use as RSL, 667

compiling SWC file for RSLs, 672

compute-digest option, 465

source-path and include-classes options, 464

compilers

compiling Flex project without Flash Builder, 11

mxmlc, 1

setting options for MXML compiler in Flash Builder, 8

compiling

application using resource modules, 696

building in localization support, 692

using Ant to compile Flex applications that use RSLs, 672–674

using component compiler (compc), 667

using Express Install for application, 680

using Flex Ant tasks, 668

using mxmlc and Ant to compile Flex applications, 670

using Rake (Ruby make tool), 674

complex assertions, using in test case, 662–663

components

accessing parent of Flex component, 23

adding to/removing from parent, setting effects for, 303–306

closing pop-up component when user clicks outside it, 153–154

creating button bar, 142–144

creating event handlers for menu-based controls, 148–149

displaying alert in application, 149–151

displaying custom pop up in custom component, 151–153

grouping radio buttons, 158–160

handling button's click event, 139–142

handling focusIn and focusOut events, 155–156

loading external SWF, 144–145

opening DropDownList with keyboard shortcut, 156–158

submitting Flex form to server-side script, 160–161

testing visual components, 649–659

creation testing, 651–652

hiding component to be tested, 658

postcreation testing, 652–654

using programmatic visual assertions, 656–658

using timers, 654–656

using calendar date input, 145–148

using s:Scroller to create scrollable container, 154–155

configuration files

passed to compilers containing information on RSLs, 673

specifying for compc compiler, 668

constraint properties for containers, 26

Consumer objects, 418, 420

ContainerController objects, 205

creating and adding to TextFlow, 206

containers, 25–77

adding Spark layout container to MX navigation container, 70–72

applying skins, 48–53

creating Spark-based ViewStack, 72–77

deep-linking via BrowserManager, 458–460

displaying children using data items, 33–36

drag and drop between data containers, 66–70

dragging and dropping visual elements between, 62–66

dynamically adding and removing child elements, 28–31

enabling scrolling, 41–46

linked, creating in TextFlow, 205–206

modifying layout of content elements in Panel, 57–59

positioning children within, 26–28

reordering child elements, 31–33

scaling children, 46–48

setting background image for BorderContainer, 53–55

tracking mouse position within, 60–62

using a control bar, 55–56
using custom item renderer in DataGroup, 36–39
using multiple item renderers in DataGroup, 39–41
content API, 79
contentBarGroup skin part, 57
contentGroup property, SkinnableContainer, 51
contentGroup skin part, 43, 57
contentHeight property, 110
contentJustify property, 85
contentMouseX and contentMouseY properties, 60
contentToGlobal( ) method, 62
ContextMenu objects, 233
ContextMenuEvent objects, 234
ContextMenuItem objects, 234
controlBarContent property, 55
    Panel container, Spark, 59
controlBarLayout property, 56
ConvolutionFilter class, 312–317
ConvolutionTween class, 314
    instantiating, 316
ConvolutionTweenEffect factory class, 314
ConvolutionTweenInstance class, 314
copylocale utility, 692
copyright information, AIR applications, 501
createCursor( ) method, 265, 335
creation testing for components, 651–652
credit card numbers, matching using regular expressions, 391
cross-domain RSLs, 465
crossdomain.xml file
    for cross-domain RSLs (example), 466
    for modules loaded from different servers, 478
cryptography
    encrypting database with password in AIR, 541–544
CSS (Cascading Style Sheets), 163
    applying skins and properties to components, 175–177
    compiling to SWF and loading using StyleManager, 192
    declaring styles, 174
    embedding fonts, 181
CSSFormatResolver objects, 191
CubicBezier segments, drawing, 119

cue points in video files, accessing and displaying, 284–287
currentTimeChange and durationChange events of VideoDisplay (Spark), 276

D

data and axis labels for charts, 617–619
data binding, 349–376
    binding property of one object to another object, 351
    binding to properties on XML source using E4X, 362–364
    creating bidirectional binding, 355
    creating customized bindable properties, 364–368
    defining Bindable metadata tag, 349
    to a function, 352–355
    to generic object, 368–370
    binding to properties using ActionScript, 356–360
    to properties on dynamic class, 370–376
    using bindable property chains, 360–362
data types
    class returned from web service, registering, 444
    registering server-side type with Flex application, 427–428
    SOAP, and corresponding ActionScript types, 432
    XML, decoding into strongly typed objects, 444–446
databases
    creating in-memory database in AIR, 540
    encrypting with password in AIR, 541
    including existing SQLite database with AIR application, 550
    storing relationships with ORM, 551–557
DataGrid controls, 247–274
    columns property, 248
    creating custom columns for, 247–250
    creating custom headers for, 255–257
    editing items in, 264–265
    enabling drag and drop, 262–264
    filtering items in, 252–255
    handling events from DataGrid and its item renderers, 258–262
    scrollToIndex( ) method, 265
    searching within and autoscrolling to match, 265–268

specifying sort functions for columns, 251–252

styleFunction property, formatting item renderer containing summary property, 269

DataGridColumn tags, 248–249
    headerRenderer property, 255
    sortCompareFunction property, 251

DataGridHeaderRender class, extending to customize DataGrid headers, 255

DataGridItemRenderer objects, 268, 270

DataGroup class, 25

DataGroup containers
    data items visually represented using item renderers, 33–36
    use of virtualization on layout delegate, 90
    using custom item renderer to render data items, 36–39
    using multiple item renderers, 39–41

dataProvider property
    of charts, 608
    DataGroup containers, 34
    editable DataGrids, 264
    List object (Spark), 223
    setting for charts, 608

dateBetween( ) method, 663

DateChooser control, 146–148

dateCompare( ) method, ObjectUtil class, 343

DateField control, 146–148

dates and time
    sorting dates in a collection, 343
    using calendar date input, 145–148

De MonsterDebugger, 666

debugging
    AIR applications, 492
    creating and monitoring expressions in Flash Builder Debugger, 675–677
    using trace statements without Flash Builder, 665

deep copy of ArrayCollection, creating, 345–347

DefaultComplexItemRenderer class, 34

DefaultItemRenderer class, Spark, 33

DefaultProperty metadata tag, 76, 333

Definition instances declared within Library tag, 136–138

depth of child elements, changing dynamically, 98–100

depth property of container elements, 32

descendant selectors (CSS), 175

description of AIR applications, 501

destination and source attributes, <fx:Binding> tag, 352

destination object (data binding), 351

digest (RSL), 465

digital certificates
    creating self-signed certificate in Flash Builder, 493
    signing AIR file with trusted certificate, 495

DisplacementEffect objects, 310

DisplacementMapAnimateInstance objects, 309

DisplacementMapFilter objects, using in Flex effect, 308–312

DisplacementMapFilterMode class, 309

DisplayObject objects
    filters Array property, 562

DisplayObject-based elements
    mask source for Graphic elements, 128

DivElement objects, 184

DockIcon objects, 574

DockItem objects
    bounce( ) method, 573

documentation, generating using ASDoc and Ant, 679

DownloadErrorEvent.DOWNLOAD_Error, 521

drag and drop
    between data containers, 66–70
    between visual containers, 62–66
    customizing drop indicator of Spark List, 238–242
    enabling dragging in Spark List, 235–238
    enabling in DataGrid, 262–264
    items in a chart, 629–631
    selectable LineSeries objects, 632

DragManager objects
    acceptDragDrop( ) method, 235
    doDrag( ) method, 235

DragSource objects
    dataForFormat( ) method, 235

drawing commands, 119

drill-down effect for columnar chart, 619–622

DropDownList, Spark
    opening with keyboard shortcut, 156–158
    skinning, 169–172

dropShadowColor and dropShadowEnabled style properties, 564
DropShadowFilter class, 562
duration property, 307
dynamic class, binding to properties on, 370–376
dynamic keyword, 371
DynamicStreamingVideoItem, Spark, 282
DynamicStreamingVideoSource, Spark, 282

E

Eclipse IDE, 2
Eclipse Java Development Tools, 678
ECMAScript for XML (E4X), 342
    defining data-binding expressions, 362–364
    navigating XML document, 437–439
    using regular expressions in queries, 439
editable property, DataGrid, 264
Effect class, 294
    pause( ) and stop( ) methods, 302
    reverse( ) and resume( ) methods, 303
    target UIComponent, 296
Effect objects
    adding to Series or Axis of a Chart, 610
    Animate objects versus, 306
    effectComplete event, 301
EffectInstance class, 293
EffectInstance objects, 309
EffectManager class, 293
effects, 293, 302
    (see also animations and effects)
    defining in MXML and in ActionScript, 295
    Halo package (mx.effects) and spark.effects package, 294
email addresses, using regular expressions to locate, 390
Embed directive, 145
<embed> (HTML) tag, 449
embedded data support with SQLite (AIR), 535
embedding Flex application into HTML page, 448
Encrypted Local Store, 535
    safeguarding files, 535–538
EntityManager class, 553
    findAll( ) method, 553
Event class, 18

clone( ) method, 19
event handlers
    creating for menu-based controls, 148–149
Event objects
    CLOSING event, 560
    preventDefault( ) method, 560
    properties accessed in listening functions, 14
    RESIZE event, 654
EventDispatcher class, 19
events
    adding event listeners in MXML, 13
    broadcast from ApplicationUpdater class, 520
    data binding on custom event rather than propertyChange event, 364–368
    defining function as bindable to, 354
    handling button's click event, 139–142
    handling events dispatched by DataGrid and its item renderers, 258–262
    handling in test case, 647–649
    listeners for VideoDisplay events, 277
    listening for keyboard event, 19
    setting events to trigger an effect, 297
    using custom events and dispatching data with events, 18
    using event bubbling, 16
executeBinding( ) method, UIComponent-based objects, 350
explicitWidth and explicitHeight properties, 96
Express Install option for applications, 680
expressions, creating and monitoring in Flash Builder Debugger, 675–677
external-library-path compiler option, 672
ExternalInterface class
    invoking ActionScript functions from JavaScript, 451
    invoking JavaScript functions from ActionScript, 450

F

facets (temporal metadata), 289
FaultEvent objects, 404
File objects
    copyTo( ) method, 551
    downloaded property, 591
    getDirectoryListingAsync( ) method, 587
    new capabilities in AIR 2, 579

openWithDefaultApplication( ) method, 579

storing binary data in AIR Encrypted Local Store, 536

filename (AIR applications), 500

fileTypes element, AIR applications, 576–578
full fileTypes node in application descriptor file, 578

fill and stroke, drawing with Path element, 119

fill mode, setting for BorderContainer background image, 55

FilledElement class
extending and overriding draw( ) method to create custom shape element, 130–134

fillMode property, BitmapImage and BitmapFill, 124

filter effects, 294

filterFunction property, 325
XMLListCollection objects, 340

filterFunction property, ArrayCollection, 253

filtering
ArrayCollection, 325–326
DataGrid items, 252–255
using ECMAScript for XML (E4X), 342

filters
dynamically setting filter for component, 294–295
using ConvolutionFilter to create animation, 312–317
using DisplacementMapFilter in Flex effect, 308–312
using Pixel Bender filter to create transition, 317–320

filters Array property, 562

finalAlpha property, 307

findFirst( ) method, IViewCursor, 265

firstIndexInView and lastIndexInView properties, 112, 114

Flash Builder
changing MXML compiler options, 8
compiling Flex project without, 11
creating a Flex project, 2
creating AIR application in Flash Builder 4, 489–492
creating Flex Library project, 7
Debugger, creating and monitoring expressions in, 675–677

Performance Profile view, examining method calls, 684

signing and exporting AIR application, 493

standalone version, installing Ant view, 678

using memory profiling to view memory snapshots, 682

Flash debug player, 666

Flash Media Server (FMS), 281

Flash Player, xv
ensuring user has correct version to view Flex application, 680
event-bubbling mechanism, 16

Flash Text Engine, 183

Flash video (.flv) files, 285

Flash XML Graphics (FXG format), 115

FlashTracer utility, 666

FlashVars variables, 448–450

flash_proxy namespace, 371

flat objects, 330

Flex Ant Tasks, installing, 668

Flex Library projects, creating, 7

FlexEvent objects
CREATION_COMPLETE event, 650
UPDATE_COMPLETE event, 654

FlexGlobals.topLevelApplication property, 24

FlexORM library, 551–557
EntityManager class, 553
metadata tags, 553

FlexPrintJob class, 702
pageWidth property, 705

FlexPrintJobScaleType class, 703

FlexUnit Framework, 635–663
creating application that uses, 636
creating application to run, 636–639
creating mock objects for testing, 659–662
creating test case, 639–642
handling events in test case, 647–649
running code before and after each text, 642–645
sharing data between test cases, 645–647
testing visual components, 649–659
using complex assertions in test case, 662–663

FlexUnitCore class, 639

flowComposer property, TextFlow objects, 202

FlowElement objects
blockProgression property, 197

retrieving from TextFlow, 194

textRotation property, 197

FlowElementMouseEvent class, 188

FlowLeafElement objects, 195

FocusEvent objects, 156

focusIn and focusOut events, handling, 155–156

Font class, enumerateFonts( ) method, 196

fonts

    determining all fonts installed on user's computer, 196

    partially embedding using CSS, 181

    using embedded fonts to display text from ideogram-based languages, 687–690

footer and header, adding when printing, 707–710

format resolvers, using custom, 206–210

formatResolver property, TextFlow objects, 191

Formatter class, 377

    format( ) method, 381

formatting

    creating custom formatter, 381–382

    using formatters and validators with TextInput controls, 378–381

forms, submitting Flex form to server-side script, 160–161

fractionOfElementInView( ) method of sequence-based layouts, 112

fragment (URLs), 454

functions

    binding to, 352–355

    binding, using BindingUtils.bindSetter( ) method, 358

<fx:Binding> tag, 352

    defining data binding expressions using property chains, 361

    twoWay property defined as true, 356

    using E4X, 363

FXG documents, symbol definitions declared in Library tag, 137

FXG format, 115

FXG fragments, 115

    creating custom standalone graphic component, 134

G

gap property, HorizontalLayout and VerticalLayout classes, 80

GET and POST methods (HTTP, 407

getElementAt( ) method, IVisualElementContainer interface, 29

getScrollPositionDeltaToElement( ) method of LayoutBase-based layouts, 112, 114

globalToContent( ) method, 62

Glow effect in MXML, 296

gradient color, displaying text in, 127–128

graphics

    adding graphic elements to TextFlow, 188–190

    applying bitmap data to graphic element as mask, 128–130

    creating custom shape element, 130–134

    creating custom standalone graphic component, 134–136

    defining and reusing graphic symbols, 136–138

    displaying bitmap data in graphic element, 124–127

    displaying gradient text, 127–128

    displaying text in graphic element, 122–124

    sizing and positioning graphic elements, 117–118

    using Path element to draw shape with fill and stroke, 118–122

group and groupName properties, Spark RadioButton, 158

Group class, 25

    removeAllElements( ) method, 29

Group components, Spark, 26

GroupBase class, Spark, 25

    getVirtualElementAt( ) method, 91

GroupBase containers

    clipAndEnableScrolling property, 42

    manipulating display list to create custom layout, 93

    using resizeMode property to lay out child elements, 46–48

GroupBase-based elements, masking of content, 128

Grouping objects, 328

GroupingCollection class

    cancelRefresh( ) method, 271, 274

refresh( ) method, 271
GroupingCollection2 class, 268
GroupingCollection2 objects, creating, 327–330
GroupingField objects, 328
groupItemRenderer property, AdvancedDataGrid, 268, 270
groupLabelFunction property, DataGrid, 268

H

H/h drawing command, 119
Halo components, 139
Halo effects, 294
Hamcrest library, using to create complex assertions, 662–663
header and footer, adding when printing, 707–710
headerRenderer property, DataGridColumn, 255
height property, 110
HGroup class, Spark, 27
hideDataEffect event attribute, series objects, 611
hideDataEffect property, charts, 619
hierarchical data provider, creating for control, 330–334
HierarchicalCollectionView objects, 268
    creating, 338–339
    methods, 337
HLODChart objects, 609
horizontalAlign property, 83
    switching between center and justify values, 85
    VerticalLayout class, 81
HorizontalLayout class, 27, 80
    columnWidth and variableColumnWidth properties, 89
    switching to VerticalLayout at runtime, 82
    verticalAlign property, 83
horizontalScrollPosition property, 108
HostComponent metadata tag, 51
    component being skinned, 164
HTML
    creating TextFlow object from, 185–187
    embedding Flex application into HTML page, 448–450
    page title, changing using BrowserManager, 453
HTTP headers, 406

HTTP proxy, creating using ServerSocket class, 599–605
HTTPService class, 403
HTTPService objects
    communicating with service returning JSON data, 408–411
    configuring, 404
    loading XML from PHP script (example), 405
    RESTful communication between Flex applications, 406
    send( ) method, returning ASyncToken, 426
    useProxy property, 407

I

IAsyncDataObject interface, 244
IAxis interface, getLabelEstimate( ) method, 632
ICollectionView interface, 321
    filterFunction property, 325
icon (custom), for AIR applications, 507
id property
    retrieving TextFlow elements by, 195
    using data objects with unique IDs, 347
ID selector (CSS), 175
IDataInput interface, 424, 570
IDataOutput interface, 424
IDataRenderer interface, 34, 36
ideogram-based languages, 687
IDropInListItemRenderer interface, 260
IEventDispatcher interface, 349, 370, 482, 697
IExternalizable interface
    AIR application storing custom class to disk, 538–540
    readExternal( ) and writeExternal( ) methods, 569
    using for custom serialization, 424–425
IFactory interface, 40, 255
IFill interface, 55
IFlexModuleFactory interface, 473
IFlowComposer interface, 202
    adding controller to instance in TextFlow, 205
IFormatResolver interface
    creating custom format resolver class that implements, 207–210
    methods, 207
IHierarchicalData interface, 268, 330, 337

getData( ) method, 338
required methods, 331
ILayoutElement interface, 80
    getElementAt( ) method, 94
    instance as value for layout control
            typicalLayoutElement property,
            90
    methods to apply 3D transformations, 106
    setLayoutBoundsPosition( ) method, 94
    setLayoutBoundsSize( ) method, 94
IList interface, 33
IListItemRenderer interface, 250, 257
IME class, 699–700
IModuleInfo interface, 475
    factory property, 479
implements keyword, 21
INavigatorContent interface, 72
includeLayout property, 658
IndexChangeEvent, 143
indexes of elements visible in container
        viewport, 112, 114
Influxis, 282
initial window settings, AIR application, 503–
        505
InlineGraphicElement objects, 189–190
input method editor (IME) devices, 698–700
INSERT SQL operation, parameterized, 545–
        548
installation folder for AIR applications, 505
InteractiveObject class
    focusIn and focusOut events, 155
    keyDown and keyUp events, 156
interfaces
    defining and implementing, 21–23
internationalization, 687
    adding international character set to
            application, 687–690
    supporting input method editor (IME)
            devices, 698–700
    using resource bundle to localize
            application, 690–693
    using resource modules for localization,
            695–698
    using ResourceManager for localization,
            694–695
invalidateDisplayList( ) method, 107
InvokeEvent objects, 578
IP addresses, matching using regular expression
        subexpressions, 395

IStroke interface, 49
item renderers
    for charts, 622–624
    CheckBoxHeaderRenderer (example), 255
    CircleItemRenderer used for LineSeries,
            633
    creating and including TextInput control for
            editable Spark List, 217–219
    creating for nested Spark Lists, 220–223
    creating for Spark List component, 216–
            217
    creating for Spark List control custom
            context menus, 234
    custom RangeRenderer used by
            DataGridColumn, 248
    custom RangeRenderer, adding sorting
            function to DataGrid, 251
    DataGridGroupItemRenderer, displaying
            hierarchical data, 268
    DataGridItemRenderer as
            groupItemRenderer, 270
    displaying data items in DataGroup
            containers, 33–36
    recycling in data element containers
            supporting virtualization, 91
    Spark ItemRenderer, using within
            DataGrid, 250
    using custom item renderer in DataGroup,
            36–39
    using multiple in DataGroup container, 39–
            41
    using owner property to dispatch event from
            parent DataGrid, 258–262
    using with PrintDataGrid component, 706
    XML item renderer for Spark List, 224
itemClick event, MenuBar control, 148–149
ItemRenderer class, Spark, 37, 216
itemRenderer property, 33, 34
    (see also item renderers)
    setting for DataGroup using MXML, 38
    setting to custom renderer for DataGroup,
            38
itemRendererFunction property, 39–41
ITextLayoutFormat objects, 207
IUID interface, 347
IViewCursor interface, 335
    findFirst( ) method, 265, 336
    methods for searching in collections, 336
IViewport interface, 42, 109

contentHeight property, 110
  implementation in Spark Scroller
    component, 154
IVisualElement interface, 28, 80
  depth property, 98
  instances as child elements in
    BorderContainer and
    SkinnableContainer, 48
IVisualElementContainer interface, 28–31, 79
  setElementIndex( ) method, 31

J

Java Message Service (JMS), 418
Java Runtime Environment (see JRE)
Java service, RemoteObject configured to use,
    416
java.io.IExternalizable API, 424
Javadoc commenting, 680
JavaScript
  embedding Flex application in HTML page,
    modifying, 449
  invoking ActionScript functions from, 451–
    453
  invoking JavaScript functions from Flex,
    450
JMS (Java Message Service), 418
JRE (Java Runtime Environment)
  path to, on Windows, 12
  setting PATH variable in Mac or Linux
    terminal shell, 13
JSON-formatted data, communicating with
    service returning, 408–411
JSON.decode( ) method, 408
justify property, 85

K

KeyboardEvent class, keyCode property, 19
KeyboardEvent objects, 156
keyDown event handler, 19
keyDown events, 156–158
keyEquivalent, NativeMenuItem objects, 572
Keyframe class, 299
keyframes property, MotionPath, 299
keyframes, defining for animation, 299–300

L

L/l drawing command, 119
labels

AxisLabelSet object, 632
  creating custom labels for charts, 617–619
languages, 515
  (see also internationalization)
  multilingual AIR installations, 512
layout, 79–114
  aligning and sizing children in layout, 83
  applying transformations using Matrix3D,
    100–102
  applying transformations using
    TransformOffsets, 102–105
  changing for Spark List, 219
  creating custom 3D layout, 105–108
  creating custom layout, 93–95
  determining visibility of elements in
    sequence-based layout, 112–114
  displaying child elements in rows and
    columns, 86
  dynamically changing depth of children, 98–
    100
  lazily creating and recycling children, 90–
    93
  positioning children horizontally or
    vertically, 80
  programmatically setting scroll position,
    108–111
  sizing child elements uniformly, 89
  switching layout management at runtime,
    81
layout containers, 25
layout delegate, 79
layout property of Spark containers, 81
LayoutBase class, 79
  extending and overriding
    updateDisplayList( ) for custom
    layout, 93–95
  extending and overriding
    updateDisplayList( ) to apply 3D
    transformations, 105–108
  measure( ) method, overriding to alter
    container dimensions, 95–98
layoutMatrix3D property, 100
libraries
  for mock objects, 659
  runtime shared libraries (see RSLs)
Library tag, symbol definitions declared in,
    136–138
library.swf files, 462
line chart, editable, creating, 631–634

Line segments, drawing, 119
LinearAxis objects, 608
LineSeries objects
    CircleItemRenderer used for, 633
    selectable property, 631
    selectable, dragging and dropping, 632
LinkElement objects, 188
linker report files, 486
links
    creating in TextFlow document, 187–188
    styling within a TextFlow, 193
Linux
    editing PATH variable to add location of
        MXML compiler, 13
    native installer file (.rpm) for AIR
        applications, 528
List component, Spark
    allowing only certain items to be selectable,
        226–228
    changing layout, 219
    creating editable List, 217–219
    creating item renderer for, 216–217
    creating nested List, 220–223
    creating right-click menu for, 233–235
    customizing drop indicator, 238–242
    displaying asynchronously loaded data,
        242
    displaying cue points for video, 286
    displaying XML data, 223–226
    enabling dragging, 235–238
    scrolling to an item, 219
    validating added data in item editor, 228–
        233
ListBase class, itemEditorInstance property,
    228
ListCollectionView class, 321, 325
listData.owner property, 262
ListViewCollection class, createCursor( )
    method, 335
LiveCycle server
    configuring HTTPService object to use,
        407
load-config option for compc, 668
loaderInfo property, using to parse appending
    URL query, 485
LoadEvent objects, bytesLoaded property, 282
local filesystem support (AIR), 535
localeChain property, 695, 698
localization

using resource bundle for, 690–693
using resource modules, 695–698
using ResourceManager to support multiple
    locales, 694–695
look-ahead and look-behind in regular
    expressions, 400
luminosityInvert and luminosityClip
    properties, Graphic element, 130

M
M/m drawing command, 119
Mac OS X
    native installer file (.dmg) for AIR
        applications, 528
Macintosh
    editing PATH variable to add MXML
        compiler, 13
    notifying user through Dock from AIR
        application, 573
major and minor tick marks, 615
maskType property, Graphic element, 128
    values set to clip, alpha, and luminosity,
        128
match( ) method, String class, 390
matrix property, ConvolutionTween, 316
Matrix3D objects, using to apply
        transformations in layout, 100–102
MD5 class, 542
measure( ) method, overriding to alter
        container dimensions, 95–98
measuredWidth and measuredHeight
        properties, 96
MediaPlayer class
    creating wrapper for ease of use with
        MXML, 287
    using to create video player, 283
MediaPlayer objects, 285
memory profiling, using with Flash Builder,
        682
MenuBar control, itemClick event, adding
        event listeners for, 148–149
menus
    keyboard shortcuts for native menu items,
        572
MessageEvent objects, 418
messaging-config.xml file, 422
metacharacters in regular expression pattern
        matching, 393
metadata

namespaces, 289
   in optimized RSLs, 468
   temporal, 288
   use in ORM, 552
metadata tags, 51
   (see also entries under individual tag names)
   FlexORM library, 553
MetadataEvent objects, 285
methods
   checking performance of, 684
   defining optional parameters for, 20
MIME types accepted by server, 601, 604
mock objects, creating for testing, 659–662
Module class, 462, 469
   ActionScript module extending, 470
   loaderInfo property, 484
   parentApplication property, 483
ModuleBase class, 462
   ActionScript module extending, 470
ModuleEvent class, 476
ModuleInfo objects, 475
ModuleLoader class, 462, 472–474
   child property, 479
ModuleManager class, 462, 474–476
   using in parent application, 480
modules
   communicating with, 479–484
   creating ActionScript-based module, 470–472
   creating MXML-based module, 468
   defined, 462
   loading from different servers, 477–479
   loading using ModuleLoader, 472–474
   loading using ModuleManager, 474–476
   passing data to, using query strings, 484–486
   using linker reports to optimize modules, 486
MotionPath objects, 306
   keyframes property, 299
   property set to matrix, 316
mouse position, tracking within container, 60–62
mouseDownOutside event, listening for on pop-up control, 153–154
MouseEvent.CLICK, 140
mouseEventToItemRenderer( ) method, 226
multilingual AIR installations, 512
MultiValueInterpolator objects, 317

MVC (Model-View-Controller) architecture, definitions of data binding, 352
MX containers, 25
   adding Spark layout container to MX navigation container, 70–72
   switching layout managers at runtime, 82
<mx:Module> tag, 469
MXML, xv
   adding event listener, 13
   assigning event listener for button click, 140
   binding properties within MXML declaration, 351
   creating module based in, 468
   defining bindable property chain, 360
   defining effects inline, 298
   FXG fragments declared directly in, 116
   FXG subset, 115
   implementing an interface, 23
   inserting itemRenderer property of DataGroup container, 38
   relation to ActionScript, 1
   standalone graphic component declared as MXML document, 135
   symbol definitions declared within a library, 137
   writing event handlers in, 15
mxmlc compiler, 1, 462
   analyzing application and outputting list of required resources, 696
   commonly-used options, 10
   compiling application SWF for application using RSLs, 673
   compiling application using resource modules, 696
   invoking from terminal window or command line, 11
   link-report option, 486
   load-externs option, 487
   runtime-shared-library-path option, 465
   setting options, 9
   using with Ant build tool, 670

N

named parameters, 544
namespaces
   flash_proxy, 371
   handling XML namespaces returned by service, 441

including in CSS type selectors, 174

metadata, 289

s (Spark components) and mx (Halo components), 139

Spark and Halo components, 139

specifying AIR version, 497

native installer

creating, 598

packaging AIR application in, 528

native operating system code, including in AIR application, 529–533

NativeApplication objects, 578

NativeMenuItem objects, keyEquivalent property, 572

NativeProcess class, 530, 593–599

isSupported property, 593

NativeProcessStartupInfo objects, 596

NativeWindow objects

notifyUser( ) method, 575

supportsNotification property, 574

navigateToURL( ) method, 447

navigation containers

adding Spark NavigatorContent container to MX navigation container, 70–72

NavigatorContent container, 71

negative look-ahead (?!), 400

negative look-behind (?<!), 400

NotificationType objects, 573, 575

notifyUser( ) method, NativeWindow objects, 575

NumberValidator objects, 385

numChildren property, 29

numeric axis label function, 617

NumericStepper, Spark, 160

O

Object class, 484

<object> (HTML) tag, 449

Object Relational Mapping (ORM), 551–557

ObjectMother class, 645–647

ObjectProxy class, 369–370, 486

objects

creating mock objects for testing, 659–662

serialization (see serialization)

ObjectUtil class

copy( ) method, 345

dateCompare( ) method, 343

Open Source Media Framework (see OSMF)

open( ) and openAsync( ) methods, SQLConnection class, 540

operating systems

adding MXML compiler to Path system variable, 12

including native code in AIR application, 529–533

integration with AIR, 559–605

adding drop shadow for custom chrome window, 561–567

checking for mounted or unmounted drives, 583

closing all open windows at once, 560–561

creating HTTP proxy using ServerSocket, 599–605

custom clipboard data formats, 568–572

deferred rendering of clipboard data, 567

deploying AIR application as native installer, 592–599

flagging downloaded files using AIR, 591

keyboard shortcuts for menu items, 572

listing of available external drives, 584–591

notifying users, 573–576

opening file with default application, 579–583

registering custom file types, 576–579

packaging AIR application in native installer, 528–529

optimizer command-line tool, 467

ORM (Object Relational Mapping), 551–557

OSMF (Open Source Media Framework), 275

creating wrapper for use with MXML, 287–288

displaying captions with your video, 288

using MediaPlayer class to create video player, 283

using to access and display cue points in videos, 284

P

padding properties for containers, 27

padding properties of layout container, 80

pageWidth and pageHeight properties, 705

Panel containers, Spark

control bars, 55
modifying layout of content elements, 57–59
Panel, Spark, 153
in PopUpAnchor, 152
pop-up when TextInput has focus, 155
ParagraphElement objects, 184
adding LinkElement object to, 188
Parallel tags, 301
how they work, 301
pausing and resuming set of effects, 302
parameters
optional, defining for methods, 20
using in SQL queries in AIR, 544–550
parentApplication property, 23, 483, 650
parentDocument property (UIComponent), 23
Path elements
using to draw shape with stroke and fill, 118–122
winding property, 120
Path systems variable, 12
pause( ) or stop( ) method, Effect class, 302
.pbj files, 319
performance of specific methods, checking, 684
PHP scripts
HTTPService object loading XML from, 406
pie charts
creating, 608
dragging and dropping items, 629–631
Pixel Bender filter, using to create transition, 317–320
pixel-shader effects, 294
polling, AMFChannel polling server for messages, 419
PollingAMFChannel, defining in service-config.xml file, 421
pop-up components
closing pop up when user clicks outside of it, 153–154
displaying custom pop up in custom component, 151–153
PopUpAnchor control, Spark, 151–153
positive look-ahead (?=), 400
positive look-behind (?<=), 400
postcreation testing for components, 652–654
postLayoutTransformOffsets property, 102

print renderers, 704
defining to produce multipage output with header and footer, 707–710
PrintDataGrid component, 705
combining with print renderer to add header and footer, 707
using with item renderer to print non-tabular text, 706
validNextPage property, 706
printing
adding header and footer, 707–710
formatting application content, 704–705
selected item in application, 702–704
unknown-length content over multiple pages, 705–707
Producer objects, 418, 420
messages sent via (example), 421
profiling, using Flex Profiler, 682
Programs menu folder, setting default for AIR applications, 506
ProgressEvent objects, 144
ProgressEvent.PROGRESS event, 523
progressive download, 281
properties, 352
(see also data binding; property names listed throughout)
bindable, 350
binding property of one object to another object, 351
properties file (localization), 690
building resource modules from, 696
creating ResourceBundle object for each file, 691
directory structure for, 691
property chains, using for data binding, 360–362
property effects, 294
propertyChange event, 350
using custom event instead in data binding, 365
PropertyChangeEvent class, 372
PropertyChangeEvent objects, 376
proxies
proxied HTTP requests and responses, 407
Proxy class, 370
creasing subclass and using E4X in setProperty( ) and getProperty( ) overrides, 371

implementation of subclass eligible for data binding (example), 372–374
pseudoselectors (CSS), 175
publish/subscribe messaging for chat applications, 418–423
PUT, POST, DELETE, and GET HTTP headers, 406

Q

Q/q drawing command, 119
QuadraticBezier segments, drawing, 119
quantifiers in regular expressions, 397
query strings, using to pass data to modules, 484–486

R

radio buttons
    validating groups of, 385–387
RadioButton component, Spark, 158
RadioButtonGroup component, Spark, 159
Rake (Ruby make tool), using to compile Flex applications, 674
RDSDispatchServlet objects, 411
Real Time Media Protocol (RTMP), 281
Rectangle class, 212
Red5 open source media server, 282
reencrypt( ) method, SQLConnection class, 541
RegExp class, 378
    test( ) method, 397
registerClassAlias( ) method, 427, 436
regular expressions
    creating using explicit character classes, 392
    matching a pattern a certain number of times, 396
    matching ends or beginnings of lines, 398
    matching valid IP addresses using subexpressions, 395
    using back-references, 398
    using character types in, 393
    using in ECMAScript for XML (E4X) queries, 439
    using look-ahead or look-behind in pattern matching, 400
    using to create international zip code validator, 382–385
    using to locate email addresses, 390

using to match credit card numbers, 391
    using to validate ISBNs, 391
RemoteClass objects, 427
RemoteObject class, 403
RemoteObject objects, 414
    configurable properties, 415
    configuring and connecting to, 415–418
remoting-config.xml file, 414
    configuring for simple chat service, 422
RemotingService objects, 414
RemoveAction class, Spark, 303
    startDelay property, 304
removeElement( ) method, IVisualElementContainer interface, 29
removeElementAt( ) method, IVisualElementContainer interface, 29
RendererExistenceEvent objects, 35, 221
ResizeMode class, 47
resizeMode property
    GroupBase containers, 46–48
    noScale value, 118
resource modules, using for localization, 695–698
ResourceBundle metadata tag, 692
ResourceBundle objects
    creating for each properties file, 691
ResourceEvent objects, 697
ResourceManager class, 694
    loadResourceModule( ) method, 697
    localeChain property, 695
Responder class, 418
rest operator (...), 21
RESTful communication between Flex applications, 406–408
RestfulX library, 408
ResultEvent objects, 404
    RemoteObject methods returning, 416
    token property, 426
resume( ) method, 303
reverse( ) method, 303
Rich Internet Application (RIA), 293
RichEditableText objects
    binding TextArea to, 190
    skin part for TextArea, 210
RichText element, 116
    content property used to supply rich-formatted text, 122

defining in MXML, 123
displaying text in, 122
gradient text using RichText element as
    mask, 127
using in FXG document, 122
rollover effect, adding to charts, 610
rowHeight property, VerticalLayout, 89
rows and columns, layout of child elements in,
    86
RSLs (runtime shared libraries), 7, 461
compiling component into SWC to use as
    RSL, 667
creating, 462–465
Flex applications that use, compiling and
    deploying with Ant, 672–674
optimizing a RSL, 467
using cross-domain RSLs, 465
RTMP (Real Time Media Protocol), 281
Ruby make tool (Rake), 674
Ruby on Rails
sending PUT command to Rails application,
    407
runtime shared libraries (see RSLs)
runtime-shared-libraries compiler option, 672
RunWith metadata tag, 642

S

Scale effect (ActionScript), setStyle( ) method,
    299
scaling print job items, 703
SchemaTypeRegistry.registerClass( ) method,
    444
screen readers, 700
Scroller component, 42
scrolling
custom layout respecting virtualization of
    data elements, 93
enabling for container using TileLayout
    rows and columns, 88
enabling in a container, 41–46
enabling within view stack, 77
to item in Spark List, 219
programmatically within layout, 108–111
Scroller object creating scroll bar in
    TextArea, 210
using s:Scroller to create scrollable
    container, 154–155
scrollToIndex( ) method, DataGrid, 265, 266
SecureAMFChannel class, 433

SecureAMFEndpoint class, 433
Security class, 477
allowDomain( ) method, 477
loadPolicyFile( ) method, 479
selectedIndex and selectedChild properties, 75
selection
controlling appearance of selected text in
    TextArea, 201
regions or items in charts, 613–615
setting in TextArea objects, 199
SelectionEvent, dispatched by TextFlow, 202
selectionMode attribute, charts, 613
SelectionState objects, 203
selectors (CSS), 174
Sequence tags, 301
pausing and resuming set of effects, 302
serialization
changes in, migrating in AIR application,
    538–540
custom, using IExternalizable interface,
    424
efficient, using AMF, 424
SeriesInterpolate effects, 611
SeriesSlide effects, 611
SeriesZoom effects, 611
using for drill-down effect in columnar
    chart, 619–622
ServerSocket class, 599–605
service-config.xml file
defining channels for messaging service,
    421
services and server-side communication, 403–
    446
adding SOAP header to WebService request,
    431
adding XMLList to XML object, 440
communicating using XMLSocket, 436
communicating with a WebService, 429–
    431
communication with server returning JSON
    data, 408–411
configuring HTTPService, 404
configuring services for application using
    BlazeDS, 411–415
custom serialization using IExternalizable
    interface, 424–425
decoding XML from web service into
    strongly typed objects, 444–446
encoding ActionScript object as XML, 442

navigating XML document in E4X, 437

parsing SOAP response from WebService, 432–433

registering server-side data type with Flex application, 427–428

sending and receiving binary data via binary socket, 435

using regular expressions in E4X queries, 439

using RESTful communication between Flex applications, 406–408

services and server-side communications

    configuring and connecting to RemoteObject, 415–418

    tracking results from multiple simultaneous service calls, 425

services-config.xml file, 412

setDataHandler( ) method, 567

setElementIndex( ) method, 31

setup method, 643–645

shaderByteCode property, 319

show and hide effects for component, 297–299

showDataEffect event attribute, series objects, 611

showDataEffect property, charts, 619

signed RSLs (.swz files), 461

SimpleMotionPath objects, 306

SimpleXMLDecoder class, 444

SimpleXMLEncoder objects, 442

sizing child elements in containers

    uniform sizing, 89

sizing child elements using alignment properties, 85

Skin class, Spark, 163

skin parts, 57

skinClass property, 49, 176

skinnable containers, providing scrolling for contents, 43–45

SkinnableContainer, Spark, 25, 48

    border and background styles, 53

    contentGroup property, 51

    creating custom skin for, 172–174

    custom skin applied to, 49

    dragging and dropping items, 64

    removeAllElements( ) method, 29

    skinClass property, 51

SkinnableContainerBase, Spark, 25

custom skin classes, setting with skinClass property, 49

SkinnableDataContainer, Spark, 48, 215

    creating custom skin for, 51

    skinClass property, 52

skinning

    applying repeating background image to application, 166–167

    applying skins and properties to components using CSS, 175–177

    chart items, 622–624

    creating button component with icon as skin part, 177–179

    creating skin for s:Button, 163–165

    creating skin for s:ButtonBar and s:ButtonBarButton, 167–169

    creating skin for s:DropDownList, 169–172

    customizing drop indicator of Spark List, 238–242

    Skin class allowing color of fill to be set by AnimateColor, 305

    Skin class created for Spark List to change layout property, 220

    Spark containers, 172–174

    TextArea control, 210–211

    video player with custom controls, 278

SkinPart metadata tag, 164

skins

    applying to a container, 48–53

    defined, 163

SkinState metadata tag, 164

SOAP

    adding SOAP header to WebService request, 431

    parsing response returned from WebService, 432–433

SOAPHeader objects, 431

Socket objects, 435

    connecting to port number lower than 1024, 436

sockets

    creating HTTP proxy using ServerSocket class, 599–605

    new capabilities in AIR 2, 599

Sort objects, 324

    passing multiple SortField objects to, 342

sortCompareFunction property, DataGridColumn, 251

SortField objects, 324
    passing multiple to Sort object, 342
sorting
    ArrayCollection items, 324
    dates in a collection, 343
    specifying sort functions for DataGrid
        columns, 251–252
    XMLListCollection objects, 340
source and destination attributes, <fx:Binding>
        tag, 352
source object (data binding), 351
SpanElement objects, 188, 194
Spark components, 139
Spark containers, 25
Spark effects, 294
spark.layouts package, 26
SparkSkin, extending with MXML to create
        custom button skin, 164–165
Spinner component, Spark, 160
SpriteVisualElement objects, 116
SQLConnection class
    open( ) and openAsync( ) methods, 540
    reencrypt( ) method, 541–544
SQLite, 535
    existing database, embedding in AIR
        application, 550
SQLStatement objects, parameters property,
        544–550
SSL (Secure Sockets Layer)
    using an AMFChannel over, 433
startDelay property, AddAction and
        RemoveAction, 304
StatusUpdateErrorEvent.UPDATE_ERROR,
        521
StatusUpdateEvent.UPDATE_STATUS, 520
StorageVolume class, 584
StorageVolumeChangeEvent objects, 584
StorageVolumeInfo class, querying with
        getStorageVolume( ) function, 585–
        591
StorageVolumeInfo.storageVolumeInfo
        objects, 583
streaming video, displaying, 281–282
StreamingAMFChannel objects, 419, 420
    defining in service-config.xml file, 421
String class
    match( ) method, 390
    methods to test regular expressions, 378
    replace( ) method, 399

stroke and fill, drawing with Path element,
        119
Style metadata tag, 179
styleName property, 175
    BorderContainer, 54
    retrieving elements in TextFlow by, 194
styles
    adding custom style properties, 179–181
    applying skins and style properties to
        components with CSS, 175–177
    creating custom selection style for objects in
        TextFlow, 191–193
    declaring new styles and properties using
        stylesheets, 174
    defined, 163
    partially embedding fonts using CSS, 181
    using Style declarations to set effects, 298
subexpressions in regular expressions, 395
Suite metadata tag, 638, 642
swapElements( ) method, 32
swapElementsAt( ) method, 32
SWC files, 2, 462
    adding to project, 3
    Flex Library project, 7
SWF files, 2, 462
    setting location for compiled SWF, 3
SWFLoader component
    loading external SWF at runtime, 144–145
    loading SWFs embedded in Flex
        application, 145
    ModuleLoader versus, 473
SWFObject library, 449, 681
.swz files (signed RSLs), 461
symbol definitions declared within Library tag,
        136–138
systemChrome attribute, 562, 564

T

tabbing reading order for accessibility, 701
tabIndex property, 701
TabNavigator objects, 458
    historyManagementEnabled parameter,
        460
teardown method, 643–645
temporal metadata, 288
TemporalFacet objects, 285
TemporalFacetEvent objects, 285
Test metadata tag, 640
TestRunnerBase class, 637

text
  displaying gradient text in graphic element, 127–128
  displaying in graphic element, 122–124
  multiple columns within TextFlow displayed by TextArea control, 211
  using custom format resolver, 206–210
Text Layout Framework (TLF), 122, 183
TextArea objects, 190
  controlling appearance of selected text, 201
  displaying vertical text, 197
  setting selection in, 199
  skinning, 210–211
TextConverter class, importToflow( ) method, 185–187
TextFlow objects, 123
  adding graphic elements to, 188–190
  blockProgression property, 199
  copying a character as bitmap, 202–204
  creating custom selection style for objects within, 191–193
  creating in ActionScript or MXML, 184
  creating linked containers in, 205–206
  creating links in, 187–188
  generating from other sources, 185–187
  highlighting last character, 212
  locating elements within, 194–195
  styling links within, 193
  textRotation, changing, 198
  using multiple columns of text, 211
TextFlowUtil class, 123
TextInput control, 146
  binding a value to, 190
TextInput control, Spark
  displaying or hiding when focus changes, 155–156
  focus on, DropDownList opened by key events, 156
TextInput controls
  using validators and formatters, 378–381
TextLayoutFormat objects, 191
  columnCount property, 211
  creating and setting hostLayout format of TextFlow, 197
  setting link formats within TextFlow, 193
TextLine objects, 202
  atomCount property, 212

drawing to BitmapData, using Matrix, 204
TextListener class, 637
textRotation property, 198
Thawte certificates, 495
tick marks, formatting for charts, 615–617
TileGroup class, Spark, 27
TileLayout class, 27, 83
  clipAndEnableScrolling property, 88
  displaying child elements in rows and columns, 86
  orientation property, 87
  requestedColumnCount property, 87
  requestedRowCount property, 87
timers, testing visual components with, 654–656
titleDisplay skin part, 57
TLF (Text Layout Framework), 122, 183
ToggleButton control, Spark, 153
ToolTip components, using to show validation errors in a form, 387–390
ToolTipManager class, 387
  destroyToolTip( ) method, 388
topLevelApplication property (FlexGlobals), 24
trace statements, using without Flash Builder, 665
transfer modes, clipboard data, 569
transform effects, 294
transformAround( ) method, 104, 107
transformations within layout
  applying using Matrix3D, 100–102
  applying using TransformOffsets, 102–105
  custom layout applying 3D transformations to all children, 105–108
TransformOffsets objects, 102
Transition objects, Spark, 303
transitions, using Pixel Bender filter to create, 317–320
transparent attribute, 562, 564
Tween objects, 307
TweenEffect objects, 306
TweenEffectInstance class, 307
  play( ) and onTweenUpdate( ) methods, 307
tweening and animated effects, 306
TweenInstance objects, 306
type selector (CSS), 174
typicalLayoutElement property, 90

U

UIComponent class
  attaching instance of MediaPlayer to, 284
  createChildren( ) method, 257
  extending to create wrapper for OSMF, 287–288
  filters property, 294
  MediaPlayer added to instance, 285
  parentApplication property, 23
  parentDocument property, 23
  properties that will play in response to actions, 297
UIComponent-based components
  contentMouseX and ContentMouseY properties, 60
  drag-and-drop support, 63
UIDUtil class, createUID( ) method, 347
unique IDs for data objects, 347
unit testing, 635–663
  creating application to run FlexUnit tests, 636–639
  creating application to use FlexUnit Framework, 636
  creating FlexUnit test case, 639–642
  creating mock objects for testing, 659–662
  handling events in test case, 647–649
  running code before and after each test, 642–645
  sharing test data between test cases, 645–647
  using complex assertions in test case, 662–663
  visual components, testing with FlexUnit, 649–659
universal selector (CSS), 174
unnamed parameters, 545
updateDisplayList( ) method, 93, 107
  overriding to apply 3D transformations, 105–108
UpdateEvent objects, 516
  broadcast by ApplicationUpdater class, 520
updates for AIR applications
  creating application updater with custom interface, 520
  creating applications with update capabilities, 514–520
  setting customUpdateUI property, 510
URL class, 289

url property
  HTTPService objects, 404
  ModuleLoader class, 473
URLLoader class, test case using, 647–649
URLRequest objects, 448
URLs
  navigating browser to new URL, 447
  parsing via BrowserManager, 454–456
  using URL fragments to control visible contents of containers, 458–460
URLUtil class, 454
URLVariables instance and sendToURL( ) method, sending Flex form data to server, 160–161
useVirtualLayout property, 90

V

V/v drawing command, 119
validation
  combo boxes and groups of radio buttons, 385–387
  showing errors using ToolTips in a form, 387–390
  using regular expressions to create international zip code validator, 382–385
  using regular expressions to validate ISBNs, 391
  using Validators and formatters with TextInput controls, 378–381
Validator class, 377
  doValidation( ) method, 382
  validateAll( ) method, 386
ValidatorResultEvent objects, 385
validNextPage property, 706
variableColumnWidth property, HorizontalLayout, 89
Vector objects
  creating typed vectors, 15
Vector of keyframe objects, 299
Vector3D objects, 105
VeriSign certificates, 495
version property
  specifying target FXG version for Graphic, 117
versions
  determining AIR application version at runtime, 512
  setting AIR application version, 500

targeting specific AIR version, 497
verticalAlign property, 83
 HorizontalLayout class, 81
VerticalLayout class, 27, 80
 horizontalAlign property, 83
 switching to HorizontalLayout at runtime, 82
verticalScrollPosition property, 108
VGroup class, Spark, 27
video, 275–292
 creating basic video player, 275
VideoDisplay component, Spark, 275
 autoPlay property, 276
 currentTimeChange and durationChange events, 276
 dispatching LoadEvent instances with bytesLoaded property, 282
VideoElement objects, 285
VideoPlayer component, Spark, 275
 creating skinnable video player, 278–281
 dispatching LoadEvent instances with bytesLoaded property, 282
 displaying streaming video, 282
videos
 accessing and displaying cue points in video file, 284–287
 creating basic video player using OSMF, 283
 creating skinned video player, 278–281
 creating wrapper for OSMF for use with MXML, 287–288
 displaying bytes loaded, 282
 displaying captions with your video, 288
 displaying playback progress, 276–278
 displaying streaming video, 281–282
viewport property, 42
ViewStack containers
 creating Spark-based ViewStack, 72–77
viewWidth and ViewHeight properties, 117
virtualization, 90–93
 programmatically using virtualized element scrolling, 110–111
 resizing of containers supporting, 98
visible property, 658
visual components, testing with FlexUnit, 649–659
Visual FlexUnit package, 658

W

web page for this book, xix
Web Services Descriptive Language (WSDL) file, 429
WebService class, 403
WebService objects
 adding SOAP header to request, 431
 communicating with, 429–431
 parsing SOAP response from, 432–433
width and height properties
 specifying for Graphic element, 117
 specifying for RichText element, 123
winding property, Path element, 120
window (initial), AIR applications, 503–505
windows
 adding drop shadow for custom chrome window in AIR, 561–567
 closing all open windows in AIR application, 560–561
Windows systems
 adding MXML compiler to Path system variable, 12
 native installer file (.exe) for AIR applications, 528
 notifications using taskbar from AIR application, 575
WSDL (Web Services Descriptive Language) file, 429
 types defined by web service, 444

X

XML
 binding to properties on XML source using E4X, 362–364
 encoding ActionScript data object as, 442
 HTTPService object loading XML from PHP script (example), 405
 namespaces returned by service, handling of, 441
 navigating a document using E4X, 437
 from web service, decoding into strongly typed objects, 444
XML namespaces (see namespaces)
XML objects, adding XMLList to, 440
xmlDecode property, HTTPService objects, 404
XMLDocument objects, 442
XMLList objects, 440

data provider for charts, 608
XMLListCollection objects, 223
    filtering and sorting, 340–342
XMLSocket class, 436

Z

Z/z drawing command, 119

About the Authors

Joshua Noble is a consultant, author, and teacher based in New York City and Portland, Oregon, and is the co-author of *Programming Interactivity* (O'Reilly), *Flex 3 Cookbook* (O'Reilly), and *ActionScript 3.0 Bible* (Wiley). He has worked with Flex and Flash on a wide range of web applications on a variety of platforms over the past six years, as well as working with PHP, Ruby, and Erlang. He also works on architectural installations and large-scale touch systems using Processing, C++, OpenCV, microcontrollers, and sensors to create reactive environments. His website is *http://thefactoryfactory.com*.

Todd Anderson is a senior software engineer for Infrared5. With over eight years of experience developing for the Flash Platform in the areas of RIA and game development, Todd has delivered web, mobile, and desktop solutions for the publishing and entertainment industries, with companies including Condé Nast Publications, Adobe, THQ, and Motorola. He is also a co-author of *AIR Create-Modify-Reuse* (Wiley Wrox) and *Flex 3 Cookbook* (O'Reilly). Currently residing in the Boston area, when he's not in front of the computer he can be seen hugging his wife, reading to his son, chasing after his dog, and trying to get back to his fine arts roots by building things on paper. Anderson runs *http://www.custardbelly.com/blog*, focusing on web, mobile, and desktop development.

Garth Braithwaite is a senior developer at Rain in Utah and specializes in Interaction Design in HTML/CSS/JS and the Flash Platform. He hosts RIA Radio, a weekly podcast for O'Reilly and InsideRIA; speaks at such conferences as 360|Flex, MAX, and Flash and the City; and teaches. Garth is an Adobe Community Professional (ACP), an Adobe Certified Instructor (ACI), an Adobe Certified Expert (ACE), and an Eagle Scout.

Marco Casario is the founder of Comtaste (*http://www.comtaste.com*), a company dedicated to exploring new frontiers in Rich Internet Applications and the convergence of the Web and the world of mobile devices. He is the author of *Flex Solutions: Essential Techniques for Flex 2 and Flex 3 Developers* (Friends of ED) and *Advanced AIR Applications* (Friends of ED). Marco often speaks at such conferences as Adobe MAX, the O'Reilly Web 2.0 Summit, FITC, the AJAXWorld Conference & Expo, 360|Flex, From A to Web, AdobeLive, and many others, details of which are on his blog at *http://casario.blogs.com*.

Rich Tretola currently holds the position of Applications Development Manager at Herff Jones, Inc. He is an award-winning Flex developer and was the lead author of *Professional Flex 2* (Wiley Wrox) and sole author of *Beginning AIR* (Wiley Wrox). He is also a contributing author on the *Adobe AIR 1.5 Cookbook* (O'Reilly). Rich has been building Internet applications for over 10 years, and has worked with Flex since the original Royale beta version was released in 2003. Other than Flex, Rich builds applications using ColdFusion, Flash, and Java. Rich is highly regarded within the Flex community as an expert in RIA and is also an Adobe Community Professional. He runs a popular Flex and AIR blog at *http://blog.EverythingFlex.com*, is the community manager of *http://InsideRIA.com*, and has been asked to be a speaker at the Adobe MAX conference for three consecutive years. For a nontechnical escape, Rich is also a co-owner of a chocolate bar manufacturing company located on Maui named WowWee Maui.

Colophon

The animal on the cover of *Flex 4 Cookbook* is the Kuhl's flying gecko (*Ptychozoon kuhli*). It and the other five species in this genus are also known as parachute geckos—the webs around their neck, legs, and chest serve to create lift when the lizard jumps between branches, and help to control landings. This particular species was named in honor of German naturalist Heinrich Kuhl, who died in Indonesia in 1821 of an infection brought on by the climate.

The flying geckos live in the tropical rainforests of Southeast Asia, almost exclusively in the trees. Their skin has a wide range of natural wood colors, and is patterned with darker bands that allow the animal to camouflage itself against tree bark. They can also change color depending on their mood. The tail's deep serrations and wide tip are defining features of the Kuhl's flying gecko. The lizard usually hunts at night, feeding solely on insects.

All geckos are able to walk on vertical surfaces and even ceilings because of the millions of microscopic hairs (called setae) on their toes, which adhere to surfaces by dragging across at an angle and creating intermolecular friction. Hanging from only one toe on a glass window, a gecko can support about eight times its weight. Strangely, however, Teflon is the only known surface that a gecko cannot stick to.

The cover image is from *Cassell's Natural History*. The cover font is Adobe ITC Garamond. The text font is Linotype Birka; the heading font is Adobe Myriad Condensed; and the code font is LucasFont's TheSansMonoCondensed.

Related Titles from O'Reilly

Web Programming

ActionScript 3.0 Cookbook

ActionScript 3.0 Design Patterns

ActionScript for Flash MX: The Definitive Guide,
  2nd Edition

Adobe AIR 1.5 Cookbook

Adobe AIR for JavaScript Developer's Pocket Guide

Advanced Rails

Ajax Design Patterns

Ajax Hacks

Ajax on Rails

Ajax: The Definitive Guide

Apache 2 Pocket Reference

Apache Cookbook, *2nd Edition*

Building Scalable Web Sites

Designing Web Navigation

Dojo: The Definitive Guide

Dynamic HTML: The Definitive Reference, *3rd Edition*

Essential ActionScript 3.0

Essential PHP Security

Ferret

Flash CS4: The Missing Manual

Flash Hacks

Head First HTML with CSS & XHTML

Head First JavaScript

Head First PHP & MySQL

High Performance Web Sites

HTTP: The Definitive Guide

JavaScript & DHTML Cookbook, *2nd Edition*

JavaScript Pocket Reference, *2nd Edition*

JavaScript: The Definitive Guide, *5th Edition*

JavaScript: The Good Parts

JavaScript: The Missing Manual

Learning ActionScript 3.0

Learning PHP and MySQL, *2nd Edition*

PHP Cookbook, *2nd Edition*

PHP Hacks

PHP in a Nutshell

PHP Pocket Reference, *2nd Edition*

Programming ColdFusion MX, *2nd Edition*

Programming Flex 2

Programming PHP, *2nd Edition*

Programming Amazon Web Services

Rails Cookbook

The ActionScript 3.0 Quick Reference Guide

Twitter API: Up and Running

Universal Design for Web Applications

Upgrading to PHP 5

Web Database Applications with PHP and MySQL,
  2nd Edition

Website Optimization

Web Site Cookbook

Webmaster in a Nutshell, *3rd Edition*

Our books are available at most retail and online bookstores.
To order direct: 1-800-998-9938 • *order@oreilly.com* • *www.oreilly.com*
Online editions of most O'Reilly titles are available by subscription at *safari.oreilly.com*

Get even more for your money.

Join the O'Reilly Community, and register the O'Reilly books you own.It's free, and you'll get:

- 40% upgrade offer on O'Reilly books
- Membership discounts on books and events
- Free lifetime updates to electronic formats of books
- Multiple ebook formats, DRM FREE
- Participation in the O'Reilly community
- Newsletters
- Account management
- 100% Satisfaction Guarantee

Signing up is easy:

1. **Go to: oreilly.com/go/register**
2. **Create an O'Reilly login.**
3. **Provide your address.**
4. **Register your books.**

Note: English-language books only

To order books online:

oreilly.com/order_new

For questions about products or an order:

orders@oreilly.com

To sign up to get topic-specific email announcements and/or news about upcoming books, conferences, special offers, and new technologies:

elists@oreilly.com

For technical questions about book content:

booktech@oreilly.com

To submit new book proposals to our editors:

proposals@oreilly.com

Many O'Reilly books are available in PDF and several ebook formats. For more information:

oreilly.com/ebooks

O'REILLY®

Spreading the knowledge of innovators

www.oreilly.com

Buy this book and get access to the online edition for 45 days—for free!

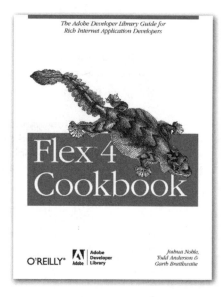

Flex 4 Cookbook
By Joshua Noble, Todd Anderson
& Garth Braithwaite
May 2010, $49.99
ISBN 9780596805616

With Safari Books Online, you can:

Access the contents of thousands of technology and business books

- Quickly search over 7000 books and certification guides
- Download whole books or chapters in PDF format, at no extra cost, to print or read on the go
- Copy and paste code
- Save up to 35% on O'Reilly print books
- **New!** Access mobile-friendly books directly from cell phones and mobile devices

Stay up-to-date on emerging topics before the books are published

- Get on-demand access to evolving manuscripts.
- Interact directly with authors of upcoming books

Explore thousands of hours of video on technology and design topics

- Learn from expert video tutorials
- Watch and replay recorded conference sessions

To try out Safari and the online edition of this book FREE for 45 days, go to *www.oreilly.com/go/safarienabled* and enter the coupon code UMEPFDB. To see the complete Safari Library, visit safari.oreilly.com.

Spreading the knowledge of innovators   safari.oreilly.com